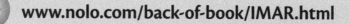

P9-DCQ-589

Download Checklists on Nolo.com

You can download the checklists in this book at:

www.nolo.com/back-of-book/IMAR.html

We'll also post updates whenever there's an important change to the law affecting this book—as well as articles and other related materials.

More Resources
from Nolo.com

Legal Forms, Books, & Software

Hundreds of do-it-yourself products—all written in plain English, approved, and updated by our in-house legal editors.

Legal Articles

Get informed with thousands of free articles on everyday legal topics. Our articles are accurate, up to date, and reader friendly.

Find a Lawyer

Want to talk to a lawyer? Use Nolo to find a lawyer who can help you with your case.

NOLO
LAW for ALL

⚖ NOLO **The Trusted Name**
(but don't take our word for it)

"In Nolo you can trust."
THE NEW YORK TIMES

"Nolo is always there in a jam as the nation's premier publisher of do-it-yourself legal books."
NEWSWEEK

"Nolo publications…guide people simply through the how, when, where and why of the law."
THE WASHINGTON POST

"[Nolo's]…material is developed by experienced attorneys who have a knack for making complicated material accessible."
LIBRARY JOURNAL

"When it comes to self-help legal stuff, nobody does a better job than Nolo…"
USA TODAY

"The most prominent U.S. publisher of self-help legal aids."
TIME MAGAZINE

"Nolo is a pioneer in both consumer and business self-help books and software."
LOS ANGELES TIMES

10th Edition

Fiancé & Marriage Visas

A Couple's Guide to U.S. Immigration

Ilona M. Bray, J.D.

Updated by Attorney Kyle A. Knapp

Tenth Edition	AUGUST 2019
Cover Design	SUSAN PUTNEY
Book Design	TERRI HEARSH
Proofreading	IRENE BARNARD
Index	UNGER INDEXING
Printing	BANG PRINTING

ISSN: 2168-6025 (print)
ISSN: 2325-3959 (online)
ISBN: 978-1-4133-2673-4 (pbk)
ISBN: 978-1-4133-2674-1 (ebook)

This book covers only United States law, unless it specifically states otherwise.
Copyright © 2001, 2004, 2005, 2006, 2008, 2010, 2012, 2014, 2016, and 2019 by Nolo.
All rights reserved. The NOLO trademark is registered in the U.S. Patent and Trademark
Office. Printed in the U.S.A.

No part of this publication may be reproduced, stored in a retrieval system, or transmitted in any
form or by any means, electronic, mechanical, photocopying, recording, or otherwise without
prior written permission. Reproduction prohibitions do not apply to the forms contained in
this product when reproduced for personal use. For information on bulk purchases or corporate
premium sales, please contact the Special Sales Department. Call 800-955-4775 or write to
Nolo, 950 Parker Street, Berkeley, California 94710.

Please note

We believe accurate, plain-English legal information should help you solve many
of your own legal problems. But this text is not a substitute for personalized
advice from a knowledgeable lawyer. If you want the help of a trained professional
—and we'll always point out situations in which we think that's a good idea—
consult an attorney licensed to practice in your state.

Acknowledgments

Special thanks to recently retired Judge Miriam Hayward, who taught me how to do these visas in the first place.

For help making sure this tenth edition is comprehensive and up to date, thanks go to updater Kyle A. Knapp, an attorney based in Ohio. I'd also like to thank the many people who contributed their knowledge and experience to this book, including attorneys Angela Bean, Camille Kim-Cook, Carl Falstrom, Kristina Gasson, Barbara Horn, Jacqueline Newman, Lynette Parker, Robert L. Herreria, and Carmen Reyes-Yossiff; the staff at the International Institute of the East Bay; and Mark Demming and Djamila Gonzalez.

Thanks also to Amien Kacou, a Florida-based attorney who lent his experience, intelligence, and sharp eye to updating past editions.

Finally, a huge round of applause to my colleagues at Nolo, for the energy they put into this project and for making the process fun: Jake Warner, Spencer Sherman, Janet Portman, Catherine Caputo, Jaleh Doane, André Zivkovich, Terri Hearsh, Susan Putney, and Toni Ihara.

About the Author

Ilona Bray, J.D., came to the practice of immigration law through her interest in international human rights issues. Before joining Nolo as legal editor in charge of immigration, she ran a solo law practice and worked for nonprofit immigration agencies including the International Institute of the East Bay (Oakland) and the Northwest Immigrant Rights Project (Seattle). Ms. Bray was also an intern in the legal office at Amnesty International's International Secretariat in London. She received her bachelor's degree in philosophy from Bryn Mawr College, and her law degree and a Master's degree in East Asian (Chinese) Studies from the University of Washington. Ms. Bray is a member of the American Immigration Lawyers Association (AILA). She has authored other books for Nolo, including *Becoming a U.S. Citizen: A Guide to the Law, Exam & Interview*, and *Effective Fundraising for Nonprofits: Real-World Strategies That Work*.

About the Updater

Kyle A. Knapp is an experienced immigration attorney who earned his law degree from Capital University Law School in 1998 and is licensed to practice in Ohio and Florida.

An important part of his practice is assisting individuals sponsor relatives for lawful permanent resident status or apply for naturalized U.S. citizenship.

Kyle also helps organizations hire non-U.S. citizens, and advises them on the requirements to ensure that their employees have authorization to work in the United States. (The former sometimes is referred to as "visa processing," while the latter is referred to as "I-9 compliance.")

His areas of expertise additionally include helping applicants obtain a wide range of nonimmigrant (temporary) and immigrant (green card or permanent resident) visas. In the nonimmigrant category, he has extensive experience with B/Visa Waiver (visitors for business or pleasure), E (treaty traders and investors), F (students), H (specialty occupation workers for individuals with relevant college degrees), J (exchange visitors), L (intracompany transferees from affiliate organizations abroad), O (individuals of extraordinary ability), R (ministers and religious workers), and TN (professional workers from Canada and Mexico under the North American Free Trade Agreement).

Find Kyle at www.knapplawco.com

Table of Contents

Glossary

Appendixes

Your Immigration Companion

"The marvel of all history is the patience with which men and women submit to burdens unnecessarily laid upon them by their governments."

—William E. Borah, former U.S. Senator from Idaho

You'll notice I haven't started this book with a quote about love or marriage. It's not that I'm a cynic—it's just that falling in love is the easy part.

Obtaining the right to live happily ever after in the United States is more complicated than even the most difficult courtship. That's because it involves more than just you, your beloved, your families, and friends. You will also be inviting the U.S. immigration authorities into your lives for as long as it takes to convince them that you are in love, want to be married, and are eligible to enter and live in the United States. And believe me, this is a lot more complicated than simply saying, "I do."

The popular perception is that U.S. citizenship comes along with an American spouse, almost automatically. The reality is quite different. There are dozens of forms, months and possibly years of legal and bureaucratic delays, and countless ways to make the process either move faster or end with a resounding "no entry" from an immigration officer. (One good piece of news, at least, is that as of 2013, same-sex couples are eligible for fiancé as well as marriage visas.)

Even after you convince the U.S. government to let you in, most often you'll get only temporary permission to marry or live in the United States. You'll have to wait a couple of years before you can get permanent residence—and even longer before you can apply to become a U.S. citizen.

I have had many clients arrive at my office after they started the application process with no preparation other than picking up the forms from U.S. Citizenship and Immigration Services (USCIS, formerly called the INS). They fled to a lawyer when the mountain of paperwork threatened to bury them. And then there were the clients who didn't look before they leaped into the application process and found themselves denied or, worse, facing deportation or removal.

None of these people had the benefit of materials that tell you, in plain English, the laws you need to understand and the way to apply for a visa or green card based on marriage. The goal of this book is to fill that gap and to be your companion through the process. "Why a whole book?" you might ask. The answer is simple: Because I'm trying to make it possible for you to get through this complicated process without getting yourself into trouble. It would be a much shorter book if I told you to fill in the forms blindly, without explaining the legal implications or the "inside scoop" on how the USCIS or consular officer will view your case.

Would it be better to hire a lawyer? Possibly. Having a lawyer is not a required part of the immigration process. Nor am I looking for your business, since I no longer actively practice immigration law. But the immigration bureaucracy has created an absurdly tangled system, in which reliable information is about as available as state secrets—and lawyers are, at the moment, the only people with some access to, or experience with, those secrets, or the contact information of people within the government.

One of the ultimate ironies is that even if you get wrong advice from a member of USCIS, you're still stuck with the consequences of having followed that advice. And the confusion accelerates every time Congress tacks amendments onto the immigration laws—which it does lately with every shift in the electorate's anti- and pro-immigrant sentiment. As a result, many immigrants end up having to hire lawyers for cases that, with information like the kind in this book, they could have handled on their own.

That said, I haven't covered every possible complication here—there are times when people really do need a lawyer's help, and I try to alert readers to these times. And if you can afford a lawyer, hiring one is a worthwhile use of your money—and this book will help you learn what to expect from your lawyer and the process as a whole.

If you decide to go without a lawyer, however, don't skip ahead. You MUST read the opening chapters, one through four, before proceeding to the chapter that best fits your individual situation.

To write this book, I have drawn on my experience with hundreds of immigrant clients, gathered stories from other lawyers, and had each edition reviewed by someone actively practicing law. I've tried to anticipate a variety of complications that readers may encounter, so that their application process will go as smoothly as possible. When all is said and done, this process is just a lot of forms and paperwork, all used to show that two decent people are in love and deserve to live together in the United States.

Get Updates and More Online

When there are important changes to the information in this book, we'll post updates online, on a page dedicated to this book:

www.nolo.com/back-of-book/IMAR.html

You'll find other useful information there, too, including copies of all the checklists found in this book as well as author blogs.

First Things First

Every year, hundreds of thousands of foreign-born people become engaged or married to U.S. citizens and permanent residents of the same or opposite sex. Just as no two romances are alike, none of these couples will have exactly the same immigration needs. Some will meet and marry overseas, then wish to move to the United States; some will meet in the United States and wish to marry and stay; and some will meet overseas and wish to come to the United States for their wedding. Each of these situations, and others, will require slightly different planning and procedures.

No matter what your situation, you have one thing in common with all the other fiancés and newlyweds (or even longtime spouses). Before you obtain the right to come to the United States, whether just to get married or to stay permanently, you will have to go through a lengthy process of submitting application forms and paperwork and meeting with government officials to prove your eligibility. The processes are not simple, but they are standard—meaning they can be done without a lawyer's help, if your case is straightforward and your marriage, or planned marriage, is real.

CAUTION

If you are or have ever been in removal (deportation) proceedings, you must see a lawyer. If the proceedings aren't yet over or are on appeal, your entire immigration situation is in the hands of the courts and you are not allowed to use the procedures described in this book. Even if the proceedings are over, you should ask a lawyer whether the outcome affects your current application.

This book will show you how to:
- decide whether you are eligible
- choose the proper visa and submit the correct paperwork
- gather all necessary documents and prepare for interviews with U.S. government officials
- create and maintain documentary proof that your marriage is real
- deal with difficult bureaucrats and delays

- get a work permit in the United States
- make it through your two-year "testing period" to get your green card
- keep and enjoy your permanent residence status, and
- know when you need professional legal help.

"Visa" and "Green Card" Can Mean More Than One Thing

We're about to start using the words "visa" and "green card" a great deal. In a few situations, their meanings are distinct and narrow, but often they overlap or are the same.

Let's start with the narrow meanings. A visa gives you the right to seek entry to the United States. Physically, it usually appears as a stamp in your passport. When this book advises you to go to the consulate to pick up your visa, it means that you'll be getting this stamp or an equivalent document that allows you to seek entry to the United States.

"Green card" is a slang term. In the narrowest usage, it is the plastic photo identification card that you receive when you become a U.S. lawful permanent resident.

Now for the broader meanings. The word visa may also be used in situations involving immigrants who are already in the United States and won't need an entry visa. That's partly because someone in the deep dark offices of the State Department may have to allocate a visa number to these immigrants, though the immigrants may never even know it. When this book talks about your "visa eligibility" or "visa availability," it's not referring to the actual visa that you pick up overseas, but about the broader, theoretical visa that the State Department will allocate to you.

The term green card also takes on broader meanings at times. It's often used, in this book and elsewhere, to refer to lawful permanent residence or lawful conditional residence. When this book talks about a "green card application" it is actually referring to one of the several application processes (adjustment of status or consular processing) that could lead to obtaining U.S. residence.

CAUTION

Here comes the jargon. We try to keep the technical vocabulary to a minimum in this book, but there are times when no other word but the technical one will do. To check on the meaning of terms like "citizen," "permanent resident," or "green card," please see the Glossary at the end of the book.

Green Cards Don't Work Like Tourist Visas

Don't expect a green card to work as a frequent travel pass. A common misconception about green cards is that they allow you unlimited travel in and out of the United States without the hassle of reapplying for visas. The result of this confusion is the practice of overseas family members of U.S. citizens or residents who want to be able to pop in for impromptu visits—they sometimes apply for green cards. But if your plan is to maintain your primary home in another country, the U.S. government may eventually figure this out and cancel your green card. The legal term for this is that you abandoned your residency. You would have to start over and apply for another one.

If, for example, you're married to a U.S. citizen or resident but plan to live in your home country for much of your early marriage, or to shuttle back and forth, you may want to wait until you're really ready to settle in the United States to apply for your permanent resident status.

A. Who Should Use This Book

You probably picked up this book because you are the fiancé or spouse of a U.S. citizen or permanent resident and you want to marry and/or live in the United States. A wedding plan or marriage certificate does not, however, automatically grant you the right to be in the United States. How you apply for permission to come to or live in the

United States depends on several factors. These include where you live now, whether you are married yet, whom you will be marrying (a U.S. citizen or lawful permanent resident), and (if you are in the country already) whether you entered the United States legally or illegally.

Upcoming chapters of this book will address various combinations of these factors separately, so that you'll understand whether and how to go forward with your application.

How We Talk to "You"

Throughout this book, we refer to the immigrant as "you," and the U.S. citizen or permanent resident as "your spouse" or "fiancé," as appropriate. That's to avoid using the corresponding legal terms "beneficiary" (the immigrant who will be getting the visa or green card) and "petitioner" (the U.S. citizen or lawful permanent resident who is sponsoring the immigrant) as much as possible. At times, however, we have no choice.

This doesn't mean that applying for your fiancé visa and/or green card won't be a joint process. You—the beneficiary—and your U.S. spouse or fiancé—the petitioner—will each have a role to play in successfully getting you the right to marry and/or live in the United States.

Also note that we spell fiancé with only one e, which technically refers only to male fiancés. This avoids using the awkward-looking "fiancé(e)." But unless we say otherwise, fiancé in this book refers to both men and women.

Both you and your spouse or fiancé should review and understand all of the paperwork and documents you submit. In fact, many couples find that it's easiest if the U.S. citizen or resident half of the couple prepares most of the paperwork, even the forms that are sent to and signed by the immigrant. This is because most of the written material must be in English and must conform to the requirements of U.S. bureaucracy.

B. Is a Fiancé or Marriage Visa the Best One for You?

Before we get too deep into the subject of this book, let's pause. You might be curious about whether there are alternate ways of getting a visa or green card—especially if you have read our early warnings about how complicated it is to get a visa or green card through marriage!

1. How Does Your Visa Option Compare to Others?

There are dozens of categories of visas and other immigration benefits for people wanting to visit or live in the United States. But none of them will get you a green card overnight or without significant effort. In fact, most experts would agree that if you are already engaged or married to a U.S. citizen or permanent resident, immigrating based on this marriage is likely to be your best bet. The eligibility criteria are reasonably straightforward and the waiting periods are generally better, or at least no worse, than for most other types of visas.

If you are married to a U.S. citizen, there is no waiting period or quota to delay your entry into the United States. You will be subject to the usual time period it takes to process your paperwork and for the government to make sure you are not excludable for any reason, such as criminal past or health problems. (See Chapter 2, Section A, for more on inadmissibility.)

Unfortunately, marriages to U.S. permanent residents don't result in such smooth sailing, immigration-wise. Spouses of permanent residents will probably have to spend time on a waiting list before their visa or green card becomes available to them (although, as we'll explain, they might in some cases become eligible for a work permit in less time). (See Chapter 2, Section A, for more on waiting periods.) However, spouses of permanent residents face shorter waits than many other family immigrant categories. For example, in early 2019, the estimated waiting period for the spouse of a

permanent resident was about two years. If the spouse also had a brother who was a U.S. citizen, he or she could also apply for a visa based on that sibling relationship, but the waiting period for that category is typically between ten and 25 years.

The only categories of people who avoid the visa waiting list are those defined as immediate relatives, which include the spouses of U.S. citizens, the unmarried children of U.S. citizens, and the parents of an adult U.S. citizen (over 21). If you don't happen to be an immediate relative, then your potential green card through marriage to a lawful permanent resident is a fine option to have.

The spouse of a permanent resident might obtain a visa more quickly than waiting for a marriage-based visa if, for example, they:

- have a potential employer in the United States
- have parents or adult children who are U.S. citizens
- would be willing to invest $500,000 or more in a U.S. business
- come from a country from which they can apply for the Diversity Visa (known as the visa lottery), or
- fear political persecution in their home country.

Any of these categories might get a person permission to enter or stay in the United States more quickly than they could as the spouse of a permanent resident. But none of them is an instant answer.

SEE AN EXPERT

If you fit into any of the categories above, you should consult an attorney. Chapter 17 contains tips on finding a good lawyer.

2. Why Can't You Start Off With a Tourist Visa?

Many fiancés and spouses immigrating from overseas wonder why they cannot simply use a tourist visa (B-2) or the Visa Waiver Program (VWP) to enter the United States. They know they will spend a long time outside the United States waiting for their proper immigrant visa, while their fiancé or spouse is living inside the United States. But they also know that a B-2 tourist visa can be gotten in a few days, and VWP entry is even easier. So why, they wonder, can't they just come to the United States using one of these, and then worry about the rest of the green card application process once they're together here?

There are two big problems with this idea. First, if you pose as a tourist or other temporary visitor with the secret intention of staying in the United States for an indefinite time, you will have committed visa fraud. Temporary (nonimmigrant) visas are meant for people who intend to stay temporarily—and then leave. The same goes for the VWP. Such forms of entry are not meant for people who plan to marry and live happily ever after in the United States.

If U.S. Citizenship and Immigration Services (USCIS, formerly called "INS") chooses to make an issue of it, your lie upon entry could lead to your losing the right to obtain a marriage-based green card and most other types of visas.

USCIS will be especially suspicious if you get married within 90 days of entering the United States. Sometimes USCIS will turn a blind eye, or you may be able to convince it that when you entered the U.S. you really planned a short stay (and only decided to marry after you arrived). If USCIS remains unconvinced, you can ask it to forgive your error, but obtaining such forgiveness (in legalese, a "waiver") is not easy and not covered in this book.

> EXAMPLE 1: Detlef enters the United States as a tourist, marries Sally (a U.S. citizen) a week later, and they apply for his green card in San Francisco. At their green card interview, the officer asks, "When did you decide to get married?" Detlef answers, "Oh, I asked Sally to marry me during a phone call last month, and when she said yes, I was so happy that I got a tourist visa, got on the next plane, and we were married in the Elvis Chapel in Las Vegas the following Monday." This is an unfortunate answer, because it practically forces the immigration officer

to notice that Detlef committed visa fraud and deny his green card.

> EXAMPLE 2: Nigel enters the United States as a tourist, marries Ellen (a U.S. citizen) four months later and they apply for his green card in New York. At the green card interview the officer asks, "What was your intention when you entered the United States?" Nigel says, "Our relationship was going very well long-distance, so I decided to travel to the United States to see Ellen in person. Frankly, it was also time for a vacation. A few weeks after I arrived, we realized we were really and truly in love. And when that feeling didn't wear off, we decided to marry." This answer has promise. Even if this couple was contemplating marriage before Nigel arrived, Nigel's candid answer, plus the fact that they waited over 90 days to get married, makes clear that Nigel didn't just use the tourist visa to get around the U.S. immigration laws.

The second problem is that if your U.S. fiancé or spouse is a permanent resident (not a citizen), you may, as mentioned above, have to wait for years until you are eligible for permanent residence or a green card. That means that if you come to the United States on a temporary visa and your permitted stay runs out, you could be here illegally for all of those years of waiting. Living here illegally would cause many problems described in detail later on. For now, just keep in mind that it could ultimately make getting a green card extremely difficult.

RESOURCE
Still curious about other visas? There are many types of visas and immigration benefits for temporary and permanent U.S. residence. Though in many cases they apply only to narrow categories of people, you might want to scan the summary provided in Appendix A. If you see any likely prospects, you can check out their advantages and disadvantages before continuing with the application covered by this book. You will find more detailed information on these visa categories in *U.S. Immigration Made Easy*, by Ilona Bray (Nolo).

C. Using a Fake Marriage to Come to the U.S.

It is illegal for anyone to get married solely for the purpose of getting, or helping someone to get, permanent residence in the United States. There are stiff fines and possible jail terms for people who are convicted of this crime. But we would be foolish not to address the fact that many people attempt to fake a marriage to obtain a green card.

⇨ **SKIP AHEAD**
If you are getting married for legitimate reasons, you can skip this section and continue reading at Section D.

If you are considering a fake, or sham, marriage, you probably already know that what you are planning is illegal. You should also know that this book is written with the assumption that you are marrying for love, not for a green card. We are not going to give you tips on making a fraudulent marriage look real. However, we will outline the risks for you.

1. What Is a Sham Marriage?

A sham marriage is one that is entered into in order to get around the U.S. immigration laws. For a marriage to be valid under the law, it is not enough that the couple had a real marriage ceremony and got all the right governmental stamps on their marriage certificate. They have to intend to live in a real marital relationship following the marriage ceremony—and prove their intention through their actions. If the couple doesn't intend to establish a life together, their marriage is a sham. (For more on what USCIS considers to be a real or bona fide marital relationship for purposes of green card eligibility, see Chapter 2, Section B.)

2. Will You Get Caught?

Detecting marriage frauds is a top priority for USCIS. Some USCIS officers still quote a survey from the 1980s that found that up to 30% of marriages between aliens and U.S. citizens are suspect. That survey has since been shown to be deeply flawed, but its legacy lives on.

In order to detect fraud, the immigration authorities require a lot of proof that a marriage is real, including more documentation than for other family-based immigration applicants. They subject marriage-based immigrants to a longer and more detailed personal interview, followed by a two-year testing period for couples who have been married less than two years upon their approval or U.S. entry.

The government will not normally follow you around or investigate your life beyond the required paperwork and the interviews it always conducts. But it has the power to look deeply into your life if the authorities get suspicious. Government inspectors can visit your home, talk to your friends, interview your employers, check out your Facebook page, and more. By requiring more of married couples than others, the government has already set up a system that gives it a lot of information about whether your marriage is real.

What is the U.S. government's view of a typical marriage? The statutes and regulations don't go into detail on this, so the following comes from a combination of court cases and attorneys' experiences.

According to USCIS, the typical couple has a fair amount in common. They share a language and religion. They live together and do things together, like take vacations, celebrate important events or holidays, and have sex and children. Typical couples also combine financial and other aspects of their lives after marriage. They demonstrate their trust in one another by sharing bank and credit card accounts and ownership of property, such as cars and houses.

The government usually expects applicants to prove that they share their lives in a way similar to what is described above. Applicants do this by providing copies of documents like rental agreements, bank account statements, and children's birth certificates. The government further tests the validity of the marriage by talking to the applicant and usually to his or her spouse. Every marriage-based applicant for a visa or green card (including fiancés), whether they are applying in the United States or overseas, will have to attend a personal interview with a U.S. government official.

U.S. government officials have developed amazing talents for discovering fraud by examining what look like insignificant details of people's lives. To ferret out lies, they have learned to cross-check dates and facts within the application forms and between the application forms and people's testimony.

> **EXAMPLE:** Rasputin has married Alice, a U.S. citizen, in the hopes of obtaining a green card. They submit an application for a green card in the United States. At Rasputin's green card interview, the officer asks for his full name, his address, and how he entered the United States. Rasputin can't believe how easy this all is. The officer goes on to ask for the dates of all of Rasputin's visits to the United States, the date of his divorce from his previous wife, and the dates of all of his children's births. Rasputin is getting bored. Then the officer notices something funny. The date of birth of Rasputin's last child by his former wife is a full year after the date of their supposed divorce. The officer becomes suspicious, and Rasputin and Alice are taken to separate rooms for fraud interviews. They are examined in minute detail about their married lives. When neither of them can remember what the other one eats for breakfast or what they did for their last birthdays, the case is denied and referred to the local Immigration Court for proceedings to deport Rasputin.

If a couple has been married for less than two years when the immigrant first receives residency, USCIS gets a second chance at testing the validity of the marriage. The immigrants in such couples don't get a permanent green card right away. Instead, the law requires that their first green card expire after another two years. (The technical term is that the immigrant has "conditional residency.")

When the two years are up, both members of the couple must file an application for the immigrant's permanent residency. They must include copies of documents showing that they are still married

and sharing the important elements of their lives. This form is mailed to a USCIS office. As USCIS knows, it is extremely difficult for members of sham marriages to keep things together for a full two years, even on paper. If the marriage appears to be a real one when the two years are up, the conversion from conditional to permanent residency won't involve an intensive investigation—the application process doesn't even include an interview if the written application looks legit.

> **EXAMPLE:** Maria married Fred, a U.S. citizen, in order to get a green card. Fred was a friend of Maria's, who simply wanted to help her out. Maria manages to get approved by the consulate at her immigrant visa interview, and enters the United States. Because their marriage is new, Maria is given two years as a conditional resident. During those two years, Maria overdraws their joint checking account three times. Fred gets angry and closes the account. Maria has an accident with their jointly owned car and it goes to the junkyard. Fred buys another car in his own name and won't let Maria drive it. Fred gets fed up and wonders why he got into this in the first place. He falls in love with someone else and insists that Maria move out. At the end of her two years of conditional residency, Maria can't get Fred to answer her phone calls. In desperation, she fills out the application form on her own, fakes Fred's signature and lists his address as her own. However, the only documents she can attach are the same bank account statements and car registration she submitted to the consulate two years ago. USCIS checks the files and notices this. They call her and Fred in for an interview. It's not long before the truth comes out and enforcement proceedings are begun.

As you see from the examples above, people who enter into sham marriages most often trip themselves up just trying to get through the standard process. It's not that USCIS can read people's minds or that it spends all its time peeking into applicants' bedrooms. They simply catch a lot of people who thought that a fake marriage was going to be easier than it really is.

References to the Immigration Laws in This Book

Throughout this book are references to the federal immigration laws that govern immigration through marriage and to the regulations that describe how USCIS will apply those laws to you. (They look like this: "I.N.A. § 319(a); 8 U.S.C. § 1430(a)," or "8 C.F.R. § 316.5.") We include these references where we feel it is important to indicate our sources for information and to help you research the immigration laws on your own. (See Chapter 17, Section H, for more detail on what these references mean and how you can look them up.)

---

3. What Happens If You Are Caught

The law pretty much speaks for itself on what happens to immigrants who commit marriage fraud. You can face prison, a fine, or both:

> *Any individual who knowingly enters into a marriage for the purpose of evading any provision of the immigration laws shall be imprisoned for not more than 5 years, or fined not more than $250,000, or both.* (I.N.A. § 275(c); 8 U.S.C. § 1325(c)).

The U.S. citizen or resident could also face criminal prosecution, including fines or imprisonment, depending on the facts of the case. They are most likely to be prosecuted for either criminal conspiracy (conspiring with the immigrant is enough; see *U.S. v. Vickerage*, 921 F.2d 143 (8th Cir. 1990)), or for establishing a "commercial enterprise" to get people green cards (see I.N.A. § 275(d); 8 U.S.C. § 1325(d)).

The extent to which these penalties will be applied depends on the specifics of each case. The government tends to reserve the highest penalties for U.S. citizens or residents engaged in major conspiracy operations, such as systematically arranging fraudulent marriages. But that doesn't mean that small-time participants in marriage fraud

can count on a soft punishment—though most immigrants will probably simply be deported and never allowed to return.

D. How to Use This Book

This book is a unique combination of legal analysis and form preparation instructions. If you're like most people, you'll be tempted to go straight to the form preparation portions of the book. After all, how many of us read the directions before we plug in a new appliance? But consider this a great big warning label: If you just "plug in" to the visa application process, it could blow up. The U.S. government may give the lucky ones a second chance, but many careless applicants have found themselves deported or prevented from coming to the United States for many years. You won't need to read every section of this book, but please figure out which ones apply to you, and read them.

First, however, a word of reassurance. Most applicants do get a second chance at bringing their application up to the government's standards if they simply leave something out. A number of people are going through the immigration process on their own, and the U.S. government is accustomed to seeing badly prepared applications. You don't need to worry that one little mistake will lead to an instant denial of your visa or green card. If there is a problem in your application that can be corrected, you'll usually be given time to correct it.

The trouble is, you could make a mistake that's irreversible—like unnecessarily revealing something that makes it look like you're ineligible. So you may as well use the advice in this book to get your application right the first time around.

1. Chapters Everyone Should Read

There are a few chapters that everyone needs to read. These include Chapters 1 and 2, which explain whether this book can help you; and whether the immigration laws might exclude you automatically for health, security, or other reasons. We also highly recommend that everyone read

Chapter 3, dealing with the income levels necessary to support a new immigrant. Lack of financial support is now one of the most common reasons for green card denials.

If your visa or green card prospects still look promising, move on to Chapter 4, which contains important tips on handling all the necessary paperwork. This is a vital chapter—the first impression that you create with your paperwork often determines how much scrutiny the government will give your application.

! **CAUTION**

Always watch for changes in the law. The U.S. Congress, USCIS, and the State Department are constantly fixing, adjusting, and updating the immigration laws, procedures, fees, and forms. We can't track you down to tell you if anything in this book is affected—you'll need to watch the news and check the Legal Updates within the Immigration section of www.nolo.com.

2. Chapters for Your Situation

After you read Chapters 1 through 4, skip to the chapter that best describes your situation. For example, as shown in "Which Chapter Is for You?" below, if you're living overseas and engaged to a U.S. citizen, you'd turn to Chapter 5. But if you're living in the United States and married to a lawful permanent resident, you'd read Chapter 12.

Each of Chapters 5 through 12 will help you analyze your immigration situation, discuss what options are available to you, and take you through any necessary preliminary procedures. If you qualify for and want to obtain a green card, you will also be coached to decide whether to apply in the United States, through a procedure called adjustment of status, or at a U.S. embassy or consulate abroad, through a procedure called consular processing, and directed to a chapter or section that explains these procedures.

You will be guided through each part of the process, using checklists designed for your immigration status. The checklists will summarize all the forms and documents that you need, and direct you to the proper forms, line-by-line discussions of how to fill out the forms, and other necessary information. Chapter 13 will instruct you on preparing for your visa or green card interview (the required final step for every applicant).

Which Chapter Is for You?			
Where is the immigrant?	**Who is the immigrant?**	**Who is the fiancé or spouse?**	**Go to Chapter**
Overseas	Fiancé	U.S. citizen	5
Overseas	Fiancé	Permanent resident	6
Overseas	Spouse	U.S. citizen	7
Overseas	Spouse	Permanent resident	8
In the U.S.	Fiancé	U.S. citizen	9
In the U.S.	Fiancé	Permanent resident	10
In the U.S.	Spouse	U.S. citizen	11
In the U.S.	Spouse	Permanent resident	12

3. Chapters for Unique or Problem Situations

Hopefully, the chapters described above will be all you need to get your visa or green card. However, things don't always happen as they should when dealing with the U.S. immigration bureaucracy. Therefore, we've included chapters to cover special situations or problems.

If you're lucky, you'll never have to read Chapter 15, Dealing With Bureaucrats, Delays, and Denials. But most people find their application takes longer than they think it should. In that case, you'll be glad to have this chapter, which also deals with what to do if your application is denied.

Finally, if your case is turning out to be much more complicated than you'd expected, you'll need to consider getting a lawyer or doing some legal research of your own. In that case, review Chapter 17.

4. Chapters to Save for Later

Even after you win a visa or new immigration status, you will still be required to follow some immigration rules. Chapter 16, After You Get Your Green Card, covers the rights and responsibilities of visa and green card holders, including you and members of your family. After all this hard work, you wouldn't want to lose your residency.

Chapter 16 also covers certain people with young marriages, whose green cards expire after a two-year testing period called "conditional residency." This chapter gives them all the instructions they need to go from conditional residency to a normal green card—that is, permanent residency.

Chapter 16 also gives you instructions on how to renew or replace the green card itself.

5. Appendixes

The appendixes to this book include a great deal of useful information, including a summary of the types of green cards and visas available to people and copies of the various handy checklists provided throughout this book.

TIP

Remember to use the checklists. No matter which immigration status you plan to pursue, it will involve lots of paperwork and documents. If you rely on the proper checklist, you should avoid missing any steps.

E. Getting the Latest Forms and Fees

This book doesn't provide immigration application forms, for good reason. The U.S. immigration authorities revise these forms so often that by the time you're using this book, chances are the form will have gone out of date—and the government could refuse to accept yours.

All the application forms you'll need—and we'll tell you exactly which ones they are—are either readily available or will be mailed to you by the immigration authorities when the time is right. Many can or must be filled out online. This book also includes filled-in samples of the most important forms.

The main sources for immigration application forms are:

- U.S. Citizenship and Immigration Services, at one of its local offices (you will have to make an appointment first); through its website, www.uscis.gov (click the "Forms" tab, then scroll down until you find the form you need); or by calling 800-870-3676, and
- the U.S. State Department, through its website, www.state.gov.

CAUTION

It's getting harder and harder to visit your local USCIS office. There are a few times when you might wish to visit a USCIS office in person, for example, to pick up local forms or ask about delays. Before 2019, applicants were able to schedule in-person ("INFOPASS") appointments through the USCIS website. However, USICS has been phasing out this function, which is due to end in September 2019. Going forward, you'll need to call the USCIS Contact Center and speak to one of its representatives. That person will either assist you by phone or schedule an in-person appointment at a local USCIS office for you. In urgent situations (such as an emergency travel document request) you can try visiting your USCIS office in person; they might or might not consent to meet with you. Bring photo identification and all documents relevant to your emergency request.

Immigration application fees, like the forms, change regularly. And most USCIS and consular applications require fees to accompany them. USCIS last raised its fees in late 2016. Be sure to check the USCIS website for the most up-to-date fees before submitting any application.

For up-to-date fees for U.S. filings, check the USCIS website at www.uscis.gov. Click on "Forms," and go to the page of the form you'll be filing. Alternatively, you could call the USCIS customer contact line at 800-375-5283.

For up-to-date fees for consular filings, check the State Department's website, www.travel.state.gov. Enter "fees for visa services" into the search box. This information may also be accessed through the U.S. State Department's Visa Services office, at 202-663-1225. The fee can be paid in dollars or in the local currency, at the current exchange rate.

CAUTION

There will be other expenses. If you're trying to figure out how much to budget for this process, don't forget the costs of required items other than the fees, such as photos, the medical exam, and having documents translated or notarized.

Are You Eligible for a Visa or Green Card?

You can think of your path toward a visa or green card as requiring you to pass through two main doors—theoretical doors, that is, though they can be harder than the wooden kind. The first door is the inadmissibility door: it can be closed on anyone whom the U.S. has decided is unfit to cross its borders. The second door is the eligibility door. It can be closed on you if you don't meet the criteria for the particular type of visa or green card for which you apply. This chapter covers these two doors.

A. Can You Enter the U.S. at All?

Whether you're coming to the United States for a short visit or to stay forever, the U.S. government has the power to tell you "no." Many people are shocked to learn that their engagement or marriage to a U.S. citizen or permanent resident is no guarantee of entry into the United States. The U.S. government has decided that certain types of people will not be allowed into the United States at all. These people are called inadmissible.

Much of your application process will involve proving that you don't fit into one of the categories of inadmissible people, primarily through answering questions and undergoing a security check and a medical exam. If you will be entering the United States on a fiancé visa, you may have to prove that you are not inadmissible twice: first, for the fiancé visa, and again if you are asking for permanent residence, as part of the green card application.

A brief list of the main grounds of inadmissibility is provided in "What Makes You Inadmissible?" below. As you'll see, the reasons concern health, criminal, security, and more specialized issues or problems. Some of the grounds make obvious sense (few would quibble about letting an international terrorist into the country); others are the topic of more controversy, such as the exclusion of people who have committed certain immigration violations.

TIP

You can read the law concerning inadmissibility yourself. The grounds for inadmissibility are in the Immigration and Nationality Act (the primary federal law covering immigrants at I.N.A. § 212(a); 8 U.S.C. § 1182). Read this Act at your local law library; or at USCIS's website at www.uscis.gov (click "Legal Resources," then "Immigration and Nationality Act"). For more information on inadmissibility in plain English, including information on exceptions or waivers, see the free articles in the immigration section of Nolo's website.

Immigrants From Overseas May Not Be Able to Bring Certain Items or Goods

When you come to the United States, you'll not only have to think about whether you'll be admitted, but whether the items that you carry on your person or in your luggage will be allowed in with you. U.S. Customs and Border Protection (CBP) regulates not only people, but also the goods and currency that all travelers bring to the United States. A CBP officer will question you and may search your luggage or even subject you to a personal search.

Certain items are completely prohibited (such as drugs and weapons); others can be brought in only in limited amounts (such as alcohol and tobacco) and others are subject to more specific restrictions or taxes. For more information, see the CBP's website at www.cbp.gov, and click "Travel," then "Clearing CBP," or ask your local U.S. consulate for more information.

The grounds of inadmissibility most likely to cause trouble for engaged or married couples include:

- You have lived or are living unlawfully in the United States, having stayed past the expiration date of your visa or entered the country illegally. (See Section A2, "Dealing With Unlawful Time in the United States," below.)

- In the past, you have committed marriage or other immigration fraud. Even if you haven't yet been found out, filing a new visa or green card application will give the immigration authorities an opportunity to snoop around a bit more.

- Your spouse is unable to support you financially, you don't have the means to support yourself in the United States, and the rest of the family won't pitch in. (An extensive discussion of the financial requirements to obtain a green card and further strategies for meeting these are set forth in Chapter 3, Meeting Income Requirements.)

- You have a communicable illness. You may request a waiver, but it involves an application and paperwork that we do not cover in this book. If you'll be applying for a K-1 fiancé visa, it will be given to you conditionally before your admission to the U.S. and will become permanent only after you've gotten married and apply to adjust status.

Under Trump "Travel Ban," Certain Countries' Citizens May Be Denied U.S. Entry

Although not a ground of inadmissibility under federal law (the I.N.A.), citizens of certain countries may be denied U.S. entry simply because of their national origin. In 2017, President Trump signed executive orders denying entry to visa holders from several Muslim-majority countries, with the stated purpose of reviewing U.S. visa-vetting procedures. Immigration and civil rights advocates immediately challenged these executive orders in several courts.

The administration issued an updated travel ban in September 2017, which restricts the ability of nationals from Iran, Libya, North Korea, Somalia, Syria, Venezuela, and Yemen to enter or immigrate to the United States. It originally also restricted nationals from Chad; this country was later taken off the list.

In June 2018, the Supreme Court held that the Trump travel ban is lawful under the President's broad powers over immigration and national security.

The ban does not affect nationals who already have U.S. lawful permanent resident status ("green card" holders). It also does not affect people seeking asylum, or refugees who have already been admitted to the United States. Finally, it will not apply to dual nationals who enter under the passport of a non-affected country.

Because challenges to the ban are still being considered in lower courts, the decision is not necessarily the end of the line. Nonetheless, the Supreme Court majority in the most recent decision stated that it is unlikely to ultimately find that the travel ban is based on religious animus against Muslims and is therefore unconstitutional. We can thus expect the ban to remain in place for the foreseeable future.

The travel ban affects people from the seven restricted countries to varying degrees. Immigrants and nonimmigrants from Iran are ineligible to enter the U.S., except with certain student and exchange visas. Libyans, Syrians, North Koreans, and Yemenis are ineligible to enter the U.S. as immigrants or nonimmigrants. Somalis cannot enter the U.S. as immigrants, but may be able to enter as nonimmigrants. Venezuelans are not banned from entering the U.S., except that restrictions apply to government officials and their family.

Nationals of all restricted countries should expect enhanced screening when entering the U.S. even if they qualify to enter.

Waivers are available, at least in theory, for people who can show that denying their entry would cause them undue hardship, would not pose a threat to national security or public safety, and would be in the national interest. Still, the vast majority of waiver requests have been denied, and only a small handful have been granted since the ban took effect.

- If you've been convicted of a crime involving alcohol, you've got double trouble. Even if the crime itself doesn't make you inadmissible, USCIS can, and often does, argue that it's a sign that you have a physical or mental disorder associated with harmful behavior—in other words, that you're inadmissible on health, rather than criminal, grounds. This is most often a problem for people with convictions for "DUI" or "DWI" (Driving Under the Influence, or Driving While Intoxicated). Other crimes such as assaults or domestic violence where alcohol or drugs were contributing factors can lead to the same result.

 SEE AN EXPERT
For any of the above situations, or if another item on the inadmissibility list seems to apply to you, you should really see a lawyer. (For information on finding an attorney see Chapter 17.)

1. You Must Pass a Medical Exam

As a test of whether you fall into a health-related ground of inadmissibility, your application for a fiancé or marriage-based visa will include a medical exam by a doctor approved by the U.S. consulate or USCIS. Your own doctor cannot do the exam unless he or she is on the government's list of approved doctors.

What Makes You Inadmissible?

With possible exceptions, the United States will not allow you to enter if you:

- have a communicable disease, such as tuberculosis
- have a physical or mental disorder that makes you harmful to others
- are likely to become a public charge (dependent on government assistance or welfare)
- are a drug abuser ("tried it more than once" in the last three years is enough for USCIS)
- have committed or been convicted of a crime of "moral turpitude" (one that's considered morally wrong or done with a bad intention)
- have been convicted of multiple crimes with a combined sentence of five years or more
- have committed or been convicted of prostitution, money laundering, human trafficking, drug trafficking, or certain other drug violations
- are the immediate family member of a drug trafficker or human trafficker and have knowingly benefited from their illicit money within the last five years
- have committed espionage or sabotage
- are a member of a totalitarian party (Communist in particular)

- are a Nazi or have participated in genocide, torture, or the recruitment of child soldiers
- have violated the immigration laws or committed immigration fraud
- falsely pretended to be a U.S. citizen
- are or have been unlawfully present in the United States or haven't obtained proper documentation or authorization to enter the United States
- were previously removed or deported from the United States
- are a polygamist (have married or lived in a relationship with more than one person at the same time)
- have committed international child abduction
- are on a J-1 or J-2 exchange visitor visa and are subject to the two-year foreign residence requirement
- have not received certain vaccines
- have violated anyone's religious freedoms while you served in government
- threaten the security or foreign policy interests of the U.S, or
- have participated in any terrorist activity or have associated with any terrorist organization.

The purpose of the exam is to make sure that you don't have any serious or communicable diseases, mental disorders, or drug problems that would make you inadmissible, and that you have had all the required vaccinations.

The Centers for Disease Control and Prevention and the Department of Health and Human Services maintain a partial list of communicable diseases, which includes infectious tuberculosis, untreated venereal and other sexually transmitted diseases, and untreated Hansen's disease (leprosy). HIV was removed from the list in 2010.

To this list may be added dangerous diseases designated by the U.S. president or the World Health Organization on an emergency basis.

Communicable diseases are not, however, the only type of condition that can make you inadmissible. The examining doctor will decide whether your condition or behavior has "posed or is likely to pose a threat to the property, safety, or welfare of the alien or others."

Vaccinations You May Need to Have

The required vaccinations presently include the ones listed below. Some of these are required only in certain age groups. If other diseases later become preventable by vaccines, they may be added to this list.

- mumps
- rubella
- measles
- polio
- tetanus and diphtheria toxoids
- pertussis
- influenza (including type B)
- hepatitis A and B
- varicella
- meningococcal disease
- pneumococcal disease, and
- rotavirus.

If you have an illness that causes you trouble but won't infect or injure others, such as heart disease, cancer, or certain mental illnesses, you won't be inadmissible on medical grounds. However, watch out for inadmissibility as a public charge if you won't be able to work and don't have medical insurance. (Chapter 3 covers inadmissibility on the grounds of lack of support.)

In order to get a green card, you must demonstrate that you have had certain vaccinations. The list of those vaccinations usually required is above. If you are entering the U.S. on a fiancé visa, however, you may postpone getting these vaccines until you are in the U.S. and you later apply for your green card.

2. Dealing With Unlawful Time in the United States

In the late 1990s, Congress decided to punish people who spend time in the United States unlawfully, without permission from the immigration authorities. It created a penalty that prevents people from coming or returning to the United States for either three years or ten years, depending on how long they stayed illegally in the country. These are usually referred to as the "time bars," or the "three- and ten-year bars."

In addition, people who lived in the United States illegally for a total, aggregate of more than a year and then left or were deported, but who returned to the United States illegally (or were caught trying to), can basically never get a green card. This is usually referred to as the "permanent bar," which we'll discuss in Subsection c, "The Permanent Bar," below. But first, let's look at the time bars that have some hope of being waived.

If you spent time in the United States unlawfully at any time after April 1997, this section could be one of the most important parts of this book for you to read and understand, no matter where you're living now.

SEE AN EXPERT

"Unlawful" is a difficult legal term. If you know that you were here without USCIS permission, it's safe to say that your stay was unlawful. But the boundaries are less clear if, for example, you were waiting for USCIS to approve or deny an application you'd filed, were in removal (Immigration Court) proceedings, or had a visa but violated its rules. For issues such as these, you'll need to consult a lawyer.

a. The Three- and Ten-Year Time Bars

The first thing to understand about the time bars is that (with rare exceptions) they are imposed only on people who are overseas and trying to return to the United States, not people who are already here and have the right to apply for their green card here by "adjusting status."

Unfortunately, a number of people have no choice but to leave the U.S. and apply for their immigrant visa and green card through an overseas U.S. consulate, either because they are already overseas, or because they are in the United States but ineligible to use the U.S. green card application procedure called adjustment of status. If you are one of these people, the time bars could delay your immigrating to the United States as follows:

- **Three Years.** If you've spent more than 180 continuous days (approximately six months) in the United States unlawfully, you could be barred from coming back for three years.
- **Ten Years.** If you've spent more than one continuous year in the United States unlawfully, you could be barred from coming back for ten years.

You could get all the way through receiving approval of your initial immigrant petition (Form I-130), submitting your follow-up paperwork, and getting an interview appointment—only to leave the United States, attend your visa interview, and have the consular official inform you that although they would love to give you a visa, the time bars prevent you from actually reentering the United States for another three or ten years. By planning ahead, however, you may be able to avoid this trap.

i. Loopholes in the Time Bar Law

Not everyone who has ever lived in the United States unlawfully will have a time bar problem. The law contains a few loopholes, as follows:

- Since the law didn't go into effect until April 1, 1997, no unlawful time before that date counts.
- None of your unlawful time when you were under the age of 18 counts against you for purposes of the three- and ten-year bars.

- The law imposes time bars only after certain lengths of "continuous" unlawful time; the time bars do not apply if no single stay lasted 180 days or more. So, generally, a few months here and there don't count, although they do add up toward the permanent bar.

Using these loopholes and some basic math, you might find that people who look like they have a time bar problem are safe after all. Here are some examples:

- Rosalie was a student in the United States from 1990 to 1995. She continued to live here unlawfully until April 1, 1997. She is not subject to the time bars because unlawful time doesn't start to count until April 1, 1997.
- Rosalie just checked her calendar and realized she stayed until July 1, 1997. But she still isn't subject to the time bars because her stay was for less than 180 continuous days after April 1, 1997.
- Juan crossed the Mexican border illegally six times in 2018, and stayed in the United States for time periods of two months each, for a total of 12 months. Now Juan wants to enter legally. The three- and ten-year time bars will not apply to him because he did not stay for more than 180 continuous days, and the permanent bar will not apply to him because his total stays did not exceed one year.
- Soraya entered the United States as a visitor on June 1, 2018 and her status expired three months later. She stayed in the United States until June 6, 2019. Soraya turned 18 on February 1, 2019. The time bars will not apply to her because only about four months of her unlawful time—less than 180 days—was while she was over the age of 18.

ii. Waivers of the Time Bar Law

If you have a time bar problem, don't just give up. If you're already married to a U.S. citizen or permanent resident, you are one of the lucky few who can ask for forgiveness, known in legal jargon as a waiver (in this case, using Form I-601). But you'll need a lawyer for this—these waivers are not easy to get. And to confuse matters further, some applicants may actually be able to apply for this waiver before, not after they leave the U.S., by using what's called the "provisional waiver" process.

Eligibility grounds for waiver of unlawful presence. To be eligible, you'll have to show that if you don't get the visa, your U.S. spouse or fiancé (or your parents, if they happen to be U.S. citizens or permanent residents) will suffer extreme hardship. And when the immigration laws say "extreme" hardship, they mean it—the sadness that your spouse will feel at your living thousands of miles away won't even begin to get your waiver application granted.

An example of a case where the government would recognize extreme hardship is one where your spouse has a severe medical problem and requires your constant attention. Financial hardship will also be taken into consideration.

If you happen to have U.S. citizen or lawful permanent resident parents living in the United States, the hardship that they would suffer upon your departure can also be counted toward a waiver. They are called your "qualifying relatives," and if you prove hardship to them, you do not need to show that your departure would cause hardship to your spouse.

How Could a Lawyer Possibly Help?

Anyone living in the United States with a time bar problem will want to get the latest information from a lawyer before making any decisions.

The lawyer could advise you, for example, whether there is any new legislation pending that would expand the right to use the adjustment of status procedure; when and if your spouse might be eligible for U.S. citizenship if your spouse is now a permanent resident (which would help you if you entered with a visa); and the current odds of being granted a waiver if you do decide to risk leaving and applying for your immigrant visa and green card through an overseas consulate. But be sure to find a lawyer who's an expert in this highly complex area.

However, hardship that your U.S. citizen or permanent resident children would suffer doesn't count (although you could argue that their suffering affects your U.S. citizen or permanent resident qualifying relative, emotionally, financially, or otherwise).

The provisional waiver of unlawful presence. These time bars put visa applicants who must apply for their visas overseas at a huge disadvantage. Until recently, these applicants have had to leave the U.S. and apply for this waiver at a U.S. consulate in order to apply for permanent residence. This carried the huge risk that their waiver would be denied, blocking their return to the United States for several years.

Fortunately, USCIS announced a 2013 change to the I-601 rules, allowing family-based and other visa applicants to seek a "provisional" or "stateside" I-601 waiver while still in the United States. If the provisional waiver is approved, they can feel relatively safe leaving the U.S. for their green card interview. If the waiver is denied, they can at least remain with family in the U.S. while they pursue any possible legal remedies—though subject to a slight risk that USCIS will place them in removal proceedings.

The applicant must not be inadmissible on any grounds other than unlawful presence in the U.S. of 180 days or more, be age 17 or older, and be (assuming the waiver is granted) otherwise eligible to receive an immigrant visa.

You must also be physically present in the U.S. at the time of submitting your provisional waiver application, which you must send to USCIS after the agency has approved your I-130 petition but before the NVC has scheduled you for an interview at a U.S. consulate. (To get the timing right, you'll need to notify the National Visa Center or NVC of your intent to apply for a provisional waiver right after you pay your immigrant visa processing fee—complexities like this are part of why we advise getting a lawyer if you'll need a waiver!)

The requirement that you be clean of any other grounds of inadmissibility turned into a huge sticking point. For a while, USCIS routinely denied every provisional waiver application in which the applicant had any hint of a criminal record—even if it was just a traffic ticket. Fortunately, after pressure by lawyers and advocates, USCIS issued (in January, 2014) a field memo telling its officers that if the applicant's criminal conviction was either for a "petty offense" or came under the "youthful offender" exception or was not a "crime of moral turpitude," then they should go forward with the application.

Only a lawyer can tell you for sure whether a criminal conviction on your record falls into one of the above categories, however, so be sure to consult with one if you're interested in a provisional waiver and face this issue. USCIS created a brand new application form for this specific waiver; instead of the regular Form I-601, you'll use Form I-601A. The fee for Form I-601A is $630. In addition, applicants under the age of 79 will need to pay the biometrics (fingerprinting) fee, $85 as of early 2019. No fee waiver requests will be considered.

You will also need to attach various documents proving eligibility, most importantly a copy of your I-130 approval notice, proof of your relationship to your qualifying relative and of his or her citizenship or resident status (if it's not your spouse), documents showing that your qualifying relative would suffer extreme hardship if you were denied the U.S. visa, and the receipt showing that you have paid the DOS-required immigrant visa processing fee.

What happens if USCIS denies your I-601A waiver request? Although you cannot appeal, you have a couple of options. One is to file a new I-601A and waiver application with USCIS during the time that your visa case is still pending with the DOS. Of course, there's little point in doing this if you don't provide new or extra information to overcome USCIS's original reason for the denial. Another option is to go ahead with your consular interview and then file the traditional waiver request on Form I-601. This, of course, risks your being unable to return to the U.S. for three or ten years if your waiver application is denied.

Also, if your provisional waiver is denied, you shouldn't worry that U.S. government agents will come knocking on your door. The DHS has specifically stated that it does "not envision initiating removal proceedings against aliens whose Form I-601As are denied or withdrawn prior to final adjudication"—unless, that is, the person "has a criminal history, has committed fraud, or otherwise poses a threat to national security or public safety."

Applying for a regular, I-601 waiver of unlawful presence. If you don't qualify to apply for a provisional waiver, you can still use the old-fashioned route, specifically leaving the U.S. for your consular interview and then submitting Form I-601 ("Application for Waiver of Grounds of Inadmissibility"), with accompanying documents proving the likelihood of extreme hardship to your qualifying relatives, to the U.S. consulate. The stakes are high, however. A denial will result in your being barred from return to the U.S. for three or ten years. Don't attempt this without the help of an experienced immigration attorney.

b. Getting Around the Time Bars by Adjusting Status

One of the strangest features of the time bars is that they apply only to people who are outside the U.S. trying to get in, not to people who are submitting applications while they are in the United States. If you have stayed in the U.S. unlawfully and you are still in the U.S. now, it's essential that, if possible, you stay here in order to avoid the time bars.

Unfortunately, only certain types of people are eligible to adjust (change) their immigration status to get a green card in the United States. The rest will have to leave the country and apply from abroad—and face the potential roadblock of the time bars.

Under current law, only three categories of marriage-based visa applicants are allowed to adjust status and receive their green card in the United States. They include people who:

Who Can Adjust Status in the United States: Summary		
	Applicant is married to a U.S. citizen	Applicant is married to a lawful U.S. permanent resident
Applicant entered the United States illegally	Cannot adjust status unless grandfathered in	Cannot adjust status unless grandfathered in under old laws
Applicant entered the United States legally and is within the expiration date of the visa or status	Okay to adjust status	Can adjust status only if an immigrant visa is immediately available (via a current Priority Date, discussed in Chapters 8 and 12); the person has not violated the terms of any visa; and the person has never worked illegally in the U.S.; or if and when spouse becomes a U.S. citizen or the person is grandfathered in
Applicant entered the United States legally but stayed past the expiration date of visa or status	Okay to adjust status if used no fraud to obtain U.S. entry visa	Cannot adjust status until and unless spouse becomes a U.S. citizen, or the person is grandfathered in

- entered the United States legally and without fraud, and are married to a U.S. citizen, in most cases, no matter how long they have overstayed their visa (I.N.A. §§ 245(a), 245(c)(2); 8 U.S.C. §§ 1255(a), 1255(c)(2))

- entered the U.S. legally, have not overstayed their visa, have never violated any visa terms or worked here illegally, and have a current Priority Date making a visa immediately available to them (Priority Dates are discussed in Chapters 8 and 12; you'll later read whichever chapter is appropriate to your situation). (See I.N.A. §§ 245(a), 245(c)(2), 245(c)(8); 8 U.S.C. §§ 1255(a); 1255(c)(2); 1255(c)(8).) This section includes people who are marrying U.S. permanent residents.

- had initial labor certification or I-130 petitions filed for them long enough ago that their cases must be decided under old laws, which allowed applicants access to the adjustment of status procedure by paying a penalty fee.

Let's look at each of these categories in more detail.

Married to a U.S. citizen and hoping to adjust status. In order to fall under the first category of people who can adjust status without leaving the United States, the applicant will have to prove that he or she entered the United States legally. Legal entries include those with a visa, under the Visa Waiver Program (but see

the caution below), with a border-crossing card, or by some other means so long as the applicant was met and allowed to enter by an official of the U.S. government. The applicant's spouse must be a U.S. citizen, not just a permanent resident.

> **EXAMPLE:** Panos came to the United States on a temporary work visa. He fell in love with Debbie, a U.S. citizen. They got married and took a long honeymoon driving around the United States. The only trouble was, Panos's employer didn't authorize that vacation and fired him—which meant that his work visa was no longer valid. While Panos tried to figure out what to do next, time ticked by. After he had been here unlawfully for six months, he heard about the time bars and panicked. But he didn't need to panic—the combination of his legal entry to the United States and his marriage to a U.S. citizen made him one of the lucky few immigrants who can apply to adjust their status at a USCIS office. Since Panos won't have to leave the United States, he won't be penalized for his unlawful stay.

It does not matter when the spouse became a U.S. citizen—the minute he or she becomes one, an applicant who entered legally becomes eligible to use the adjustment of status procedure. This is true even if the person has overstayed the visa and been staying in the United States illegally.

CAUTION

Visa waiver entrants should check in with an attorney. Up until recently, USCIS was inconsistent when dealing with adjustment of status (green card) applications from Visa Waiver Program (VWP) entrants. Some offices required a "compelling reason" to even consider processing them. However, all field offices should now be accepting adjustment applications from immediate-relative applicants who came into the U.S. on a visa waiver, whether or not they apply within their 90-day period of legal status. In fact, to avoid allegations of visa fraud, anyone whose relationship with the U.S. petitioner began *before* their U.S. entry will need to overstay the 90 days before applying for adjustment. Nevertheless, if a VWP overstay is picked up by ICE and put into removal proceedings before having had a chance to submit the adjustment application, that person cannot adjust status at all, and has no ability to fight removal. Also, if USCIS denies an adjustment application from a VWP entrant, it will order that person to depart the country without first placing him or her into removal proceedings for a second chance before an immigration judge! An exception exists for applicants within the Ninth Circuit of the federal court system. If they filed the Form I-485 adjustment of status application during their 90 days in valid VWP status, they may be placed into removal proceedings after a USCIS denial and allowed to present their case to an immigration judge.

Married to a U.S. permanent resident and hoping to adjust status. It is rare for spouses of permanent residents to be able to use the adjustment of status procedure. To do so, you would have to prove that:

- your most recent entry into the U.S. was legal
- you have not violated the terms of your recent entry visa or any other past visa
- you never worked illegally in the U.S., and
- you are immediately eligible to apply for permanent residence, meaning you've already spent the months or years required on the government's waiting list, there is a visa number available to you, and the government is ready to let you take the final steps toward applying for your green card.

It would be highly unusual for anyone with a time bar problem to fit into this category. Even for people with no time bar problem, this combination of circumstances rarely occurs, but it could.

EXAMPLE: Megumi enters the United States as a student to enroll at UCLA. She falls in love with Shigeru, a U.S. permanent resident, and they marry six months later. He immediately files an initial petition with USCIS and Megumi is put on the waiting list. Five years later, while she's still working toward her degree, she reaches the top of the list and is allowed to apply for a green card. Since she has been legally in the United States, has not violated her student visa, and now has a visa number currently available to her, she can adjust her status to permanent resident in the United States.

Adjustment of status possibilities for petitions filed long ago and before certain deadlines. To fall into the third category, a family member or employer must have started the immigration process for you a long time ago. In the mid-1990s, Congress passed a piece of legislation called "Section 245(i)" of the immigration law. Section 245(i) said that anyone who was eligible for a green card, even if they entered illegally or were only married to a lawful permanent resident, could use the adjustment of status procedure so long as they paid a large penalty fee. It didn't matter how they entered the U.S. or whom they married. Section 245(i) allowed many people to avoid the hassle of leaving the U.S. to do consular processing—and if it had remained on the law books, would have allowed a number of people to avoid the time bars.

But in 1998 Congress decided not to renew Section 245(i). The only people who can still use it are those for whom an employer or family member began their immigration process (such as by filing a labor certification or Form I-130) before certain dates. We will cover Form I-130 later, but briefly, it is the first filing that any couple submits, and your U.S. citizen or permanent resident wife or husband would probably be the one who submitted it for you. You would probably know if one had been submitted for you. Ideally, you would have an approved I-130. But if your petition was mistakenly denied for some reason, you may still be able to use the petition to adjust your status to permanent resident (though you would likely need a lawyer's help for this).

You can be grandfathered in and allowed to use the old Section 245(i) if your I-130 (or a labor certification by employer) was submitted to the INS (as USCIS was then called) either:

- Before January 14, 1998 (the day § 245(i) was originally allowed to expire), or
- Between January 14, 1998 and April 30, 2001, if you can prove that you were physically present in the United States on December 21, 2000 (the day the legislation temporarily renewing § 245(i) was signed).

If your husband or wife did not submit an I-130 for you by one of these two dates, you may not be out of luck yet. In a wonderful policy move, USCIS has said that it will allow you to use an I-130 or labor certification filed by anyone on your behalf. If you had a prospective employer or a close family member (such as a parent, child, or brother) who tried to start the immigration process for you by filing a case before one of the dates listed above, that filing is transferable. It can become your ticket to using the adjustment of status procedure to apply for a green card in the United States based on your current marriage.

To make use of the option of being grandfathered in under Section 245(i), you'll still have to pay a hefty penalty fee, currently $1,000 (I.N.A. § 245(i); 8 U.S.C. § 1255(i)).

If you are eligible to adjust status—that is, apply for your green card in the United States—you would be wise to take advantage of this procedure, especially if you have a time bar problem. Do not leave the United States until your adjustment of status application is pending and you have received what's called "Advance Parole" (explained in Chapter 14).

c. The Permanent Bar

The permanent bar applies to certain people who spend a total of one year's unlawful time in the United States or have been ordered deported (even after spending less than one year there). If such a person then leaves and returns or attempts to return to the United States illegally (without a visa or other permission) he or she becomes permanently inadmissible to the United States.

This law is one of the harshest aspects of the immigration laws. (It is found at I.N.A. § 212(a)(9)(C); 8 U.S.C. § 1182(a)(9)(C).)

Unlike the three- and ten-year time bars, the permanent bar applies only to people who have entered the United States illegally, or are trying to. If the total of all their previous stays is one year or more, then that person will never be allowed back into the United States or given a green card when they apply for one here.

The law took effect on April 1, 1997, so no illegal time before that date counts. Also, an applicant can request a waiver (official forgiveness), but only after a full ten years have passed since leaving the United States. And you cannot avoid the penalty by staying in the United States to adjust status.

EXAMPLE 1: Cosimo came to the United States in 2016 on a three-month tourist visa. He stayed past the visa's expiration date and didn't leave until 2018; so he accrued over one year of illegal time. Then he went to Canada and lived there for a while. But he missed his U.S. citizen girlfriend, so he came back with a friend, who hid him in the back of his truck. Cosimo and his girlfriend married and he applied for a green card. However, the combination of his previous stay and his subsequent illegal entry is poison. He is subject to the permanent bar and cannot get a green card through his wife unless he spends the next ten years outside of the United States, remains married, and successfully convinces the U.S. government to forgive him.

EXAMPLE 2: Jorge lives in Mexico, near the El Paso border. He is a pro at crossing illegally and picking up odd jobs on both sides of the border. Between April 1, 1997 and July 2017 he crossed the border illegally at least 17 times and stayed between two weeks and three months each time. The combination of all his stays, however, adds up to more than a year. When he marries his U.S. citizen girlfriend in July 2019 and tries to apply for a green card, he is hit with the permanent bar. Only if he can stay out and stay married for ten years can he apply for a waiver to return and claim permanent residency.

Here on a Temporary Employment Visa? The Risks of Applying for a Green Card

Are you already in the U.S. on an employment-based visa, and now want to apply for a green card through marriage? Be careful: Becoming a permanent resident can be trickier than you might expect.

Most employment-based visas are "nonimmigrant" visas. This means that the visa was granted on the understanding that, after you have finished working in the U.S. for a predefined period, you would return to your home country. When you applied for your employment-based visa, you likely assured the consular officer that you intended to leave the U.S. once your work was done.

Starting the immigrant visa process and applying for a green card is a bit like setting off fireworks around you. Not only does the process draw a lot of attention, it also signals your intention to stay in the U.S. permanently. You probably already recognize the problem: Although you promised the consulate, under oath, that you would eventually leave the U.S., your green card application is a break in that promise. This can have serious consequences. Not only could immigration authorities (depending on the facts of your situation) charge you with lying to a consular officer, they can also revoke your employment-based visa and remove your ability to work in the United States.

Thankfully, the U.S. government recognized that disallowing all nonimmigrant workers from seeking permanent residence in the U.S. through marriage could be incredibly burdensome. Certain nonimmigrant visas benefit from a concept called "dual intent." This allows nonimmigrant workers to intend to eventually leave the U.S.—while seeking a green card and permanent residence all at the same time. This is perhaps one of the strangest legal concepts in all of U.S. immigration law. Regardless, the benefit to you is obvious: If you're in the U.S. on an employment-based visa that allows dual intent, you can pursue permanent residence and not worry.

Only certain types of employment-based visas benefit from dual intent. They include the H-1B, L-1, and to a lesser extent, E-1, E-2, and O-1 visas. If you are in the U.S. on an employment-based visa that does not allow dual intent, try speaking with your employer about possible sponsorship under one of the visa types that does. For more specific questions, consult an immigration attorney.

SEE AN EXPERT

If you think you might be subject to the permanent bar, see a lawyer immediately. Chapter 17 has tips on finding a good attorney.

d. Proving You Didn't Stay Unlawfully

The first question anyone asks when they hear about the time bars is, "How will anyone know? The United States is a huge country, and even with space-age technology, its government can't possibly trace who was living there and when."

For one thing, the U.S. government keeps travel records of all noncitizens who are lawfully admitted to the U.S. (but don't have a green card), by using Form I-94. People who overstay their permitted time under a visa or visa waiver can be identified on this basis.

But the real question to ask is, "What happens if they suspect that I was here illegally?" Because as soon as there is a hint that you might have lived in the United States illegally, it becomes your problem. You have to prove to the U.S. government that you didn't live there illegally, not the other way around. People in this situation must come up with copies of their plane tickets, rent receipts, credit card statements, pay stubs, medical records, school transcripts, and more, all to prove that they were in the United States until a certain date and then left.

EXAMPLE: Siri came to the United States from Norway on a six-month tourist visa in March 2018, but didn't leave until January of 2019—a four-month overstay. Her U.S. citizen boyfriend then petitioned for her as his fiancé. Everything was going fine until she went to the U.S. consulate in Norway for the final interview to get her fiancé visa. Siri explained the four-month overstay, knowing that this wasn't long enough to subject her to any penalty, not even the three-year bar. But the consulate demanded proof that she wasn't in the United States longer than four months. Siri had lived with her parents after she got home and had thrown out her plane tickets. She had no paperwork with her to prove when she had returned to Norway. Luckily, the consulate gave her more time and she eventually came up with a copy of her frequent flier statement showing the date of her travel, as well as a prescription that she got in February 2019 in Oslo. The visa was granted.

TIP
If you have spent any time in the United States since 1997, make sure you are prepared to prove that you returned home on time. Begin gathering all relevant documents now, such as rent receipts, plane tickets, credit card statements, and more.

B. Are You Eligible for a Fiancé or Marriage-Based Visa or Green Card?

Section A above should have helped you determine whether you can get through the first door, which screens who is admissible to the United States. Now we're moving to the second door: Are you eligible for the particular type of visa or green card that you are seeking? This book covers two basic choices: the fiancé visa and the marriage-based visa or green card.

Remember, we're not yet talking about the procedures to get these visas and green cards—this will come later. Of course, since we haven't gotten to the procedures yet, you might feel uncertain about which visa you'll be using. For now, it is safe to assume that you will be applying for a fiancé visa only if you are presently living overseas and are engaged to a U.S. citizen (but not a permanent resident, since there are no fiancé visas for people engaged to permanent residents) and want to hold your wedding in the United States. Everyone else should apply for a marriage-based visa or green card. (In the unlikely event that you later decide that you want or need the other visa, don't worry—the eligibility criteria are so similar that you won't have wasted your time.)

SKIP AHEAD
Everyone applying for a marriage-based visa or green card, not a fiancé visa, skip ahead to Section 3.

1. The Legal Requirements for a K-1 Fiancé Visa

A fiancé visa will get you into the United States to get married. To be eligible for a fiancé visa, you do not have to intend to live permanently in the U.S. after your marriage. Whether you decide to stay in the U.S. and apply for a green card is up to you. (If you know in advance that you won't be staying in the U.S., however, you could apply for a tourist visa instead—but see Chapter 5 for more on the risks and benefits of using that visa.)

In order to be eligible for a fiancé visa, the law requires that you:

- intend to marry a U.S. citizen (see Subsections a and b, below)
- have met your intended spouse in person within the last two years (though this can be waived based on cultural customs or extreme hardship; see Subsection c), and
- are legally able to marry (see Subsection d).

You'll need to provide more than just your assurances. Part of the application process involves submitting convincing documents showing that your intentions match these eligibility criteria. This task has become harder under the Trump administration, which has targeted K-1 visa applicants for extra scrutiny, believing this visa is a legal "loophole" allowing terrorists to gain U.S. entry. Approval rates of the K-1 visa are reportedly down by a third.

a. You Must Intend to Marry

The requirement that you intend to marry might seem obvious—you wouldn't be applying for a fiancé visa otherwise. But the U.S. government will want proof that you've made actual plans, such as a place, a type of ceremony or proceedings (even if the proceedings are only in front of a judge), and more. We'll talk more about how to provide this evidence in the chapter matching your individual situation, below.

TIP

Make your wedding plans flexible. You can't know exactly how long it will take to get the fiancé visa, but you'll have to hold your wedding within 90 days of entering the United States. Before you sign any contracts for catering, photographic, or other services, discuss the situation with them and build some flexibility into your contracts or agreements in case the date needs to change.

b. Your Intended Spouse Must Be a U.S. Citizen

To be eligible for a fiancé visa, the person that you plan to marry must be a citizen, not a permanent resident, of the United States. A U.S. citizen is someone who either was:

- born in the United States or its territories
- became a citizen through application and testing (called naturalization), or
- acquired or derived citizenship through a family member. (Acquisition and derivation of citizenship are complex areas of the law. In general, however, people may acquire citizenship by being born abroad to one or two U.S. citizen parents; they may derive citizenship if they are lawful permanent residents first and one of their parents is or becomes a U.S. citizen.)

RESOURCE

To learn more about acquired and derived citizenship: See the free article "U.S. Citizenship by Birth or Through Parents," on Nolo's website at www.nolo.com. Or see *U.S. Immigration Made Easy*, by Ilona Bray (Nolo).

Unlike some countries, the United States does not require that its citizens carry any sort of national identity card. People who are U.S. citizens may have different types of documents that prove their status, such as a birth certificate, a U.S. passport, or a naturalization certificate. We'll talk more in later chapters about how your spouse can obtain documentary proof of citizenship that will satisfy the immigration authorities.

CAUTION

Permanent residents of the United States—also known as green card holders—are not U.S. citizens. If your spouse is only a permanent resident, he or she can petition to obtain permanent residency for you, but your marriage must already have taken place—there are no fiancé visas available to you.

c. You Must Have Met in Person Within the Last Two Years

To protect against sham marriages, the law also requires that you and your intended have met in person within the last two years in order to be eligible for a fiancé visa. These days, a surprising number of couples fall in love over the Internet. Such couples will need to make sure they schedule at least one in-person meeting in the two years before submitting a petition for the fiancé visa (Form I-129F). Even a brief meeting may be sufficient.

In some countries, prospective husbands and wives customarily do not meet before their wedding. If one or both of you come from a country where such a meeting would not be acceptable, you may find the meeting requirement a bit of a hurdle. Fortunately, if you provide documentation of the prevailing customs in your country, USCIS may overlook this requirement.

EXAMPLE: Dimple, a 21-year-old native and resident of India, is engaged to Athar, a naturalized U.S. citizen. Athar is 29 years old and lives and works in California. Athar remembers seeing Dimple playing in a nearby courtyard when they were both children in India. They have exchanged recent photos and their parents, who are very traditional, have approved a marriage. Athar and Dimple will have no problem with two of the three eligibility criteria: they intend to marry (they can show evidence of wedding arrangements in California) and they are legally able to marry (for example, neither is underage, and neither is already married to someone else). But they don't meet the third eligibility criterion, since they haven't personally met within the last two years. To overcome this obstacle, in their application they include a letter from their religious leader, sworn statements by their parents, and other documents showing that they come from families and a culture where arranged marriage without a face-to-face meeting is an important and accepted practice. USCIS may waive the in-person meeting requirement.

Expect skepticism from USCIS, however. Most cultures allow some level of in-person meeting between the potential bride and groom, and USCIS knows it. If there is any precedent within the culture of allowing in-person meetings, USCIS will deny the waiver.

The meeting requirement may also be waived if the U.S. citizen spouse can show that arranging a physical meeting would result in extreme hardship to him or her. This exception is usually granted only in cases where the U.S. citizen suffers from severe medical problems that would make an overseas visit difficult.

> **EXAMPLE:** Tom is a U.S. citizen confined to a wheelchair. He has severe environmental and food allergies. It is unsafe for him to leave the controlled environment of his home. He is also an Internet junkie and has been corresponding with Kathy, a native of Australia, for the last three years. They have exchanged not only emails, but photos and even videos, and have decided to marry. By providing copies of their communications with one another, as well as a letter from Tom's doctor and copies of his medical records, the couple may be able to obtain a waiver of the meeting requirement so that Kathy can enter the United States as a fiancé.

> ! **CAUTION**
> **Seeking a waiver of the two-year meeting requirement will delay visa approval.** The waiver review often adds five to 12 months to the process. Even if you have a strong case, USCIS might well deny your initial waiver application, thus forcing you through an appeal process, which adds even more time.

Financial concerns are not usually considered sufficient to prove extreme hardship. In fact, the very request could make USCIS think the U.S. petitioner is in no financial position to sponsor an immigrant. (Remember that the U.S. consulate will require the fiancé to demonstrate that he or she is not inadmissible as a likely "public charge.")

Dangerous country conditions are also rarely grounds for a successful "extreme hardship" waiver of the meeting requirement. Even if your fiancé lives somewhere that's unsafe for a U.S. citizen to visit, USCIS can deny the waiver on grounds that the two of you should be able to meet in a neutral third country. Even if your fiancé's country only rarely issues travel permits to any country, USCIS will most likely not consider this an extreme hardship.

The bottom line is that the bar to demonstrating extreme hardship to the U.S. citizen is high. Simply showing that meeting in person would be inconvenient, more expensive, or more difficult is not going to suffice.

d. You Must Be Legally Able to Marry

Last but not least, to be eligible for a fiancé visa there must not be any legal barrier to your getting married. You may not have to provide anything at all to satisfy this requirement if you're an adult who's never been previously married and you're not a blood relative of your fiancé. This requirement is primarily directed at couples in which:

- one person is underage
- one person has been previously married and needs to prove that that marriage was legally ended, or
- the two members of the couple are related by blood.

Age. If one of you is under the age of 18, you may be considered underage. Your legal ability to marry will depend on the laws of the state where you plan to get married. Each of the 50 U.S. states sets its own rules, and you will need to research them. For example, you may find that in one state you must be 18 years of age to marry, while in another you can marry younger if you can show the consent of your parents.

Previous marriages. If you or your fiancé have been previously married, you will not be given a fiancé visa until you prove that that marriage was legally ended, for example by death, divorce, or annulment. This is usually easily proven, by obtaining copies of records from the court or local civic records office. If your divorce or annulment occurred overseas, the U.S. government will recognize it as long as it is recognized in the country where it took place, and as long as at least one of the divorcing parties had a residence in the place where the divorce took place.

Blood relationship. If you and your fiancé are blood relations, your legal ability to marry will depend on the laws of the state where you plan to get married. You will need to research these rules. You'll find that all states prohibit marrying your sister or brother (sibling), half sibling, parent, grandparent, great grandparent, child, grandchild, great grandchild, aunt, uncle, niece, or nephew. But some states have additional prohibitions, such as marrying your first cousin.

2. Your Children's Eligibility for a K-2 Visa

Your unmarried children under the age of 21, whether or not they are the biological children of your U.S. citizen fiancé, may be eligible to accompany you to the United States on your fiancé visa (they'll get "K-2" visas) and apply for green cards. Children include not only your natural children, but your adopted children and children born out of wedlock, if your home country legally recognizes them as yours.

Don't be confused by the fact that already-married applicants need to prove that their children fit the definition of "stepchildren," by showing that the parents' marriage took place before the children turned 18. You, as a fiancé visa applicant, don't need to fit those criteria. The only reason we even mention it is that immigration officials themselves sometimes get confused about it and try to deny K-2 fiancé visas to children who are over 18 but still under age 21. (If this happens to you, understand that the official has gotten the laws mixed up, and suggest reading 8 C.F.R. § 214.2(k)(6)(ii).)

Your children will have to go through the same (or a very similar) application process as you. They'll have to prove that they are not inadmissible and that they will be financially supported along with you. This book will give you an overview of the application procedures that your children will have to follow, but will not cover them in great detail.

For your planning purposes, however, note that the children must remain unmarried and under age 21 right up to the day they enter the United States on their K-2 visas. Fortunately, if you alert the immigration authorities to an upcoming 21st birthday, they can usually speed up the application process for you. (Unfortunately, a law you may have heard of called the Child Status Protection Act does not protect children on fiancé visas from the loss of visa rights caused by turning 21.)

> **CAUTION**
> **Check your own country's law on taking your children if their other parent is staying behind.** If you are planning to bring children to the United States who are not the biological children of your fiancé, it will be up to you to comply with any custody requirements. Even if the children are legally in your custody, you may need to get written consent from the other parent for you to take the children out of your country.

3. The Legal Requirements for a Marriage-Based Visa or Green Card

If you are already married to a U.S. citizen or permanent resident, you will apply for a marriage-based visa or green card. To be legally eligible, you and your spouse must show that you are:

- legally married (see Subsection a, below)
- in a bona fide marriage (see Subsection b, below)
- married to a U.S. citizen or lawful permanent resident (see Subsection c, below), and
- that neither you nor your spouse are married to anyone else (see Subsection d, below).

a. You Are Legally Married

To qualify for a marriage-based visa or green card, you must be legally married. A legal marriage is one that is officially recognized by the government in the country or state where you were married. This usually means that an official record of your marriage has been made or can be obtained from some public office.

For this reason, domestic partnerships, in which a couple lives together but have not formalized their relationship, are not normally recognized for immigration purposes. However, if you have lived together in a place that recognizes common law marriages, you may be able to show that you met the requirements for your marriage to be legally recognized in that state or country. We do not cover common law situations in this book. If you are in this circumstance, you may want to consult an attorney.

You do not need to have been married in the United States for your marriage to be legal. It is perfectly acceptable if you marry in your home country or in the luxurious or adventurous travel destination of your choice.

If you're part of a same-sex couple, make sure that not only does the country in question recognize same-sex marriages, but that it does so in a form that the U.S. government also recognizes. Consult an immigration attorney for details. You'll also find help from the article entitled "Where Can We Marry?" on the Immigration Equality website (immigrationequality.org).

A variety of marriage procedures are also recognized, from church weddings to customary tribal practices. But note that both you and your spouse must have actually attended your wedding ceremony—so-called "proxy" marriages, where another person stands in for the bride or groom, are not recognized by the U.S. government unless the couple later consummates the marriage, meaning they have sexual relations.

If you have not yet married, make sure you are eligible to do so. The state or federal government where you intend to marry may have legal restrictions on who can marry. In the United States, each of the 50 states establishes its own marriage rules. For example, in some states you must be 18 years of age to marry, while in others you can marry younger if you can have the consent of your parents. Only some states recognize same-sex marriages. If you and your spouse are related by blood, you'll also need to do some research. You'll find that all states prohibit marrying your sister or brother (sibling), half sibling, parent, grandparent, great grandparent, child, grandchild, great grandchild, aunt, uncle, niece, or nephew. But some states have additional prohibitions, such as marrying your first cousin.

Finally, you will need to provide a document to show you were legally married—most commonly, a marriage certificate issued by a legitimate governmental agency. A piece of paper from a church or a ship's captain won't, on its own, be enough to establish that you really are married. How you'll go about providing the appropriate documentation will be covered in later chapters.

b. Your Marriage Is "Bona Fide"

A bona fide marriage is one in which the two people intend, from the start, to establish a life together. Although this can mean different things to different people, one thing is clear: A marriage entered into for the sole purpose of getting the immigrant a green card is not bona fide. (It's called a "sham" or "fraudulent" marriage, and uncovering these relationships is a top USCIS priority.) When it comes to deciding whether a marriage is bona fide, USCIS is pretty strict.

EXAMPLE 1: Yoko has been studying in the United States for four years. She would like to stay permanently, but can't find an employer to sponsor her. A classmate tells her that for $5,000, he'll marry her and take care of sponsoring her as an immigrant. If Yoko agrees, this will be a classic case of marriage fraud.

EXAMPLE 2: Ermelinda and Joe are very close friends, who have occasionally had sexual relations, but are not now romantically involved. Ermelinda came to the United States on a student visa. However, because she dropped out of school, she no longer has any legal status or right to remain in the United States. When Ermelinda is threatened with deportation, Joe, a U.S. citizen, would like to help her. He figures he can live with her for a few years and then move on. Joe and Ermelinda get married. In the eyes of USCIS, this is marriage fraud.

EXAMPLE 3: Viktor and Bert have been living together in the United States since not long after Viktor came here on a student visa, two years ago. They are in love and have talked about marriage, but were nagged by doubts as to whether their marriage would work out. But when Viktor's student status ran out, he realized he'd either have to marry Bert or leave and return to Russia. They marry and apply for his green card. This case is basically bona fide, since the relationship is real—but they will need to be careful in presenting it at the eventual green card interview. Viktor and Bert shouldn't offer up information about their doubts about the marriage. If this subject does arise, they'll emphasize their intention to make their marriage last.

c. You Married a Citizen or Permanent Resident of the United States

There are only two classes of people living in the United States who can obtain permanent residency or green cards for their spouses through the process described in this book: U.S. citizens and U.S. lawful permanent residents (green card holders). People with temporary rights to live in the United States (such as visas or work permits) cannot petition for their spouse to become a permanent resident.

i. Determining Whether Your Spouse Is a U.S. Citizen

Your spouse may have become a U.S. citizen in a variety of ways, including the following:

- being born in the United States or its territories
- becoming a citizen through application and testing (called naturalization), or
- acquiring or deriving citizenship through a family member. (Acquisition and derivation of citizenship are complex areas of the law. In general, however, people may acquire citizenship by being born abroad to one or two U.S. citizen parents; they may derive citizenship if they become lawful permanent residents first and then their parents are or become U.S. citizens.)

RESOURCE
Want to learn more about acquired and derived citizenship? Visit Nolo's website at www.nolo.com, see *U.S. Immigration Made Easy*, by Ilona Bray (Nolo), or ask your local nonprofit organization serving immigrants for more information.

Unlike some countries, the United States does not require that its citizens carry any sort of national identity card. People who are U.S. citizens may have different types of documents that prove their status, such as a birth certificate, a U.S. passport, or a naturalization certificate. We'll talk more in later chapters about how your spouse can obtain documentary proof of his or her citizenship that will satisfy the immigration authorities.

ii. Determining Whether Your Spouse Is a U.S. Lawful Permanent Resident

A lawful permanent resident is someone with a legally obtained green card. This means that the person has a right to live in the United States permanently and may eventually become a U.S. citizen. The spouses of permanent residents are eligible for a green card.

You should know, however, that the fact that your spouse has a green card now doesn't guarantee that he or she will have it forever. Permanent residence can be lost, for example, if the person makes his or her home outside the United States or commits certain crimes or other acts that cause USCIS to begin removal proceedings and order deportation. If your spouse lost permanent residence, you would also lose your right to immigrate through your marriage.

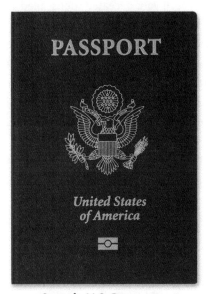

Sample U.S. Passport

CAUTION

A green card is not the same thing as an Employment Authorization Document, border crossing card, or SENTRI card. If your spouse carries a card with any of these titles, he or she is not a permanent resident. These cards grant the temporary right either to work in or gain entry to the United States. You can't get a green card through someone who only has one of these cards.

Sample U.S. Green Card

d. This Is Your and Your Spouse's Only Marriage

Most people would love to leave their previous marriages far behind them. However, the U.S. government doesn't make it that easy if you want to enter this country via a new marriage. Any previous marriages must have ended by legal means—such as death, divorce, or annulment—and you'll have to present the official documents to prove it. Otherwise, USCIS will wonder whether your first marriage is still your active and real one—making your new marriage just a sham to get a green card.

We'll talk more in later chapters about how to obtain the appropriate documents to prove a prior marriage has ended.

4. Your Children's Eligibility

Your foreign-born children, whether or not they are the biological children of your petitioning spouse, may be eligible to obtain green cards along with you. It won't happen automatically, however. They will have to go through the same or a very similar application process as you do. They'll have to prove that they are not inadmissible and that they will be financially supported along with you.

If your children are unmarried and under age 21, they will (with very few exceptions, as you'll see below) be placed in the same category of applicant as you. The result will be that they get a visa or green card at the same time as you do.

If your children are married or over age 21, they may or may not be able to get a visa, and any visa they might get will take years longer than yours to obtain. Their eligibility will depend in part on whether your spouse is a U.S. citizen or a permanent resident, as discussed in Subsections b and c, below.

a. Who Counts as a Child

Some of the visa possibilities for your children will depend on a biological parent-child relationship between your new citizen or permanent resident spouse and your child. Luckily, immigration law also recognizes certain nonbiological parent-child relationships, and includes the following as "children."

What If Your Spouse Dies Before You Get Your Green Card?

The last thing you probably need—or want—to worry about right now is whether your U.S. petitioner will pass away unexpectedly while you're in middle of the green card application process. For anyone affected by the untimely passing of a U.S. citizen spouse, however, at least know that in 2009, Congress changed the law to allow the surviving spouse of a U.S. citizen to petition for him- or herself, regardless of the length of the marriage prior to the spouse's death. This changed the old law, which had required the couple to have been married for at least two years at the time the U.S. citizen died in order for the surviving spouse to self-petition.

If you find yourself in this position, make sure you file your self-petition within two years of your U.S. citizen spouse's death.

You may include your children who are under 21 years old on the petition. You will still have to show that you and your spouse had a bona fide marriage, and that you have not remarried.

If you are the spouse of a deceased lawful permanent resident, you cannot self-petition the way the spouse of a deceased U.S. citizen can, but there are some other "survivor benefits" in the new law that might help you. If your deceased spouse filed a petition for you, you (and your children) may be able to adjust status once your Priority Date becomes current, despite the death of your spouse. If you are outside the country, under certain conditions USCIS may grant "humanitarian reinstatement" of the I-130 petition and may allow you to get your immigrant visa through consular processing.

Consult an immigration attorney for help and the latest information.

- Your children who have become the stepchildren of your petitioning spouse, as long as your marriage took place before the child turned 18. Children who were born out of wedlock or legally adopted by you will qualify.
- Children born to unmarried parents. This provision might come in handy if you and your spouse had a child before you were married, but the child doesn't qualify as your spouse's stepchild because the marriage took place after the child's 18th birthday. If your petitioning spouse is the child's mother, the case is handled just like any other. If the petitioner is the child's father, however, he will have to prove that he was the biological father, and either had a bona fide (real) relationship with the child before the child turned 21 (such as living together or financial support), or took legal steps to formally "legitimate" the child before its 18th birthday. At the time of legitimation, the child must have been in the legal custody of the father.

b. Children's Visa Eligibility If Your Spouse Is a U.S. Citizen

If your spouse is a U.S. citizen and your unmarried children under 21 are his or her biological children or legal stepchildren (you married when they were under age 18), they qualify for green cards as his or her immediate relatives. Immediate relatives are given high legal priority, with no quotas or waiting periods to slow their receipt of a green card. Their green card should be approved at the same time as yours (provided they remain unmarried).

If any of your children marry before they receive their visa or green card, they will automatically drop into category 3 of the Visa Preference System, which is subject to even longer waiting periods than category 1. (For more details, see Chapter 6 and Chapter 16, Section D, "Sponsoring Other Family Members.")

What if one of your children turns 21 before receiving a visa or green card? Formerly, they would have dropped into category 1 of the Visa Preference System, but that was changed with the Child Status

Protection Act of 2002. As long as a child was under 21 when the I-130 petition was filed, the child will still be considered an immediate relative even after turning 21.

c. Children's Visa Eligibility If Your Spouse Is a Permanent Resident

If your spouse has a U.S. green card, your children who are unmarried and under age 21 are considered derivative beneficiaries. As a practical matter, this means that your children won't need a separate initial petition in order to be included in your immigration process. Unlike many other applicants, they also won't need to prove that your spouse is their parent or even stepparent, because they are riding on your application. (Eventually, however, they will have to fill out some forms of their own.) They will share your place on the visa/green card waiting list, and most likely get a visa at the same time as you (provided they remain unmarried).

Your children who have gotten married will not be able to immigrate to the United States at the same time as you. They will have no visa options until your spouse becomes a U.S. citizen and files an I-130 petition for them in category 3 of the Visa Preference System (which has a very long waiting period). Of course, to do this, your spouse would have to prove that he or she is the child's legal stepparent or biological parent.

Another issue to be aware of is how turning 21 will affect your child's eligibility for a visa or green card. If your child turns 21 before his or her Priority Date has become current (that is, before visas are being allotted to people who applied at the same time as you), the child could, in theory, "age out," or drop into a lower Visa Preference category (2B), with a longer waiting period. Thanks to the Child Status Protection Act (CSPA) however, a child can actually turn 21 without turning 21 in the eyes of the law! That's because the law allows you to subtract from the child's age the amount of time that it took USCIS to approve your family's immigrant petition.

For children who turn 21 after their Priority Date becomes current, the news is better—they can keep their 2A status—but there's a catch. The child who has turned 21 must submit his or her green card application within a year of when the Priority Date became current—just another good reason to keep a close watch on the *Visa Bulletin*.

For more details on how your children could move between visa categories, see Chapter 8 or 12, below, depending on which chapter matches your situation. (Also see Chapter 16, Section D, "Sponsoring Other Family Members," for help with children who aren't eligible to immigrate at the same time as you.)

CAUTION

If your spouse becomes a U.S. citizen, the picture changes. You will need to review Section 4b, above, to determine your children's visa eligibility.

NEXT STEP

At this point you should know whether you are eligible to apply for a marriage or a fiancé visa. If you are, read Chapters 3 and 4 before turning to the chapter that explains your application process in detail.

Meeting Income Requirements

Not everyone marries a millionaire, unfortunately (or not). Before any fiancé or spouse can immigrate, the U.S. citizen or permanent resident half of the couple must reveal his or her financial situation to the immigration authorities. The purpose is to show enough money to support the immigrant and to prevent him or her from becoming a public charge (the legal term for receiving government assistance or going on welfare). Any immigrant who appears likely to rely on publicly funded programs that support poor people is inadmissible. Requiring this showing of financial support is a way of testing the immigrant's admissibility.

Every U.S. fiancé or spouse petitioning for an immigrant must fill out a government form called an Affidavit of Support. Sponsors of fiancés use the Form I-134 affidavit; sponsors of spouses use Form I-864 (even if they earlier filled out a Form I-134). By filling out either form, your U.S. fiancé or spouse becomes what is known as your sponsor. As you'll see, however, additional people can also serve as financial sponsors.

A number of fiancé and green card applications are held up over the issue of whether the U.S. citizen or resident half of the couple can financially support the immigrant. The government has a very specific idea of how much money it takes to support someone.

But even if your fiancé or spouse fills out the Affidavit of Support in a manner that shows that his or her income and assets meet this government-established minimum, the consulates and USCIS have the power to look at the bigger picture and decide that you are likely to become a public charge anyway. For example, your application could be denied if you have chronic health problems, are elderly, or your fiancé or spouse's income barely meets the minimum and you appear to be unemployable.

TIP

Married U.S. citizens with long work histories and long marriages may be able to avoid filling out an Affidavit of Support (Form I-864). The reason is that their obligations to act as sponsors end after the immigrant has worked 40 quarters (about ten years)—but, in an interesting twist, immigrants can be credited with work done by their U.S. citizen spouses while they were married. So, if your U.S. citizen spouse has worked 40 quarters in the U.S. during your marriage, he or she need not fill out Form I-864. Though it's the rare married couple who will have gone this many years without applying for a green card, this exception is highly useful for those to whom it applies. Use Form I-864W (available at www.uscis.gov) to help determine whether you are able to avoid the Form I-864 requirement and to show the immigration authorities if you are in fact exempt.

A. Meeting the Minimum Requirements

The minimum financial requirements for Affidavits of Support are determined according to the U.S. government's *Poverty Guidelines* chart, reproduced below and found on immigration Form I-864P.

Green card applicants must show that their sponsor is able to support them at 125% of the *Poverty Guidelines*.

Also, the baseline amounts are somewhat different for sponsors living in Alaska and Hawaii than for those in the 48 contiguous states, Washington DC, Puerto Rico, the U.S. Virgin Islands, Guam, and the Commonwealth of the Northern Mariana Islands:

According to the Department of State, fiancé applicants need only to show that their sponsor is able to support them at 100% of the *Poverty Guidelines*. However, because the Affidavit of Support stays in the fiancé applicant's file, it is to the fiancé's advantage if the sponsor can already show an income level at or above the 125% guideline. That way, when (and if) the fiancé later applies for a green card, the financial requirement will have already been met. In addition, some consular officers are particularly strict in dealing with fiancé visas, and consider the 125% level that will be required when you apply for your green card. Other officers may simply apply the "eyeball" test for fiancés—if you look young and healthy, you're in.

2019 HHS Poverty Guidelines for Affidavit of Support

Means-Tested Public Benefits

Excerpted from online Form I-864P, at www.uscis.gov/i-864p.

Federal Means-Tested Public Benefits: To date, federal agencies administering benefit programs have determined that federal means-tested public benefits include food stamps, Medicaid, Supplemental Security Income (SSI), Temporary Assistance for Needy Families (TANF), and the State Child Health Insurance Program (SCHIP).

State Means-Tested Public Benefits: Each state will determine which, if any, of its public benefits are means-tested. If a state determines that it has programs which meet this definition, it is encouraged to provide notice to the public on which programs are included. Check with the state public assistance office to determine which, if any, state assistance programs have been determined to be state means-tested public benefits

Programs Not Included: The following federal and state programs are not included as means-tested benefits:

- Emergency Medicaid;
- Short-term, non-cash emergency relief;
- Services provided under the National School Lunch and Child Nutrition Acts;
- Immunizations and testing and treatment for communicable diseases;
- Student assistance under the Higher Education Act and the Public Health Service Act;
- Certain forms of foster-care or adoption assistance under the Social Security Act;
- Head Start programs;
- Means-tested programs under the Elementary and Secondary Education Act; and
- Job Training Partnership Act programs.

For the 48 Contiguous States, the District of Columbia, Puerto Rico, the U.S. Virgin Islands, Guam, and the Commonwealth of the Northern Mariana Islands:

Sponsor's Household Size	100% of HHS Poverty Guidelines	125% of HHS Poverty Guidelines
	For sponsors on active duty in the U.S. armed forces who are petitioning for their spouse or child	*For all other sponsors*
2	$16,910	$21,137
3	$21,330	$26,662
4	$25,750	$32,187
5	$30,170	$37,712
6	$34,590	$43,237
7	$39,010	$48,762
8	$43,430	$54,287
	Add $4,420 for each additional person	**Add $5,525 for each additional person**

2019 HHS Poverty Guidelines for Affidavit of Support (continued)

For Alaska:

Sponsor's Household Size	100% of HHS Poverty Guidelines	125% of HHS Poverty Guidelines
	For sponsors on active duty in the U.S. armed forces who are petitioning for their spouse or child	*For all other sponsors*
2	$21,130	$26,412
3	$26,660	$33,325
4	$32,190	$40,237
5	$37,720	$47,150
6	$43,250	$54,062
7	$48,780	$60,975
8	$54,310	$67,887
	Add $5,530 for each additional person	**Add $6,912 for each additional person**

For Hawaii:

Sponsor's Household Size	100% of HHS Poverty Guidelines	125% of HHS Poverty Guidelines
	For sponsors on active duty in the U.S. armed forces who are petitioning for their spouse or child	*For all other sponsors*
2	$19,460	$24,325
3	$24,540	$30,675
4	$29,620	$37,025
5	$34,700	$43,375
6	$39,780	$49,725
7	$44,860	$56,075
8	$49,940	$62,425
	Add $5,080 for each additional person	**Add $6,350 for each additional person**

! CAUTION

The *Poverty Guidelines* chart changes regularly. The federal government usually updates it in February or March of each year, and the immigration authorities start to follow it two months later. When you attend your visa or green card interview, you will have to meet the most current guidelines.

1. The U.S. Increasingly Demands More Than Minimum Income

In 2018, the U.S. Department of State issued new guidance saying that the I-864 Affidavit of Support will no longer carry the weight it once did, and thus might not be enough to demonstrate that the immigrant will not become a public charge (use welfare or other financial-need-based government assistance). If you have used any public benefits in the past, you will have to demonstrate that "the totality of circumstances," including your age, health, family status, assets, education, and work experience demonstrate that you will not become a public charge if admitted to the United States. Furthermore, the new regulations allow the consular officer to look at the U.S. sponsor's past use of public benefits in this analysis.

With regard to people applying for adjustment of status in the U.S. (with USCIS), as of early 2019, new regulations concerning public charge had been proposed, but had not yet gone into effect.

2. How to Read the *Poverty Guidelines* Chart

For green card and immigrant visa applications, the sponsor's income and assets must at least be enough to support the people who depend financially on the sponsor (also called household members or dependents), at 125% of the income level that the government believes puts a person into poverty. (Again, that number turns to 100% for fiancé visa applicants.) An exception is made for members of the U.S. Armed Forces, who need only reach 100% of the *Poverty Guidelines* levels when sponsoring someone for a green card.

To count the dependents who must be covered, add up the following:

- the sponsor
- the currently entering immigrant or immigrants (if children are also applying)
- any other immigrants for whom the sponsor has signed an I-864
- all minor children of the sponsor (whether or not listed as dependents on the sponsor's tax return and regardless of where they live), and
- all other persons listed as dependents on the sponsor's tax return (whether or not they are family members).

Once you have calculated the number of household members and dependents, refer to the *Poverty Guidelines* chart. In the far left column, locate the line showing the number of people for whom the sponsor is responsible. Then look to the appropriate column to find how much the sponsor must show in income and assets.

Assets (such as savings, houses, or cars) are only counted at one-fifth of their current market value, or one-third if you're immigrating as the spouse or child of a U.S. citizen, after subtraction of debt liabilities, mortgages, and liens. Assets must also be readily convertible into cash (within one year). For example, if the sponsor owns a luxury house with major structural damage, there may not be a market for the house because no one wants to buy it. USCIS may decide that, even though the sponsor paid a million dollars for the house, this asset doesn't count—because it cannot be converted into cash within one year.

! CAUTION

Job offers with anticipated salaries don't count. If you are applying for your fiancé or immigrant visa from overseas, a job offer with a set salary in the United States might help a little, but it won't make up for a shortfall in your sponsor's ability to meet the *Poverty Guidelines* minimum.

USCIS also says that income you (the immigrant) earn overseas can't be counted, since you probably won't be able to keep such a job once you come to the United States. Finally, any income that you gained through unauthorized employment in the U.S. (when you didn't have a legal right or USCIS permission to work) can't be counted either.

3. Special Advice for Fiancé Visa Applicants

Because fiancé visas are, technically, only temporary, your U.S. citizen spouse's financial situation isn't seen as such a big deal. The Department of State says that the U.S. citizen sponsor needs only to demonstrate an income equal to, or greater than, 100% of the federal *Poverty Guidelines*. In contrast, when you eventually apply for your green card, your U.S. citizen petitioner will have to show an income equal to or greater than 125% of the *Poverty Guidelines*. Each consulate has a lot of discretion, however, in evaluating the income needed for a fiancé visa to be approved.

If you're having trouble meeting the consulate's standards for getting your fiancé visa, one option is to have another family member or friend in the United States agree to serve as a joint sponsor. A joint sponsor is someone who agrees to share responsibility for your financial support with your primary sponsor, up to the full amount of your support. If your sponsor can't support you, the joint sponsor can be held 100% responsible for your support—the joint sponsor is not allowed to choose a percentage or limit on how much he or she will support you.

Joint sponsors can indicate their willingness to help support you by signing an Affidavit of Support on Form I-134 (different from the Form I-864 used by green card applicants).

Both the advantage and the disadvantage of the Form I-134 Affidavit of Support is that it is not considered to have much legal weight. In other words, although the government could take a sponsor to court to enforce it, it never seems to do so—probably because it realizes it wouldn't win. That's an advantage because it allows you to easily persuade someone to sign the form, without endangering his or her financial future. It's also a disadvantage—since the consular officials know

that the affidavit is hardly worth the paper it's written on, they may disregard the joint sponsor. For this reason, if you go the joint sponsor route, you might want to supplement the person's affidavit with a letter or a sworn statement expressing his or her heartfelt commitment to supporting you.

4. Special Advice for Green Card Applicants

Before exploring your options for meeting the *Poverty Guidelines* support levels or any higher level required by USCIS or a consulate, you need to understand more about the legal implications of the Form I-864 Affidavit of Support. If you can bear it, also try reading all the instructions that come with the form.

Some lucky sponsors now get to use a new, considerably simpler Form I-864EZ rather than the Form I-864. If your sponsor is sponsoring only you, and if your sponsor's income alone is enough to satisfy the *Poverty Guidelines*, read the rest of this chapter regarding your sponsor's general obligations, but be sure to use this easier form!

a. The Sponsor's Obligations

The Form I-864 Affidavit of Support is a legally enforceable contract, meaning that either the government or you, the sponsored immigrant, can take the sponsor to court if the sponsor fails to provide adequate support for you. When the government sues the sponsor, it collects enough money to reimburse any public agencies that have given public benefits to you, the immigrant. When the immigrant sues, he or she collects cash support up to 125% of the amount listed in the U.S. government's *Poverty Guidelines* (as shown in the chart in Form I-864P).

The sponsor's responsibility begins when the sponsored immigrant becomes a permanent resident and lasts until the immigrant becomes a U.S. citizen, has earned 40 work quarters credited toward Social Security (a work quarter is about three months, so this means about ten years of work), dies, or permanently leaves the United

States. If you've been living in the U.S. and earned work credits before applying for your green card, those count toward the 40.

In fact, work done by your U.S. spouse during your marriage can be counted toward these 40 quarters.

CAUTION
A sponsor remains legally obligated even after a divorce. Yes, a divorced immigrant spouse could decide to sit on a couch all day and sue the former spouse for support. The sponsor may wish to have the immigrant sign a separate contract agreeing not to do this, but it's unclear whether courts will enforce such a contract.

b. Who Can Be a Financial Sponsor

Your spouse and/or additional sponsor(s) must meet three requirements to be a sponsor. Each sponsor must be:

- a U.S. citizen, national, or permanent resident
- at least 18 years of age, and
- live in the United States or a U.S. territory or possession.

As a practical matter, of course, the sponsor will have to be in good shape financially to get you into the country. Even if your spouse's income and assets are lower than the *Poverty Guidelines* demand, however, he or she must fill out and sign an Affidavit of Support—but will have to look for additional sponsors to help you immigrate.

Take particular note of the third requirement if the two of you are presently living overseas. If your U.S. citizen spouse is not currently living in the U.S., the I-864 will be approved only if he or she can show that this is a temporary absence, that he or she has maintained ties to the U.S., and that he or she intends to reestablish domicile there no later than the date that you are admitted as a permanent resident. Some of the ways the U.S. citizen can show having maintained ties to the U.S. include having paid state or local taxes, kept U.S. bank accounts, kept a permanent U.S. mailing address, or voted in U.S. elections. Some of the ways the U.S. citizen can show intent to reestablish a domicile in the U.S.

with you include leasing or buying a place to live together, opening a joint bank account with you, looking for a job, and the like. Different consulates are more and less strict about this, however, so your spouse should talk to someone at the consulate before making any major decisions.

If your sponsoring spouse can't meet the required income level alone, there are other possibilities. You may be able to enlist the help of members of your sponsor's household, as explained below in Subsection c. Or, you may find someone independent of the sponsor's household, as explained in Subsection d.

CAUTION
Sponsors who try to run away will face fines. The government has anticipated that some sponsors might try to escape their financial obligation by simply moving and leaving no forwarding address. That's why the law says that the sponsor must report a new address to USCIS on Form I-865 within 30 days of moving. If that does not happen, the sponsor will face fines of between $250 and $2,000; or $5,000 if the sponsor knows the immigrant has collected benefits.

c. How Household Members Can Help Out

If your spouse cannot meet the financial minimum on his or her own, the first step is to see if another member of his or her household is willing to contribute income and assets to the mix. A household member is someone who:

- was listed as a dependent or joint filer on the sponsor's latest tax return, or
- is related to and shares a residence (home) with the sponsor.

The household member agrees to support the immigrant by signing a supplemental Form I-864A. One nice thing about using a household member's income is that it has to be only enough to make up the shortfall in the main sponsor's income (see examples below).

However, the potential household joint sponsors should realize that if for any reason the main sponsor doesn't support the immigrant, the joint sponsors can be called upon for the full support amount. (The form itself supposedly warns the signer with the following legal jargon: "I, the Household Member, … Agree to be jointly and severally liable for payment of any and all obligations owed by the sponsor ….") It's a lot to ask someone to sign onto such a long-term, substantial legal obligation.

> **EXAMPLE:** Lara is a U.S. citizen, sponsoring her husband, Dr. Z, who will be immigrating from Russia. Lara lives with her elderly mother and two adopted children. That means that Lara has to prove she can support a total of five people. For five people, the 2019 *Poverty Guidelines* chart mandates that she show $37,712 in income and assets. Lara earns $27,712 a year as a translator and has no assets, so she's $10,000 short. Will she and Dr. Z be parted forever? Not if:
>
> - Lara's mother (who is a household member) has an emerald ring that she could sell within a year for $50,000 (five times the shortfall of $10,000) or more, and Mom is willing to sign an I-864A; or
> - One of Lara's adopted children works, he happens to earn $10,000 (or more) a year, and he is willing to sign a Form I-864A.
>
> Notice that if Lara were using her own assets to make up the difference between the *Poverty Guidelines* and her income, she would need only assets equal to three times the missing amount, because she is a U.S. citizen sponsoring her spouse. The other household members, however, must show that they have assets equal to five times the missing amount.

Immigrating spouses who live in the United States and are eligible to apply for adjustment of status have an advantage over those coming from overseas. Their income can be counted along with their spouse/sponsors' if they are living in the same household and their income came from authorized employment and is expected to continue from the same source after they become a permanent resident. It's as if they were another household joint sponsor. (They also won't need to sign Form I-864A unless they are agreeing to support children who are immigrating with them.)

Even if the immigrant hasn't been living in the sponsor's household, the immigrant's assets (but not income) can be added to the pot as well (again, minus debts, mortgages, and liens and at one-fifth the assets' value).

> **EXAMPLE:** Now assume that Dr. Z from the earlier example has a country house outside of St. Petersburg on which he owes four million rubles (or $50,000 in U.S. dollars). He could sell it within a year for the U.S. equivalent of $100,000. Subtracting the $50,000 debt, this gives him $50,000, which conveniently enough, is five times the shortfall of $10,000. Dr. Z's contribution of assets would serve to make Lara's Affidavit of Support sufficient under the current *Poverty Guidelines* requirements.

d. How an Independent Joint Sponsor Can Help Out

If no one in the sponsor's household can help boost the sponsor's income and assets, you can look for a joint sponsor outside the household to fill out and sign an additional Form I-864. Each sponsor needs to meet the basic sponsorship requirements as explained above in Subsection a. An independent joint sponsor must also be pretty well off financially.

Unlike household joint sponsors, joint sponsors who live outside the household will need to earn enough to cover the entire *Poverty Guidelines* minimum requirement for their own household *and* for the incoming immigrant or immigrants (if children will also be coming). The joint sponsor cannot simply make up the main sponsor's shortfall. It's as if they were the only sponsor. Like the household joint sponsor, an independent sponsor can be held 100% responsible for supporting the immigrant.

> **CAUTION**
> **No matter what, the main petitioner must fill out a Form I-864.** All the possibilities that we're discussing to overcome the petitioner's insufficient income do not change the fact that he or she must complete and submit the Affidavit of Support form.

If there is more than one incoming immigrant, there can be up to two joint sponsors. This can be helpful, for example, where the incoming immigrants include an adult and two children, and neither of the joint sponsors earn enough to meet the minimum *Poverty Guidelines* for all three immigrants. As long as one of these joint sponsors earns enough to meet the *Poverty Guidelines* minimum for one immigrant, and the other joint sponsor earns enough to meet the *Poverty Guidelines* minimum for the other two immigrants, the I-864 requirements are met.

Although independent joint sponsors must meet the entire *Poverty Guidelines* minimum on their own, they at least will not be responsible for supporting people in the immigrant's household other than the immigrant(s). To meet the *Poverty Guidelines* requirements as a joint sponsor, don't just add up the number of people in the two households. Instead, add only the number of people in the joint sponsor's household plus the number of new immigrants.

> **EXAMPLE:** Imagine now that Dr. Z has a long-lost cousin, Leonid, who's an unmarried U.S. citizen, age 32, living in Seattle, who claims his parents as dependents. The cousin earns $34,000 a year from his espresso cart. The cousin is willing to sign a separate Form I-864 as a joint sponsor on Dr. Z's behalf. The minimum Leonid would have to earn to be a joint sponsor according to the 2019 *Poverty Guidelines* would be $32,187, to cover himself, Dr. Z, and his (Leonid's) two parents. Leonid qualifies as a joint sponsor.

If the immigrant is also bringing in children to the United States, a last resort might have to be to leave some or all of the children behind for the moment. Once the immigrant arrives and begins earning an income, he or she (or potentially the U.S. spouse) can petition to bring the children over—and will be able to use his or her new income to meet the minimum requirements.

> **EXAMPLE:** Imagine that Dr. Z has two children from a previous marriage. They raise the minimum amount Lara must earn (in 2019) to $48,762 (for seven people in total). If she cannot reach that level or find someone to sign on for joint sponsorship,

Dr. Z may have to leave his children behind for now. Once he gets established in the United States and begins earning income, Lara can petition for the children separately (as stepchildren, so long as her marriage took place before the children turned 18), using Dr. Z's new U.S. income to meet the shortfall. (They'll need to make sure the children aren't about to turn age 21 and fall into another visa category; see Chapter 8 or 12 for details.)

e. Should You Ask Family Members to Help?

The reaction of many applicants with inadequate financial resources is to ask another family member to pitch in and sign an additional Affidavit of Support (Form I-864). Think long and hard before doing this—and advise your family member to consult a lawyer before signing.

The Affidavit of Support is a binding, long-term contract, with ramifications the signer might not immediately realize. For example, the cosponsor will be obligated to continue supporting the immigrant spouse even if the couple divorces, or to support the immigrant in the event that the immigrant has a disabling accident. Even if these U.S. family members love and want to support the incoming immigrant, having to either support the immigrant directly or reimburse the U.S. government for large sums of welfare or public assistance money probably won't be a satisfying way of expressing that love. Try to keep your family members off the hook as much as possible.

TIP
This book does not discuss the availability of public benefits to immigrants. Immigration law is federal, and doesn't prevent individual states from setting up special assistance programs that help immigrants. Indeed, some states make limited medical care, pregnancy care, or supplemental food available to low-income immigrants. If you're facing severe economic problems, the best thing to do is contact a nonprofit that serves immigrants to see what help is out there and how you can make use of it without jeopardizing your immigration status.

B. Applicants Who Must Show More Than Minimum Income

It's rare for a consulate or USCIS to ask you to show that your sponsor earns or owns *more* than the government's minimum requirements as announced in the *Poverty Guidelines*.

However, certain immigrants may have to produce sponsors who can exceed the minimum income requirement. Elderly applicants and those with severe health problems that might prevent them from working or result in large medical bills fall into this group. Finding additional sponsors as described in Subsections a and b, above, might be enough to help you overcome these added requirements. But if they're not, by all means consult an attorney.

C. Increasing Your Sponsor's Income to Meet the Minimum

What if all of the above advice still isn't enough to get your spouse and cosponsors past the income requirement? Some couples don't have assets, household members, family, or friends that they can look to for financial support. To make up for financial shortfalls, the U.S. citizen spouse, or the immigrant if living in the United States, may have to find an additional job or a job with better pay and benefits.

Improving your financial situation may not be easy. It may mean moving to another city, dropping out of school for a while, or giving up enjoyable work or time with the children.

Luckily, after you are approved for your green card there is no obligation that you or your spouse stay with the new job. USCIS will not send inspectors to your or your spouse's workplace or check up on you.

If you and your family can survive on less than the U.S. government thinks possible, that's your choice—so long as you do not go on means-based public assistance for the first five years after your green card approval. The way the law works, you wouldn't face any repercussions for postapproval reductions in your family's income until and unless you tried to apply

for public benefits. You would probably be denied the benefits—or forced to pay them back later.

If you don't find out until your visa or green card interview that you can't be approved without showing more financial support, you will usually be given a time limit to send in new evidence. The time limit may approach all too quickly while your spouse looks for a better job, health insurance, or other source of family support. If the deadline is about to pass and you have nothing new to show, at least send a letter saying that you are still interested in pursuing your application. Ask for more time to provide the requested documents (you usually will not be reinterviewed).

If you are in the United States, it is especially important to send such a letter, because once USCIS denies your application, it will transfer your case to the Immigration Court for removal proceedings. The consulates and USCIS will generally give you a total of six months to a year after your interview before they declare your application dead.

Have a Backup Plan

You won't know whether the government will ask you for an unusually high level of proven income and assets until you're in the visa or green card interview. If you're caught by surprise, don't worry—they'll always give you more time to provide new or further evidence that you'll be supported. But there are a couple of advantages to advance planning if you know that your case is a marginal one.

One advantage, of course, is that having extra documents or affidavits on hand may shorten the time before your case is approved. Another is that cases that aren't approved at the interview tend to get greater scrutiny when they're evaluated later by the interviewers and their supervisors. If you're understandably reluctant to turn in an extra Affidavit of Support from a joint sponsor, you can always keep it in your back pocket and give it to the interviewer only if he or she tells you she'll need it to approve your case.

4

The Right Way to Prepare, Collect, and Manage the Paperwork

As you've probably figured out by now, you're going to have to collect and keep track of a lot of paperwork. This chapter will give you instructions on how to keep the paperwork organized, and how to make sure that all documents are of a type and quality that USCIS and the consulates will accept (Sections A and B). We also tell you how to locate and translate some of the documents that you'll need to support your application (Section C). And finally, Section D explains how to protect your application before you mail it from being lost by the U.S. government.

(For where to get the latest forms, see Chapter 1.)

A. Getting Organized

Start by setting up a good system to keep track of all the forms and documents that you'll need during this application process. There is no feeling worse than being in front of an impatient government official while you desperately go through piles of stuff looking for that one vital slip of paper. Take our word for it, you'll need a lot more than one jumbo folder.

We suggest using manila file folders and putting them in a box or drawer (or use a series of large envelopes or an accordion file). Label one folder or envelope Original Documents, for things like your birth certificate, marriage certificate, and USCIS or consular approval notices. Keep this file in a very safe place (such as a safe deposit box at your local bank). Be sure to remember to retrieve your originals in time to take them to your interview.

Label the other files or envelopes according to which packets, forms, or documents they contain. If you're applying for a green card within the United States, you might label one folder I-130 Petition; another Adjustment of Status Packet; another Interview Materials (containing copies of the documents you'll want to take to your interview); and another Old Drafts/Copies. Similarly, if you're applying from overseas, one folder might be labeled I-130 Petition, another Mailed to Consulate, another Affidavit of Support and Financial Documents, another Interview Materials, and the rest as described above.

You should also keep a separate file for correspondence from USCIS or the consulate. Include in this file your handwritten notes on any phone conversations you've had with USCIS or consular personnel. Don't forget to write the date on your notes, so you can refer to them later in further correspondence.

How Nightmarish Can It Get?

Maybe you'll turn in your application and everything will go like clockwork: USCIS and consular files all in order, approval received on time. Educating yourself about the process and preparing everything carefully certainly improves your chances. But we wouldn't be doing our job if we didn't warn you about how the government bureaucracy can chew up and spit out even the best-prepared application.

Every immigration lawyer has his or her favorite horror stories. For instance, there was the client whose I-130 petitions were lost by USCIS—so after many months, the lawyer filed new petitions and canceled the checks that went with the lost ones. But USCIS then found the old petitions, tried to cash the "lost" checks and to collect from the client for the bank charges when the checks bounced.

Then there was the woman who waited over six months for USCIS to approve her work permit—only to have them finally send her a work permit with someone else's name and photo. By the time that finally got straightened out, the work permit had expired and USCIS forced her to apply, and pay again, for a new one.

And let's not forget the woman who nearly got stuck outside the United States because USCIS refused to renew her Refugee Travel Document on the nonsensical grounds that she hadn't provided a valid address in the application. (She had, and it was the same address that USCIS had been using to correspond with her for years.)

What can you do about such absurd and Orwellian horrors? Mostly just know in advance that they may happen to you, leave time to deal with them, and keep copies of everything.

As you're preparing your forms and documents, attach our checklists on the outside of each folder or envelope and check the boxes off as the items have been completed and put inside. When you've finished filling a folder or envelope, take out some of the old drafts or items you've decided not to use and move them to the Old Drafts/Copies folder, so as not to clutter up the materials you'll take to your interview. Carefully write "final copy, mailed xx/xx/20xx" (you fill in the date) on the top of the copy of the application or petition you've mailed to USCIS or the consulate.

B. How to Prepare USCIS and Consular Forms

Now, let's make sure the government doesn't return your forms for technical reasons. Follow these instructions for printing and filling out the forms.

1. Form Names, Numbers, and Dates

The government refers to its forms not by their name or title, but by the tiny numbers in the lower left or right corner. For example, if you look at the sample form in Chapter 7 entitled Petition for Alien Relative, you'll see I-130 there at the bottom. And because USCIS uses these numbers, we usually do, too.

Another thing you'll find in the corner is the date the form was issued. That's an important date, because once USCIS issues a later version (which it frequently does), you'll usually need to use the later one. That means that for every form you plan to submit, you should check the USCIS website just before actually mailing it. (Go to www.uscis.gov, click "Forms" and you will find a list you can scroll down by form number.)

After you have submitted the form, you can stop worrying—you won't need to redo it even if USCIS issues a new form before your application has been decided.

2. Instructions That Come With the Forms

USCIS provides instructions with each form. Save yourself a little postage and don't send the instruction pages back to them when the time comes to submit your application. USCIS wants only the part of the form you fill in. Sadly, the instructions are often hard to understand (that's why we wrote this book) and at times they even contain information that is wrong or misleading.

3. Filing Fees

Many of the immigration forms require you to pay a fee in order to file them. (No, you can't get your money back if your case is not approved.) Definitely double-check the fees at the USCIS website at www.uscis.gov before submitting anything, or call its information line at 800-375-5283.

You can pay the fees by credit card, personal check, or money order, made out to the "U.S. Department of Homeland Security." Don't send cash! To make sure they see your check, paperclip or staple it to the upper left-hand corner of your main application form.

Although you can combine all the amounts owed for one person into one check (for example, adding up the application fee and the biometrics fee) it's better not to combine fees for the whole family when applying together. That's because if one person's application has a mistake, USCIS will send the entire package back to you if you've sent in only one check, delaying the process. With separate checks, they're more likely to start the process rolling and send a letter regarding the mistake or missing item.

4. Hand or Online?

Many immigration forms can be filled out on the computer. (And in cases involving overseas fiancés and spouses, visa application forms have to be filled out and submitted entirely online.) Where using the computer is optional, however, realize that it's not always as convenient as you'd expect. The online version of the form may not save—you may have to do the whole form in one sitting. Fortunately, in many cases, you can download the form and save it onto your own computer.

If you need extra space to answer a particular question, write "see attached" in the space provided, then check whether the form comes with its own supplementary page for adding information. If not, write your answer on a separate sheet of paper. Make sure that sheet of paper includes your name and date of birth, as well as the form number and question number.

If you won't be using a computer, the next best thing is to print the form and fill it out using a typewriter. But don't do this if you're an inaccurate typist—USCIS uses special scanners to read forms and documents, and these will not properly read information that is greyed out, highlighted or corrected using correction fluid or tape.

Also keep that in mind if you handwrite your answers (which you must do using black ink), USCIS recommends that, if you make a mistake, you start fresh with a new form.

5. Questions That Don't Apply to You

If a question just doesn't fit your situation, write "N/A" (not applicable). Or, if the answer is "none," as in "number of children," answer "none."

Try not to mix these two up—it irritates the government officials reading your application. But if you're not sure how or whether to answer a question, seek skilled legal help (Chapter 17 gives you information on finding a good lawyer).

6. Tell the Truth

There will be many temptations to lie in this process—to hide a ground of inadmissibility, ignore a previous marriage, or avoid questions about previous visits to the United States, for example. But lying to the government or even omitting

information can get you in bigger trouble than the problem you are lying about. And you've never seen anyone angrier than a USCIS or State Department official who discovers that you've lied to them.

If you feel you just can't complete the form without hiding a certain piece of information—or you really don't know how to answer or explain a key question—see a lawyer. The lawyer may be able to show you how to be truthful in a way that doesn't risk having your application denied.

7. What's Your Name?

The easiest thing on a form should be filling out your name, right? Not in this bureaucratic morass. USCIS will want not only your current name, but on certain of its forms, "other names used." Here are some important things to get straight before you start writing your name(s) in the forms to follow:

- **Married name.** If you've just married and changed your last name as part of your marriage, use your married name. But women shouldn't feel pressured into taking on a married name for the sake of the green card application. By now USCIS is well aware that not all women change their name when they marry. They will not look upon keeping your name as a sign that your marriage is a sham. Nor does having different last names seem to cause any confusion in the processing of your application (after all, USCIS thinks of you as a number, not a name).

- **Current name.** When your current name is requested, it is best to insert the name you currently use for legal purposes. This will normally be the name on your bank account, driver's license, and passport. If you've always gone by a nickname (for example, your name is Richard but you always use the common nickname "Dick"), it's okay to fill in the application as "Dick," as long as you list "Richard" where the form asks for other names used. This will avoid confusion when USCIS compares your application form with the accompanying documents (your employer, for example, may write a letter saying "Dick worked here ...."). But there's no way to avoid a little confusion, since your birth certificate will still say Richard.

- **Legal name changes.** If you've actually done a court-ordered legal name change, include a copy of the court order, to help dispel some of the inevitable confusion. If you have changed your name without a court order (by simply beginning to use a different name and using it consistently, which is legal in many states) and you use your changed name for all legal purposes, list it as your current name.

- **Other names.** The category for "other names used" could include nicknames. USCIS will want to know about nicknames that might have made their way onto your various legal documents (or criminal record). You should also include names by which you have been commonly known, especially as an adult. However, "pet" names such as "sweetie-pie" need not be included. Nor should unwanted childhood nicknames. For example, if your name is Roberto Malfi but your oh-so-clever high school buddies called you "Mafia," best forget about it.

- **Previous married names.** If you have been married previously, don't forget to list your name from that marriage in the boxes requesting other names used.

8. Be Consistent

As you might have guessed from the previous section, it's important not to cause confusion when filling out the forms. At worst, not getting your facts straight can cause the person reviewing your application to think you cannot be believed.

For example, you might live with a group of friends but use your parents' address to get mail. Notice the places on the forms that ask for your actual residence, and the places on the forms that ask for your mailing address. Be careful to answer correctly and consistently in response.

C. How to Obtain Needed Documents

You would be lucky if forms were the only paperwork you had to worry about—but no, there are documents, too. At a minimum, you are going to need your long-form, government-issued birth certificate to complete your visa or green card application. You will also need your marriage certificate, if you're past the fiancé stage. You may also need other documents, such as death certificate, divorce decree, and your spouse's birth certificate or U.S. passport.

When it's time for your visa or green card approval, you will need a passport from your own country (either to travel to the United States or to hold a stamp showing your residence status). If you get married in your home country and you change your name, make sure your passport is either updated or is still considered valid with your maiden name in it. Make sure the passport won't expire soon, either. It will need to be valid for at least six months after you enter the United States or receive permanent residence at a USCIS office within the United States.

Within the United States, official copies of birth, death, marriage, and divorce certificates or decrees can usually be obtained from the Vital Records office (called the Registrar's or Recorder's office in some areas) of the appropriate county or locality. Even if you already have your own copy of these items, it's a good idea to request a certified copy. That's because your copy may not have been given all the official governmental stamps necessary for USCIS to accept it as authentic.

You can find more details on the National Center for Health Statistics website at www.cdc.gov/nchs. There are also services that will order your vital records for a fee, such as www.VitalChek.com.

U.S. passports are available to U.S. citizens through the State Department; see www.travel.state.gov (click " Get a U.S. Passport").

Outside of the United States, records should be obtained from official, government sources wherever possible. The sources that USCIS and the State

Department consider acceptable are listed in the State Department's *Foreign Affairs Manual* (FAM). It's accessible at www.usvisas.state.gov. (Scroll down and click "Fees/Reciprocity" then "Visa Issuance Fee - Reciprocity Tables," then select the country about which you want information.) U.S. law libraries may also be able to locate copies of the FAM for you.

If you are overseas and do not have Web access, talk to your local U.S. consulate about what form of record will be acceptable, particularly if you need to document an event for which your government does not issue certificates.

1. Translate Non-English Documents

If the documents you are submitting are in a language other than English, you will need to submit both:

- a copy of the original document, and
- a certified, word-for-word translation (summaries are not acceptable).

This is particularly true if you're submitting the document to a USCIS office; consulates can often deal with documents that are in the language of that country (their instructions will usually tell you if they can't).

There is no need to hire a certified translator. Any trustworthy friend who is fluent in English and the language of the document and is not your close relative can do the job. That person should simply type out the translated text, then add at the bottom:

I certify that I am competent to translate from [*the language of the document*] to English and that the above [*identify the document and to whom it pertains; for example, "Birth Certificate of Maritza Malakoff"*] is a correct and true translation to the best of my knowledge and belief.

Signed: _____[*translator's full name*]_____

Address: _____

Telephone: _____

Date: _____

If you prefer, you can hire a professional translator, who should also add the same certification at the bottom of the translation.

2. Substitute for Unavailable Documents

If you cannot obtain a needed document, USCIS may, under some circumstances, accept another type of evidence. For example, if your birth certificate was destroyed in a fire, USCIS may accept in its place school records or sworn statements by people who knew you to prove your date of birth.

USCIS instructions included with Forms I-129F (for the fiancé petition) and I-130 (the immigrant petition) outline the other types of evidence that USCIS accepts. If you substitute a new type of evidence for a missing document, you should also include a statement from the local civil authorities explaining why the original document is unavailable.

3. Homemade Documents

One form of substitute document that you may need to use is a sworn declaration. For example, you might need to ask a friend or family member to prepare one affirming your date and place of birth. If so, emphasize to the person that fancy legal language is not as important as detailed facts when it comes to convincing an immigration official to accept this person's word in place of an official document.

Someone could write, for example, "I swear that Francois was born in Paris in 1962 to Mr. and Mrs. Marti." But it would be much more compelling for them to write, "I swear that I am Francois's older brother. I remember the morning that my mother brought him home from the hospital in 1962 (I was then five years old), and we grew up together in our parents' home (Mr. and Mrs. Xavier Marti) in Paris."

The full declaration should be longer and contain more details than this example. The more details that are offered, the more likely USCIS or the consulate is to accept the declaration as the truth.

To start the declaration, the person should state his or her complete name and address, as well as country of citizenship. At the bottom of the declaration, the person should write:

> I swear, under penalty of perjury, that the foregoing is true and correct to the best of my knowledge.
>
> Signed: _____
>
> Date: _____

**Declaration in Support of
Application of Guofeng Zheng**

I, Shaoling Liu, hereby say and declare as follows:

1. I am a U.S. permanent resident, residing at 222 Rhododendron Drive, Seattle, WA 98111. My telephone number is 206-555-1212. I have been living in the United States since January 2, 1999.

2. I am originally from Mainland China, where I grew up in the same town (called Dahuo, in Suzhou province) as Guofeng Zheng.

3. I knew Guofeng's first wife, Meihua. I attended their wedding, and had dinner at their home several times. I also remember when Meihua fell ill with cancer. She was sick for many months before passing away on October 31, 1998.

4. I received the news of Meihua's death a few days later, in early November of 1998. I knew the doctor who had treated her, and he was very sad that his treatments had failed. I also attended Meihua's funeral on November 7th. Her ashes are buried in the local cemetery.

5. I am also aware that the municipal records office, where all deaths are recorded, burnt down in the year 2002. I myself had difficulty with this, when I tried to get a copy of my mother's birth certificate last year.

I swear, under penalty of perjury, that the foregoing is true and correct to the best of my knowledge.

Signed: _Shaoling Liu_

Date: _August 4, 2019_

If preparing sworn declarations seems like too much to accomplish, you could hire a lawyer for this task only. Above is a sample of a full sworn declaration, written to prove that an immigrant who is applying through marriage is no longer married to his first wife, due to her death. (Remember, when writing your own declaration, tailor it to your situation—don't follow the wording of the sample too closely.)

Don't confuse a declaration with an affidavit. An affidavit is very similar—a written statement that the author dates and signs—but it has one additional feature. Affidavits are notarized, which means that they are signed in front of someone who is authorized by the government to attest to, or certify, the authenticity of signatures. When you bring a declaration to a notary, that person will ask for identification, such as your passport or driver's license, to make sure that you are the person whose signature is called for on the declaration. You sign the declaration in the presence of the notary, who makes a note of this in his or her notary book. The notary also places a stamp, or seal, on your document.

As you can see, affidavits are more formal and more trouble than simple declarations. An affidavit is not required for substitute documents such as we're describing now—but if you want to make the document look more official, and know where to find a notary, you might want to take the extra trouble. If an immigration process described in this book requires an affidavit, we'll alert you.

D. Before You Mail an Application

There are three rules to remember before you mail anything to USCIS, consulate, or other government office:

1. Make copies.
2. Mail your applications by a traceable method.
3. Don't mail anything that you can't replace.

We'll explain the reasons for these maxims—and how to follow them.

1. Make Complete Copies

When you've at last finished filling out a packet of required immigration forms; and if you won't be filing online your first instinct will be to seal them in an envelope, pop them in the mail, and forget about them for awhile. That could waste all of your hard work.

Find a photocopy machine and make copies of every page of every application, as well as any photos, documents, checks, and money orders. Make color copies of color documents, if possible. Carefully keep these in your records. This will help you recreate these pages and items if they're lost in the mail or in the overstuffed files of some government office. It may also help convince USCIS or the consulate to take another look for the lost items.

2. Mail by a Traceable Method

In any government agency, things get lost. The sorting of newly arrived applications seems to be a common time for them to disappear. If this happens to your application, it can become important to prove that you mailed it in the first place.

In the United States, you can go to the Post Office and pay extra to use Priority Mail for all your applications or correspondence with USCIS or the consulates. You can use the receipt to convince USCIS or the consulate to look for the application if it gets misplaced. Another option is to use a courier service such as FedEx or DHL. (In fact, it may be your best option if mailing from overseas.) These automatically offer receipts and tracking. In that case, however, be sure not to send your submission to a USCIS post office box. Only the U.S. Postal Service is authorized to deliver to a P.O. box.

Most service centers provide alternate addresses for delivery by courier.

3. If You Want It Back, Don't Send It

Many immigration applications require that certain documents be attached (paper-clipping them to the form is fine). Some documents must be included in packets of forms you must file and others brought to interviews. Whatever you do, *don't send originals* to USCIS unless it's absolutely clear that you have no choice.

The National Visa Center might explicitly ask for the originals of certain documents, and will not forward your case to the consulate until it receives them. Whenever you send an original, however, be sure to make a copy for yourself first.

If USCIS or the National Visa Center (or consulate) does not explicitly request an original document, simply photocopy any document (as long as the original is the official version), and send the copy. The USCIS or consular officer will have a chance to view the originals when you bring them to your interview. It's best to write the word "COPY" in red letters at the top, and to add the following text, right on the front of the copy, if there's room:

Copies of documents submitted are exact photocopies of unaltered original documents and I understand that I may be required to submit original documents to an immigration or consular official at a later date.

Signature: _____

Typed or printed name: _____

Date: _____

Always make photocopies on one-sided, 8½" × 11" paper. Some applicants have been known to try to create exact copies of things by cutting the image out of the full page of paper—creating, for example, a tiny photocopied green card. The government doesn't appreciate these minicopies.

By the same token, 8½" × 14" paper (or larger) doesn't fit well into the government's files—use a photocopy machine that will reduce your document image to 8½" × 11", if possible.

Overseas Fiancés of U.S. Citizens

f you are not yet married, your intended spouse is a U.S. citizen, and you are living overseas, you will have a choice among visa options. Depending on your own preference or the length of time each will take to obtain, you can choose to pursue:

- a fiancé visa (for readers who won't marry until they come to the U.S.), explained in Section A
- a marriage-based visa (for readers who decide to marry overseas and then apply to come to the U.S.), explained in Section B, or
- a tourist visa (if you just want to marry in the U.S. and return home), explained in Section C.

This chapter explains these options in detail. In Section D, we'll help you decide which is best for you. If you decide to get married overseas, we'll send you on to Chapter 7, where the application process for a spouse of a U.S. citizen is explained. Or, if you decide that a quick trip to the U.S. for the wedding, followed by a return to your home country, is all that you need, we'll discuss the tourist visa process, though not in great detail (Section E). And for those of you who are engaged to be married and want to come to the U.S. for the wedding, Sections F, G, and H give you the information you need to prepare the applications and obtain your fiancé visa.

A. The Fiancé Visa Option

Since you are presently a fiancé, the most obvious option is the fiancé visa. If you need to review whether you would be eligible for a fiancé visa, see Chapter 2, Section B. A fiancé visa allows you to enter the United States, marry within 90 days, and apply for your green card in the United States. Your unmarried children under age 21 are eligible to accompany you.

There are no quotas or limits on the number of people who can obtain fiancé visas and subsequent green cards through marriage to a U.S. citizen. A fiancé visa can take anywhere from six months to a year or more to obtain—depending on how backed up the various offices dealing with your file are.

1. You Must Marry in the U.S.

A fiancé visa gives you no choice but to hold your marriage ceremony in the United States. In fact, you'll have to get married fairly quickly if you plan to go on to apply for a U.S. green card. Although technically you have 90 days to get married, waiting until the latter part of that time period is risky, because even after you're married, it may take weeks to get the all-important marriage certificate that you'll need to apply for your green card.

Couples often ask whether their overseas marriage really counts, or wonder why they can't just get married for a second time after entering on a fiancé visa.

Unfortunately, once you're legally married, no matter where the marriage took place, you no longer qualify for a traditional, K-1 fiancé visa.

Married couples do have other options, however, assuming you're planning to apply for U.S. permanent residency. (See Section B, below.)

> **TIP**
> **Wedding ceremonies that don't result in legally binding marriages won't stand in your way.** If you don't feel right leaving home unmarried, see if you can arrange for a religious or other ceremony that won't be recorded or recognized by your country's civil authorities. USCIS does not recognize these as valid marriages. You will need to have a legal marriage in the United States once you get there.

2. The Green Card Application Will Be Separate

Fiancés wishing to live in the United States will need to get married within the 90 days that they're allowed in the United States on the fiancé visa, and then file the application for a green card using a procedure called adjustment of status. Your marriage alone does not extend your period of authorized stay past the original 90 days. Once you file your application for adjustment of status, however, you are legally authorized to stay in the

U.S. while the government makes a decision on the application. This application procedure involves even more paperwork than the fiancé visa.

Most USCIS offices schedule adjustment of status interviews within a few months of when the application is filed.

B. The Marriage-Based Visa Option

The second option is for you to get married outside of the United States, before applying for any visa. In that case you would be eligible to apply for an immigrant visa as the immediate relative of your U.S. citizen spouse. (If you need to review whether you would be eligible for a marriage-based immigrant visa, see Chapter 2, Section B.)

You would use your immigrant visa to enter the United States and become a U.S. resident immediately.

There are no quotas or limits on the number of people who can obtain visas or green cards through marriage to a U.S. citizen. A marriage-based immigrant visa usually takes around one year to obtain. Although the procedural steps are very similar to those for obtaining a traditional, K-1 fiancé visa, the application itself is somewhat more demanding.

> **CAUTION**
> **This book does not discuss the K-3 visa.** At one time, this hybrid visa was offered as a way to speed up the process of U.S. entry for spouses of U.S. citizens. It allowed them to get the equivalent of a fiancé visa for U.S. entry (despite being already married) and then complete the green card application in the United States. However, USCIS delays in processing K-3s made it no improvement on existing visa possibilities—and so the K-3 visa is now largely considered dead.

C. The Tourist Visa Option

A third option is available to fiancés who want to hold their marriage ceremony in the United States, but do not wish to live there after the ceremony.

They can apply for a tourist visa at a local U.S. consulate. A tourist visa usually takes between a few days and ten weeks to obtain.

However, using a tourist visa carries certain risks, primarily the possibility of being denied entry at the U.S. border. (These risks are explained more fully in Section E, below.)

D. Choosing Among the Visa Options

Your choice of visa may be based simply on where you wish to hold your wedding.

- If your heart is set on marrying in the United States and remaining there, a fiancé visa is probably the most appropriate.
- If you would like to marry in the United States and return to your home country to live, either a fiancé visa or a tourist visa would be appropriate.
- If you want to get married in your home country, and want to enter the U.S. as a permanent resident, then a marriage-based immigrant visa should suit you well.

1. Immigrant Visas Can Take the Longest to Get

Of all your visa options permitting you U.S. entry, you'll probably wait longest for a marriage-based immigrant visa, because it represents the completion of your quest for permanent residence. Accordingly, the consular officers who decide your immigrant visa will have to review more than one set of paperwork, and you will have to go through various procedural hoops, before the visa can be approved.

By contrast, the K-1 fiancé visa is considered a short-term visa. This means that it has fewer requirements than the marriage-based immigrant visa. Accordingly, there are fewer opportunities for a consular officer to delay your application for more information.

Short-term visas also have fewer consequences for the U.S. government—the K-1 visa has a 90-day limit, and offers no guarantees that you'll be approved for a green card. USCIS and the consulates know that they'll get a second look at you if and when you apply for the actual green card.

This doesn't mean that K-1 fiancé visas are given out like free candy—in fact, the internal rules tell consular officers to give fiancé visa applications almost as hard a look as marriage-based immigrant visa applications. Nevertheless, most attorneys find that USCIS and the consulates make smoother and quicker decisions on K-1 fiancé, as opposed to marriage-based immigrant visa applications.

At the time this book went to print, the initial petitions that start the process on all of these types of cases—that is, the Form I-130 for people who will enter the U.S. as permanent residents, and the Form 1-129F for people who will enter on either the K-1 or the K-3 visa—were being processed by USCIS within approximately five to ten months, depending on which service center is handling it. Once USCIS has forwarded the petition to the consulate, however, people with nonimmigrant petitions—K-1s and K-2s—are often interviewed more quickly and are able to enter the U.S. sooner than those who will be entering as permanent residents. Case processing times for K-1 visas are typically 5.5 to 7.5 months.

In sum, if you plan to remain in the United States permanently and your main consideration is which visa will get you into the United States the fastest, the traditional K-1 fiancé visa may be your best bet.

> **CAUTION**
>
> **If you have children between the ages of 18 and 21 who are not the natural children or stepchildren of your U.S. spouse-to-be, choose a fiancé visa (K-1 or K-3).** Due to a strange twist in the immigration laws, children under 21 can accompany a fiancé on their visa, but only children whose parents married while they were under 18 can qualify as stepchildren for purposes of getting an immigrant visa.

2. Fiancé Visa Applications Require Less Financial Support Information

The biggest difference between the nonimmigrant fiancé and immigrant marriage visa applications concerns your fiancé's ability to support you financially. Although fiancé applicants as well as marriage visa applicants must both prove that they'll be supported in the United States, fiancés usually do so using the Form I-134, Affidavit of Support. Form I-134 is fairly simple to prepare and is not considered legally binding—even if the government took you (the sponsor) to court to enforce it, it would probably lose.

By contrast, if you were applying for a marriage-based immigrant visa, your spouse would definitely have to submit an Affidavit of Support on Form I-864. This form is several pages long, demands detailed financial information, and is legally binding. The U.S. government takes it seriously and scrutinizes it carefully. Problems with Form I-864 are a frequent cause of delays in approving immigrant visas.

If you apply for a fiancé visa, you can probably (depending on the consulate where you live) avoid submitting the Form I-864 until you are already in the U.S. (where it will be a required part of your green card application). Chapter 3 contains detailed explanations of the workings of Form I-864.

3. Fiancé Visas Involve More Paperwork and Expense

If your primary concern is how much paperwork you'll have to deal with, you should know that getting a K-1 fiancé visa adds an extra step to the green card application process compared to a marriage-based immigrant visa application. Even after you've gotten the fiancé visa and entered the United States, you'll have to prepare and submit another heavy round of paperwork for a green card, as much as if you'd just gotten married in the first place and applied for an immigrant visa through the U.S. consulate. And the green card application in the United States will probably take another four or five months to be approved.

Another concern is money. With K-1 visas, you'll finish the process by adjusting status in the United States—where the fees are much higher than if you were doing everything overseas. The difference is currently nearly $600 per person.

4. Problems Are Easier to Resolve With Fiancé Visas

Once an immigrant visa application gets postponed overseas, things get difficult—neither your fiancé nor any lawyer whom you hire is going to have an easy time reaching the consular officials. The officials can get away with some fairly arbitrary behavior because of their isolation. This could, of course, also happen with your fiancé visa application, but because the process is shorter and easier, the chances are less.

Next Step

You want to get a K-1 fiancé visa and marry in the U.S.:	Continue on to Section F, below.
You want a tourist visa to hold a wedding in the United States and then return home:	Read Section E, below.
You want to get married overseas and apply for an immigrant visa:	See Chapter 7.

E. How to Use a Tourist Visa

If you want only to get married in the United States —but not live there—you can apply for a visitor or tourist visa, known as a B-2 visa. The application process is probably the easiest and fastest in the immigration law world. However, it carries certain risks.

First, there is the risk that you may unwittingly get the visa under false pretenses. You must make sure to tell the consular officer that you intend to use the visa in order to get married to a U.S. citizen. Otherwise, USCIS may later claim that you obtained the visa through fraud (pretending to be "only" a tourist), which can prevent you from getting a green card if you want one later. And then you'll have to also convince the consular official that you really, truly plan to leave the U.S. after you've gotten married, rather than sticking around and applying for a U.S. green card. (Making that argument could be tough, but it's not impossible.)

Second, you could face problems at the U.S. border when you enter. Even after you've convinced the consular officer that your intention after marrying is to return to your home country (or even if you are traveling on a tourist visa obtained long before you planned on getting married), you'll still have to convince the U.S. border official. If you get a reasonable official, this should be no problem— your use of a tourist visa is perfectly legal.

If you get an official who is inclined to be suspicious, however, it's another matter. The border officials can keep you out if they think you've used fraud to obtain the visa, such as having lied about your intentions to return home after the wedding. (In fact, border officials can keep you out for simply failing to submit enough evidence of your intent to return. The burden is on you, and there is no appeal.) Once you've been removed this way, you may be prevented from reentering the United States for five years. The border officials have reason to be suspicious, since many people have used tourist visas as a way to enter the United States precisely for the purpose of applying for a green card there.

To prepare for the possibility of meeting a skeptical border official, you can bring along some of the following to demonstrate your plan to return home (these are the same things you would have shown the consular officer in order to get the visitor visa):

- a copy of your lease or rental agreement
- a letter from your employer stating that you are expected back by a certain date
- copies of birth certificates from close family members remaining behind, and
- copy of return ticket.

Also make sure there is nothing in your luggage to contradict this evidence. If your luggage is searched and the official realizes you are carrying enough prescription medication for a three-year stay and a letter from your fiancé saying, "Can't wait until you are here and we can settle down in our new house," you will find yourself on the next return plane.

We can't decide for you whether it's better to use a tourist or a fiancé visa if you're only coming to the United States to hold your wedding and then leave. If you don't like risk, and the cost of your plane ticket is high or will wipe out your savings, the fiancé visa might be more appropriate for you. With a fiancé visa, the border officer doesn't have to worry about whether your secret intention is to remain in the United States and apply for a green card, because you would have every right, under the fiancé visa, to do just that.

On the other hand, the fiancé visa takes much longer to get, and there is no way to remove every element of risk. Even with a fiancé visa, your entry to the United States depends on the perception and decision of a single border patrol official. It's as simple as that.

F. The K-1 Fiancé Visa Application Process

If you are reading this section, it means that you are not married yet and have decided that you want, and are eligible for, a fiancé visa. Let's get to the nuts and bolts of the fiancé visa application process. The amount of paperwork and the number of forms and appointments that you'll have to deal with can be daunting, bewildering, and frustrating. But countless other immigrants have made it through, and so can you.

TIP
Don't be discouraged by mounds of paperwork —but do get it right. Read Chapter 4 on how to organize yourself to make sure you keep good track of the paperwork involved in the visa process. That chapter also gives detailed instructions on how to enter the requested information.

Obtaining a K-1 fiancé visa involves three major steps:

Step 1: Your U.S. citizen fiancé submits a fiancé petition to USCIS.

Step 2: USCIS sends your approval to the National Visa Center (NVC) which advises you which consulate it's forwarding your case to, and

Step 3: You fill out an online form, then attend an interview at a U.S. consulate and receive your visa.

In rare instances, some couples have to attend a fraud interview if the government has doubts about their intended marriage being the real thing. This could happen either as part of Step One or after Step Three.

Below we describe, in detail, what happens at each of these steps.

Stay Put During the Application Process

Once this process has started, you're better off if you don't change addresses or take any long trips. USCIS or the consulate could send you a request for more information or call you in for your interview at any time. Missing such a notification could result in long delays in getting your visa application back on track.

If you do change addresses, be sure to notify the last USCIS or consular office you heard from. But don't assume they'll pay attention. USCIS and the consulates are notorious for losing change-of-address notifications. So, as a backup plan, have your mail forwarded or check in regularly with the new people living in your former home.

Many couples wish that they could take a quick trip to the United States while waiting for the fiancé visa to be granted. Unfortunately, once you've submitted any part of your fiancé visa application, you're unlikely to be granted a tourist visa. This is because the consulate will likely believe that your real intention in using the tourist visa is to get married and then apply for your green card in the United States, which is an inappropriate use of the tourist visa and could be considered visa fraud.

---

1. Step One: The Initial Fiancé Petition

The first person that the U.S. government wants to hear from in this process is your U.S. citizen fiancé. He or she will be responsible for preparing what's called a petition for alien fiancé. The purpose of this petition is to alert the immigration authorities that your fiancé is planning to marry you and willing to participate in your visa application. You play a minor role at this step, but should help your U.S. fiancé gather certain information and documents.

Checklist for K-1 Fiancé Petition

☐ USCIS Form I-129F (see Subsection F1a, below, for line-by-line instructions)

☐ Form G-1145 (optional, but useful so that you'll receive an email or text notification from USCIS after it gets your application)

☐ A color photo of you (passport style)

☐ A color photo of your U.S. fiancé (passport style)

☐ Fee (currently $535; double-check at www.uscis.gov) and if paying by credit card, Form G-1450, Authorization for Credit Card Transactions

☐ Proof of the U.S. citizenship of U.S petitioner: a birth certificate, passport, naturalization certificate, or Report of Birth Abroad of a United States Citizen (see Chapter 4, Section C, on "How to Obtain Needed Documents")

☐ Proof that the two of you are legally able to marry (see Chapter 2, Section B, to review)

☐ A statement written by U.S. citizen petitioner describing how you met (see Subsection F1b, below)

☐ Proof that the two of you have met in person within the last two years, or that you qualify for an exception to this requirement (see Subsection F1b, below)

☐ Additional proof that the two of you truly intend to marry, whether or not you have met in person (see Subsection F1b, below)

☐ If the U.S. citizen petitioner has ever been convicted of certain crimes, certified copies of police and court records showing the outcome (get a lawyer's help)

☐ If the U.S. citizen has filed two or more K-1 petitions for other immigrants in the past (no matter how long ago), or had a K-1 petition approved for another immigrant within the two years before filing your petition, a letter requesting a waiver (get a lawyer's help)

We'll go through how to prepare and assemble the various forms and documents, one by one. To keep track of them all, refer to the Fiancé Petition Checklist, above. A few items on this checklist are self-explanatory, so they aren't discussed in the following text.

a. Line-by-Line Instructions for K-1 Fiancé Petition Forms

This section will give precise instructions for filling out the forms that are listed on the Fiancé Petition Checklist. The U.S. citizen fiancé should be handling the original forms and paperwork, but should send you copies of the drafts to review and discuss. Whoever reads these instructions should also have a copy of the appropriate form in hand.

> **CAUTION**
> **Don't confuse your forms.** Form I-129F is the proper one to use for a fiancé petition. There is another USCIS form called simply I-129, without the letter F. It is completely different (and much longer), so don't confuse the two or you'll be sorry!

i. Form I-129F

The following instructions refer to the version of the form dated 11/04/18, expiring 11/30/2020.

> **WEB RESOURCE**
> **This form is available on the USCIS website at www.uscis.gov/i-129f.** A sample filled-in version of the relevant pages of this form is shown below.

Form I-129F starts by asking for information about the U.S. citizen petitioner, then asks for information about the immigrating fiancé.

Part 1. Information About You

Questions 1-3: The U.S. citizen petitioner will have an A-number only if he or she once held a green card (permanent residence). If the U.S. citizen has ever filed a petition with USCIS, he or she might have a USCIS Online Account Number. The U.S. citizen will have a Social Security number and should enter it under Question 3.

Sample Form I-129F, Petition for Alien Fiancé(e)—Page 1

<table>
<tr><td colspan="2">**Petition for Alien Fiancé(e)**
Department of Homeland Security
U.S. Citizenship and Immigration Services</td><td>**USCIS**
Form I-129F
OMB No. 1615-0001
Expires 11/30/2020</td></tr>
</table>

For USCIS Use Only	Fee Stamp	Action Block
Case ID Number		
A-Number		
G-28 Number		

☐ The petition is approved for status under Section 101(a)(15)(K). It is valid for 4 months and expires on: _____

Extraordinary Circumstances Waiver
☐ Approved   Reason
☐ Denied   _____

General Waiver	**Mandatory Waiver**	**AMCON:** _____
☐ Approved Reason ☐ Denied ____	☐ Approved Reason ☐ Denied ____	☐ Personal Interview ☐ Previously Forwarded ☐ Document Check ☐ Field Investigation

Initial Receipt	**Relocated** Received	**Completed** Approved	**Remarks**	**IMBRA disclosure to the beneficiary required?**
Resubmitted	Sent	Returned		☐ Yes ☐ No

► **START HERE - Type or print in black ink.**

Part 1. Information About You

1. Alien Registration Number (A-Number) (if any)
► A- [ ][ ][ ][ ][ ][ ][ ][ ][ ]

2. USCIS Online Account Number (if any)
► [ ][ ][ ][ ][ ][ ][ ][ ][ ][ ][ ][ ]

3. U.S. Social Security Number (if any)
► 1 2 3 4 5 6 7 8 9

Select **one** box below to indicate the classification you are requesting for your beneficiary:

4.a. ☒ Fiancé(e) (K-1 visa)

4.b. ☐ Spouse (K-3 visa)

5. If you are filing to classify your spouse as a K-3, have you filed Form I-130?   ☐ Yes   ☐ No

Your Full Name

6.a. Family Name (Last Name)   BEACH

6.b. Given Name (First Name)   Sandra

6.c. Middle Name   Leah

Other Names Used

Provide all other names you have ever used, including aliases, maiden name, and nicknames. If you need extra space to complete this section, use the space provided in **Part 8. Additional Information**.

7.a. Family Name (Last Name)   (None)

7.b. Given Name (First Name)

7.c. Middle Name

Your Mailing Address   (USPS ZIP Code Lookup)

8.a. In Care Of Name

8.b. Street Number and Name   114 Fulton St.

8.c. ☒ Apt. ☐ Ste. ☐ Flr.   6E

8.d. City or Town   New York

8.e. State   NY   **8.f.** ZIP Code   10038

8.g. Province

8.h. Postal Code

8.i. Country   U.S.A.

8.j. Is your current mailing address the same as your physical address?   ☒ Yes   ☐ No

If you answered "No," provide your physical address in **Item Numbers 9.a. - 9.h.**

Sample Form I-129F, Petition for Alien Fiancé(e)—Page 2

Part 1. Information About You (continued)

Your Address History

Provide your physical addresses for the last five years, whether inside or outside the United States. Provide your current address first if it is different from your mailing address in **Item Numbers 8.a. - 8.i.** If you need extra space to complete this section, use the space provided in **Part 8. Additional Information**.

Physical Address 1

9.a. Street Number and Name

9.b. ☐ Apt. ☐ Ste. ☐ Flr.

9.c. City or Town

9.d. State   **9.e.** ZIP Code

9.f. Province

9.g. Postal Code

9.h. Country

10.a. Date From (mm/dd/yyyy)

10.b. Date To (mm/dd/yyyy)   PRESENT

Physical Address 2

11.a. Street Number and Name

11.b. ☐ Apt. ☐ Ste. ☐ Flr.

11.c. City or Town

11.d. State ▼   **11.e.** ZIP Code

11.f. Province

11.g. Postal Code

11.h. Country

12.a. Date From (mm/dd/yyyy)

12.b. Date To (mm/dd/yyyy)

Your Employment History

Provide your employment history for the last five years, whether inside or outside the United States. Provide your current employment first. If you need extra space to complete this section, use the space provided in **Part 8. Additional Information**.

Employer 1

13. Full Name of Employer

    Helport Foundation

14.a. Street Number and Name   87 W. 57th St

14.b. ☐ Apt. ☐ Ste. ☐ Flr.

14.c. City or Town   New York

14.d. State NY ▼   **14.e.** ZIP Code 10039

14.f. Province

14.g. Postal Code

14.h. Country   U.S.A.

15. Your Occupation (specify)

    Executive Assistant

16.a. Employment Start Date (mm/dd/yyyy)   02/15/2013

16.b. Employment End Date (mm/dd/yyyy)

Employer 2

17. Full Name of Employer

18.a. Street Number and Name

18.b. ☐ Apt. ☐ Ste. ☐ Flr.

18.c. City or Town

18.d. State ▼   **18.e.** ZIP Code

18.f. Province

18.g. Postal Code

18.h. Country

19. Your Occupation (specify)

Sample Form I-129F, Petition for Alien Fiancé(e)—Page 3

Part 1. Information About You (continued)

20.a. Employment Start Date (mm/dd/yyyy) [   ]

20.b. Employment End Date (mm/dd/yyyy) [   ]

Other Information

21. Gender ☐ Male ☒ Female

22. Date of Birth (mm/dd/yyyy) [12/20/1990]

23. Marital Status
☒ Single ☐ Married ☐ Divorced ☐ Widowed

24. City/Town/Village of Birth
[Horseheads]

25. Province or State of Birth
[New York]

26. Country of Birth
[U.S.A.]

Information About Your Parents

Parent 1's Information

27.a. Family Name (Last Name) [Beach]

27.b. Given Name (First Name) [michael]

27.c. Middle Name [James]

28. Date of Birth (mm/dd/yyyy) [05/02/1962]

29. Gender ☒ Male ☐ Female

30. Country of Birth
[U.S.A.]

31.a. City/Town/Village of Residence
[Horseheads]

31.b. Country of Residence
[U.S.A.]

Parent 2's Information

32.a. Family Name (Last Name) [Beach]

32.b. Given Name (First Name) [Samantha]

32.c. Middle Name [Anne]

33. Date of Birth (mm/dd/yyyy) [01/05/1960]

34. Gender ☐ Male ☒ Female

35. Country of Birth
[U.S.A.]

36.a. City/Town/Village of Residence
[Horseheads]

36.b. Country of Residence
[U.S.A.]

37. Have you ever been previously married?
☐ Yes ☒ No

If you answered "Yes" to **Item Number 37.**, provide the names of each spouse and the date that each prior marriage ended in **Item Numbers 38.a. - 39.** If you need extra space to complete this section, use the space provided in **Part 8. Additional Information**.

Name of Previous Spouse

38.a. Family Name (Last Name) [   ]

38.b. Given Name (First Name) [   ]

38.c. Middle Name [   ]

39. Date Marriage Ended (mm/dd/yyyy) [   ]

Your Citizenship Information

You are a U.S. citizen through (select **only one** box):

40.a. ☒ Birth in the United States

40.b. ☐ Naturalization

40.c. ☐ U.S. citizen parents

41. Have you obtained a Certificate of Naturalization or a Certificate of Citizenship in your own name?
☐ Yes ☐ No

If you answered "Yes" to **Item Number 41.**, complete **Item Numbers 42.a. - 42.c.**

Sample Form I-129F, Petition for Alien Fiancé(e)—Page 4

Part 1. Information About You (continued)

42.a. Certificate Number

42.b. Place of Issuance

42.c. Date of Issuance (mm/dd/yyyy)

Additional Information

43. Have you ever filed Form I-129F for any other beneficiary? ☐ Yes ☒ No

If you answered "Yes" to **Item Number 43.**, provide the responses to **Item Number 44. - 46.** for each previous beneficiary. If you need to provide information for more than one beneficiary, use the space provided in **Part 8. Additional Information**.

44. A-Number (if any) ► A-

45.a. Family Name (Last Name)

45.b. Given Name (First Name)

45.c. Middle Name

46. Date of Filing (mm/dd/yyyy)

47. What action did USCIS take on Form I-129F (for example, approved, denied, revoked)?

48. Do you have any children under 18 years of age? ☐ Yes ☒ No

If you answered "Yes" to **Item Number 48.**, provide the ages for your children under 18 years of age in **Item Numbers 49.a. - 49.b.**

Provide the ages for your children under 18 years of age. If you need extra space to complete this section, use the space provided in **Part 8. Additional Information**.

49.a. Age

49.b. Age

Provide all U.S. states and foreign countries in which you have resided since your 18th birthday.

Residence 1

50.a. State NY

50.b. Country
U.S.A.

Residence 2

51.a. State

51.b. Country

Part 2. Information About Your Beneficiary

1.a. Family Name (Last Name) Hollis

1.b. Given Name (First Name) Nigel

1.c. Middle Name Ian

2. A-Number (if any) ► A-

3. U.S. Social Security Number (if any) ►

4. Date of Birth (mm/dd/yyyy) 08/17/1990

5. Gender ☒ Male ☐ Female

6. Marital Status ☐ Single ☐ Married ☒ Divorced ☐ Widowed

7. City/Town/Village of Birth
Port Navas

8. Country of Birth
U.K.

9. Country of Citizenship or Nationality
U.K.

Other Names Used

Provide all other names you have ever used, including aliases, maiden name, and nicknames. If you need extra space to complete this section, use the space provided in **Part 8. Additional Information**.

10.a. Family Name (Last Name)

10.b. Given Name (First Name)

10.c. Middle Name

Sample Form I-129F, Petition for Alien Fiancé(e)—Page 5

Part 2. Information About Your Beneficiary (continued)

Mailing Address for Your Beneficiary

11.a. In Care Of Name

11.b. Street Number and Name — 123 Limestone Way

11.c. ☒ Apt. ☐ Ste. ☐ Flr. — 7

11.d. City or Town — Penzance

11.e. State ▼ **11.f.** ZIP Code

11.g. Province — Cornwall

11.h. Postal Code — TR 197 NL

11.i. Country — U.K.

Your Beneficiary's Address History

Provide your beneficiary's physical addresses for the last five years, whether inside or outside the United States. Provide your beneficiary's current address first if it is different from the mailing address in **Item Numbers 11.a. - 11.i.** If you need extra space to complete this section, use the space provided in **Part 8. Additional Information.**

Beneficiary's Physical Address 1

12.a. Street Number and Name

12.b. ☐ Apt. ☐ Ste. ☐ Flr.

12.c. City or Town

12.d. State ▼ **12.e.** ZIP Code

12.f. Province

12.g. Postal Code

12.h. Country

13.a. Date From (mm/dd/yyyy)

13.b. Date To (mm/dd/yyyy) — PRESENT

Beneficiary's Physical Address 2

14.a. Street Number and Name

14.b. ☐ Apt. ☐ Ste. ☐ Flr.

14.c. City or Town

14.d. State ▼ **14.e.** ZIP Code

14.f. Province

14.g. Postal Code

14.h. Country

15.a. Date From (mm/dd/yyyy)

15.b. Date To (mm/dd/yyyy)

Your Beneficiary's Employment History

Provide your employment history for the last five years, whether inside or outside the United States. Provide your current employment first. If you need extra space to complete this section, use the space provided in **Part 8. Additional Information**.

Beneficiary's Employer 1

16. Full Name of Employer

Outbound Design

17.a. Street Number and Name — 222 Heather Lane

17.b. ☐ Apt. ☐ Ste. ☐ Flr.

17.c. City or Town — Penzance

17.d. State ▼ **17.e.** ZIP Code

17.f. Province — Cornwall

17.g. Postal Code — TR 197 NL

17.h. Country — U.K.

18. Beneficiary's Occupation (specify)

Sportswear Designer

19.a. Employment Start Date (mm/dd/yyyy) — 08/02/2014

19.b. Employment End Date (mm/dd/yyyy)

Sample Form I-129F, Petition for Alien Fiancé(e)—Page 6

Part 2. Information About Your Beneficiary (continued)

Beneficiary's Employer 2

20. Full Name of Employer

21.a. Street Number and Name

21.b. ☐ Apt. ☐ Ste. ☐ Flr.

21.c. City or Town

21.d. State ▼ **21.e.** ZIP Code

21.f. Province

21.g. Postal Code

21.h. Country

22. Beneficiary's Occupation (specify)

23.a. Employment Start Date (mm/dd/yyyy)

23.b. Employment End Date (mm/dd/yyyy)

Information About Your Beneficiary's Parents

Parent 1's Information

24.a. Family Name (Last Name) Hollis
24.b. Given Name (First Name) Sarah
24.c. Middle Name Rose

25. Date of Birth (mm/dd/yyyy) 04/07/1965

26. Gender ☐ Male ☒ Female

27. Country of Birth U.K.

28.a. City/Town/Village of Residence York

28.b. Country of Residence U.K.

Parent 2's Information

29.a. Family Name (Last Name) Hollis
29.b. Given Name (First Name) Kevin
29.c. Middle Name Andrew

30. Date of Birth (mm/dd/yyyy) 01/12/1961

31. Gender ☒ Male ☐ Female

32. Country of Birth U.K.

33.a. City/Town/Village of Residence York

33.b. Country of Residence U.K.

Other Information About Your Beneficiary

34. Has your beneficiary ever been previously married? ☒ Yes ☐ No

If you answered "Yes" to **Item Number 34.**, provide the names of each prior spouse and the date each prior marriage ended in **Item Numbers 35.a. - 36.** If you need to provide information for more than one spouse, use the space provided in **Part 8. Additional Information.**

Name of Previous Spouse

35.a. Family Name (Last Name) Simpson
35.b. Given Name (First Name) Jane
35.c. Middle Name Marie

36. Date Marriage Ended (mm/dd/yyyy) 05/02/2016

37. Has your beneficiary ever been in the United States? ☐ Yes ☒ No

If your beneficiary is currently in the United States, complete **Item Numbers 38.a. - 38.h.**

38.a. He or she last entered as a (for example, visitor, student, exchange alien, crewman, stowaway, temporary worker, without inspection):

38.b. I-94 Arrival-Departure Record Number ▶

38.c. Date of Arrival (mm/dd/yyyy)

Sample Form I-129F, Petition for Alien Fiancé(e)—Page 7

Part 2. Information About Your Beneficiary (continued)

38.d. Date authorized stay expired or will expire as shown on Form I-94 or I-95 (mm/dd/yyyy)

38.e. Passport Number

38.f. Travel Document Number

38.g. Country of Issuance for Passport or Travel Document

38.h. Expiration Date for Passport or Travel Document (mm/dd/yyyy)

39. Does your beneficiary have any children?
☐ Yes ☒ No

If you answered "Yes" to **Item Number 39.**, provide the following information about each child. If you need to provide information for more than one child, use the space provided in **Part 8. Additional Information.**

Children of Beneficiary

40.a. Family Name (Last Name)

40.b. Given Name (First Name)

40.c. Middle Name

41. Country of Birth

42. Date of Birth (mm/dd/yyyy)

43. Does this child reside with your beneficiary?
☐ Yes ☐ No

If the child does not reside with your beneficiary, provide the child's physical residence.

44.a. Street Number and Name

44.b. ☐ Apt. ☐ Ste. ☐ Flr.

44.c. City or Town

44.d. State

44.e. ZIP Code

44.f. Province

44.g. Postal Code

44.h. Country

Address in the United States Where Your Beneficiary Intends to Live

45.a. Street Number and Name 14 Fulton St

45.b. ☒ Apt. ☐ Ste. ☐ Flr. 6E

45.c. City or Town New York

45.d. State NY **45.e.** ZIP Code 10038

46. Daytime Telephone Number
212-555-1313

Your Beneficiary's Physical Address Abroad

47.a. Street Number and Name 123 Limestone Way

47.b. ☒ Apt. ☐ Ste. ☐ Flr. 7

47.c. City or Town Penzance

47.d. Province NY Cornwall

47.e. Postal Code TR 197 N2

47.f. Country U.K.

48. Daytime Telephone Number
123-412-3456

Your Beneficiary's Name and Address in His or Her Native Alphabet

49.a. Family Name (Last Name)

49.b. Given Name (First Name)

49.c. Middle Name

50.a. Street Number and Name

50.b. ☐ Apt. ☐ Ste. ☐ Flr.

50.c. City or Town

50.d. Province

50.e. Postal Code

50.f. Country

Sample Form I-129F, Petition for Alien Fiancé(e)—Page 8

Part 2. Information About Your Beneficiary (continued)

51. Is your fiancé(e) related to you?

☐ Yes ☒ No ☐ N/A, beneficiary is my spouse

52. Provide the nature and degree of relationship (for example, third cousin or maternal uncle).

53. Have you and your fiancé(e) met in person during the two years immediately before filing this petition?

☒ Yes ☐ No ☐ N/A, beneficiary is my spouse

If you answered "Yes" to **Item Number 53.**, describe the circumstances of your in-person meeting in **Item Number 54.** Attach evidence to demonstrate that you were in each other's physical presence during the required two year period.

If you answered "No," explain your reasons for requesting an exemption from the in person meeting requirement in **Item Number 54.** and provide evidence that you should be exempt from this requirement. Refer to **Part 2., Item Numbers 53. - 54.** of the **Specific Instructions** section of the Instructions for additional information about the requirement to meet. If you need extra space to complete this section, use the space provided in **Part 8. Additional Information**.

54. See attached statement

International Marriage Broker (IMB) Information

55. Did you meet your beneficiary through the services of an IMB? ☐ Yes ☒ No

If you answered "Yes" to **Item Number 55.**, provide the IMB's contact information and Website information below. In addition, attach a copy of the signed, written consent form the IMB obtained from your beneficiary authorizing your beneficiary's personal contact information to be released to you.

56. IMB's Name (if any)

57.a. Family Name of IMB (Last Name)

57.b. Given Name of IMB (First Name)

58. Organization Name of IMB

59. Website of IMB

60.a. Street Number and Name

60.b. ☐ Apt. ☐ Ste. ☐ Flr.

60.c. City or Town

60.d. Province

60.e. Postal Code

60.f. Country

61. Daytime Telephone Number

Consular Processing Information

Your beneficiary will apply for a visa abroad at the U.S. Embassy or U.S. Consulate at:

62.a. City or Town

London

62.b. Country

U.K.

Part 3. Other Information

Criminal Information

NOTE: These criminal information questions must be answered even if your records were sealed, cleared, or if anyone, including a judge, law enforcement officer, or attorney, told you that you no longer have a record. If you need extra space to complete this section, use the space provided in **Part 8. Additional Information**.

1. Have you **EVER** been subject to a temporary or permanent protection or restraining order (either civil or criminal)? ☐ Yes ☒ No

Have you EVER been arrested or convicted of any of the following crimes:

2.a. Domestic violence, sexual assault, child abuse, child neglect, dating violence, elder abuse, stalking or an attempt to commit any of these crimes? (See **Part 3. Other Information, Item Numbers 1. - 3.c.** of the Instructions for the full definition of the term "domestic violence.") ☐ Yes ☒ No

Sample Form I-129F, Petition for Alien Fiancé(e)—Page 9

Part 3. Other Information (continued)

2.b. Homicide, murder, manslaughter, rape, abusive sexual contact, sexual exploitation, incest, torture, trafficking, peonage, holding hostage, involuntary servitude, slave trade, kidnapping, abduction, unlawful criminal restraint, false imprisonment, or an attempt to commit any of these crimes? ☐ Yes ☒ No

2.c. Three or more arrests or convictions, not from a single act, for crimes relating to a controlled substance or alcohol? ☐ Yes ☒ No

NOTE: If you were ever arrested or convicted of any of the specified crimes, you must submit certified copies of all court and police records showing the charges and disposition for every arrest or conviction. You must do so even if your records were sealed, expunged, or otherwise cleared, and regardless of whether anyone, including a judge, law enforcement officer, or attorney, informed you that you no longer have a criminal record. If you need extra space to complete this section, use the space provided in **Part 8. Additional Information**.

If you have provided information about a conviction for a crime listed in **Item Numbers 2.a. - 2.c.** and you were being battered or subjected to extreme cruelty at the time of your conviction, select all of the following that apply to you:

3.a. ☐ I was acting in self-defense.

3.b. ☐ I violated a protection order issued for my own protection.

3.c. ☐ I committed, was arrested for, was convicted of, or pled guilty to a crime that did not result in serious bodily injury and there was a connection between the crime and me having been battered or subjected to extreme cruelty.

4.a. Have you ever been arrested, cited, charged, indicted, convicted, fined, or imprisoned for breaking or violating any law or ordinance in any country, excluding traffic violations (unless a traffic violation was alcohol- or drug-related or involved a fine of $500 or more)? ☐ Yes ☐ No

4.b. If the answer to **Item Number 4.a.** is "Yes," provide information about each of those arrests, citations, charges, indictments, convictions, fines, or imprisonments in the space below. If you were the subject of an order of protection or restraining order and believe you are the victim, please explain those circumstances and provide any evidence to support your claims. Include the dates and outcomes. If you need extra space to complete this section, use the space provided in **Part 8. Additional Information**.

Multiple Filer Waiver Request Information

Refer to **Part 3. Types of Waivers** in the **Specific Instructions** section of the Instructions for an explanation of the filing waivers.

Indicate which one of the following waivers you are requesting:

5.a. ☐ Multiple Filer, No Permanent Restraining Orders or Convictions for a Specified Offense (**General Waiver**)

5.b. ☐ Multiple Filer, Prior Permanent Restraining Orders or Criminal Conviction for Specified Offense (**Extraordinary Circumstances Waiver**)

5.c. ☐ Multiple Filer, Prior Permanent Restraining Order or Criminal Convictions for Specified Offense Resulting from Domestic Violence (**Mandatory Waiver**)

5.d. ☐ Not applicable, beneficiary is my spouse or I am not a multiple filer

Part 4. Biographic Information

1. Ethnicity (Select **only one** box)
☐ Hispanic or Latino
☒ Not Hispanic or Latino

2. Race (Select **all applicable** boxes)
☒ White
☐ Asian
☐ Black or African American
☐ American Indian or Alaska Native
☐ Native Hawaiian or Other Pacific Islander

3. Height   Feet 5 ▼   Inches 6 ▼

4. Weight   Pounds 1 4 0

5. Eye Color (Select **only one** box)
☐ Black   ☐ Blue   ☒ Brown
☐ Gray   ☐ Green   ☐ Hazel
☐ Maroon   ☐ Pink   ☐ Unknown/Other

6. Hair Color (Select **only one** box)
☐ Bald (No hair)   ☐ Black   ☐ Blond
☒ Brown   ☐ Gray   ☐ Red
☐ Sandy   ☐ White   ☐ Unknown/Other

Sample Form I-129F, Petition for Alien Fiancé(e)—Page 10

Part 5. Petitioner's Statement, Contact Information, Declaration, Certification, and Signature

NOTE: Read the **Penalties** section of the Form I-129F Instructions before completing this part.

Petitioner's Statement

NOTE: Select the box for either **Item Number 1.a.** or **1.b.** If applicable, select the box for **Item Number 2.**

1.a. ☒ I can read and understand English, and I have read and understand every question and instruction on this petition and my answer to every question.

1.b. ☐ The interpreter named in **Part 6.** read to me every question and instruction on this petition and my answer to every question in

[   ] ,

a language in which I am fluent, and I understood everything.

2. ☐ At my request, the preparer named in **Part 7.**,

[   ] ,

prepared this petition for me based only upon information I provided or authorized.

Petitioner's Contact Information

3. Petitioner's Daytime Telephone Number

[202-444-1212]

4. Petitioner's Mobile Telephone Number (if any)

[212-555-1313]

5. Petitioner's Email Address (if any)

[sandrab@email.com]

Petitioner's Declaration and Certification

Copies of any documents I have submitted are exact photocopies of unaltered, original documents, and I understand that USCIS may require that I submit original documents to USCIS at a later date. Furthermore, I authorize the release of any information from any and all of my records that USCIS may need to determine my eligibility for the immigration benefit that I seek.

I furthermore authorize release of information contained in this petition, in supporting documents, and in my USCIS records, to other entities and persons where necessary for the administration and enforcement of U.S. immigration law.

I understand that USCIS may require me to appear for an appointment to take my biometrics (fingerprints, photograph, and/or signature) and, at that time, if I am required to provide biometrics, I will be required to sign an oath reaffirming that:

1) I reviewed and understood all of the information contained in, and submitted with, my petition; and

2) All of this information was complete, true, and correct at the time of filing.

I certify, under penalty of perjury, that all of the information in my petition and any document submitted with it were provided or authorized by me, that I reviewed and understand all of the information contained in, and submitted with my petition, and that all of this information is complete, true, and correct.

Petitioner's Signature

6.a. Petitioner's Signature

➡ [*Sandra L. Beach*]

6.b. Date of Signature (mm/dd/yyyy) [09/01/2019]

NOTE TO ALL PETITIONERS: If you do not completely fill out this petition or fail to submit required documents listed in the Instructions, USCIS may deny your petition.

Part 6. Interpreter's Contact Information, Certification, and Signature

Provide the following information about the interpreter.

Interpreter's Full Name

1.a. Interpreter's Family Name (Last Name)

[   ]

1.b. Interpreter's Given Name (First Name)

[   ]

2. Interpreter's Business or Organization Name (if any)

[   ]

Interpreter's Mailing Address

3.a. Street Number and Name [   ]

3.b. ☐ Apt. ☐ Ste. ☐ Flr. [   ]

3.c. City or Town [   ]

3.d. State [▼] **3.e.** ZIP Code [   ]

3.f. Province [   ]

3.g. Postal Code [   ]

3.h. Country [   ]

Sample Fiancé Meeting Statement—Attachment to Form I-129F

FILED BY SANDRA BEACH ON BEHALF OF NIGEL HOLLIS

STATEMENT OF MEETING AND INTENT TO MARRY

I met my fiancé 18 months ago, while visiting a college friend who has settled in England. My friend Carrie had been telling me for months that she wanted to introduce me to Nigel, because of our offbeat senses of humor and shared interest in long-distance swimming. I've had bad experiences with friends trying to set me up before, so I didn't take it very seriously. But when vacation plans took me to England, I let her arrange for me and Nigel to meet over lunch at a pub.

To my amazement, we clicked right away. We had a lot to talk about—he had completed an English Channel swim a few months before, and I'm hoping to swim the Channel next year. Both of us have built our lives around swimming, which sometimes leaves little time for other things, including relationships. We compared notes on training techniques, equipment, dealing with cold water, rip tides, and more.

Our lunch lasted all afternoon and into the evening. By the end of that evening, I considered Nigel a friend, and someone I could very easily fall in love with.

Nigel and I spent almost all my remaining week's vacation together. Poor Carrie joked that her plan had backfired, because I spent embarrassingly little time at her house. By the end of the week, we both knew this was headed toward a serious relationship.

Since then, Nigel and I have corresponded almost constantly by email, and call each other twice a week. During one long phone call, we decided to get married.

It was difficult deciding where we would live after marrying—Nigel has a beautiful cottage in Cornwall, and I could happily live in England. However, my mother is in poor health, and ever since my father passed away last year, she has relied on my help, so we agreed to make our home in New York.

As proof that Nigel and I are in love and plan to marry, I am attaching copies of his plane tickets to New York; photos of the two of us together; copies of our telephone bills and some of our emails; copies of catering and other contracts showing that the two of us plan to marry in July; and copies of our travel itinerary for New Zealand, where we will honeymoon.

Signed: _Sandra Leah Beach_
Sandra Beach

Date: _1/2/2019_

Question 4: Check the box indicating whether you're filing for a K-1 visa (petitioning for someone you intend to marry but have not yet married) or K-3 visa (petitioning for someone you have already married).

Question 5: Answer only if applying for a K-3 visa (already married). You'll want to be able to answer "yes" to having already filed an I-130 family-based immigrant petition for the foreign-born spouse; it's a requirement.

Question 6: The U.S. citizen petitioner enters his or her name.

Question 7: The U.S. citizen enters any names previously used. If the citizen was married before and used another name then, add it here.

Question 8: Self-explanatory.

Questions 9-12: Fill in all the U.S. citizen petitioner's addresses from the last five years. If the mailing and physical addresses are the same, the form will not allow you to fill in when you began living at the current address. If the citizen has lived at more than one address in the last five years, include the start and end dates of each. Enter additional addresses that do not fit on the main form in Part 8.

Questions 13-20: Fill in U.S. citizen petitioner's employment history from the last five years. If he or she has had more than two jobs during this time, enter the additional addresses in Part 8.

Questions 21-26: Answer basic biographic questions about the U.S. citizen. If he or she was married before but is now divorced, check "divorced" instead of "single." Make sure not to check "married" if applying for the K-1 visa.

Questions 27-36: Answer basic biographic information about the U.S. citizen's parents. If lacking pieces of information, say "unknown."

Question 37: Answer whether the U.S. citizen has been previously married.

Questions 38-39: Enter name(s) of the U.S. citizen's prior spouse(s). These marriages must have ended before sponsoring someone for a K-1 visa. **Date Marriage Ended** means the date the divorce became final, not the date of splitting up or ceasing to live together. USCIS will accept only a final divorce.

Question 40: A U.S. citizen born in the U.S. should check option 40.a. One who had a green card (permanent residence) and then naturalized to become a citizen should check option 40.b. One not born on U.S. soil but was a U.S. citizen at birth due to having U.S. citizen parents should check option 40.c.

Questions 41-42: A U.S. citizen sponsor who was not a citizen at birth must include information about his or her Certificate of Naturalization. Make sure the current name matches the name on the certificate.

Questions 43-47: A U.S. citizen spouse who has filed a K-1 visa in the past must include information on that person here. For filings of more than one K-1 visa in the past, enter that information in Part 8. USCIS may deny the K-1 petition if the U.S. petitioner has filed too many K-1 visa requests in the past, or may require applying for a waiver.

Questions 48-49: The citizen must state how many children under the age of 18 he or she has, and their ages. This refers to all children, whether born of this relationship or a previous one, and whether or not they were born in the United States.

Questions 50-51: Self-explanatory, referring to U.S. citizen.

Part 2. Information About Your Beneficiary

Now the questions concern the foreign-born fiancé (the "beneficiary") instead of the U.S. citizen petitioner.

Questions 1-9: Self-explanatory biographical information.

Question 10: Fill in any names the beneficiary previously used here. If the person was previously married and used another name during that time, include it here.

Questions 11-15: Fill in the foreign beneficiary's addresses from the last five years. If there are more than three, all must still be listed, using Part 8.

Questions 16-23: Fill in the foreign beneficiary's employment history from the last five years. If there were more than two jobs in the past five years, all must still be listed, using Part 8.

Questions 24-33: Answer basic biographic information about the foreign beneficiary's parents. If lacking any pieces of information, answer "unknown."

Questions 34-36: Enter the name(s) of any of the foreign beneficiary's former spouse(s). Prior marriages must have ended before a U.S. fiancé can successfully sponsor someone. Make sure that under **Date Marriage Ended** you give the date the divorce became final, not the date the couple split up or stopped living together. USCIS will accept only a final divorce as proof that the marriage ended.

Question 37: Enter "yes" if the foreign beneficiary has ever been to the United States, even if for only a short time as a tourist.

Questions 38-39: Leave these boxes empty, since the beneficiary is not in the United States.

Questions 40-44: If the foreign beneficiary has children, whether born of this relationship or a previous one, and whether the children were born in or out of the U.S., fill in their information here.

Questions 45-46: Hopefully the intended address where the beneficiary will live in the U.S. is the same as that of the U.S. citizen fiancé, or USCIS will raise questions. If the K-1 beneficiary will spend some time away from the married home, such as for school or for work, consider the married home to be the permanent address. If there is a compelling reason to have a completely separate residence, however, attach documents to explain why, or consult with a lawyer.

Questions 47-48: Self-explanatory—the beneficiary's address in the home country.

Questions 49-50: If the beneficiary's native language uses a non-Roman script (for example, Russian, Chinese, or Arabic) write the name and address in that script.

Question 51-52: If the beneficiary and U.S. fiancé are related by blood, make sure that a marriage between you is legally allowed in the geographic state where you plan to marry. (See Chapter 2, Section B1, "The Legal Requirements for a K-1 Fiancé Visa.")

Questions 53-54: It's wise to attach a page to fully answer this question; see our sample Fiancé Meeting Statement. Note that this is also where you'd need to explain any reason why you are instead requesting a waiver of the personal meeting requirement. Although the main purpose is to show that you've fulfilled the personal meeting requirement, this is a fine opportunity to include extra detail about your life with your fiancé to show USCIS that this is a real relationship. No need to sound like a lawyer; and definitely provide enough personal detail for USCIS to see you didn't just copy a sample statement out of a book!

Questions 55-61: Responding to concern that so-called "mail order" spouses (who met through the services of an international matchmaking agency) are especially susceptible to domestic violence and abuse, Congress passed the International Marriage Brokers Regulation Act of 2005 (IMBRA). IMBRA requires you to state here whether you met your fiancé or spouse through an international marriage broker, and if so, to give information about the broker.

Question 62: Enter name of U.S. consulate with a visa processing office in your country; or if none exists, the one with the power to handle visa requests from your country. (Don't worry too much about getting it wrong; USCIS will redirect your application when it approves the petition.) You can write "Please Cable" in this section, in an effort to speed up USCIS's notification to the consulate after your petition is approved.

Part 3. Other Information

Now the questions again refer to the U.S. citizen petitioner.

Questions 1-4: A U.S. citizen petitioner who has a history of violent crime, stalking, child abuse, crime relating to alcohol, or controlled substance abuse may have to reveal this to USCIS. The petitioner should see an attorney if there is any question about whether this section applies. You, the immigrant, will also be told of any relevant history.

Question 5: This needs to be filled out only if the U.S. petitioner has previously filed two or more I-129F petitions for other foreign-born fiancés. Definitely get a lawyer's help if this is the case—USCIS will deny the petition unless you make a convincing request for a waiver of the "multiple filing restriction."

Sample Form G-1145, e-Notification of Application/Petition Acceptance

e-Notification of Application/Petition Acceptance

Department of Homeland Security
U.S. Citizenship and Immigration Services

USCIS
Form G-1145

What Is the Purpose of This Form?

Use this form to request an electronic notification (e-Notification) when U.S. Citizenship and Immigration Services accepts your immigration application. This service is available for applications filed at a USCIS Lockbox facility.

General Information

Complete the information below and clip this form to the first page of your application package. You will receive one e-mail and/or text message for each form you are filing.

We will send the e-Notification within 24 hours after we accept your application. Domestic customers will receive an e-mail and/or text message; overseas customers will only receive an e-mail. Undeliverable e-Notifications cannot be resent.

The e-mail or text message will display your receipt number and tell you how to get updated case status information. It will not include any personal information. The e-Notification does not grant any type of status or benefit; rather it is provided as a convenience to customers.

USCIS will also mail you a receipt notice (I-797C), which you will receive within 10 days after your application has been accepted; use this notice as proof of your pending application or petition.

USCIS Privacy Act Statement

AUTHORITIES: The information requested on this form is collected pursuant to section 103(a) of the Immigration and Nationality Act, as amended INA section 101, et seq.

PURPOSE: The primary purpose for providing the information on this form is to request an electronic notification when USCIS accepts immigration form. The information you provide will be used to send you a text and/or email message.

DISCLOSURE: The information you provide is voluntary. However, failure to provide the requested information may prevent USCIS from providing you a text and/or email message receipting your immigration form.

ROUTINE USES: The information provided on this form will be used by and disclosed to DHS personnel and contractors in accordance with approved routine uses, as described in the associated published system of records notices [**DHS/USCIS-007 - Benefits Information System and DHS/USCIS-001 - Alien File (A-File) and Central Index System (CIS),** which can be found at **www.dhs.gov/privacy**]. The information may also be made available, as appropriate for law enforcement purposes or in the interest of national security.

Complete this form and clip it on top of the first page of your immigration form(s).

Applicant/Petitioner Full Last Name	Applicant/Petitioner Full First Name	Applicant/Petitioner Full Middle Name
BEACH	Sandra	Leah

Email Address	Mobile Phone Number (Text Message)
sandrab@email.com	212-555-1313

Part 4. Biographic Information

Fill in information for U.S. citizen petitioner.

Part 5. Petitioner's Statement, Contact Information, Declaration, and Signature

The U.S. citizen must sign and date the form.

Part 6. Interpreter's Contact Information, Certification, and Signature

Fill in this section if you used an interpreter to fill in the form, and make sure the interpreter signs it.

Part 7. Contact Information, Declaration, and Signature of the Person Preparing this Petition, if Other Than the Petitioner

This need not be filled in if you just got a little help from a friend. This section is mainly for lawyers or agencies that fill out these forms on others' behalf.

ii. Form G-1145

This optional form is very simple to fill out. Enter the U.S. citizen's name and contact information. By doing so, you will trigger USCIS to notify the U.S. citizen electronically when the application has been received. Be sure to clip Form G-1145 to the top of your packet when mailing everything to USCIS.

> **WEB RESOURCE**
> **This form is available on the USCIS website at www.uscis.gov/g-1145.** Above is a sample filled-in version of this form.

b. Documents That Must Accompany Your Fiancé Petition

You need to do more than just fill in the blanks for your I-129F. The government wants additional written proof of two issues—that the two of you have met in person within the last two years, and that you really intend to marry. This section contains detailed instructions about how to satisfy these requirements. It also describes some of the miscellaneous requirements, such as photos and fees.

i. Proof That You Have Met in Person or Qualify for an Exception

If you and your fiancé have met in person, look for documents that will illustrate your meetings. Documents from a neutral, outside source such as an airline or landlord are best. Some possibilities are:

- dated photos of you together
- copies of plane tickets (including boarding passes) that you used to meet each other
- copies of your passports showing the stamps from when you traveled to see each other, and
- credit card receipts showing that you spent money at the same place and same time.

If you and your fiancé have not met in person, include documentation that will prove that this was for religious or medical reasons, such as

- a letter from your parents
- a letter from your religious guide
- a detailed letter from a medical professional, and
- copies of relevant medical records.

ii. Additional Proof That You Intend to Marry

Now that you've found a way to prove that you and your fiancé have met, you need to go one step further and show that you plan to marry. Some possible documents to gather are:

- a statement by you (the immigrant beneficiary) affirming your intent to marry (see sample below)
- copies of cards and letters between you discussing your marriage plans (it's okay to block out the most intimate sections)
- copies of phone bills showing that you called each other
- wedding announcements, and
- evidence of other wedding arrangements (such as a letter from the religious leader or justice of the peace who will perform the ceremony, contracts for catering, photography, rented chairs, dishes, or other equipment, flowers, and musical entertainment).

Sample Beneficiary Statement of Intent to Marry

Nigel Hollis
123 Limestone Way
Penzance, Cornwall, U.K.
TR197NL

USCIS
P.O. Box 660151
Dallas, TX 75266

August 1, 2019

Re: Beneficiary's Statement of Intent to Marry

Dear USCIS,

I, Nigel Ian Hollis, am engaged to marry Sandra Leah Beach. I hereby state that I am legally able and willing to marry Ms. Beach and intend to do so within 90 days of my arrival in the United States using the K-1 visa for which we are currently petitioning.

If you have any questions regarding this matter, do not hesitate to contact me.

Sincerely,

Nigel Ian Hollis

---

iii. Proof That You're Legally Able to Marry

If you're an adult who's never been previously married and you're not a blood relative of your fiancé, and your fiancé hasn't been previously married, you may not have to attach any documents under this category. (See Chapter 2, Section B, for details.) In many couples, however, one of the two people has been previously married, in which case you will need to prove that that marriage was legally ended. To do so, attach copies of such documents as:

- divorce decree
- annulment decree, or
- death certificate.

iv. Additional Items to Accompany Fiancé Petition

In addition, your fiancé petition will need to include the following:

- **Proof of the U.S. citizenship status of your petitioning spouse.** Depending on how your spouse became a citizen, this might include a copy of a birth certificate, passport, certificate of naturalization, certificate of citizenship, or Form FS-240 (Consular Report of Birth Abroad).

- **Photos.** You must submit one passport-style color photograph of yourself and ideally one passport-style color photograph of your fiancé. (Or, the fiancé can wait, and present photos at the consular interview.) The photos must be two by two inches in size, showing your current appearance, and taken within 30 days of filing the petition. They must have a white background, be glossy, unretouched, and not mounted. Passport style means showing your full face from the front, with a plain white or off-white background—and your face must measure between one inch and 1⅜ inches from the bottom of your chin to the top of your head. For more information, see the State Department website at www.travel.state.gov; click "Get U.S. Visas," then "Photo Requirements." However, USCIS regulations permit you to submit a photo that doesn't completely follow the instructions if you live in a country where such photographs are unavailable or are cost prohibitive.

- **Fee.** The 2019 fee for an I-129F petition for a K-1 visa is $535. However, USCIS fees go up fairly regularly, so double-check them at www.uscis.gov or by calling 800-375-5283. Make checks or money orders payable to U.S. Department of Homeland Security (don't send cash). Or, if paying by credit card, fill out Form G-1450, Authorization for Credit Card Transactions, available at www.uscis.gov/g-1450.

v. Document Requirements If U.S. Citizen Has a Criminal Record

If the U.S. citizen petitioner has ever been convicted of any violent crime, sexual assault, or a crime involving domestic violence or substance abuse (a more complete list of crimes is provided in the instructions to Form I-129F), he or she must submit certified copies of all police and court records showing the outcome. This is required even if the records were sealed or otherwise cleared. All of this information (except for victim's names) will be passed on to the immigrant during the consular interview. Get a lawyer's help in this instance.

vi. Waiver Request If U.S. Citizen Has Filed Previous I-129fs

To prevent abuse of immigrants, the law limits the number of times a U.S. citizen can petition for a K-1 (but not a K-3) fiancé. If the U.S. citizen has filed two or more K-1 petitions for other immigrants in the past (no matter how long ago), or had a K-1 petition approved for another immigrant within the two years before filing your petition, the U.S. citizen must request a waiver (official forgiveness) from USCIS.

To succeed with the waiver request, your best bet is to show unusual circumstances, such as the death (by natural causes, of course) of the prior immigrant. If the U.S. citizen has a history of violent crime, the waiver will be denied.

The procedure for requesting a waiver is to attach a signed and dated letter to Form I-129F, along with any supporting evidence. However, we strongly recommend getting a lawyer's help with your waiver request.

c. Where to Send the Fiancé Petition

When your U.S. citizen fiancé has finished the Fiancé Petition, the next step is to send it to the USCIS Dallas Lockbox Facility. The address will be the same whether your U.S. citizen fiancé resides in the United States or abroad.

If sending the petition by the U.S. Postal Service, the address is:

USCIS
P.O. Box 660151
Dallas, TX 75266

If sending the petition by express mail or a courier service, the address is:

USCIS
Attn: I-129F
2501 South State Highway 121 Business
Suite 400
Lewisville, TX 75067

Your U.S. citizen fiancé should also photocopy and send a copy of the Fiancé Petition to you. File it carefully with your other records and familiarize yourself with the answers so you'll be prepared to explain anything on it during your upcoming visa interview.

d. What Will Happen After Sending in the Fiancé Petition

A few weeks after sending in the Fiancé Petition, USCIS should mail your U.S. citizen fiancé a notice titled Notice of Action and numbered I-797C (see sample below). This notice will tell you to check the USCIS website for information on how long the petition is likely to remain in processing (usually at least two to six months). Until that date, USCIS will ignore any letters asking what is going on.

USCIS lockbox facilities are like walled fortresses. You can't visit them and it's impossible to speak with the person working on your case. If the petition is delayed past the processing time predicted (and delays are fairly normal), you can contact USCIS to try to get the petition back on track by calling 800-375-5283, where a live person will take your question from 8 a.m. until 8 p.m. Eastern time. Although the person you speak with will most likely not be able to tell you anything useful during that phone call, he or she should start an inquiry for you and tell you when you can expect a response. The USCIS representative may even schedule an in-person appointment for you at your local USCIS field office. Alternatively, you can submit the inquiry yourself directly, as an e-Request on USCIS's website (https://egov.uscis.gov/e-request/Intro.do).

Sample Receipt Notice Form for I-129F

Department of Homeland Security
U.S. Citizenship and Immigration Services

I-797C, Notice of Action

THE UNITED STATES OF AMERICA

RECEIPT NUMBER		CASE TYPE I129F	
WAC-19-041-00000		PETITION FOR FIANCE(E)	

RECEIVED DATE	PRIORITY DATE	PETITIONER	
August 5, 2019		BEACH, SANDRA	

NOTICE DATE	PAGE	BENEFICIARY	
August 10, 2019	1 of 1	HOLLIS, NIGEL	

ILONA BRAY
RE: NIGEL IAN HOLLIS
950 PARKER ST.
BERKELEY, CA 94710

Notice Type: Receipt Notice

Amount received: $ 535.00

Receipt notice - If any of the above information is incorrect, call customer service immediately.

Processing time - Processing times vary by kind of case.
- You can check our current processing time for this kind of case on our website at **uscis.gov**.
- On our website you can also sign up to get free e-mail updates as we complete key processing steps on this case.
- Most of the time your case is pending the processing status will not change because we will be working on others filed earlier.
- We will notify you by mail when we make a decision on this case, or if we need something from you. If you move while this case is pending, call customer service when you move.
- Processing times can change. If you don't get a decision or update from us within our current processing time, check our website or call for an update.

If you have questions, check our website or call customer service. Please save this notice, and have it with you if you contact us about this case.

Notice to all customers with a pending I-130 petition - USCIS is now processing Form I-130, Petition for Alien Relative, as a visa number becomes available. Filing and approval of an I-130 relative petition is only the first step in helping a relative immigrate to the United States. Eligible family members must wait until there is a visa number available before they can apply for an immigrant visa or adjustment of status to a lawful permanent resident. This process will allow USCIS to concentrate resources first on cases where visas are actually available. This process should not delay the ability of one's relative to apply for an immigrant visa or adjustment of status. Refer to **www.state.gov/travel** <http://www.state.gov/travel> to determine current visa availability dates. For more information, please visit our website at www.uscis.gov or contact us at 1-800-375-5283.

Always remember to call customer service if you move while your case is pending. If you have a pending I-130 relative petition, also call customer service if you should decide to withdraw your petition or if you become a U.S. citizen.

Please see the additional information on the back. You will be notified separately about any other cases you filed.
U.S. CITIZENSHIP & IMMIGRATION SVC
CALIFORNIA SERVICE CENTER
P.O. BOX 30111
LAGUNA NIGUEL CA 92607-0111
Customer Service Telephone: (800) 375-5283

Form I-797C (Rev. 08/31/04) N

Sample Approval Notice Form for I-129F

Department of Homeland Security
U.S. Citizenship and Immigration Services

I-797, Notice of Action

THE UNITED STATES OF AMERICA

RECEIPT NUMBER		CASE TYPE I129F
WAC-19-041-00000		PETITION FOR FIANCE(E)
RECEIPT DATE August 5, 2019	**PRIORITY DATE**	**PETITIONER** BEACH, SANDRA
NOTICE DATE February 10, 2020	**PAGE** 1 of 1	**BENEFICIARY** HOLLIS, NIGEL

ILONA BRAY
RE: NIGEL IAN HOLLIS
950 PARKER ST.
BERKELEY, CA 94710

Notice Type: Approval Notice

Valid from 02/10/2020 to 06/10/2020

The above petition has been approved. We have sent the original visa petition to the Department of State National Visa Center (NVC), 32 Rochester Avenue, Portsmouth, NH 03801-2909. The INS has completed all action; further inquiries should be directed to the NVC.

The NVC now processes all approved fiance(e) petitions. The NVC processing should be complete within two to four weeks after receiving the petition from INS. The NVC will create a case record with your petition information. NVC will then send the petition to the U.S. Embassy or Consulate where your fiance(e) will be interviewed for his or her visa.

You will receive notification by mail when NVC has sent your petition to the U.S. Embassy or Consulate. The notification letter will provide you with a unique number for your case and the name and address of the U.S. Embassy or Consulate where your petition has been sent.

If it has been more than four weeks since you received this approval notice and you have not received notification from NVC that your petition has been forwarded overseas, please call NVC at (603) 334-0700. Please call between 8:00am-6:45pm Eastern Standard Time. You will need to enter the INS receipt number from this approval notice into the automated response system to receive information on your petition.

THIS FORM IS NOT A VISA NOR MAY IT BE USED IN PLACE OF A VISA.

Please see the additional information on the back. You will be notified separately about any other cases you filed.
U.S. CITIZENSHIP & IMMIGRATION SVC
CALIFORNIA SERVICE CENTER
P. O. BOX 30111
LAGUNA NIGUEL CA 92607-0111
Customer Service Telephone: (800) 375-5283

Form I-797 (Rev. 01/31/05) N

Sample NVC Notice Transferring Fiancé Visa Case to Consulate

August 16, 2019

Dear Petitioner:

The State Department's National Visa Center has recently received an approved I-129F petition filed on behalf of your spouse. This letter is to let you know that within a week the petition will be forwarded to the visa-issuing post overseas that is responsible for processing visa cases originating in the country where you were married.

Our records show that you filed the I-129F petition for:

Name of Spouse:

USCIS Receipt Number: MSC09

Case Number: SAA2015
The case must be processed at:

     Post: SANAA
           EMBASSY OF THE UNITED STATES
           P.O. BOX 22347, DHAHR HIMYAR ZONE
           SHERATON HOTEL DIST, SANAA
           REPUBLIC OF YEMEN

Your spouse will soon receive a packet with instructions from the consular section at this post on how to apply for the K1 visa at that post and what documents will be required. For further information on the K1 visa process, please consult our Website at: http://travel.state.gov.

Sincerely,

Bureau of Consular Affairs

Fianceé Visa Application Process

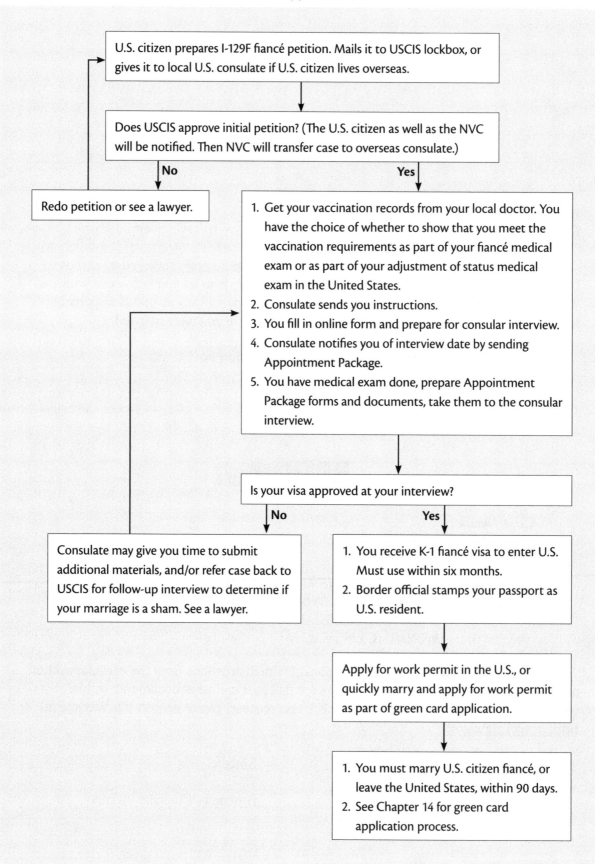

U.S. citizen prepares I-129F fiancé petition. Mails it to USCIS lockbox, or gives it to local U.S. consulate if U.S. citizen lives overseas.

Does USCIS approve initial petition? (The U.S. citizen as well as the NVC will be notified. Then NVC will transfer case to overseas consulate.)

No

Yes

Redo petition or see a lawyer.

1. Get your vaccination records from your local doctor. You have the choice of whether to show that you meet the vaccination requirements as part of your fiancé medical exam or as part of your adjustment of status medical exam in the United States.
2. Consulate sends you instructions.
3. You fill in online form and prepare for consular interview.
4. Consulate notifies you of interview date by sending Appointment Package.
5. You have medical exam done, prepare Appointment Package forms and documents, take them to the consular interview.

Is your visa approved at your interview?

No

Yes

Consulate may give you time to submit additional materials, and/or refer case back to USCIS for follow-up interview to determine if your marriage is a sham. See a lawyer.

1. You receive K-1 fiancé visa to enter U.S. Must use within six months.
2. Border official stamps your passport as U.S. resident.

Apply for work permit in the U.S., or quickly marry and apply for work permit as part of green card application.

1. You must marry U.S. citizen fiancé, or leave the United States, within 90 days.
2. See Chapter 14 for green card application process.

Unfortunately, if you write a letter to USCIS you are not likely to get a response, other than a boilerplate letter telling you to call the 800 number or to make an online appointment.

If USCIS needs additional documentation to complete the Fiancé Petition, it will send the U.S. citizen a letter asking for it. Strictly follow any deadlines given by USCIS if you receive such a letter.

Once the petition is approved (see the sample Approval Notice below), the service center will notify the U.S. citizen fiancé and transfer your case to the National Visa Center (NVC). The NVC will take care of some processing matters, then transfer your file to the U.S. consulate in your home country. The NVC will notify you when the case has been transferred (see sample below).

e. Using the Checklist for the K-1 Fiancé Petition

When you put it all together, the Fiancé Petition involves two or three forms and some supporting documents, as detailed on the above checklist. As you fill out and prepare your paperwork, mark off the items that you've found or finished on your checklist. This will be the best way to make sure you haven't forgotten anything.

CHECKLIST

Appendix B includes instructions on where to get a copy of the Fiancé Petition Checklist online.

2. Step Two: Fiancé Arranges for Consular Interview

Once the U.S. consulate receives the NVC notice of the approval of your Fiancé Petition, it will send you further instructions.

Don't delay, since the approval of your Fiancé Petition is good for only four months (though the consulate can give you one four-month extension). If you don't proceed within the required time frame, you'll have to start over at Step One.

The NVC will advise the fiancé to take two important steps, namely:

1. Fill out Form DS-160 online and get a receipt number, and
2. Use that receipt number to schedule an interview with the local U.S. consulate.

If you've read older accounts of how to get a fiancé visa, you may have seen mention of various paper forms, such as DS-230, DS-156, and DS-156K. These were phased out in late 2013, so you need not worry about them.

DS-160 is a fairly straightforward application, but you will need access to the Internet and at least some command of the English language. There is no paper version of the form (for which reason, we do not supply a sample in this book.)

By naming your location and nationality on the Bureau of Consular Affairs website, you can read the questions and guidance in your native language, but you will still need to supply all your answers in English.

Each applicant for a K visa (including any accompanying children) will need to complete a separate Form DS-160. You, as the parent, can complete the form for any of your children under age 16.

CAUTION

Plan ahead in case you can't complete Form DS-160 in one sitting. When you start filling out this online form, you'll be given a personal Application ID. Write this down! It will allow you to retrieve a saved version of your DS-160 in case you do not complete it the first time through or it "times out," perhaps due to a faulty Internet connection. It will also help to have as much of the required information on hand as possible, plus your photo.

You will be asked for personal information such as any names used, date and place of birth, address, phone number and email, any national identification or other numbers, and passport information. You will also be asked about your U.S. travel plans: your expected date of U.S. arrival, names of any travel companions, previous U.S. travel history and contacts, family information, and work and educational history.

You'll also need to have a recent and clear digital photograph of yourself to upload.

Although you don't need to print the application for submission, do so for your records. You WILL need a copy of the confirmation page and DS-160 barcode to bring to your interview at the U.S. consulate. It will allow the consular officer to upload your application.

Your next step is to schedule an interview at the U.S. consulate nearest you. You will need your receipt number and DS-160 barcode number in order to schedule the interview. To get instructions specific to your local consulate, go to www.usembassy.gov and look for the sections on nonimmigrant or K visa interviews.

3. Step Three: Fiancé Attends Visa Interview

For the final step in the fiancé visa application process, the consulate will send you one more form (called an I-134) and instructions (including one for the medical exam) in advance of your upcoming interview.

Your Appointment Package may contain forms and instructions specially prepared by your local consulate and therefore not covered in this book. Always use the forms provided by the consulate if they are different from the ones in this book.

> **CAUTION**
> **If you know or are advised by the U.S. consulate that you have a criminal record,** consult a lawyer right away, no matter how minor the crime.

a. Line-by-Line Form Instructions for Form I-134

Form I-134 is filled out by the U.S. citizen to show the U.S. government that the citizen can and will support you financially. Not all consulates require the use of Form I-134 as part of the fiancé visa application, though all will require some evidence that you won't need to go on welfare or receive other government assistance.

If you have children immigrating with you, the children won't need separate Forms I-134; listing them in Question 3 is sufficient.

> **WEB RESOURCE**
> **This form is available on the USCIS website at www.uscis.gov/i-134.** Below is a sample filled-in version of the relevant pages of this form.

What this form doesn't tell you is that the government can be very strict in its opinion of how much income it takes to support someone. Read Chapter 3 for further discussion of how to satisfy the government's requirements. After your U.S. citizen fiancé is done filling in the blanks on this form, refer to the instructions at the bottom of this section to find out if the amount is sufficient. If it isn't, go back to Chapter 3 for suggestions.

One very important difference between the Affidavit of Support for a fiancé (Form I-134) and the Affidavit of Support that eventually needs to be used at time of adjustment of status (Form I-864) is that the income requirements are different. For the Form I-134, the petitioner needs to show that his or her income is at least 100% of amounts listed per family size in the federal *Poverty Guidelines*. For the Form I-864, the petitioner needs to show an income of at least 125% of amounts listed in the *Poverty Guidelines*.

The Form I-134 becomes part of your permanent record, however, and consular officers are aware that you will have to meet the 125% requirement just a few months later when you adjust your status to permanent resident. Therefore, we recommend that, if possible, you show that your spouse meets the 125% requirement even at this point.

The following instructions refer to the version of Form I-134 created on 02/03/19, expiring on 02/28/2021.

Part I. Information About You (the Sponsor)

Questions 1-5: Self-explanatory, calling for the U.S. citizen to fill in name and address.

Questions 6-7: Self-explanatory.

Sample Form I-134, Affidavit of Support—Page 1

Affidavit of Support

Department of Homeland Security
U.S. Citizenship and Immigration Services

USCIS
Form I-134
OMB No. 1615-0014
Expires 02/28/2021

▶ **START HERE - Type or print in black ink.**

Part 1. Information About You (the Sponsor)

Your Full Name

1.a. Family Name (Last Name) — BEACH

1.b. Given Name (First Name) — Sandra

1.c. Middle Name — Leah

Other Names Used

List all other names you have ever used, including aliases, maiden name, and nicknames. If you need extra space to complete this section, use the space provided in **Part 7. Additional Information**.

2.a. Family Name (Last Name) — None

2.b. Given Name (First Name)

2.c. Middle Name

Sponsor's Mailing Address   *(USPS ZIP Code Lookup)*

3.a. In Care Of Name

3.b. Street Number and Name — 114 Fulton St.

3.c. ☒ Apt. ☐ Ste. ☐ Flr. — 6E

3.d. City or Town — New York

3.e. State — NY   **3.f.** ZIP Code — 10038

3.g. Province

3.h. Postal Code

3.i. Country — U.S.A.

4. Are your mailing address and physical address the same?
☒ Yes ☐ No

If you answered "No" to **Item Number 4.**, provide your physical address in **Item Numbers 5.a. - 5.h.**

Sponsor's Physical Address

5.a. Street Number and Name

5.b. ☐ Apt. ☐ Ste. ☐ Flr.

5.c. City or Town

5.d. State   **5.e.** ZIP Code

5.f. Province

5.g. Postal Code

5.h. Country

Other Information

6. Date of Birth (mm/dd/yyyy) — 10/20/1990

7.a. Town or City of Birth — Horseheads

7.b. Country of Birth — U.S.A.

8. Alien Registration Number (A-Number) (if any)
▶ A-

9. U.S. Social Security Number (if any)
▶ 1 2 3 4 5 6 7 8 9

10. USCIS Online Account Number (if any)
▶

Citizenship or Residency or Status

If you are not a U.S. citizen based on your birth in the United States, or a non-citizen U.S. national based on your birth in American Samoa (including Swains Island), answer the following as appropriate:

11.a. ☐ I am a U.S. citizen through naturalization. My Certificate of Naturalization number is

11.b. ☐ I am a U.S. citizen through parent(s) or marriage. My Certificate of Citizenship number is

Form I-134 02/13/19

Page 1 of 8

Sample Form I-134, Affidavit of Support—Page 2

Part 1. Information About You (the Sponsor) (continued)

11.c. ☐ I derived my U.S. citizenship by another method. (Provide an explain in **Part 7. Additional Information**.)

11.d. ☐ I am a lawful permanent resident of the United States. My A-Number is
► A- ☐☐☐☐☐☐☐☐☐

11.e. ☐ I am a lawfully admitted nonimmigrant. My Form I-94, Arrival-Departure Record Number is
► ☐☐☐☐☐☐☐☐☐☐☐

12. I am ☐ years of age and have resided in the United States since (Date) (mm/dd/yyyy) ☐

Part 2. Information About the Beneficiary

This affidavit is executed on behalf of the following person:

1.a. Family Name (Last Name) | Hollis

1.b. Given Name (First Name) | Nigel

1.c. Middle Name | Ian

2. Date of Birth (mm/dd/yyyy) | 08/17/1990

3. Gender ☒ Male ☐ Female

4. A-Number (if any)
► A- ☐☐☐☐☐☐☐☐☐

5. Country of Citizenship or Nationality | U.K.

6. Marital Status
☐ Single or Single, Never Married
☐ Married
☒ Divorced
☐ Widowed
☐ Legally Separated
☐ Marriage Annulled
☐ Other ☐

7. Relationship to Sponsor | Fiancé

Beneficiary's Physical Address

8.a. Street Number and Name | 123 Limestone Way

8.b. ☒ Apt. ☐ Ste. ☐ Flr. | 7

8.c. City or Town | Penzance

8.d. State ☐ **8.e.** ZIP Code ☐

8.f. Province | Cornwall

8.g. Postal Code | TR 197 NL

8.h. Country | U.K.

Beneficiary's Spouse (accompanying or following to join beneficiary)

9.a. Family Name (Last Name)

9.b. Given Name (First Name)

9.c. Middle Name

10. Date of Birth (mm/dd/yyyy)

11. Gender ☐ Male ☐ Female

Beneficiary's Children

Child 1

12.a. Family Name (Last Name)

12.b. Given Name (First Name)

12.c. Middle Name

13. Date of Birth (mm/dd/yyyy)

14. Gender ☐ Male ☐ Female

Child 2

15.a. Family Name (Last Name)

15.b. Given Name (First Name)

15.c. Middle Name

16. Date of Birth (mm/dd/yyyy)

17. Gender ☐ Male ☐ Female

If you need additional space to complete this section, use the space provided in **Part 7. Additional Information**.

Sample Form I-134, Affidavit of Support—Page 3

Part 3. Other Information About the Sponsor

Employment Information

I am currently:

1.a. ☒ Employed as a/an `Executive Assistant`

1.a.1. Name of Employer (if applicable)

`Helport Foundation`

1.b. ☐ Self employed as a/an

Current Employer Address (if employed)

2.a. Street Number and Name `87 W 57th St`

2.b. ☐ Apt. ☐ Ste. ☐ Flr.

2.c. City or Town `New York`

2.d. State `NY` ⊘ **2.e.** ZIP Code `10039`

2.f. Province

2.g. Postal Code

2.h. Country `U.S.A.`

Income and Asset Information

3. My annual income is $ `45,000`

(If self-employed, I have attached a copy of my last income tax return or report of commercial rating concern which I certify to be true and correct to the best of my knowledge and belief. See Instructions for nature of evidence of net worth to be submitted.)

4. Balance of all my savings and checking accounts in United States-based financial institutions

$ `8,200`

5. Value of my other personal property

$ `7,500`

6. Market value of my stocks and bonds

$ `0`

I have listed my stocks and bonds in **Part 7. Additional Information** (or attached a list of them), which I certify to be true and correct to the best of my knowledge and belief.

7.a. I have life insurance in the sum of $ `0`

7.b. With a cash surrender value of

$ `0`

Real Estate Information

8.a. I own real estate valued at $ `0`

8.b. I have mortgages or other debts amounting to

$ `0`

My real estate is located at:

9.a. Street Number and Name

9.b. ☐ Apt. ☐ Ste. ☐ Flr.

9.c. City or Town

9.d. State ⊘ **9.e.** ZIP Code

Dependents' Information

The following persons are dependent upon me for support. If you need extra space to complete this section, use the space provided in **Part 7. Additional Information**.

10.a. Family Name (Last Name)

10.b. Given Name (First Name)

10.c. Middle Name

11. Relationship to Me:

12. Date of Birth (mm/dd/yyyy)

13. This person is:

☐ Wholly Dependent On Me For Support

☐ Partially Dependent On Me For Support

14.a. Family Name (Last Name)

14.b. Given Name (First Name)

14.c. Middle Name

15. Relationship to Me:

16. Date of Birth (mm/dd/yyyy)

Sample Form I-134, Affidavit of Support—Page 4

Part 3. Other Information About the Sponsor (continued)

17. This person is:

☐ Wholly Dependent On Me For Support

☐ Partially Dependent On Me For Support

18.a. Family Name (Last Name)

18.b. Given Name (First Name)

18.c. Middle Name

19. Relationship to Me:

20. Date of Birth (mm/dd/yyyy)

21. This person is:

☐ Wholly Dependent On Me For Support

☐ Partially Dependent On Me For Support

I have previously submitted affidavit(s) of support for the following person(s). (If none, write "None" in the space for name below.)

22.a. Family Name (Last Name)

22.b. Given Name (First Name)

22.c. Middle Name

23. Date Submitted (mm/dd/yyyy)

24.a. Family Name (Last Name)

24.b. Given Name (First Name)

24.c. Middle Name

25. Date Submitted (mm/dd/yyyy)

I have submitted a visa petition(s) to U.S. Citizenship and Immigration Services on behalf of the following persons. (If none, write "None" in the space for name below.)

26.a. Family Name (Last Name)

26.b. Given Name (First Name)

26.c. Middle Name

27. Relationship to Me:

28. Date of Birth (mm/dd/yyyy)

29. Date of Filing (mm/dd/yyyy)

30.a. Family Name (Last Name)

30.b. Given Name (First Name)

30.c. Middle Name

31. Relationship to Me:

32. Date of Birth (mm/dd/yyyy)

33. Date of Filing (mm/dd/yyyy)

34.a. Family Name (Last Name)

34.b. Given Name (First Name)

34.c. Middle Name

35. Relationship to Me:

36. Date of Birth (mm/dd/yyyy)

37. Date of Filing (mm/dd/yyyy)

38. I ☐ intend ☐ do not intend to make specific contributions to the support of the person(s) named in **Part 2**.

(If you select "intend," indicate the exact nature and duration of the contributions you intend to make in **Part 7. Additional Information.** For example, if you intend to furnish room and board, state for how long and, if money, state the amount in U.S. dollars and whether it is to be given in a lump sum, weekly or monthly, and for how long.)

Sample Form I-134, Affidavit of Support—Page 5

Part 4. Sponsor's Statement, Contact Information, Certification, and Signature

NOTE: Read the Penalties section of the Form I-134 Instructions before completing this part.

Sponsor's Statement

NOTE: Select the box for either **Item Number 1.a.** or **1.b.** If applicable, select the box for **Item Number 2.**

1.a. ☒ I can read and understand English, and I have read and understand every question and instruction on this affidavit and my answer to every question.

1.b. ☐ The interpreter named in **Part 5.** read to me every question and instruction on this affidavit and my answer to every question in

_____,

a language in which I am fluent and I understood everything.

2. ☐ At my request, the preparer named in **Part 6.**,

_____,

prepared this affidavit for me based only upon information I provided or authorized.

Sponsor's Contact Information

3. Sponsor's Daytime Telephone Number

212-444-1212

4. Sponsor's Mobile Telephone Number (if any)

213-555-1313

5. Sponsor's Email Address (if any)

sandrab@email.com

Sponsor's Certification

Copies of any documents I have submitted are exact photocopies of unaltered, original documents, and I understand that USCIS or the Department of State may require that I submit original documents to USCIS or the Department of State at a later date. Furthermore, I authorize the release of any information from any of my records that USCIS or the Department of State may need to determine my eligibility for the immigration benefit I seek.

I further authorize release of information contained in this affidavit, in supporting documents, and in my USCIS or the Department of State records to other entities and persons where necessary for the administration and enforcement of U.S. immigration laws.

I understand that USCIS may require me to appear for an appointment to take my biometrics (fingerprints, photograph, and/or signature) and, at that time, if I am required to provide biometrics, I will be required to sign an oath reaffirming that:

1) I reviewed and provided or authorized all of the information in my affidavit;

2) I understood all of the information contained in, and submitted with, my affidavit; and

3) All of this information was complete, true, and correct at the time of filing.

I certify, under penalty of perjury, that I provided or authorized all of the information in my affidavit, I understand all of the information contained in, and submitted with, my affidavit, and that all of this information is complete, true, and correct.

That this affidavit is made by me to assure the U.S. Government that the person named in **Part 2.** will not become a public charge in the United States.

That I am willing and able to receive, maintain, and support the person named in **Part 2.** I am ready and willing to deposit a bond, if necessary, to guarantee that such persons will not become a public charge during his or her stay in the United States, or to guarantee that the above named persons will maintain his or her nonimmigrant status, if admitted temporarily, and will depart prior to the expiration of his or her authorized stay in the United States.

That I understand that Form I-134 is an "undertaking" under section 213 of the Immigration and Nationality Act, and I may be sued if the persons named in **Part 2.** become a public charge after admission to the United States.

That I understand that Form I-134 may be made available to any Federal, State, or local agency that may receive an application from the persons named in **Part 2.** for Food Stamps, Supplemental Security Income, or Temporary Assistance to Needy Families.

That I understand that if the person named in **Part 2.** does apply for Food Stamps, Supplemental Security Income, or Temporary Assistance for Needy Families, my own income and assets may be considered in deciding the person's application. How long my income and assets may be attributed to the persons named in **Part 2.** is determined under the statutes and rules governing each specific program.

I acknowledge that I have read the section entitled **Sponsor and Beneficiary Liability** in the Instructions for this affidavit, and am aware of my responsibilities as a sponsor under the Social Security Act, as amended, and the Food Stamp Act, as amended.

Sponsor's Signature

6.a. Sponsor's Signature

Sandra L. Beach

6.b. Date of Signature (mm/dd/yyyy)

01/01/2019

Questions 8-10: A U.S. citizen petitioner will have an A-number only if he or she once held a green card (permanent residence). The U.S. citizen will have a Social Security Number and should enter it in Question 9. A U.S. citizen who filed a past petition with USCIS might have a USCIS Online Account Number.

Questions 11-12: The U.S. citizen answers how he or she obtained citizenship. If born in the U.S., there's no need to answer these questions. A citizen who once had a green card (permanent residence) and then was naturalized should check option 11.a. One not born on U.S. soil but who was nevertheless a U.S. citizen at birth due to having U.S. citizen parents should check 11.b. One who obtained citizenship through another method should check option 11.c and then explain it in Part 7. (No U.S. citizen should fill in 11.d, 11.e, or 12.)

Part 2. Information About the Beneficiary

Now you are answering questions about the foreign-born fiancé instead of the U.S. citizen petitioner.

Questions 1-5: Self-explanatory.

Questions 6-7: "Marital Status" should, of course, be "single," "divorced," "widowed," or anything other than "married," since the foreign beneficiary is coming to the U.S. for the specific purpose of getting married. "Relationship to Sponsor" asks what relation the fiancé has to the U.S. citizen. Enter "fiancé" if the intending immigrant is a man, "fiancée" if the intending immigrant is a woman.

Question 8: Fill in immigrant's address, presumably overseas.

Questions 9-17: The lines for "spouse" should be left blank or filled in with "N/A." If any children will be immigrating at the same time, enter their information here.

Part 3. Other Information About the Sponsor

Now the questions again refer to the U.S. citizen petitioner.

Questions 1-2: The U.S. citizen must enter information about where he or she works.

Questions 3-9: The U.S. citizen enters income and assets. If the U.S. citizen's income is sufficient for

the Form I-134, the Department of State will not care about assets, so the U.S. citizen won't really need to list them all. Assets become important, however, in cases where the U.S. citizen's income does not meet the *Poverty Guidelines* levels. For "value of my other personal property," the U.S. citizen need not consider every item owned. An approximate total value of cars, jewelry, appliances, and equipment (TV, refrigerator, computer, camera, and so forth) will do. Nor does the citizen have to provide proof of ownership—yet. But when it comes time for the green card application in the U.S., the citizen sponsor will have to prove ownership of any assets used to show financial capacity, so it's best not to exaggerate on Form I-134.

Questions 10-21: Anyone whom the sponsor has listed on his/her tax returns should be listed here.

Questions 22-25: This question attempts to find out whether the U.S. citizen is overextending him- or herself financially. A citizen who has filled out this form or Form I-864 (the Affidavit of Support used in green card applications) on behalf of any other immigrant must fill in these lines.

Questions 26-38: For the same reasons underlying Questions 22-25, the U.S. government wants to know whether the U.S. citizen is planning to sponsor anyone else, having filed an I-130 petition on the person's behalf. Even if the foreign fiancé is the only person being sponsored, the U.S. citizen should fill in his or her name here, with the notation "subject of this affidavit." For Question 38, you would likely want to check "do not intend to make specific contributions to the support" of the fiancé. That's because it's mostly people sponsoring short-term visitors (like tourists) who would want to limit what they plan to provide during the person's U.S. stay.

Part 4. Sponsor's Statement, Contact Information, Certification, and Signature

Questions 1-2: Check box 1.a. if the U.S. citizen filled in the form unassisted. Box 1.b. is the appropriate one if the citizen filled in the form with the help of an interpreter. Check box 2 only if a lawyer or agency filled in the form.

Questions 3-5: U.S. citizen's phone numbers and email.

Sponsor's Certification. The U.S. citizen should be sure, before signing the form, that to the best of his or her knowledge, the answers provided are correct.

Parts 5 and 6.

If you used a lawyer, interpreter, or preparer from a professional agency, that person will complete these portions of the form.

b. Document Instructions for Appointment Package

This section contains detailed instructions about some of the documents on the Checklist for Fiancé Appointment Package in Subsection e, below.

i. Copy of U.S. Citizen's Most Recent Federal Tax Return

As part of proving that your fiancé can support you financially, he or she will probably be asked to provide federal tax-filing information—at least one year's worth, and maybe three. There is no need to include state tax information.

The consulate prefers to see the tax return in the form of IRS transcripts (an IRS-generated summary of the return that your U.S. citizen fiancé filed), which your U.S. fiancé can request either online or by mail, following the instructions on the IRS website at: www.irs.gov/individuals/get-transcript.·

If for some reason that doesn't work, you can submit photocopies of tax returns—just don't forget to include the W-2 forms. Also, if the sponsor wasn't legally required to submit a tax return, perhaps because his or her income was too low, submit a written explanation of this.

TIP

We're advising you to prepare more than the minimum financial documents. Technically, you're supposed to be asked for only one year's tax returns, and that's it. But because some consulates ask for more, it makes sense to be ready with additional years' tax returns plus a bank and employer letter.

Is the Total Support Amount Sufficient?

Technically, Form I-134 only covers your first 90 days in the United States, so the consulate may not require your U.S. citizen fiancé to show a certain income level—despite the fact that they've asked him or her to fill out this form. However, it's wise to look at the *Poverty Guidelines* chart to see what income level is required for fiancés (100% of the *Poverty Guidelines*) and even what income level you will have to show at the time of your adjustment of status (125%).

Go back to the form you've filled out and follow these steps.

1. Remember, it is the U.S. citizen's income that is most important. Compare that income to the *Poverty Guidelines* chart located in Chapter 3, Section A (after checking for a more recent version at uscis.gov, on Form I-864P). In the left column, find the line corresponding to the number of people that the U.S. citizen is responsible for supporting. Now look to the right column. That's the total amount of income that the U.S. government will want to see when you apply for your green card. If your U.S. citizen fiancé's income comfortably reaches that level, you are fine, and the U.S. citizen should not have to also list assets.

2. If your U.S. citizen fiancé's income does not reach the level required by the *Poverty Guidelines*, total up additional assets.

3. Subtract the mortgages and other debts from the assets' worth and divide that total by three.

4. Add the figure to the amount of income. How does this figure compare to the total amount of income that the U.S. government will want to see when you apply for your green card? Check this, and if it still does not reach that level, reread Chapter 3.

Fortunately, by the time you've reached your U.S. green card interview, you will have had a work permit for several months, and can hopefully find a job and contribute to the household income.

ii. Letter From U.S. Citizen's Bank(s) Confirming Account(s)

The U.S. citizen should ask all of his or her banks reported on page one of Form I-134 to draft simple letters confirming the accounts. The letters can be addressed "To Whom It May Concern," and should state the date the account was opened, the total amount deposited over the last year, and the present balance.

Banks will often (without your asking) also state an average balance. Be aware that if this is much lower than the present amount, the consulate will wonder whether the U.S. citizen got a quick loan from a friend to make the financial situation look more impressive.

Some consulates prefer a recent bank statement instead.

iii. Employer Letter

Here is a sample of a letter from the sponsor's employer. This letter should accompany Form I-134.

Sample Letter From Employer

Hitting the Road Trucking
222 Plaza Place
Outthereville, MA 90000

May 22, 20xx

To Whom It May Concern:

Ron Goodley has been an employee of Hitting the Road Trucking since September 4, 20xx, a total of over five years. He has a full-time position as a driver. His salary is $45,000 per year. This position is permanent, and Ron's prospects for performance-based advancement and salary increases are excellent.

Very truly yours,

Bob Bossman

Bob Bossman
Personnel Manager
Hitting the Road Trucking

iv. The Medical Exam

To prove that you are not inadmissible for medical reasons, you will have to present the results of a medical exam done by a doctor approved by the U.S. consulate. Your Appointment Package will give you complete instructions on where and when to visit the appropriate clinic or doctor. It's best to go around a week before your interview, so as to allow time for the test results to come in. And allow several hours for the appointment. There will be a base fee of about $150, plus additional fees for X-rays and tests.

When you go for your medical exam, make sure to bring the following:

- a form you fill out describing your medical history, if requested
- your visa appointment letter
- the doctor's fee
- your vaccination records, and
- photo identification—the doctor must make sure you don't send a healthier person in your place. You may also be requested to bring a passport-style photo.

The doctor will examine you, ask you questions about your medical and psychiatric history and drug use, and test you (including blood tests and chest X-rays). Pregnant women can (if they bring proof of pregnancy) refuse the chest X-ray until after the baby is born if they have no symptoms of tuberculosis.

As a fiancé, you are not required to fulfill the vaccination requirements at the time of your medical examination for a fiancé visa. These vaccinations are required when you apply for a green card (adjust status) following your marriage, however, so you might decide to get them out of the way at this time.

When the laboratory results are in, the doctor will fill out the appropriate form and may return it to you in a sealed envelope. DO NOT open the envelope—this will invalidate the results. In some countries, the doctor will send your results straight to the consulate. The doctor should supply you with a separate copy of your results, or tell you whether any illnesses showed up.

c. Where You'll Take Your Appointment Package

On the day of your interview, you will be expected to arrive at the consulate with forms and documents in hand, according to the consulate's instructions. After you've attended your interview and been approved, the consulate will give you a visa to enter the United States.

Ideally you'll receive the visa within a few days of your interview, but recent delays for FBI and CIA security checks have been adding weeks to the process, especially for people with common names.

Actually, your visa will be a thick, sealed envelope, stuffed full of most of the forms and documents that you've submitted over the course of this process.

CAUTION

Do not open the envelope! Your visa envelope must be presented to a U.S. border official before it is opened. If you open it, the immigration officials will probably assume that you've tampered with it. At best, the border official might send you back to the consulate for another try; at worst, he or she might accuse you of visa fraud and use summary exclusion powers to prohibit you from entering the United States for the next five years.

To prepare, read Chapter 13, Interviews With USCIS or Consular Officials.

Also prepare to go through a security checkpoint before entry to the U.S. consulate, as most now require (similar to most busy airports). Portable

---

Checklist for Fiancé Appointment Package

- ☐ Confirmation page and bar code, showing that you (and any accompanying family members) completed an online Form DS-160
- ☐ Original USCIS Notice of Action approving your K-1, or fiancé, petition
- ☐ A complete copy of your Fiancé Petition (the items in the checklist in Section F1, above) in case USCIS did not forward it to the consulate
- ☐ Originals of documents submitted in connection with the I-129F petition, such as your fiancé's U.S. birth certificate and proof that any previous marriages were legally ended
- ☐ Form I-134, Affidavit of Support, if the consulate requested it (see line-by-line instructions in Subsection F3a, above)
- ☐ Documents to accompany Form I-134, including:
  - ☐ Proof of U.S. citizen's employment (see sample letter in Subsection F3b, above)
  - ☐ Copy of U.S. citizen's most recent federal tax return(s) (see further discussion in Subsection F3b, above)
- ☐ Letter from U.S. citizen's bank(s) confirming the account(s) (see further discussion in Subsection F3b, above)
- ☐ A valid passport from your home country, good for at least six months

- ☐ Your original birth certificate
- ☐ An original police clearance certificate, if this is available in your country (the instructions from the consulate will tell you)
- ☐ Three additional photographs of you, the immigrating fiancé (according to the consulate's photo instructions)
- ☐ Fingerprints (you'll receive instructions from the consulate)
- ☐ Results of your medical examination, in an unopened envelope, unless the doctor sent the results directly to the consulate (see Chapter 2, Section A, for more on the medical exam)
- ☐ Additional documents proving your relationship (to cover the time period since submitting the fiancé petition), such as copies of:
  - ☐ phone bills showing calls to one another
  - ☐ correspondence between you
  - ☐ photos taken together while one fiancé visited the other
- ☐ Any other items or forms requested by the consulate
- ☐ Visa Application fee (currently $265). In some countries, you may also be charged an issuance fee if your visa is approved.

electronics, like portable music players, mobile phones, or digital cameras, are usually not allowed at the consulate; leave them at home. Carry all of your visa and application documents—and there will be a lot of them—in a clear, plastic folder or something similar, so that consulate security can easily identify your materials as safe.

d. After You Receive Your K-1 Fiancé Visa

Once you receive your fiancé visa, you'll have six months to enter the United States. At the U.S. port of entry, the border officer will examine the contents of your visa envelope and ask you a few questions.

Though this part shouldn't be a problem, don't treat it lightly. If the official spots a reason that you shouldn't have been given the fiancé visa, he or she has the power—called expedited removal—to deny your entry right there. You would have no right to a lawyer or a hearing, but would simply have to turn around and find a flight or other means of transport home. And you wouldn't be allowed back for five years (unless the border officials allowed you to withdraw the application before they officially denied it, which is entirely at their discretion).

After advice like this, the hardest thing to hear is "just stay calm." It may be impossible to control your beating heart—but whatever you do, don't start speaking more than is necessary. The worst thing someone could do at this stage is to make a nervous little joke like, "Yeah, I'll see if I still like him, and maybe I'll marry him." Border officials are not known for their sense of humor, and a statement like this could be used as a reason to deny your entry.

Assuming all goes well, the border official will stamp your passport with your K-1 fiancé status, and enter the 90-day duration of your visa into a database.

e. When to Marry and Apply for Your Green Card

You should start working on your green card application as soon as you arrive in the United States. Once your 90 days expires, you will not be authorized to remain in the U.S. until such time as you file the green card application. (For complete instructions, see Chapter 14.)

In fact, it's a good idea to get married fairly soon after your arrival. Doing so will give you the maximum amount of time after your marriage to prepare the green card application (which is even longer than the fiancé visa application). Also assume that the local government authorities may take a while (up to three months) to produce their final version of your marriage certificate, which you'll need for the green card application.

Contact your local (usually county) Registrar, Recorder, or Vital Records office before you get married to find out their time estimate. Ask whether there is any way to speed up the process. In some areas, couples have found that by hand-carrying the certificate that they receive at the wedding ceremony to the county office, they can shave weeks off the processing time.

f. Using the Checklist for Your Fiancé Appointment Package

Which forms you are required to prepare for your fiancé visa Appointment Package may vary among consulates. The ones listed on the checklist above are those most commonly required. You can strike off any that you don't receive from the consulate, and proceed to use the checklist as usual.

CHECKLIST
Appendix B includes instructions on where to get a copy of this checklist online.

G. How to Have Your Children and Pets Accompany You

Although your whole family cannot immigrate right now, U.S. laws and regulations do recognize the need for certain of your loved ones to accompany you to the United States and live there with you, including your children and certain pets.

1. Your Children

If you have unmarried children under age 21 who are interested in accompanying you to the United States and applying for green cards, review Chapter 2 to make sure they fit the basic eligibility requirements. This book does not cover in detail the application process for children. However, it is very similar to your own visa application process. Once you've become familiar with the process, handling your children's applications should not be difficult. We'll give you some tips here to get you started.

All you have to do at the beginning of the fiancé visa application process is to include your children's names on the fiancé petition (Form I-129F). The consular officials should then send you extra sets of any required materials for the children.

Your children will probably be asked to attend your consular interview with you (although some consulates permit younger children to stay at home). The children will receive their visas on the same day you do. The technical name for their visa will be K-2. The materials that children are normally asked to bring to the visa interview include:

- child's long-form birth certificate
- child's police record (if the child is over age 16)
- child's passport (unless your country permits the children to be included on your passport)
- two photos of child passport-style, and
- medical exam results.

Even if your children don't accompany you when you first enter as a fiancé, they can join you under the same visa for a year after yours was approved. (Just make sure they remain unmarried and are still under the age of 21.) If they decide to follow you, they will need to contact the U.S. consulate. The consulate will verify your initial visa approval, ask your children to fill in the same forms that you did, interview them regarding their admissibility, and hopefully grant them a visa.

The children will need to submit their green card applications in the United States before their visa expires. (For further information on the children's green card ("adjustment of status") applications, see Chapter 14.)

If you have children who would just like to come for your wedding ceremony, they may be able to obtain a tourist visa. Talk to your local U.S. consulate about the application procedure.

2. Your Pets

Good news for your dog and cat, who may not have learned to sign their names yet—they won't need a visa. Bringing pets into the United States is not an immigration law matter. But before bringing any pets to the United States, you will need to check into U.S. customs restrictions. In general, pets will be allowed in if they are in good health and have had all the proper vaccinations. Certain more specific restrictions apply, however. For example, monkeys aren't allowed into the United States at all, and some states don't allow certain animals. Check with your local U.S. consulate for details, or read more at www.cbp.gov (enter "pets" into the search box, which will bring up a publication called "Pets and Wildlife").

H. Your 90 Days on a K-1 Fiancé Visa

If you're reading this after getting your K-1 fiancé visa, congratulations! But don't stop reading. It's important to understand how to protect and enjoy your visa and how to continue the process toward obtaining a green card, if you plan to make your home in the United States.

1. Are You Permitted to Work?

In theory, fiancés have the right to work in the United States during the 90-day duration of their visa. In practice, taking advantage of this right is more complicated than it sounds.

Sample Form I-765, Application for Employment Authorization—Page 1

Application For Employment Authorization

Department of Homeland Security
U.S. Citizenship and Immigration Services

USCIS
Form I-765
OMB No. 1615-0040
Expires 05/31/2020

For USCIS Use Only	
☐ **Authorization/Extension Valid From** _____	**Fee Stamp**
☐ **Authorization/Extension Valid Through** _____	
Alien Registration Number A- ☐☐☐☐☐☐☐☐☐	**Action Block**
Remarks	

To be completed by an attorney or Board of Immigration Appeals (BIA)-accredited representative (if any).	☐ **Select this box if Form G-28 is attached.**	**Attorney or Accredited Representative USCIS Online Account Number** (if any) ☐☐☐☐☐☐☐☐☐☐☐☐☐

▶ **START HERE - Type or print in black ink.**

Part 1. Reason for Applying

I am applying for (select **only one** box):

1.a. ☒ Initial permission to accept employment.

1.b. ☐ Replacement of lost, stolen, or damaged employment authorization document, or correction of my employment authorization document **NOT DUE** to U.S. Citizenship and Immigration Services (USCIS) error.

> **NOTE:** Replacement (correction) of an employment authorization document due to USCIS error does not require a new Form I-765 and filing fee. Refer to **Replacement for Card Error** in the **What is the Filing Fee** section of the Form I-765 Instructions for further details.

1.c. ☐ Renewal of my permission to accept employment. (Attach a copy of your previous employment authorization document.)

Part 2. Information About You

Your Full Legal Name

1.a. Family Name (Last Name) `HOLLIS`

1.b. Given Name (First Name) `Nigel`

1.c. Middle Name `Ian`

Other Names Used

Provide all other names you have ever used, including aliases, maiden name, and nicknames. If you need extra space to complete this section, use the space provided in **Part 6. Additional Information**.

2.a. Family Name (Last Name) `None`

2.b. Given Name (First Name)

2.c. Middle Name

3.a. Family Name (Last Name)

3.b. Given Name (First Name)

3.c. Middle Name

4.a. Family Name (Last Name)

4.b. Given Name (First Name)

4.c. Middle Name

Sample Form I-765, Application for Employment Authorization—Page 2

Part 2. Information About You (continued)

Your U.S. Mailing Address

5.a. In Care Of Name (if any)

5.b. Street Number and Name `114 Fulton Street`

5.c. ☒ Apt. ☐ Ste. ☐ Flr. `6E`

5.d. City or Town `New York`

5.e. State `NY ▼`   **5.f.** ZIP Code `10038`

(USPS ZIP Code Lookup)

6. Is your current mailing address the same as your physical address?   ☒ Yes   ☐ No

NOTE: If you answered "No" to **Item Number 6.**, provide your physical address below.

U.S. Physical Address

7.a. Street Number and Name

7.b. ☐ Apt. ☐ Ste. ☐ Flr.

7.c. City or Town

7.d. State   **7.e.** ZIP Code

Other Information

8. Alien Registration Number (A-Number) (if any)
▶ A-

9. USCIS Online Account Number (if any)
▶

10. Gender   ☒ Male   ☐ Female

11. Marital Status
☐ Single   ☐ Married   ☒ Divorced   ☐ Widowed

12. Have you previously filed Form I-765?
☐ Yes   ☒ No

13.a. Has the Social Security Administration (SSA) ever officially issued a Social Security card to you?
☐ Yes   ☒ No

NOTE: If you answered "No" to **Item Number 13.a.**, skip to **Item Number 14.** If you answered "Yes" to **Item Number 13.a.**, provide the information requested in **Item Number 13.b.**

13.b. Provide your Social Security number (SSN) (if known).
▶

14. Do you want the SSA to issue you a Social Security card? (You must also answer "Yes" to **Item Number 15.**, **Consent for Disclosure**, to receive a card.)
☒ Yes   ☐ No

NOTE: If you answered "No" to **Item Number 14.**, skip to **Part 2., Item Number 18.a.** If you answered "Yes" to **Item Number 14.**, you must also answer "Yes" to **Item Number 15.**

15. **Consent for Disclosure:** I authorize disclosure of information from this application to the SSA as required for the purpose of assigning me an SSN and issuing me a Social Security card.   ☒ Yes   ☐ No

NOTE: If you answered "Yes" to **Item Numbers 14. - 15.**, provide the information requested in **Item Numbers 16.a. - 17.b.**

Father's Name

Provide your father's birth name.

16.a. Family Name (Last Name) `HOLLIS`

16.b. Given Name (First Name) `Kevin`

Mother's Name

Provide your mother's birth name.

17.a. Family Name (Last Name) `HOLLIS`

17.b. Given Name (First Name) `Sarah`

Your Country or Countries of Citizenship or Nationality

List all countries where you are currently a citizen or national. If you need extra space to complete this item, use the space provided in **Part 6. Additional Information**.

18.a. Country
`UK`

18.b. Country

Sample Form I-765, Application for Employment Authorization—Page 3

Part 2. Information About You (continued)

Place of Birth

List the city/town/village, state/province, and country where you were born.

19.a. City/Town/Village of Birth

Port Navas

19.b. State/Province of Birth

Cornwall

19.c. Country of Birth

UK

20. Date of Birth (mm/dd/yyyy)   08/17/1990

Information About Your Last Arrival in the United States

21.a. Form I-94 Arrival-Departure Record Number (if any)

▶ 1 2 3 4 5 6 7 8 9 1 2

21.b. Passport Number of Your Most Recently Issued Passport

123456789

21.c. Travel Document Number (if any)

123456789

21.d. Country That Issued Your Passport or Travel Document

UK

21.e. Expiration Date for Passport or Travel Document (mm/dd/yyyy)   01/01/2022

22. Date of Your Last Arrival Into the United States, On or About (mm/dd/yyyy)   05/01/2019

23. Place of Your Last Arrival Into the United States

JFK Intl Airport

24. Immigration Status at Your Last Arrival (for example, B-2 visitor, F-1 student, or no status)

K-1

25. Your Current Immigration Status or Category (for example, B-2 visitor, F-1 student, parolee, deferred action, or no status or category)

K-1

26. Student and Exchange Visitor Information System (SEVIS) Number (if any)

▶ N-

Information About Your Eligibility Category

27. **Eligibility Category.** Refer to the **Who May File Form I-765** section of the Form I-765 Instructions to determine the appropriate eligibility category for this application. Enter the appropriate letter and number for your eligibility category below (for example, (a)(8), (c)(17)(iii)).

(   ) (a) (6)

28. **(c)(3)(C) STEM OPT Eligibility Category.** If you entered the eligibility category **(c)(3)(C)** in **Item Number 27.**, provide the information requested in **Item Numbers 28.a - 28.c.**

28.a. Degree

28.b. Employer's Name as Listed in E-Verify

28.c. Employer's E-Verify Company Identification Number or a Valid E-Verify Client Company Identification Number

29. **(c)(26) Eligibility Category.** If you entered the eligibility category (c)(26) in **Item Number 27.**, provide the receipt number of your H-1B spouse's most recent Form I-797 Notice for Form I-129, Petition for a Nonimmigrant Worker.

▶

30. **(c)(8) Eligibility Category.** If you entered the eligibility category (c)(8) in **Item Number 27.**, have you **EVER** been arrested for and/or convicted of any crime?

☐ Yes ☐ No

NOTE: If you answered "Yes" to **Item Number 30.**, refer to **Special Filing Instructions for Those With Pending Asylum Applications (c)(8)** in the **Required Documentation** section of the Form I-765 Instructions for information about providing court dispositions.

31.a. **(c)(35) and (c)(36) Eligibility Category.** If you entered the eligibility category (c)(35) in **Item Number 27.**, please provide the receipt number of your Form I-797 Notice for Form I-140, Immigrant Petition for Alien Worker. If you entered the eligibility category (c)(36) in **Item Number 27.**, please provide the receipt number of your spouse's or parent's Form I-797 Notice for Form I-140.

▶

31.b. If you entered the eligibility category (c)(35) or (c)(36) in **Item Number 27.**, have you **EVER** been arrested for and/or convicted of any crime?   ☐ Yes ☐ No

NOTE: If you answered "Yes" to **Item Number 31.b.**, refer to **Employment-Based Nonimmigrant Categories, Items 8. - 9.**, in the **Who May File Form I-765** section of the Form I-765 Instructions for information about providing court dispositions.

Sample Form I-765, Application for Employment Authorization—Page 4

Part 3. Applicant's Statement, Contact Information, Declaration, Certification, and Signature

NOTE: Read the **Penalties** section of the Form I-765 Instructions before completing this section. You must file Form I-765 while in the United States.

Applicant's Statement

NOTE: Select the box for either **Item Number 1.a.** or **1.b.** If applicable, select the box for **Item Number 2.**

1.a. ☒ I can read and understand English, and I have read and understand every question and instruction on this application and my answer to every question.

1.b. ☐ The interpreter named in **Part 4.** read to me every question and instruction on this application and my answer to every question in

[   ] ,

a language in which I am fluent, and I understood everything.

2. ☐ At my request, the preparer named in **Part 5.**,

[   ] ,

prepared this application for me based only upon information I provided or authorized.

Applicant's Contact Information

3. Applicant's Daytime Telephone Number

[1234123456]

4. Applicant's Mobile Telephone Number (if any)

[   ]

5. Applicant's Email Address (if any)

[nigelh@email.com]

6. ☐ Select this box if you are a Salvadoran or Guatemalan national eligible for benefits under the ABC settlement agreement.

Applicant's Declaration and Certification

Copies of any documents I have submitted are exact photocopies of unaltered, original documents, and I understand that USCIS may require that I submit original documents to USCIS at a later date. Furthermore, I authorize the release of any information from any and all of my records that USCIS may need to determine my eligibility for the immigration benefit that I seek.

I furthermore authorize release of information contained in this application, in supporting documents, and in my USCIS records, to other entities and persons where necessary for the administration and enforcement of U.S. immigration law.

I understand that USCIS may require me to appear for an appointment to take my biometrics (fingerprints, photograph, and/or signature) and, at that time, if I am required to provide biometrics, I will be required to sign an oath reaffirming that:

1) I reviewed and understood all of the information contained in, and submitted with, my application; and

2) All of this information was complete, true, and correct at the time of filing.

I certify, under penalty of perjury, that all of the information in my application and any document submitted with it were provided or authorized by me, that I reviewed and understand all of the information contained in, and submitted with, my application and that all of this information is complete, true, and correct.

Applicant's Signature

7.a. Applicant's Signature

➡  *Nigel I. Hollis*

7.b. Date of Signature (mm/dd/yyyy) [01/01/2019]

NOTE TO ALL APPLICANTS: If you do not completely fill out this application or fail to submit required documents listed in the Instructions, USCIS may deny your application.

Part 4. Interpreter's Contact Information, Certification, and Signature

Provide the following information about the interpreter.

Interpreter's Full Name

1.a. Interpreter's Family Name (Last Name)

[   ]

1.b. Interpreter's Given Name (First Name)

[   ]

2. Interpreter's Business or Organization Name (if any)

[   ]

a. Whether You Should Apply for a Work Permit

You can work in the United States only if, after entering, you apply for and receive a work permit. This is known by USCIS as an Employment Authorization Document, and it's a small plastic card with your photo on it. For application procedures, see Subsection b, below; but first, keep reading for the reasons you might not want to apply.

The problem with applying for a work permit is that USCIS service centers routinely take from 45 to 90 days to issue them. This means that your chances of receiving your work permit while you're still eligible for it, as the holder of a fiancé visa, are slim.

You might be better off just getting to work on your adjustment of status application and submitting it as soon as possible after you are married. Once you submit your adjustment of status application, you will still probably wait anywhere from 60 to 90 days for your work permit—but it will last many months longer, and won't require paying a separate fee.

b. How to Apply for a Work Permit

If you still want to apply for a work permit, use Form I-765, Application for Employment Authorization.

 WEB RESOURCE
This form is available on the USCIS website at www.uscis.gov/i-765. Above is a sample filled-in version of the relevant pages of this form.

These instructions refer to the version of Form I-765 created 05/31/2018, expiring 5/31/2020.

Part 1. Reason for Applying

Assuming this is your first work permit, under **"I am applying for,"** check box 1.a, initial "permission to Accept Employment."

Part 2. Information About You

Questions 1-11: Self-explanatory.

Question 12: Answer "no" if this is your first time filing for a work permit in the United States.

Questions 13-15: If you have never been issued a Social Security card, you can apply for it here. Check that you would like the Social Security Administration (SSA) to issue you a card (Question 14). The Social Security card is supposed to arrive soon after your work permit. If it doesn't, you can request one at your nearest SSA office.

Questions 16-17: Enter biographic information about your parents.

Questions 18-20: Enter information about your background and home country.

Questions 21-26: Presumably you entered the U.S. using your K-1 visa; fill in the information about your entry here. In Question 25, your answer is likely "K-1 fiancé" (if male) or "K-1 fiancée" (if female).

Question 27: Your eligibility category is (a)(6).

Questions 28-31: Leave these questions blank or enter "N/A," to indicate that they do not apply to you.

Part 3. Applicant's Statement, Contact Information, Declaration, Certification, and Signature

Questions 1-2: Check box 1.a. if you filled in the form yourself. Check box 1.b. if you filled in the form with the help of an interpreter. Check box 2 only if a lawyer or agency filled in the form for you.

Questions 3-6: Fill in your phone and email information.

Question 7: Sign and date the form.

Parts 4 and 5.

If you used a lawyer, interpreter, or preparer from a professional agency, that person will fill in these portions of the form.

When you're finished, mail the form, the fee (currently $410), two passport-style photos, and proof of your fiancé visa status (such as a copy of your approval notice, the stamp in your passport, and your I-94 card) to the appropriate USCIS service center. The addresses of the service centers are on the USCIS website (look under "Family-Based Nonimmigrants.")

Previously, it was possible to file your Form I-765 electronically, through the USCIS website. However, USCIS discontinued this "e-Filing" system in 2015.

c. How to Get a Social Security Number

With the employment stamp in your passport or your new work permit in your wallet, you can visit your local Social Security office to get a Social Security number. You'll need this number before you start work—your employer will ask for it in order to file taxes on your behalf. To find your local Social Security office, check your phone book in the federal government pages or look on the Social Security Administration's website at www.ssa.gov. You'll need to show them either your K-1 fiancé visa or your work permit.

2. Are You Permitted to Leave the United States?

If you are planning to make your home in the United States, don't count on leaving for the five months or more that it will take to get your U.S. residency.

a. You Can Use Your K-1 Visa Only Once

A fiancé visa is good for only one entry, so you can't go out and come back on it. If an emergency comes up before your marriage and you have to leave, try to make time to apply for a travel document ("Advance Parole") at your local USCIS office, using Form I-131 (available on the USCIS website). If you leave without a travel document, the consulate may be able to revalidate your visa back in your home country, but they'll take a hard look at your situation first. You could end up having to start over with a new fiancé petition.

b. Leaving After You've Applied for a Green Card: Advance Parole

In theory, once you've turned in your green card application, any departure from the United States automatically cancels that application. However, if you obtain special permission—called Advance Parole—the application won't be cancelled while you're away. Obtaining Advance Parole is usually fairly easy. Instructions for this application are included in Chapter 14, Section D.

Advance Parole only keeps your application alive while you're gone, it doesn't guarantee your reentry to the United States. Any time you ask to enter the United States, the border officer has a chance to keep you out if he or she determines you are inadmissible. Consult a lawyer before leaving if this is a possible concern.

3. What Rights Do Family Members Have?

Your children who accompanied you on your fiancé visa have basically the same immigration-related rights as you. They must either leave within the 90 days on their K-2 visas or, after you've married, file applications for green cards along with you.

In order to obtain green cards, each child must submit a separate application. At no point in the process can they be included automatically within your application. However, if you and your children submit your green card applications at the same time, you'll normally be scheduled to attend your green card interview together. (For guidance on preparing green card applications for your children, see Chapter 14.)

4. Can You Renew or Extend Your K-1 Fiancé Visa Status?

A K-1 fiancé visa cannot be renewed. You are expected to get married within 90 days or leave the United States.

But if something happens and you weren't able to marry within the 90 days, go ahead and marry (if the marriage is still what you want). As long as USCIS hasn't caught up with you before you're ready to submit the application, you should be able to apply for your green card through normal procedures, as explained below.

a. Filing Late for Your Green Card

If you marry after the 90 days permitted by your fiancé visa, your spouse will have to submit an I-130 petition on your behalf. (It's similar to Form I-129F, but for married couples.) Because you're already legally in the U.S., however, the I-130 can be submitted with the rest of your green card application to USCIS. Form I-130 shows your eligibility to immigrate (this time as the immediate relative (spouse) of a U.S. citizen, rather than as a fiancé) and your spouse's willingness to support your application. (Instructions for preparing the I-130 as the spouse of a U.S. citizen living in the United States are included in Chapter 11.)

Another consequence of marrying after the 90-day expiration of your visa is that you will be living in the United States unlawfully. Although this is a serious concern, it is unlikely that the immigration enforcement authorities will search you out anytime soon. They have higher enforcement priorities than going after people who will ultimately have the right to a green card, but are simply late in applying for it.

CAUTION

Don't even think of leaving the United States if you've stayed six or more months past the expiration date on your fiancé visa. If your 90 days is up and you still haven't filed your green card or adjustment of status application, you are in the United States unlawfully. However, leaving the U.S. and starting the process over could be the worst thing to do at this point. If you have stayed in the United States more than six months beyond your visa expiration date, leaving would subject you to laws preventing your return for three or ten years. (See Chapter 2, Section A.)

b. Filing in Immigration Court for Your Green Card

If you're late in getting married and turning in your green card application, and the immigration authorities do catch up with you and place you in removal proceedings, it's not a complete disaster. You can apply for your green card in Immigration Court. The application paperwork is mostly the same. However, the law requires the judges to look even harder at your case than a USCIS officer would. That means you will have to do extra work to convince the judge that despite your late marriage, this marriage is bona fide, not a sham.

SEE AN EXPERT

If you're called into Immigration Court, you'll need a lawyer's help. Going to court requires some knowledge of official court procedures, and the lawyer can help you prepare extra evidence that your marriage is bona fide.

Overseas Fiancés of U.S. Permanent Residents

f you are the fiancé of a U.S. lawful permanent resident (someone who is not a citizen) and you currently live outside the United States, your options are limited, whether you want to stay in the United States for a short time or permanently. There are no fiancé visas available for foreign nationals wishing to marry U.S. permanent residents. Fiancé visas are only available to people coming to the United States to marry U.S. citizens.

Don't lose hope, however. There are three ways to get yourself into the United States if you are the fiancé of a permanent resident. You can:

- Marry your fiancé first, then begin the entry process as a spouse of a permanent resident. This method is described in Section A.
- Wait until your fiancé becomes a U.S. citizen, and begin your entry process as a fiancé of a citizen. Section B covers this approach, or
- Come to the United States on a tourist visa and get married here (with the idea of returning home afterward). This strategy is described in Section C.

Each of these options has drawbacks, unfortunately. It may not be feasible to have your fiancé travel to you so that you can get married—and if you feel strongly about having your wedding in the U.S., this may not be what you want. And even after you're married, it will take a while before you can move to the United States. Waiting for your fiancé to become a citizen may take a similarly long time. And entering as a tourist will get you in—but you'll have to leave within six months. But these methods are the best we can offer, so take a look and see what's best for you.

CAUTION

If the U.S. petitioner has a criminal record, see an attorney. Under the Adam Walsh Child Protection and Safety Act of 2006, U.S. citizens and lawful permanent residents who have been convicted of any "specified offense against a minor" are prohibited from filing a family-based immigrant petition on behalf of any beneficiary (whether a child or not). USCIS will run security checks on all petitions and may call the petitioner in for fingerprinting. If the petitioner has a conviction for one of the specified offenses against a minor, then the petition will not be approved unless USCIS determines that the U.S. petitioner poses no risk to the beneficiary.

A. The Marriage Visa Option

If you plan to live in the United States permanently, the first thing you should do is to get married. It doesn't matter where you get married. You can have the ceremony in your home country, a third country, or in the United States, if you can get a tourist visa to come here (see Section C below for more on tourist visas).

After you are married, you will be eligible to immigrate to the United States as the spouse of a permanent resident. But first you will have to wait—and wait. Only a limited number of visas are given to spouses of U.S. permanent residents each year, and the demand for these visas is far greater than the supply. (For more on the waiting periods and other aspects of the process of applying as the spouse of a permanent resident see Chapter 8.) It can take several years to secure a visa this way.

You can't get on the waiting list for a marriage-based visa until you are married. But as soon as your spouse has your marriage certificate in hand, he or she can submit an I-130 petition that puts you in line. Unfortunately, you will not be allowed to live in the United States while you wait. You should marry as soon as possible in order to secure your place on the list.

B. If Your Fiancé or Spouse Becomes a U.S. Citizen

If your permanent resident fiancé or spouse becomes a U.S. citizen, your ability to obtain a fiancé or marriage-based visa improves tremendously. The process of obtaining a visa itself takes time, but there are no waiting periods for beginning the process if you are the foreign-born fiancé or spouse of a U.S. citizen.

The quicker your fiancé or spouse becomes a citizen, the quicker you can enter the United States. Unless your fiancé faces some serious impediment to citizenship—like not knowing English or having a criminal record—he or she can help your immigration application by applying for citizenship as soon as possible. A permanent resident can apply for U.S. citizenship five years after getting a green card (unless he or she qualifies for one of various exceptions). In fact, USCIS currently permits people to submit the application three months before the end of the required years (but no more than three months before, or they'll reject the application as premature).

There are other requirements to become a U.S. citizen, such as being of good moral character, having lived in the United States for at least half of the previous five years, being able to speak, read, and write English, and passing a test covering U.S. history and government.

RESOURCE

Need more information on the process and requirements of applying for U.S. citizenship? See the USCIS website at www.uscis.gov and *Becoming a U.S. Citizen: A Guide to the Law, Exam & Interview*, by Ilona Bray (Nolo).

The decision whether to apply for U.S. citizenship is a personal one. Your fiancé may not be interested in U.S. citizenship, perhaps out of a sense of allegiance to his or her home country. Having a green card does allow your fiancé to live in the United States permanently (though a permanent resident can lose the right to a green card, by living outside the United States for too long, committing crimes, or otherwise becoming deportable).

Your fiancé should know, however, that dual citizenship may be a possibility—if his or her home country allows it, so will the United States.

1. If You're Still Unmarried When Your Fiancé Becomes a Citizen

As the fiancé of a U.S. citizen, you will be eligible to apply for a fiancé visa. This will permit you to enter the United States, marry within 90 days, and apply for your green card in the United States. By applying as a fiancé, you'll avoid the waiting list for foreign spouses married to U.S. permanent residents (see Chapter 8 for more on the waiting lists).

However, unless you are extremely certain that your fiancé is about to become a citizen, it might be wiser to marry now and apply as the spouse of a permanent resident (see Section A, above). Your spouse's citizenship could be delayed or denied—leaving you nowhere. You would then have to marry and join the waiting list later than you otherwise could have.

2. If You're Already Married When Your Spouse Becomes a Citizen

The moment your spouse obtains citizenship, you become what is called an immediate relative. That means that you are immediately eligible for a marriage-based visa to enter the United States and obtain permanent residence, although the application process itself often takes about a year.

You can apply for entry as an immediate relative no matter where you are in the immigration process. So, for example, if your spouse filed the application to put you on the visa waiting list when he or she was a permanent resident (Form I-130), all you'll have to do is tell USCIS about the grant of citizenship for you to jump off the waiting list and move forward in your progress toward a green card.

C. Fiancés Coming as Tourists

Fiancés who only want to hold their marriage ceremony in the United States, knowing that they will not be permitted to remain here to apply for a green card, may be able to obtain a tourist visa (also called a visitor or B-2 visa). This is done at your local U.S. consulate. The application for a tourist visa is not terribly complicated, and usually takes between one day and six weeks to obtain. You will be given up to a six months' permitted stay.

1. Problems Getting a Tourist Visa

Obtaining and using a tourist visa isn't a sure thing. First, you must convince the consular officer that you really plan to leave your new spouse and return home when your visa expires.

You might be tempted to lie and say you are coming only as a tourist, not to get married. This is a bad idea. If the consular official or immigration officer at the border catches you in this lie, it will reinforce the suspicion that your true intention is to live in the United States permanently. You could be denied the tourist visa and accused of visa fraud—which would make it difficult, if not impossible, to eventually obtain your green card.

To convince a skeptical consular official that you intend to return to your home country, bring along documents like:

- a copy of your lease or rental agreement
- a letter from your employer stating that you are expected back by a certain date, and
- copies of birth certificates from close family members remaining behind.

2. Problems at the U.S. Border With a Tourist Visa

Even after obtaining your tourist visa, you could face problems at the U.S. border. Even if the consular officer in your home country believed your plan to return home, the border official might not. If you meet with a reasonable official, this should be no problem—your use of a tourist visa is perfectly legal.

If you get an official who is inclined to be suspicious, however, it's another matter. The border officials have what are called expedited removal powers. This means that they can keep you out if they think you've used fraud, such as lying about your intentions to return home after the wedding.

The border official has reason to be suspicious, since many people have used tourist visas as a way to enter the United States precisely for the purpose of living here illegally while they wait to apply for their green card. Once you've been kept out of the United States this way, you may be prevented from returning for five years.

To prepare for the possibility of meeting a wary border official, bring along the same things you showed the consular officer in order to get the visitor visa, explained above in Section 1. Also make sure there is nothing in your luggage to contradict this evidence. If your luggage is searched and the official realizes you are carrying enough prescription medication for a three-year stay and a letter from your fiancé saying, "Can't wait until you are here and we can settle down in our new house," you will find yourself on the next return plane.

Unfortunately, there is no way to remove every element of risk—your entry to the United States depends on the perception and decision of a single border patrol official. It's as simple as that. The prospect of your marriage in the U.S. might raise less suspicion than would be the case if you were the fiancé of a U.S. citizen (because spouses of permanent residents have no immediate path to a green card), but you should be just as prepared.

3. Staying in the U.S. on a Tourist Visa

No matter how you entered the United States, it will be natural for you to want to stay there with your new spouse after your marriage. You may even know people who have entered on tourist visas and ultimately been able to apply for a green card. However, this is not a workable plan, particularly for the spouses of lawful permanent residents as opposed to U.S. citizens.

As you may know, spouses of U.S. permanent residents are normally not eligible to stay in the United States during the years they are on the waiting list for a green card. And even if they do stay, they must leave the United States in most circumstances to perform the final step of the process, visiting a U.S. consulate to obtain an immigrant visa leading to permanent resident status. So even if you managed to stay in the United States illegally, you would, as the spouse of a permanent resident, have to return to a U.S. consulate eventually.

"No problem," you might think, "I'll take my chances on living in the United States illegally until then." But the U.S. Congress thought of this possibility too, and created a law to make you think twice. Once you leave to pick up your marriage-based visa at the U.S. consulate in your home country, the law will prevent you from coming back to the United States for a long time. (See Chapter 2, Section A.) If your illegal stay lasts six months or more, you won't be allowed back into the United States for three years. If your stay extends for one year or more, you will be kept out for ten years. That's a strong incentive to comply with the laws and wait for your immigrant visa outside the United States.

On the other hand, if your spouse becomes a U.S. citizen, and you've stayed in the United States as a tourist without getting caught, the law does allow you to file your green card (adjustment of status) application in the United States, without leaving. Since you wouldn't have to leave, you wouldn't face the time bars described above, which are only handed down once you're outside the United States.

But you could have another problem. You could be denied your green card (or at least have to apply for a waiver first) for having misused your tourist visa, pretending to be a mere tourist when your intention was to stay in the United States permanently. You would need a lawyer's help to apply for a waiver of your visa fraud.

Next Step

If you decide to get a tourist visa:	Learn the procedures from your local U.S. consulate. The application form is fairly simple. You will need to convince the consulate that you will return home after the wedding.
If you marry (abroad or in the U.S.) and file for permanent resident status:	See Chapter 8 covering overseas spouses of lawful permanent residents.
If you marry (abroad or in the U.S.) and your spouse becomes a U.S. citizen:	See Chapter 7 for overseas spouses of U.S. citizens.

Overseas Spouses of U.S. Citizens

I f you are married to a U.S. citizen and are living overseas, you are called an "immediate relative" in immigration law terminology. Your road to a green card should be fairly smooth. There are no waiting periods or quotas for people in your category. Your U.S. entry visa and green card are available to you as soon as you can get through the application procedures, which usually takes many months.

A marriage-based visa or green card is available to anyone whose marriage to a U.S. citizen is real and legally valid, and who is not inadmissible for any other reason. (See Chapter 2, Section B, if you need to review the complete eligibility criteria.)

This chapter assumes that you will be seeking an immigrant visa based on your marriage, rather than an alternative known as a "K-3" visa. This is a hybrid of the fiancé visa, allowing married couples to arrange for the foreign-born spouse to enter the U.S. as a nonimmigrant and then apply for a green card after arriving in the United States. It was meant to speed up the process—but has for the most part failed to do so, and adds a good deal of expense. For that reason the K-3 visa is widely considered "dead," and we do not cover it in this book.

If you've been married for less than two years when you either arrive in the United States on an immigrant visa (or are approved for a green card (adjustment of status) after arriving on a K-3 visa), you will begin life in America as a conditional resident. Your conditional residency will expire after a two-year "testing" period. Ninety days or less before the expiration date, you will have to apply for permanent status by filing Form I-751. (See Chapter 16 for information about removing the condition on your residence.)

Stay Put During the Application Process

Once this process has started, you're better off if you don't change addresses or take any long trips. USCIS or the consulate could send you a request for more information or call you in for your interview at any time. Missing such a notification could result in long delays in getting your visa application back on track.

If you do change addresses, be sure to send notification to the last USCIS or consular office you heard from. But don't assume they'll pay attention. USCIS and the consulates are notorious for losing change-of-address notifications. So, as a backup plan, make sure to have your mail forwarded or check in regularly with the new people living in your former home.

Many couples wish that they could take a quick trip to the United States while waiting for their immigrant visa to be granted. Unfortunately, once you've submitted any part of your immigrant visa application, you're unlikely to be granted a tourist visa. This is because the consulate will probably believe that your real intention in using the tourist visa is to apply for your green card in the United States, which is an inappropriate use of the tourist visa and could be considered visa fraud.

USCIS will review your file at that time and might decide to interview you and your spouse, to find out whether your marriage is real. If USCIS determines your marriage is not real, you could lose your status entirely and have to leave the United States.

If your marriage is already two years old when you either arrive at the U.S. border (with an immigrant visa) or get approved for a green card (after a K-3 entry), you will receive permanent residency and won't have to worry about your status expiring (although the actual card will need to be replaced once every ten years).

Applying for Immigrant Visa (Overseas Spouses of U.S. Citizens)

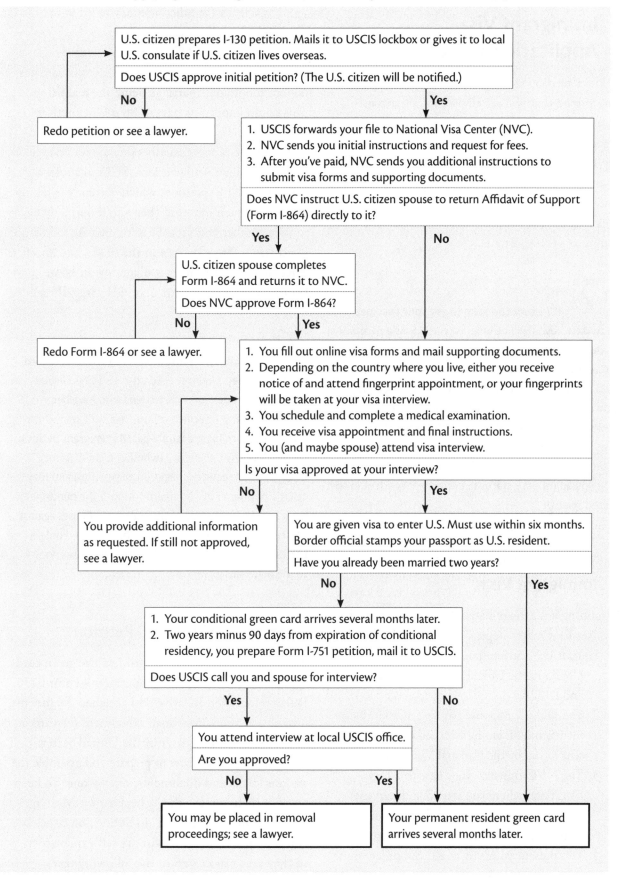

A. The Marriage-Based Immigrant Visa Application Process

If you're reading this section, it means that you have determined that you are eligible for a marriage-based immigrant visa and are ready to find out exactly how to get it. But first, a warning: This application process is a bit like harnessing yourself to a turtle. It's going to move slowly, and to succeed you'll have to hang on for the whole bumpy ride. This chapter gives you a map for that ride and clues you in to a few shortcuts.

> **TIP**
>
> **It's never too soon to get your vaccinations up to date.** If you will be entering the U.S. as a permanent resident, then before you enter, you'll have to prove that you've had all the necessary vaccinations. (The ones you'll need are listed in Chapter 2, Section A.) Check with your local doctor now so that you're not stuck later waiting weeks while a series of shots is administered. If you are entering the U.S. on a K-3/K-4 visa, you are not required to prove that you've had all the necessary vaccinations until you adjust your status to permanent resident in the United States.

1. The Four Steps to an Immigrant Visa

Obtaining a marriage-based visa and green card involves four major steps:

1. Your U.S. citizen spouse submits a petition to USCIS in the United States using Forms I-130 and I-130A.
2. You and your spouse pay fees, gather documents, and fill out forms based on instructions sent to you by the National Visa Center (NVC).
3. The NVC transfers your case to a U.S. consulate, where you attend an interview (in your home country) and receive your immigrant visa (then or soon after), and
4. You present your visa at a U.S. border where it is examined. Assuming you are approved, your passport will be stamped for U.S. residency (in other words, you get your green card status).

In rare instances, USCIS will ask your spouse to attend a "fraud interview" if it or the consulate has doubts about your marriage being the real thing. This could happen as part of Step One or after Step Three.

This entire process usually takes approximately 12 months. First you wait for USCIS to approve your initial I-130 petition, which currently is taking about five to ten months. Then you'll normally have to wait another two months to receive the follow-up instructions (Step Two) from the NVC, and another three months until the consulate in your home country calls you for your interview (Step Three).

> **CAUTION**
>
> **If the U.S. petitioner has a criminal record, see an attorney.** Under the Adam Walsh Child Protection and Safety Act of 2006, U.S. citizens who have been convicted of any "specified offense against a minor" are prohibited from filing a family-based immigrant petition on behalf of any beneficiary (whether a child or not). USCIS will run security checks on all petitions and may call the petitioner in for fingerprinting. If the petitioner has a conviction for one of the specified offenses against a minor, then the petition will not be approved unless USCIS determines that the U.S. petitioner poses no risk to the beneficiary.

2. Step One: The I-130 Petition

The U.S. citizen spouse will initiate the green card application process by filing a petition—Form I-130, Petition for Alien Relative and attached documents—with a USCIS "lockbox," which will forward it to a USCIS service center in the United States.

We'll go through how to prepare and assemble the various forms and documents, one by one. To keep track of them all, use the "Checklist for Marriage-Based Immigrant Petition" in Subsection c, below. A few items on this checklist are self-explanatory, so they aren't discussed in the following text.

a. Line-by-Line Instructions for Form I-130 Petition

This section will give precise instructions for filling out the three forms that are required in Step One. Before proceeding, take a look at the general instructions for filling in USCIS immigration forms in Chapter 4.

i. Form I-130

Form I-130 is one of the most important ones in your immigration process. It will be the U.S. spouse's first opportunity to explain who each of you is, where you live, and why you qualify for a visa.

Don't be thrown off by the fact that the form addresses your spouse as "you"—after all, it's the U.S. spouse who fills out this form.

WEB RESOURCE

Form I-130 is available on the USCIS website, at www.uscis.gov/i-130. Below is a sample filled-in version of the relevant pages of this form.

Part A

Question 1: Check the first box, "Spouse."

Questions 2–3: Since you are petitioning for a spouse, do not check any boxes here.

Question 4: If the petitioning U.S. spouse gained permanent residence through adoption (immigrated to the U.S. before becoming a citizen), check "Yes." But no matter which box is checked, it won't affect the application, since this question is mainly directed at people immigrating through parent/child relationships—something not covered in this book.

Part 2

Question 1: A U.S. citizen petitioner will have an A-number (Alien Registration Number) only if he or she once held a green card (permanent residence).

Question 2: A U.S. citizen petitioner who has filed a past petition with USCIS may have received a USCIS Online Account Number, and should enter it here.

Question 3: A U.S. citizen will have a Social Security number, and should fill it in here.

Question 4: The petitioning spouse should enter his/her full name. Use current married name if it was changed at the time of your marriage. (See "What's Your Name?" in Chapter 4, Section B).

Question 5: The U.S. petitioner should enter any names previously used. If the citizen was married before and used another name during that time, enter it here.

Questions 6-9: Self-explanatory.

Questions 10-15: Fill in the U.S. citizen's addresses from the last five years. If the citizen has lived at more than one address during these years, include the start and end dates of the other addresses.

Question 16: Answer how many times the petitioner has been married, including this time.

Question 17: This refers only to the petitioning spouse's most recent marital status, so check only married, even if there was a previous divorce.

Questions 18–19: Self-explanatory.

Questions 20-23: Put the name of the petitioner's current spouse (the immigrant) first and then any past spouses next. Leave blank or enter "N/A" under the date marriage ended for your current marriage. The question of when the U.S. spouse's prior marriage ended is intended to make sure your current marriage is valid. If the petitioning spouse's prior marriage(s) ended after your present marriage began, yours is not a lawful marriage. But it may not be necessary to run to a lawyer. Assuming that the divorce has since become final, you can simply correct the problem by remarrying. (If there was fraud involved in your hasty marriage, consult a lawyer before proceeding.)

Questions 24-35: Answer basic biographic information about the petitioning U.S. citizen's parents. If lacking any information about a parent, enter "unknown."

Question 36: Self-explanatory.

Question 37: State how the U.S. citizen petitioner gained citizenship.

Questions 38–39: If the petitioning spouse is a naturalized U.S. citizen (meaning someone who wasn't born a citizen, but became one after an application and exam), this number can be found at the top right-hand side of the naturalization certificate. The date and place issued are also shown on the certificate.

Sample Form I-130, Petition for Alien Relative—Page 1

Petition for Alien Relative

Department of Homeland Security
U.S. Citizenship and Immigration Services

USCIS
Form I-130
OMB No. 1615-0012
Expires 02/28/2021

For USCIS Use Only	Fee Stamp	Action Stamp

A-Number

A-

Initial Receipt

Resubmitted

Relocated	**Section of Law/Visa Category**
Received	☐ 201(b) Spouse - IR-1/CR-1 ☐ 203(a)(1) Unm. S/D - F1-1 ☐ 203(a)(2)(B) Unm. S/D - F2-4
Sent	☐ 201(b) Child - IR-2/CR-2 ☐ 203(a)(2)(A) Spouse - F2-1 ☐ 203(a)(3) Married S/D - F3-1
Completed	☐ 201(b) Parent - IR-5 ☐ 203(a)(2)(A) Child - F2-2 ☐ 203(a)(4) Brother/Sister - F4-1

Approved	Petition was filed on (Priority Date mm/dd/yyyy):	☐ Field Investigation	☐ Personal Interview	☐ 204(a)(2)(A) Resolved
Returned	PDR request granted/denied - New priority date (mm/dd/yyyy):	☐ Previously Forwarded	☐ Pet. A-File Reviewed	☐ I-485 Filed Simultaneously
		☐ 203(g) Resolved	☐ Ben. A-File Reviewed	☐ 204(g) Resolved

Remarks

At which USCIS office (e.g., NBC, VSC, LOS, CRO) was Form I-130 adjudicated? _____

To be completed by an attorney or accredited representative (if any).

☐ **Select this box if Form G-28 is attached.**	**Volag Number** (if any)	**Attorney State Bar Number** (if applicable)	**Attorney or Accredited Representative USCIS Online Account Number** (if any)

▶ **START HERE** - Type or print in black ink.

If you need extra space to complete any section of this petition, use the space provided in **Part 9. Additional Information.**
Complete and submit as many copies of Part 9., as necessary, with your petition.

Part 1. Relationship (You are the Petitioner. Your relative is the Beneficiary)

1. I am filing this petition for my (Select **only one** box):

   ☒ Spouse   ☐ Parent   ☐ Brother/Sister   ☐ Child

2. If you are filing this petition for your child or parent, select the box that describes your relationship (Select **only one** box):

   ☐ Child was born to parents who were married to each other at the time of the child's birth

   ☐ Stepchild/Stepparent

   ☐ Child was born to parents who were not married to each other at the time of the child's birth

   ☐ Child was adopted (not an Orphan or Hague Convention adoptee)

3. If the beneficiary is your brother/sister, are you related by adoption?   ☐ Yes   ☐ No

4. Did you gain lawful permanent resident status or citizenship through adoption?   ☐ Yes   ☒ No

Part 2. Information About You (Petitioner)

1. Alien Registration Number (A-Number) (if any)

   ▶ A-

2. USCIS Online Account Number (if any)

   ▶

3. U.S. Social Security Number (if any)

   ▶ a a a a a a a a a

Your Full Name

4.a.	Family Name (Last Name)	mancini
4.b.	Given Name (First Name)	Alberto
4.c.	Middle Name	Ilario

Sample Form I-130, Petition for Alien Relative—Page 2

Part 2. Information About You (Petitioner) (continued)

Other Names Used (if any)

Provide all other names you have ever used, including aliases, maiden name, and nicknames.

5.a. Family Name (Last Name)

5.b. Given Name (First Name)

5.c. Middle Name

Other Information

6. City/Town/Village of Birth

Los Angeles

7. Country of Birth

USA

8. Date of Birth (mm/dd/yyyy)   03/30/1978

9. Sex   ☒ Male   ☐ Female

Mailing Address   *(USPS ZIP Code Lookup)*

10.a. In Care Of Name

10.b. Street Number and Name   800 Broadway

10.c. ☐ Apt. ☐ Ste. ☐ Flr.

10.d. City or Town   Lindenhurst

10.e. State   NY   **10.f.** ZIP Code   11757

10.g. Province

10.h. Postal Code

10.i. Country

USA

11. Is your current mailing address the same as your physical address?   ☒ Yes   ☐ No

If you answered "No" to **Item Number 11.**, provide information on your physical address in **Item Numbers 12.a. - 13.b.**

Address History

Provide your physical addresses for the last five years, whether inside or outside the United States. Provide your current address first if it is different from your mailing address in **Item Numbers 10.a. - 10.i.**

Physical Address 1

12.a. Street Number and Name

12.b. ☐ Apt. ☐ Ste. ☐ Flr.

12.c. City or Town

12.d. State   ▼   **12.e.** ZIP Code

12.f. Province

12.g. Postal Code

12.h. Country

13.a. Date From (mm/dd/yyyy)

13.b. Date To (mm/dd/yyyy)   **PRESENT**

Physical Address 2

14.a. Street Number and Name

14.b. ☐ Apt. ☐ Ste. ☐ Flr.

14.c. City or Town

14.d. State   ▼   **14.e.** ZIP Code

14.f. Province

14.g. Postal Code

14.h. Country

15.a. Date From (mm/dd/yyyy)

15.b. Date To (mm/dd/yyyy)

Your Marital Information

16. How many times have you been married?   ▶   2

17. Current Marital Status

☐ Single, Never Married   ☒ Married   ☐ Divorced

☐ Widowed   ☐ Separated   ☐ Annulled

Sample Form I-130, Petition for Alien Relative—Page 3

Part 2. Information About You (Petitioner) (continued)

18. Date of Current Marriage (if currently married) (mm/dd/yyyy)

Place of Your Current Marriage (if married)

19.a. City or Town

19.b. State

19.c. Province

19.d. Country

Names of All Your Spouses (if any)

Provide information on your current spouse (if currently married) first and then list all your prior spouses (if any).

Spouse 1

20.a. Family Name (Last Name)   Mancini

20.b. Given Name (First Name)   Terese

20.c. Middle Name   Marcia

21. Date Marriage Ended (mm/dd/yyyy)

Spouse 2

22.a. Family Name (Last Name)   Colombo

22.b. Given Name (First Name)   Andrea

22.c. Middle Name   Luisa

23. Date Marriage Ended (mm/dd/yyyy)   03/07/2000

Information About Your Parents

Parent 1's Information

Full Name of Parent 1

24.a. Family Name (Last Name)   Mancini

24.b. Given Name (First Name)   Angela

24.c. Middle Name   Sofia

25. Date of Birth (mm/dd/yyyy)   03/01/1952

26. Sex   ☐ Male   ☒ Female

27. Country of Birth   USA

28. City/Town/Village of Residence   Lindenhurst

29. Country of Residence   USA

Parent 2's Information

Full Name of Parent 2

30.a. Family Name (Last Name)   Mancini

30.b. Given Name (First Name)   Mario

30.c. Middle Name   Luca

31. Date of Birth (mm/dd/yyyy)   02/01/1945

32. Sex   ☒ Male   ☐ Female

33. Country of Birth   Italy

34. City/Town/Village of Residence   Lindenhurst

35. Country of Residence   USA

Additional Information About You (Petitioner)

36. I am a (Select **only one** box):

☒ U.S. Citizen   ☐ Lawful Permanent Resident

If you are a U.S. citizen, complete Item Number 37.

37. My citizenship was acquired through (Select **only one** box):

☒ Birth in the United States

☐ Naturalization

☐ Parents

38. Have you obtained a Certificate of Naturalization or a Certificate of Citizenship?   ☐ Yes   ☐ No

If you answered "Yes" to **Item Number 38.**, complete the following:

39.a. Certificate Number

39.b. Place of Issuance

39.c. Date of Issuance (mm/dd/yyyy)

Sample Form I-130, Petition for Alien Relative—Page 4

Part 2. Information About You (Petitioner) (continued)

If you are a lawful permanent resident, complete **Item Numbers 40.a. - 41.**

40.a. Class of Admission

40.b. Date of Admission (mm/dd/yyyy)

Place of Admission

40.c. City or Town

40.d State

41. Did you gain lawful permanent resident status through marriage to a U.S. citizen or lawful permanent resident?

☐ Yes ☐ No

Employment History

Provide your employment history for the last five years, whether inside or outside the United States. Provide your current employment first. If you are currently unemployed, type or print "Unemployed" in **Item Number 42.**

Employer 1

42. Name of Employer/Company

Bob's Diner

43.a. Street Number and Name

195 W. Montauk Hwy

43.b. ☐ Apt. ☐ Ste. ☐ Flr.

43.c. City or Town

Lindenhurst

43.d. State NY **43.e.** ZIP Code 11757

43.f. Province

43.g. Postal Code

43.h. Country

USA

44. Your Occupation

Shift manager

45.a. Date From (mm/dd/yyyy) 05/05/2009

45.b. Date To (mm/dd/yyyy) **PRESENT**

Employer 2

46. Name of Employer/Company

47.a. Street Number and Name

47.b. ☐ Apt. ☐ Ste. ☐ Flr.

47.c. City or Town

47.d. State **47.e.** ZIP Code

47.f. Province

47.g. Postal Code

47.h. Country

48. Your Occupation

49.a. Date From (mm/dd/yyyy)

49.b. Date To (mm/dd/yyyy)

Part 3. Biographic Information

NOTE: Provide the biographic information about you, the petitioner.

1. Ethnicity (Select **only one** box)

☐ Hispanic or Latino

☒ Not Hispanic or Latino

2. Race (Select **all applicable** boxes)

☒ White

☐ Asian

☐ Black or African American

☐ American Indian or Alaska Native

☐ Native Hawaiian or Other Pacific Islander

3. Height Feet 6 Inches 1

4. Weight Pounds 1 8 5

5. Eye Color (Select **only one** box)

☐ Black ☐ Blue ☒ Brown

☐ Gray ☐ Green ☐ Hazel

☐ Maroon ☐ Pink ☐ Unknown/Other

Sample Form I-130, Petition for Alien Relative—Page 5

Part 3. Biographic Information (continued)

6. Hair Color (Select **only one** box)

- [ ] Bald (No hair)
- [X] Black
- [ ] Blond
- [ ] Brown
- [ ] Gray
- [ ] Red
- [ ] Sandy
- [ ] White
- [ ] Unknown/Other

Part 4. Information About Beneficiary

1. Alien Registration Number (A-Number) (if any)

▶ A-

2. USCIS Online Account Number (if any)

▶

3. U.S. Social Security Number (if any)

▶

Beneficiary's Full Name

4.a. Family Name (Last Name) — mancini

4.b. Given Name (First Name) — Terese

4.c. Middle Name — marcia

Other Names Used (if any)

Provide all other names the beneficiary has ever used, including aliases, maiden name, and nicknames.

5.a. Family Name (Last Name) — moreno, Brambantio

5.b. Given Name (First Name) —

5.c. Middle Name —

Other Information About Beneficiary

6. City/Town/Village of Birth

Venice

7. Country of Birth

Italy

8. Date of Birth (mm/dd/yyyy) — 02/15/1982

9. Sex — [ ] Male [X] Female

10. Has anyone else ever filed a petition for the beneficiary?

[ ] Yes [X] No [ ] Unknown

NOTE: Select "Unknown" *only* if you do not know, and the beneficiary also does not know, if anyone else has ever filed a petition for the beneficiary.

Beneficiary's Physical Address

If the beneficiary lives outside the United States in a home without a street number or name, leave **Item Numbers 11.a.** and **11.b.** blank.

11.a. Street Number and Name — 108 Piazza d'Azeglio

11.b. [ ] Apt. [ ] Ste. [ ] Flr.

11.c. City or Town — Venice

11.d. State ▼ **11.e.** ZIP Code

11.f. Province — Veneto

11.g. Postal Code — 99999

11.h. Country

Italy

Other Address and Contact Information

Provide the address in the United States where the beneficiary intends to live, if different from **Item Numbers 11.a. - 11.h.** If the address is the same, type or print "SAME" in **Item Number 12.a.**

12.a Street Number and Name — 800 Broadway

12.b. [ ] Apt. [ ] Ste. [ ] Flr.

12.c. City or Town — Lindenhurst

12.d. State NY ▼ **12.e.** ZIP Code 11757

Provide the beneficiary's address outside the United States, if different from **Item Numbers 11.a. - 11.h.** If the address is the same, type or print "SAME" in **Item Number 13.a.**

13.a. Street Number and Name — SAME

13.b. [ ] Apt. [ ] Ste. [ ] Flr.

13.c. City or Town

13.d. Province

13.e. Postal Code

13.f. Country

14. Daytime Telephone Number (if any)

0121234

Sample Form I-130, Petition for Alien Relative—Page 6

Part 4. Information About Beneficiary (continued)

15. Mobile Telephone Number (if any)

16. Email Address (if any)

Beneficiary's Marital Information

17. How many times has the beneficiary been married?

▶ 2

18. Current Marital Status

☐ Single, Never Married ☒ Married ☐ Divorced

☐ Widowed ☐ Separated ☐ Annulled

19. Date of Current Marriage (if currently married) (mm/dd/yyyy)

01/01/2019

Place of Beneficiary's Current Marriage (if married)

20.a. City or Town Venice

20.b. State

20.c. Province Veneto

20.d. Country Italy

Names of Beneficiary's Spouses (if any)

Provide information on the beneficiary's current spouse (if currently married) first and then list all the beneficiary's prior spouses (if any).

Spouse 1

21.a. Family Name (Last Name) mancini

21.b. Given Name (First Name) Alberto

21.c. Middle Name Ilario

22. Date Marriage Ended (mm/dd/yyyy)

Spouse 2

23.a. Family Name (Last Name) moreno

23.b. Given Name (First Name) Giovanni

23.c. Middle Name

24. Date Marriage Ended (mm/dd/yyyy) 07/10/2008

Information About Beneficiary's Family

Provide information about the beneficiary's spouse and children.

Person 1

25.a. Family Name (Last Name) mancini

25.b. Given Name (First Name) Alberto

25.c. Middle Name Ilario

26. Relationship Spouse

27. Date of Birth (mm/dd/yyyy) 03/30/1978

28. Country of Birth USA

Person 2

29.a. Family Name (Last Name) moreno

29.b. Given Name (First Name) Giovanna

29.c. Middle Name Lucia

30. Relationship Daughter

31. Date of Birth (mm/dd/yyyy) 06/01/2005

32. Country of Birth Italy

Person 3

33.a. Family Name (Last Name)

33.b. Given Name (First Name)

33.c. Middle Name

34. Relationship

35. Date of Birth (mm/dd/yyyy)

36. Country of Birth

Sample Form I-130, Petition for Alien Relative—Page 7

Part 4. Information About Beneficiary (continued)

Person 4

37.a. Family Name (Last Name)

37.b. Given Name (First Name)

37.c. Middle Name

38. Relationship

39. Date of Birth (mm/dd/yyyy)

40. Country of Birth

Person 5

41.a. Family Name (Last Name)

41.b. Given Name (First Name)

41.c. Middle Name

42. Relationship

43. Date of Birth (mm/dd/yyyy)

44. Country of Birth

Beneficiary's Entry Information

45. Was the beneficiary **EVER** in the United States?

☐ Yes ☒ No

If the beneficiary is currently in the United States, complete **Items Numbers 46.a. - 46.d.**

46.a. He or she arrived as a (Class of Admission):

46.b. Form I-94 Arrival-Departure Record Number

▶

46.c. Date of Arrival (mm/dd/yyyy)

46.d. Date authorized stay expired, or will expire, as shown on Form I-94 or Form I-95 (mm/dd/yyyy) or type or print "D/S" for Duration of Status

47. Passport Number

48. Travel Document Number

49. Country of Issuance for Passport or Travel Document

50. Expiration Date for Passport or Travel Document (mm/dd/yyyy)

Beneficiary's Employment Information

Provide the beneficiary's current employment information (if applicable), even if they are employed outside of the United States. If the beneficiary is currently unemployed, type or print "Unemployed" in **Item Number 51.a.**

51.a. Name of Current Employer (if applicable)

Self-employed

51.b. Street Number and Name

108 Piazza d'Azeglio

51.c. ☐ Apt. ☐ Ste. ☐ Flr.

51.d. City or Town

Venice

51.e. State ▼ **51.f.** ZIP Code

51.g. Province

Veneto

51.h. Postal Code

99999

51.i. Country

Italy

52. Date Employment Began (mm/dd/yyyy)

08/06/2010

Additional Information About Beneficiary

53. Was the beneficiary **EVER** in immigration proceedings?

☐ Yes ☒ No

54. If you answered "Yes," select the type of proceedings and provide the location and date of the proceedings.

☐ Removal ☐ Exclusion/Deportation

☐ Rescission ☐ Other Judicial Proceedings

55.a. City or Town

55.b. State

56. Date (mm/dd/yyyy)

Sample Form I-130, Petition for Alien Relative—Page 8

Part 4. Information About Beneficiary (continued)

If the beneficiary's native written language does not use Roman letters, type or print his or her name and foreign address in their native written language.

57.a. Family Name (Last Name) `N/A`

57.b. Given Name (First Name)

57.c. Middle Name

58.a. Street Number and Name

58.b. ☐ Apt. ☐ Ste. ☐ Flr.

58.c. City or Town

58.d. Province

58.e. Postal Code

58.f. Country

If filing for your spouse, provide the last address at which you physically lived together. If you never lived together, type or print, "Never lived together" in Item Number 59.a.

59.a. Street Number and Name `Never lived together`

59.b. ☐ Apt. ☐ Ste. ☐ Flr.

59.c. City or Town

59.d. State ▼   **59.e.** ZIP Code

59.f. Province

59.g. Postal Code

59.h. Country

60.a. Date From (mm/dd/yyyy)

60.b. Date To (mm/dd/yyyy)

The beneficiary is in the United States and will apply for adjustment of status to that of a lawful permanent resident at the U.S. Citizenship and Immigration Services (USCIS) office in:

61.a. City or Town

61.b. State ▼

The beneficiary will not apply for adjustment of status in the United States, but he or she will apply for an immigrant visa abroad at the U.S. Embassy or U.S. Consulate in:

62.a. City or Town `Rome`

62.b. Province

62.c. Country `Italy`

NOTE: Choosing a U.S. Embassy or U.S. Consulate outside the country of the beneficiary's last residence does not guarantee that it will accept the beneficiary's case for processing. In these situations, the designated U.S. Embassy or U.S. Consulate has discretion over whether or not to accept the beneficiary's case.

Part 5. Other Information

1. Have you **EVER** previously filed a petition for this beneficiary or any other alien?   ☐ Yes   ☒ No

If you answered "Yes," provide the name, place, date of filing, and the result.

2.a. Family Name (Last Name)

2.b. Given Name (First Name)

2.c. Middle Name

3.a. City or Town

3.b. State

4. Date Filed (mm/dd/yyyy)

5. Result (for example, approved, denied, withdrawn)

If you are also submitting separate petitions for other relatives, provide the names of and your relationship to each relative.

Relative 1

6.a. Family Name (Last Name) `moreno`

6.b. Given Name (First Name) `Giovanni`

6.c. Middle Name `Lucia`

7. Relationship `Stepdaughter`

Sample Form I-130, Petition for Alien Relative—Page 9

Part 5. Other Information (continued)

Relative 2

8.a. Family Name
(Last Name)

8.b. Given Name
(First Name)

8.c. Middle Name

9. Relationship

WARNING: USCIS investigates the claimed relationships and verifies the validity of documents you submit. If you falsify a family relationship to obtain a visa, USCIS may seek to have you criminally prosecuted.

PENALTIES: By law, you may be imprisoned for up to 5 years or fined $250,000, or both, for entering into a marriage contract in order to evade any U.S. immigration law. In addition, you may be fined up to $10,000 and imprisoned for up to 5 years, or both, for knowingly and willfully falsifying or concealing a material fact or using any false document in submitting this petition.

Part 6. Petitioner's Statement, Contact Information, Declaration, and Signature

NOTE: Read the **Penalties** section of the Form I-130 Instructions before completing this part.

Petitioner's Statement

NOTE: Select the box for either **Item Number 1.a.** or **1.b.** If applicable, select the box for **Item Number 2.**

1.a. ☒ I can read and understand English, and I have read and understand every question and instruction on this petition and my answer to every question.

1.b. ☐ The interpreter named in **Part 7.** read to me every question and instruction on this petition and my answer to every question in

[   ],

a language in which I am fluent. I understood all of this information as interpreted.

2. ☐ At my request, the preparer named in **Part 8.**,

[   ],

prepared this petition for me based only upon information I provided or authorized.

Petitioner's Contact Information

3. Petitioner's Daytime Telephone Number

212-222-9822

4. Petitioner's Mobile Telephone Number (if any)

5. Petitioner's Email Address (if any)

alberbom@email.com

Petitioner's Declaration and Certification

Copies of any documents I have submitted are exact photocopies of unaltered, original documents, and I understand that USCIS may require that I submit original documents to USCIS at a later date. Furthermore, I authorize the release of any information from any of my records that USCIS may need to determine my eligibility for the immigration benefit I seek.

I further authorize release of information contained in this petition, in supporting documents, and in my USCIS records to other entities and persons where necessary for the administration and enforcement of U.S. immigration laws.

I understand that USCIS may require me to appear for an appointment to take my biometrics (fingerprints, photograph, and/or signature) and, at that time, if I am required to provide biometrics, I will be required to sign an oath reaffirming that:

1) I provided or authorized all of the information contained in, and submitted with, my petition;

2) I reviewed and understood all of the information in, and submitted with, my petition; and

3) All of this information was complete, true, and correct at the time of filing.

I certify, under penalty of perjury, that all of the information in my petition and any document submitted with it were provided or authorized by me, that I reviewed and understand all of the information contained in, and submitted with, my petition, and that all of this information is complete, true, and correct.

Petitioner's Signature

6.a. Petitioner's Signature (sign in ink)

➡ Alberto I. Mancini

6.b. Date of Signature (mm/dd/yyyy)   03/01/2019

NOTE TO ALL PETITIONERS: If you do not completely fill out this petition or fail to submit required documents listed in the Instructions, USCIS may deny your petition.

Question 40: U.S. citizens can write "N/A" here.

Question 41: If the petitioning spouse checks "yes" here to indicate having received U.S. permanent residence through marriage, calculate how long it has been since the U.S. spouse's approval for permanent residence. A petitioning spouse who immigrated through marriage cannot petition a new spouse for five years, unless the first spouse died or the U.S. spouse can prove by "clear and convincing evidence" that the previous marriage was bona fide (real). USCIS is concerned that the first marriage was just a sham, with the long-term goal of getting both of you into the United States by piggybacking on a sham marriage. To prove that the first marriage was bona fide, enclose documentary evidence showing that the couple shared a life, such as shared rent receipts or a mortgage, club memberships, children's birth certificates, utility bills, and insurance agreements. As for what makes for "clear and convincing" evidence, this is one of those legal standards that is easy to state but hard to pin down. A spouse in this situation may have a hard time persuading a suspicious government official that the previous marriage was bona fide.

Questions 42-49: Fill in the petitioner's employment history from the last five years. If he or she has had more than two jobs in the past five years, all must be listed. Attach additional employment in Part 9 on page 12.

Part 3

Questions 1–5: Provide basic biographic information about the U.S. citizen petitioner.

Part 4

Now the questions refer to you, the immigrant beneficiary.

Question 1: The Alien Registration Number is an eight- or nine-digit number following a letter A that USCIS (or the formerly named INS) would have assigned an immigrant who previously applied for permanent (or, in some cases, temporary) residence or was in deportation/removal proceedings. Of course, if that previous application was denied because the immigrant was found inadmissible or lied on that application, call a lawyer before going any further.

Question 2: An immigrant who has ever filed a petition with USCIS might have a USCIS Online Account Number.

Question 3: An immigrant won't have a Social Security number without having lived in the United States with a work permit, a visa allowing work, or U.S. residence.

Question 4: Current name.

Question 5: Enter any names the immigrant previously used, including during a previous marriage.

Questions 6–10: Self-explanatory.

Question 11: Immigrant's current address outside of the United States.

Questions 12–13: Self-explanatory. Hopefully, the immigrant intends to live at the U.S. spouse's address, or USCIS will raise questions.

Questions 14–16: Self-explanatory.

Question 17: Answer how many times the immigrant has been married, including this time.

Question 18: This refers only to recent marital status, so check only married, even if there was a previous divorce.

Questions 19–20: Self-explanatory.

Questions 21–24: Name current spouse first and any past spouses next. Put "N/A" under the date marriage ended for your current marriage. The question of when any prior marriage(s) ended is intended to make sure your current marriage is valid. If prior marriage(s) ended after your present marriage began, yours is not a lawful marriage. But if the divorce has since become final, you can likely cure the problem by remarrying. (If there was fraud involved in your hasty marriage, consult a lawyer before proceeding.)

Questions 25–44: Although the U.S. spouse is already covered in this application, it's safest to list him or her again before listing children, if any. This means all children, including any by previous relationships.

Question 45: If the immigrant has ever been to the United States, even for a short time as a tourist, check "Yes."

Questions 46–50: Because the immigrant is currently overseas, there's no need to complete these questions.

Questions 51–52: Fill in the immigrant's current employment information. If not working, enter "unemployed" or "student," if applicable.

Questions 53–56: If the immigrant has ever been in Immigration Court (removal or deportation) proceedings, consult a lawyer before continuing. The immigrant might be inadmissible to the United States or need a special waiver.

Questions 57–58: If the immigrant's native language uses a non-Roman script (for example, Russian, Chinese, or Arabic), you will need to write the name and address in that script.

Questions 59–60: If you've ever lived together, put the last address here.

Question 61: Because the immigrant is currently overseas, there's no need to complete these questions.

Question 62: Enter the name of the U.S. consulate with a visa processing office in the immigrant's country; or if none exists, the one with the power to handle visa requests from there. (Don't worry too much about getting it wrong; USCIS will redirect the application when it approves the petition.)

Part 5

Now we're back to questions about the petitioning spouse.

Questions 1–5: This is meant to uncover the U.S. spouse's history (if any) of petitioning other immigrants to come to the United States. As you can probably imagine, a petitioning spouse who has a history of short marriages to people whom he/she then helped to obtain green cards, can expect a major marriage fraud investigation. Consult a lawyer before proceeding.

Questions 6–9: This refers to other petitions being submitted simultaneously (for example, for the immigrant's children from this or other marriages), so that USCIS can process the petitions together.

Part 6

The U.S. citizen petitioner should fill out this section with contact information and signature.

Parts 7 and 8

These are for a preparer or interpreter helping fill out the form. If filling out the application unassisted, write "N/A" here. A little typing assistance or advice from a friend doesn't count— the only people who need to complete this line are lawyers or agencies who fill out these forms on others' behalf or offer translation services.

ii. Form I-130A

You (the immigrant spouse beneficiary) must fill out this form. The purpose is to give the U.S. government information with which to check your background. Most of the questions are self-explanatory. If you really can't remember or are unable to find out an exact date, enter what you can remember, such as the year. Alternatively, you can say "unknown," but if you overuse the "unknowns," USCIS may return the application for another try.

WEB RESOURCE
Form I-130A is available on the USCIS website, at www.uscis.gov/i-130. Below is a sample filled-in version of the relevant pages of this form.

Part 1

Question 1: The Alien Registration Number is an eight- or nine-digit number following a letter A that USCIS (or the formerly named INS) would have assigned to you if you previously applied for permanent (or, in some cases, temporary) residence or been in deportation/removal proceedings. Of course, if that previous application was denied because you were inadmissible or you lied on that application, you should call a lawyer before going any further.

Question 2: If you filed a petition with USCIS in the past, you might have a USCIS Online Account Number.

Sample Form I-130A, Supplemental Information for Spouse Beneficiary—Page 1

Supplemental Information for Spouse Beneficiary

Department of Homeland Security
U.S. Citizenship and Immigration Services

**USCIS
Form I-130A**
OMB No. 1615-0012
Expires 02/28/2021

To be completed by an attorney or accredited representative (if any).			
☐ **Select this box if Form G-28 is attached.**	**Volag Number** (if any)	**Attorney State Bar Number** (if applicable)	**Attorney or Accredited Representative USCIS Online Account Number** (if any)

▶ **START HERE - Type or print in black ink.**

The purpose of this form is to collect additional information for a spouse beneficiary of Form I-130, Petition for Alien Relative. If your spouse is a U.S. citizen, lawful permanent resident, or non-citizen U.S. national who is filing Form I-130 on your behalf, you must complete and sign Form I-130A, Supplemental Information for Spouse Beneficiary, and submit it with the Form I-130 filed by your spouse. If you reside overseas, you still must complete Form I-130A, but you do not need to sign the form.

Part 1. Information About You (Spouse Beneficiary)

1. Alien Registration Number (A-Number) (if any)
▶ A-

2. USCIS Online Account Number (if any)
▶

Your Full Name

3.a. Family Name (Last Name) Mancini
3.b. Given Name (First Name) Terese
3.c. Middle Name Maria

Address History

Provide your physical addresses for the last five years, whether inside or outside the United States. Provide your current address first. If you need extra space to complete this section, use the space provided in **Part 7. Additional Information**.

Physical Address 1

4.a. Street Number and Name 108 Piazza d'Azeglio
4.b. ☐ Apt. ☐ Ste. ☐ Flr.
4.c. City or Town Venice
4.d. State ▼ **4.e.** ZIP Code
4.f. Province Veneto
4.g. Postal Code 99999
4.h. Country
Italy

5.a. Date From (mm/dd/yyyy) 08/15/2014
5.b. Date To (mm/dd/yyyy) PRESENT

Physical Address 2

6.a. Street Number and Name
6.b. ☐ Apt. ☐ Ste. ☐ Flr.
6.c. City or Town
6.d. State ▼ **6.e.** ZIP Code
6.f. Province
6.g. Postal Code
6.h. Country

7.a. Date From (mm/dd/yyyy)
7.b. Date To (mm/dd/yyyy)

Last Physical Address Outside the United States

Provide your last address outside the United States of more than one year (even if listed above).

8.a. Street Number and Name 108 Piazza d'Azeglio
8.b. ☐ Apt. ☐ Ste. ☐ Flr.
8.c. City or Town Venice
8.d. Province Veneto
8.e. Postal Code 99999
8.f. Country
Italy

Sample Form I-130A, Supplemental Information for Spouse Beneficiary—Page 2

Part 1. Information About You (The Spouse Beneficiary)

9.a. Date From (mm/dd/yyyy) — `08/14/2014`

9.b. Date To (mm/dd/yyyy) — `Present`

Information About Parent 1

Full Name of Parent 1

10.a. Family Name (Maiden Name) — `Gallo`

10.b. Given Name (First Name) — `Magdalena`

10.c. Middle Name — `Aurora`

11. Date of Birth (mm/dd/yyyy) — `04/24/1968`

12. Sex — ☐ Male ☒ Female

13. City/Town/Village of Birth — `Venice`

14. Country of Birth — `Italy`

15. City/Town/Village of Residence — `Venice`

16. Country of Residence — `Italy`

Information About Parent 2

Full Name of Parent 2

17.a. Family Name (Last Name) — `Brabantio`

17.b. Given Name (First Name) — `Francisco`

17.c. Middle Name — `Matteo`

18. Date of Birth (mm/dd/yyyy) — `08/02/1961`

19. Sex — ☒ Male ☐ Female

20. City/Town/Village of Birth —

21. Country of Birth — `Venice`

22. City/Town/Village of Residence — `deceased`

23. Country of Residence — `deceased`

Part 2. Information About Your Employment

Provide your employment history for the last five years, whether inside or outside the United States. Provide your current employment first. If you are currently unemployed, type or print "Unemployed" in **Item Number 1.** below. If you need extra space to complete this section, use the space provided in **Part 7. Additional Information**.

Employment History

Employer 1

1. Name of Employer/Company — `Self-employed`

2.a. Street Number and Name — `108 Piazza d'Azeglio`

2.b. ☐ Apt. ☐ Ste. ☐ Flr.

2.c. City or Town — `Venice`

2.d. State — ▼ **2.e.** ZIP Code

2.f. Province

2.g. Postal Code — `99999`

2.h. Country — `Italy`

3. Your Occupation — `Freelance writer`

4.a. Date From (mm/dd/yyyy) — `08/06/2010`

4.b. Date To (mm/dd/yyyy) — **PRESENT**

Employer 2

5. Name of Employer/Company

6.a. Street Number and Name

6.b. ☐ Apt. ☐ Ste. ☐ Flr.

6.c. City or Town

6.d. State — ▼ **6.e.** ZIP Code

6.f. Province

6.g. Postal Code

6.h. Country

Sample Form I-130A, Supplemental Information for Spouse Beneficiary—Page 3

Part 2. Information About Your Employment (continued)

7. Your Occupation

8.a. Date From (mm/dd/yyyy)

8.b. Date To (mm/dd/yyyy)

Part 3. Information About Your Employment Outside the United States

Provide your last occupation outside the United States if not shown above. If you never worked outside the United States, provide this information in the space provided in **Part 7. Additional Information**.

1. Name of Employer/Company

2.a. Street Number and Name

2.b. ☐ Apt. ☐ Ste. ☐ Flr.

2.c. City or Town

2.d. State ▼   2.e. ZIP Code

2.f. Province

2.g. Postal Code

2.h. Country

3. Your Occupation

4.a. Date From (mm/dd/yyyy)

4.b. Date To (mm/dd/yyyy)

Part 4. Spouse Beneficiary's Statement, Contact Information, Certification, and Signature

NOTE: Read the **Penalties** section of the Form I-130 and Form I-130A Instructions before completing this part.

Spouse Beneficiary's Statement

NOTE: Select the box for either **Item Number 1.a.** or **1.b.** If applicable, select the box for **Item Number 2.**

1.a. ☒ I can read and understand English, and I have read and understand every question and instruction on this form and my answer to every question.

1.b. ☐ The interpreter named in **Part 5.** read to me every question and instruction on this form and my answer to every question in

[blank], a language in which I am fluent, and I understood everything.

2. ☐ At my request, the preparer name in **Part 6.**,

[blank], prepared this form for me based only upon information I provided or authorized.

Spouse Beneficiary's Contact Information

3. Spouse Beneficiary's Daytime Telephone Number

764-290-7645

4. Spouse Beneficiary's Mobile Telephone Number (if any)

5. Spouse Beneficiary's Email Address (if any)

teresem@email.com

Spouse Beneficiary's Certification

Copies of any documents I have submitted are exact photocopies of unaltered, original documents, and I understand that USCIS may require that I submit original documents to USCIS at a later date. Furthermore, I authorize the release of any information from any of my records that USCIS may need to determine my eligibility for the immigration benefit I seek.

I further authorize release of information contained in this form, in supporting documents, and in my USCIS records to other entities and persons where necessary for the administration and enforcement of U.S. immigration laws.

I certify, under penalty of perjury, that I provided or authorized all of the information in this form, I understand all of the information contained in, and submitted with, my form, and that all of this information is complete, true, and correct.

Spouse Beneficiary's Signature

6.a. Spouse Beneficiary's Signature (sign in ink)

➡ *Terese M. Mancini*

6.b. Date of Signature (mm/dd/yyyy)   03/01/2019

NOTE TO ALL SPOUSE BENEFICIARIES: If you do not completely fill out this form or fail to submit required documents listed in the Instructions, USCIS may deny the Form I-130 filed on your behalf.

Sample I-130 Receipt Notice

Department of Homeland Security
U.S. Citizenship and Immigration Services

Form I-797C, Notice of Action

THIS NOTICE DOES NOT GRANT ANY IMMIGRATION STATUS OR BENEFIT.

NOTICE TYPE	NOTICE DATE
Receipt	August 15, 2019

CASE TYPE	USCIS ALIEN NUMBER
I-130, Petition for Alien Relative	

RECEIPT NUMBER	RECEIVED DATE	PAGE
MSC-19-047-00000	May 15, 2019	1 of 1

PRIORITY DATE	PREFERENCE CLASSIFICATION	DATE OF BIRTH
May 15, 2019	201 B INA SPOUSE OF USC	February 15, 1982

Ilona Bray
RE: TERESE MARIA MANCINI
950 PARKER STREET
BERKELEY,CA 94710

PAYMENT INFORMATION:

Application/Petition Fee:	$535.00
Biometrics Fee:	$0.00
Total Amount Received:	$535.00
Total Balance Due:	$0.00

APPLICANT/PETITIONER NAME AND MAILING ADDRESS

The I-130, Petition for Alien Relative has been received by our office for the following beneficiaries and is in process:

Name	Date of Birth	Country of Birth	Class (If Applicable)
MANCINI, TERESE MARIA	02/15/1982	Italy	

Please verify your personal information listed above and immediately notify the USCIS National Customer Service Center at the phone number listed below if there are any changes.

Please note that if a priority date is printed on this notice, the priority does not reflect earlier retained priority dates.

If you have questions about possible immigration benefits and services, filing information, or USCIS forms, please call the USCIS National Customer Service Center (NCSC) at **1-800-375-5283**. If you are hearing impaired, please call the NCSC TDD at **1-800-767-1833**. Please also refer to the USCIS website: www.uscis.gov.

If you have any questions or comments regarding this notice or the status of your case, please contact our customer service number.

You will be notified separately about any other case you may have filed.

USCIS Office Address:

USCIS
Nebraska Service Center
P.O. Box 82521
Lincoln, NE 68501-2521

USCIS Customer Service Number:

(800)375-5283
ATTORNEY COPY

If this is an interview or biometrics appointment notice, please see the back of this notice for important information.

Form I-797C 07/11/14 Y

Sample I-130 Approval Notice

Department of Homeland Security
U.S. Citizenship and Immigration Services

I-797, Notice of Action

THE UNITED STATES OF AMERICA

RECEIPT NUMBER		CASE TYPE I130 PETITION FOR ALIEN RELATIVE
MSC-19-047-00000		

RECEIPT DATE	PRIORITY DATE	PETITIONER
August 15, 2019	May 15, 2019	MANCINI, ALBERTO

NOTICE DATE	PAGE	BENEFICIARY
April 11, 2020	1 of 1	MANCINI, TERESE

Ilona Bray
RE: TERESE MARIA MANCINI
950 PARKER STREET
BERKELEY,CA 94710

Notice Type: Approval Notice
Section: Husband or wife of U.S. Citizen,
201(b) INA

This notice is to advise you of action taken on this case. The official notice has been mailed according to the mailing preferences noted on the Form G-28, Notice of Entry of Appearance as Attorney or Accredited Representative. Any relevant documentation was mailed according to the specified mailing preferences.

The above petition has been approved. The petition indicates that the person for whom you are petitioning is in the United States and will apply for adjustment of status. He or she should contact the local USCIS office to obtain Form I-485, Application for Permanent Residence. A copy of this notice should be submitted with the application.

If the person for whom you are petitioning decides to apply for a visa outside the United States based on this petition, the petitioner should file Form I-824, Application for Action on an Approved Application or Petition, to request that we send the petition to the Department of State National Visa Center (NVC).

The NVC processes all approved immigrant visa petitions that require consular action. The NVC also determines which consular post is the appropriate consulate to complete visa processing. It will then forward the approved petition to that consulate.

The approval of this visa petition does not in itself grant any immigration status and does not guarantee that the alien beneficiary will subsequently be found to be eligible for a visa, for admission to the United States, or for an extension, change, or adjustment of status.

This courtesy copy may not be used in lieu of official notification to demonstrate the filing or processing action taken on this case.

THIS FORM IS NOT A VISA AND MAY NOT BE USED IN PLACE OF A VISA.

NOTICE: Although this application/petition has been approved, USCIS and the U.S. Department of Homeland Security reserve the right to verify the information submitted in this application, petition and/or supporting documentation to ensure conformity with applicable laws, rules, regulations, and other authorities. Methods used for verifying information may include, but are not limited to, the review of public information and records, contact by correspondence, the internet, or telephone, and site inspections of businesses and residences. Information obtained during the course of verification will be used to determine whether revocation, rescission, and/or removal proceedings are appropriate. Applicants, petitioners, and representatives of record will be provided an opportunity to address derogatory information before any formal proceeding is initiated.

Please see the additional information on the back. You will be notified separately about any other cases you filed.
NEBRASKA SERVICE CENTER
U. S. CITIZENSHIP & IMMIG SERVICE
P.O. BOX 82521
LINCOLN   NE   68501-2521
Customer Service Telephone: 800-375-5283

Form I-797 (Rev. 01/31/05) N

Question 3: Enter your current full name; use your married name if it was changed at the time you wed.

Questions 4-9: Fill in all your addresses from the last five years. If you have more than two, enter the additional addresses in Part 7. Make sure to include the start and end dates of all previous addresses. Your "last address outside the United States" might be your current address; that's all right, enter it again.

Questions 10-23: Answer basic biographic information about your parents. If lacking any pieces of information, say "unknown."

Part 2

Questions 1-8: Fill in your current employment information for the last five years, no matter which country you worked in. If you are not working, enter "unemployed" or "student," if applicable. If you had more than two jobs in the past five years, put them in Part 7.

Part 3

Include information about your most recent employment outside of the U.S. if it's not already listed in Part 2.

Part 4

Fill out this section with your contact information and signature.

Parts 5 and 6

These are for a preparer or interpreter helping fill out the form to fill out. If doing your own application, write "N/A" here.

b. Documents to Have on Hand for I-130 Petition

The I-130 petition asks for supporting documents and payment along with the form. You're not done until you have gathered together the following:

- **Proof of the U.S. citizen status of your petitioning spouse.** Depending on how your spouse became a citizen, he or she should copy a birth certificate, passport, certificate of naturalization, or Form FS-240 (Consular Report of Birth Abroad).

- **Proof that you're legally married.** This should include at a minimum a copy of your marriage certificate, most likely from a government source (see Chapter 4, Section C, for details). In addition, if either you or your spouse have been previously married, you must include proof that these marriages were terminated, such as a copy of a death, divorce, or annulment certificate.

- **Proof that the marriage is bona fide.** Include a select few items of evidence to show that your marriage is not a sham, but a real relationship. For instance, copies of documents showing you've spent time or lived together (such as a lease or mortgage agreement, bills sent to the house, and letters sent to the house for each spouse) are all good, as are copies of joint financial accounts (bank and credit statements, loans, insurance policies). Of less weight are things like joint memberships and photos taken with friends and family; you might want to save these for your interview, when the issue of bona fide marriage will come up again.

- **Photos.** Attach two color passport photos of yourself, and two of your spouse. The photos should be in color, 2 x 2 inches in size, taken within the past six months, showing your current appearance. "Passport style" means that the photo shows your full face from the front, with a plain white or off-white background—and your face must measure between one inch and 1⅜ inches from the bottom of your chin to the top of your head. (For more information, see the State Department website.) However, USCIS regulations permit you to submit a photo that doesn't completely follow the instructions if you live in a country where such photographs are unavailable or are cost prohibitive.

- **Fees.** The current fee for an I-130 petition is $535. However, these fees go up fairly regularly, so double-check this on the USCIS website at www.uscis.gov, or by calling USCIS at 800-375-5283.

c. Using the Checklist for Step One, I-130 Petition

When you put it all together, the petition that your spouse files for Step One will include three forms and some supporting documents, photos, and a fee, as explained above and detailed on the following checklist. As you fill out and prepare your paperwork, mark off the items that you've found or finished on your checklist. This will be the best way to make sure you haven't forgotten anything.

Checklist for Marriage-Based Immigrant Petition

This checklist shows every form, document, and other item needed for the initial petition that your spouse, with your help, will assemble and submit to USCIS.

☐ Form I-130 (see line-by-line instructions in Subsection A2a, above)

☐ Form I-130A, Supplemental Information on Spouse Beneficiary (see line-by-line instructions in subsection A2a, above)

☐ Documents to accompany Form I-130:

   ☐ Copy of your marriage certificate (see Chapter 4, Section C, on obtaining such documents)

   ☐ Proof of bona fide marriage, such as copies of joint mortgage or rental agreements, bank and credit card accounts, insurance, and more.

   ☐ Proof of the U.S. citizen status of your petitioning spouse (see Subsection A2b, above)

   ☐ Proof of termination of all previous marriages, such as a copy of a death, divorce, or annulment certificate (see Chapter 4, Section C, on how to obtain vital documents)

☐ Two color photos of you

☐ Two color photos of your spouse

☐ Fee: currently $535 but double-check this at www.uscis.gov/i-130

✓ **CHECKLIST**
Appendix B includes instructions on where to get a copy of this checklist online.

d. Where to Send Form I-130 Petition

After having prepared and assembled all the forms and other items from the checklist above, make photocopies for your records. Send the whole petition to a USCIS office called a "lockbox" for the region where the U.S. spouse lives. (The lockbox will process the fee payment then forward the petition to a USCIS service center.)

If your spouse is mailing this in the United States, a courier service or Priority Mail is usually the safest way to send it. The receipt will prove that USCIS received the petition and help convince it to track it down if it's misplaced. The lockbox address is below. You can double-check this information on the USCIS website.

If your spouse lives overseas, he or she should ask the local U.S. consulate where to send the I-130 petition. In most cases, it's to the USCIS Chicago Lockbox.

e. What Happens After Sending in the Form I-130 Petition

A few weeks after the U.S. spouse sends in your petition, he or she should get a receipt notice from a different USCIS processing center (see sample Form I-797C above). The receipt notice will explain how to check the USCIS website for information on how long the application is likely to remain in processing—currently up to about ten months, but processing times can change, so checking the USCIS website is a good idea. Do so by going to www.uscis.gov, and clicking "Check Processing Times." Select "Form I-130" then your service center from the dropdown list (look at the bottom of your Form I-797C). Look under the classification "U.S. citizen filing for a spouse, parent, or child under 21." The service center with jurisdiction over your case is based on where the U.S. citizen lives.

Where to Send the Form I-130 Petition			
If the U.S. petitioner lives in:			**Send Form I-130 to:**
Alaska American Samoa Arizona California Colorado Florida Guam Hawaii Idaho	Kansas Montana Nebraska Nevada New Mexico North Dakota Northern Mariana Islands Oklahoma	Oregon Puerto Rico South Dakota Texas Utah Virgin Islands Washington Wyoming	**USCIS Phoenix Lockbox** For U.S. Postal Service (USPS) deliveries: 　USCIS ATTN: I-130 　P.O. Box 21700 　Phoenix, AZ 85036 For courier deliveries: 　USCIS 　Attn: I-130 　1820 E. Skyharbor Circle S 　Suite 100 　Phoenix, AZ 85034
Alabama Arkansas Connecticut Delaware District of Columbia Georgia Illinois Indiana Iowa Kentucky Louisiana	Maine Maryland Massachusetts Michigan Minnesota Mississippi Missouri New Hampshire New Jersey New York	North Carolina Ohio Pennsylvania Rhode Island South Carolina Tennessee Vermont Virginia West Virginia Wisconsin	**USCIS Chicago Lockbox** For U.S. Postal Service: 　USCIS 　P.O. Box 804625 　Chicago, IL 60680-4107 For courier deliveries: 　USCIS 　Attn: I-130 　131 South Dearborn–3rd Floor 　Chicago, IL 60603-5517

If the U.S. petitioner lives outside the U.S., send Form I-130 to:

USCIS Chicago Lockbox

For U.S. Postal Service (USPS) deliveries:
　USCIS
　P.O. Box 804625
　Chicago, IL 60680-4104

For courier deliveries:
　USCIS
　Attn: I-130
　131 South Dearborn-3rd Floor
　Chicago, IL 60603-5517

TIP

Look for your receipt number. When you get your USCIS receipt, you will see this number in the upper left-hand corner. You can use this number to check the status of your case online by going to www.uscis.gov, and clicking "Check Case Status." When you do this, you will also be able to create a USCIS account, which will allow you to receive updates about your case. If you sign up for either the email updates or the text messaging, you will still receive information about your case by regular mail.

Until the completion time predicted by the USCIS website, USCIS will ignore any inquiries from you or your spouse asking what is going on. These processing centers seem like walled fortresses. You can't visit them, nor talk to a live person there. (See Chapter 15 for what to do if you don't get a timely answer from USCIS.) If USCIS needs additional documentation to complete your application, it will send your spouse a letter asking for it.

Likewise, if USCIS considers denying the case based on negative evidence obtained by other means, it will send your spouse a letter informing you and giving you an opportunity to respond. Eventually your spouse will either receive an approval or a denial of the visa petition.

i.   If the I-130 Petition Is Denied

If the petition is denied, USCIS will tell you the reason for the denial. The fastest thing to do is to fix the problem and try again. For example, if the denial came because your petitioning spouse did not appear to be actually divorced from a previous spouse, your spouse would need to see a lawyer and obtain new and better documentation showing that there was a final divorce. Then he or she can file a new petition.

ii.   If the I-130 Petition Is Approved

When your petition is approved, your spouse will receive a notice from the USCIS processing center. An example of a visa petition approval notice is shown above. As you can see, it's nothing fancy. But it is an important document. Make a few photocopies of it and store these and the original in safe places.

At the same time that USCIS notifies your spouse of the approval of your petition, it will forward your case to the National Visa Center (NVC) in New Hampshire. This office will take over and guide you through Step Two.

3. Step Two: Pay Fees, Prepare Forms and Documents

Next, you, the immigrant, will receive instructions from the NVC. The NVC will ask you to visit the Consular Electronic Application Center (CEAC) at https://ceac.state.gov/ceac and complete Form DS-261, Online Choice of Address and Agent. Log in using the invoice number that the NVC sent you either by mail or email. This is a fairly simple form—but bear in mind that by choosing an "agent," you're essentially deciding where all the important mail from the U.S. government

regarding your immigration should go—to you at your overseas address, or to someone else, most likely your petitioner in the U.S. (if you're not using an attorney).

If mail service from the U.S. has been at all unreliable where you live, or if you might be moving before your visa interview, it's safest to choose your petitioner as agent, or to indicate that you'd rather be contacted by email. Since the majority of the steps you'll need to take on your petition are online, it makes sense to enroll in email notifications.

After you submit the DS-261, you will receive some information about filing fees. The NVC will send the U.S. family member petitioner a bill for the Affidavit of Support review ($120) and send either you or your agent a bill for the immigrant visa processing fee (currently $325). If any family members who are included on your petition are immigrating with you, you'll need to pay a separate filing fee of $325 for each. However, all family members can be included on the one $120 filing fee for the Affidavit of Support.

The NVC prefers that you pay these fees online, by entering your checking account number and bank routing number. That's also the best way to ensure that your fees get credited to your account, and that all your documents are kept together.

However, if you don't have a checking account, you will need to pay by mail, using a bank check or money order. Have your visa bill handy: It contains a bar code that the NVC will need in order to credit your fee to your application.

After paying your fees, you will need to submit DS-260, the online immigrant visa application. You can find a sample on the Department of State website; go to usvisas.state.gov and click "All Forms," then look for "DS-260" and click "Preview a sample DS-260." The form asks a number of biographical questions, such as all names used, all addresses where you have lived, your work and educational history, and family member information. You will also be asked questions to determine your admissibility to the United States.

You will again need your NVC invoice number and receipt number in order to complete this form. You can save your DS-260 on your computer and come back to it later. You will need to complete the form in English, using solely English characters, so have someone ready to help you if you might need it.

You'll be asked for all your addresses since the age of 16 and the exact dates that you lived there. If an answer does not apply to you (such as U.S. Social Security number), you will be given the option to choose "Does Not Apply."

After you submit the DS-260, print the confirmation page and bring it to your interview. Although you are not required to do so, it doesn't hurt to print out a copy of the entire form as well, so that you can refer to it when needed.

After the NVC is satisfied that you have submitted the necessary documentation and have paid all your fees, it will schedule an interview date and transfer your visa file to the appropriate U.S. consulate or embassy.

a. Line-by-Line Instructions for Step Two Forms

Here are instructions for preparing the most important forms that will be required of you at this stage.

i. Form I-864

Form I-864, the Affidavit of Support, is the primary form that your spouse and any joint sponsor will use to prove that he, she, or they are willing and able to support you. (You might need a joint sponsor to assist in supporting you if your spouse's income and assets aren't high enough to reach the government's guidelines, as covered in Chapter 3.)

TIP

Some sponsors can use a simpler version of Form I-864. If the sponsor has enough income so that he or she doesn't need to resort to assets or other help to sponsor the immigrant(s), it's okay to use Form I-864EZ, available at www.uscis.gov/forms.

Before you fill out this form, look again at Chapter 3, Meeting Income Requirements, which explains how USCIS will evaluate your finances and those of your spouse. This chapter gives you strategies on meeting the minimum requirements if your own resources are too low. The following subsection, "Financial Documents to Have on Hand," gives you information on how to create, assemble, or prepare the supporting documentation that you may need to attach to the forms discussed below.

TIP

U.S. citizens with long work histories and long marriages may be able to avoid filling out an Affidavit of Support (Form I-864). The reason is that their obligations to act as sponsors end after the immigrant has worked 40 quarters (about ten years, depending on earnings amounts)—but, in an interesting twist, the immigrants can be credited with work done by their U.S. citizen spouses while they were married. So, if your U.S. citizen spouse has worked 40 quarters in the U.S. during your marriage, he or she need not fill out Form I-864. Though it's the rare married couple who will have gone this many years without applying for a green card, the exception is highly useful for those to whom it applies. You will need to submit Form I-864W (available from www.uscis.gov/i-864W) in order to claim this exception (and attach a Social Security Statement as proof).

WEB RESOURCE

Form I-864 is available on the USCIS website at www.uscis.gov/i-864. Below is a sample filled-in version of the relevant pages of this form. Note that our sample assumes that the sponsor has an adult child from a previous relationship, who agrees to contribute to the household income in order to raise it to the necessary level.

Because this form may be filled out either by your spouse or by a joint sponsor, the instructions below usually refer to the "sponsor," which refers to either of them.

Sample Form I-864 Affidavit of Support Under Section 213A of the Act—Page 1

Affidavit of Support Under Section 213A of the INA
Department of Homeland Security
U.S. Citizenship and Immigration Services

USCIS Form I-864
OMB No. 1615-0075
Expires 03/31/2020

For USCIS Use Only

Affidavit of Support Submitter	Section 213A Review	Number of Support Affidavits in File
☐ Petitioner	☐ MEETS requirements ☐ DOES NOT MEET requirements	☐ 1 ☐ 2
☐ 1st Joint Sponsor		**Remarks**
☐ 2nd Joint Sponsor	Reviewed By:_____	
☐ Substitute Sponsor	Office: _____	
☐ 5% Owner	Date (mm/dd/yyyy): _____	

To be completed by an attorney or accredited representative (if any).

☐ Select this box if Form G-28 or G-28I is attached.

Attorney State Bar Number (if applicable)

Attorney or Accredited Representative USCIS Online Account Number (if any)

► **START HERE** - Type or print in black ink.

Part 1. Basis For Filing Affidavit of Support

I, Alberto Ilario Mancini, am the sponsor submitting this affidavit of support because (Select **only one** box):

1.a. ☒ I am the petitioner. I filed or am filing for the immigration of my relative.

1.b. ☐ I filed an alien worker petition on behalf of the intending immigrant, who is related to me as my

1.c. ☐ I have an ownership interest of at least 5 percent in

which filed an alien worker petition on behalf of the intending immigrant, who is related to me as my

1.d. ☐ I am the only joint sponsor.

1.e. ☐ I am the ☐ first ☐ second of two joint sponsors.

1.f. ☐ The original petitioner is deceased. I am the substitute sponsor. I am the intending immigrant's

NOTE: If you are filing this form as a sponsor, you must include proof of your U.S. citizenship, U.S. national status, or lawful permanent resident status.

Part 2. Information About the Principal Immigrant

1.a. Family Name (Last Name): MANCINI

1.b. Given Name (First Name): Teresa

1.c. Middle Name: Maria

Mailing Address   (USPS ZIP Code Lookup)

2.a. In Care Of Name

2.b. Street Number and Name: 108 Piazza d Azeglio

2.c. ☐ Apt. ☐ Ste. ☐ Flr.

2.d. City or Town: Venice

2.e. State   **2.f.** ZIP Code

2.g. Province: Veneto

2.h. Postal Code: 99999

2.i. Country: Italy

Other Information

3. Country of Citizenship or Nationality: Italy

4. Date of Birth (mm/dd/yyyy): 02/15/1982

5. Alien Registration Number (A-Number) (if any) ► A-

6. USCIS Online Account Number (if any) ►

7. Daytime Telephone Number: 7642907645

Form I-864   03/06/18

Page 1 of 10

Sample Form I-864 Affidavit of Support Under Section 213A of the Act—Page 2

Part 3. Information About the Immigrants You Are Sponsoring

1. I am sponsoring the principal immigrant named in **Part 2.**

    ☒ Yes ☐ No (Applicable only if you are sponsoring family members in **Part 3.** as the second joint sponsor or if you are sponsoring family members who are immigrating more than six months after the principal immigrant)

2. ☐ I am sponsoring the following family members immigrating at the same time or within six months of the principal immigrant named in **Part 2.** (Do not include any relative listed on a separate visa petition.)

3. ☐ I am sponsoring the following family members who are immigrating more than six months after the principal immigrant.

Family Member 1

4.a. Family Name (Last Name)

4.b. Given Name (First Name)

4.c. Middle Name

5. Relationship to Principal Immigrant

6. Date of Birth (mm/dd/yyyy)

7. Alien Registration Number (A-Number) (if any)
    ► A-

8. USCIS Online Account Number (if any)
    ►

Family Member 2

9.a. Family Name (Last Name)

9.b. Given Name (First Name)

9.c. Middle Name

10. Relationship to Principal Immigrant

11. Date of Birth (mm/dd/yyyy)

12. Alien Registration Number (A-Number) (if any)
    ► A-

13. USCIS Online Account Number (if any)
    ►

Family Member 3

14.a. Family Name (Last Name)

14.b. Given Name (First Name)

14.c. Middle Name

15. Relationship to Principal Immigrant

16. Date of Birth (mm/dd/yyyy)

17. Alien Registration Number (A-Number) (if any)
    ► A-

18. USCIS Online Account Number (if any)
    ►

Family Member 4

19.a. Family Name (Last Name)

19.b. Given Name (First Name)

19.c. Middle Name

20. Relationship to Principal Immigrant

21. Date of Birth (mm/dd/yyyy)

22. Alien Registration Number (A-Number) (if any)
    ► A-

23. USCIS Online Account Number (if any)
    ►

Family Member 5

24.a. Family Name (Last Name)

24.b. Given Name (First Name)

24.c. Middle Name

25. Relationship to Principal Immigrant

26. Date of Birth (mm/dd/yyyy)

27. Alien Registration Number (A-Number) (if any)
    ► A-

28. USCIS Online Account Number (if any)
    ►

Sample Form I-864 Affidavit of Support Under Section 213A of the Act—Page 3

Part 3. Information About the Immigrants You Are Sponsoring (continued)

29. Enter the total number of immigrants you are sponsoring on this affidavit which includes the principal immigrant listed in **Part 2.**, any immigrants listed in **Part 3.**, **Item Numbers 1. - 28.** and (if applicable), any immigrants listed for these questions in **Part 11. Additional Information.** Do not count the principal immigrant if you are only sponsoring family members entering more than 6 months after the principal immigrant.

| 1 |

Part 4. Information About You (Sponsor)

Sponsor's Full Name

1.a. Family Name (Last Name) `MANCINI`

1.b. Given Name (First Name) `Alberto`

1.c. Middle Name `Ilario`

Sponsor's Mailing Address

2.a. In Care Of Name

2.b. Street Number and Name `800 Broadway`

2.c. ☐ Apt. ☐ Ste. ☐ Flr.

2.d. City or Town `Lindenhurst`

2.e. State `NY` ▼ **2.f.** ZIP Code `11757`

2.g. Province

2.h. Postal Code

2.i. Country `USA`

3. Is your current mailing address the same as your physical address? ☒ Yes ☐ No

If you answered "No" to **Item Number 3.**, provide your physical address in **Item Numbers 4.a. - 4.h.**

Sponsor's Physical Address

4.a. Street Number and Name

4.b. ☐ Apt. ☐ Ste. ☐ Flr.

4.c. City or Town

4.d. State **4.e.** ZIP Code

4.f. Province

4.g. Postal Code

4.h. Country

Other Information

5. Country of Domicile
`USA`

6. Date of Birth (mm/dd/yyyy) `03/30/1970`

7. City or Town of Birth
`Los Angeles`

8. State or Province of Birth
`California`

9. Country of Birth
`USA`

10. U.S. Social Security Number (Required)
▶

Citizenship or Residency

11.a. ☒ I am a U.S. citizen.

11.b. ☐ I am a U.S. national.

11.c. ☐ I am a lawful permanent resident.

12. Sponsor's A-Number (if any)
▶ A-

13. Sponsor's USCIS Online Account Number (if any)
▶

Military Service (To be completed by petitioner sponsors only.)

14. I am currently on **active duty** in the U.S. Armed Forces or U.S. Coast Guard. ☐ Yes ☒ No

Sample Form I-864 Affidavit of Support Under Section 213A of the Act—Page 4

For USCIS Use Only	

Part 5. Sponsor's Household Size

NOTE: Do not count any member of your household more than once.

Persons you are sponsoring in this affidavit:

1. Provide the number you entered in **Part 3.**, **Item Number 29.** [1]

Persons NOT sponsored in this affidavit:

2. Yourself. [1]

3. If you are currently married, enter "1" for your spouse. [ ]

4. If you have dependent children, enter the number here. [ ]

5. If you have any other dependents, enter the number here. [ ]

6. If you have sponsored any other persons on Form I-864 or Form I-864EZ who are now lawful permanent residents, enter the number here. [ ]

7. **OPTIONAL:** If you have siblings, parents, or adult children with the same principal residence who are combining their income with yours by submitting Form I-864A, enter the number here. [1]

8. Add together **Part 5.**, **Item Numbers 1. - 7.** and enter the number here.

    Household Size: [3]

Part 6. Sponsor's Employment and Income

I am currently:

1. [X] Employed as a/an

    Shift Manager

2. Name of Employer 1

    Bobs Diner

3. Name of Employer 2 (if applicable)

    [ ]

4. [ ] Self-Employed as a/an (Occupation)

    [ ]

5. [ ] Retired Since (mm/dd/yyyy) [ ]

6. [ ] Unemployed Since (mm/dd/yyyy) [ ]

7. My current individual annual income is:

    $ 22,000.00

Income you are using from any other person who was counted in your household size, including, in certain conditions, the intending immigrant. (See Form I-864 Instructions.) Please indicate name, relationship, and income.

Person 1

8. Name

    Stella Mancini

9. Relationship

    daughter

10. **Current Income** $ 18,000.00

Person 2

11. Name

    [ ]

12. Relationship

    [ ]

13. **Current Income** $ [ ]

Person 3

14. Name

    [ ]

15. Relationship

    [ ]

16. **Current Income** $ [ ]

Person 4

17. Name

    [ ]

18. Relationship

    [ ]

19. **Current Income** $ [ ]

Sample Form I-864 Affidavit of Support Under Section 213A of the Act—Page 5

For USCIS Use Only	Household Size ☐ 1 ☐ 2 ☐ 3 ☐ 4 ☐ 5 ☐ 6 ☐ 7 ☐ 8 ☐ 9 ☐ Other _____	Poverty Guideline Year: _2 0____ Poverty Line: $ _____	Remarks

Part 6. Sponsor's Employment and Income (continued)

20. **My Current Annual Household Income** (Total all lines from **Part 6. Item Numbers 7., 10., 13., 16.,** and **19.**; the total will be compared to Federal Poverty Guidelines on Form I-864P.) $ | 40,000.00 |

21. ☒ The people listed in **Item Numbers 8., 11., 14.,** and **17.** have completed Form I-864A. I am filing along with this affidavit all necessary Form I-864As completed by these people.

22. ☐ One or more of the people listed in **Item Numbers 8., 11., 14.,** and **17.** do not need to complete Form I-864A because he or she is the intending immigrant and has no accompanying dependents.

Name
| |

Federal Income Tax Return Information

23.a. Have you filed a Federal income tax return for each of the three most recent tax years? ☒ Yes ☐ No

NOTE: You **MUST** attach a photocopy or transcript of your Federal income tax return for only the most recent tax year.

23.b. ☐ (Optional) I have attached photocopies or transcripts of my Federal income tax returns for my second and third most recent tax years.

My total income (adjusted gross income on Internal Revenue Service (IRS) Form 1040EZ) as reported on my Federal income tax returns for the most recent three years was:

		Tax Year	Total Income
24.a.	Most Recent	2018	$ 22,000.00
24.b.	2nd Most Recent	2017	$ 20,000.00
24.c.	3rd Most Recent	2016	$ 19,500.00

25. ☐ I was not required to file a Federal income tax return as my income was below the IRS required level and I have attached evidence to support this.

Part 7. Use of Assets to Supplement Income (Optional)

If your income, or the total income for you and your household, from **Part 6., Item Numbers 20.** or **24.a. - 24.c.,** exceeds the Federal Poverty Guidelines for your household size, **YOU ARE NOT REQUIRED** to complete this **Part 7.** Skip to **Part 8.**

Your Assets (Optional)

1. Enter the balance of all savings and checking accounts.
$ | |

2. Enter the net cash value of real-estate holdings. (Net value means current assessed value minus mortgage debt.)
$ | |

3. Enter the net cash value of all stocks, bonds, certificates of deposit, and any other assets not already included in **Item Number 1.** or **Item Number 2.**
$ | |

4. Add together **Item Numbers 1. - 3.** and enter the number here. **TOTAL:** $ | |

Assets from Form I-864A, Part 4., Item Number 3.d., for:

5.a. Name of Relative
| |

5.b. Your household member's assets from Form I-864A (optional). $ | |

Assets of the principal sponsored immigrant (optional).

The principal sponsored immigrant is the person listed in **Part 2., Item Numbers 1.a. - 1.c.** Only include the assets if the principal immigrant is being sponsored by this affidavit of support.

6. Enter the balance of the principal immigrant's savings and checking accounts. $ | |

7. Enter the net cash value of all the principal immigrant's real estate holdings. (Net value means investment value minus mortgage debt.) $ | |

8. Enter the current cash value of the principal immigrant's stocks, bonds, certificates of deposit, and other assets not included in **Item Number 6.** or **Item Number 7.**
$ | |

Sample Form I-864 Affidavit of Support Under Section 213A of the Act—Page 6

For USCIS Use Only	Household Size	Poverty Guideline	Sponsor's Household Income *(Page 5, Line 10)*	Remarks
	☐ 1 ☐ 2 ☐ 3 ☐ 4 ☐ 5 ☐ 6 ☐ 7 ☐ 8 ☐ 9 ☐ Other_____	Year: 2 0____ Poverty Line: $_____	$_____ *The total value of all assets, line 10, must equal 5 times (3 times for spouses and children of USC's, or 1 time for orphans to be formally adopted in the U.S.) the difference between the poverty guidelines and the sponsor's household income, line 10.*	

Part 7. Use of Assets to Supplement Income (Optional) (continued)

9. Add together **Item Numbers 6. - 8.** and enter the number here. $ [_____]

Total Value of Assets

10. Add together **Item Numbers 4., 5.b.,** and **9.** and enter the number here.

TOTAL: $ [_____]

Part 8. Sponsor's Contract, Statement, Contact Information, Declaration, Certification, and Signature

NOTE: Read the **Penalties** section of the Form I-864 Instructions before completing this part.

Sponsor's Contract

Please note that, by signing this Form I-864, you agree to assume certain specific obligations under the Immigration and Nationality Act (INA) and other Federal laws. The following paragraphs describe those obligations. Please read the following information carefully before you sign Form I-864. If you do not understand the obligations, you may wish to consult an attorney or accredited representative.

What is the Legal Effect of My Signing Form I-864?

If you sign Form I-864 on behalf of any person (called the intending immigrant) who is applying for an immigrant visa or for adjustment of status to a lawful permanent resident, and that intending immigrant submits Form I-864 to the U.S. Government with his or her application for an immigrant visa or adjustment of status, under INA section 213A, these actions create a contract between you and the U.S. Government. The intending immigrant becoming a lawful permanent resident is the consideration for the contract.

Under this contract, you agree that, in deciding whether the intending immigrant can establish that he or she is not inadmissible to the United States as a person likely to become a public charge, the U.S. Government can consider your income and assets as available for the support of the intending immigrant.

What If I Choose Not to Sign Form I-864?

The U.S. Government cannot make you sign Form I-864 if you do not want to do so. But if you do not sign Form I-864, the intending immigrant may not become a lawful permanent resident in the United States.

What Does Signing Form I-864 Require Me To Do?

If an intending immigrant becomes a lawful permanent resident in the United States based on a Form I-864 that you have signed, then, until your obligations under Form I-864 terminate, you must:

A. Provide the intending immigrant any support necessary to maintain him or her at an income that is at least 125 percent of the Federal Poverty Guidelines for his or her household size (100 percent if you are the petitioning sponsor and are on active duty in the U.S. Armed Forces or U.S. Coast Guard, and the person is your husband, wife, or unmarried child under 21 years of age); and

B. Notify U.S. Citizenship and Immigration Services (USCIS) of any change in your address, within 30 days of the change, by filing Form I-865.

What Other Consequences Are There?

If an intending immigrant becomes a lawful permanent resident in the United States based on a Form I-864 that you have signed, then, until your obligations under Form I-864 terminate, the U.S. Government may consider (deem) your income and assets as available to that person, in determining whether he or she is eligible for certain Federal means-tested public benefits and also for state or local means-tested public benefits, if the state or local government's rules provide for consideration (deeming) of your income and assets as available to the person.

This provision does **not** apply to public benefits specified in section 403(c) of the Welfare Reform Act such as emergency Medicaid, short-term, non-cash emergency relief; services provided under the National School Lunch and Child Nutrition Acts; immunizations and testing and treatment for communicable diseases; and means-tested programs under the Elementary and Secondary Education Act.

What If I Do Not Fulfill My Obligations?

If you do not provide sufficient support to the person who becomes a lawful permanent resident based on a Form I-864 that you signed, that person may sue you for this support.

Sample Form I-864 Affidavit of Support Under Section 213A of the Act—Page 7

Part 8. Sponsor's Contract, Statement, Contact Information, Declaration, Certification, and Signature (continued)

If a Federal, state, local, or private agency provided any covered means-tested public benefit to the person who becomes a lawful permanent resident based on a Form I-864 that you signed, the agency may ask you to reimburse them for the amount of the benefits they provided. If you do not make the reimbursement, the agency may sue you for the amount that the agency believes you owe.

If you are sued, and the court enters a judgment against you, the person or agency that sued you may use any legally permitted procedures for enforcing or collecting the judgment. You may also be required to pay the costs of collection, including attorney fees.

If you do not file a properly completed Form I-865 within 30 days of any change of address, USCIS may impose a civil fine for your failing to do so.

When Will These Obligations End?

Your obligations under a Form I-864 that you signed will end if the person who becomes a lawful permanent resident based on that affidavit:

- **A.** Becomes a U.S. citizen;
- **B.** Has worked, or can receive credit for, 40 quarters of coverage under the Social Security Act;
- **C.** No longer has lawful permanent resident status and has departed the United States;
- **D.** Is subject to removal, but applies for and obtains, in removal proceedings, a new grant of adjustment of status, based on a new affidavit of support, if one is required; or
- **E.** Dies.

NOTE: Divorce **does not** terminate your obligations under Form I-864.

Your obligations under a Form I-864 that you signed also end if you die. Therefore, if you die, your estate is not required to take responsibility for the person's support after your death. However, your estate may owe any support that you accumulated before you died.

Sponsor's Statement

NOTE: Select the box for either **Item Number 1.a.** or **1.b.** If applicable, select the box for **Item Number 2.**

1.a. ☒ I can read and understand English, and I have read and understand every question and instruction on this affidavit and my answer to every question.

1.b. ☐ The interpreter named in **Part 9.** read to me every question and instruction on this affidavit and my answer to every question in

[   ],

a language in which I am fluent, and I understood everything.

2. ☐ At my request, the preparer named in **Part 10.**,

[   ],

prepared this affidavit for me based only upon information I provided or authorized.

Sponsor's Contact Information

3. Sponsor's Daytime Telephone Number

2122221212

4. Sponsor's Mobile Telephone Number (if any)

5. Sponsor's Email Address (if any)

albertom@email.com

Sponsor's Declaration and Certification

Copies of any documents I have submitted are exact photocopies of unaltered, original documents, and I understand that USCIS or the U.S. Department of State (DOS) may require that I submit original documents to USCIS or DOS at a later date. Furthermore, I authorize the release of any information from any and all of my records that USCIS or DOS may need to determine my eligibility for the benefit that I seek.

I furthermore authorize release of information contained in this affidavit, in supporting documents, and in my USCIS or DOS records, to other entities and persons where necessary for the administration and enforcement of U.S. immigration law.

I certify, under penalty of perjury, that all of the information in my affidavit and any document submitted with it were provided or authorized by me, that I reviewed and understand all of the information contained in, and submitted with, my affidavit and that all of this information is complete, true, and correct.

- **A.** I know the contents of this affidavit of support that I signed;
- **B.** I have read and I understand each of the obligations described in **Part 8.**, and I agree, freely and without any mental reservation or purpose of evasion, to accept each of those obligations in order to make it possible for the immigrants indicated in **Part 3.** to become lawful permanent residents of the United States;
- **C.** I agree to submit to the personal jurisdiction of any Federal or state court that has subject matter jurisdiction of a lawsuit against me to enforce my obligations under this Form I-864;

Sample Form I-864 Affidavit of Support Under Section 213A of the Act—Page 8

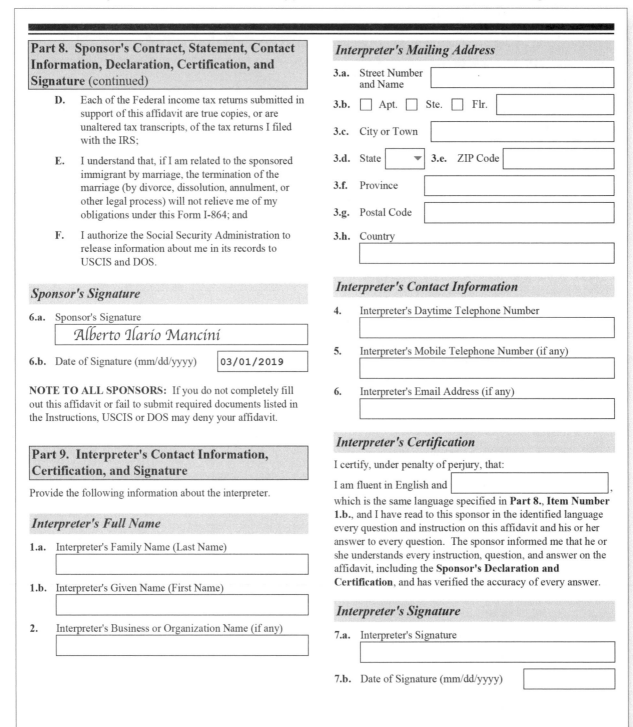

Part 8. Sponsor's Contract, Statement, Contact Information, Declaration, Certification, and Signature (continued)

D. Each of the Federal income tax returns submitted in support of this affidavit are true copies, or are unaltered tax transcripts, of the tax returns I filed with the IRS;

E. I understand that, if I am related to the sponsored immigrant by marriage, the termination of the marriage (by divorce, dissolution, annulment, or other legal process) will not relieve me of my obligations under this Form I-864; and

F. I authorize the Social Security Administration to release information about me in its records to USCIS and DOS.

Sponsor's Signature

6.a. Sponsor's Signature

Alberto Ilario Mancini

6.b. Date of Signature (mm/dd/yyyy) 03/01/2019

NOTE TO ALL SPONSORS: If you do not completely fill out this affidavit or fail to submit required documents listed in the Instructions, USCIS or DOS may deny your affidavit.

Part 9. Interpreter's Contact Information, Certification, and Signature

Provide the following information about the interpreter.

Interpreter's Full Name

1.a. Interpreter's Family Name (Last Name)

1.b. Interpreter's Given Name (First Name)

2. Interpreter's Business or Organization Name (if any)

Interpreter's Mailing Address

3.a. Street Number and Name

3.b. ☐ Apt. ☐ Ste. ☐ Flr.

3.c. City or Town

3.d. State ▼ **3.e.** ZIP Code

3.f. Province

3.g. Postal Code

3.h. Country

Interpreter's Contact Information

4. Interpreter's Daytime Telephone Number

5. Interpreter's Mobile Telephone Number (if any)

6. Interpreter's Email Address (if any)

Interpreter's Certification

I certify, under penalty of perjury, that:

I am fluent in English and [   ],
which is the same language specified in **Part 8.**, **Item Number 1.b.**, and I have read to this sponsor in the identified language every question and instruction on this affidavit and his or her answer to every question. The sponsor informed me that he or she understands every instruction, question, and answer on the affidavit, including the **Sponsor's Declaration and Certification**, and has verified the accuracy of every answer.

Interpreter's Signature

7.a. Interpreter's Signature

7.b. Date of Signature (mm/dd/yyyy)

Parts 1-4

These sections are self-explanatory, with the following notes:

- **In Part 1,** spouses check box 1.a; any other nice friends who are separately filling in this form as joint sponsors check either box 1.d or box 1.e.
- **In Part 2,** all the information requested refers to the immigrant, including the mailing address. For Question 6, you're unlikely to have a USCIS Online Account Number; unless you registered in order to file certain forms online.
- **In Part 3,** note that there's a place to list children. You don't need to name children who were born in the United States, because the sponsor has no obligation to support them (at least not under the immigration laws, though they will be counted elsewhere within this form to test the sponsor's overall financial capacity). Similarly, you shouldn't name children who are immigrating with you. Because each of them had their own petition (Form I-130), each is considered a "principal immigrant" and needs a separate Form I-864 prepared for him or her.
- **In Part 4,** note that the sponsor's physical address must be in the United States in order for him or her to be eligible as a financial sponsor. In theory, if your petitioner lives outside the U.S., he or she can meet this requirement by showing the steps taken to return to the U.S. and make the U.S. his or her residence as soon as you enter. Such steps might include finding U.S. employment, locating a place to live, and registering children in U.S. schools. The Affidavit of Support should also show that the petitioner has made arrangements to give up residence outside the United States.

Part 5, Sponsor's household size

Remember not to count anyone twice! In other words, there's no need to put a "1" in question 3, because you've already counted your spouse.

Part 6, Sponsor's income and employment

The sponsor needs to fill in information about his or her employment here. Self-employment is fine. Be aware that if a self-employed sponsor has underreported income in the past, the earnings shown may not be sufficient to support you. In that case, the sponsor will need to file an amended tax return and pay a penalty before the newly reported income is accepted as meeting the guidelines for sponsorship.

Question 7: Here, the sponsor is supposed to enter the income shown on his or her most recent tax return. But what if the sponsor's income has risen since filing those taxes? In that case, the sponsor should enter the more recent income figure, but put an asterisk (an *) next to it. Then find some white space somewhere on the page and write "this figure reflects present earnings, not earnings shown on tax return; see supporting documentation." The documentation the sponsor is already providing, such as an employer's letter, should be enough to show current income.

Questions 8–12: These questions are important for sponsors whose income is not enough by itself, but who will be using the income of members of their household to help meet the *Poverty Guidelines* minimum requirements. Unless any one of these household members is the actual immigrant, they must plan to complete a separate agreement with the sponsor, using Form I-864A. The total income from the sponsor and household members goes in Question 15.

Part 7, Use of Assets to Supplement Income

The sponsor needs to complete this section only if his or her income wasn't enough by itself to meet the *Poverty Guidelines* requirements. If the sponsor needs to add assets, he or she may include such items as a house, car, or boat, but should remember to subtract debts, mortgages, and liens before writing down their value. And remember that the value of these assets will later be divided by three before being used to meet the *Poverty Guidelines* minimum. (Or divided by five if someone other than the U.S. citizen spouse is filling out the form.)

If some of the assets being used to meet the minimum belong to a household member, enter the household member's name in Question 5, along with the total amount the assets are worth.

If some of the assets being used to meet the minimum belong to the immigrant, state their value in Questions 6-8.

Be sure to attach documents to prove the ownership, location, and value of any assets claimed.

If the combination of the sponsor's available income and one third of the sponsor's and/or the immigrant's assets don't yet meet the *Poverty Guidelines* minimum, you'll still need to hand in this Affidavit. But you'll definitely want to look for a joint sponsor or a participating household member.

Part 8, Sponsor's Contract

Unlike past versions of this form, the sponsor's signature no longer needs to be witnessed by a notary public.

ii. Form I-864A

Not every immigrant needs to submit this form. It is only required if, on the main Form I-864, the sponsor had to use the income of members of the sponsor's household to meet the *Poverty Guidelines*. In that case, these household member(s) will need to fill out portions of Form I-864A. The sponsor must attach the Form I-864A to the main Form I-864.

WEB RESOURCE
Form I-864A is available on the USCIS website at www.uscis.gov/i-864a. Below is a sample filled-in version of the relevant pages of this form.

Part I: Mostly self-explanatory; to be filled out by the household member. For Question 8, the household member is unlikely to have a USCIS ELIS Account Number; unless, that is, he or she registered in order to file certain USCIS forms online. However, the ELIS system is largely nonfunctional at the moment.

Part 5: This part is filled out and signed by the main sponsor (the U.S. citizen spouse). Just fill in the names of the immigrants being sponsored and don't worry about the legal language.

Part 6: This is where the household member will fill in and sign the form.

iii. Form I-864W

Only a few lucky people will be able to use this form, namely those who are exempt from the Affidavit of Support requirement because the immigrant has either:

- worked lawfully for 40 Social Security quarters (approximately ten years) in the U.S.
- been married while the U.S. spouse worked for 40 Social Security quarters, or
- a combination of the above.

The deal is that a financial sponsor's responsibility lasts until the immigrant has (among other possibilities) earned 40 work quarters credited toward Social Security. A work quarter is approximately three months, but it depends partly on how much you earn. So if you've already reached that amount of work on your own, through lawful employment—perhaps while in the U.S. as a student or H-1B worker—there's no point in the sponsor filling out an Affidavit of Support for you. And, in an interesting twist, you can be credited for work done by your U.S. spouse if it was during your marriage.

You'll need to prove to USCIS how many quarters of work your spouse or you has done. Contact Social Security about getting a certified statement with this information.

Because Form I-864W is fairly easy to fill out, we won't include a sample here. The form is available at www.uscis.gov/i.864w. In Part 2, you would check the first box.

b. Financial Documents to Have on Hand

To prove that your spouse or additional sponsors are able and willing to support you, the consulate will require detailed, up-to-date information from trustworthy sources. The types of documents they look for are described below.

Sample Form I-864A, Contract Between Sponsor and Household Member—Page 1

	Contract Between Sponsor and Household Member	**USCIS**
	Department of Homeland Security	**Form I-864A**
	U.S. Citizenship and Immigration Services	OMB No. 1615-0075
		Expires 03/31/2020

For Government Use Only

This Form I-864A relates to a household member who:

☐ **IS** the intending immigrant ☐ **IS NOT** the intending immigrant

Reviewed By: _____

Location: _____ Date (mm/dd/yyyy): _____

To be completed by an attorney or accredited representative (if any).	☐ **Select this box if Form G-28 or G-28I is attached.**	**Attorney State Bar Number** (if applicable)	**Attorney or Accredited Representative USCIS Online Account Number** (if any)

▶ **START HERE - Type or print in black ink.**

Part 1. Information About You (the Household Member)

Full Name

1.a. Family Name (Last Name) `Mancini`

1.b. Given Name (First Name) `Stella`

1.c. Middle Name `Beatrice`

Mailing Address *(USPS ZIP Code Lookup)*

2.a. In Care Of Name

2.b. Street Number and Name `800 Broadway`

2.c. ☐ Apt. ☐ Ste. ☐ Flr.

2.d. City or Town `Lindenhurst`

2.e. State `NY` **2.f.** ZIP Code `11757`

2.g. Province

2.h. Postal Code

2.i. Country `USA`

3. Is your current mailing address the same as your physical address? ☒ Yes ☐ No

If you answered "No" to **Item Number 3.**, provide your physical address.

Physical Address

4.a. Street Number and Name

4.b. ☐ Apt. ☐ Ste. ☐ Flr.

4.c. City or Town

4.d. State **4.e.** ZIP Code

4.f. Province

4.g. Postal Code

4.h. Country

Other Information

5. Date of Birth (mm/dd/yyyy) `03/06/1998`

Place of Birth

6.a. City or Town `Syracuse`

6.b. State or Province `New York`

6.c. Country `USA`

7. U.S. Social Security Number (if any) ▶ `2 1 2 2 2 9 8 2 2`

8. USCIS Online Account Number (if any) ▶

Sample Form I-864A, Contract Between Sponsor and Household Member—Page 2

Part 2. Your (the Household Member's) Relationship to the Sponsor

Select **Item Number 1.a., 1.b., or 1.c.**

1.a. ☐ I am the intending immigrant and also the sponsor's spouse.

1.b. ☐ I am the intending immigrant and also a member of the sponsor's household.

1.c. ☒ I am **not** the intending immigrant. I am the sponsor's household member. I am related to the sponsor as his/her:

☐ Spouse

☒ Son or Daughter (at least 18 years of age)

☐ Parent

☐ Brother or Sister

☐ Other Dependent (Specify)

Part 3. Your (the Household Member's) Employment and Income

I am currently:

1. ☐ Employed as a/an

2. Name of Employer Number 1

3. Name of Employer Number 2 (if applicable)

4. ☒ Self employed as a/an

Freelance graphic designer

5. ☐ Retired from (Company Name)

Since (mm/dd/yyyy)

6. ☐ Unemployed since (mm/dd/yyyy)

7. **My current individual annual income is:**

$ **18,000.00**

Part 4. Your (the Household Member's) Federal Income Tax Information and Assets

1.a. Have you filed a Federal income tax return for each of the three most recent tax years? ☒ Yes ☐ No

NOTE: You **MUST** attach a photocopy or transcript of your Federal income tax return for only the most recent tax year.

1.b. ☐ (Optional) I have attached photocopies or transcripts of my Federal income tax returns for my second and third most recent tax years.

My total income (adjusted gross income on IRS Form 1040EZ) as reported on my Federal income tax returns for the most recent three years was:

	Tax Year		Total Income
2.a. Most Recent	2018	$	18,000.00
2.b. 2nd Most Recent	2017	$	18,500.00
2.c. 3rd Most Recent	2016	$	17,500.00

My assets (complete only if necessary).

3.a. Enter the balance of all cash, savings, and checking accounts. $

3.b. Enter the net cash value of real-estate holdings. (Net value means assessed value minus mortgage debt.) $

3.c. Enter the cash value of all stocks, bonds, certificates of deposit, and other assets not listed on **Item Numbers 3.a.** or **3.b.** $

3.d. Add together **Item Numbers 3.a., 3.b.,** and **3.c.** and enter the number here. $

Part 5. Sponsor's Promise, Statement, Contact Information, Declaration, Certification, and Signature

NOTE: Read the **Penalties** section of the Form I-864A Instructions before completing this part.

I, THE SPONSOR,

Alberto Ilario Mancini,
(Print Name)

in consideration of the household member's promise to support the following intending immigrants and to be jointly and severally liable for any obligations I incur under the affidavit of support, promise to complete and file an affidavit of support on behalf of the following named intending immigrants.

2
(Indicate Number)

Sample Form I-864A, Contract Between Sponsor and Household Member—Page 3

Part 5. Sponsor's Promise, Statement, Contact Information, Declaration, Certification, and Signature (continued)

Intending Immigrant Number 1

Name

1.a. Family Name (Last Name)   `Mancini`

1.b. Given Name (First Name)   `Terese`

1.c. Middle Name   `Maria`

2. Date of Birth (mm/dd/yyyy)   `02/15/1982`

3. Alien Registration Number (A-Number, if any)
▶ A-

4. U.S. Social Security Number (if any)
▶

5. USCIS Online Account Number (if any)
▶

Intending Immigrant Number 2

Name

6.a. Family Name (Last Name)

6.b. Given Name (First Name)

6.c. Middle Name

7. Date of Birth (mm/dd/yyyy)

8. Alien Registration Number (A-Number, if any)
▶ A-

9. U.S. Social Security Number (if any)
▶

10. USCIS Online Account Number (if any)
▶

Intending Immigrant Number 3

Name

11.a. Family Name (Last Name)

11.b. Given Name (First Name)

11.c. Middle Name

12. Date of Birth (mm/dd/yyyy)

13. Alien Registration Number (A-Number, if any)
▶ A-

14. U.S. Social Security Number (if any)
▶

15. USCIS Online Account Number (if any)
▶

Intending Immigrant Number 4

Name

16.a. Family Name (Last Name)

16.b. Given Name (First Name)

16.c. Middle Name

17. Date of Birth (mm/dd/yyyy)

18. Alien Registration Number (A-Number, if any)
▶ A-

19. U.S. Social Security Number (if any)
▶

20. USCIS Online Account Number (if any)
▶

Intending Immigrant Number 5

Name

21.a. Family Name (Last Name)

21.b. Given Name (First Name)

21.c. Middle Name

22. Date of Birth (mm/dd/yyyy)

23. Alien Registration Number (A-Number, if any)
▶ A-

24. U.S. Social Security Number (if any)
▶

25. USCIS Online Account Number (if any)
▶

Sponsor's Statement

NOTE: Select the box for either **Item Number 26.a.** or **26.b.** If applicable, select the box for **Item Number 27.**

26.a. ☒ I can read and understand English, and I have read and understand every question and instruction on this contract and my answer to every question.

Sample Form I-864A, Contract Between Sponsor and Household Member—Page 4

Part 5. Sponsor's Promise, Statement, Contact Information, Declaration, Certification, and Signature (continued)

26.b. ☐ The interpreter named in **Part 7.** read to me every question and instruction on this contract and my answer to every question in

_____

a language in which I am fluent, and I understood everything.

27. ☐ At my request, the preparer named in **Part 8.**,

_____

prepared this contract for me based only upon information I provided or authorized.

Sponsor's Contact Information

28. Sponsor's Daytime Telephone Number

2122229822

29. Sponsor's Mobile Telephone Number (if any)

_____

30. Sponsor's Email Address (if any)

albertom@email.com

Sponsor's Declaration and Certification

Copies of any documents I have submitted are exact photocopies of unaltered, original documents, and I understand that U.S. Citizenship and Immigration Services (USCIS) or the U.S. Department of State (DOS) may require that I submit original documents to USCIS or DOS at a later date. Furthermore, I authorize the release of any information from any and all of my records that USCIS or DOS may need to determine my eligibility for the immigration benefit that I seek.

I furthermore authorize release of information contained in this contract, in supporting documents, and in my USCIS or DOS records, to other entities and persons where necessary for the administration and enforcement of U.S. immigration law.

I certify, under penalty of perjury, that all of the information in my contract and any document submitted with it were provided or authorized by me, that I reviewed and understand all of the information contained in, and submitted with, my contract and that all of this information is complete, true, and correct.

Sponsor's Signature

31.a. Sponsor's Signature

Alberto Ilario Mancini

31.b. Date of Signature   (mm/dd/yyyy)   07/06/2019

NOTE TO ALL SPONSORS: If you do not completely fill out this contract or fail to submit required documents listed in the Instructions, USCIS may deny your contract.

Part 6. Your (the Household Member's) Promise, Statement, Contact Information, Declaration, Certification, and Signature

NOTE: Read the **Penalties** section of the Form I-864A Instructions before completing this part.

I, THE HOUSEHOLD MEMBER,

Stella Beatrice Mancini ,
(Print Name)

in consideration of the sponsor's promise to complete and file an affidavit of support on behalf of the above named intending immigrants.

| 1 |

(Print number of intending immigrants noted in **Part 5. Sponsor's Promise, Statement, Contact Information, Declaration, Certification and Signature.**)

A. Promise to provide any and all financial support necessary to assist the sponsor in maintaining the sponsored immigrants at or above the minimum income provided for in the Immigration and Naturalization Act (INA) section 213A(a)(1)(A) (not less than 125 percent of the Federal Poverty Guidelines) during the period in which the affidavit of support is enforceable;

B. Agree to be jointly and severally liable for payment of any and all obligations owed by the sponsor under the affidavit of support to the sponsored immigrants, to any agency of the Federal Government, to any agency of a state or local government, or to any other private entity that provides means-tested public benefits;

C. Certify under penalty under the laws of the United States that the Federal income tax returns submitted in support of the contract are true copies or unaltered tax transcripts filed with the Internal Revenue Service;

D. **Consideration where the household member is also the sponsored immigrant:** I understand that if I am the sponsored immigrant and a member of the sponsor's household that this promise relates only to my promise to be jointly and severally liable for any obligation owed by the sponsor under the affidavit of support to any of my dependents, to any agency of the Federal Government, to any agency of a state or local government, or to any other private entity that provides means-tested public benefits and to provide any and all financial support necessary to assist the sponsor in maintaining any of my dependents at or above the minimum income provided for in INA section 213A(a)(1)(A) (not less than 125 percent of the Federal Poverty Guideline) during the period which the affidavit of support is enforceable.

Sample Form I-864A, Contract Between Sponsor and Household Member—Page 5

Part 6. Your (the Household Member's) Promise, Statement, Contact Information, Declaration, Certification, and Signature (continued)

E. I understand that, if I am related to the sponsored immigrant or the sponsor by marriage, the termination of the marriage (by divorce, dissolution, annulment, or other legal process) will not relieve me of my obligations under this Form I-864A.

F. I authorize the Social Security Administration to release information about me in its records to the Department of State and U.S. Citizenship and Immigration Services (USCIS).

Your (the Household Member's) Statement

NOTE: Select the box for either **Item Number 1.a.** or **1.b.** If applicable, select the box for **Item Number 2.**

1.a. ☒ I can read and understand English, and I have read and understand every question and instruction on this contract and my answer to every question.

1.b. ☐ The interpreter named in **Part 7.** read to me every question and instruction on this contract and my answer to every question in

_____,

a language in which I am fluent, and I understood everything.

2. ☐ At my request, the preparer named in **Part 8.,**

_____,

prepared this contract for me based only upon information I provided or authorized.

Your (the Household Member's) Contact Information

3. Your (the Household Member's) Daytime Telephone Number

2122229822

4. Your (the Household Member's) Mobile Telephone Number (if any)

2122211111

5. Your (the Household Member's) Email Address (if any)

stella33@email.com

Your (the Household Member's) Declaration and Certification

Copies of any documents I have submitted are exact photocopies of unaltered, original documents, and I understand that USCIS or DOS may require that I submit original documents to USCIS or DOS at a later date. Furthermore, I authorize the release of any information from any and all of my records that USCIS or DOS may need to determine my eligibility for the immigration benefit that I seek.

I furthermore authorize release of information contained in this contract, in supporting documents, and in my USCIS or DOS records, to other entities and persons where necessary for the administration and enforcement of U.S. immigration law.

I certify, under penalty of perjury, that all of the information in my contract and any document submitted with it were provided or authorized by me, that I reviewed and understand all of the information contained in, and submitted with, my contract and that all of this information is complete, true, and correct.

Your (the Household Member's) Signature

6.a. Your (the Household Member's) Printed Name

Stella Beatrice Mancini

6.b. Your (the Household Member's) Signature

Stella Beatrice Mancini

6.c. Date of Signature (mm/dd/yyyy) 7/6/2019

NOTE TO ALL HOUSEHOLD MEMBERS: If you do not completely fill out this contract or fail to submit required documents listed in the Instructions, USCIS may deny your contract.

Part 7. Interpreter's Contact Information, Certification, and Signature

Provide the following information about the interpreter.

Interpreter's Full Name

1.a. Interpreter's Family Name (Last Name)

1.b. Interpreter's Given Name (First Name)

2. Interpreter's Business or Organization Name (if any)

i.   Documents to Accompany Form I-864

Form I-864 asks for several supporting documents. If your spouse is relying on a joint sponsor (outside the household), that person should also be told to assemble a set of these documents:

- **A copy of your spouse/sponsor's federal income tax transcripts for the last one to three years.** Don't include state tax forms. The immigration authorities prefer to see federal tax returns in the form of Internal Revenue Service (IRS) transcripts (an IRS-generated summary of the return that was filed). The fastest way to get such a transcript is from the IRS website at www.irs.gov/Individuals/Get-Transcript. If for some reason that doesn't work, you can submit photocopies of tax returns—just don't forget to include the W-2 forms. And if the sponsor wasn't legally required to submit a tax return, perhaps because his or her income was too low, submit a written explanation of this.

- **Proof of your sponsor's current employment.** Start with a letter from the sponsor's employer describing the dates of employment, nature of the job, wages/salary, time worked per week, and prospects for advancement. (See the sample employer letter below.) Also include copies of pay stubs covering the last six months, or the most recent stub if it shows cumulative pay. If the sponsor is self-employed, a tax return is acceptable, but it's a good idea to add a business license, copies of current receipts, or other supporting documents.

- **A list of assets (the sponsor's and/or the immigrant's), if they must be used to meet the** *Poverty Guidelines'* **minimum.** There is no form to use for creating this list. Simply prepare (on a typewriter or word processor) a list or table with the following information:
    - a brief description of the item
    - current value
    - remaining debt (if any), and

- a brief description of the document you've attached to prove ownership.

- **Proof of ownership of assets (the sponsor's and/ or the immigrant's), if any were listed.** The Instructions to Form I-864 do a good job of detailing which documents will be accepted as proof of ownership of assets, in Part 7. Use of Assets to Supplement Income. The value must be the likely sale price, not how much the sponsor paid for the property. For real estate, you can use a tax assessment to show the value. If the assessment seems too low, or for property other than real estate, the sponsor can hire a professional appraiser to prepare an estimate and report. For cars, the value listed in the *Kelley Blue Book* is acceptable (online at www.kbb.com). The sponsor must also document the amount of any debt remaining on the property. If no debt remains, submit proof of final payment.

Sample Letter Showing Sponsor's Employment

Hitting the Road Trucking
222 Plaza Place
Outthereville, MA 90000
May 22, 20xx

To Whom It May Concern:

Ron Goodley has been an employee of Hitting the Road Trucking since September 4, 20xx, a total of over five years. He has a full-time position as a driver. His salary is $45,000 per year. This position is permanent, and Ron's prospects for performance-based advancement and salary increases are excellent.

Very truly yours,
Bob Bossman
Bob Bossman
Personnel Manager
Hitting the Road Trucking

CAUTION
You may need to update your information later. By the time you get to your visa interview, circumstances may have changed for your sponsor, joint sponsor, or household joint sponsor. For example, if the sponsor or joint sponsor have new or different employment, bring a job letter and copies of recent pay stubs; and if a new tax year has begun, bring copies of the sponsor(s)' most recent tax returns or transcripts.

ii. Documents to Accompany Form I-864A

You will submit Form I-864A only if your spouse needs to rely on the financial contributions of members of his or her household. Form I-864A also requires several supporting documents. These include not only proof of the joint sponsors' financial capacity, but proof that they live with and are related to the main sponsor.

- **Proof that the household joint sponsors live with the primary sponsor.** Such proof can include a copy of the rental agreement showing the household member's name, and copies of items that show the same address as the sponsor (such as a driver's license, copies of school records, copies of utility bills, or personal correspondence).

- **Proof that the household joint sponsors are related to the primary sponsor (if they're not already listed as relations on the sponsor's tax return).** The best way to prove this family relationship is through birth certificates. If, for example, the sponsor and household joint sponsor are parent and child, the child's birth certificate will do. If they are brother and sister, providing both birth certificates will work (as long as the certificates show that they share the same parent or parents). If the birth certificates don't make the family relationships clear, look for other official documents such as court or school records to confirm the parent-child links.

- **Copies of the household joint sponsors' tax returns for the last one to three years.** As with the primary sponsor, the government prefers to see IRS-generated tax transcripts.

- **Proof of the household joint sponsors' employment.** This can include a letter from their employer confirming employment, as in the sample above, and recent pay stubs.

- **A list of the household joint sponsors' assets if they must be used to meet the *Poverty Guidelines'* minimum.** There is no form for creating this list. Using a typewriter or word processor, the household joint sponsors should prepare a list or table with the following information:
  - brief description of item
  - current value
  - remaining debt (if any), and
  - brief description of the document attached to prove ownership.

- **Proof of ownership of household joint sponsors' assets, if any were listed.**

- **A list of the benefits programs and dates of receipt if the household joint sponsors or their dependents have used financial need-based public benefits in the last three years.**

c. Other Documents to Prepare

You'll be asked to prepare various other documents for the NVC and for your consular interview, such as your birth certificate, marriage certificate, passport, and police certificates from countries where you've lived. These will be well explained in the instructions you receive, so we won't review them further here.

You'll need to obtain a police certificate (hopefully showing your clean record) only if such certificates are available in your country. For country-specific information on how to obtain proper police certification, birth and marriage certificates, and divorce decrees, visit www.travel.state.gov and click "U.S. Visas" then "Immigrate" then "The Immigrant Visa Process," then, on the flowchart, click "Collect Supporting Forms and Documents to the NVC."

If you don't have a clean record, see a lawyer.

d. Documenting That Your Marriage Is Bona Fide

You may be asked for evidence that your marriage is a real one, not a sham. Gather and photocopy as many of the following items as possible:

- rental agreements, leases, or mortgages showing that you have lived together and/or have leased or bought property in both spouses' names
- hotel and airplane receipts showing trips that you have taken together or to visit one another
- text or phone records showing your conversations
- copies of letters and emails between you
- your mutual child's birth certificate or a doctor's report saying that you are pregnant
- joint bank statements
- joint credit card statements
- evidence that one spouse has made the other a beneficiary on his/her life or health insurance or retirement account
- auto registrations showing joint ownership and/or addresses
- joint club memberships
- receipts for gifts that you purchased for one another (these should be items that are normally considered gifts, such as flowers, candy, jewelry, and art)
- letters from friends and family to each or both of you, mailed to an address where you were living together, and
- photos of you and your spouse taken before and during your marriage, including at your wedding (the government knows wedding pictures can be faked, but some officers enjoy seeing them anyway). The photos should, if possible, include parents and other relatives from both families. Write the date the picture was taken and a brief description of what the photo shows on the back (or underneath, if you're photocopying them). Don't bother with the wedding or other videos; there won't be time or a space to view them. And keep them clean—no need for intimate scenes!

e. Using the Checklist for Forms and Documents

Although you must fill out only a few forms, you and your spouse will be responsible for pulling together a great deal of supporting documents, financial and otherwise. It will be particularly important to use the checklist to keep track of everything.

All the checklist items concerning Form I-864 apply whether it's your spouse filling it out or a joint sponsor who is willing to assist in supporting you; see Chapter 3 for more on joint sponsorship.

> **CHECKLIST**
> Appendix B includes instructions on where to get a copy of this checklist online.

4. Step Three: Attend Your Visa Interview

On the appointed day, you and your petitioning spouse (if he or she can possibly make it—it's optional) will go to a U.S. consulate for an interview. See a detailed description of the interview and how to prepare for it in Chapter 13.

Which consulate you go to depends on where you're from and where you live now. If you've been living (legally) in a country that is not your country of citizenship, you'll probably be told to work with the consulate in the country where you now live. If your country of residence doesn't have diplomatic relations with the United States, the NVC will name another consulate to handle your case. (And if you'll be getting a K-3 visa, you'll need to go to the consulate in the country where you were married.)

At a minimum, you'll need to bring to your interview:

- envelope contains results of your medical exam (described below)
- evidence that your marriage is bona fide (as described in Subsection 3d, above)
- financial documents to bring the Affidavit of Support up to date if it was prepared many months ago, and
- your passport, valid for at least six months.

Checklist for Immigrant Visa Forms and Documents

This checklist lists the forms, documents, and other items that you and your spouse will need to assemble.

☐ Confirmation page and bar code, showing that you (and any accompanying family members) completed an online Form DS-260

☐ Form I-864, Affidavit of Support (see Subsection A3a, above, for line-by-line instructions)

☐ Documents to accompany Form I-864 (see Subsection A3b, above):

  ☐ A copy of your spouse/sponsor's federal income tax transcripts for the last one to three years

  ☐ Proof of your sponsor's current employment

  ☐ A list of assets, (the sponsor's and/or the immigrant's) if they must be used to meet the *Poverty Guidelines'* minimum

  ☐ Proof of ownership of assets (the sponsor's and/or the immigrant's), if any were listed

  ☐ If sponsor or sponsor's dependents have used financial need-based public benefits in the last three years, a list of the programs and dates of receipt

☐ Form I-864A, Contract Between Sponsor and Household Member (only needed if sponsor's income is insufficient; see line-by-line instructions to Form I-864A in Subsection A3a, above)

☐ Documents to accompany Form I-864A (see Subsection A3b, above):

  ☐ Proof that the household joint sponsors live with the primary sponsor

  ☐ Proof that the household joint sponsors are related to the primary sponsor (if they're not already listed as dependents on the sponsor's tax return)

☐ Copies of the household joint sponsors' tax transcripts for the last one to three years

☐ Proof of the household joint sponsors' employment

☐ Proof of ownership of household joint sponsors' assets, if any were listed

☐ If the household joint sponsors or their dependents have used financial need-based public benefits in the last three years, a list of the benefits programs and dates of receipt

☐ If you're exempt from the Affidavit of Support requirement, Form I-864W, together with a certified statement of your Social Security earnings history

☐ Other documents:

  ☐ Original and one photocopy of your birth certificate (see Chapter 4, Section C, for how to obtain vital documents)

  ☐ Original and one photocopy of your marriage certificate (see Chapter 4, Section C, for how to obtain vital documents)

  ☐ If applicable, original and one photocopy of proof of termination of all previous marriages, such as a death, divorce, or annulment certificate

  ☐ Original USCIS notice of approved I-130 (Form I-797)

  ☐ Two color photographs of you (passport style)

  ☐ Police certificate, if available in your country

  ☐ Military records, if applicable

  ☐ Court and prison records, if applicable

☐ Fees (currently $325) (if not already paid to the NVC)

a. The Medical Exam

To prove that you are not inadmissible for medical reasons, you will have to present the results of a medical exam done by a doctor approved by the U.S. consulate. Your appointment notice will give you complete instructions on where and when to visit the appropriate clinic or doctor. There will be a basic fee (the exact amount of which depends on the country and the doctor), plus other fees for tests and any needed vaccinations.

When you go for your medical exam, make sure to bring the following:

- your visa appointment letter
- the doctor's fee
- a form you fill out describing your medical history, if requested
- your vaccination records, and
- photo identification—the doctor must make sure you don't send a healthier person in your place. You may also be requested to bring a passport-style photo.

The doctor will examine you, ask you questions about your medical and psychiatric history and drug use, and test you (including blood tests and chest X-rays). Pregnant women can (with proof of pregnancy) refuse the chest X-ray until after the baby is born if they have no symptoms of tuberculosis.

When the laboratory results are in, the doctor will fill out the appropriate form and return it to you in a sealed envelope or forward it directly to the consulate. DO NOT open the envelope—this will invalidate the results. The doctor should supply you with a separate copy of your results, or tell you whether any illnesses showed up.

b. Fingerprinting

At your interview, you'll probably also need to have your fingerprints taken. Depending on the country where you are applying, the consulate could also send you a date and location for having them taken in advance. After your appointment, you'll have to wait until your prints have cleared with the U.S. FBI and other security agencies. After that, assuming you have no criminal record, your case can continue forward. (See Chapter 2 regarding how a criminal record can make you inadmissible to the U.S.)

5. Step Four: At the Border

Assuming all goes well at the visa interview, you will be given an immigrant visa. But wait—you're not a U.S. resident yet. You'll have six months to use the visa to enter the United States.

TIP

If you're about to reach your two-year wedding anniversary, don't rush to enter the United States. An immigrating spouse whose marriage is less than two years old when he or she becomes a U.S. resident receives conditional, not permanent residency. USCIS will reexamine the marriage after another two years. So if your marriage is nearly two years old when you get your visa to enter the United States, make the most of that six-month entry window and wait to enter until your two-year wedding anniversary has passed. That way, you'll enter as a permanent resident. Point out your anniversary date to the border official, to be sure that he or she stamps your passport for permanent, not conditional, residence.

Sample Conditional Residence Stamp

At the border, airport, or other port of entry, a U.S. border officer will open the sealed envelope containing your visa documents and do a last check to make sure you haven't used fraud. The border officer has expedited removal powers, which means he or she can turn you right around and send you home if he or she sees anything wrong in your packet or with your answers to his or her questions. When the officer is satisfied that everything is in order, he or she will stamp your passport to show that you're now a U.S. resident (see reproduction of this stamp above—the CR-1 means that this person entered as a conditional resident).

If your marriage is less than two years old on that day, the border officer will make you a conditional resident; if your marriage is older than two years, you'll be made a permanent resident.

Your actual green card should arrive within 45 days after you pay your USCIS Immigrant Fee ($220). If you receive conditional residence, you'll want to read Chapter 16, Section G. In about 21 months, you'll have to file an application with USCIS asking to convert this into permanent residency.

B. How to Have Your Children and Pets Accompany You

Although your whole family cannot immigrate right now, U.S. laws and regulations do recognize the need for certain of your loved ones to accompany you to the United States and live there with you, including your children and certain pets.

> **⚠ CAUTION**
>
> **Check your own country's law on taking your children if their other parent is staying behind.** If you will be bringing children to the United States who are not the biological children of your U.S. spouse, or who became the adopted children of another person, it will be up to you to comply with any custody requirements. Even if the children are legally in your custody, you may need to get written consent from the other parent for you to take the children out of the country. U.S. consular officials may also require proof that you have legal custody of your children.

1. Your Children on an Immigrant Visa

Your foreign-born children, whether they are the biological children or the stepchildren of your petitioning spouse, may be eligible to obtain green cards through him or her. (For the fundamentals of children's eligibility, see Chapter 2, Section B.)

If the children are unmarried and were under age 21 when their I-130 petition was filed, they will have to go through the identical four steps described in Section A, above. As part of these steps, you must prove that the children are not only yours, but are also your spouse's biological children or legal stepchildren, that they are not inadmissible, and that they will be financially supported along with you.

Children who were over age 21 when their I-130 petition was filed, or who don't qualify as stepchildren or are married, will not be able to immigrate to the United States at the same time as you. As a U.S. citizen, your spouse may file petitions for them if they are his or her biological children or legal stepchildren, but they will be subject to quotas and waiting periods. This book does not cover how to file these petitions.

This section contains a brief overview of the procedures for immigrating children, but complete details (especially line-by-line instructions on filling out the forms) are outside the scope of this book. Once you've filled in all the paperwork described in this book, you will have a good basis of knowledge with which to fill in these forms for your children; or you might be more comfortable using a lawyer.

To start the process, your U.S. citizen spouse will need to fill in a separate petition (Form I-130) for each child. However, the children do not need to have their photos included in the petition. Include copies of your and your spouse's marriage certificate, but also include copies of the children's birth certificates to show the family relationships.

At the Step Two (NVC) stage, you will have to submit a Form DS-260 for each of your children (the same online form you filled in for yourself).

When it's time for your interview, the children will have to submit all the same documents as you, including separately filled out versions of the Affidavit of Support (Form I-864). Of course, you'll want to make sure that the income and assets shown are sufficient to cover them. Children under the age of 16 will not need to submit a police certificate.

You can expect to attend your interviews together. The children probably won't have to answer more than one or two questions.

2. Your Pets

Good news for your dog and cat, who may not have learned to sign their names yet—they won't need a visa. Bringing pets into the United States is not an immigration law matter. But before bringing any pets to the United States, you will need to check into U.S. customs restrictions. In general, pets will be admitted if they are in good health and have had all the proper vaccinations. There are some restrictions, however. For example, certain states don't allow specific animals, and monkeys aren't allowed into the United States at all. Check with your local U.S. consulate for details, or read more on the Web at www.cbp.gov (enter "pets" into the search box, which will bring up a "Pets and Wildlife" page, where you'll find a publication called "Bringing Pets and Wildlife into the United States").

SKIP AHEAD

For what to do after you have obtained your visa and entered the United States, see Chapter 16.

Overseas Spouses of Lawful Permanent Residents

A marriage-based visa or green card is available to anyone who is living overseas, married to a U.S. permanent resident, and whose marriage is real and legally valid. In addition, the person must not be inadmissible to the United States for any of the reasons covered in Chapter 2, Section A. To confirm that you are eligible for a marriage-based green card, review Chapter 2, Section B.

Unfortunately, there are many people like you—known as a preference relative—but few available visas year by year. After your spouse files an application to start the process, you will become one of many prospective immigrants on a long and somewhat mysterious waiting list. This wait will add, on average, almost two years to the often twelve-month-long application process. You will most likely have to wait outside the United States. (Read Section A2, later in this chapter, for how to estimate your wait.)

The only good thing about this long wait is that, when you ultimately are allowed to enter the United States, your residence status will be permanent. Here's why: Immigrants who enter the United States before completing two years of marriage are given only conditional residence. USCIS puts their marriage through a two-year testing period to make sure the marriage is not a sham, and makes a final decision on the green card (granting permanent residency) only after those two years are up. Since it is normally unlikely that the spouse of a permanent resident will get through the application and waiting within two years of your marriage, you may not have to go through this two-year testing period.

Your immigration application will be handled initially by USCIS offices in the United States and later will be transferred to a U.S. consulate in your home country. We'll explain the various steps involved in this application process in this chapter.

> **CAUTION**
>
> **If your U.S. permanent resident spouse has made his or her home outside the United States, that permanent residence may now be lost.** Permanent residents are expected to make their primary home in the United States. Any absence longer than six months will definitely raise questions. Before you rely on your permanent resident spouse to petition for you, make sure this isn't a problem. (See Chapter 16 for more on how permanent residents can lose their residency this way.)

A. The Immigrant Visa Application Process

If you are reading this section, it means that you have determined that you are eligible for a marriage-based visa and are ready to find out exactly how to get it. But first, a warning: This application process is a bit like harnessing yourself to a turtle. It's going to move slowly, and to succeed you'll have to hang on for the whole bumpy ride. This chapter gives you a map for that ride and offers a few shortcuts.

Obtaining an immigrant visa and green card through a permanent resident spouse involves five major steps:

Step 1: Your spouse submits a petition (Form I-130) to USCIS.

Step 2: Your petition is approved, your file is transferred to the National Visa Center (NVC) in the United States, and you wait for a visa to become available to you.

Step 3: When a visa is about to become available, the NVC sends you instructions.

Step 4: You attend an interview at a U.S. consulate in your home country, which later gives you your immigrant visa.

Step 5: You present your visa at a U.S. border, where it is examined and you are approved and stamped for U.S. residency.

In addition to the steps above, a few couples (or more likely the U.S.-based spouse) are required to attend a "fraud interview" if the government has doubts about their marriage being the real thing. This could happen either as part of Step One or after Step Four, above.

Applying for Immigrant Visa Overseas (Spouses of Permanent Residents)

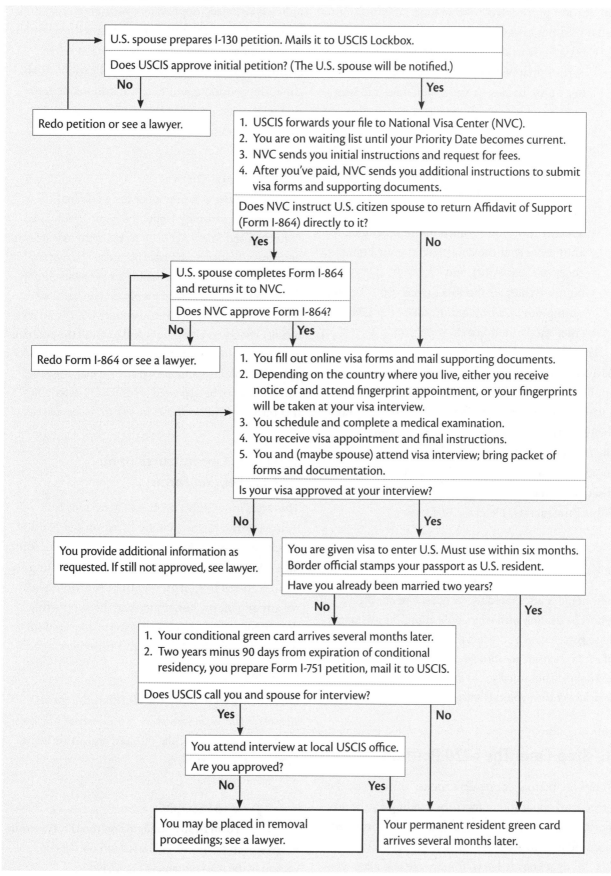

Now you may have a clearer picture of why your application process will take so long. The total time often (but not always) includes:

- between several months to two years for approval of the initial petition (Step One) (USCIS is not in a hurry, because it knows you'll need to wait until a visa is available to you, as described next)
- another year or two at least before a visa is available to you (Step Two)
- another month at least—or possibly many months —to receive the follow-up instructions (Step Three) from the National Visa Center (NVC)
- another few months until you're scheduled for an interview at the consulate in your home country (Step Four), and
- no more than six months before you take your immigrant visa in hand, to take Step Five and enter the United States.

These time periods are mere educated guesses, based on averages over the last few years. Your application could go faster or slower, depending on a variety of factors including the current demand for visas, the complexities of your own case, and the efficiency and workload of the U.S. consulate in your country. (Potential issues and hassles are discussed in more detail in Chapter 15, Dealing With Bureaucrats, Delays, and Denials.)

> **CAUTION**
> **The urgency you feel to get settled into your new home is not shared by the government officials who'll be dealing with your application.** They've long since gotten used to the fact that they have thousands of applications to get through. Once in a while, a miracle will happen; but usually your green card application will take longer than you ever imagined.

1. Step One: The I-130 Petition

Your U.S. permanent resident spouse will initiate the green card application process by sending a petition—Form I-130, Petition for Alien Relative and attached documents—to a USCIS office. This petition asks USCIS to acknowledge your marriage and allow you to go forward with green card processing.

Approval of the I-130 petition does not mean you're guaranteed approval of your green card, however. Like every immigrant, you will eventually have to file your own, extensive portion of the immigrant visa and green card application. At that time, the consulate will take a hard look at your financial situation and other factors that might disqualify you from entering the United States.

> **CAUTION**
> **If the U.S. petitioner has a criminal record, see an attorney.** Under the Adam Walsh Child Protection and Safety Act of 2006, U.S. citizens and lawful permanent residents who have been convicted of any "specified offense against a minor" are prohibited from filing a family-based immigrant petition on behalf of any beneficiary (whether a child or not). USCIS will run security checks on all petitions and may call the petitioner in for fingerprinting. If the petitioner has a conviction for one of the specified offenses against a minor, then the petition will not be approved unless USCIS determines that the U.S. petitioner poses no risk to the beneficiary.

a. Line-by-Line Instructions for I-130 Petition Forms

This section will give precise instructions for filling out the forms that are listed on the petition checklist in Subsection e, below. Before proceeding, take a look at the general instructions on filling in USCIS forms in Chapter 4. In Subsection b, below, we advise you on how to gather the supporting documentary proof and other items required for Form I-130, such as photos and filing fees.

i. Form I-130

Don't be thrown off by the fact that the form addresses the U.S. spouse as "you"—after all, it's the U.S. spouse who fills out and signs this form. Now for the questions.

> **WEB RESOURCE**
> **Form I-130 is available on the USCIS website at www.uscis.gov/i-130.** Below is a sample filled-in version of the relevant pages of this form.

Part A

Question 1: Check the first box, "Spouse."

Questions 2-3: Since you are petitioning for a spouse, do not check any boxes here.

Question 4: If the petitioning spouse gained permanent residence through adoption, check "Yes." But no matter which box you check, it won't affect the application, since this question is mainly directed at people immigrating through parent/child relationships—something not covered in this book.

Part 2

Question 1: A U.S. permanent resident petitioner will have an A-number (Alien Registration Number) shown on the green card.

Question 2: A U.S. petitioner who has filed a past petition with USCIS may have received a USCIS Online Account Number, and should enter it here.

Question 3: A U.S. permanent resident should have a Social Security number, and fill it in here.

Question 4: The petitioning U.S. spouse must enter his/her full name. Use current married name if it was changed at the time of your marriage. (If unclear on which name to use, see "What's Your Name?" in Chapter 4, Section B.)

Question 5: The U.S. petitioner should enter any names previously used. One who was married before and used another name during that time must enter it here.

Questions 6-9: Self-explanatory.

Questions 10-15: Fill in the permanent resident's addresses from the last five years. If there have been more than two addresses, enter the additional ones in Part 9. Make sure to include the start and end dates of all the addresses before the current one.

Question 16: State how many times the petitioner has been married, including this time.

Question 17: This refers only to the petitioning spouse's most recent marital status. Check "Married" even if there was a previous divorce.

Question 18-19: Self-explanatory.

Questions 20-23: Put the name of the petitioner's current (immigrating) spouse first and then any past spouses next. Leave blank or put "N/A" under the date marriage ended for your current marriage. If the petitioning spouse's prior marriage(s) ended after your present marriage began, yours is not a lawful marriage. If you've just discovered that the divorce wasn't final when your marriage took place, it may not be necessary to run to a lawyer. Assuming that the divorce has since become final, you can correct the problem by remarrying. (If there was fraud involved in your hasty marriage, consult a lawyer.)

Questions 24-35: Answer basic biographic information about the petitioning U.S. permanent resident's parents. If lacking any pieces of information, enter "unknown."

Question 36: Self-explanatory.

Questions 37-39: Leave blank, since the U.S. spouse is not yet a citizen.

Question 40: Some of the information requested here is on the U.S. petitioner's green card. (See the illustration below.) The date of admission shown on the older cards usually starts with the year, so that Dec. 3, 1998 would be 981203. The city is in code on the old cards: for example, SFR is San Francisco, BUF is Buffalo, and LIN is the service center in Lincoln, Nebraska. If it's a newer card, figure out where the petitioner entered the U.S. with an immigrant visa or was approved for a green card. Class of Admission asks for the type of visa or remedy through which the person got permanent residence, such as a Fourth Preference visa or political asylum.

Green Card (Front)

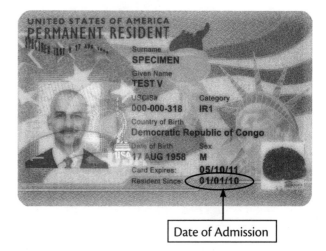

Date of Admission

Sample Form I-130, Petition for Alien Relative—Page 1

Petition for Alien Relative

Department of Homeland Security
U.S. Citizenship and Immigration Services

**USCIS
Form I-130**
OMB No. 1615-0012
Expires 02/28/2021

For USCIS Use Only		
A-Number		
A-		
Initial Receipt		
Resubmitted		

Fee Stamp

Action Stamp

Relocated	**Section of Law/Visa Category**		
Received	☐ 201(b) Spouse - IR-1/CR-1	☐ 203(a)(1) Unm. S/D - F1-1	☐ 203(a)(2)(B) Unm. S/D - F2-4
Sent	☐ 201(b) Child - IR-2/CR-2	☐ 203(a)(2)(A) Spouse - F2-1	☐ 203(a)(3) Married S/D - F3-1
Completed	☐ 201(b) Parent - IR-5	☐ 203(a)(2)(A) Child - F2-2	☐ 203(a)(4) Brother/Sister - F4-1

Approved	Petition was filed on (Priority Date mm/dd/yyyy):	☐ Field Investigation	☐ Personal Interview	☐ 204(a)(2)(A) Resolved
		☐ Previously Forwarded	☐ Pet. A-File Reviewed	☐ I-485 Filed Simultaneously
Returned	PDR request granted/denied - New priority date (mm/dd/yyyy):	☐ 203(g) Resolved	☐ Ben. A-File Reviewed	☐ 204(g) Resolved
Remarks				

At which USCIS office (e.g., NBC, VSC, LOS, CRO) was Form I-130 adjudicated? _____

To be completed by an attorney or accredited representative (if any).			
☐ **Select this box if Form G-28 is attached.**	**Volag Number** (if any)	**Attorney State Bar Number** (if applicable)	**Attorney or Accredited Representative USCIS Online Account Number** (if any)

▶ **START HERE** - Type or print in black ink.

> If you need extra space to complete any section of this petition, use the space provided in **Part 9. Additional Information.** **Complete and submit as many copies of Part 9., as necessary, with your petition.**

Part 1. Relationship (You are the Petitioner. Your relative is the Beneficiary)

1. I am filing this petition for my (Select **only one** box):

   ☒ Spouse ☐ Parent ☐ Brother/Sister ☐ Child

2. If you are filing this petition for your child or parent, select the box that describes your relationship (Select **only one** box):

   ☐ Child was born to parents who were married to each other at the time of the child's birth

   ☐ Stepchild/Stepparent

   ☐ Child was born to parents who were not married to each other at the time of the child's birth

   ☐ Child was adopted (not an Orphan or Hague Convention adoptee)

3. If the beneficiary is your brother/sister, are you related by adoption? ☐ Yes ☐ No

4. Did you gain lawful permanent resident status or citizenship through adoption? ☐ Yes ☒ No

Part 2. Information About You (Petitioner)

1. Alien Registration Number (A-Number) (if any)

   ▶ A- 2 2 3 3 4 4 5 5 5

2. USCIS Online Account Number (if any)

   ▶

3. U.S. Social Security Number (if any)

   ▶ 1 2 3 1 2 3 1 2 3

Your Full Name

4.a. Family Name (Last Name) Debden

4.b. Given Name (First Name) Alice

4.c. Middle Name Ann

Sample Form I-130, Petition for Alien Relative—Page 2

Part 2. Information About You (Petitioner) (continued)

Other Names Used (if any)

Provide all other names you have ever used, including aliases, maiden name, and nicknames.

5.a. Family Name (Last Name) — madison

5.b. Given Name (First Name) —

5.c. Middle Name —

Other Information

6. City/Town/Village of Birth — Dublin

7. Country of Birth — Ireland

8. Date of Birth (mm/dd/yyyy) — 03/30/1978

9. Sex — ☐ Male   ☒ Female

Mailing Address   *(USPS ZIP Code Lookup)*

10.a. In Care Of Name —

10.b. Street Number and Name — 432 Fairfax St.

10.c. ☒ Apt. ☐ Ste. ☐ Flr. — A

10.d. City or Town — Alexandria

10.e. State — VA   **10.f.** ZIP Code — 22314

10.g. Province —

10.h. Postal Code —

10.i. Country — USA

11. Is your current mailing address the same as your physical address?   ☒ Yes ☐ No

If you answered "No" to **Item Number 11.**, provide information on your physical address in **Item Numbers 12.a. - 13.b.**

Address History

Provide your physical addresses for the last five years, whether inside or outside the United States. Provide your current address first if it is different from your mailing address in **Item Numbers 10.a. - 10.i.**

Physical Address 1

12.a. Street Number and Name —

12.b. ☐ Apt. ☐ Ste. ☐ Flr. —

12.c. City or Town —

12.d. State —   **12.e.** ZIP Code —

12.f. Province —

12.g. Postal Code —

12.h. Country —

13.a. Date From (mm/dd/yyyy) —

13.b. Date To (mm/dd/yyyy) — PRESENT

Physical Address 2

14.a. Street Number and Name —

14.b. ☐ Apt. ☐ Ste. ☐ Flr. —

14.c. City or Town —

14.d. State —   **14.e.** ZIP Code —

14.f. Province —

14.g. Postal Code —

14.h. Country —

15.a. Date From (mm/dd/yyyy) —

15.b. Date To (mm/dd/yyyy) —

Your Marital Information

16. How many times have you been married? ▶ 2

17. Current Marital Status

☐ Single, Never Married   ☒ Married   ☐ Divorced

☐ Widowed   ☐ Separated   ☐ Annulled

Sample Form I-130, Petition for Alien Relative—Page 3

Part 2. Information About You (Petitioner) (continued)

18. Date of Current Marriage (if currently married) (mm/dd/yyyy) `03/05/2018`

Place of Your Current Marriage (if married)

19.a. City or Town `London`

19.b. State `▼`

19.c. Province

19.d. Country `UK`

Names of All Your Spouses (if any)

Provide information on your current spouse (if currently married) first and then list all your prior spouses (if any).

Spouse 1

20.a. Family Name (Last Name) `Lindsey`

20.b. Given Name (First Name) `Edmund`

20.c. Middle Name `Alexander`

21. Date Marriage Ended (mm/dd/yyyy)

Spouse 2

22.a. Family Name (Last Name) `Madison`

22.b. Given Name (First Name) `David`

22.c. Middle Name

23. Date Marriage Ended (mm/dd/yyyy) `09/22/2005`

Information About Your Parents

Parent 1's Information

Full Name of Parent 1

24.a. Family Name (Last Name) `Debden`

24.b. Given Name (First Name) `Elizabeth`

24.c. Middle Name `Ann`

25. Date of Birth (mm/dd/yyyy) `07/01/1952`

26. Sex ☐ Male ☒ Female

27. Country of Birth `Ireland`

28. City/Town/Village of Residence `Dublin`

29. Country of Residence `Ireland`

Parent 2's Information

Full Name of Parent 2

30.a. Family Name (Last Name) `Debden`

30.b. Given Name (First Name) `Marcus`

30.c. Middle Name `George`

31. Date of Birth (mm/dd/yyyy)

32. Sex ☒ Male ☐ Female

33. Country of Birth `Ireland`

34. City/Town/Village of Residence `Dublin`

35. Country of Residence `Ireland`

Additional Information About You (Petitioner)

36. I am a (Select **only one** box):
☐ U.S. Citizen ☒ Lawful Permanent Resident

If you are a U.S. citizen, complete Item Number 37.

37. My citizenship was acquired through (Select **only one** box):

☐ Birth in the United States

☐ Naturalization

☐ Parents

38. Have you obtained a Certificate of Naturalization or a Certificate of Citizenship? ☐ Yes ☒ No

If you answered "Yes" to **Item Number 38.**, complete the following:

39.a. Certificate Number

39.b. Place of Issuance

39.c. Date of Issuance (mm/dd/yyyy)

Sample Form I-130, Petition for Alien Relative—Page 4

Part 2. Information About You (Petitioner) (continued)

If you are a lawful permanent resident, complete **Item Numbers 40.a. - 41.**

40.a. Class of Admission

IRI

40.b. Date of Admission (mm/dd/yyyy) 01/01/2012

Place of Admission

40.c. City or Town

Dulles

40.d State VA ▼

41. Did you gain lawful permanent resident status through marriage to a U.S. citizen or lawful permanent resident?

☒ Yes ☐ No

Employment History

Provide your employment history for the last five years, whether inside or outside the United States. Provide your current employment first. If you are currently unemployed, type or print "Unemployed" in **Item Number 42.**

Employer 1

42. Name of Employer/Company

Alexandria Quartet Potters

43.a. Street Number and Name 100 King St.

43.b. ☐ Apt. ☐ Ste. ☐ Flr.

43.c. City or Town Alexandria

43.d. State VA ▼ **43.e.** ZIP Code 22314

43.f. Province

43.g. Postal Code

43.h. Country

USA

44. Your Occupation

Potter

45.a. Date From (mm/dd/yyyy) 05/01/2012

45.b. Date To (mm/dd/yyyy) **PRESENT**

Employer 2

46. Name of Employer/Company

47.a. Street Number and Name

47.b. ☐ Apt. ☐ Ste. ☐ Flr.

47.c. City or Town

47.d. State ▼ **47.e.** ZIP Code

47.f. Province

47.g. Postal Code

47.h. Country

48. Your Occupation

49.a. Date From (mm/dd/yyyy)

49.b. Date To (mm/dd/yyyy)

Part 3. Biographic Information

NOTE: Provide the biographic information about you, the petitioner.

1. Ethnicity (Select **only one** box)

☐ Hispanic or Latino
☒ Not Hispanic or Latino

2. Race (Select **all applicable** boxes)

☒ White
☐ Asian
☐ Black or African American
☐ American Indian or Alaska Native
☐ Native Hawaiian or Other Pacific Islander

3. Height Feet 5 ▼ Inches 3 ▼

4. Weight Pounds 1 5 0

5. Eye Color (Select **only one** box)

☐ Black ☐ Blue ☐ Brown
☐ Gray ☒ Green ☐ Hazel
☐ Maroon ☐ Pink ☐ Unknown/Other

Sample Form I-130, Petition for Alien Relative—Page 5

Part 3. Biographic Information (continued)

6. Hair Color (Select **only one** box)

   ☐ Bald (No hair) ☐ Black ☒ Blond
   ☐ Brown ☐ Gray ☐ Red
   ☐ Sandy ☐ White ☐ Unknown/Other

Part 4. Information About Beneficiary

1. Alien Registration Number (A-Number) (if any)

   ▶ A-[ ][ ][ ][ ][ ][ ][ ][ ][ ]

2. USCIS Online Account Number (if any)

   ▶ [ ][ ][ ][ ][ ][ ][ ][ ][ ][ ][ ][ ]

3. U.S. Social Security Number (if any)

   ▶ [ ][ ][ ][ ][ ][ ][ ][ ][ ]

Beneficiary's Full Name

4.a. Family Name (Last Name)   Lindsey

4.b. Given Name (First Name)   Edmund

4.c. Middle Name   Alexander

Other Names Used (if any)

Provide all other names the beneficiary has ever used, including aliases, maiden name, and nicknames.

5.a. Family Name (Last Name)

5.b. Given Name (First Name)

5.c. Middle Name

Other Information About Beneficiary

6. City/Town/Village of Birth

   London

7. Country of Birth

   UK

8. Date of Birth (mm/dd/yyyy)   11/21/1977

9. Sex   ☒ Male ☐ Female

10. Has anyone else ever filed a petition for the beneficiary?

    ☐ Yes ☒ No ☐ Unknown

    NOTE: Select "Unknown" *only* if you do not know, and the beneficiary also does not know, if anyone else has ever filed a petition for the beneficiary.

Beneficiary's Physical Address

If the beneficiary lives outside the United States in a home without a street number or name, leave **Item Numbers 11.a.** and **11.b.** blank.

11.a. Street Number and Name   10 Walden Rd.

11.b. ☐ Apt. ☐ Ste. ☐ Flr.

11.c. City or Town   London

11.d. State ▼   11.e. ZIP Code

11.f. Province

11.g. Postal Code   SW1 1AA

11.h. Country

   UK

Other Address and Contact Information

Provide the address in the United States where the beneficiary intends to live, if different from **Item Numbers 11.a. - 11.h.** If the address is the same, type or print "SAME" in **Item Number 12.a.**

12.a. Street Number and Name   432 Fairfax St.

12.b. ☒ Apt. ☐ Ste. ☐ Flr.   A

12.c. City or Town   Alexandria

12.d. State   VA ▼   12.e. ZIP Code   22314

Provide the beneficiary's address outside the United States, if different from **Item Numbers 11.a. - 11.h.** If the address is the same, type or print "SAME" in **Item Number 13.a.**

13.a. Street Number and Name

13.b. ☐ Apt. ☐ Ste. ☐ Flr.

13.c. City or Town

13.d. Province

13.e. Postal Code

13.f. Country

14. Daytime Telephone Number (if any)

   442 073 631323

Sample Form I-130, Petition for Alien Relative—Page 6

Part 4. Information About Beneficiary (continued)

15. Mobile Telephone Number (if any)

16. Email Address (if any)

lealexander@email.com

Beneficiary's Marital Information

17. How many times has the beneficiary been married? ▶

18. Current Marital Status

☐ Single, Never Married ☒ Married ☐ Divorced

☐ Widowed ☐ Separated ☐ Annulled

19. Date of Current Marriage (if currently married) (mm/dd/yyyy) 03/05/2018

Place of Beneficiary's Current Marriage (if married)

20.a. City or Town London

20.b. State ▼

20.c. Province

20.d. Country UK

Names of Beneficiary's Spouses (if any)

Provide information on the beneficiary's current spouse (if currently married) first and then list all the beneficiary's prior spouses (if any).

Spouse 1

21.a. Family Name (Last Name) Debden

21.b. Given Name (First Name) Alice

21.c. Middle Name Anne

22. Date Marriage Ended (mm/dd/yyyy)

Spouse 2

23.a. Family Name (Last Name)

23.b. Given Name (First Name)

23.c. Middle Name

24. Date Marriage Ended (mm/dd/yyyy)

Information About Beneficiary's Family

Provide information about the beneficiary's spouse and children.

Person 1

25.a. Family Name (Last Name) Debden

25.b. Given Name (First Name) Alice

25.c. Middle Name Anne

26. Relationship Spouse

27. Date of Birth (mm/dd/yyyy) 03/03/1978

28. Country of Birth Ireland

Person 2

29.a. Family Name (Last Name)

29.b. Given Name (First Name)

29.c. Middle Name

30. Relationship

31. Date of Birth (mm/dd/yyyy)

32. Country of Birth

Person 3

33.a. Family Name (Last Name)

33.b. Given Name (First Name)

33.c. Middle Name

34. Relationship

35. Date of Birth (mm/dd/yyyy)

36. Country of Birth

Sample Form I-130, Petition for Alien Relative—Page 7

Part 4. Information About Beneficiary (continued)

Person 4

37.a. Family Name (Last Name)

37.b. Given Name (First Name)

37.c. Middle Name

38. Relationship

39. Date of Birth (mm/dd/yyyy)

40. Country of Birth

Person 5

41.a. Family Name (Last Name)

41.b. Given Name (First Name)

41.c. Middle Name

42. Relationship

43. Date of Birth (mm/dd/yyyy)

44. Country of Birth

Beneficiary's Entry Information

45. Was the beneficiary **EVER** in the United States?

☐ Yes ☒ No

If the beneficiary is currently in the United States, complete **Items Numbers 46.a. - 46.d.**

46.a. He or she arrived as a (Class of Admission):

46.b. Form I-94 Arrival-Departure Record Number

▶

46.c. Date of Arrival (mm/dd/yyyy)

46.d. Date authorized stay expired, or will expire, as shown on Form I-94 or Form I-95 (mm/dd/yyyy) or type or print "D/S" for Duration of Status

47. Passport Number

48. Travel Document Number

49. Country of Issuance for Passport or Travel Document

50. Expiration Date for Passport or Travel Document (mm/dd/yyyy)

Beneficiary's Employment Information

Provide the beneficiary's current employment information (if applicable), even if they are employed outside of the United States. If the beneficiary is currently unemployed, type or print "Unemployed" in **Item Number 51.a.**

51.a. Name of Current Employer (if applicable)

London Underground

51.b. Street Number and Name

55 Broadway

51.c. ☐ Apt. ☐ Ste. ☐ Flr.

51.d. City or Town   London

51.e. State ☐   **51.f.** ZIP Code

51.g. Province

51.h. Postal Code   SW1H0BP

51.i. Country

UK

52. Date Employment Began (mm/dd/yyyy)

07/14/2012

Additional Information About Beneficiary

53. Was the beneficiary **EVER** in immigration proceedings?

☐ Yes ☒ No

54. If you answered "Yes," select the type of proceedings and provide the location and date of the proceedings.

☐ Removal ☐ Exclusion/Deportation

☐ Rescission ☐ Other Judicial Proceedings

55.a. City or Town

55.b. State ☐

56. Date (mm/dd/yyyy)

Sample Form I-130, Petition for Alien Relative—Page 8

Part 4. Information About Beneficiary (continued)

If the beneficiary's native written language does not use Roman letters, type or print his or her name and foreign address in their native written language.

57.a. Family Name (Last Name)

57.b. Given Name (First Name)

57.c. Middle Name

58.a. Street Number and Name

58.b. ☐ Apt. ☐ Ste. ☐ Flr.

58.c. City or Town

58.d. Province

58.e. Postal Code

58.f. Country

If filing for your spouse, provide the last address at which you physically lived together. If you never lived together, type or print, "Never lived together" in Item Number 59.a.

59.a. Street Number and Name — 10 Walden Rd

59.b. ☐ Apt. ☐ Ste. ☐ Flr.

59.c. City or Town — London

59.d. State ☐▼ **59.e.** ZIP Code

59.f. Province

59.g. Postal Code

59.h. Country — UK

60.a. Date From (mm/dd/yyyy) — 11/01/2015

60.b. Date To (mm/dd/yyyy) — 04/15/2016

The beneficiary is in the United States and will apply for adjustment of status to that of a lawful permanent resident at the U.S. Citizenship and Immigration Services (USCIS) office in:

61.a. City or Town

61.b. State ☐▼

The beneficiary will not apply for adjustment of status in the United States, but he or she will apply for an immigrant visa abroad at the U.S. Embassy or U.S. Consulate in:

62.a. City or Town

62.b. Province

62.c. Country

NOTE: Choosing a U.S. Embassy or U.S. Consulate outside the country of the beneficiary's last residence does not guarantee that it will accept the beneficiary's case for processing. In these situations, the designated U.S. Embassy or U.S. Consulate has discretion over whether or not to accept the beneficiary's case.

Part 5. Other Information

1. Have you **EVER** previously filed a petition for this beneficiary or any other alien? ☐ Yes ☒ No

If you answered "Yes," provide the name, place, date of filing, and the result.

2.a. Family Name (Last Name)

2.b. Given Name (First Name)

2.c. Middle Name

3.a. City or Town

3.b. State

4. Date Filed (mm/dd/yyyy)

5. Result (for example, approved, denied, withdrawn)

If you are also submitting separate petitions for other relatives, provide the names of and your relationship to each relative.

Relative 1

6.a. Family Name (Last Name)

6.b. Given Name (First Name)

6.c. Middle Name

7. Relationship

Sample Form I-130, Petition for Alien Relative—Page 9

Part 5. Other Information (continued)

Relative 2

8.a. Family Name
(Last Name)

8.b. Given Name
(First Name)

8.c. Middle Name

9. Relationship

WARNING: USCIS investigates the claimed relationships and verifies the validity of documents you submit. If you falsify a family relationship to obtain a visa, USCIS may seek to have you criminally prosecuted.

PENALTIES: By law, you may be imprisoned for up to 5 years or fined $250,000, or both, for entering into a marriage contract in order to evade any U.S. immigration law. In addition, you may be fined up to $10,000 and imprisoned for up to 5 years, or both, for knowingly and willfully falsifying or concealing a material fact or using any false document in submitting this petition.

Part 6. Petitioner's Statement, Contact Information, Declaration, and Signature

NOTE: Read the **Penalties** section of the Form I-130 Instructions before completing this part.

Petitioner's Statement

NOTE: Select the box for either **Item Number 1.a.** or **1.b.** If applicable, select the box for **Item Number 2.**

1.a. ☒ I can read and understand English, and I have read and understand every question and instruction on this petition and my answer to every question.

1.b. ☐ The interpreter named in **Part 7.** read to me every question and instruction on this petition and my answer to every question in

_____,
a language in which I am fluent. I understood all of this information as interpreted.

2. ☐ At my request, the preparer named in **Part 8.**,

_____,
prepared this petition for me based only upon information I provided or authorized.

Petitioner's Contact Information

3. Petitioner's Daytime Telephone Number

703-555-1212

4. Petitioner's Mobile Telephone Number (if any)

5. Petitioner's Email Address (if any)

aliced@email.com

Petitioner's Declaration and Certification

Copies of any documents I have submitted are exact photocopies of unaltered, original documents, and I understand that USCIS may require that I submit original documents to USCIS at a later date. Furthermore, I authorize the release of any information from any of my records that USCIS may need to determine my eligibility for the immigration benefit I seek.

I further authorize release of information contained in this petition, in supporting documents, and in my USCIS records to other entities and persons where necessary for the administration and enforcement of U.S. immigration laws.

I understand that USCIS may require me to appear for an appointment to take my biometrics (fingerprints, photograph, and/or signature) and, at that time, if I am required to provide biometrics, I will be required to sign an oath reaffirming that:

1) I provided or authorized all of the information contained in, and submitted with, my petition;

2) I reviewed and understood all of the information in, and submitted with, my petition; and

3) All of this information was complete, true, and correct at the time of filing.

I certify, under penalty of perjury, that all of the information in my petition and any document submitted with it were provided or authorized by me, that I reviewed and understand all of the information contained in, and submitted with, my petition, and that all of this information is complete, true, and correct.

Petitioner's Signature

6.a. Petitioner's Signature (sign in ink)

➡ *Alice Anne Debden*

6.b. Date of Signature (mm/dd/yyyy)   03/01/2019

NOTE TO ALL PETITIONERS: If you do not completely fill out this petition or fail to submit required documents listed in the Instructions, USCIS may deny your petition.

Question 41: A petitioning U.S. spouse who checks "yes" here, to indicate having received U.S. permanent residence through marriage, must calculate how long it has been since the approval for permanent residence. A petitioning spouse who immigrated through marriage cannot petition for a new spouse for five years, unless the first spouse died or the U.S. spouse can prove by "clear and convincing evidence" that the previous marriage was bona fide (real). USCIS is concerned that the first marriage was just a sham, with the long-term goal of getting both of you into the United States by piggybacking on a sham marriage. To prove that the first marriage was bona fide, enclose documentary evidence showing that the couple shared a life, such as shared rent receipts, club memberships, children's birth certificates, utility bills, and insurance agreements. Will USCIS find this evidence to be "clear and convincing"? Unfortunately, this legal standard is easy to state but hard to pin down or apply. The bottom line is that the U.S. spouse has a lot of proving to do to persuade a suspicious government official that the previous marriage was bona fide.

Questions 42-49: Fill in the U.S. petitioner's employment history from the last five years. If there have been more than two jobs, list the ones that don't fit in Part 9.

Part 3:

Questions 1-5: Provide basic biographic information on the U.S. petitioner.

Part 4

Now the questions refer to you, the immigrant beneficiary.

Question 1: The Alien Registration Number is an eight- or nine-digit number following a letter A that USCIS assigns to immigrants who've previously applied for permanent or, in some cases, temporary residence; or been in deportation/removal proceedings. (Of course, if the previous application was denied because the immigrant was found inadmissible or lied on that application, call a lawyer before going any further.)

Question 2: If you have ever filed a petition with USCIS, you may have a USCIS Online Account Number.

Question 3: If immigrant has no Social Security number, write "None." An immigrant probably wouldn't have a Social Security number without having lived in the United States with a work permit, a visa allowing work, or U.S. residence.

Question 4: Your current name.

Question 5: Enter any names you have previously used. If you were previously married and used another name then, include it here.

Questions 6-10: Self-explanatory.

Question 11: Your current address outside of the United States.

Questions 12-13: Self-explanatory. Hopefully, your intended address will be the same as that of your spouse, or USCIS may raise questions.

Questions 14-16: Self-explanatory.

Question 17: Answer how many times you have been married, including this time.

Question 18: This refers only to your most recent marital status, so check "married," even if there was a previous divorce.

Questions 19-20: Self-explanatory.

Questions 21-24: Name current spouse first and then any past spouses. Put "N/A" under the date marriage ended for your current marriage. The question of when any prior marriage(s) ended is intended to make sure your current marriage is valid. If your prior marriage(s) ended after your present marriage began, yours is not a lawful marriage. If you have just discovered that the divorce wasn't final when your marriage took place, it may not be necessary to run to a lawyer. Assuming that the divorce has since become final, you can correct the problem by remarrying. (If there was fraud involved in your hasty marriage, consult a lawyer before proceeding.)

Questions 25-44: Although the U.S. spouse is already covered in this application, it's safest to list him or her again before listing children, if any. This means all children, including any by previous relationships.

Question 45: If the immigrant has ever been to the United States, even for a short time as a tourist, check "Yes."

Questions 46-50: Because the immigrant is currently overseas, you do not need to complete these questions about U.S. entry documents and passport.

Questions 51-52: Fill in current employment information. If the immigrant is not working, enter "unemployed" or "student," if applicable.

Questions 53-56: If the would-be immigrant has ever been in Immigration Court (removal or deportation) proceedings, consult a lawyer before continuing. He or she may be inadmissible to the U.S. or need a special waiver.

Questions 57-58: If the immigrant's native language uses a non-Roman script (for example, Russian, Chinese, or Arabic), you will need to write the name and address in that script.

Questions 59-60: If you've ever lived together, put the last address here. If not, write "N/A" or "never lived together."

Question 61: Because the immigrant is currently overseas, you do not need to answer this.

Question 62: Enter the name of the U.S. consulate with a visa processing office in the immigrant's country; or if none exists, the one with the power to handle visa requests from your country. (Don't worry about getting it wrong; USCIS will redirect the application when it approves the petition.)

Part 5

Now we're back to questions about the petitioning spouse.

Questions 1-5: These are meant to uncover the permanent resident spouse's history (if any) of petitioning other immigrants to come to the United States. A petitioning spouse who has a history of short marriages to people whom he/she then helped to obtain green cards should expect a major marriage fraud investigation. Consult a lawyer before proceeding.

Questions 6-9: These refer to other petitions being submitted simultaneously (for example, for the immigrant's children from this or other marriages),

so that USCIS can process the petitions together. Enter the children's names here.

Part 6

The U.S. permanent resident petitioner should fill out this section with contact information and signature.

Parts 7 and 8

If filling this form out unassisted, write "N/A" here. A little typing assistance or advice from a friend doesn't count—the only people who need to complete this line are lawyers or agencies who fill out forms on others' behalf or offer translation services.

ii. Form I-130A

The information you (the immigrant) supply on this form will allow the U.S. government to check your background. Most of the form is self-explanatory.

If you really can't remember or are unable to find out an exact date, enter whatever you can remember, such as the year. Alternately, you can simply say "unknown," but if you overuse the "unknowns" USCIS may return your entire application for another try.

> **WEB RESOURCE**
> **Form I-130A is available on the USCIS** website at www.uscis.gov/i-130. Below is a sample filled-in version of the relevant pages of this form (done by the immigrating half of the couple).

Part 1

Question 1: The Alien Registration Number is an eight- or nine-digit number following a letter A that USCIS (or the formerly named INS) would have assigned if you (the immigrant) previously applied for permanent (or, in some cases, temporary) residence or were in deportation/removal proceedings. Of course, if that previous application was denied because you were inadmissible or lied on that application, call a lawyer before going any further.

Question 2: An immigrant who filed a past petition with USCIS might have a USCIS Online Account Number.

Sample Form I-130A, Supplemental Information for Spouse Beneficiary–Page 1

Supplemental Information for Spouse Beneficiary		**USCIS Form I-130A**
Department of Homeland Security		OMB No. 1615-0012
U.S. Citizenship and Immigration Services		Expires 02/28/2021

To be completed by an attorney or accredited representative (if any).			
☐ **Select this box if Form G-28 is attached.**	**Volag Number** (if any)	**Attorney State Bar Number** (if applicable)	**Attorney or Accredited Representative USCIS Online Account Number** (if any)

▶ **START HERE - Type or print in black ink.**

The purpose of this form is to collect additional information for a spouse beneficiary of Form I-130, Petition for Alien Relative. If your spouse is a U.S. citizen, lawful permanent resident, or non-citizen U.S. national who is filing Form I-130 on your behalf, you must complete and sign Form I-130A, Supplemental Information for Spouse Beneficiary, and submit it with the Form I-130 filed by your spouse. If you reside overseas, you still must complete Form I-130A, but you do not need to sign the form.

Part 1. Information About You (Spouse Beneficiary)

1. Alien Registration Number (A-Number) (if any)

▶ A-

2. USCIS Online Account Number (if any)

▶

Your Full Name

3.a. Family Name (Last Name) Lindsey

3.b. Given Name (First Name) Edmund

3.c. Middle Name Alexander

Address History

Provide your physical addresses for the last five years, whether inside or outside the United States. Provide your current address first. If you need extra space to complete this section, use the space provided in **Part 7. Additional Information.**

Physical Address 1

4.a. Street Number and Name 10 Walden Rd

4.b. ☐ Apt. ☐ Ste. ☐ Flr.

4.c. City or Town London

4.d. State ▼ **4.e.** ZIP Code

4.f. Province

4.g. Postal Code SW1 1AA

4.h. Country UK

5.a. Date From (mm/dd/yyyy) 09/01/2006

5.b. Date To (mm/dd/yyyy) **PRESENT**

Physical Address 2

6.a. Street Number and Name

6.b. ☐ Apt. ☐ Ste. ☐ Flr.

6.c. City or Town

6.d. State ▼ **6.e.** ZIP Code

6.f. Province

6.g. Postal Code

6.h. Country

7.a. Date From (mm/dd/yyyy)

7.b. Date To (mm/dd/yyyy)

Last Physical Address Outside the United States

Provide your last address outside the United States of more than one year (even if listed above).

8.a. Street Number and Name 10 Walden Rd

8.b. ☐ Apt. ☐ Ste. ☐ Flr.

8.c. City or Town London

8.d. Province

8.e. Postal Code SW1 1AA

8.f. Country UK

Sample Form I-130A, Supplemental Information for Spouse Beneficiary–Page 2

Part 1. Information About You (The Spouse Beneficiary)

9.a. Date From (mm/dd/yyyy)

9.b. Date To (mm/dd/yyyy)

Information About Parent 1

Full Name of Parent 1

10.a. Family Name (Maiden Name): Lindsey

10.b. Given Name (First Name): Thomas

10.c. Middle Name: Andrew

11. Date of Birth (mm/dd/yyyy): 10/22/1955

12. Sex: ☒ Male ☐ Female

13. City/Town/Village of Birth: London

14. Country of Birth: UK

15. City/Town/Village of Residence: London

16. Country of Residence: UK

Information About Parent 2

Full Name of Parent 2

17.a. Family Name (Last Name): Herries

17.b. Given Name (First Name): Janice

17.c. Middle Name: Rose

18. Date of Birth (mm/dd/yyyy): 08/17/1959

19. Sex: ☐ Male ☒ Female

20. City/Town/Village of Birth: Haddington

21. Country of Birth: UK

22. City/Town/Village of Residence: London

23. Country of Residence: UK

Part 2. Information About Your Employment

Provide your employment history for the last five years, whether inside or outside the United States. Provide your current employment first. If you are currently unemployed, type or print "Unemployed" in **Item Number 1.** below. If you need extra space to complete this section, use the space provided in **Part 7. Additional Information**.

Employment History

Employer 1

1. Name of Employer/Company: London Underground

2.a. Street Number and Name: 55 Broadway

2.b. ☐ Apt. ☐ Ste. ☐ Flr.

2.c. City or Town: London

2.d. State: ▼   2.e. ZIP Code

2.f. Province

2.g. Postal Code: SW1H 0BD

2.h. Country: UK

3. Your Occupation: Asst. Fleets manager

4.a. Date From (mm/dd/yyyy): 07/15/2010

4.b. Date To (mm/dd/yyyy): PRESENT

Employer 2

5. Name of Employer/Company

6.a. Street Number and Name

6.b. ☐ Apt. ☐ Ste. ☐ Flr.

6.c. City or Town

6.d. State: ▼   6.e. ZIP Code

6.f. Province

6.g. Postal Code

6.h. Country

Sample Form I-130A, Supplemental Information for Spouse Beneficiary–Page 3

Part 2. Information About Your Employment (continued)

7. Your Occupation

8.a. Date From (mm/dd/yyyy)

8.b. Date To (mm/dd/yyyy)

Part 3. Information About Your Employment Outside the United States

Provide your last occupation outside the United States if not shown above. If you never worked outside the United States, provide this information in the space provided in **Part 7. Additional Information**.

1. Name of Employer/Company

2.a. Street Number and Name

2.b. ☐ Apt. ☐ Ste. ☐ Flr.

2.c. City or Town

2.d. State ▼ **2.e.** ZIP Code

2.f. Province

2.g. Postal Code

2.h. Country

3. Your Occupation

4.a. Date From (mm/dd/yyyy)

4.b. Date To (mm/dd/yyyy)

Part 4. Spouse Beneficiary's Statement, Contact Information, Certification, and Signature

NOTE: Read the **Penalties** section of the Form I-130 and Form I-130A Instructions before completing this part.

Spouse Beneficiary's Statement

NOTE: Select the box for either **Item Number 1.a.** or **1.b.** If applicable, select the box for **Item Number 2.**

1.a. ☒ I can read and understand English, and I have read and understand every question and instruction on this form and my answer to every question.

1.b. ☐ The interpreter named in **Part 5.** read to me every question and instruction on this form and my answer to every question in

a language in which I am fluent, and I understood everything.

2. ☐ At my request, the preparer name in **Part 6.**,

prepared this form for me based only upon information I provided or authorized.

Spouse Beneficiary's Contact Information

3. Spouse Beneficiary's Daytime Telephone Number

442073631323

4. Spouse Beneficiary's Mobile Telephone Number (if any)

5. Spouse Beneficiary's Email Address (if any)

lealexander@email.com

Spouse Beneficiary's Certification

Copies of any documents I have submitted are exact photocopies of unaltered, original documents, and I understand that USCIS may require that I submit original documents to USCIS at a later date. Furthermore, I authorize the release of any information from any of my records that USCIS may need to determine my eligibility for the immigration benefit I seek.

I further authorize release of information contained in this form, in supporting documents, and in my USCIS records to other entities and persons where necessary for the administration and enforcement of U.S. immigration laws.

I certify, under penalty of perjury, that I provided or authorized all of the information in this form, I understand all of the information contained in, and submitted with, my form, and that all of this information is complete, true, and correct.

Spouse Beneficiary's Signature

6.a. Spouse Beneficiary's Signature (sign in ink)

➡ *Edmund A. Lindsey*

6.b. Date of Signature (mm/dd/yyyy) 03/01/2019

NOTE TO ALL SPOUSE BENEFICIARIES: If you do not completely fill out this form or fail to submit required documents listed in the Instructions, USCIS may deny the Form I-130 filed on your behalf.

Question 3: Enter your full, current name. Use your married name if it was changed at the time you wed.

Questions 4-9: Fill in all your addresses from the last five years. Any that don't fit can be included in Part 7. If you have lived at more than one address in the last five years, make sure to include the start and end dates of the other addresses.

Questions 10-23: Answer basic biographic information about your parents. If you do not know any answers, enter "unknown."

Part 2

Questions 1-8: Fill in your current job information (inside or outside the U.S.) for the last five years. If you are not working, enter "unemployed" or "student," if applicable. If you have had more than two jobs in the past five years, attach additional information in Part 7.

Part 3

Include information about your most recent employment outside of the U.S. if it's not already listed in Part 2.

Part 4

Fill out this section with your contact information and signature.

b. Documents to Have on Hand for I-130 Petition

The I-130 petition asks you to submit supporting documents along with the form. Among these are the following, which are listed on the Checklist in Subsection e:

- **Proof of the U.S. permanent resident status of your petitioning spouse.** To prove permanent residency, your spouse should make a copy of his or her green card (front and back). If your spouse hasn't yet been issued a green card, a copy of the stamp placed in his or her passport indicating permanent residence will be sufficient. Or, your spouse can submit a copy of the Form I-797 notice approving his or her permanent resident status, if issued one.

- **Proof that you're legally married.** This should include at a minimum a copy of your marriage certificate, most likely from a government source (see Chapter 4, Section C, for details). In addition, if either you or your spouse have been previously married, you must include proof that these marriages were terminated, such as a copy of a death, divorce, or annulment certificate.

- **Proof that the marriage is bona fide.** Include a select few items of evidence to show that your marriage is not a sham, but a real spousal relationship. For instance, copies of documents showing you've spent time or lived together (such as a lease or mortgage agreement, bills sent to the house, and letters sent to the house for each spouse) are good, as are copies of joint financial accounts (bank and credit statements, loans, insurance policies). Of less weight are things like joint memberships and photos taken with friends and family; you might want to save these for the in-person interview, when the issue of bona fide marriage will come up again.

- **Photos.** You and your spouse must each submit two color passport-style photos, 2 x 2 inches in size, taken within the past six months, showing your current appearances. Passport style means that the photo shows your full face from the front, with a plain white or off-white background—and your face must measure between one inch and $1\frac{3}{8}$ inches from the bottom of your chin to the top of your head. For more information, see the State Department website. However, USCIS regulations permit you to submit a photo that doesn't completely follow the instructions if you live in a country where such photographs are unavailable or are cost prohibitive.

- **Fees.** The current fee for an I-130 petition is $535. However, these fees go up fairly regularly, so double-check this on the USCIS website at www.uscis.gov, or by calling USCIS at 800-375-5283.

Where to Send the Form I-130 Petition			
If the U.S. petitioner lives in:			**Send Form I-130 to:**

Alaska
American Samoa
Arizona
California
Colorado
Florida
Guam
Hawaii
Idaho
	Kansas
	Montana
	Nebraska
	Nevada
	New Mexico
	North Dakota
	Northern Mariana Islands
	Oklahoma
		Oregon
		Puerto Rico
		South Dakota
		Texas
		Utah
		Virgin Islands
		Washington
		Wyoming
			USCIS Phoenix Lockbox
			For U.S. Postal Service (USPS) deliveries:
			  USCIS ATTN: I-130
			  P.O. Box 21700
			  Phoenix, AZ 85036
			For courier deliveries:
			  USCIS
			  Attn: I-130
			  1820 E. Skyharbor Circle S
			  Suite 100
			  Phoenix, AZ 85034

Alabama
Arkansas
Connecticut
Delaware
District of Columbia
Georgia
Illinois
Indiana
Iowa
Kentucky
Louisiana
	Maine
	Maryland
	Massachusetts
	Michigan
	Minnesota
	Mississippi
	Missouri
	New Hampshire
	New Jersey
	New York
		North Carolina
		Ohio
		Pennsylvania
		Rhode Island
		South Carolina
		Tennessee
		Vermont
		Virginia
		West Virginia
		Wisconsin
			USCIS Chicago Lockbox
			For U.S. Postal Service:
			  USCIS
			  P.O. Box 804625
			  Chicago, IL 60680-4107
			For courier deliveries:
			  USCIS
			  Attn: I-130
			  131 South Dearborn–3rd Floor
			  Chicago, IL 60603-5517

If the U.S. petitioner lives outside the U.S., send Form I-130 to:			

USCIS Chicago Lockbox
For U.S. Postal Service (USPS) deliveries:
  USCIS
  P.O. Box 804625
  Chicago, IL 60680-4107
		For courier deliveries:
		  USCIS
		  Attn: I-130
		  131 South Dearborn-3rd Floor
		  Chicago, IL 60603-5517	

c. Where to Send I-130 Petition

After your spouse has prepared and assembled all the forms and other items from the checklist below, (including the I-130A and photos that you'll have to send him or her) your spouse should make photocopies for your records. Then your spouse must send the packet to the USCIS "lockbox" office for the region where he or she lives. Priority mail is the safest way to send anything to USCIS.

The address is below. You can double-check this information on the USCIS website.

If your spouse lives outside the United States or its territories, he or she should contact the nearest U.S. consulate about where to send the petition.

d. What Happens After Sending in the Form I-130 Petition

A few weeks after your spouse sends in your petition, he or she should get a receipt notice from a USCIS service center (a different office from the lockbox the I-130 was sent to—the lockbox will have forwarded the file to a USCIS service center). The receipt notice will tell you to check the USCIS

Sample I-130 Receipt Notice

Department of Homeland Security U.S. Citizenship and Immigration Services	**Form I-797C, Notice of Action**

THIS NOTICE DOES NOT GRANT ANY IMMIGRATION STATUS OR BENEFIT.

NOTICE TYPE **Receipt**	NOTICE DATE **August 20, 2019**

CASE TYPE **I130 IMMIGRANT PETITION FOR RELATIVE, FIANCE(E), OR ORPHAN**	USCIS ALIEN NUMBER

RECEIPT NUMBER **WAC-19-054-00000**	RECEIVED DATE **August 6, 2019**	PAGE **1 of 1**

PRIORITY DATE	PREFERENCE CLASSIFICATION **203(a)(2) (A) INA SPOUSE OF LPR**	DATE OF BIRTH **November 21, 1977**

ILONA BRAY
RE: EDMUND ALEXANDER LINDSEY
950 PARKER STREET
BERKELEY, CA 94710

PAYMENT INFORMATION:

Application/Petition Fee:	$535.00
Biometrics Fee:	$0.00
Total Amount Received:	$535.00
Total Balance Due:	$0.00

APPLICANT/PETITIONER NAME AND MAILING ADDRESS

The I-130, Petition for Alien Relative has been received by our office for the following beneficiaries and is in process:

Name	Date of Birth	Country of Birth	Class (If Applicable)
LINDSEY, EDMUND ALEXANDER	11/21/1977	U.K.	

Please verify your personal information listed above and immediately notify the USCIS National Customer Service Center at the phone number listed below if there are any changes.

Please note that if a priority date is printed on this notice, the priority does not reflect earlier retained priority dates.

If you have questions about possible immigration benefits and services, filing information, or USCIS forms, please call the USCIS National Customer Service Center (NCSC) at **1-800-375-5283**. If you are hearing impaired, please call the NCSC TDD at **1-800-767-1833**. Please also refer to the USCIS website: www.uscis.gov.

If you have any questions or comments regarding this notice or the status of your case, please contact our customer service number.

You will be notified separately about any other case you may have filed.

USCIS Office Address:	USCIS Customer Service Number:
USCIS Nebraska Service Center P.O. Box 82521 Lincoln, NE 68501-2521	(800)375-5283 ATTORNEY COPY

If this is an interview or biometrics appointment notice, please see the back of this notice for important information. | Form I-797C 07/11/14 Y

Sample I-130 Approval Notice

Department of Homeland Security
U.S. Citizenship and Immigration Services

I-797, Notice of Action

THE UNITED STATES OF AMERICA

RECEIPT NUMBER		CASE TYPE	IMMIGRANT PETITION FOR RELATIVE, FIANCE(E), OR ORPHAN
WAC-19-054-00000			
RECEIPT DATE	PRIORITY DATE	PETITIONER	
December 15, 2020	August 15, 2019	LINDSEY, EDMUND	
NOTICE DATE	PAGE	BENEFICIARY	
APRIL 1 1, 2021		DEBDEN, ALICE	

ILONA BRAY RE: EDMUND ALEXANDER LINDSEY 950 PARKER STREET BERKELEY, CA 94710	Notice Type: Approval Notice Section: Husband or wife of U.S. permanent resident, 203(a)(2)(A)(e) INA

This notice is to advise you of action taken on this case. The official notice has been mailed according to the mailing preferences noted on the Form G-28, Notice of Entry of Appearance as Attorney or Accredited Representative. Any relevant documentation was mailed according to the specified mailing preferences.

The above petition has been approved. The petition indicates that the person for whom you are petitioning is in the United States and will apply for adjustment of status. He or she should contact the local USCIS office to obtain Form I-485, Application for Permanent Residence. A copy of this notice should be submitted with the application.

If the person for whom you are petitioning decides to apply for a visa outside the United States based on this petition, the petitioner should file Form I-824, Application for Action on an Approved Application or Petition, to request that we send the petition to the Department of State National Visa Center (NVC).

The NVC processes all approved immigrant visa petitions that require consular action. The NVC also determines which consular post is the appropriate consulate to complete visa processing. It will then forward the approved petition to that consulate.

The approval of this visa petition does not in itself grant any immigration status and does not guarantee that the alien beneficiary will subsequently be found to be eligible for a visa, for admission to the United States, or for an extension, change, or adjustment of status.

This courtesy copy may not be used in lieu of official notification to demonstrate the filing or processing action taken on this case.

THIS FORM IS NOT A VISA AND MAY NOT BE USED IN PLACE OF A VISA.

NOTICE: Although this application/petition has been approved, USCIS and the U.S. Department of Homeland Security reserve the right to verify the information submitted in this application, petition and/or supporting documentation to ensure conformity with applicable laws, rules, regulations, and other authorities. Methods used for verifying information may include, but are not limited to, the review of public information and records, contact by correspondence, the internet, or telephone, and site inspections of businesses and residences. Information obtained during the course of verification will be used to determine whether revocation, rescission, and/or removal proceedings are appropriate. Applicants, petitioners, and representatives of record will be provided an opportunity to address derogatory information before any formal proceeding is initiated.

Please see the additional information on the back. You will be notified separately about any other cases you filed.
NEBRASKA SERVICE CENTER
U. S. CITIZENSHIP & IMMIG SERVICE
P.O. BOX 82521
LINCOLN   NE   68501-2521
Customer Service Telephone: 800-375-5283

Form I-797 (Rev. 01/31/05) N

website for information on how long the application is likely to remain in processing. A sample receipt notice is included below.

In a way, how long your I-130 petition spends in processing doesn't matter. As soon as the petition is received by USCIS, you've established your place in line (known as your Priority Date, which we'll discuss in Section 2, below). And no matter when the petition is approved, you'll have to wait from that Priority Date until a visa becomes available to you. For that reason, USCIS sometimes takes its time making a decision on these petitions—the wait was between five and 25 months when this book went to press.

You can check current processing times when your spouse files by going to the USCIS website at www.uscis.gov and clicking "Check Processing Times." Select Form I-130, then your service center from the dropdown list (look at the bottom of your Form I-797C), click "Get processing time," look under the classification "Permanent resident filing for a spouse, parent, or child under 21."

If your petition is within the normal processing time, USCIS will ignore any inquiry from you or your spouse asking about its progress. These service centers seem like walled fortresses—you can't visit them, and it's impossible to speak with the person who's actually working on your case. If you still don't have a decision on your case after USCIS's normal processing time has passed, then call 800-375-5283, where a live person will take your questions from 8 a.m. to 9 p.m. Eastern time.

Although the person you speak with will most likely not be able to tell you anything useful during that phone call, he or she will start an inquiry for you and tell you when to expect a response. Alternatively, you can submit the inquiry yourself directly as an e-Request on USCIS's website (https:// egov.uscis.gov/e-request/Intro.do). (See Chapter 15 for more on what to do if you don't get a timely answer from the USCIS service center.) If USCIS needs additional documentation to complete your application, it will send your spouse a Request for Evidence (RFE) asking for it. Similarly, if USCIS considers denying the case based on negative evidence obtained by other means, it will notify your spouse and give an opportunity to respond.

Eventually, your spouse will receive an approval or a denial of the petition.

i. If the Petition Is Denied

If the petition is denied, the fastest thing to do is to fix the problem and try again. For example, if the denial was because your petitioning spouse did not appear to be actually divorced from a previous spouse, your spouse will need to see a lawyer and obtain new and better documentation showing that there had been a final divorce. Then your spouse can file a new petition.

ii. If the I-130 Petition Is Approved

When your I-130 petition is approved, your spouse will receive a notice from the USCIS service center. An example of a petition approval notice is shown below. As you can see, it's nothing fancy. But it is an important document. Make a few photocopies of it and store these and the original in safe places. Note the "Priority Date" listed in the box of that name—that is the date that USCIS received the I-130 petition your spouse filed for you, and that date will become very important in determining your place on the waiting list, as discussed in Section 2, below.

At the same time that the USCIS service center notifies your spouse of the approval of your petition, it will forward your case to the National Visa Center (NVC) in New Hampshire. This office will then take over and maintain your file through Step Two.

e. Using the Checklist for Step One, I-130 Petition

When you put it all together, the petition that your spouse files will include three forms and some supporting documents, photos, and a fee, as detailed on the checklist below. As you fill out and prepare your paperwork, mark off the items that you've found or finished with on your checklist.

CHECKLIST
Appendix B includes instructions on where to get a copy of this checklist online.

Checklist for I-130 Petition by Lawful Permanent Resident

☐ Form I-130 (see line-by-line instructions in Subsection A1a, above)

☐ Documents to accompany Form I-130:

  ☐ Proof of the U.S. permanent resident status of your petitioning spouse (see Subsection A1b, above)

  ☐ Copy of your marriage certificate (see Chapter 4, Section C, for how to obtain such documents)

  ☐ Proof of bona fide marriage, such as copies of joint mortgage or rental agreements, bank and credit card accounts, insurance, and more

  ☐ Copies of proof of termination of all previous marriages, yours or your spouse's, such as certificates of death, divorce, or annulment

  ☐ Two color photos of you (passport style)

  ☐ Two color photos of your spouse (passport style)

  ☐ Fee: currently $535 (see Subsection A1b, above)

☐ Form I-130A, Supplemental Information on Spouse Beneficiary (see line-by-line instructions in subsection A1a, above)

---

2. Step Two: The Waiting Period (Your "Priority Date")

Visa waiting periods are not set periods of time. Some attorneys tell their clients, "It will probably be two years"—then when two years go by and the visa hasn't come through, the clients worry that something has gone wrong. The truth is that waiting periods are only partly predictable. They depend on visa supply and demand, combined with monthly decisions by the U.S. government.

You won't know for sure how long you'll have to wait until your wait is almost over. This section will help you to understand the mechanics of this wait and how to deal with it.

a. Preference Categories

As the spouse of a lawful permanent resident, you're known as a "preference relative." The U.S. government ranks preference relatives, usually giving visas quicker to those at the top. As you'll see, you are in the second category down ("2A" or "F2A"). This means that the U.S. government has allotted a higher priority to your visa than to those of the people in categories 3 and 4. Here is how the preferences are arranged:

- **First Preference:** The unmarried sons or daughters of a U.S. citizen who are over 21 and are therefore no longer considered children. (If they were still children, they could qualify as immediate relatives, who are immediately eligible for visas.)
- **Second Preference:** The second preference category, which is where you fit, is actually made up of two subcategories, each with different waiting periods. In subcategory 2A are spouses or unmarried sons or daughters under age 21 of a permanent resident (green card holder). In subcategory 2B are the unmarried sons and daughters *over* age 21 of a permanent resident (they usually wait longer than 2As).
- **Third Preference:** The married sons or daughters, any age, of a U.S. citizen.
- **Fourth Preference:** The brothers or sisters of a U.S. citizen. The citizen must be age 21 or older.

b. How Visas Are Allotted Year by Year

Each year, the U.S. government allots a certain number of immigrant visas in each preference category. For purposes of visa allocation, the government follows its fiscal year, which starts and ends in October. This might affect you if the government runs out of visas for your category before October. You'll know at that point that you have no chance of advancing on the waiting list until the "new year" begins October 1.

Currently, the total worldwide numbers are:

- **First Preference:** 23,400, plus any visas not used for fourth preference

- **Second Preference:** 114,200, with 77% of these going to category 2A, 23% to category 2B
- **Third Preference:** 23,400, plus any not used for first and second preference, and
- **Fourth Preference:** 65,000 plus any not used for the first three preferences.

This may sound like a lot of visas, but far more people want immigrant visas than can get them every year. The government gives out visas month by month, making sure never to go over the annual limit.

There are also limits on the number of visas allowed for any one country. No more than 7% of the total visas each year can go to any one country, and often the percentage turns out to be less.

There are more complexities to the allocation and numbers of these visas, but a full understanding of these numbers won't help you speed up your waiting time. The important thing to know is how to chart your own place on the visa waiting list.

c. How to Chart Your Place on the Waiting List

It would be nice if you could just call the government and ask how long you have to wait for your green card. No such luck. Instead, the State Department publishes a monthly *Visa Bulletin*, the one source of information on visa waiting periods. The *Visa Bulletin* is accessible online at www.travel.state.gov (click "U.S. Visas" then "Check the Visa Bulletin").

The *Visa Bulletin* comes out monthly, around the middle of the month, but not on any particular day. Due to recent changes, it now includes two sections, instead of one: Section A ("Application Final Action

Dates"), which shows the "visa cutoff dates" for immigrants who are eligible to *receive* a green card or visa (as explained below) and Section B ("Dates for Filing"), which shows cutoff dates for immigrants eligible to *begin* their portion of the application process for the green card or visa. Below is a sample of what a family-based chart in the *Visa Bulletin* looks like.

Although it's confusing at first glance, you will be able to make your way through this chart. Here's how:

1. Locate your preference category (2A or F2A) in the left column.
2. Locate your country across the top. China, India, Mexico, and the Philippines often have their own columns because of the large number of applicants—as a result, people from these countries wait longer than others. All other countries are included in the second column called "All Chargeability Areas Except Those Listed."
3. Draw a line across from your preference category (2A or F2A) and down from your country of origin. Where the two lines cross is what is called the visa cutoff or final action date—the key date that you will compare with your own Priority Date to chart your progress.

Every prospective immigrant has his or her own Priority Date—the date that USCIS first received their I-130. Your Priority Date is on the approval notice you received after the initial approval of your Form I-130 petition. Prospective immigrants whose Priority Dates are at or earlier than the cutoff date listed in Section B of that month's bulletin should

Final Action Dates for March 2019					
Family-Sponsored	All Chargeability Areas Except Those Listed	CHINA—mainland born	INDIA	MEXICO	PHILIPPINES
F1	22OCT11	22OCT11	22OCT11	01AUG97	01APR07
F2A	08JAN17	08JAN17	08JAN17	15DEC16	08JAN17
F2B	01AUG12	01AUG12	01AUG12	22SEP97	22JUL07
F3	08SEP06	08SEP06	08SEP06	15JAN96	01JAN96
F4	22SEP05	22SEP05	08JUL04	08FEB98	01JAN96

soon be contacted by NVC to start the process, while those whose Priority Dates are at or earlier than the cutoff date listed in Section A of that month's bulletin will become eligible to receive visas or green cards.

The earlier your Priority Date, the better off you are, because it means you are in line ahead of other applicants. But as you can see, the current cutoff date doesn't tell you how long it will be before your own visa or green card is issued.

Look again at the example of the USCIS approval notice in Subsection 1d, above. The Priority Date is in the middle of the second line, and says August 15, 2019. The following examples will help you understand how to read the *Visa Bulletin* chart.

> **EXAMPLE 1:** Toshiko is a citizen of Japan, married to a U.S. permanent resident.
>
> Toshiko's husband submitted an I-130 for her several years ago and she received a Priority Date of January 1, 2017. What does Toshiko learn by looking at the *Visa Bulletin* chart below? After locating the box for Japan (under All Chargeability Areas) in category 2A, she sees that the Priority Date in Section A that is now current is January 8, 2017.
>
> That means that Toshiko, with her Priority Date of January 1, 2017, is now eligible for a visa. If you're confused by the fact that Toshiko's Priority Date isn't an exact match with the *Visa Bulletin* final action date, look at it this way: Earlier is always better. Toshiko's husband actually submitted her I-130 a few days before some other people who also became current under this month's *Visa Bulletin*. If this process were like taking a number at the bakery counter, she would have become eligible for her visa (or get to choose her doughnut) a little before the people with January 8 Priority Dates. But the *Visa Bulletin* jumps by days, and weeks, worth of Priority Dates every month, so people get lumped into larger groups. Anyone with a Priority Date of January 8, 2017 or earlier is therefore considered to have become visa eligible, or "current."

> **EXAMPLE 2:** Yumiko is also a citizen of Japan, who got married to a U.S. permanent resident more recently than Toshiko in the example above.

Yumiko's husband submitted her I-130 on January 30, 2018, so that is now her Priority Date.

What does Yumiko learn by looking at the *Visa Bulletin* chart? She must look at the same box as Toshiko did, to see that the current final action date is January 8, 2017. But Yumiko's Priority Date is certainly not current, and she is not yet eligible for a visa. It's safe to say there are a number of people in line ahead of her, and thus a likely wait of about a year ahead.

If you follow the *Visa Bulletin* chart month by month, you might notice a couple of odd things. Sometimes the government gets backed up with visa applications and the final action dates just don't change. In the example above, it could be that Toshiko's Priority Date actually became current a month earlier—but she forgot to check it then, and the number didn't change. Sometimes the cutoff dates get stuck for months at a time, while the government deals with a backlog of visa applications. If the government hits a huge logjam, you may even see the cutoff dates go backwards.

Another odd thing you might see is a box that contains the letter C or U, instead of a date. The letter C (for "current") means there are plenty of visas in that category and no one has to wait. It's as if everyone's Priority Date suddenly were current.

The letter U (for "unavailable") is the opposite; it means that all the visas have been used up for that year. If, for example, this were February 2017, and Yumiko saw a U in her category 2A box, she'd know she could forget about getting closer to a visa until October 2019 (when the new year starts in the visa allocation process).

d. Figuring How Long You Will Wait

To roughly determine how long you will have to wait for a visa, you can subtract the cutoff date on the current month's *Visa Bulletin* chart from today's date. That will tell you the approximate length of time that other applicants are now waiting for a visa—though this method is complicated by the fact that they applied during a different time period than you, and demand in your category may have risen or fallen during that time. There is no exact science to computing your probable wait.

e. How to Deal With the Long Wait

You will probably feel like nothing at all is happening during the years that you wait for your visa to become available. But in fact, the Priority Dates will be inching forward, and there are steps that you should be taking to make sure that you can claim your visa as soon as it becomes available.

i. Organizing Your Papers and Checking the *Visa Bulletin*

After your U.S. permanent resident spouse files an I-130 petition for you, you will get your own approval notice; looking much like the one shown in Subsection 1d, above. The approval notice will show your Priority Date. Take careful note of the date and keep the notice in a safe place.

Look in the current *Visa Bulletin* to get an idea of how long your wait will be. Then start checking the bulletin regularly, so you can find out as soon as you are current and can make sure that the U.S. government realizes that you are current and still alive and interested, as explained below.

> **TIP**
>
> **You can ask to have the *Visa Bulletin* sent to you monthly, by email.** This is a great way to make sure you don't forget to check how your Priority Date is advancing. Complete instructions can be found toward the bottom of any *Visa Bulletin*.

ii. If You Change Addresses

Don't rely solely on the U.S. government to tell you when your Priority Date is current—the National Visa Center does a fine job, but a few files may get buried in the shuffle. And, you're guaranteed not to hear from them if they don't know where to find you. Also, under rare circumstances, such as a major change in the U.S. immigration laws, the government may send out mass mailings that you also wouldn't want to miss.

If either you or your petitioning spouse change addresses, the place to contact is the National Visa Center (NVC), which keeps your case file until your Priority Date is close to being current. You can advise the NVC of your new address by calling 603-334-0700 or searching for "Ask NVC" online and filling out its public inquiry form.

iii. What to Do When Your Priority Date Is Current

One day, your Priority Date will become current—in other words, you'll finally see the exact date of your original application, or a later date, on the *Visa Bulletin* Final Action chart. Then you'll know that it's time for you to move forward in the process of getting your visa or green card.

When you see that your Priority Date is current, don't wait for the government to call you. If you don't hear from them within a few weeks, contact the National Visa Center and ask it to send you the appropriate paperwork.

iv. What Happens If No One Notices Your Current Priority Date

Some immigrants forget to check the *Visa Bulletin*, and their Priority Date becomes current without their noticing. Sometimes, the NVC has tried to notify them, but has only an old address. Or, the NVC may have failed to keep track of the person's file. These problems can delay or destroy a person's hopes of immigrating.

You have one year after your Priority Date becomes current (in Section A of the *Visa Bulletin*) to pursue your visa or green card. If you do not, the government assumes you have abandoned it—and will give your visa to the next person in line. You may have an argument for getting the visa back if the government completely failed to contact you, but it's better to avoid such situations altogether. Keep track of your own Priority Date and follow the procedures in Subsection iii, directly above, as soon as your date, or a later date, is listed in Section B of the *Visa Bulletin*.

f. How to Get Your Children Onto the Waiting List

Like other immigrants, you can bring certain family members along when you come to the United States. Your children who are unmarried and under age 21 qualify as what are called derivative beneficiaries. See Chapter 2, Section B, to review who counts as a child.

As a practical matter, this means that your children won't need a separate I-130 petition to start off the process. Simply by being named on your Form I-130, they will share your Priority Date and place on the waiting list. (Eventually, however, they will have to fill out some forms of their own.)

As you'll see in Section B, below, children can lose their derivative beneficiary status. For example, if your spouse becomes a U.S. citizen, or if children turn 21 or get married, the children would no longer be considered derivative beneficiaries and would have to find another way to immigrate. Section B, below, tells you which of these situations can be cured and how to cure them.

g. If the Permanent Resident Petitioner Dies

Under previous law, if you were the spouse of a permanent resident who died before you could immigrate, the petition was canceled and you could no longer become a permanent resident.

However, in October of 2009, Congress changed the law so that under certain conditions, the petition that was filed by your now-deceased spouse may still be decided on. Assuming you are outside the United States, if the petition was approved prior to your spouse's death, "humanitarian reinstatement" provisions may allow the petition to remain valid, and you may be allowed to continue with the application through the U.S. consulate.

Unlike the spouse of a U.S. citizen, however, this law does not allow you to petition for yourself if your spouse never filed the petition.

If you are in the unfortunate situation of dealing with the untimely death of the petitioner in your immigration case, consult an immigration attorney.

h. Problems getting a tourist visa or entering the U.S. with a tourist visa

If your Priority Date is current under Section B of the *Visa Bulletin*, you can begin the visa-application process. But doing so could lengthen the time during which you are unable to travel to the U.S. while waiting to become eligible for the green card. This is because once you've submitted your immigrant visa application, you have demonstrated that you're an intending immigrant, and thus are unlikely to be granted a tourist visa (or entry under an old tourist visa).

> **CAUTION**
>
> **Grandchildren can't come along.** If your derivative beneficiary children have children of their own, those children (your grandchildren) will not be considered your derivative beneficiaries. The law says that no one can be the derivative of someone who is already a derivative beneficiary. In this circumstance, the grandchildren would have to stay behind for at least a few years—a heartbreaking situation for some families.

i. Changing Visa Preference Categories

It is possible for people to move into a different preference category, which will speed up or delay their waiting time. For example, you might get a visa quicker—by moving to the immediate relative category—if your spouse became a U.S. citizen.

Or, life changes could push you out of your visa category and into a lower one or out of the race altogether. This section explains the most typical situations affecting married couples and shows you how to keep or improve on your visa category. (For situations affecting only your children, see Section B, below.)

i. If a Permanent Resident Petitioner Becomes a Citizen

If the petitioning spouse becomes a citizen, it is normally good news for the immigrant. You go from category 2A straight to immediate relative. This means that you jump off the waiting list and immediately move forward with your visa processing.

If your permanent resident spouse already meets the legal requirements for U.S. citizenship, he or she might be wise to apply as soon as possible. Most permanent residents can apply within five years of receiving their residence (or four years after entering as a refugee or receiving political asylum). They must also be of good moral character, meet certain U.S. residency requirements, and be able to pass a test on the English language and U.S. history and government. (If you know that your spouse is going to become a U.S. citizen very soon, read Chapter 7 covering overseas spouses of U.S. citizens.)

If your petitioner becomes a citizen, advise the National Visa Center (NVC). It will upgrade your status to immediate relative.

You'll need to first search "Ask NVC" online and fill out its public inquiry form. Include your case number in the subject line and attach (as a PDF or JPG file) a copy of your U.S. passport or naturalization certificate. The sample text below will help you craft the text of the email.

Sample Email Text Requesting Upgrade to Immediate Relative

Dear Sir/Madam:

I am the petitioner in the above case. I recently became a U.S. citizen. A copy of my citizenship certificate is attached. Please upgrade my wife, Marta Moscow, from category 2A to immediate relative, and proceed with consular processing.

Thank you.

Sam Washington
123 Salmon Way
Seattle, WA 98105
(206) 555-1212

 RESOURCE
Need more information on the eligibility and procedural requirements for obtaining U.S. citizenship? See the USCIS website at www.uscis.gov or *Becoming a U.S. Citizen: A Guide to the Law, Exam & Interview,* by Ilona Bray (Nolo).

SKIP AHEAD
If your spouse becomes a citizen and you have children who will be immigrating with you, be sure to read Section B, below. For certain children, immigrating may now become more difficult.

ii. If the Petitioner and Beneficiary Divorce

If you and your spouse get divorced before you apply for your immigrant visa or green card, you are out of luck. The petition is canceled and you and your derivative beneficiaries lose your green card eligibility.

There is an exception for immigrants who are victims of emotional or physical abuse by their spouse. They can file a special self-petition (Form I-360) any time until the divorce becomes final or for two years afterward, if they can show that the divorce was related to the domestic violence. (These self-petitions are not covered in this book. Talk to a U.S. nonprofit organization or consult an attorney. See Chapter 17 for suggestions on how to locate nonprofits and good attorneys.)

iii. If a Beneficiary Dies

If you were to die, your children would lose their opportunity for a visa as well—unless your spouse has filed or can file a separate petition for them in category 2A or 2B.

If your family is in this situation, the U.S. permanent resident petitioner should ask USCIS to "recapture" the deceased parent's Priority Date when the permanent resident submits the new petitions. If USCIS assigns the deceased parent's date to the children, the children won't have to start the waiting game all over.

iv. If a U.S. Petitioner Loses Permanent Resident Status

If the permanent resident petitioner loses the right to live in the United States, the immigrating applicants lose the right to become residents there also. In theory, permanent residence or a green card gives a person the right to live in the United States permanently—but this right can be taken away. If, for example the petitioner spends many months overseas, USCIS may decide that he or she abandoned U.S. residency and refuse to let him or her reclaim it. Or, if the petitioner commits certain crimes, permanent residency could be taken away and he or she could be deported.

Even if a permanent resident has had a crime on record for a long time, it may not be safe. Recent laws have allowed USCIS to deport people for crimes that would not have made them deportable when the crime was committed. Since the goal of the law is to reunite families, it makes sense that the government would refuse to grant immigrant visas to the family members of former permanent residents.

j.   Should You Wait Until Your Spouse Is a U.S. Citizen?

Applicants sometimes ask, "If I can avoid the Visa Preference System by waiting for my spouse to become a U.S. citizen, shouldn't I do so and avoid the quotas and waiting period?" The answer is no, you don't really gain anything by waiting, and you may actually lose time if your spouse's citizenship gets delayed.

You don't gain anything, because your spouse will have to submit the petition sometime, even after she or he becomes a U.S. citizen. The form is the same, whether your spouse is a citizen or permanent resident. Your approval notice will remain good even after your spouse becomes a citizen. Besides this, the longer you wait, the higher the application fee is likely to go (it's already $535). Finally, you can't predict for sure when your spouse will actually become a citizen—and you will lose time until that happens.

Let's take an imaginary permanent resident spouse named Kari. She is only one year away from being eligible to apply for citizenship. Her immigrating spouse, Sven, might think it's better to wait until she's a citizen before she files the I-130 on his behalf. But after Kari turns in the citizenship application, she waits another year before her interview. Then the officer tells her, "I can't approve this until you show me proof of all your divorces, and you need to amend your last year's tax return and pay back the extra tax that you owe to show me that you have good moral character." This takes time to pull together, and Kari waits several months more for the final approval.

You can see how things might drag on. Even after your spouse is approved for citizenship, it could be a few months more before he or she attends the ceremony making him or her a U.S. citizen. By waiting for your spouse to attain U.S. citizenship, you could end up waiting even longer than you would have as a Preference Relative.

3.   Step Three: Pay Fees, Prepare Forms and Documents

One day, your Priority Date will become current. If the National Visa Center doesn't contact you within a matter of weeks, go back to Subsection 2e regarding how to contact it.

Once the NVC sees that your Priority Date is current, it will ask you to visit the Consular Electronic Application Center (CEAC) at https://ceac.state.gov/ceac and complete Form DS-261, Online Choice of Address and Agent. Log in using the invoice number that the NVC sent you. This is a simple form—but by choosing an "agent," as the form asks for, you're essentially deciding where all the important mail from the U.S. government regarding your immigration should go—to you, at your overseas address, or to someone else, most likely your petitioner in the U.S. (if you're not using an attorney).

If mail service from the U.S. has been at all unreliable where you live, or if you might be moving before your visa interview, it's safest to choose your U.S. petitioner as agent, or to indicate that you'd rather be contacted by email. Since the majority of the steps you'll need to take on your petition are online, it makes sense to enroll in email notifications.

> **CAUTION**
> **If you used this book for Step One, you probably need a new edition now.** In the years that you waited for your Priority Date to become current, the immigration laws or procedures may have changed. Check with Nolo's customer service department regarding how to obtain a new edition.

After you submit the DS-261, you will receive some information about filing fees. The NVC will send the U.S. family-member petitioner a bill for the Affidavit of Support review ($120) and send either you or your agent a bill for the immigrant visa processing fee (currently $325). If any family members included on your I-130 petition are immigrating with you, you'll need to pay a separate filing fee of $325 for each. However, all family members can be included on the one $120 filing fee for the Affidavit of Support.

The NVC prefers that you pay these fees online, by entering your checking account number and bank routing number. That's also the best way to ensure that your fees get properly credited to your account and that all your documents are kept together.

However, if you don't have a checking account, you will need to pay by mail, using a bank check or money order. Have your visa bill handy: It contains a bar code that the NVC will need in order to credit your fee to your application.

After paying your fees, you will need to submit DS-260, the online immigrant visa application. You can find a sample on the Department of State website; go to https://ceac.state.gov/ceac, then look for "DS-260." The form asks a number of biographical questions, such as all names used, all addresses where you have lived, your work and educational history, and family member information. You will also be asked questions to determine your admissibility to the United States.

You will again need your NVC invoice number and receipt number in order to complete this form. You can save your DS-260 on your computer and come back to it later. You will need to complete the form in English, using solely English characters, so have someone ready to help you if you might need it.

This online form isn't much different from the paper one that preceded it (known as DS-230), except that it requires a lot more detail. You'll be asked for all your addresses since the age of 16 and the exact dates that you lived there. Make sure that all your answers correspond with the answers you gave on previous forms. If an answer does not apply to you (such as U.S. Social Security number), you will be given the option to choose "Does Not Apply."

After you submit the DS-260, print the confirmation page and bring it to your interview. Although you are not required to do so, it doesn't hurt to print out a copy of the entire form as well, so that you can refer to it when needed.

After the NVC is satisfied that you have submitted the necessary documentation and have paid all your fees, it will schedule an interview date and transfer your visa file to the appropriate U.S. consulate or embassy.

> **TIP**
> **It's never too soon to get your vaccinations up to date.** Before you're allowed to enter the United States, you'll have to prove that you've had all the necessary vaccinations, as listed in Chapter 2, Section A. Check with your local doctor now so that you're not stuck later waiting weeks while a series of shots is administered.

a. Line-by-Line Instructions for Step Three Forms

Here are instructions for preparing the most important forms that will be required of you at this stage.

i. Form I-864

Form I-864, the Affidavit of Support, is the primary form that your spouse and any joint sponsor will use to prove that he, she, or they are willing and able to support you. (You might also need a joint sponsor to assist in supporting you if your spouse's income and assets aren't high enough to reach the government's guidelines, as covered in Chapter 3.)

> **TIP**
> **Some sponsors can use a simpler version of Form I-864.** If the sponsor has enough income so that he or she doesn't need to resort to assets or other help to sponsor the immigrant(s), it's okay to use Form I-864EZ. And for those lucky couples who have been married long enough that the immigrant can be credited with 40 quarters of work through the U.S. citizen spouse, fill out Form I-864W to tell USCIS that you don't need to fill out an Affidavit of Support at all. Both forms are available at www.uscis.gov/forms.

Be sure to read Chapter 3, Section A, before beginning to fill in this form. The chapter contains analysis of the legal implications of this form and your strategy in filling it out.

WEB RESOURCE
Form I-864 is available on the USCIS website at www.uscis.gov/i-864. Below is a sample filled-in version of the relevant pages of this form. Note that our sample assumes that the sponsor has a child of her own, from a previous relationship, who agrees to contribute to the household income.

Because this form may be filled in either by your spouse or by a joint sponsor, the instructions below usually refer to the "sponsor," which refers to either of them.

These sections are self-explanatory, with the following notes:

- **In Part 1,** spouses check box 1; friends who are separately filling in this form as joint sponsors check either box 1.d or box 1.e.

- **In Part 2,** all the information requested refers to the immigrant, including the mailing address. If you live overseas and haven't spent time in the U.S., it is unlikely that you would have an A-Number (issued by USCIS) to enter here. For Question 6, you're unlikely to have a USCIS Online Account Number; unless, that is, you registered in order to file certain USCIS forms online. However, the ELIS system is largely nonfunctional at the moment.

- **In Part 3,** note that the list of children should include only those who will be immigrating with the immigrant spouse. If you mention any other children here, it will mean that the sponsor is agreeing to be sued if he or she fails to support them. In particular, it is unnecessary to name children who were born in the United States, because the sponsor has no obligation to support them (at least not under the immigration laws, though they will be counted elsewhere within this form to test the sponsor's overall financial capacity).

- **In Part 4,** note that the sponsor's physical address must be in the United States in order for him or her to be eligible as a financial sponsor. If the sponsor is not currently living in the U.S., the I-864 will be approved only with a showing that he or she is abroad temporarily, has maintained ties to the U.S., and intends to reestablish domicile in the U.S. no later than the date that you are admitted to the U.S. as a permanent resident.

Some of the ways your spouse can show having maintained ties to the U.S. include having paid state or local taxes, maintained bank accounts in the U.S., and maintained a permanent U.S. mailing address. (Of course, if a permanent resident has been outside the U.S. for more than a year at a time without first getting USCIS permission, or has made so many short trips outside the U.S. for the last few years that he or she appears to be living outside the U.S. and only visiting, that person may be in danger of having the U.S. government decide that he or she has abandoned the right to permanent residence. That would be a disaster and the petition for you would be revoked.)

Part 5, Sponsor's household size

This section is self-explanatory. Remember not to count anyone twice! In other words, there's no need to put a "1" in question 3, because you've already counted your spouse.

Part 6, Sponsor's income and employment

The sponsor needs to fill in information about his or her employment here. Self-employment is fine. Be aware that if a self-employed sponsor has underreported income in the past, the earnings shown may not be sufficient to support you. In that case, the sponsor will need to file an amended tax return and pay a penalty before the newly reported income is accepted as meeting the guidelines for sponsorship.

Sample Form I-864, Affidavit of Support Under Section 213A of the Act—Page 1

Affidavit of Support Under Section 213A of the INA

Department of Homeland Security
U.S. Citizenship and Immigration Services

USCIS
Form I-864
OMB No. 1615-0075
Expires 03/31/2020

For USCIS Use Only	Affidavit of Support Submitter	Section 213A Review	Number of Support Affidavits in File
	☐ Petitioner	☐ MEETS requirements ☐ DOES NOT MEET requirements	☐ 1 ☐ 2
	☐ 1st Joint Sponsor		**Remarks**
	☐ 2nd Joint Sponsor	Reviewed By:_____	
	☐ Substitute Sponsor	Office: _____	
	☐ 5% Owner	Date (mm/dd/yyyy): _____	

To be completed by an attorney or accredited representative (if any).	☐ Select this box if Form G-28 or G-28I is attached.	Attorney State Bar Number (if applicable)	Attorney or Accredited Representative USCIS Online Account Number (if any)

▶ **START HERE - Type or print in black ink.**

Part 1. Basis For Filing Affidavit of Support

I, `Alice Anne Debden` ,
am the sponsor submitting this affidavit of support because
(Select **only one** box):

1.a. ☒ I am the petitioner. I filed or am filing for the immigration of my relative.

1.b. ☐ I filed an alien worker petition on behalf of the intending immigrant, who is related to me as my

1.c. ☐ I have an ownership interest of at least 5 percent in

which filed an alien worker petition on behalf of the intending immigrant, who is related to me as my

1.d. ☐ I am the only joint sponsor.

1.e. ☐ I am the ☐ first ☐ second of two joint sponsors.

1.f. ☐ The original petitioner is deceased. I am the substitute sponsor. I am the intending immigrant's

NOTE: If you are filing this form as a sponsor, you must include proof of your U.S. citizenship, U.S. national status, or lawful permanent resident status.

Part 2. Information About the Principal Immigrant

1.a. Family Name (Last Name) `LINDSEY`

1.b. Given Name (First Name) `Edmund`

1.c. Middle Name `Alexander`

Mailing Address   *(USPS ZIP Code Lookup)*

2.a. In Care Of Name

2.b. Street Number and Name `10 Walden Rd`

2.c. ☐ Apt. ☐ Ste. ☐ Flr.

2.d. City or Town `London`

2.e. State ____ **2.f.** ZIP Code _____

2.g. Province

2.h. Postal Code

2.i. Country `UK`

Other Information

3. Country of Citizenship or Nationality `UK`

4. Date of Birth (mm/dd/yyyy) `11/21/1977`

5. Alien Registration Number (A-Number) (if any)
▶ A-

6. USCIS Online Account Number (if any)
▶

7. Daytime Telephone Number
`0212345678`

Sample Form I-864, Affidavit of Support Under Section 213A of the Act—Page 2

Part 3. Information About the Immigrants You Are Sponsoring

1. I am sponsoring the principal immigrant named in **Part 2.**

    [X] Yes [ ] No (Applicable only if you are sponsoring family members in **Part 3.** as the second joint sponsor or if you are sponsoring family members who are immigrating more than six months after the principal immigrant)

2. [ ] I am sponsoring the following family members immigrating at the same time or within six months of the principal immigrant named in **Part 2.** (Do not include any relative listed on a separate visa petition.)

3. [ ] I am sponsoring the following family members who are immigrating more than six months after the principal immigrant.

Family Member 1

4.a. Family Name (Last Name)

4.b. Given Name (First Name)

4.c. Middle Name

5. Relationship to Principal Immigrant

6. Date of Birth (mm/dd/yyyy)

7. Alien Registration Number (A-Number) (if any)
   ▶ A-

8. USCIS Online Account Number (if any)
   ▶

Family Member 2

9.a. Family Name (Last Name)

9.b. Given Name (First Name)

9.c. Middle Name

10. Relationship to Principal Immigrant

11. Date of Birth (mm/dd/yyyy)

12. Alien Registration Number (A-Number) (if any)
    ▶ A-

13. USCIS Online Account Number (if any)
    ▶

Family Member 3

14.a. Family Name (Last Name)

14.b. Given Name (First Name)

14.c. Middle Name

15. Relationship to Principal Immigrant

16. Date of Birth (mm/dd/yyyy)

17. Alien Registration Number (A-Number) (if any)
    ▶ A-

18. USCIS Online Account Number (if any)
    ▶

Family Member 4

19.a. Family Name (Last Name)

19.b. Given Name (First Name)

19.c. Middle Name

20. Relationship to Principal Immigrant

21. Date of Birth (mm/dd/yyyy)

22. Alien Registration Number (A-Number) (if any)
    ▶ A-

23. USCIS Online Account Number (if any)
    ▶

Family Member 5

24.a. Family Name (Last Name)

24.b. Given Name (First Name)

24.c. Middle Name

25. Relationship to Principal Immigrant

26. Date of Birth (mm/dd/yyyy)

27. Alien Registration Number (A-Number) (if any)
    ▶ A-

28. USCIS Online Account Number (if any)
    ▶

Sample Form I-864, Affidavit of Support Under Section 213A of the Act—Page 3

Part 3. Information About the Immigrants You Are Sponsoring (continued)

29. Enter the total number of immigrants you are sponsoring on this affidavit which includes the principal immigrant listed in **Part 2.**, any immigrants listed in **Part 3.**, **Item Numbers 1. - 28.** and (if applicable), any immigrants listed for these questions in **Part 11. Additional Information**. Do not count the principal immigrant if you are only sponsoring family members entering more than 6 months after the principal immigrant.

| 1 |

Part 4. Information About You (Sponsor)

Sponsor's Full Name

1.a. Family Name (Last Name) `DEBDEN`

1.b. Given Name (First Name) `Alice`

1.c. Middle Name `Anne`

Sponsor's Mailing Address

2.a. In Care Of Name

2.b. Street Number and Name `432 Fairfax Street`

2.c. ☒ Apt. ☐ Ste. ☐ Flr. `A`

2.d. City or Town `Alexandria`

2.e. State `VA` ▼ **2.f.** ZIP Code `22314`

2.g. Province

2.h. Postal Code

2.i. Country `USA`

3. Is your current mailing address the same as your physical address? ☒ Yes ☐ No

If you answered "No" to **Item Number 3.**, provide your physical address in **Item Numbers 4.a. - 4.h.**

Sponsor's Physical Address

4.a. Street Number and Name

4.b. ☐ Apt. ☐ Ste. ☐ Flr.

4.c. City or Town

4.d. State **4.e.** ZIP Code

4.f. Province

4.g. Postal Code

4.h. Country

Other Information

5. Country of Domicile `USA`

6. Date of Birth (mm/dd/yyyy) `03/03/1978`

7. City or Town of Birth `Dublin`

8. State or Province of Birth

9. Country of Birth `Ireland`

10. U.S. Social Security Number (Required) ► `1 2 3 1 2 1 2 3 4`

Citizenship or Residency

11.a. ☐ I am a U.S. citizen.

11.b. ☐ I am a U.S. national.

11.c. ☒ I am a lawful permanent resident.

12. Sponsor's A-Number (if any) ► A- `0 2 2 3 3 4 4 5 5`

13. Sponsor's USCIS Online Account Number (if any) ►

Military Service (To be completed by petitioner sponsors only.)

14. I am currently on **active duty** in the U.S. Armed Forces or U.S. Coast Guard. ☐ Yes ☐ No

Sample Form I-864, Affidavit of Support Under Section 213A of the Act—Page 4

For USCIS Use Only	

Part 5. Sponsor's Household Size

NOTE: Do not count any member of your household more than once.

Persons you are sponsoring in this affidavit:

1. Provide the number you entered in **Part 3., Item Number 29.** `1`

Persons NOT sponsored in this affidavit:

2. Yourself. `1`

3. If you are currently married, enter "1" for your spouse.

4. If you have dependent children, enter the number here.

5. If you have any other dependents, enter the number here.

6. If you have sponsored any other persons on Form I-864 or Form I-864EZ who are now lawful permanent residents, enter the number here.

7. **OPTIONAL:** If you have siblings, parents, or adult children with the same principal residence who are combining their income with yours by submitting Form I-864A, enter the number here. `1`

8. Add together **Part 5., Item Numbers 1. - 7.** and enter the number here.

   Household Size: `3`

Part 6. Sponsor's Employment and Income

I am currently:

1. ☒ Employed as a/an

   `Potter`

2. Name of Employer 1

   `Alexandria Quartet Potters`

3. Name of Employer 2 (if applicable)

4. ☐ Self-Employed as a/an (Occupation)

5. ☐ Retired Since (mm/dd/yyyy)

6. ☐ Unemployed Since (mm/dd/yyyy)

7. My current individual annual income is:

   $ `18,500.00`

Income you are using from any other person who was counted in your household size, including, in certain conditions, the intending immigrant. (See Form I-864 Instructions.) Please indicate name, relationship, and income.

Person 1

8. Name

   `Louisa Jane Madison`

9. Relationship

   `Daughter`

10. **Current Income** $ `38,000.00`

Person 2

11. Name

12. Relationship

13. **Current Income** $

Person 3

14. Name

15. Relationship

16. **Current Income** $

Person 4

17. Name

18. Relationship

19. **Current Income** $

Sample Form I-864, Affidavit of Support Under Section 213A of the Act—Page 5

For USCIS Use Only	**Household Size** ☐ 1 ☐ 2 ☐ 3 ☐ 4 ☐ 5 ☐ 6 ☐ 7 ☐ 8 ☐ 9 ☐ Other_____	**Poverty Guideline** Year: _2 0____ Poverty Line: $_____	**Remarks**

Part 6. Sponsor's Employment and Income (continued)

20. **My Current Annual Household Income** (Total all lines from **Part 6. Item Numbers 7.**, **10.**, **13.**, **16.**, and **19.**; the total will be compared to Federal Poverty Guidelines on Form I-864P.) $ `56,500.00`

21. ☒ The people listed in **Item Numbers 8.**, **11.**, **14.**, and **17.** have completed Form I-864A. I am filing along with this affidavit all necessary Form I-864As completed by these people.

22. ☐ One or more of the people listed in **Item Numbers 8.**, **11.**, **14.**, and **17.** do not need to complete Form I-864A because he or she is the intending immigrant and has no accompanying dependents.

Name

Federal Income Tax Return Information

23.a. Have you filed a Federal income tax return for each of the three most recent tax years? ☒ Yes ☐ No

NOTE: You **MUST** attach a photocopy or transcript of your Federal income tax return for only the most recent tax year.

23.b. ☐ (Optional) I have attached photocopies or transcripts of my Federal income tax returns for my second and third most recent tax years.

My total income (adjusted gross income on Internal Revenue Service (IRS) Form 1040EZ) as reported on my Federal income tax returns for the most recent three years was:

	Tax Year	Total Income
24.a. Most Recent	2018	$ 18,500.00
24.b. 2nd Most Recent	2017	$ 18,000.00
24.c. 3rd Most Recent	2016	$ 15,000.00

25. ☐ I was not required to file a Federal income tax return as my income was below the IRS required level and I have attached evidence to support this.

Part 7. Use of Assets to Supplement Income (Optional)

If your income, or the total income for you and your household, from **Part 6.**, **Item Numbers 20.** or **24.a.** - **24.c.**, exceeds the Federal Poverty Guidelines for your household size, **YOU ARE NOT REQUIRED** to complete this **Part 7**. Skip to **Part 8.**

Your Assets (Optional)

1. Enter the balance of all savings and checking accounts. $

2. Enter the net cash value of real-estate holdings. (Net value means current assessed value minus mortgage debt.) $

3. Enter the net cash value of all stocks, bonds, certificates of deposit, and any other assets not already included in **Item Number 1.** or **Item Number 2.** $

4. Add together **Item Numbers 1.** - **3.** and enter the number here. **TOTAL:** $

Assets from Form I-864A, Part 4., Item Number 3.d., for:

5.a. Name of Relative

5.b. Your household member's assets from Form I-864A (optional). $

Assets of the principal sponsored immigrant (optional).

The principal sponsored immigrant is the person listed in **Part 2.**, **Item Numbers 1.a.** - **1.c.** Only include the assets if the principal immigrant is being sponsored by this affidavit of support.

6. Enter the balance of the principal immigrant's savings and checking accounts. $

7. Enter the net cash value of all the principal immigrant's real estate holdings. (Net value means investment value minus mortgage debt.) $

8. Enter the current cash value of the principal immigrant's stocks, bonds, certificates of deposit, and other assets not included in **Item Number 6.** or **Item Number 7.** $

Sample Form I-864, Affidavit of Support Under Section 213A of the Act—Page 6

	Household Size	Poverty Guideline	Sponsor's Household Income *(Page 5, Line 10)*	Remarks
For USCIS Use Only	☐ 1 ☐ 2 ☐ 3 ☐ 4 ☐ 5 ☐ 6 ☐ 7 ☐ 8 ☐ 9 ☐ Other_____	Year: 2 0 ____ Poverty Line: $ _____	$ _____ *The total value of all assets, line 10, must equal 5 times (3 times for spouses and children of USC's, or 1 time for orphans to be formally adopted in the U.S.) the difference between the poverty guidelines and the sponsor's household income, line 10.*	

Part 7. Use of Assets to Supplement Income (Optional) (continued)

9. Add together **Item Numbers 6. - 8.** and enter the number here. $ [_____]

Total Value of Assets

10. Add together **Item Numbers 4., 5.b.,** and **9.** and enter the number here.

    TOTAL: $ [_____]

Part 8. Sponsor's Contract, Statement, Contact Information, Declaration, Certification, and Signature

NOTE: Read the **Penalties** section of the Form I-864 Instructions before completing this part.

Sponsor's Contract

Please note that, by signing this Form I-864, you agree to assume certain specific obligations under the Immigration and Nationality Act (INA) and other Federal laws. The following paragraphs describe those obligations. Please read the following information carefully before you sign Form I-864. If you do not understand the obligations, you may wish to consult an attorney or accredited representative.

What is the Legal Effect of My Signing Form I-864?

If you sign Form I-864 on behalf of any person (called the intending immigrant) who is applying for an immigrant visa or for adjustment of status to a lawful permanent resident, and that intending immigrant submits Form I-864 to the U.S. Government with his or her application for an immigrant visa or adjustment of status, under INA section 213A, these actions create a contract between you and the U.S. Government. The intending immigrant becoming a lawful permanent resident is the consideration for the contract.

Under this contract, you agree that, in deciding whether the intending immigrant can establish that he or she is not inadmissible to the United States as a person likely to become a public charge, the U.S. Government can consider your income and assets as available for the support of the intending immigrant.

What If I Choose Not to Sign Form I-864?

The U.S. Government cannot make you sign Form 1-864 if you do not want to do so. But if you do not sign Form I-864, the intending immigrant may not become a lawful permanent resident in the United States.

What Does Signing Form I-864 Require Me To Do?

If an intending immigrant becomes a lawful permanent resident in the United States based on a Form I-864 that you have signed, then, until your obligations under Form I-864 terminate, you must:

A. Provide the intending immigrant any support necessary to maintain him or her at an income that is at least 125 percent of the Federal Poverty Guidelines for his or her household size (100 percent if you are the petitioning sponsor and are on active duty in the U.S. Armed Forces or U.S. Coast Guard, and the person is your husband, wife, or unmarried child under 21 years of age); and

B. Notify U.S. Citizenship and Immigration Services (USCIS) of any change in your address, within 30 days of the change, by filing Form I-865.

What Other Consequences Are There?

If an intending immigrant becomes a lawful permanent resident in the United States based on a Form I-864 that you have signed, then, until your obligations under Form I-864 terminate, the U.S. Government may consider (deem) your income and assets as available to that person, in determining whether he or she is eligible for certain Federal means-tested public benefits and also for state or local means-tested public benefits, if the state or local government's rules provide for consideration (deeming) of your income and assets as available to the person.

This provision does **not** apply to public benefits specified in section 403(c) of the Welfare Reform Act such as emergency Medicaid, short-term, non-cash emergency relief; services provided under the National School Lunch and Child Nutrition Acts; immunizations and testing and treatment for communicable diseases; and means-tested programs under the Elementary and Secondary Education Act.

What If I Do Not Fulfill My Obligations?

If you do not provide sufficient support to the person who becomes a lawful permanent resident based on a Form I-864 that you signed, that person may sue you for this support.

Sample Form I-864, Affidavit of Support Under Section 213A of the Act—Page 7

Part 8. Sponsor's Contract, Statement, Contact Information, Declaration, Certification, and Signature (continued)

If a Federal, state, local, or private agency provided any covered means-tested public benefit to the person who becomes a lawful permanent resident based on a Form I-864 that you signed, the agency may ask you to reimburse them for the amount of the benefits they provided. If you do not make the reimbursement, the agency may sue you for the amount that the agency believes you owe.

If you are sued, and the court enters a judgment against you, the person or agency that sued you may use any legally permitted procedures for enforcing or collecting the judgment. You may also be required to pay the costs of collection, including attorney fees.

If you do not file a properly completed Form I-865 within 30 days of any change of address, USCIS may impose a civil fine for your failing to do so.

When Will These Obligations End?

Your obligations under a Form I-864 that you signed will end if the person who becomes a lawful permanent resident based on that affidavit:

- **A.** Becomes a U.S. citizen;
- **B.** Has worked, or can receive credit for, 40 quarters of coverage under the Social Security Act;
- **C.** No longer has lawful permanent resident status and has departed the United States;
- **D.** Is subject to removal, but applies for and obtains, in removal proceedings, a new grant of adjustment of status, based on a new affidavit of support, if one is required; or
- **E.** Dies.

NOTE: Divorce **does not** terminate your obligations under Form I-864.

Your obligations under a Form I-864 that you signed also end if you die. Therefore, if you die, your estate is not required to take responsibility for the person's support after your death. However, your estate may owe any support that you accumulated before you died.

Sponsor's Statement

NOTE: Select the box for either **Item Number 1.a.** or **1.b.** If applicable, select the box for **Item Number 2.**

1.a. ☒ I can read and understand English, and I have read and understand every question and instruction on this affidavit and my answer to every question.

1.b. ☐ The interpreter named in **Part 9.** read to me every question and instruction on this affidavit and my answer to every question in

[_____],

a language in which I am fluent, and I understood everything.

2. ☐ At my request, the preparer named in **Part 10.**,

[_____],

prepared this affidavit for me based only upon information I provided or authorized.

Sponsor's Contact Information

3. Sponsor's Daytime Telephone Number

7035551212

4. Sponsor's Mobile Telephone Number (if any)

7035512222

5. Sponsor's Email Address (if any)

alideb@email.com

Sponsor's Declaration and Certification

Copies of any documents I have submitted are exact photocopies of unaltered, original documents, and I understand that USCIS or the U.S. Department of State (DOS) may require that I submit original documents to USCIS or DOS at a later date. Furthermore, I authorize the release of any information from any and all of my records that USCIS or DOS may need to determine my eligibility for the benefit that I seek.

I furthermore authorize release of information contained in this affidavit, in supporting documents, and in my USCIS or DOS records, to other entities and persons where necessary for the administration and enforcement of U.S. immigration law.

I certify, under penalty of perjury, that all of the information in my affidavit and any document submitted with it were provided or authorized by me, that I reviewed and understand all of the information contained in, and submitted with, my affidavit and that all of this information is complete, true, and correct.

- **A.** I know the contents of this affidavit of support that I signed;
- **B.** I have read and I understand each of the obligations described in **Part 8.**, and I agree, freely and without any mental reservation or purpose of evasion, to accept each of those obligations in order to make it possible for the immigrants indicated in **Part 3.** to become lawful permanent residents of the United States;
- **C.** I agree to submit to the personal jurisdiction of any Federal or state court that has subject matter jurisdiction of a lawsuit against me to enforce my obligations under this Form I-864;

Sample Form I-864, Affidavit of Support Under Section 213A of the Act—Page 8

Part 8. Sponsor's Contract, Statement, Contact Information, Declaration, Certification, and Signature (continued)

D. Each of the Federal income tax returns submitted in support of this affidavit are true copies, or are unaltered tax transcripts, of the tax returns I filed with the IRS;

E. I understand that, if I am related to the sponsored immigrant by marriage, the termination of the marriage (by divorce, dissolution, annulment, or other legal process) will not relieve me of my obligations under this Form I-864; and

F. I authorize the Social Security Administration to release information about me in its records to USCIS and DOS.

Sponsor's Signature

6.a. Sponsor's Signature

Alice Anne Debden

6.b. Date of Signature (mm/dd/yyyy) `04/01/2019`

NOTE TO ALL SPONSORS: If you do not completely fill out this affidavit or fail to submit required documents listed in the Instructions, USCIS or DOS may deny your affidavit.

Part 9. Interpreter's Contact Information, Certification, and Signature

Provide the following information about the interpreter.

Interpreter's Full Name

1.a. Interpreter's Family Name (Last Name)

1.b. Interpreter's Given Name (First Name)

2. Interpreter's Business or Organization Name (if any)

Interpreter's Mailing Address

3.a. Street Number and Name

3.b. ☐ Apt. ☐ Ste. ☐ Flr.

3.c. City or Town

3.d. State ▼ **3.e.** ZIP Code

3.f. Province

3.g. Postal Code

3.h. Country

Interpreter's Contact Information

4. Interpreter's Daytime Telephone Number

5. Interpreter's Mobile Telephone Number (if any)

6. Interpreter's Email Address (if any)

Interpreter's Certification

I certify, under penalty of perjury, that:

I am fluent in English and _____ , which is the same language specified in **Part 8.**, **Item Number 1.b.**, and I have read to this sponsor in the identified language every question and instruction on this affidavit and his or her answer to every question. The sponsor informed me that he or she understands every instruction, question, and answer on the affidavit, including the **Sponsor's Declaration and Certification**, and has verified the accuracy of every answer.

Interpreter's Signature

7.a. Interpreter's Signature

7.b. Date of Signature (mm/dd/yyyy)

Question 7: Here, the sponsor is supposed to enter the income shown on his or her most recent tax return. But what if the sponsor's income has risen since filing those taxes? In that case, the sponsor should enter the more recent income figure, but put an asterisk (an *) next to it. Then find some white space somewhere on the page and write "this figure reflects present earnings, not earnings shown on tax return; see supporting documentation." The documentation the sponsor is already providing, such as an employer's letter, should be enough to show current income.

Questions 8-22: These questions are important for sponsors whose income is not enough by itself, but who will be using the income of members of their household to help meet the *Poverty Guidelines* minimum requirements. Unless any one of these household members is the actual immigrant, they must plan to complete a separate agreement with the sponsor, using Form I-864A. The total income from the sponsor and household members goes in Question 15.

Part 7, Use of Assets to Supplement Income

The sponsor needs to complete this section only if his or her income wasn't enough by itself to meet the *Poverty Guidelines* requirements. If the sponsor needs to add assets and he or she includes such items as a house, car, or boat, remember to subtract debts, mortgages, and liens before writing down their value. And remember that the value of these assets will later be divided by five before being used to meet the *Poverty Guidelines* minimum.

If some of the assets being used to meet the minimum belong to a household member, enter the household member's name in Question 5, along with the total amount the assets are worth. If some of the assets being used to meet the minimum belong to the immigrant, describe these in Questions 6-8 (and of course attach documents to prove the assets' ownership, location, and value).

If the combination of the sponsor's available income and one-fifth of the sponsor's and/or the immigrant's assets don't yet meet the *Poverty Guidelines* minimum, you'll still need to hand in this Affidavit. But you'll definitely want to look for a joint sponsor or a participating household member.

Part 8, Sponsor's Contract

Unlike past versions of this form, the sponsor's signature no longer needs to be witnessed by a notary public.

> **TIP**
>
> **Need to prepare Affidavits for several family members at once?** If the sponsor is bringing in more than one person (you and your children) in the same process and based on the same Form I-130, he or she can simply copy Form I-864 (with supporting documents) the appropriate number of times after signing it.

ii. Form I-864A

Not every immigrant needs to submit Form I-864A. It is required only if, on the main Form I-864, the sponsor had to use the income of members of his or her own household to meet the *Poverty Guidelines*. In that case, the sponsor will have to ask these persons to fill in portions of Form I-864A. The sponsor must then attach the Form I-864A to the main Form I-864.

> **WEB RESOURCE**
>
> **Form I-864A is available on the USCIS website at www.uscis.gov/i-864a.** Below is a sample filled-in version of the relevant pages of this form.

Parts 1-4: Mostly self-explanatory; filled out by household member. For Question 8, the household member is unlikely to have a USCIS Online Account Number; unless, that is, he or she registered in order to file certain USCIS forms online.

Part 5: This part is filled out and signed by the petitioning sponsor.

Part 6: Filled out and signed by the household member.

Sample Form I-864A, Contract Between Sponsor and Household Member—Page 1

Contract Between Sponsor and Household Member
Department of Homeland Security
U.S. Citizenship and Immigration Services

USCIS
Form I-864A
OMB No. 1615-0075
Expires 03/31/2020

For Government Use Only

This Form I-864A relates to a household member who:

☐ **IS** the intending immigrant   ☐ **IS NOT** the intending immigrant

Reviewed By: _____

Location: _____ Date (mm/dd/yyyy): _____

To be completed by an attorney or accredited representative (if any).	☐ **Select this box if Form G-28 or G-28I is attached.**	**Attorney State Bar Number** (if applicable)	**Attorney or Accredited Representative USCIS Online Account Number** (if any)

▶ **START HERE - Type or print in black ink.**

Part 1. Information About You (the Household Member)

Full Name

1.a. Family Name (Last Name)   `MADISON`

1.b. Given Name (First Name)   `Louisa`

1.c. Middle Name   `Jane`

Mailing Address   *(USPS ZIP Code Lookup)*

2.a. In Care Of Name

2.b. Street Number and Name   `432 Fairfax Street`

2.c. ☒ Apt. ☐ Ste. ☐ Flr. `A`

2.d. City or Town   `Alexandria`

2.e. State `VA` **2.f.** ZIP Code `22314`

2.g. Province

2.h. Postal Code

2.i. Country   `USA`

3. Is your current mailing address the same as your physical address? ☒ Yes ☐ No

If you answered "No" to **Item Number 3.**, provide your physical address.

Physical Address

4.a. Street Number and Name

4.b. ☐ Apt. ☐ Ste. ☐ Flr.

4.c. City or Town

4.d. State   **4.e.** ZIP Code

4.f. Province

4.g. Postal Code

4.h. Country

Other Information

5. Date of Birth (mm/dd/yyyy)   `10/18/1995`

Place of Birth

6.a. City or Town   `Dublin`

6.b. State or Province

6.c. Country   `Ireland`

7. U.S. Social Security Number (if any)   ▶ `4 0 4 4 4 4 0 0 4`

8. USCIS Online Account Number (if any)   ▶

Sample Form I-864A, Contract Between Sponsor and Household Member—Page 2

Part 2. Your (the Household Member's) Relationship to the Sponsor

Select **Item Number 1.a., 1.b.,** or **1.c.**

1.a. ☐ I am the intending immigrant and also the sponsor's spouse.

1.b. ☐ I am the intending immigrant and also a member of the sponsor's household.

1.c. ☒ I am **not** the intending immigrant. I am the sponsor's household member. I am related to the sponsor as his/her:

   ☐ Spouse

   ☒ Son or Daughter (at least 18 years of age)

   ☐ Parent

   ☐ Brother or Sister

   ☐ Other Dependent (Specify)

   _____

Part 3. Your (the Household Member's) Employment and Income

I am currently:

1. ☒ Employed as a/an

   `Bookkeeper`

2. Name of Employer Number 1

   `Hutt Tax Service`

3. Name of Employer Number 2 (if applicable)

   _____

4. ☐ Self employed as a/an

   _____

5. ☐ Retired from (Company Name)

   _____

   Since (mm/dd/yyyy) _____

6. ☐ Unemployed since (mm/dd/yyyy) _____

7. **My current individual annual income is:**

   $ `38,000.00`

Part 4. Your (the Household Member's) Federal Income Tax Information and Assets

1.a. Have you filed a Federal income tax return for each of the three most recent tax years?   ☒ Yes   ☐ No

NOTE: You **MUST** attach a photocopy or transcript of your Federal income tax return for only the most recent tax year.

1.b. ☐ (Optional) I have attached photocopies or transcripts of my Federal income tax returns for my second and third most recent tax years.

My total income (adjusted gross income on IRS Form 1040EZ) as reported on my Federal income tax returns for the most recent three years was:

	Tax Year		Total Income
2.a. Most Recent	2018	$	38,000.00
2.b. 2nd Most Recent	2017	$	21,000.00
2.c. 3rd Most Recent	2016	$	15,000.00

My assets (complete only if necessary).

3.a. Enter the balance of all cash, savings, and checking accounts. $ _____

3.b. Enter the net cash value of real-estate holdings. (Net value means assessed value minus mortgage debt.) $ _____

3.c. Enter the cash value of all stocks, bonds, certificates of deposit, and other assets not listed on **Item Numbers 3.a.** or **3.b.** $ _____

3.d. Add together **Item Numbers 3.a., 3.b.,** and **3.c.** and enter the number here. $ _____

Part 5. Sponsor's Promise, Statement, Contact Information, Declaration, Certification, and Signature

NOTE: Read the **Penalties** section of the Form I-864A Instructions before completing this part.

I, THE SPONSOR,

`Alice Anne Debden`   ,

(Print Name)

in consideration of the household member's promise to support the following intending immigrants and to be jointly and severally liable for any obligations I incur under the affidavit of support, promise to complete and file an affidavit of support on behalf of the following named intending immigrants.

1

(Indicate Number)

Sample Form I-864A, Contract Between Sponsor and Household Member—Page 3

Part 5. Sponsor's Promise, Statement, Contact Information, Declaration, Certification, and Signature (continued)

Intending Immigrant Number 1

Name

1.a. Family Name (Last Name)   `LINDSEY`

1.b. Given Name (First Name)   `Edmund`

1.c. Middle Name   `Alexander`

2. Date of Birth (mm/dd/yyyy)   `11/21/1977`

3. Alien Registration Number (A-Number, if any)
▶ A-

4. U.S. Social Security Number (if any)
▶

5. USCIS Online Account Number (if any)
▶

Intending Immigrant Number 2

Name

6.a. Family Name (Last Name)

6.b. Given Name (First Name)

6.c. Middle Name

7. Date of Birth (mm/dd/yyyy)

8. Alien Registration Number (A-Number, if any)
▶ A-

9. U.S. Social Security Number (if any)
▶

10. USCIS Online Account Number (if any)
▶

Intending Immigrant Number 3

Name

11.a. Family Name (Last Name)

11.b. Given Name (First Name)

11.c. Middle Name

12. Date of Birth (mm/dd/yyyy)

13. Alien Registration Number (A-Number, if any)
▶ A-

14. U.S. Social Security Number (if any)
▶

15. USCIS Online Account Number (if any)
▶

Intending Immigrant Number 4

Name

16.a. Family Name (Last Name)

16.b. Given Name (First Name)

16.c. Middle Name

17. Date of Birth (mm/dd/yyyy)

18. Alien Registration Number (A-Number, if any)
▶ A-

19. U.S. Social Security Number (if any)
▶

20. USCIS Online Account Number (if any)
▶

Intending Immigrant Number 5

Name

21.a. Family Name (Last Name)

21.b. Given Name (First Name)

21.c. Middle Name

22. Date of Birth (mm/dd/yyyy)

23. Alien Registration Number (A-Number, if any)
▶ A-

24. U.S. Social Security Number (if any)
▶

25. USCIS Online Account Number (if any)
▶

Sponsor's Statement

NOTE: Select the box for either **Item Number 26.a.** or **26.b.** If applicable, select the box for **Item Number 27.**

26.a. ☒ I can read and understand English, and I have read and understand every question and instruction on this contract and my answer to every question.

Sample Form I-864A, Contract Between Sponsor and Household Member—Page 4

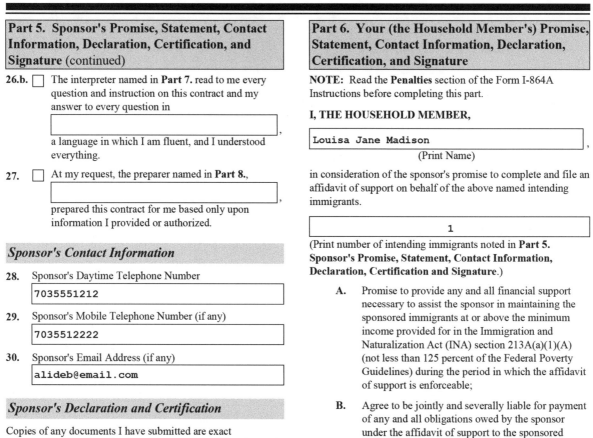

Part 5. Sponsor's Promise, Statement, Contact Information, Declaration, Certification, and Signature (continued)

26.b. ☐ The interpreter named in **Part 7.** read to me every question and instruction on this contract and my answer to every question in

[_____],

a language in which I am fluent, and I understood everything.

27. ☐ At my request, the preparer named in **Part 8.**,

[_____],

prepared this contract for me based only upon information I provided or authorized.

Sponsor's Contact Information

28. Sponsor's Daytime Telephone Number

7035551212

29. Sponsor's Mobile Telephone Number (if any)

7035512222

30. Sponsor's Email Address (if any)

alideb@email.com

Sponsor's Declaration and Certification

Copies of any documents I have submitted are exact photocopies of unaltered, original documents, and I understand that U.S. Citizenship and Immigration Services (USCIS) or the U.S. Department of State (DOS) may require that I submit original documents to USCIS or DOS at a later date. Furthermore, I authorize the release of any information from any and all of my records that USCIS or DOS may need to determine my eligibility for the immigration benefit that I seek.

I furthermore authorize release of information contained in this contract, in supporting documents, and in my USCIS or DOS records, to other entities and persons where necessary for the administration and enforcement of U.S. immigration law.

I certify, under penalty of perjury, that all of the information in my contract and any document submitted with it were provided or authorized by me, that I reviewed and understand all of the information contained in, and submitted with, my contract and that all of this information is complete, true, and correct.

Sponsor's Signature

31.a. Sponsor's Signature

Alice Anne Debden

31.b. Date of Signature (mm/dd/yyyy) 04/01/2019

NOTE TO ALL SPONSORS: If you do not completely fill out this contract or fail to submit required documents listed in the Instructions, USCIS may deny your contract.

Part 6. Your (the Household Member's) Promise, Statement, Contact Information, Declaration, Certification, and Signature

NOTE: Read the **Penalties** section of the Form I-864A Instructions before completing this part.

I, THE HOUSEHOLD MEMBER,

Louisa Jane Madison

(Print Name)

in consideration of the sponsor's promise to complete and file an affidavit of support on behalf of the above named intending immigrants.

| 1 |

(Print number of intending immigrants noted in **Part 5. Sponsor's Promise, Statement, Contact Information, Declaration, Certification and Signature**.)

A. Promise to provide any and all financial support necessary to assist the sponsor in maintaining the sponsored immigrants at or above the minimum income provided for in the Immigration and Naturalization Act (INA) section 213A(a)(1)(A) (not less than 125 percent of the Federal Poverty Guidelines) during the period in which the affidavit of support is enforceable;

B. Agree to be jointly and severally liable for payment of any and all obligations owed by the sponsor under the affidavit of support to the sponsored immigrants, to any agency of the Federal Government, to any agency of a state or local government, or to any other private entity that provides means-tested public benefits;

C. Certify under penalty under the laws of the United States that the Federal income tax returns submitted in support of the contract are true copies or unaltered tax transcripts filed with the Internal Revenue Service;

D. **Consideration where the household member is also the sponsored immigrant:** I understand that if I am the sponsored immigrant and a member of the sponsor's household that this promise relates only to my promise to be jointly and severally liable for any obligation owed by the sponsor under the affidavit of support to any of my dependents, to any agency of the Federal Government, to any agency of a state or local government, or to any other private entity that provides means-tested public benefits and to provide any and all financial support necessary to assist the sponsor in maintaining any of my dependents at or above the minimum income provided for in INA section 213A(a)(1)(A) (not less than 125 percent of the Federal Poverty Guideline) during the period which the affidavit of support is enforceable.

Sample Form I-864A, Contract Between Sponsor and Household Member—Page 5

Part 6. Your (the Household Member's) Promise, Statement, Contact Information, Declaration, Certification, and Signature (continued)

E. I understand that, if I am related to the sponsored immigrant or the sponsor by marriage, the termination of the marriage (by divorce, dissolution, annulment, or other legal process) will not relieve me of my obligations under this Form I-864A.

F. I authorize the Social Security Administration to release information about me in its records to the Department of State and U.S. Citizenship and Immigration Services (USCIS).

Your (the Household Member's) Statement

NOTE: Select the box for either **Item Number 1.a.** or **1.b.** If applicable, select the box for **Item Number 2.**

1.a. ☒ I can read and understand English, and I have read and understand every question and instruction on this contract and my answer to every question.

1.b. ☐ The interpreter named in **Part 7.** read to me every question and instruction on this contract and my answer to every question in

_____ , a language in which I am fluent, and I understood everything.

2. ☐ At my request, the preparer named in **Part 8.**,

_____ , prepared this contract for me based only upon information I provided or authorized.

Your (the Household Member's) Contact Information

3. Your (the Household Member's) Daytime Telephone Number

7035551212

4. Your (the Household Member's) Mobile Telephone Number (if any)

7051234567

5. Your (the Household Member's) Email Address (if any)

louisjm@email.com

Your (the Household Member's) Declaration and Certification

Copies of any documents I have submitted are exact photocopies of unaltered, original documents, and I understand that USCIS or DOS may require that I submit original documents to USCIS or DOS at a later date. Furthermore, I authorize the release of any information from any and all of my records that USCIS or DOS may need to determine my eligibility for the immigration benefit that I seek.

I furthermore authorize release of information contained in this contract, in supporting documents, and in my USCIS or DOS records, to other entities and persons where necessary for the administration and enforcement of U.S. immigration law.

I certify, under penalty of perjury, that all of the information in my contract and any document submitted with it were provided or authorized by me, that I reviewed and understand all of the information contained in, and submitted with, my contract and that all of this information is complete, true, and correct.

Your (the Household Member's) Signature

6.a. Your (the Household Member's) Printed Name

Louisa Jane Madison

6.b. Your (the Household Member's) Signature

Louisa Jane Madison

6.c. Date of Signature (mm/dd/yyyy) 04/01/2019

NOTE TO ALL HOUSEHOLD MEMBERS: If you do not completely fill out this contract or fail to submit required documents listed in the Instructions, USCIS may deny your contract.

Part 7. Interpreter's Contact Information, Certification, and Signature

Provide the following information about the interpreter.

Interpreter's Full Name

1.a. Interpreter's Family Name (Last Name)

1.b. Interpreter's Given Name (First Name)

2. Interpreter's Business or Organization Name (if any)

iii. Form I-864W

Only a few lucky people will be able to use this form, namely those who are exempt from the Affidavit of Support requirement because the immigrant has either:

- worked lawfully for 40 Social Security quarters (approximately ten years) in the U.S.
- been married while the U.S. spouse worked for 40 Social Security quarters, or
- a combination of the above.

The deal is that a financial sponsor's responsibility lasts until the immigrant has (among other possibilities) earned 40 work quarters credited toward Social Security. A work quarter is approximately three months, but it depends partly on how much you earn. So if you've already reached the 40 quarters on your own, through lawful employment—perhaps while in the U.S. as a student or H-1B worker—there's no point in the sponsor filling out an Affidavit of Support for you. And, in an interesting twist, you can be credited for work done by the U.S. spouse if it was during your marriage.

You'll need to prove to USCIS how many quarters of work the U.S. spouse or immigrant has done. Contact Social Security about getting a certified statement with this information.

Because Form I-864W is fairly easy to fill out, we won't include a sample here. The form is available at www.uscis.gov/i-864w. In Part 2, Reason for Exemption, you would check the first box.

b. Financial Documents to Have on Hand

When it comes to proving your sponsor's capacity to support you financially, the consulate will require detailed, up-to-date information from trustworthy sources, as detailed below.

i. Documents to Accompany Form I-864

Form I-864 asks for several supporting documents. If your spouse is relying on a joint sponsor (someone outside the household), that person should also be told to assemble a set of these documents:

- **A copy of your spouse/sponsor's federal income tax transcripts for the last one to three years.**

Don't include state tax forms. The immigration authorities prefer to see federal tax returns in the form of Internal Revenue Service (IRS) transcripts (an IRS-generated summary of the return that was filed). The fastest way to get such a transcript is from the IRS website at www.irs.gov/Individuals/Get-Transcript. If for some reason that doesn't work, you can submit photocopies of tax returns—just don't forget to include the W-2 forms. Also, if the sponsor wasn't legally required to submit a tax return, perhaps because his or her income was too low, submit a written explanation of this.

- **Proof of your sponsor's current employment.** Start with a letter from the sponsor's employer describing the dates of employment, nature of the job, wages/salary, time worked per week, terms, and prospects for advancement. The sample letter below shows how one employer described a sponsor's job and compensation. Also include copies of pay stubs covering the last six months, or the most recent stub if it shows cumulative pay. If the sponsor is self-employed, a tax return is acceptable, but it's a good idea to add a business license, copies of current receipts, or other supporting documents.

- **A list of assets, (the sponsor's and/or the immigrant's) if they must be used to meet the** *Poverty Guidelines'* **minimum.** There is no form to use for creating this asset list. Using a typewriter or word processor, prepare a list or table giving:
  - a brief description of the item
  - the item's current value
  - remaining debt (if any), and
  - a brief description of the document you've attached to prove ownership (see below).

- **Proof of ownership of assets (the sponsor's and/or the immigrant's), if any were listed.** The instructions to Form I-864 do a good job of detailing which documents will be accepted as proof of ownership of assets, in Part 7. The value must be the likely sale price, not how much the sponsor paid for the property. For real estate, you can use a tax assessment to show the value. If the assessment seems too low, or for property other than real estate, the sponsor can hire a professional appraiser to prepare an estimate and report. For cars, the value listed in the *Kelley Blue Book* is acceptable (online at www.kbb.com). The sponsor must also document the amount of any debt remaining on the property. If no debt remains, submit proof of final payment.

Sample Letter Showing Sponsor's Employment

Alexandria Quartet Potters
123 Fourth Street
Alexandria, VA 22315
May 22, 20xx

To Whom It May Concern:

Alice Debden has been an employee of Alexandria Quartet Potters since September 4, 20xx, a total of over five years. She has a full-time position as a ceramist. Her salary is $18,500 per year. This position is permanent, and Alice's prospects for performance-based advancement and salary increases are excellent.

Very truly yours,

Bob Bossman

Bob Bossman
Personnel Manager
Alexandria Quartet Potters

CAUTION
You may need to update your information later. By the time you get to your visa interview, circumstances may have changed for your sponsor, joint sponsor, or household joint sponsor. For example, if the sponsor or joint sponsor have new or different employment, bring a job letter and copies of recent pay stubs; and if a new tax year has begun, bring copies of the sponsor(s)' most recent tax returns or transcripts.

ii. Documents to Accompany Form I-864A

Form I-864A, the contract between your spouse and any household joint sponsors who are willing to contribute financially, also requires several supporting documents. These include not only proof of the joint sponsors' financial capacity, but proof that they live with and are related to the main sponsor.

- **Proof that the household joint sponsors live with the primary sponsor.** To satisfy this requirement, you can include a copy of the joint mortgage or rental agreement showing the household member's name and copies of items that show the same address as the sponsor (such as a driver's license, copies of school records, copies of utility bills, or personal correspondence).
- **Proof that the household joint sponsors are related to the primary sponsor (if they're not already listed as relations on the sponsor's tax return).** The best way to prove this family relationship is through birth certificates. For example, if the sponsor and household joint sponsor are parent and child, the child's birth certificate will do. If they are brother and sister, providing both birth certificates will work (as long as the certificates show that they share the same parent or parents). If the birth certificates don't make the family relationships clear, look for other official documents such as court or school records to confirm the parent-child links.
- **Copies of the household joint sponsors' tax returns for the last one to three years.** IRS-generated tax transcripts are best.
- **Proof of the household joint sponsors' employment.** A letter from the employer confirming employment and recent pay stubs work well for this.
- **A list of the household joint sponsors' assets if they must be used to meet the *Poverty Guidelines'* minimum.** There is no form to use for creating this list. The household joint sponsors should simply prepare (on a typewriter or word processor) a list or table giving:
  - a brief description of the item
  - its current value

- remaining debt (if any), and
- brief description of the document that has been attached to prove the sponsor owns the asset.

- **Proof of ownership of household joint sponsors' assets, if any were listed.**
- **A list of the benefit programs and dates of receipt if the household joint sponsor or their dependents have used financial need-based public benefits in the last three years.**

c. Other Documents to Prepare

You'll be asked to prepare various other documents for the NVC and for your consular interview, such as your birth certificate, marriage certificate, passport, and police certificates from countries where you've lived. These will be well explained in the instructions you receive, so we won't review them further here.

You need to obtain a police certificate (hopefully showing your clean record) only if such certificates are available in your country. For country-specific information on how to obtain proper police certification, birth and marriage certificates, and divorce decrees, visit https://travel.state.gov and click "U.S. Visas," then "Immigrate," then "The Immigrant Visa Process," then "Collect and Submit Forms and Documents to the NVC," then, "Step 5: Collect Supporting Documents."

If you don't have a clean record, see a lawyer.

d. Documents Proving Your Marriage Is Bona Fide

You must present evidence that your marriage is a real one, not a sham. Gather and photocopy as many of the following items as possible:

- rental agreements, leases, or mortgages showing that you have lived together and/or have leased or bought property in both spouses' names
- hotel and airplane receipts showing trips that you have taken together or to visit one another
- phone bills showing your conversations; copies of letters, texts, and emails

- your mutual child's birth certificate, or a doctor's report saying that you are pregnant or seeking fertility treatment
- joint bank statements
- joint credit card statements
- evidence that one spouse has made the other a beneficiary on his/her life or health insurance or retirement account
- auto registrations showing joint ownership and/or addresses
- joint club memberships
- receipts from gifts that you purchased for one another (these should be obvious gift-type purchases, like from a flower shop or candy store)
- letters from friends and family to each or both of you mailed at an address where you were living together, and
- photos of you and your spouse taken before and during your marriage, including at your wedding (the government knows wedding pictures can be faked, but some officers enjoy seeing them anyway). The photos should, if possible, include parents and other relatives from both families. Write the date taken and a brief description of what the photo shows on the back (or underneath, if you're printing out digital copies). Don't bother with the wedding or other videos—there won't be time or a space to view them. And keep them clean—no need for intimate scenes!

e. Using the Checklist for Step Three Interview Preparation

This checklist notes every form, document, and other item that you and your spouse will need to assemble in preparation for your immigrant visa interview.

 CHECKLIST

Appendix B includes instructions on where to get a copy of this checklist online.

Checklist for Immigrant Visa Forms and Documents

☐ Confirmation page and bar code, showing that you (and any accompanying family members) completed an online Form DS-260

☐ Form I-864, Affidavit of Support (see Subsection A3a(i), above, for line-by-line instructions)

☐ Documents to accompany Form I-864 (see Subsection A3b(i), above):

   ☐ A copy of your spouse/sponsor's federal income tax transcripts for the last one to three years

   ☐ Proof of your sponsor's current employment

   ☐ A list of assets, (the sponsor's and/or the immigrant's) if they're being used to meet the *Poverty Guidelines*' minimum

   ☐ Proof of ownership of assets (the sponsor's and/or the immigrant's), if any were listed

   ☐ If sponsor or sponsor's dependents have used financial need-based public benefits in the last three years, a list of the programs and dates of receipt

☐ Form I-864A, Contract Between Sponsor and Household Member (only needed if sponsor's income is insufficient; see line-by-line instructions in Subsection A3a(ii), above)

☐ Documents to accompany Form I-864A (see Subsection A3b(ii), above):

   ☐ Proof that the household joint sponsors live with the primary sponsor

   ☐ Proof that the household joint sponsors are related to the primary sponsor (if they're not already listed as dependents on the sponsor's tax return)

☐ Copies of the household joint sponsors' tax transcripts for the last one to three years

☐ Proof of the household joint sponsors' employment

☐ Proof of ownership of household joint sponsors' assets, if any were listed

☐ If the household joint sponsors or their dependents have used financial need-based public benefits in the last three years, a list of the benefits programs and dates of receipt

☐ If you're exempt from the Affidavit of Support requirement, Form I-864W, together with a certified statement of your Social Security earnings history

☐ Additional documents to accompany forms:

   ☐ Original and one photocopy of your birth certificate (see Chapter 4, Section C, for how to obtain vital documents)

   ☐ Original and one photocopy of your marriage certificate (see Chapter 4, Section C, for how to obtain vital documents)

   ☐ If applicable, original and one photocopy of proof of termination of all previous marriages, such as certificates of death, divorce, or annulment

   ☐ Original USCIS notice of approved I-130 (Form I-797)

   ☐ Two color photographs of you (passport style)

   ☐ Police certificate, if available in your country

   ☐ Military records, if applicable

   ☐ Court and prison records, if applicable

   ☐ Fees (currently $325 unless already paid to the NVC)

4. Step Four: Attend Your Visa Interview

On the appointed day, you and your U.S. petitioning spouse (if he or she can possibly make it) will go to the consulate for an interview. (See a detailed description of the interview and how to prepare for it in Chapter 13.)

Which consulate you go to depends on where you're from and where you live now. If you've been living (legally) in a country that is not your country of citizenship, you'll probably be told to work with the consulate in the country where you now live. If your country of residence doesn't have diplomatic relations with the United States, the NVC will name another consulate to handle your case.

At a minimum, you'll need to bring to your interview:

- ☐ the results of your medical exam (described below)
- ☐ evidence that your marriage is bona fide (as described in Subsection 3d, above)
- ☐ financial documents to bring the Affidavit of Support up to date if it was prepared many months ago, and
- ☐ your passport, valid for at least six more months.

a. The Medical Exam

To prove that you are not inadmissible for medical reasons, you will have to present the results of a medical exam done by a doctor approved by the U.S. consulate. Your appointment notice will give you complete instructions on where and when to visit the appropriate clinic or doctor. There will be a basic fee (the exact amount of which will depend on the country and the doctor) plus more for tests and any vaccinations.

When you go for your medical exam, make sure to bring the following:

- your visa appointment letter
- the doctor's fee
- a form you fill out describing your medical history, if requested
- your vaccination records, and
- photo identification—the doctor must make sure you don't send a healthier person in your place. You may also be requested to bring a passport-style photo.

The doctor will examine you, ask you questions about your medical and psychiatric history and drug use, and test you (including blood tests and chest X-rays). Pregnant women can refuse the chest X-ray until after the baby is born if they have no symptoms of tuberculosis. When the laboratory results are in, the doctor will fill out the appropriate form and either send it directly to the consulate or return it to you in a sealed envelope. DO NOT open the envelope—this will invalidate the results. The doctor should supply you with a separate copy of your results, or tell you whether any illnesses showed up.

b. Fingerprints

Your fingerprints will be taken at your interview, unless you live in a country where this process can be completed in advance (in which case, you will receive a date and location from the consulate).

5. Step Five: At the Border

Assuming all goes well at the visa interview, you will be given an immigrant visa in a sealed envelope (which you must NOT open). But wait—you're not a U.S. resident yet. You'll have six months to use the visa to enter the United States.

At the border, airport, or other port of entry a U.S. border officer will open the sealed envelope containing your visa documents and do a last check to make sure you haven't used fraud. The border officer has expedited removal powers, which means he or she can turn you right around and send you home if he or she sees anything wrong in your packet or with your answers to his questions. Once satisfied that everything is in order, the officer will stamp your passport to show that you're now a U.S. resident (see reproduction of this stamp below; yours will probably have slightly different codes written on it).

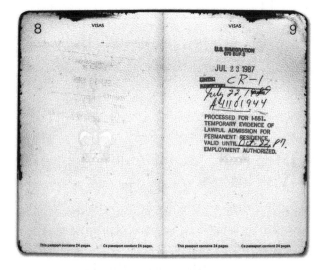

Sample Conditional Residence Stamp

In the unlikely event that you have been married for less than two years on that day, the border officer will make you a conditional resident. In about 21 months, conditional residents will have to file an application with USCIS to convert to permanent residency. (For more information, see Chapter 16, Section G.)

Your actual green card should arrive within 45 days after you pay your USCIS Immigrant Fee ($220).

B. How to Have Your Children and Pets Accompany You

Although your whole family cannot immigrate right now, U.S. laws and regulations do recognize the need for certain of your loved ones to accompany you to the United States and live there with you, including your children and certain pets.

1. Children of the Immigrant Spouse

Your unmarried foreign-born children, whether they are the biological children or the stepchildren of your U.S. permanent resident spouse, may be eligible to obtain green cards. It won't happen automatically, however. A complete review of the application procedures for children is outside the scope of this book. However, once you've filled in all the paperwork described in this book, you will have a good basis of knowledge with which to fill in these forms for your children; or you might be more comfortable using a lawyer.

See Chapter 2, Section B, for a review of which of your children might be eligible to immigrate. After their Priority Dates become current, your children will have to go through the identical visa application steps described in Section A, above (either with you or separately). You will also have to prove that the children are not inadmissible and that they will be financially supported along with you.

a. Application Procedures for Children

This section contains an overview of the procedures for immigrating children. The following is intended as guidance for people who feel comfortable undertaking this process on their own.

To start the process (Step One), your U.S. permanent resident spouse will need either to name the children on your Form I-130 or fill in a separate petition (Form I-130) for each child. It is particularly advisable to fill in a separate Form I-130 for children who are likely to turn 21 in the next five years if your spouse might apply for U.S. citizenship (see discussion in Subsection d, below). In cases where your spouse does file a separate I-130 for a child, it is unnecessary to include photos (these are only required of spouses, not children). But do include your and your spouse's marriage certificate, as well as the children's birth certificates, to show the family relationships.

If your children have the same Priority Date as you, they will wait the same amount of time for a visa to become available. However, children who turn 21 before their Priority Date becomes current may drop into a separate waiting category (2B); although, thanks to the Child Status Protection Act, you can subtract from the child's age the amount of time it took USCIS to approve his or her I-130 petition. Children who get married will drop out of the process altogether.

After you've received your fee instructions from the NVC and paid, you will have to submit a separate Form DS-260 for each child.

> CAUTION
> **Check your own country's law on taking your children if their other parent is staying behind.** If you will be bringing children to the United States who are not the biological children of your U.S. spouse, or who became the adopted children of another person, it will be up to you to comply with any custody requirements. Even if the children are legally in your custody, you may need to get written consent from the other parent for you to take the children out of the country. U.S. consular officials may also require proof that you have legal custody of your children.

The children will have to submit all the same documents as you, except they can simply submit photocopies of the Affidavit of Support (Form I-864). Of course, you'll want to make sure that their names are listed on the I-864 and that the income and assets shown are sufficient to cover them (see discussion of income requirements in Chapter 3). Children under the age of 16 will not need to submit a police certificate.

You can expect to attend your interviews together, though the children probably won't have to answer more than one or two questions.

b. What Happens When a Child Beneficiary Turns 21

If there is a chance that your child might turn 21 *before* his or her Priority Date becomes current, watch out! The minute a child hits the 21st birthday, he will automatically drop into a different visa category, from 2A to 2B. The child can, however, subtract from his or her age the amount of time it took USCIS to approve the initial petition.

This is a protection created in 2002 by the Child Status Protection Act (CSPA). Basically, you have to wait until two events have occurred: your family's petition has been approved, and the child's Priority Date has become current. At that time, you add up the number of days that the petition was pending with USCIS, and subtract it from the child's actual age. If the result of the calculation is a number less than 21, the child may continue with his or her green card application. (Act quickly, however; the child has only a year after becoming eligible to submit the green card application.)

> **EXAMPLE 1:** Nengah's mother marries a U.S. permanent resident named Frank when Nengah is 17 years old. Immediately after, Frank files a petition for the mother that includes Nengah as a derivative. USCIS takes five years to approve the petition, which coincidentally happens right around the time their Priority Date becomes current. By now, Nengah is 22 years old—which, in theory, should drop her into category 2B. Fortunately, under the CSPA, she can subtract the five years that it took USCIS to approve the petition—which puts her age back under 21. As long as Nengah files for permanent residence within one year of becoming eligible, her case should be approved.

> **EXAMPLE 2:** Kareem's father marries a U.S. permanent resident woman named Alyssa when Kareem is 17 years old. Immediately after, Alyssa files a petition for the father that includes Kareem as a derivative. It takes USCIS only one year to approve the petition. However, another five years pass before Kareem and his father's Priority Date becomes current. By this time, Kareem is 23 years old. Kareem can subtract only one year from his age of 23, which makes him legally 22 years old under the CSPA formula, and thus ineligible to adjust status under category 2A—he'll drop to category 2B and face a longer wait before immigrating.

If the CSPA doesn't help and your child does drop into category 2B, he or she will face a wait of several years before being eligible for a visa. This problem is known as "aging out." (However, if your child turns 21 after your spouse has become a U.S. citizen, his or her prospects may be brighter, as discussed below in Subsection d and Chapter 2, Section B.)

It can be very stressful when a child beneficiary is close to getting his or her visa or green card and is about to turn 21. But until your family's Priority Date has become current, or your spouse becomes a U.S. citizen, there's nothing you can do.

c. What Happens When a Child Beneficiary Marries

In preference categories 2A (children of permanent residents, under age 21) and 2B (children of permanent residents, over age 21), the beneficiaries must be unmarried. If your children marry, their beneficiary status is revoked forever. Their only hope is for you or your spouse to become a U.S. citizen and file a new petition for them later.

If you plan to bring along your children in either the 2A or 2B categories, make sure to advise them not to marry until after they get their green card. (USCIS may not find out about the marriage now, but it often catches such cases when the immigrant applies for U.S. citizenship—and then it strips them of their green card.)

d. What Happens to Your Children When Your Spouse Becomes a U.S. Citizen

As you remember from Section A2, above, if your spouse becomes a U.S. citizen it may help you immigrate more quickly. The same is true for your children's immigration—but there's a twist. Children of U.S. citizens need to have their own petitions (Forms I-130) on file with USCIS in order to immigrate as children of a U.S. citizen. They can't enjoy the benefits of that parent's new citizenship if they are merely named on their immigrating parent's petition.

When this whole process began, your spouse may have simply entered your children's names on the I-130 petition for you—which would have been enough for them to immigrate if he or she had remained a permanent resident. To put this in more technical terms, your children were eligible to immigrate as your derivative beneficiaries when your spouse was a permanent resident, but once your spouse became a U.S. citizen, they lost their derivative beneficiary status. They now need to have I-130 petitions of their own.

Fortunately, it's not too late for your spouse to file separate petitions for your children even after becoming a citizen. So long as the children are still unmarried, under age 21, and are your spouse's natural children or legal stepchildren (that is, the marriage took place before they turned 18), they qualify as immediate relatives just like you. As immediate relatives, they will be able to immigrate at the same time as you. It may take several months for the new petitions to be approved, but for most children, it should all work out in the end. However, there are three groups of children who are, to varying degrees, still left out in the cold: those who have married, those who are not your spouse's legal stepchildren, and those who have turned 21.

Children who have married. Your children who have married could not have immigrated with you when your spouse was a permanent resident, so your spouse's citizenship doesn't actually make their situation worse. In fact, it could improve their situation if your spouse is the children's natural father or legal stepfather, because your spouse can file a petition for them in the third preference category.

Children who are not your spouse's legal stepchildren. As part of filing new I-130 petitions for your children, your spouse will have to prove that he or she has a direct relationship with each child, either as natural parent or legal stepparent. To be their legal stepparent, your spouse will have to show that your marriage took place before the child turned 18. If it didn't, then that child cannot immigrate until you yourself become a permanent resident and file a second preference petition for your child.

Children who have turned 21. If your child has turned 21 and no separate I-130 petition was filed for him or her, you're in for some extra work. As with your other children, your U.S. citizen spouse can file a new, separate petition if he or she is the child's natural parent or legal stepparent—but if you don't alert USCIS to the situation, your child won't become an immediate relative like you. Instead, the child will be put into the first preference visa category, which is subject to annual quotas. The child will get a Priority Date, but it will be at the very end of the first preference waiting list.

> **EXAMPLE:** Ricardo, a U.S. permanent resident, filed an I-130 petition for his Mexican wife Soledad and their four children on January 2, 2008. Soledad got an approval notice showing her January 2, 2008 Priority Date. Because the children were named on the I-130 petition and Ricardo was a permanent resident, USCIS knew that the children were derivative beneficiaries and shared Soledad's Priority Date. But on February 3, 2012 Ricardo was sworn in as a U.S. citizen. No more derivative beneficiaries for this family; Ricardo must file a separate I-130 for each child. He does so, on February 10, 2012. That works fine for three of his children, who are under age 21—as minor, unmarried children of a U.S. citizen, they are still immediate relatives and immediately eligible for a visa, just like their mother. But the fourth child, Jorge, has since turned 21.

Letter Requesting Recaptured Priority Date

111 Seaside Lane

Orlando, FL 32801

June 1, 20xx

USCIS

P.O. Box XXX

[See Appendix B for the complete address of the USCIS office serving your geographic region.]

RE: Petitioner: Ricardo Torres

Beneficiary: Jorge Torres

I-130 Petition with Priority Date Recapture Request

Dear Sir/Madam:

I am the Petitioner named above. Enclosed please find an I-130 petition for the above-named Beneficiary (my son) with supporting documents, including:

1. Copy of my son's birth certificate

2. Copy of his mother's and my marriage certificate

3. Copy of my citizenship certificate

4. Fee of $535 (money order).

In addition, please note that I am requesting a recapture of an earlier Priority Date for this application. My son was formerly a Derivative Beneficiary on an approved petition that I filed for his mother in 20xx, with Priority Date January 2, 20xx. I recently became a U.S. citizen, and so my son lost his derivative status.

Please grant my son the earlier, January 2, 20xx, Priority Date on the approval of this I-130 petition. In support of this request, I also enclose the following:

1. Copy of original I-130, showing my son's name

2. Copy of USCIS notice approving this I-130, with January 2, 20xx, Priority Date.

Thank you for your attention to this matter.

Very truly yours,

Ricardo Torres

Ricardo Torres

Jorge's Priority Date is now February 10, 2012. If you look on the *Visa Bulletin* chart in Section A2, above, you'll see that in his category, Mexico first preference, the current Priority Date is August 1, 1997. Jorge is facing an approximate 21-year wait for a visa. If Ricardo had planned ahead and filed a separate I-130 for Jorge in 2008 when he filed for the rest of the family, he could have shaved at least four years off Jorge's wait.

But this isn't fair! True enough. Luckily, there is a remedy for children in this situation. When your U.S. citizen spouse files the new petition, he or she can ask the USCIS service center not to put the child at the bottom of the waiting list, but to give him or her the same Priority Date as the rest of the family, even in this new category. In other words, your spouse asks USCIS to pretend that a separate I-130 petition was submitted for the over-21-year-old at the same time that the petition for the whole family was submitted, perhaps years ago.

This is called "recapturing" a Priority Date. Below is a sample letter showing how to ask for a recapture. The petitioner also needs to include complete copies of the original I-130 petition, the original USCIS approval notice showing the family's old Priority Date, and the petitioner's citizenship certificate.

Approval of recaptured dates is supposed to be automatic. Unfortunately, the USCIS service centers sometimes pay no attention to such requests—even if you write the most compelling letter and include complete documentation. You might get an approval notice showing a new Priority Date rather than your family's old one. Your main recourse would be to write many letters trying to get USCIS to correct the date. As a last resort, you might consider contacting the USCIS Ombudsman (www.dhs.gov/case-assistance).

TIP

Plan ahead—submit separate I-130 petitions for any children who will soon turn 21. If you are at the beginning of the immigration process, have children who may turn 21 before the process ends, and your spouse is likely to apply for U.S. citizenship, you can avoid the hassles involved in recapturing Priority Dates. Your spouse should simply file separate petitions for them from the outset.

2. Your Pets

Good news for your dog and cat, who may not have learned to sign their names yet—they won't need a visa. Bringing pets into the United States is not an immigration law matter. But before bringing any pets to the United States, check into U.S. customs restrictions. In general, pets will be allowed in if they are in good health and have had all the proper vaccinations. Some restrictions apply, however. For example, some states do not permit certain kinds of animals, and monkeys aren't allowed into the United States at all. Check with your local U.S. consulate for details, or read more at www.cbp.gov (enter "pets" into the search box, which will bring up a page called "Pets and Wildlife," on which you'll find a publication called "Bringing Pets and Wildlife into the United States").

SKIP AHEAD

For what to do after you have obtained your visa and entered the United States, see Chapter 16.

Fiancés in the U.S. Engaged to U.S. Citizens

f you are in the United States—legally or illegally—and are engaged to marry a U.S. citizen, you are one step away from being, in immigration law lingo, an immediate relative. Of all the different classes of applicants for U.S. visas, immediate relatives will get them the quickest.

That one step, however, is to get married. Once you are married, a green card should be available to you as soon as you can get through the application procedures. There are no limits to the numbers of immediate relatives allowed to apply for permanent residence each year, and the only waiting period is the time it takes for your paperwork to be processed by the U.S. immigration authorities.

If you marry and apply as an immediate relative, the application process you'll use and where you'll live during the process—in the U.S. or abroad—depends on whether you entered the United States legally or illegally. For example, if you entered legally (and nonfraudulently) with a tourist visa but stayed beyond the expiration date, you have entered the country legally and may apply for your visa here. On the other hand, if you entered without permission, such as by crossing at an unguarded point on the U.S. border, you entered illegally and must apply from abroad. Start by reading Section A to see whether your entry is considered legal or illegal, then move on to the sections that match your current situation.

Because of the benefits of being an immediate relative, there is very little reason to delay your marriage. However, be aware that getting married within 60 days of your U.S. entry will raise suspicions (especially if you entered the U.S. on a tourist visa or visa waiver and plan to apply for the green card within the U.S.)

This chapter will discuss all your immigration options, including returning home and applying for either a fiancé visa or a marriage-based immigrant or nonimmigrant visa. Once you decide what procedure you want to use, you'll be directed to the appropriate chapter to begin the process.

A. Did You Enter Legally or Illegally?

If you entered the United States with permission of the U.S. authorities, you entered legally. Whether you got that permission in advance or were simply allowed in when you arrived, the important thing is that you were personally met and allowed to enter by an officer of the U.S. border control. This could occur either at the border itself or at some other port of entry such as an airport, seaport, or bus station. The usual ways people enter legally are:

- with a visa, such as a tourist, student, or temporary worker visa
- with a border crossing card (a special pass allowing regular entries), and
- under the Visa Waiver Program, where citizens of certain countries are allowed to enter the U.S. as tourists by showing their passport, without first obtaining an entry visa.

! CAUTION
Your entry must pass the fraud test, too.
As discussed in Chapter 1, Section B2, using a tourist or other nonimmigrant visa to enter the U.S. with a specific plan of applying for a marriage-based green card is considered visa fraud. You may be disqualified from receiving the green card as a result.

An illegal entry is, naturally, the opposite of a legal entry. People entering illegally have failed to obtain permission to enter. They may pay someone to sneak them across the U.S. border, wait until the dead of night and find an unguarded point on the U.S. border, or conceal themselves in the trunk of someone's car. USCIS says that they entered "without inspection," which means that they weren't personally met and approved for entry by a U.S. border control official. (USCIS refers to such people as "EWIs," pronounced "ee-wee," which stands for entry without inspection.) People who entered the United States without inspection, or illegally, will have a very difficult time obtaining a green card.

> SKIP AHEAD
>
> **If you entered the United States by crossing the border illegally, skip ahead to Section C.**

B. Fiancés Who Entered the U.S. Legally

This section explains the entry options for foreign nationals who entered the United States legally and still live there. If this describes your situation, you have a choice among three immigration paths:

- Get married and immediately apply for your green card at a USCIS office (even if the expiration date of your visa has passed). This path is explained below in Section 1.
- Leave the United States before you have overstayed your visa by six months or more and apply at a U.S. consulate to return on a fiancé visa. This choice is explained below in Section 2.
- Leave the United States before you have overstayed your visa by six months or more, get married, and apply at a U.S. consulate to return on an immigrant visa (green card) or nonimmigrant visa (a special version of the fiancé visa for married couples). This option is explained below in Section 3.

> CAUTION
>
> **If you overstay your visa.** If you have stayed in the United States without permission for six months or more at any time since April 1, 1997, you should avoid leaving at all until you have a green card. That's because you could be barred from returning for three or ten years, depending how long you overstayed. (See Chapter 2, Section A, for more on this issue.)

1. Overview of the U.S. Marriage-Based Green Card Option

If you and your U.S. citizen fiancé get married, you will, as someone who entered legally and non-fraudulently, be one of few immigrants eligible to stay in the United States while you apply and wait for your green card. The fact that you entered the United States legally and that your spouse is a U.S. citizen is in most cases a magic combination. It allows you to get your green card through a procedure called adjustment of status. Using this procedure, you can apply for permanent residence without leaving the United States, even if you have stayed past the date when you were originally supposed to leave (which is most likely the expiration date of your visa).

> **EXAMPLE:** Marbelita came to the United States in May, on a tourist visa. While enjoying the view from the Empire State Building, she struck up a conversation with Bill, a U.S. citizen. They fell in love, and Marbelita couldn't bear to leave when her tourist visa expired in July. She and Bill married in August. Although she is now in the United States illegally, the combination of her legal entry and Bill's status as a U.S. citizen allows her to apply for her green card (adjustment of status) at a local USCIS office. (Also important in this scenario is that, because Marbelita met Bill only after her arrival in the U.S., there should be no suspicion that she misused a tourist visa so as to gain U.S. entry, marry him, and get a green card.) As soon as Marbelita submits that application, her stay will become legal and she and Bill can live together in the United States while awaiting approval of her green card. Of course, there are other hurdles they must cross, including convincing USCIS that their marriage is real and not simply a way for Marbelita to stay in the United States.

There are many benefits to staying in the United States during the application process. You will avoid being separated from your spouse and will receive a permit to work while you wait to attend the final green card interview at a local USCIS office. Although your spouse will be required to accompany you to that interview (which is not required of overseas applicants), this is actually an advantage, both for moral support and because a large part of the discussion may concern your spouse's ability to support you financially.

And unlike overseas interviews, at a stateside interview you can bring an attorney with you if your case has become complicated during the application process. For instance, if you realize that you might fall into a ground of inadmissibility, you'll need a lawyer's help to argue that it doesn't apply.

a. Why Entry on a Temporary Visa Might Pose a Problem

If you used a temporary visa—such as a tourist visa—to enter the United States, planning all along to get married, you might find yourself facing accusations of visa fraud if you apply to adjust status in the United States. Particularly if you knew your spouse before arriving in the United States, and you used a temporary visa to enter, USCIS is likely to be suspicious. At the interview where your green card would normally be approved, USCIS might question you about whether your real intention when you arrived was to apply for permanent residence after your marriage. Unless you entered on a fiancé visa, the discovery that this was your real intention will lead USCIS to demand that you file an additional application requesting a waiver or forgiveness of your visa fraud. (See Chapter 1, Section B2, if you think you might be in this category.)

Of course, if you met your spouse after you arrived in the United States, this won't be a problem. And even for other couples, uncertainties about their marriage plans, as well as the length of time they waited to get married or to begin the green card application process (at least 60 days after entry is best), often satisfy USCIS that they didn't misuse an entry visa.

b. Two-Year Testing Period for New Marriages

You must be married for two years to obtain a permanent green card. Since most people will apply for their adjustment of status soon after marrying, they will first be given a conditional green card, which is valid for only two years. You won't be kicked out of the country after the two years—provided you don't forget to file the next application. This is

an application for a permanent green card, which sometimes involves an interview to allow USCIS to take a second look at whether your marriage is real. (See Chapter 16, Section G, for more on this issue.)

c. Your Children

Your unmarried children under age 21 may be eligible to submit applications to adjust status along with you, if your marriage to the U.S. citizen takes place when they are still under 18. Your spouse will also need to file separate petitions on their behalf (as his or her stepchildren).

SKIP AHEAD

If you are certain that you wish to marry and adjust status in the United States, go straight to Chapter 11 for instructions on the first step, the I-130 petition to be filed by your spouse.

2. Overview of the Fiancé Visa Option

As long as you leave the United States before overstaying your visa by six months or more, your planned marriage to a U.S. citizen should qualify you for a fiancé ("K-1") visa in order to return. (See Chapter 2, Section B, for the eligibility requirements for a fiancé visa.)

If you overstay by six months or more or have stayed in the United States illegally for six continuous months at any time after April 1997, however, this option disappears. You will need a waiver (official government forgiveness) of your illegal stay in order to return before three or ten years are up. As a fiancé applying for a K-1 visa, your waiver could be approved only conditionally until your marriage to the petitioner in the United States. Follow the steps in Section C2b, below.

If you decide to leave and apply for a fiancé visa, it will allow you to enter the United States, marry within 90 days, and apply for your green card in the United States. Your unmarried children under age 21 will be eligible to accompany you. There are no quotas or limits on the number of people who can obtain fiancé visas and subsequently green cards through marriage to a U.S. citizen. A fiancé visa usually takes at least six months to obtain.

a. K-1 Visa or a U.S. Marriage Only

A fiancé visa gives you no choice but to hold your marriage ceremony in the United States. Couples often ask whether their overseas marriage really counts, or wonder why they can't just get married for a second time after entering on a fiancé visa.

Unfortunately, once you're legally married, no matter where the marriage occurred, you no longer qualify for a fiancé (K-1) visa. You must apply for U.S. entry as the spouse of a U.S. citizen.

TIP

Wedding ceremonies that don't result in legally binding marriages won't stand in your way. If you don't feel right leaving home unmarried, see if you can arrange for a religious or other ceremony that will not be legally recognized or registered in your country. USCIS does not recognize these as valid marriages. You will need to have a legal marriage in the United States once you get here.

b. The Green Card Application Will Be Separate

Fiancés wishing to live in the United States will need to marry and apply for their green card within the 90 days they are allowed to stay in the United States on their K-1 fiancé visa, using a procedure called adjustment of status. This application procedure usually takes between five months and a year to complete and involves even more paperwork than the fiancé visa.

SKIP AHEAD

If you are certain that you wish to leave the United States and apply for a fiancé visa overseas, go straight to Chapter 5, Section F, for further instructions. This petition can be filed before or after you leave the United States.

3. Overview of the Marriage-Based Visa (Consular) Option

For most married applicants, adjustment of status in the United States is the preferred way to obtain permanent residence. However, a second option for people who haven't overstayed their visa by six months or more is to leave the United States and apply for a green card at a U.S. consulate overseas.

Although the procedural steps to apply for a green card are very similar to those for obtaining a fiancé visa, the application itself is somewhat more demanding. At the final interview, you can be accompanied by your spouse if you wish, but not by an attorney.

It makes sense to apply for your U.S. residency at a consulate only if doing so will significantly speed up the green-card approval process, or perhaps to avoid suspicions of tourist visa fraud. The adjustment of status process in the United States usually takes between many months to a year. The application process for a green card through a consulate may take a year, but some consulates are much more efficient and will approve an application within months.

(By the way, another visa option for married couples at U.S. consulates is a K-3 nonimmigrant visa, but it doesn't get you a green card—it only gets you back into the United States, where you have to spend another four or five months applying for your green card. That means it's probably not a good option for you.)

Contact the U.S. consulate in your home country (and ask other immigrants about their experience with that consulate) to find out how long the consulate takes for green card application and approval.

To find out how long it is taking your local USCIS office to process applications for adjustment of status, go www.uscis.gov and click "Check Processing Times." In the "Form" box, choose I-485. Then choose your local field office from the "Field Office or Service Center" drop-down menu, and click "Get processing time."

CAUTION

Carry proof of when you depart the United States. If you decide to apply for your green card at a U.S. consulate, your history of U.S. visits will trigger a request that you prove you left on time. Collect and keep all evidence, such as your plane tickets, store receipts, medical records, credit card statements, and anything else relevant. (See Chapter 2, Section A, for the rules on and penalties for overstaying a U.S. visa by six months or more.)

a. Two-Year Testing Period for New Marriages

You must be married for two years to obtain a permanent green card. Since most people will apply for their immigrant visa and green card soon after marrying, they will be given only a conditional green card, which is valid for two years. You won't be kicked out of the country after the two years—provided you don't forget to file the next application. This is an application for a permanent green card, which sometimes involves an interview to allow USCIS to take a second look at whether your marriage is real. (See Chapter 16, Section G, for more on this issue.)

b. Your Children

Your unmarried children under age 21 may be eligible to submit applications for immigrant visas along with you if your marriage to the U.S. citizen takes place when they are still under 18. Your spouse will also need to file separate petitions on their behalf (as his or her stepchildren).

SKIP AHEAD

If you are certain that you wish to leave the United States and apply overseas, go straight to Chapter 7 for instructions on the first step, the I-130 petition to be filed by your spouse. This petition can be filed before or after you leave the United States.

4. If You Have Children 18–21

If you have children between the ages of 18 and 21 who are not the biological children or stepchildren of your spouse and you want to bring them to the United States, you should, if possible, leave the U.S. and apply for a fiancé visa. Due to a nonsensical twist in the immigration laws, children under 21 can accompany a fiancé on his or her visa and then apply for a green card, but only children whose parents married when the child was under 18 can qualify as stepchildren and accompany a just-married spouse on an immigrant visa or apply for a green card.

Don't even think of leaving the United States if, after April 1, 1997, you or your children have overstayed your right to be there by six months or more, on this visa or any other visa. You could be barred from reentering the United States for up to ten years under these circumstances. (See the discussion of time bars in Chapter 2, Section A.)

C. Fiancés Who Entered the U.S. Illegally

This section explains the immigration choices for foreign nationals who entered the United States illegally and still live there. If you've come to the United States illegally more than once, spent a total of a year or more during your previous visits, and/or were deported at the end of a visit, see an attorney before going any further. You may be permanently barred from immigrating to the United States. (See Chapter 2, Section A, for further review of the permanent bar.)

Assuming these difficulties don't apply to you, there are three options for you to consider if you entered the United States illegally and are engaged to marry a U.S. citizen. You can:

- Marry, stay, and find a way to adjust your status to permanent resident in the United States. This rare and unlikely path is explained below in Section 1.
- Marry and leave, then apply for an immigrant visa to return. If you stayed illegally in the United States for more than six months, apply for a waiver (forgiveness) of your illegal stay. (The new "provisional waiver" might yield an approval of your application even before you

leave the U.S. for your consular interview.) If the waiver is denied, and you have left the U.S., you may be barred from returning for three or ten years. This choice is covered in Section 2, below.

- Leave the United States before you have been here illegally for six months and apply at a U.S. consulate to return on a fiancé visa. This option is described in Section 3, below.

1. Marry and Adjust Status in the United States

As the fiancé of a U.S. citizen, you are theoretically one step away from being an immediate relative—an immigrant who is immediately eligible for a green card. You will be an immediate relative as soon as you get married. Unfortunately, your eligibility may not get you a green card anytime soon. The trouble is that only certain categories of immigrants are allowed to apply for their green card in the United States (using the procedure called adjustment of status). People who entered the United States without being inspected and admitted by a U.S. official are not among them.

However, a very few people might be lucky enough to fall into an exception, based on having started the application process before the laws changed and made them ineligible. You may be eligible to adjust status in the United States if an employer filed a labor certification on your behalf or a family member (whether it was your spouse or someone else) filed an immigrant petition (Form I-130) on your behalf either:

- before January 14, 1998, or
- between January 14, 1998 and April 30, 2001, if you can also prove that you were physically present in the United States on December 21, 2000.

If your labor certification or petition was approved, or was denied only because of a mistake by USCIS, you may be allowed to adjust status in the United States. (For more details on this issue, see Chapter 2, Section A.)

If you fall into this exception, your best bet is to get married and file for adjustment of status in the United States. (But you should really consult with an immigration attorney to confirm your eligibility.) This is especially true if you have stayed in the United States for more than six months. If you were to leave and try to apply for your green card at a U.S. consulate overseas, the consulate could punish your illegal stay by preventing your return to the United States for three or ten years.

(In the alternative, if you have DACA, see Chapter 11, Section C1.)

SKIP AHEAD
If you are sure this option will work for you, proceed directly to Chapter 11, Section D, for instructions on how to begin the application process.

2. Marry, Leave, and Apply for an Immigrant Visa to Return

If, as is likely, you do not fall into one of the exceptional categories of immigrants who are allowed to stay in the United States to use the adjustment of status procedure, you must decide whether you can get a visa overseas at a U.S. consulate. This will depend on how long you have stayed illegally in the United States.

If you have not stayed in the United States more than six months, proceed to Subsection a, below. If you have stayed in the United States illegally longer than six months, proceed to Subsection b below.

a. If You Have Stayed Illegally for Less Than Six Months

If you don't fit into the exceptions described in Section C1 above, but you haven't yet stayed in the United States illegally for more than six months, your safest bet is to get married and leave before that date rolls around. Leaving now will at least protect you from being found inadmissible based on your unlawful presence.

After leaving, you can get a marriage-based immigrant visa because of your immediate relative status (spouse of a U.S. citizen). This may mean many months of separation from your spouse while you wait overseas for your green card to be approved. But months of separation now might be better than being denied a green card later, if you stay too long illegally in the United States.

> ⊘ **CAUTION**
>
> **Carry proof of when you depart the United States.** If you decide to apply for your green card at a U.S. consulate, your history of U.S. visits will trigger a request that you prove how much time you spent there. Collect and keep all evidence, such as your plane tickets, store receipts, medical records, credit card statements, and anything else relevant. (See Chapter 2, Section A, for the rules on and penalties for staying in the U.S. illegally for six months or more.)

> ⇨ **SKIP AHEAD**
>
> **If you are sure you will use this option,** go to Chapter 7 for further instructions on your immigration process.

b. If You Have Stayed Illegally for More Than Six Months

If you are not eligible to apply for a green card (adjust status) in the United States upon marrying, and you have stayed illegally in the United States for more than six months, you are in a tough situation. You can't get a green card by staying in the United States; but if you leave, you face being barred from reentering the United States—for three years if your stay was between six months and a year, and for ten years if your stay was more than one year.

You should see an attorney, and not just any immigration lawyer. Look for an attorney who has actual experience with this problem. The attorney can help you consider whether you can ask the U.S. government to forgive your illegal stay. Previously, applicants for this waiver (called an "I-601") would have to leave the U.S. and apply at a U.S. consulate along with their application for permanent residence. This carried the significant risk that their waiver might be denied, blocking their return to the United States for either three or ten years, depending on the length of their unlawful stay.

However, USCIS now allows applicants to apply for a "provisional," I-601A waiver while still in the United States. That way, they can wait for an approval of their waiver before leaving for their consular interview. USCIS has not been generous in approving these provisional waivers, however, so your best bet is to get help from an attorney.

To get a waiver, you'll have to prove that the denial of your visa would cause extreme hardship to your U.S. spouse or children—and when the law says extreme, it means much more than the sadness your spouse and children will feel at your being thousands of miles away. The classic case of extreme hardship is someone whose U.S. citizen spouse has severe medical problems that require the other spouse's constant attention.

There is another option, which we don't recommend. You could stay in the United States illegally, hoping that the immigration laws change in your favor and make you eligible for a green card. Many couples have done this, but it is a huge gamble. Recent changes in the immigration laws have made them harsher, not gentler, on immigrants; and there is no sign that this trend will change.

But none of us have a crystal ball, and some families find it unthinkable to separate now, come what may later. If you take this option, however, you must be aware that you will likely never obtain legal residence in the United States and will face the ever-present possibility of being caught, deported, and prevented from reentering the United States for at least ten years.

3. Leave and Apply for a K-1 Fiancé Visa to Return

If you have been in the United States for less than six months and you have not married, you can consider leaving and applying for a K-1 fiancé visa to return. Stay over six months, however, and this option disappears. You will need a waiver (official government forgiveness) of your illegal stay in order to return before three or ten years are up. As a fiancé applying for a K-1 visa, your waiver could be approved only conditionally until your marriage to the petitioner in the United States. Follow the steps in Section b, above.

Assuming you haven't stayed six months illegally, your planned marriage to a U.S. citizen should qualify you for a fiancé visa. (See Chapter 2, Section B, for the eligibility requirements.) A fiancé visa will allow you to enter the United States, marry within 90 days, and apply for your green card in the United States. Your unmarried children under age 21 will be eligible to accompany you.

There are no quotas or limits on the number of people who can obtain fiancé visas and subsequent green cards through marriage to a U.S. citizen. A fiancé visa usually takes at least six months to obtain.

a. K-1 Visa Is for U.S. Marriage Only

A K-1 fiancé visa gives you no choice but to hold your marriage ceremony in the United States. Couples often ask whether their overseas marriage really counts, or wonder why they can't just get married for a second time after entering on a fiancé visa. Unfortunately, once you're legally married, no matter where the marriage occurred, you no longer qualify for a K-1 fiancé visa and you must apply for U.S. residency as the spouse of a U.S. citizen.

You may also have heard about an alternative visa, call the K-3 visa, available to already-married couples. The K-3 visa is a special form of fiancé visa, which allows a married immigrant to enter the United States as a temporary nonimmigrant, and then complete a green card application process after arriving in the United States. However, because they tend to save

neither time nor money, we do not recommend or discuss them in detail within this book.

> **TIP**
> **Wedding ceremonies that don't result in legally binding marriages won't stand in your way.** If you don't feel right leaving home unmarried, see if you can arrange for a religious or other ceremony that will not be legally recognized or registered in your country. USCIS does not recognize these as valid marriages. You will need to have a legal marriage in the United States once you get there.

b. The Green Card Application Will Be Separate

Fiancés wishing to live in the United States will need to marry and apply for their green card during the 90 days they are allowed to stay in the United States on their K-1 fiancé visa, using a procedure called adjustment of status. This application procedure usually takes between five months and a year to complete and involves even more paperwork than the fiancé visa.

4. If You Have Children 18–21

If you have children between the ages of 18 and 21 who are not the biological children or stepchildren of your spouse, and you want to bring them to the United States, you should, if possible, leave the U.S. and apply for a fiancé visa. Due to a nonsensical twist in the immigration laws, children under 21 can accompany a fiancé on his or her visa, but only children whose parents married while the child was under 18 can qualify as stepchildren and accompany a just-married spouse on an immigrant visa or apply for a green card.

Don't even think of leaving the United States if you or your children have stayed there illegally for six months or more, at any time since April 1, 1997. You could be barred from reentering the United States for up to ten years under these circumstances. (See the discussion of time bars in Chapter 2, Section A.)

Next Step If You Entered The U.S. Legally

If you decide to get married and apply for your green card in the United States:	See Chapter 11 covering spouses of U.S. citizens living in the U.S. Go to Section D, which covers the first application.
If you decide to leave the United States unmarried before overstaying by six months or more, and apply for a K-1 fiancé visa:	See Chapter 5, Section F, for fiancé visa application procedures.
If you decide to marry (abroad or in the U.S.), leave the United States, and apply for an immigrant visa:	See Chapter 7 for marriage-based visa application procedures.
If none of the above options work:	See an attorney; Chapter 17 contains tips on finding a good one.

Next Step If You Entered The U.S. Illegally

If you decide to get married and are legally allowed to adjust in the United States:	See Chapter 11 for spouses of U.S. citizens living in the United States. Go to Section D, which covers the first application.
If you have not stayed illegally for more than six months and decide to leave the United States and apply for a fiancé visa:	See Chapter 5, Section F, regarding fiancé visa application procedures.
If you have not stayed illegally for more than six months and decide to leave the United States and apply for a marriage-based immigrant visa:	See Chapter 7 regarding marriage visa application procedures for overseas spouses of U.S. citizens.
If none of the above options work:	See an attorney; Chapter 17 contains tips on finding a good one.

Fiancés in the U.S. Engaged to Permanent Residents

I f you are in the United States—legally or illegally—and are engaged to marry a U.S. lawful permanent resident, you are not immediately eligible to obtain permanent residence (a green card) on this basis. Only foreign nationals married to *U.S. citizens* are immediately eligible for permanent residence.

No one will stop you from getting married in the United States—in fact, getting married will take you one step closer to a green card, by allowing you to get on the waiting list for one. But there are quotas for the number of spouses of permanent residents who are allowed green cards each year, which means there are long waiting lists. Many newlyweds will have to live outside the United States while their names sit on a waiting list for a marriage-based visa—a wait of at least a year or two.

During that time, you might be able to wait in (or travel regularly to) the U.S. on a temporary visa. But anyone entering the country on (or applying for) a tourist visa, in particular, might face suspicions of intending to stay permanently.

The key to knowing how and where—in the U.S. or overseas—you'll get your green card is whether you entered the United States legally or illegally. For example, if you entered with permission, such as with a tourist visa, but stayed beyond the expiration date, you have entered the country legally and may eventually be able to get your green card in the United States. On the other hand, if you entered illegally, for example by crossing secretly at an unguarded point, you lose certain important procedural rights—you may have to leave the United States right away if you want to get a green card later.

Start by reading Section A to see whether your entry is considered legal or illegal, then move to the subsections that match your current situation.

A. Did You Enter Legally or Illegally?

If you entered the United States with permission of the U.S. authorities, you entered legally. Whether you got that permission in advance or were simply allowed in when you arrived, the important thing is that you were personally met and allowed to enter by an officer of the U.S. border control. This could occur either at the border itself or at some other port of entry such as an airport, seaport, or bus station. The usual ways people enter legally are:

- with a visa (a tourist, student, or temporary worker visa, for example)
- with a border crossing card (a special pass allowing regular entries), or
- under the Visa Waiver Program (where citizens of certain countries are allowed to enter the U.S. as tourists by showing their passport, without first obtaining an entry visa).

CAUTION
Your entry must pass the fraud test, too. As discussed in Chapter 1, Section B2, using a tourist or other nonimmigrant visa to enter the U.S. with a specific plan of applying for a marriage-based green card is considered visa fraud. You may be disqualified from receiving the green card as a result.

An illegal entry is, naturally, the opposite of a legal entry. People entering illegally have failed to obtain permission to enter. They may pay someone to sneak them across the U.S. border, wait until the dead of night and find an unguarded point on the U.S. border, or conceal themselves in the trunk of someone else's car. USCIS says that they entered "without inspection," which means that they weren't personally met and approved for entry by a U.S. border control official. (USCIS refers to such people as "EWIs," pronounced "ee-wee," which stands for entry without inspection.) The immigration laws make getting a green card very difficult for people who entered the United States without inspection, or illegally.

SKIP AHEAD
If you entered the United States by crossing the border illegally, skip ahead to Section C.

B. Fiancés Who Entered the U.S. Legally

This section explains the immigration options for foreign nationals who entered the United States legally, as defined in Section A above, and still live there. Even if you are living in the U.S. illegally now, this section is for you.

Before we discuss your actual visa options, let's sweep away one myth. A fiancé visa is not an option for you. Fiancé visas are not given to fiancés of permanent residents, and they're not given to people already inside the United States. They are only available to the fiancés of U.S. citizens living overseas.

This said, you do have two options. You can:

- wait until your fiancé becomes a U.S. citizen, then apply for a fiancé or a marriage-based visa, as explained below in Section 1, or
- marry your fiancé and request a green card as the spouse of a lawful permanent resident, covered in Section 2.

> **CAUTION**
>
> **Don't delay.** If you are close to the end of your legal stay in the United States you must act quickly. Despite your planned marriage, it may be necessary to leave the United States very soon in order to get a green card later. (See Chapter 2, Section A, for more on the consequences of visa overstays.)

1. If Your Fiancé Becomes a U.S. Citizen

In order to become a U.S. citizen, your fiancé must have been a U.S. permanent resident for five years (with some exceptions), lived in the United States for at least half of those years, be of good moral character, and pass an exam covering the English language as well as U.S. history and government. (To learn more about becoming a U.S. citizen, see the USCIS website at www.uscis.gov or *Becoming*

a U.S. Citizen: A Guide to the Law, Exam & Interview, by Ilona Bray (Nolo).)

To help speed your progress toward a green card, your fiancé should look into the requirements for U.S. citizenship, and apply as soon as he or she can. After your fiancé obtains U.S. citizenship, you can, for example:

- get married and immediately apply for your green card at a USCIS office (even if the expiration date of your visa has passed)
- leave the United States before overstaying your visa by six months or more and apply at a U.S. consulate to return on a fiancé visa, or
- leave the United States before overstaying your visa by six months or more and, once you're married, apply at a U.S. consulate to return on an immigrant visa (green card).

These and other options are discussed fully in Chapter 9, covering fiancés of U.S. citizens living in the United States.

> **CAUTION**
>
> **Be careful about leaving the U.S. if you have an expired visa or status.** If you have stayed six months or more past the expiration date of your visa, try to avoid the options that involve leaving the United States before obtaining your permanent resident status. You could be barred from returning to the United States for three or ten years, depending how long you overstayed. (See Chapter 2, Section A, for more on this issue.)

2. If You Marry Your Permanent Resident Fiancé

If you marry your permanent resident fiancé while in the United States or abroad, you become what the immigration law calls a preference relative. This means that you become eligible for permanent residence in the United States—but not right away. There are annual quotas and long waiting lists for people in this category. You will not be able to legally live in the United States with your spouse during the waiting period unless you have another type of visa that allows you to stay the entire time. Your options boil down to the following:

- stay in the United States legally (if your nonimmigrant visa lasts long enough to get you through the waiting period) and then adjust your status to permanent resident in the United States
- stay in the United States illegally, hoping to adjust your status to green card holder in the United States, most likely after your spouse becomes a citizen
- leave the United States before you have overstayed your visa by six months or more, wait overseas, then apply for a green card at a U.S. consulate
- leave the United States after you have overstayed your visa by more than six months but less than one year (thereby avoiding the more severe ten-year time bar), wait overseas, then apply for a green card at a U.S. consulate, or
- leave the United States after you have overstayed your visa by more than six months or a year, wait overseas, then apply for your green card and request a waiver (forgiveness) of your overstay at a U.S. consulate. (Or, you can apply for a waiver before having to leave the U.S.; for more on this "provisional waiver" procedure, see Chapter 9, Section C2b.)

Learn more about each of the above options in Chapter 12 covering spouses of U.S. permanent residents.

C. Fiancés Who Entered the U.S. Illegally

The advice in this section is for foreign fiancés living in the United States after crossing the border illegally. If you are close to having stayed illegally for six months in the United States, you must act quickly. When you ultimately go to a U.S. consulate to apply for your green card, you could face severe penalties if you've passed the six-month mark. You may not be able to return to the United States for up to ten years. (See Chapter 2, Section A, for more on these consequences.)

CAUTION

If this is your second time (or more) in the United States and you spent a total of a year or more during your previous visits and/or were deported at the end of a visit, see an attorney before going any further. You may be permanently barred from immigrating to the United States. (See Chapter 2, Section A, for further review of the permanent bar.)

Before we discuss your actual visa options, let's sweep away one myth. A fiancé visa is not an option for you. Fiancé visas are not given to fiancés of permanent residents, and they're not given to people already inside the United States. They are available only to the fiancés of U.S. citizens living overseas.

This said, you do have a choice of methods for immigrating to the United States:

- wait until your fiancé becomes a U.S. citizen, then apply for a fiancé or a marriage-based visa (either of which will probably involve leaving the United States first and getting a waiver), as explained in Section 1, or
- marry your fiancé and request a green card application as the spouse of a lawful permanent resident (which will probably involve leaving the United States first and getting a waiver), as explained in Section 2.

CAUTION

Be careful about leaving the United States if you have stayed illegally for six months or more. If you have, try to avoid the options that involve leaving before obtaining your permanent resident status. You could be barred from returning to the United States for three or ten years, depending how long you stayed illegally. (See Chapter 2, Section A, for more on this issue.)

1. If Your Fiancé Becomes a U.S. Citizen

In order to become a U.S. citizen, your fiancé must have been a U.S. permanent resident for five years (with some exceptions), lived in the United States for at least half of those years, be of good moral character, and pass an exam covering the English language as well as U.S. history and government. To learn more about becoming a U.S. citizen, see the USCIS website at www.uscis.gov or *Becoming a U.S. Citizen: A Guide to the Law, Exam & Interview*, by Ilona Bray (Nolo).

To help speed your progress toward a green card, your fiancé should look into the requirements for U.S. citizenship and apply as soon as he or she can. After your fiancé obtains U.S. citizenship, you can, for example:

- marry and leave, then apply for an immigrant visa to return. If you stayed illegally in the United States for more than six months, accompany your application with a request for a waiver (forgiveness) of your illegal stay. Get a lawyer's help with this—if the waiver is denied, you may be barred from returning for three or ten years.
- leave the United States before you have been here illegally for six months and apply at a U.S. consulate to return on a fiancé visa.

These and other options are discussed fully in Chapter 9, covering fiancés of U.S. citizens living in the United States.

2. If You Marry Your Permanent Resident Fiancé

If you marry your permanent resident fiancé while in the United States or abroad, you become a so-called preference relative. That means you will become eligible for permanent residence in the United States. But there are annual quotas and long waiting lists for people in this category. You also will not be able to legally live in the United States with your spouse during the waiting period (unless you were able to apply for another immigration program that allowed you to stay legally for a time, such as political asylum or deferred action, but this is unlikely).

Because of your illegal entry, you will probably not be allowed to apply for your green card inside the United States, even after your long wait. Your four options are to:

- stay in the United States illegally, hoping to adjust your status to permanent residence through USCIS, probably through an eventual change in the laws, or because your husband or wife became a U.S. citizen
- leave the United States before you have stayed illegally for six months or more, wait out your waiting period (when your "Priority Date" is current), and apply for your green card through a U.S. consulate overseas
- leave the United States after you have stayed illegally for more than six months but less than a year, wait out your waiting period as well as your three-year inadmissibility period, and apply for your green card through a U.S. consulate overseas, or
- if you have stayed illegally for more than a year, apply for your green card along with a request for waiver of your illegal stay, through a U.S. consulate overseas.

Learn more about these options in Chapter 12, covering spouses of U.S. permanent residents living in the United States.

Next Step If You Entered The U.S. Legally

Your fiancé will become a U.S. citizen:	See Chapter 9 covering fiancés of U.S. citizens living in the United States.
You will marry soon:	See Chapter 12 covering spouses of U.S. permanent residents living in the United States.

Next Step If You Entered The U.S. Illegally

Your fiancé will become a U.S. citizen:	See Chapter 9 covering fiancés of U.S. citizens living in the United States.
You will marry soon:	See Chapter 12 covering spouses of lawful permanent residents living in the United States.

Spouses of U.S. Citizens, Living in the U.S.

If you are married to a U.S. citizen, you are what is called an "immediate relative" in USCIS terminology. There are no limits on the number of immediate relatives allowed to apply for permanent residence each year. The only waiting period is the time it takes for your paperwork to be processed by the U.S. government. A green card will be available to you just as soon as you can get through the application procedures—but watch out, this is where things can get complicated.

Even though you are in the United States now, you may have to leave and apply for your green card overseas. The key to knowing how and where you'll get your green card is whether you entered the United States legally or illegally. Here's how it works: If you entered with permission, such as with a student or tourist visa (and with the intent to be a tourist, not to misuse the visa by applying for a green card), you have entered the country legally. That's true even if you stayed beyond the visa expiration date. Your road to a green card should be fairly smooth—you should be able to stay in the United States for your entire application process, which will take about a year.

On the other hand, if you entered illegally, for example by crossing secretly at an unguarded border point, you lose certain important procedural rights—you may have to leave the United States and apply for your green card at a U.S. consulate abroad—which could be difficult, depending on how long you have lived in the United States after that illegal entry. Start by reading Section A to see whether your entry is considered legal or illegal, then move to the subsections that match your current situation.

> **!** **CAUTION**
> **Your entry must pass the fraud test, too.**
> As discussed in Chapter 1, Section B2, using a tourist or other nonimmigrant visa to enter the U.S. with a specific plan of applying for a marriage-based green card is considered visa fraud. You may be disqualified from receiving the green card as a result.

A. Did You Enter Legally or Illegally?

If you entered the United States with permission of the U.S. authorities, you entered legally. Whether you got that permission in advance or were simply allowed in when you arrived, the important thing is that you were personally met and allowed to enter by an officer of the U.S. border control. This could occur either at the border itself or at some other port of entry such as an airport, seaport, or bus station. The usual ways people enter legally are:

- with a visa (a tourist, student, or temporary worker visa, for example)
- with a border crossing card (a special pass allowing regular entries), or
- under the Visa Waiver Program or VWP (where citizens of certain countries are allowed to enter the U.S. as tourists by showing their passport, without first obtaining an entry visa).

An illegal entry is, naturally, the opposite of a legal entry. People entering illegally have failed to obtain permission to enter. They may pay someone to sneak them across the U.S. border, wait until the dead of night and find an unguarded point on the U.S. border, or conceal themselves in the trunk of someone else's car. USCIS says that they entered "without inspection," which means that they weren't personally met and approved for entry by a U.S. border control official. (USCIS refers to such people as "EWIs," pronounced "ee-wee," which stands for entry without inspection.) The immigration laws make getting a green card very difficult for people who entered the United States without inspection, or illegally.

> **!** **CAUTION**
> **Even if you are married to a U.S. citizen, there are reasons USCIS could reject your application and move to deport you.** (See Chapter 2, Section A, for a discussion of the grounds of inadmissibility and review Chapter 2, Section B, to make sure you meet the basic eligibility criteria for a green card.)

SKIP AHEAD
If you entered the United States by crossing the border illegally, skip ahead to Section C.

B. Spouses Who Entered the U.S. Legally

This section is for foreign nationals married to U.S. citizens and living in the United States after entering legally. There are two ways to apply for your green card. You might have a choice to either:

- stay in the United States and submit an application to adjust status to permanent residence at a local USCIS office, as explained in Section 1, below, or
- leave the United States before you have overstayed your visa by six months or more and apply for your immigrant visa/green card at an overseas U.S. consulate, as covered in Section 2.

1. Stay in the U.S. to Apply

The fact that you entered the United States legally and that your spouse is a U.S. citizen is a magic combination. It should allow you to get your green card through a procedure called adjustment of status (unless you tried to create your own magic by misusing an entry visa, as described in Subsection 1a, below).

Using this procedure, you can apply for permanent residence without leaving the United States, even if you have stayed past the date when you were originally supposed to leave (which is most likely the expiration date shown on your I-94 card).

> **EXAMPLE:** Marbelita came to the United States in May, on a tourist visa. While enjoying the view from the Empire State Building, she struck up a conversation with Bill, a U.S. citizen. They fell in love and Marbelita couldn't bear to leave when her tourist visa expired in July. She and Bill married in August. Although she is now in the United States

illegally, the combination of her legal entry and Bill's status as a U.S. citizen allows her to apply for her green card (adjustment of status) through a local USCIS office. As soon as Marbelita submits that application, her stay will become legal and she and Bill can live together in the United States while awaiting approval of her green card. Of course, there are other hurdles they must cross, including convincing USCIS that their marriage is real and not simply a way for Marbelita to stay in the United States.

There are many benefits to staying in the United States during the application process. You won't be separated from your spouse, and will receive a permit to work while you wait to attend the final green card interview at a local USCIS office. Although your spouse will be required to accompany you to that interview (which is not required for interviews attended by immigrants coming from overseas), having your spouse present is an advantage, both for moral support and because a large part of the discussion will be your spouse's ability to support you financially.

And, unlike an overseas interview, you can bring an attorney with you—which you might want to do if your case has become complicated during the application process. You may want a lawyer, for example, if you realize that you might fall into a ground of inadmissibility (see Chapter 17 for more on how to find and use a lawyer).

a. Why Entry on a Temporary Visa Might Pose a Problem

If you used a temporary visa—such as a B-2 tourist visa or a visa waiver—to enter the United States, planning all along to get married, you might find yourself facing accusations of visa fraud if you apply to adjust status in the United States. Particularly if you knew your spouse before arriving in the United States and used a temporary visa or the VWP to enter, USCIS is likely to be suspicious. At the interview where your green card would normally be approved, USCIS might question you about whether your real intention when you arrived was to apply for permanent residence after your marriage. Unless you entered on a fiancé visa, the discovery that this was your real intention will lead USCIS to demand that you file an additional application requesting a waiver or forgiveness of your visa fraud. (See Chapter 1, Section B2, if you think you might be in this category. Also see Chapter 2, Section A.2.a for issues concerning overstaying a VWP entry: In short, you might need to overstay the 90 days to show you didn't intend marriage upon entry; but you become instantly removable if ICE arrests you after those 90 days are over.) This really happens, so watch out!

Of course, if you met your spouse after you arrived in the United States, this won't be a problem. And even for other couples, uncertainties about their marriage plans as well as the length of time they waited to get married or to begin the green card application process—at least 90 days after entry is best—often satisfy USCIS that they didn't misuse an entry visa.

> **EXAMPLE:** After a whirlwind romance in Belgium, Zachary (a U.S. citizen) proposed to Angela and she accepted. Not wanting to be parted for long, Angela used her tourist visa to enter the United States. She told the airport official only that she was taking a vacation to see friends. Angela and Zachary then married at City Hall. When she applied to adjust status, however, the USCIS interviewing officer immediately noticed the timing of the marriage and asked about her intentions upon entering the United States. When Angela fumbled with her answers, the officer stopped the interview and said she would need to apply for a waiver of her apparent visa fraud before the application could continue. Angela is now facing having to pay a lawyer to submit an application that might not in the end succeed, in which case she would be deported and barred from returning to the U.S. for many years.

! **CAUTION**

Watch out if you're in the U.S. on an employment-based visa. If you entered the U.S. on one of certain types of employment-based visas, applying for a green card through your U.S. citizen spouse puts you at risk of losing your visa status. (See the discussion called, "Here on a Temporary Employment Visa? The Risks of Applying for a Green Card," in Chapter 2, Section A.)

b. Two-Year Testing Period for New Marriages

You must be married for two years to obtain a permanent green card. If you apply before your marriage is two years old, you'll get a conditional card, good for only two years. Since most people apply for their green card soon after marrying, they get a conditional green card.

You won't be kicked out of the country after the two years—provided you don't forget to file the next application. This is an application for a permanent green card (using Form I-751), which sometimes involves an interview to allow USCIS to take a second look at whether your marriage is real. (See Chapter 16, Section G, for more on this issue.)

c. Your Children

Your unmarried children under age 21 may also be eligible to apply for green cards if your marriage to the U.S. citizen took place when they were under 18 (see Chapter 2, Section B, if you have children).

d. Introduction to the Application Process in the U.S.

Getting a marriage-based green card is normally a two-step process. First, the U.S. spouse submits a petition (Form I-130) telling USCIS that he or she wants to help someone immigrate. After USCIS approves this petition, the prospective immigrant submits an application for permanent residence (a green card), showing that he or she is interested and eligible to immigrate.

But for the spouse of a U.S. citizen who entered the country legally, the process usually gets condensed into one step. Your spouse's petition and your green card application can be filed together. Nevertheless, we cover the petition and your green card application in separate sections: Section D, below, covers the I-130 petition, and Chapter 14 covers the remainder of your green card application. You should have no trouble following the instructions in both sections and then combining the I-130 petition and green card application before submitting them to USCIS.

SKIP AHEAD

If you're ready to get to work on the petition, jump to Section D below for complete instructions.

2. Leave and Apply at an Overseas Consulate

For most married applicants who entered the U.S. legally, staying in the U.S. and adjusting status is the preferred way to obtain permanent residence. However, a second option for people who haven't overstayed their visa by six months or more is to leave the United States and apply for a green card at a U.S. consulate overseas.

At the time this book went to press, applications to adjust status in the U.S. were taking around 12 months, depending on the USCIS office. Applying at a consulate could actually be a quicker way to get your green card. Or you might prefer to apply at a consulate if you need to leave the U.S. right away and cannot wait for the processing of an adjustment of status application and a travel permit. Although the application process through an overseas consulate can take close to a year, some consulates are much more efficient and can approve you for a green card in a matter of months.

Contact the U.S. consulate in your home country to find out how long its application and approval process takes. Also, ask other immigrants about their experience with that consulate.

To compare that to how long your local USCIS office is taking to process applications for adjustment of status, go www.uscis.gov, click "Check Processing Times," then select "Form I-485" and choose your local field office from the drop-down menu and click "Get processing time."

Keep in mind that if your application gets delayed or the consulate asks you to supplement your application before it will approve it, your overseas stay could last longer.

There are some immigrants who should not leave the U.S. to apply for their green card, no matter how efficient their consulate will be. These are the people who have stayed past the expiration date on their visa by six months or more. Such people could be found inadmissible and prevented from returning for three or ten years, as described in Chapter 2, Section A.

> EXAMPLE: Asma is in the United States on a student visa, and recently married Fred, a U.S. citizen. Asma's elderly mother lives alone in Ethiopia, under very difficult circumstances. Asma is her mother's only hope to leave Ethiopia. Once Asma becomes a U.S. citizen, she can file an immediate relative petition for her mother to immigrate. But Asma can't apply for U.S. citizenship until she has been a U.S. resident for three years— so she needs that green card approval as soon as possible. In her case, it may be worthwhile to compare processing times between her local USCIS office and the U.S. consulate in Ethiopia. Asma understands that if she stays past the expiration of her student visa by six months or more, she should not even consider leaving the United States to apply for her green card, since she might face penalties of three or ten years, depending on how long she overstayed.

! CAUTION

Carry proof of when you depart the United States. If you decide to apply for your green card at a U.S. consulate, your history of U.S. visits will trigger a request that you prove you left on time. Collect and keep all evidence, such as your plane tickets, store receipts, medical records, credit card statements, and anything else relevant. (See Chapter 2, Section A, for the rules on and penalties for overstaying a U.S. visa by six months or more.)

a. Two-Year Testing Period for New Marriages

You must be married for two years to obtain a permanent green card. If you use your immigrant visa to enter the U.S. before your marriage is two years old, you'll get a conditional card, good for only two years. Since most people will apply for their green card soon after marrying, they will get a conditional green card.

You won't be kicked out of the country after the two years—provided you don't forget to file the next application (on Form I-751). This is an application for a permanent green card, which sometimes involves an interview to allow USCIS to take a second look at whether your marriage is real. (See Chapter 16, Section G, for more on this issue.)

b. Your Children

Your unmarried children under age 21 may also be eligible for immigrant visas and green cards if your marriage to the U.S. citizen took place when they were under 18 (see Chapter 2, Section B, if you have children).

⇨ SKIP AHEAD

If you are certain that you wish to leave the United States and apply overseas, go straight to Section D below. This section contains instructions on the first step, the I-130 petition to be filed by your spouse. This petition can be filed before or after you leave the United States.

C. Spouses Who Entered the U.S. Illegally

This section is for foreign nationals living in the United States after an unlawful entry. Unfortunately, your path to a green card is a difficult one, involving unattractive choices. Before explaining them in detail, we need to warn readers to see an attorney if:

- you've entered the U.S. illegally two or more times and
- the total amount of illegal time in the U.S. totals one year or more; or
- you've been deported (removed).

These would-be immigrants may be permanently barred from immigrating to the United States. See Chapter 2, Section A, for further information about the permanent bar.

Now, for those of you who have entered illegally only once, or whose previous illegal entries and stays total less than one year, here are your choices. As the spouse of a U.S. citizen, you are known as an immediate relative. A visa or green card is theoretically available as soon as you can get through the application procedures. Unfortunately, the procedures themselves make it difficult or impossible to get a green card.

Unless you fall into a rare exception, you will not be allowed to apply for your green card at a USCIS office in the United States. But if you leave after living here illegally for more than six months, you risk having the consulate punish you by refusing to let you return to the United States for three or ten years. (Chapter 2 has a full discussion of these time bars.)

To avoid being punished by the time bars, you need to act carefully and quickly. You have three options to consider:

- see if you fit into an exception and can apply to change your status to green card holder in the United States; this path is covered below in Section 1

- leave the United States before you have been here six months and apply to an overseas U.S. consulate to return immediately with an immigrant visa; this option is explained below in Section 2, or
- apply for a waiver of your illegal stay along with an immigrant visa to return after your interview at a U.S. consulate; this choice is explained in Section 3.

1. Can You Adjust Your Status in the U.S.?

Most married immigrants want to get their green card without leaving the United States. But in the late 1990s, the U.S. Congress made it far more difficult for immigrants to fulfill that hope. Only certain categories of immigrants are now allowed to apply for their green card in the United States using the adjustment of status procedure. People who entered the United States illegally are normally not among them.

However, a very few people will be lucky enough to fall into an exception to these laws if they started the application process before the laws changed. The key is whether a prospective employer filed a labor certification on your behalf or a close family member of yours, even if it wasn't your spouse, filed an immigrant petition (Form I-130) on your behalf either:

- before January 14, 1998, or
- between January 14, 1998 and April 30, 2001, if you can prove that you were physically present in the United States on December 21, 2000.

If the labor certification or petition was approved (or denied only because of a mistake by USCIS), you may be allowed to adjust your status to permanent resident without leaving the United States. (See Chapter 2, Section A, for details.)

If you fall into this exception, by all means plan to change (adjust) your status to green card holder in the United States. This is especially true if you have stayed in the United States illegally for more than six months. If you were to leave and try to apply for your green card at a U.S. consulate, the officials could punish you for your illegal stay by preventing your return for three or ten years.

SKIP AHEAD

If you are sure you will be able to adjust status in the United States, go to Section D, below for the first step.

If you don't fall into this exception but are determined not to leave the United States at all, your main option (which we don't recommend) is to stay illegally, hoping that the immigration laws will change in your favor. Many couples have chosen this route, but it is a huge gamble. If you chose this option, you must be aware that you may never obtain legal residence in the United States and will face the ever-present possibility of being caught, deported, and prevented from returning to the United States for at least ten years. The "provisional waiver" described in Chapter 2, however, may help you safely leave for a green card interview at a U.S. consulate.

TIP

If you have DACA status, could you leave and return to the U.S. on Advance Parole? Only your most recent entry to the U.S. needs to have been legal in order to adjust status via an immediate relative. Therefore, immigration attorneys have come up with a clever possibility for people with Deferred Action for Childhood Arrivals (DACA) status: to apply for Advance Parole, then leave and return before applying to adjust. It has worked—but this is an area of the law that's in flux, and leaving the U.S. is also risky (you could be barred from return based on any of a number of grounds of inadmissibility), so ABSOLUTELY speak with an experienced immigration attorney if you're interested in this route.

2. Leave the U.S. Before Six Months Have Passed

If you don't fit into an exception as described in Section 1, above, but you haven't yet stayed in the United States illegally for more than six months, your safest bet is to leave the United States before that date rolls around. Leaving now would protect you from having a three-year bar assessed against you when you later visit the U.S. consulate overseas to apply for your green card (and from a ten-year bar if you stayed illegally for more than a year).

As the overseas spouse of a U.S. citizen, you can get a marriage-based immigrant visa based on your immediate relative status. This may mean many months of separation from your spouse while you wait overseas for your green card to be approved; but months of separation now might be better than three or ten years of separation later. (See Chapter 7 for instructions on how to apply overseas for an immigrant visa as the spouse of a U.S. citizen.)

> **CAUTION**
>
> **Make sure you can prove you stayed illegally for less than six months.** When the time comes to apply for your green card, the consulate will want to see proof of how long you stayed illegally in the United States. Collect and keep all evidence, such as your plane tickets, store receipts, medical records, credit card statements, and anything else relevant.

> **SKIP AHEAD**
>
> **If you are certain that you wish to leave the United States and apply overseas, go straight to Section D, below.** This section contains instructions on the first step, the I-130 petition to be filed by your spouse. This petition can be filed before or after you leave the United States.

3. If Six or More Months Have Passed, Apply for a Waiver

If you are not eligible to adjust status in the United States, but your unlawful stay was long enough that you would face a three- or ten-year bar on returning if you left, see an attorney. (See Chapter 2 for more on the three- and ten-year bars, and Chapter 17 for tips on finding a good attorney.) The attorney can help you decide whether applying for a marriage-based visa along with a waiver of the time bars (in other words, forgiveness of your unlawful stay) is a realistic option.

It's not easy to get a waiver. You'll have to convince the immigration authorities that if your visa were denied, it would cause extreme hardship to your U.S. spouse or parents (if they happen to be U.S. citizens or permanent residents). And when the law says extreme, it means much more than the sadness your spouse and/or parents will feel at your being thousands of miles away. The classic case of extreme hardship is someone whose U.S. citizen spouse has severe medical problems that require the other spouse's constant attention.

The "provisional waiver" described in Chapter 2, however, may at least help you get an answer and thus safely leave for a green card interview at a U.S. consulate.

If your waiver request is granted, you will then be able to make a short trip for your consular interview, then return to the U.S. as a permanent resident, without having to wait the additional three to ten years that you would have waited without the waiver.

> **SEE AN EXPERT**
>
> **Time bar waivers are complex and require a lot of documents.** Look for an attorney who has had experience preparing and arguing for them.

D. The First Application: I-130 Petition

Your U.S. citizen spouse initiates the green card application process by preparing a petition— Form I-130, Petition for Alien Relative, and attached documents. Your spouse can start and submit this any time, before or after you have left the United States.

With the I-130 petition, you're asking USCIS to acknowledge that you're married and to let you go forward with green card processing. Approval of the petition does not guarantee approval of your green card. This is only the first step in the process. Your portion of the application is still to come, and you will have to pass all the tests USCIS gives before allowing someone to live in the United States permanently.

We'll go through how to prepare and assemble the various forms and documents, one by one. To keep track of them all, refer to the checklist in Section 5, below. A few items on this checklist are self-explanatory, so they aren't discussed in the following text.

Before proceeding, take a look at the general instructions for filling in USCIS forms in Chapter 4. Also, as you read these instructions, have a copy of the appropriate form in hand.

> **CAUTION**
>
> **If the U.S. petitioner has a criminal record, see an attorney.** Under the Adam Walsh Child Protection and Safety Act of 2006, U.S. citizens and lawful permanent residents who have been convicted of any "specified offense against a minor" are prohibited from filing a family-based immigrant petition on behalf of any beneficiary (whether a child or not). USCIS will run security checks on all petitions and may call the petitioner in for fingerprinting. If the petitioner has a conviction for one of the specified offenses against a minor, then the petition will not be approved unless USCIS determines that the U.S. petitioner poses no risk to the beneficiary.

1. Form I-130

Form I-130 is one of the most important ones in your immigration process. It will be the U.S. spouse's first opportunity to explain who each of you is, where you live, and why you qualify for a visa.

Don't be thrown off by the fact that the form addresses the U.S. citizen spouse as "you"—after all, it's the U.S. spouse who fills out and signs this form.

> **WEB RESOURCE**
>
> **Form I-130 is available on the USCIS website at www.uscis.gov/i-130.** Below is a sample filled-in version of the relevant pages of this form.

Part A

Question 1: Check the first box, "Spouse."

Questions 2-3: Since you are petitioning for a spouse, do not check any boxes here.

Question 4: If the petitioning U.S. spouse gained U.S. permanent residence through adoption before becoming a citizen, check "Yes." But no matter which box is checked, it won't affect the application, since this question is mainly directed at people immigrating through parent/child relationships—something not covered in this book.

Part 2

Question 1: A U.S. citizen petitioner will have an A-number (Alien Registration Number) only if he or she once held a green card (permanent residence).

Question 2: A U.S. citizen petitioner who has filed a past petition with USCIS may have received a USCIS Online Account Number, and should enter it here.

Question 3: A U.S. citizen will have a Social Security number, and should fill it in here.

Question 4: The petitioning spouse must enter his or her full name. Use a current married name if it was changed at the time of your marriage. (See "What's Your Name?" in Chapter 4, Section B.)

Question 5: The U.S. petitioner should enter any names previously used. If the citizen was married before and used another name during that time, enter it here.

Questions 6-9: Self-explanatory.

Questions 10-15: Fill in the U.S. citizen's addresses from the last five years. If the citizen has lived at more than one address during these years, include the start and end dates of the other addresses.

Question 16: Answer how many times the petitioner has been married, including this time.

Question 17: This question refers only to the petitioning spouse's most recent marital status. He or she should check only "married," even if there was a previous divorce.

Sample Form I-130, Petition for Alien Relative—Page 1

Petition for Alien Relative

Department of Homeland Security
U.S. Citizenship and Immigration Services

USCIS
Form I-130
OMB No. 1615-0012
Expires 02/28/2021

For USCIS Use Only		
A-Number	Fee Stamp	Action Stamp

A- [ ][ ][ ][ ][ ][ ][ ][ ]

Initial Receipt

Resubmitted

Relocated — **Section of Law/Visa Category**

Received
☐ 201(b) Spouse - IR-1/CR-1   ☐ 203(a)(1) Unm. S/D - F1-1   ☐ 203(a)(2)(B) Unm. S/D - F2-4

Sent
☐ 201(b) Child - IR-2/CR-2   ☐ 203(a)(2)(A) Spouse - F2-1   ☐ 203(a)(3) Married S/D - F3-1

Completed
☐ 201(b) Parent - IR-5   ☐ 203(a)(2)(A) Child - F2-2   ☐ 203(a)(4) Brother/Sister - F4-1

Approved — Petition was filed on (Priority Date mm/dd/yyyy):
☐ Field Investigation   ☐ Personal Interview   ☐ 204(a)(2)(A) Resolved
☐ Previously Forwarded   ☐ Pet. A-File Reviewed   ☐ I-485 Filed Simultaneously

Returned — PDR request granted/denied - New priority date (mm/dd/yyyy):
☐ 203(g) Resolved   ☐ Ben. A-File Reviewed   ☐ 204(g) Resolved

Remarks

At which USCIS office (e.g., NBC, VSC, LOS, CRO) was Form I-130 adjudicated? _____

To be completed by an attorney or accredited representative (if any).

☐ **Select this box if Form G-28 is attached.** | **Volag Number** (if any) | **Attorney State Bar Number** (if applicable) | **Attorney or Accredited Representative USCIS Online Account Number** (if any)

▶ **START HERE - Type or print in black ink.**

> If you need extra space to complete any section of this petition, use the space provided in **Part 9. Additional Information.**
> **Complete and submit as many copies of Part 9., as necessary, with your petition.**

Part 1. Relationship (You are the Petitioner. Your relative is the Beneficiary)

1. I am filing this petition for my (Select **only one** box):

☒ Spouse   ☐ Parent   ☐ Brother/Sister   ☐ Child

2. If you are filing this petition for your child or parent, select the box that describes your relationship (Select **only one** box):

☐ Child was born to parents who were married to each other at the time of the child's birth

☐ Stepchild/Stepparent

☐ Child was born to parents who were not married to each other at the time of the child's birth

☐ Child was adopted (not an Orphan or Hague Convention adoptee)

3. If the beneficiary is your brother/sister, are you related by adoption?   ☐ Yes   ☐ No

4. Did you gain lawful permanent resident status or citizenship through adoption?   ☐ Yes   ☐ No

Part 2. Information About You (Petitioner)

1. Alien Registration Number (A-Number) (if any)
▶ A- [ ][ ][ ][ ][ ][ ][ ][ ]

2. USCIS Online Account Number (if any)
▶ [ ][ ][ ][ ][ ][ ][ ][ ][ ][ ][ ][ ]

3. U.S. Social Security Number (if any)
▶ [1][1][1][1][1][1][1][1][1]

Your Full Name

4.a. Family Name (Last Name)   MIHOV

4.b. Given Name (First Name)   Grun

4.c. Middle Name   Branimir

Sample Form I-130, Petition for Alien Relative—Page 2

Part 2. Information About You (Petitioner) (continued)

Other Names Used (if any)

Provide all other names you have ever used, including aliases, maiden name, and nicknames.

5.a. Family Name (Last Name)

5.b. Given Name (First Name)

5.c. Middle Name

Other Information

6. City/Town/Village of Birth

Hershey

7. Country of Birth

USA

8. Date of Birth (mm/dd/yyyy) | 03/30/1992

9. Sex ☒ Male ☐ Female

Mailing Address

10.a. In Care Of Name

10.b. Street Number and Name | 68 Watertown Blvd.

10.c. ☒ Apt. ☐ Ste. ☐ Flr. | 12

10.d. City or Town | Erie

10.e. State | PA **10.f.** ZIP Code | 19380

10.g. Province

10.h. Postal Code

10.i. Country | USA

11. Is your current mailing address the same as your physical address? ☒ Yes ☐ No

If you answered "No" to **Item Number 11.**, provide information on your physical address in **Item Numbers 12.a. - 13.b.**

Address History

Provide your physical addresses for the last five years, whether inside or outside the United States. Provide your current address first if it is different from your mailing address in **Item Numbers 10.a. - 10.i.**

Physical Address 1

12.a. Street Number and Name

12.b. ☐ Apt. ☐ Ste. ☐ Flr.

12.c. City or Town

12.d. State | **12.e.** ZIP Code

12.f. Province

12.g. Postal Code

12.h. Country

13.a. Date From (mm/dd/yyyy)

13.b. Date To (mm/dd/yyyy)

Physical Address 2

14.a. Street Number and Name | 68 Watertown Blvd.

14.b. ☒ Apt. ☐ Ste. ☐ Flr. | 12

14.c. City or Town | Erie

14.d. State | PA **14.e.** ZIP Code | 19380

14.f. Province

14.g. Postal Code

14.h. Country | USA

15.a. Date From (mm/dd/yyyy) | 11/01/2012

15.b. Date To (mm/dd/yyyy) | present

Your Marital Information

16. How many times have you been married? ▶ | 1

17. Current Marital Status

☐ Single, Never Married ☒ Married ☐ Divorced

☐ Widowed ☐ Separated ☐ Annulled

Sample Form I-130, Petition for Alien Relative—Page 3

Part 2. Information About You (Petitioner) (continued)

18. Date of Current Marriage (if currently married) (mm/dd/yyyy) `12/17/2017`

Place of Your Current Marriage (if married)

19.a. City or Town `Hershey`

19.b. State `PA`

19.c. Province

19.d. Country `USA`

Names of All Your Spouses (if any)

Provide information on your current spouse (if currently married) first and then list all your prior spouses (if any).

Spouse 1

20.a. Family Name (Last Name) `MIHOV`

20.b. Given Name (First Name) `Anda`

20.c. Middle Name `Marina`

21. Date Marriage Ended (mm/dd/yyyy) `n/a`

Spouse 2

22.a. Family Name (Last Name) `n/a`

22.b. Given Name (First Name)

22.c. Middle Name

23. Date Marriage Ended (mm/dd/yyyy)

Information About Your Parents

Parent 1's Information

Full Name of Parent 1

24.a. Family Name (Last Name) `MIHOV`

24.b. Given Name (First Name) `Georg`

24.c. Middle Name

25. Date of Birth (mm/dd/yyyy) `01/31/1965`

26. Sex ☒ Male ☐ Female

27. Country of Birth `USA`

28. City/Town/Village of Residence `Pittsburgh`

29. Country of Residence `USA`

Parent 2's Information

Full Name of Parent 2

30.a. Family Name (Last Name) `MIHOV`

30.b. Given Name (First Name) `Jane`

30.c. Middle Name

31. Date of Birth (mm/dd/yyyy) `03/15/1960`

32. Sex ☐ Male ☒ Female

33. Country of Birth `USA`

34. City/Town/Village of Residence `Pittsburgh`

35. Country of Residence `USA`

Additional Information About You (Petitioner)

36. I am a (Select **only one** box):
    ☒ U.S. Citizen ☐ Lawful Permanent Resident

If you are a U.S. citizen, complete Item Number 37.

37. My citizenship was acquired through (Select **only one** box):
    ☒ Birth in the United States
    ☐ Naturalization
    ☐ Parents

38. Have you obtained a Certificate of Naturalization or a Certificate of Citizenship? ☐ Yes ☐ No

If you answered "Yes" to **Item Number 38.**, complete the following:

39.a. Certificate Number

39.b. Place of Issuance

39.c. Date of Issuance (mm/dd/yyyy)

Sample Form I-130, Petition for Alien Relative—Page 4

Part 2. Information About You (Petitioner) (continued)

If you are a lawful permanent resident, complete **Item Numbers 40.a. - 41.**

40.a. Class of Admission

n/a

40.b. Date of Admission (mm/dd/yyyy)

Place of Admission

40.c. City or Town

40.d State

41. Did you gain lawful permanent resident status through marriage to a U.S. citizen or lawful permanent resident?

☐ Yes ☐ No

Employment History

Provide your employment history for the last five years, whether inside or outside the United States. Provide your current employment first. If you are currently unemployed, type or print "Unemployed" in **Item Number 42.**

Employer 1

42. Name of Employer/Company

Chocolate Company, Inc.

43.a. Street Number and Name

One Chocolate Way

43.b. ☐ Apt. ☐ Ste. ☐ Flr.

43.c. City or Town

Hershey

43.d. State   PA   **43.e.** ZIP Code   17033

43.f. Province

43.g. Postal Code

43.h. Country

USA

44. Your Occupation

Accountant

45.a. Date From (mm/dd/yyyy)   06/15/2012

45.b. Date To (mm/dd/yyyy)   present

Employer 2

46. Name of Employer/Company

n/a

47.a. Street Number and Name

47.b. ☐ Apt. ☐ Ste. ☐ Flr.

47.c. City or Town

47.d. State   **47.e.** ZIP Code

47.f. Province

47.g. Postal Code

47.h. Country

48. Your Occupation

49.a. Date From (mm/dd/yyyy)

49.b. Date To (mm/dd/yyyy)

Part 3. Biographic Information

NOTE: Provide the biographic information about you, the petitioner.

1. Ethnicity (Select **only one** box)

☐ Hispanic or Latino
☒ Not Hispanic or Latino

2. Race (Select **all applicable** boxes)

☒ White
☐ Asian
☐ Black or African American
☐ American Indian or Alaska Native
☐ Native Hawaiian or Other Pacific Islander

3. Height   Feet   5   Inches   10

4. Weight   Pounds   1   7   0

5. Eye Color (Select **only one** box)

☐ Black   ☒ Blue   ☐ Brown
☐ Gray   ☐ Green   ☐ Hazel
☐ Maroon   ☐ Pink   ☐ Unknown/Other

Sample Form I-130, Petition for Alien Relative—Page 5

Part 3. Biographic Information (continued)

6. Hair Color (Select **only one** box)

☐ Bald (No hair) ☐ Black ☐ Blond
☒ Brown ☐ Gray ☐ Red
☐ Sandy ☐ White ☐ Unknown/Other

Part 4. Information About Beneficiary

1. Alien Registration Number (A-Number) (if any)

▶ A- ☐☐☐☐☐☐☐☐☐

2. USCIS Online Account Number (if any)

▶ ☐☐☐☐☐☐☐☐☐☐☐☐

3. U.S. Social Security Number (if any)

▶ 3 8 7 3 3 8 8 7 7

Beneficiary's Full Name

4.a. Family Name (Last Name) Mihov

4.b. Given Name (First Name) Anda

4.c. Middle Name Marina

Other Names Used (if any)

Provide all other names the beneficiary has ever used, including aliases, maiden name, and nicknames.

5.a. Family Name (Last Name) Michelski

5.b. Given Name (First Name)

5.c. Middle Name

Other Information About Beneficiary

6. City/Town/Village of Birth

Sofia

7. Country of Birth

Bulgaria

8. Date of Birth (mm/dd/yyyy) 06/28/1991

9. Sex ☐ Male ☒ Female

10. Has anyone else ever filed a petition for the beneficiary?

☐ Yes ☒ No ☐ Unknown

NOTE: Select "Unknown" *only* if you do not know, and the beneficiary also does not know, if anyone else has ever filed a petition for the beneficiary.

Beneficiary's Physical Address

If the beneficiary lives outside the United States in a home without a street number or name, leave **Item Numbers 11.a.** and **11.b.** blank.

11.a. Street Number and Name 68 Watertown Blvd

11.b. ☒ Apt. ☐ Ste. ☐ Flr. 12

11.c. City or Town Erie

11.d. State PA **11.e.** ZIP Code 19380

11.f. Province

11.g. Postal Code

11.h. Country

USA

Other Address and Contact Information

Provide the address in the United States where the beneficiary intends to live, if different from **Item Numbers 11.a. - 11.h.** If the address is the same, type or print "SAME" in **Item Number 12.a.**

12.a Street Number and Name SAME

12.b. ☐ Apt. ☐ Ste. ☐ Flr.

12.c. City or Town

12.d. State **12.e.** ZIP Code

Provide the beneficiary's address outside the United States, if different from **Item Numbers 11.a. - 11.h.** If the address is the same, type or print "SAME" in **Item Number 13.a.**

13.a. Street Number and Name 42, Raiska Gradina St.

13.b. ☐ Apt. ☐ Ste. ☐ Flr.

13.c. City or Town Sofia

13.d. Province

13.e. Postal Code

13.f. Country

Bulgaria

14. Daytime Telephone Number (if any)

6105551122

Sample Form I-130, Petition for Alien Relative—Page 6

Part 4. Information About Beneficiary (continued)

15. Mobile Telephone Number (if any)

5061235555

16. Email Address (if any)

mihov123@email.com

Beneficiary's Marital Information

17. How many times has the beneficiary been married? ▶ 1

18. Current Marital Status

☐ Single, Never Married   ☒ Married   ☐ Divorced

☐ Widowed   ☐ Separated   ☐ Annulled

19. Date of Current Marriage (if currently married) (mm/dd/yyyy)

12/17/2017

Place of Beneficiary's Current Marriage (if married)

20.a. City or Town   Hershey

20.b. State   PA

20.c. Province

20.d. Country   USA

Names of Beneficiary's Spouses (if any)

Provide information on the beneficiary's current spouse (if currently married) first and then list all the beneficiary's prior spouses (if any).

Spouse 1

21.a. Family Name (Last Name)   Mihov

21.b. Given Name (First Name)   Grun

21.c. Middle Name   Branimir

22. Date Marriage Ended (mm/dd/yyyy)   n/a

Spouse 2

23.a. Family Name (Last Name)   n/a

23.b. Given Name (First Name)

23.c. Middle Name

24. Date Marriage Ended (mm/dd/yyyy)

Information About Beneficiary's Family

Provide information about the beneficiary's spouse and children.

Person 1

25.a. Family Name (Last Name)   Mihov

25.b. Given Name (First Name)   Grun

25.c. Middle Name   Branimir

26. Relationship

27. Date of Birth (mm/dd/yyyy)   03/17/1992

28. Country of Birth   USA

Person 2

29.a. Family Name (Last Name)

29.b. Given Name (First Name)

29.c. Middle Name

30. Relationship

31. Date of Birth (mm/dd/yyyy)

32. Country of Birth

Person 3

33.a. Family Name (Last Name)

33.b. Given Name (First Name)

33.c. Middle Name

34. Relationship

35. Date of Birth (mm/dd/yyyy)

36. Country of Birth

Sample Form I-130, Petition for Alien Relative—Page 7

Part 4. Information About Beneficiary (continued)

Person 4

37.a. Family Name (Last Name)

37.b. Given Name (First Name)

37.c. Middle Name

38. Relationship

39. Date of Birth (mm/dd/yyyy)

40. Country of Birth

Person 5

41.a. Family Name (Last Name)

41.b. Given Name (First Name)

41.c. Middle Name

42. Relationship

43. Date of Birth (mm/dd/yyyy)

44. Country of Birth

Beneficiary's Entry Information

45. Was the beneficiary **EVER** in the United States?

☒ Yes ☐ No

If the beneficiary is currently in the United States, complete **Items Numbers 46.a. - 46.d.**

46.a. He or she arrived as a (Class of Admission):

H-1B

46.b. Form I-94 Arrival-Departure Record Number

▶ 1 2 3 2 3 1 2 3 1 1 1

46.c. Date of Arrival (mm/dd/yyyy) 11/04/2018

46.d. Date authorized stay expired, or will expire, as shown on Form I-94 or Form I-95 (mm/dd/yyyy) or type or print "D/S" for Duration of Status

09/30/2020

47. Passport Number

BG0000

48. Travel Document Number

49. Country of Issuance for Passport or Travel Document

Bulgaria

50. Expiration Date for Passport or Travel Document (mm/dd/yyyy)

06/30/2025

Beneficiary's Employment Information

Provide the beneficiary's current employment information (if applicable), even if they are employed outside of the United States. If the beneficiary is currently unemployed, type or print "Unemployed" in **Item Number 51.a.**

51.a. Name of Current Employer (if applicable)

Berlitz Cultural Center

51.b. Street Number and Name Penn Center

51.c. ☐ Apt. ☒ Ste. ☐ Flr. 800

51.d. City or Town Pittsburgh

51.e. State PA   **51.f.** ZIP Code 15276

51.g. Province

51.h. Postal Code

51.i. Country

USA

52. Date Employment Began (mm/dd/yyyy)

12/06/2017

Additional Information About Beneficiary

53. Was the beneficiary **EVER** in immigration proceedings?

☐ Yes ☒ No

54. If you answered "Yes," select the type of proceedings and provide the location and date of the proceedings.

☐ Removal   ☐ Exclusion/Deportation

☐ Rescission   ☐ Other Judicial Proceedings

55.a. City or Town

55.b. State

56. Date (mm/dd/yyyy)

Sample Form I-130, Petition for Alien Relative—Page 8

Part 4. Information About Beneficiary (continued)

If the beneficiary's native written language does not use Roman letters, type or print his or her name and foreign address in their native written language.

57.a. Family Name (Last Name) [ ]

57.b. Given Name (First Name) [ ]

57.c. Middle Name [ ]

58.a. Street Number and Name [ ]

58.b. ☐ Apt. ☐ Ste. ☐ Flr. [ ]

58.c. City or Town [ ]

58.d. Province [ ]

58.e. Postal Code [ ]

58.f. Country [ ]

If filing for your spouse, provide the last address at which you physically lived together. If you never lived together, type or print, "Never lived together" in Item Number 59.a.

59.a. Street Number and Name [68 Watertown Blvd.]

59.b. ☐ Apt. ☒ Ste. ☐ Flr. [12]

59.c. City or Town [Erie]

59.d. State [PA] **59.e.** ZIP Code [19380]

59.f. Province [ ]

59.g. Postal Code [ ]

59.h. Country [USA]

60.a. Date From (mm/dd/yyyy) [11/01/2015]

60.b. Date To (mm/dd/yyyy) [present]

The beneficiary is in the United States and will apply for adjustment of status to that of a lawful permanent resident at the U.S. Citizenship and Immigration Services (USCIS) office in:

61.a. City or Town [Pittsburgh]

61.b. State [PA]

The beneficiary will not apply for adjustment of status in the United States, but he or she will apply for an immigrant visa abroad at the U.S. Embassy or U.S. Consulate in:

62.a. City or Town [ ]

62.b. Province [ ]

62.c. Country [ ]

NOTE: Choosing a U.S. Embassy or U.S. Consulate outside the country of the beneficiary's last residence does not guarantee that it will accept the beneficiary's case for processing. In these situations, the designated U.S. Embassy or U.S. Consulate has discretion over whether or not to accept the beneficiary's case.

Part 5. Other Information

1. Have you **EVER** previously filed a petition for this beneficiary or any other alien? ☐ Yes ☒ No

If you answered "Yes," provide the name, place, date of filing, and the result.

2.a. Family Name (Last Name) [ ]

2.b. Given Name (First Name) [ ]

2.c. Middle Name [ ]

3.a. City or Town [ ]

3.b. State [ ]

4. Date Filed (mm/dd/yyyy) [ ]

5. Result (for example, approved, denied, withdrawn) [ ]

If you are also submitting separate petitions for other relatives, provide the names of and your relationship to each relative.

Relative 1

6.a. Family Name (Last Name) [ ]

6.b. Given Name (First Name) [ ]

6.c. Middle Name [ ]

7. Relationship [ ]

Sample Form I-130, Petition for Alien Relative—Page 9

Part 5. Other Information (continued)

Relative 2

8.a. Family Name
(Last Name)

8.b. Given Name
(First Name)

8.c. Middle Name

9. Relationship

WARNING: USCIS investigates the claimed relationships and verifies the validity of documents you submit. If you falsify a family relationship to obtain a visa, USCIS may seek to have you criminally prosecuted.

PENAL TIES: By law , you may be imprisoned for up to 5 years or fined $250,000, or both, for entering into a marriage contract in order to evade any U.S. immigration law. In addition, you may be fined up to $10,000 and imprisoned for up to 5 years, or both, for knowingly and willfully falsifying or concealing a material fact or using any false document in submitting this petition.

Part 6. Petitioner's Statement, Contact Information, Declaration, and Signature

NOTE: Read the **Penalties** section of the Form I-130 Instructions before completing this part.

Petitioner's Statement

NOTE: Select the box for either **Item Number 1.a.** or **1.b.** If applicable, select the box for **Item Number 2.**

1.a. ☒ I can read and understand English, and I have read and understand every question and instruction on this petition and my answer to every question.

1.b. ☐ The interpreter named in **Part 7.** read to me every question and instruction on this petition and my answer to every question in

_____,
a language in which I am fluent. I understood all of this information as interpreted.

2. ☐ At my request, the preparer named in **Part 8.**,

_____,
prepared this petition for me based only upon information I provided or authorized.

Petitioner's Contact Information

3. Petitioner's Daytime Telephone Number

6105551212

4. Petitioner's Mobile Telephone Number (if any)

5. Petitioner's Email Address (if any)

grun@email.com

Petitioner's Declaration and Certification

Copies of any documents I have submitted are exact photocopies of unaltered, original documents, and I understand that USCIS may require that I submit original documents to USCIS at a later date. Furthermore, I authorize the release of any information from any of my records that USCIS may need to determine my eligibility for the immigration benefit I seek.

I further authorize release of information contained in this petition, in supporting documents, and in my USCIS records to other entities and persons where necessary for the administration and enforcement of U.S. immigration laws.

I understand that USCIS may require me to appear for an appointment to take my biometrics (fingerprints, photograph, and/or signature) and, at that time, if I am required to provide biometrics, I will be required to sign an oath reaffirming that:

  1) I provided or authorized all of the information contained in, and submitted with, my petition;

  2) I reviewed and understood all of the information in, and submitted with, my petition; and

  3) All of this information was complete, true, and correct at the time of filing.

I certify, under penalty of perjury, that all of the information in my petition and any document submitted with it were provided or authorized by me, that I reviewed and understand all of the information contained in, and submitted with, my petition, and that all of this information is complete, true, and correct.

Petitioner's Signature

6.a. Petitioner's Signature (sign in ink)

➡ *Grun Mihov*

6.b. Date of Signature (mm/dd/yyyy)   04/11/2019

NOTE TO ALL PETITIONERS: If you do not completely fill out this petition or fail to submit required documents listed in the Instructions, USCIS may deny your petition.

Questions 18-19: Self-explanatory.

Question 20-23: Put the name of the U.S. petitioner's current spouse (the immigrant) first and then any past spouses next. Leave blank or enter "N/A" under the date marriage ended for your current marriage. This question of when the U.S. spouse's prior marriage ended is intended to make sure your current marriage is valid. If the petitioning spouse's prior marriage(s) ended after your present marriage began, yours is not a lawful marriage. If the petitioning spouse has just discovered that the divorce wasn't final when your marriage took place, it may not be necessary to run to a lawyer. Assuming that the divorce has since become final, you can correct the problem by remarrying. (If there was fraud involved in your hasty marriage, consult a lawyer before proceeding.)

Questions 24-35: Answer basic biographic information about the petitioning U.S. citizen's parents. If lacking any pieces of information, enter "unknown."

Question 36: Self-explanatory.

Question 37: State how the U.S. citizen petitioner obtained citizenship.

Questions 38-39: If the petitioning spouse is a naturalized U.S. citizen (meaning he or she wasn't born a citizen, but had to apply and take a citizenship exam), this number is on the top right-hand side of the naturalization certificate. The date and place issued are also shown on the certificate.

Question 40: U.S. citizens can write "N/A" here.

Question 41: If the petitioning spouse checks "Yes" here, to indicate having received U.S. permanent residence through marriage, calculate how long it has been since the U.S. spouse's approval for permanent residence. A petitioning spouse who him- or herself immigrated through marriage cannot petition for a new spouse for five years after approval, unless the first spouse died or there is "clear and convincing evidence" that the previous marriage was bona fide (real). USCIS is concerned that the first marriage was just a sham, with the long-term goal of getting both of you into the United States by piggybacking on a sham marriage.

To prove that the first marriage was bona fide, enclose documentary evidence, such as shared rent receipts, club memberships, children's birth certificates, utility bills, and insurance agreements showing that the couple shared a life together. As for what makes for "clear and convincing evidence," it means a high bar to persuade a suspicious government official that the previous marriage was bona fide.

Questions 42-49: Fill in U.S. petitioner's employment history from the last five years. For more than two jobs in the past five years, use Part 9 to list the ones that don't fit.

Part 3

Questions 1-5: Provide basic biographic information about the U.S. citizen petitioner.

Part 4

Question 1: The Alien Registration Number is an eight- or nine-digit number following a letter A that USCIS (or the former INS) will have assigned to an immigrant who previously applied for immigration benefits, or was in deportation/removal proceedings. (If the previous application was denied because the immigrant was found inadmissible, or lied on that application, call a lawyer before going any further.)

Question 2: Someone who filed a past petition with USCIS might have a USCIS Online Account Number.

Question 3: An immigrant shouldn't have a Social Security number without having had a work permit, a visa allowing work, or U.S. residence.

Question 4: Enter current name.

Question 5: Enter any names the immigrant previously used. If the immigrant was married before and used another name then, include it here.

Questions 6-10: Self-explanatory.

Question 11: Immigrant's current address in the United States.

Questions 12-16: Assuming you've filled in the immigrant's U.S. addresses in Part 11, you need not fill out Part 12. But for an immigrant who has an overseas address and will be living there while completing this application for U.S. residence, enter that address and phone number here.

Question 17: Answer how many times the immigrant has been married, including this time.

Question 18: This refers only to most recent marital status, so check "married," even if there was a previous divorce.

Questions 19-20: Self-explanatory.

Questions 21-24: Name immigrant's current spouse first (the U.S. petitioner) and any past spouses next. Enter "N/A" under the date marriage ended for your current marriage. The question of when any prior marriage(s) ended is intended to make sure your current marriage is valid. If prior marriage(s) ended after your present marriage began, yours is not a lawful marriage. If you have just discovered that the divorce wasn't final when your marriage took place, it may not be necessary to run to a lawyer. Assuming that the divorce has since become final, you can correct the problem by remarrying. (If there was fraud involved in your hasty marriage, consult a lawyer before proceeding.)

Questions 25-44: Although the U.S. spouse is already covered in this application, it's safest to list him or her again before listing children, if any. This means all children, including any by previous relationships.

Question 45: Because you are in the U.S. now, you must check "Yes."

CAUTION

If the immigrant must leave the United States to get green card approval, be careful here. This section gives the government information on when the immigrant was living in the United States—perhaps unlawfully. It could lead to being punished for the illegal stay with a three- or ten-year bar on reentry (see Chapter 2, which explains the time bars in detail). Ideally, if the immigrant has already left the United States when the U.S. spouse sends this in, there will be no need to answer the question.

If the immigrant entered legally. In Question 46.a, state the type of visa used to enter the United States, such as F-1 student or Visa Waiver (if the immigrant came from a country from which no formal U.S. revised visa is required). For 46.b, c, and d, the I-94 may be a little white or green card that the consulate or the border official gave the immigrant upon arrival; the number is on the card. The date the stay expires or expired should be on the I-94 (or in rare cases, in the passport). An immigrant who entered the U.S. in 2013 or thereafter, may not have received an actual I-94 card, as was once the norm. You will instead need to download the I-94 information from the U.S. Customs and Border Protection (CBP) website at www.cbp.gov/i94. Note that this date is different than the expiration date on your original visa.

If the immigrant entered illegally. Write "without inspection in 46.a."

Questions 51-52: Fill in the immigrant's current employment information. For an immigrant who is not working, enter "unemployed" or "student," if applicable.

Questions 53-56: If you have ever been in Immigration Court (removal or deportation) proceedings, consult a lawyer before continuing. You may be inadmissible to the United States or need a special waiver.

Questions 57-58: If the immigrant's native language uses a non-Roman script (for example, Russian, Chinese, or Arabic), you will need to write the name and address in that script.

Questions 59-60: If you are living together or have done so in the past, enter the last address here. But if the immigrant will be leaving the United States after living here unlawfully, this is another time to be careful—the information about how long you and your spouse lived at the same address could be used against you.

Questions 61-62:

If the immigrant entered legally. If planning to take advantage of the option to stay in the United States to adjust status, enter the closest city and state with a U.S. immigration office. Add the name of the consulate from the immigrant's last country of residence, as a backup.

For an immigrant choosing to return to the home country and apply through a U.S. consulate, do not fill out Question 62.

If the immigrant entered illegally. Unless an exception allows the immigrant to stay in the United States to apply for the green card, he or she will complete the application at a U.S. consulate. No need to fill out Question 62.

Part 5: Other Information.

Now we're back to questions about the U.S. petitioning spouse.

Questions 1-2: As you can probably imagine, if the petitioning U.S. spouse has a history of short marriages to people whom he/she then helped get green cards, USCIS will conduct a major marriage fraud investigation. See a lawyer (Chapter 17 has more on how to find and use a lawyer). If also submitting petitions for children, however, this is where to enter their names and relationship to the U.S. spouse (such as child or stepchild). This will result in USCIS processing all of the petitions together.

Part 6

The U.S. citizen petitioner should fill out this section with contact information and signature.

Parts 7 and 8

These are for a preparer or interpreter helping to fill out the form. If filling out the application unassisted, write "N/A" here. A little typing assistance or advice from a friend doesn't count— the only people who need to complete this line are lawyers or agencies who fill out these forms on others' behalf or offer translation services.

2. Form I-130A

You (the immigrant spouse beneficiary) must fill out this form. The purpose is to give the U.S. government information with which to check your background. Most of the questions are self-explanatory. If you really can't remember or are unable to find out an exact date, enter what you can remember, such as the year. Alternatively, you can say "unknown," but if you overuse the "unknowns," USCIS may return the application for another try.

WEB RESOURCE

Form I-130A is available on the USCIS website, at www.uscis.gov/i-130. Below is a sample filled-in version of the relevant pages of this form.

Part 1

Question 1: The Alien Registration Number is an eight- or nine-digit number following a letter A that USCIS (or the formerly named INS) would have assigned to you if you'd previously applied for permanent (or, in some cases, temporary) residence or been in deportation/removal proceedings. Of course, if that previous application was denied because you were inadmissible or lied on that application, you should call a lawyer before going any further.

Question 2: If you have ever filed a petition with USCIS you may have a USCIS Online Account Number. If so, fill it in here.

Question 3: Enter your last full, current name. Use your married name if it was changed at the time you wed.

Questions 4-9: Fill in all your addresses from the last five years. If you have more than two, enter additional addresses in Part 7. Make sure to include the start and end dates of all previous addresses.

Questions 10-23: Answer basic biographic information about your parents. If lacking any pieces of information, say "unknown."

Part 2

Questions 1-8: Fill in your current employment information for the last five years, no matter which country you worked in. If not working, enter "unemployed" or "student," if applicable. If you had more than two jobs in the past five years, enter the extras in Part 7.

Part 3

Include information about your most recent employment outside of the U.S. if it's not already listed in Part 2.

Part 4

Fill out this section with your contact information and signature.

Parts 5 and 6

These are for a preparer or interpreter helping fill out the form. If doing your own application, write "N/A" here.

Sample Form I-130A, Supplemental Information—Page 1

Supplemental Information for Spouse Beneficiary

Department of Homeland Security

U.S. Citizenship and Immigration Services

USCIS Form I-130A

OMB No. 1615-0012
Expires 02/28/2021

To be completed by an attorney or accredited representative (if any).			
☐ Select this box if Form G-28 is attached.	**Volag Number** (if any)	**Attorney State Bar Number** (if applicable)	**Attorney or Accredited Representative USCIS Online Account Number** (if any)

▶ **START HERE - Type or print in black ink.**

The purpose of this form is to collect additional information for a spouse beneficiary of Form I-130, Petition for Alien Relative. If your spouse is a U.S. citizen, lawful permanent resident, or non-citizen U.S. national who is filing Form I-130 on your behalf, you must complete and sign Form I-130A, Supplemental Information for Spouse Beneficiary, and submit it with the Form I-130 filed by your spouse. If you reside overseas, you still must complete Form I-130A, but you do not need to sign the form.

Part 1. Information About You (Spouse Beneficiary)

1. Alien Registration Number (A-Number) (if any)
   ▶ A-

2. USCIS Online Account Number (if any)
   ▶

Your Full Name

3.a. Family Name (Last Name): Mihov

3.b. Given Name (First Name): Anda

3.c. Middle Name: Marina

Address History

Provide your physical addresses for the last five years, whether inside or outside the United States. Provide your current address first. If you need extra space to complete this section, use the space provided in **Part 7. Additional Information.**

Physical Address 1

4.a. Street Number and Name: 68 Watertown Blvd

4.b. ☒ Apt. ☐ Ste. ☐ Flr. 12

4.c. City or Town: Erie

4.d. State: PA   4.e. ZIP Code: 19380

4.f. Province:

4.g. Postal Code:

4.h. Country: USA

5.a. Date From (mm/dd/yyyy): 11/01/2015

5.b. Date To (mm/dd/yyyy): PRESENT

Physical Address 2

6.a. Street Number and Name: n/a

6.b. ☐ Apt. ☐ Ste. ☐ Flr.

6.c. City or Town:

6.d. State: 6.e. ZIP Code:

6.f. Province:

6.g. Postal Code:

6.h. Country:

7.a. Date From (mm/dd/yyyy):

7.b. Date To (mm/dd/yyyy):

Last Physical Address Outside the United States

Provide your last address outside the United States of more than one year (even if listed above).

8.a. Street Number and Name: 42, Raiska Gradina St.

8.b. ☐ Apt. ☐ Ste. ☐ Flr.

8.c. City or Town: Sofia

8.d. Province:

8.e. Postal Code:

8.f. Country: Bulgaria

Form I-130A 02/13/19

Page 1 of 6

Sample Form I-130A, Supplemental Information—Page 2

Part 1. Information About You (The Spouse Beneficiary)

9.a. Date From (mm/dd/yyyy) | 02/01/2010

9.b. Date To (mm/dd/yyyy) | 10/31/2017

Information About Parent 1

Full Name of Parent 1

10.a. Family Name (Maiden Name) | Borisova

10.b. Given Name (First Name) | Anastasia

10.c. Middle Name

11. Date of Birth (mm/dd/yyyy) | 03/10/1972

12. Sex ☐ Male ☒ Female

13. City/Town/Village of Birth | Sofia

14. Country of Birth | Bulgaria

15. City/Town/Village of Residence | Sofia

16. Country of Residence | Bulgaria

Information About Parent 2

Full Name of Parent 2

17.a. Family Name (Last Name) | Michelski

17.b. Given Name (First Name) | Liski

17.c. Middle Name

18. Date of Birth (mm/dd/yyyy) | 12/24/1968

19. Sex ☒ Male ☐ Female

20. City/Town/Village of Birth | Sofia

21. Country of Birth | Bulgaria

22. City/Town/Village of Residence | Sofia

23. Country of Residence | Bulgaria

Part 2. Information About Your Employment

Provide your employment history for the last five years, whether inside or outside the United States. Provide your current employment first. If you are currently unemployed, type or print "Unemployed" in **Item Number 1.** below. If you need extra space to complete this section, use the space provided in **Part 7. Additional Information**.

Employment History

Employer 1

1. Name of Employer/Company

Berlitz Cultural Center

2.a. Street Number and Name | Penn Center

2.b. ☐ Apt. ☒ Ste. ☐ Flr. | 800

2.c. City or Town | Pittsburgh

2.d. State | PA **2.e.** ZIP Code | 15276

2.f. Province

2.g. Postal Code

2.h. Country | USA

3. Your Occupation | Language Teacher

4.a. Date From (mm/dd/yyyy) | 12/06/2017

4.b. Date To (mm/dd/yyyy) | present

Employer 2

5. Name of Employer/Company | n/a

6.a. Street Number and Name

6.b. ☐ Apt. ☐ Ste. ☐ Flr.

6.c. City or Town

6.d. State **6.e.** ZIP Code

6.f. Province

6.g. Postal Code

6.h. Country

Sample Form I-130A, Supplemental Information—Page 3

Part 2. Information About Your Employment (continued)

7. Your Occupation

8.a. Date From (mm/dd/yyyy)

8.b. Date To (mm/dd/yyyy)

Part 3. Information About Your Employment Outside the United States

Provide your last occupation outside the United States if not shown above. If you never worked outside the United States, provide this information in the space provided in **Part 7. Additional Information**.

1. Name of Employer/Company

   Czech Cultural Center

2.a. Street Number and Name

   123 Sveta Serdika Str.

2.b. ☐ Apt. ☐ Ste. ☐ Flr.

2.c. City or Town

   Sofia

2.d. State   2.e. ZIP Code

2.f. Province

2.g. Postal Code

2.h. Country

   Bulgaria

3. Your Occupation

   Language Teacher

4.a. Date From (mm/dd/yyyy)   08/01/2011

4.b. Date To (mm/dd/yyyy)   10/01/2017

Part 4. Spouse Beneficiary's Statement, Contact Information, Certification, and Signature

NOTE: Read the **Penalties** section of the Form I-130 and Form I-130A Instructions before completing this part.

Spouse Beneficiary's Statement

NOTE: Select the box for either **Item Number 1.a.** or **1.b.** If applicable, select the box for **Item Number 2.**

1.a. ☒ I can read and understand English, and I have read and understand every question and instruction on this form and my answer to every question.

1.b. ☐ The interpreter named in **Part 5.** read to me every question and instruction on this form and my answer to every question in

   a language in which I am fluent, and I understood everything.

2. ☐ At my request, the preparer name in **Part 6.**,

   prepared this form for me based only upon information I provided or authorized.

Spouse Beneficiary's Contact Information

3. Spouse Beneficiary's Daytime Telephone Number

   6105551122

4. Spouse Beneficiary's Mobile Telephone Number (if any)

   5061235555

5. Spouse Beneficiary's Email Address (if any)

   mihov123@email.com

Spouse Beneficiary's Certification

Copies of any documents I have submitted are exact photocopies of unaltered, original documents, and I understand that USCIS may require that I submit original documents to USCIS at a later date. Furthermore, I authorize the release of any information from any of my records that USCIS may need to determine my eligibility for the immigration benefit I seek.

I further authorize release of information contained in this form, in supporting documents, and in my USCIS records to other entities and persons where necessary for the administration and enforcement of U.S. immigration laws.

I certify, under penalty of perjury, that I provided or authorized all of the information in this form, I understand all of the information contained in, and submitted with, my form, and that all of this information is complete, true, and correct.

Spouse Beneficiary's Signature

6.a. Spouse Beneficiary's Signature (sign in ink)

   ➡ *Anda M. Mihov*

6.b. Date of Signature (mm/dd/yyyy)   04/11/2019

NOTE TO ALL SPOUSE BENEFICIARIES: If you do not completely fill out this form or fail to submit required documents listed in the Instructions, USCIS may deny the Form I-130 filed on your behalf.

3. Documents to Assemble for I-130 Petition

The I-130 petition asks you to submit supporting documents and payment along with the form. You're not done with this form until you have gathered together the following:

- **Proof of the U.S. citizen status of your petitioning spouse.** Depending on how your spouse became a citizen, he or she should copy a birth certificate, passport, certificate of naturalization, or Form FS-240 (Consular Report of Birth Abroad).
- **Proof that you're legally married.** This should include at a minimum a copy of your marriage certificate, most likely from a government source (see Chapter 4, Section C, for details). In addition, if either you or your spouse have been previously married, you must include proof that these marriages were terminated, such as a copy of a death, divorce, or annulment certificate.
- **Proof that the marriage is bona fide.** Include a select few items of evidence to show that your marriage is not a sham, but a real marital relationship. For instance, copies of documents showing you've spent time or lived together (such as a lease or mortgage agreement, bills sent to the house, and letters sent to the house for each spouse) are good, as are copies of joint financial accounts (bank and credit statements, loans, insurance policies). Of less weight are things like joint memberships and photos taken with friends and family; you might want to save these for your interview, when the issue of bona fide marriage will come up again.
- **Photos.** You must each submit two color, passport-style photos, 2 x 2 inches in size, taken within the past six months, showing your current appearance. Passport style means that the photo shows your full face from the front, with a plain white or off-white background—and your face must measure between one inch and 1⅜ inches from the bottom of your chin to the top of your head. For more information, see the State Department website at www.travel.state.gov. However, USCIS regulations permit you to submit a photo that doesn't completely follow the instructions if you live in a country where such photographs are unavailable or are cost prohibitive.
- **Fees.** The current fee for an I-130 petition is $535. However, these fees go up fairly regularly, so double-check this on the USCIS website at www.uscis.gov, or by calling USCIS at 800-375-5283.

4. Where to Send Form I-130 Petition

Where you'll send your Form I-130 petition will depend on whether you'll be allowed to complete your green card (adjustment of status) application in the United States or will be leaving to apply through an overseas U.S. consulate.

a. If You Will Be Adjusting Your Status in the U.S.

If you will be adjusting your status in the United States (either because you entered legally or because you can use an earlier-filed petition as your entry ticket to adjusting status), you can file the Form I-130 at the same time you file your adjustment of status forms, so don't send it anywhere yet! Simply keep the completed I-130 petition until you have completed your green card application.

SKIP AHEAD
Applicants who will be adjusting status in the United States can now skip to Chapter 14.

Where to Send the Form I-130 Petition

If the U.S. petitioner lives in:			Send Form I-130 to:
Alaska	Kansas	Oregon	**USCIS Phoenix Lockbox**
American Samoa	Montana	Puerto Rico	For U.S. Postal Service (USPS) deliveries:
Arizona	Nebraska	South Dakota	USCIS ATTN: I-130
California	Nevada	Texas	P.O. Box 21700
Colorado	New Mexico	Utah	Phoenix, AZ 85036
Florida	North Dakota	Virgin Islands	For courier deliveries:
Guam	Northern Mariana Islands	Washington	USCIS
Hawaii	Oklahoma	Wyoming	Attn: I-130
Idaho			1820 E. Skyharbor Circle S
			Suite 100
			Phoenix, AZ 85034
Alabama	Maine	North Carolina	**USCIS Chicago Lockbox**
Arkansas	Maryland	Ohio	For U.S. Postal Service:
Connecticut	Massachusetts	Pennsylvania	USCIS
Delaware	Michigan	Rhode Island	P.O. Box 804625
District of Columbia	Minnesota	South Carolina	Chicago, IL 60680-4107
Georgia	Mississippi	Tennessee	For courier deliveries:
Illinois	Missouri	Vermont	USCIS
Indiana	New Hampshire	Virginia	Attn: I-130
Iowa	New Jersey	West Virginia	131 South Dearborn–3rd Floor
Kentucky	New York	Wisconsin	Chicago, IL 60603-5517
Louisiana			

If the U.S. petitioner lives outside the U.S., send Form I-130 to:

USCIS Chicago Lockbox

For U.S. Postal Service (USPS) deliveries:
  USCIS
  P.O. Box 804625
  Chicago, IL 60680-4107

For courier deliveries:
  USCIS
  Attn: I-130
  131 South Dearborn-3rd Floor
  Chicago, IL 60603-5517

b. If You Will Be Completing the Process Overseas

If you will ultimately be leaving the United States to apply for your green card through a U.S. consulate, your spouse must send the Form I-130 and all its attachments to a USCIS office called a "lockbox" that serves the region where he or she lives. That office will then forward your petition to a USCIS service center, which will make the final decision approving or denying it. The form can be sent in any time, before or after you leave the United States.

Your spouse should make a copy of everything being sent (including the checks and photographs). Priority mail is typically the safest way to send anything to USCIS. The address is above (and on the USCIS website). Once USCIS has approved the I-130, it will transfer your file to the National Visa Center (NVC), which will link you up with an overseas U.S. consulate.

5. What Happens After You Mail in Form I-130 Petition

Your spouse will get a receipt notice from USCIS a few weeks after the petition is mailed. The notice will tell you to check the USCIS website for information on how long the application is likely to remain in processing, which is currently about 12 months.

As long as your petition is not beyond the "normal processing time," USCIS will ignore any inquiries from you or your spouse asking what is going on. USCIS lockbox offices and service centers seem like walled fortresses—you can't visit them, and it's impossible to talk with the person working on your case. If USCIS needs additional documentation to complete your application, it will send your spouse a letter asking for it. (See Chapter 15 for what to do if you don't get a timely answer from USCIS.) Likewise, if USCIS considers denying the case based on negative evidence obtained by other means, it will send your spouse a letter informing you and giving an opportunity to respond.

Eventually your spouse will receive a denial or an approval of the I-130 petition.

a. If the I-130 Petition Is Denied

If the I-130 petition is denied, USCIS will give a reason. The fastest thing to do is to fix the problem and try again.

For example, if the denial is because your petitioning spouse did not appear to be divorced from his or her previous spouse, your spouse will need to see a lawyer and obtain new and better documentation showing that there was a final divorce. Then your spouse can file a new I-130 petition.

b. If the I-130 Petition Is Approved

Assuming your case is approved, your spouse will receive a notice from the USCIS service center. An example of an I-130 petition approval notice is shown below. As you can see, it's nothing fancy. But it is an important document. Make a few photocopies of it and store these and the original in safe places.

As you'll see when you get to the next step, you'll use a copy of the approval notice as part of your green card application.

6. Using the Checklist for Step One, I-130 Petition

This checklist shows every form, document, and other item needed for the initial petition that your spouse, with your help, will assemble and submit to USCIS.

> **CHECKLIST**
>
> **Instructions on where to obtain an online version of this checklist are available in Appendix B.**

Checklist for Immigrant Petition by U. S. Citizen

- ☐ Form I-130 (see line-by-line instructions in Section D1, above)
- ☐ Form I-130A, Supplemental Information on Spouse Beneficiary
- ☐ Documents to accompany Form I-130 (photocopies only):
  - ☐ Your marriage certificate (see Chapter 4, Section C, on obtaining vital documents)
  - ☐ Proof of the U.S. citizenship status of your petitioning spouse, such as a birth certificate, passport, certificate of naturalization, or Form FS-240 (Consular Report of Birth Abroad)
  - ☐ Proof of termination of all previous marriages, such as certificates of death, divorce, or annulment (see Chapter 4, Section C, regarding how to obtain vital documents)
  - ☐ Proof of bona fide marriage, such as copies of joint mortgage or rental agreements, bank and credit card accounts, insurance, and more
  - ☐ Two color photos of you, passport style
  - ☐ Two color photos of your spouse (passport style), and
  - ☐ Fees: Currently $535 for an I-130, but double-check this at www.uscis.gov or call 800-375-5283

Sample I-130 Receipt Notice

Department of Homeland Security U.S. Citizenship and Immigration Services	**Form I-797C, Notice of Action**

THIS NOTICE DOES NOT GRANT ANY IMMIGRATION STATUS OR BENEFIT.

NOTICE TYPE Receipt	NOTICE DATE April 23, 2019
CASE TYPE I-130 PETITION FOR ALIEN RELATIVE	USCIS ALIEN NUMBER
RECEIPT NUMBER MSC-19-041-00000	RECEIVED DATE April 21, 2019	PAGE 1 of 1
PRIORITY DATE	PREFERENCE CLASSIFICATION 201 B INA SPOUSE OF USC	DATE OF BIRTH September 26, 1960

ILONA BRAY
RE: ANDA M. MIHOV
950 PARKER STREET
BERKELEY, CA 94710

PAYMENT INFORMATION:

Application/Petition Fee:	$535.00
Biometrics Fee:	$0.00
Total Amount Received:	$535.00
Total Balance Due:	$0.00

APPLICANT/PETITIONER NAME AND MAILING ADDRESS

The I-130, Petition for Alien Relative has been received by our office for the following beneficiaries and is in process:

Name	Date of Birth	Country of Birth	Class (If Applicable)
MIHOV, ANDA M	09/26/1960	BULGARIA	

Please verify your personal information listed above and immediately notify the USCIS National Customer Service Center at the phone number listed below if there are any changes.

Please note that if a priority date is printed on this notice, the priority does not reflect earlier retained priority dates.

If you have questions about possible immigration benefits and services, filing information, or USCIS forms, please call the USCIS National Customer Service Center (NCSC) at **1-800-375-5283**. If you are hearing impaired, please call the NCSC TDD at **1-800-767-1833**. Please also refer to the USCIS website: www.uscis.gov.

If you have any questions or comments regarding this notice or the status of your case, please contact our customer service number.

You will be notified separately about any other case you may have filed.

USCIS Office Address:

USCIS
Nebraska Service Center
P.O. Box 82521
Lincoln, NE 68501-2521

USCIS Customer Service Number:

(800)375-5283
ATTORNEY COPY

If this is an interview or biometrics appointment notice, please see the back of this notice for important information.   Form I-797C 07/11/14 Y

Sample I-130 Approval Notice

Department of Homeland Security
U.S. Citizenship and Immigration Services

I-797, Notice of Action

THE UNITED STATES OF AMERICA

RECEIPT NUMBER MSC-19-047-00000		CASE TYPE I130 IMMIGRANT PETITION FOR RELATIVE, FIANCE(E), OR ORPHAN
RECEIPT DATE April 21, 2019	PRIORITY DATE	PETITIONER MIHOV, GRUN
NOTICE DATE October 11, 2019	PAGE	BENEFICIARY MIHOV, ANDA

ILONA BRAY
RE: ANDA MIHOV
950 PARKER STREET
BERKELEY, CA 94710

Notice Type: Approval Notice

Section: Husband or wife of U.S. citizen, 201(b)(2)(A)(i) INA

This notice is to advise you of action taken on this case. The official notice has been mailed according to the mailing preferences noted on the Form G-28, Notice of Entry of Appearance as Attorney or Accredited Representative. Any relevant documentation was mailed according to the specified mailing preferences.

The above petition has been approved. The petition indicates that the person for whom you are petitioning is in the United States and will apply for adjustment of status. He or she should contact the local USCIS office to obtain Form I-485, Application for Permanent Residence. A copy of this notice should be submitted with the application.

If the person for whom you are petitioning decides to apply for a visa outside the United States based on this petition, the petitioner should file Form I-824, Application for Action on an Approved Application or Petition, to request that we send the petition to the Department of State National Visa Center (NVC).

The NVC processes all approved immigrant visa petitions that require consular action. The NVC also determines which consular post is the appropriate consulate to complete visa processing. It will then forward the approved petition to that consulate.

The approval of this visa petition does not in itself grant any immigration status and does not guarantee that the alien beneficiary will subsequently be found to be eligible for a visa, for admission to the United States, or for an extension, change, or adjustment of status.

This courtesy copy may not be used in lieu of official notification to demonstrate the filing or processing action taken on this case.

THIS FORM IS NOT A VISA AND MAY NOT BE USED IN PLACE OF A VISA.

NOTICE: Although this application/petition has been approved, USCIS and the U.S. Department of Homeland Security reserve the right to verify the information submitted in this application, petition and/or supporting documentation to ensure conformity with applicable laws, rules, regulations, and other authorities. Methods used for verifying information may include, but are not limited to, the review of public information and records, contact by correspondence, the internet, or telephone, and site inspections of businesses and residences. Information obtained during the course of verification will be used to determine whether revocation, rescission, and/or removal proceedings are appropriate. Applicants, petitioners, and representatives of record will be provided an opportunity to address derogatory information before any formal proceeding is initiated.

Please see the additional information on the back. You will be notified separately about any other cases you filed.
NEBRASKA SERVICE CENTER
U. S. CITIZENSHIP & IMMIG SERVICE
P.O. BOX 82521
LINCOLN   NE   68501-2521
Customer Service Telephone: 800-375-5283

Form I-797 (Rev. 01/31/05) N

Next Step If You Entered The U.S. Illegally

If you are grandfathered into being allowed to adjust status in the United States:	See Chapter 14 regarding adjustment of status application procedures.
If you leave the United States before six months are up:	See Chapter 7, starting at Section A4, on consular processing procedures.
If you will have spent more than six months in the U.S. and plan to apply for a waiver:	See an attorney; Chapter 17 contains tips on finding a good one.

Next Step If You Entered The U.S. Legally

You will be applying for your green card in the United States:	See Chapter 14 on applying to adjust your status to permanent resident.
You will be applying for your green card overseas:	See Chapter 7, starting at Section A4, on consular processing procedures.

Spouses of Permanent Residents, in the U.S.

f you are in the United States—legally or illegally—and you are married to a U.S. lawful permanent resident, you are not immediately eligible to obtain permanent residence. Only foreign nationals married to U.S. citizens are immediately eligible for permanent residence.

As the spouse of a permanent resident, you are known as a preference relative. There are quotas on the number of preference relatives who are allowed green cards each year, which means there are long waiting lists. Your spouse can, and should, put you on the waiting list for a green card right away.

But you might be on the waiting list for at least a year or two. And no matter what your circumstances, it probably won't be legal for you to live in the United States while you wait (unless you happen to have a nonimmigrant visa or other status that will last for all those years).

The key to how and where you'll get your green card is whether you entered the United States legally or illegally. If you entered illegally, you lose certain important rights. Start by reading Section A to see whether your entry is considered legal or illegal, then move on to the subsections that match your current situation.

A. Did You Enter Legally or Illegally?

If you entered the United States with permission of the U.S. authorities, you entered legally. Whether you got that permission in advance or were simply allowed in when you arrived, the important thing is that you were personally met and allowed to enter by an officer of the U.S. border control. This might have occurred at the border itself or some other port of entry, such as an airport, seaport, or bus station. The usual ways people enter legally are:

- with a visa (a tourist, student, or temporary worker visa, for example)
- with a border crossing card (a special pass allowing regular entries), or
- under the Visa Waiver Program (whereby citizens of certain countries are allowed to

enter the U.S. as tourists by showing only their passport, without first obtaining an entry visa).

An illegal entry is, naturally, the opposite of a legal entry. People entering illegally have failed to obtain permission to enter. They may pay someone to sneak them across the U.S. border, wait until night and find an unguarded point on the U.S. border, or conceal themselves in the trunk of a car. USCIS says that they entered "without inspection," which means that they weren't personally met and approved for entry by a U.S. border control official. (USCIS refers to such people as "EWIs," pronounced "ee-wee," which stands for entry without inspection.) The immigration laws make getting a green card very difficult for people who entered the United States without inspection, or illegally.

SKIP AHEAD
If you entered the United States by crossing the border illegally, skip ahead to Section C.

B. Spouses Who Entered Legally

This section explains the immigration choices for foreign nationals who entered the United States legally and still live here. It applies to those of you who have overstayed your visa as well as those who are still within the visa's time limit.

1. Options and Strategies

USCIS expects the application process for every spouse of a permanent resident—even those who happen to be in the United States already—to follow this sequence:

1. Your permanent resident spouse puts you on the waiting list for a green card by filing a petition on Form I-130.
2. You wait overseas for an average of a few years until you reach the top of the waiting list.
3. You apply for an immigrant visa at a U.S consulate in your home country.

4. Only when you have your immigrant visa do you come to the United States to claim your green card.

Unfortunately, what USCIS expects and what immigrant applicants want are often two different things. We're guessing that since you are already in the United States, you would like to stay here with your spouse while you apply for your green card. Many couples have stayed illegally in the past, and for brief periods Congress allowed them to apply for their green cards here—but these laws are gone (although a very few people can still take advantage of them; see Section 3, below).

It will be difficult or impossible for the spouses of permanent residents living in the United States to remain in the United States while they complete the application process for a green card. Nevertheless, the options outlined below will cover every possible way to get your green card in the United States and will tell you how and where to apply if you can't.

CAUTION
The six-month problem. If you've already stayed in the United States for 180 days or more beyond the expiration of your permitted stay, you have a very good reason to look for a way to get your green card without leaving the United States. If you leave the country and apply for permission to come back as a permanent resident, you can be prevented from entering the United States for three or ten years even if you are otherwise entitled to a green card through marriage (see Chapter 2, Section A, to review the time bar penalties for illegal stays).

The spouse of a U.S. lawful permanent resident has five options (though we don't recommend all of them, as you'll see in the subsequent discussion):

- stay in the United States legally (if your permitted stay, most likely under a nonimmigrant visa, lasts long enough to get you through the waiting period) and adjust your status to permanent resident in the United States; this option is covered in Section 2, below

- stay in the United States illegally, hoping for a way to adjust your status to green card holder in the United States; this path is explained in Section 3

- leave the United States before you have overstayed your visa by six months or more, wait overseas, then apply for a green card at a U.S. consulate; this possibility is explained in Section 4

- leave the United States after you have overstayed your visa by more than six months but less than one year, wait out your waiting period at the same time that you serve your three-year penalty for overstaying, then apply for a green card at a U.S. consulate; this possibility is explained in Section 5, or

- after you have overstayed your visa by more than six months or a year, apply for the waiver before having to leave the U.S., then apply for your green card at a U.S. consulate; this option is described in Section 6.

2. Stay in the U.S. Legally

If you can make your current permitted stay (perhaps with the visa you used to enter the United States) last for the full amount of time that you spend on the waiting list for a green card, you may be able to apply for your green card without leaving the United States. However, that's hard to do, and all of the following will need to be true when your waiting period is over and it's time for you to apply for your green card:

- you entered the United States legally

- you have never been out of lawful U.S. immigration status

- you have never worked illegally in the United States, and

- your visa waiting period is over and you are immediately eligible to apply for your green card.

CAUTION
If you are already out of lawful immigration status or have worked illegally, skip to Section 3, below. If you're uncertain, consult an attorney (see Chapter 17 for tips on finding a good lawyer.)

If your current stay (as probably shown on your I-94) has not expired and you haven't worked illegally, your spouse should file an initial petition for you as soon as possible. This is the I-130 that will put you on the waiting list for a green card. (See Section D below for how to prepare and submit this.) You should have no problem getting USCIS approval to put you on the waiting list. Then the important question is: Will your current status (student, temporary worker, or some other) really last long enough to get you through the waiting period?

If you are on a tourist visa, the answer is probably no. Your permitted tourist stay probably lasts no more than six months, with the possibility of one six-month extension. And having a spousal petition pending may make it difficult to obtain such an extension.

That's normally not long enough for a visa to become available in your category (2A)—though the waits vary, so do some checking before you make any decisions. If you are on some other visa, such as a student or temporary worker visa, you may have a decent chance. In fact, academic student visas can be extended by moving on to a more advanced program; and some temporary worker visas can be renewed. Just be sure not to work illegally, which would destroy your eligibility to adjust status.

Keep in mind that the fact of your having a spousal petition filed on your behalf could come up at the border, if you travel outside the United States. This, too, could jeopardize your status.

CAUTION

Watch out if you're in the U.S. on a work-based visa. If you entered the U.S. on any of certain types of employment-based visas, applying for a green card through your U.S. spouse puts you at risk of losing your visa status. (See the discussion called, "Here on a Temporary Employment Visa? The Risks of Applying for a Green Card," in Chapter 2, Section A.)

SEE AN EXPERT

A full discussion of which visas are renewable and how long you can make them last is outside the scope of this book. You might wish to consult with an attorney.

You may also benefit from recent changes in how cases are processed during the waiting period. As explained in more detail in Section D below, these changes may allow you to begin the green card application months before a visa becomes available to you. This would be beneficial because, as explained in Chapter 14, having a green card application pending would automatically allow you to stay in the U.S. and apply for a work permit.

If your visa or status runs out and you are still on the waiting list, what should you do? You will need to make an educated guess at how much longer you will be on the waiting list (see Section E below for help). If your wait is probably going to be another six months or more from the date your visa expires, you would be best advised to leave the United States within those six months to avoid facing a three- or ten-year bar on reentering (be sure to save proof of your departure date, such as a plane ticket). You could try returning to the United States with another temporary visa, but the U.S. consulate is unlikely to grant one, knowing that your true intention is to stay in the United States permanently (which the consulate may view as a fraudulent misuse of the temporary visa).

Another issue is to consider when your spouse will become a U.S. citizen. Once he or she becomes a citizen, you move off the waiting list and can apply for a green card right away, no matter how long you overstayed. But you will be living in the United States illegally between the time your visa runs out and when you turn in your green card application. If USCIS or DHS happens to catch you, it could deport you. (See Section 3 below for a discussion of living in the United States illegally and for more on the benefits of your spouse becoming a citizen.)

If you do need to finish your wait in your home country, you will ultimately apply for your green card through a U.S. consulate. So long as you didn't stay unlawfully in the United States for more than six continuous months, this is not a risky procedure. Hopefully, you won't have to wait overseas for long.

SKIP AHEAD

If an option described in this section definitely fits your situation, go to Section D below for the next step.

3. Stay in the U.S. Illegally

It is illegal to stay in the United States past the expiration of any temporary visa or without any status while you are on the waiting list for a green card. However, a number of people take this risk. The people most likely to do so are those who know or believe that an exception to the law allows them access to a local USCIS office to apply for their green card (adjustment of status) at the end of their wait. For these few people, taking the risk of waiting illegally may have a big payoff at the end, because there will be no penalty for their illegal stay when they apply to adjust status. By contrast, any applicant who goes to a U.S. consulate to apply for a green card is exposed to penalties for their illegal stay—a three- or ten-year bar on returning to the United States, depending on the length of their stay. Still, staying in the United States illegally is a gamble that we only describe, not recommend.

CAUTION

People who attempt to stay in the United States illegally can be picked up and placed in removal proceedings at any time. Marriage to a permanent resident will not be enough by itself to protect you from deportation. For more on the risks, see Subsection 3c, below.

Some people choose to wait illegally in the United States knowing that they won't be permitted to adjust their status at the end of the waiting period. Their only hope is that the immigration laws will change in their favor. This is a huge gamble—recent changes in the immigration laws have made them harsher, not gentler on immigrants. But none of us has a crystal ball, and some immigrant families find it unthinkable to separate now, come what may later.

There are two categories of people who might be allowed to adjust their status to permanent resident at a USCIS office, even after their visa has run out and they have stayed illegally. These are people who not only entered legally (perhaps with a visa) but whose spouses become U.S. citizens during the waiting period, and people who fall into narrow exceptions within the immigration laws.

a. If Your Spouse Becomes a U.S. Citizen

If your permanent resident spouse becomes a U.S. citizen, your situation will dramatically improve. For this reason, your spouse should be planning now for U.S. citizenship.

i. Move Off the Waiting List and Adjust Status

When your spouse becomes a U.S. citizen, you (as a legal entrant) become eligible to adjust your status to permanent resident in the United States right away. This is true even if your spouse becomes a citizen after your visa runs out and you've stayed in the United States illegally, no matter how long your illegal stay. You would move off the green card waiting list and become what is known as an immediate relative.

You'll become eligible for a green card just as soon as you can get through the rest of the application procedures. And you won't have to leave the United States to apply for that green card. Because you entered the United States legally and your spouse is a U.S. citizen, you are eligible to file your green card application in the United States, using the adjustment of status procedure. But if you have children with whom you intend to immigrate, be careful: changing your visa category could complicate their case (see Section E6, below).

CAUTION

Don't leave the United States until your green card is approved. Having your spouse become a U.S. citizen doesn't solve everything. If you stayed illegally for more than six months in the United States after the expiration of your visa and before turning in your green card application, watch out. Leaving the United States before your green card is approved will subject you to bars on reentry of three or ten years.

ii. When Your Spouse Can Apply for Citizenship

A permanent resident can apply for U.S. citizenship five years after approval for residence (with some exceptions).

Unless your spouse faces some serious impediment to citizenship—such as not knowing English or having a criminal record—he or she should probably apply for citizenship as soon as possible. USCIS permits people to submit the application three months before the end of their waiting period—but no more than three months, or USCIS will reject the application.

RESOURCE

Want more information on the process and requirements of applying for U.S. citizenship? See the USCIS website at www.uscis.gov, or *Becoming a U.S. Citizen: A Guide to the Law, Exam & Interview*, by Ilona Bray (Nolo).

b. A Few People Can Adjust Status in the U.S.

A very few people living illegally in the United States might be lucky enough to fall into an exception to the immigration laws and be allowed to change their status to permanent resident at a local USCIS office. The key is whether an employer filed a labor certification on your behalf or a family member (even if it wasn't your spouse) filed an immigrant petition on your behalf, either:

- before January 14, 1998, or
- between January 14, 1998 and April 30, 2001, if you can also prove that you were physically present in the United States on December 21, 2000.

If that labor certification or I-130 petition was approved, or if it was denied only because of a mistake by the INS (as USCIS was then called), then you will be "grandfathered in" under the old laws and allowed to change your status to permanent resident at a USCIS office. Immigrants who can take advantage of the time windows mentioned above are among the lucky few who won't have to travel to a U.S. consulate to apply for their green card. (For more details on the grandfathering clauses, see Chapter 2, Section A.)

This grandfathering exception only lets you submit and receive a decision on your green card application at a USCIS office as opposed to an overseas consulate. It doesn't mean that you can stay in the United States illegally while on the waiting list (for permission to submit the green card application). But many people take the risk of staying, in order to be with their spouse during the application process. (The immigration authorities don't normally search these people out, but can deport them if they happen to find them.)

If you get to the end of the waiting period without being ordered to leave the U.S., you'll be allowed to apply for your green card.

The opportunity to adjust status in the United States is especially valuable to people who have already stayed for more than six months past the expiration date of their visa. If they leave the United States, they can be kept out for three or ten years. (See Chapter 2, Section A.)

c. The Risks of Staying Illegally

If you decide to stay in the United States illegally, you will be taking some chances. Immigration and Customs Enforcement (ICE) so far has not made any major efforts to catch waiting spouses of permanent residents—but this could change. In addition, you could be picked up in a raid, or after someone with a grudge has tipped off ICE to your whereabouts.

If you are picked up, you could be removed (deported)—and hit with a ten-year bar on returning to the United States. Your marriage to a U.S. permanent resident won't help you if you are still on the waiting list for a visa. It could only help you if you were immediately eligible to apply for your green card, either because your waiting period was over or your spouse had become a U.S. citizen.

SEE AN EXPERT

If you are discovered by ICE, get a lawyer right away. The lawyer can fully evaluate your case and possibly defend you against deportation. Whatever you do, don't ignore the summons to go to court (also known as a Notice to Appear or NTA)—doing so could destroy your chances of getting a green card later.

4. Leave Before You Have Overstayed by Six Months or Less

If you haven't stayed more than six months past the expiration date of your I-94 or other right to be here (such as having entered under the Visa Waiver Program), your safest bet is to leave the United States before that date rolls around. It is particularly important to think about when you are going to leave if you won't be allowed to submit your green card application to a USCIS office (because your situation does not fit into Subsection 3a or 3b, above).

If you must leave, it's better to leave sooner rather than later. Remember, if you leave before you have overstayed for six months, there are no penalties. But if you've overstayed by 180 to 365 continuous days, you can be barred from returning to the United States for three years. If you overstay for more than a year, you can be barred for ten years.

CAUTION

Make sure you can prove you overstayed by less than 180 days. When the time comes to apply for your green card, the consulate will want proof of how long you stayed illegally in the United States. Collect and keep all evidence, such as your plane tickets, store receipts, medical records, credit card statements, and anything else relevant to show that you left the United States before six months was up.

After you are overseas and your waiting period is over or your spouse becomes a U.S. citizen, you can receive a green card through normal procedures at an overseas consulate. Obviously, this may also mean many months or years of separation from your spouse while you wait overseas to rise to the top of the waiting list. But that might be better than ten years of separation (because of a time bar penalty) later.

5. Leave After You Have Overstayed by More Than Six Months But Less Than One Year

If you have stayed past the expiration date of your permitted stay under a visa by more than six months but less than year, the law would only bar you from returning to the United States for a three-year period. If you left the United States now, you could work off your three-year penalty at the same time as you wait to reach the top of the waiting list and are allowed to apply for your immigrant visa and green card.

CAUTION

Make sure you can prove you overstayed by less than one year. When the time comes to apply for your green card, the consulate will want to see proof of how long you stayed illegally in the United States. Collect and keep all evidence, such as your plane tickets, store receipts, medical records, credit card statements, and anything else relevant to show that you left before a year was up.

6. After You Have Overstayed a Year or More, Apply for a Waiver

If you have stayed in the United States more than a year after your permitted stay expired and cannot apply for a green card there, you should, to avoid being prevented from returning to the United States for ten years, ask USCIS to forgive your illegal time in the United States. This is called asking for an I-601 "provisional" or "stateside" waiver. This allows the application for forgiveness of your illegal stay to be decided before you leave the United States. This waiver-application procedure is best handled by an experienced immigration attorney.

The attorney can give you a sense of how likely it is that your waiver will be approved. There are certainly no guarantees. To get approved, you will have to show that your not receiving a visa will cause extreme hardship to your spouse in the United States and/or, if you happen to have a U.S. citizen or permanent resident parent in the U.S., to him or her—and when the law says extreme, it means much more than the sadness they will feel at your being thousands of miles away. The classic case of extreme hardship is someone whose U.S. spouse or parent has severe medical or emotional problems that require the immigrating spouse's constant attention. Financial hardship will also be taken into account

With a waiver, you can return to the United States as soon as your waiting period is over and you get through the immigrant visa/green card application process. (The latter usually takes about one year.)

SEE AN EXPERT

These waivers are complex and require preparing and collecting many documents. Look for an attorney who has experience with them. (See Chapter 17 for tips on finding a good attorney.)

C. Spouses Who Entered Illegally

This section is for foreign nationals living in the United States after entering illegally. Unfortunately, your path to a green card is a difficult one, involving unattractive choices. Before explaining them in detail, we need to warn readers to see an attorney if:

- you've entered the U.S. illegally two or more times and
- the total amount of illegal time in the U.S. is one year or more; or
- you've been deported.

These would-be immigrants may be permanently barred from immigrating to the United States. (See Chapter 2, Section A, for further information about the permanent bar.)

1. Options and Strategies for Illegal Entrants

USCIS expects the application process for every spouse of a permanent resident—even those already living in the United States—to follow this sequence:

1. Your permanent resident spouse puts you on the waiting list for a green card by filing a petition on Form I-130.
2. You wait overseas (for an average of up to five years) until you reach the top of the waiting list.
3. You apply for an immigrant visa at a U.S consulate in your home country.
4. Only when you have your immigrant visa do you come to the United States to claim your green card.

But what USCIS expects and what immigrant applicants want are often two different things. We're guessing that since you are already in the United States, you would like to stay here with your spouse while you apply for your green card. Many couples have stayed illegally in the past, and for brief periods of time Congress allowed them to apply for their green cards here—but these laws are gone (although a few people can still take advantage of them; see Section 2, below).

It will be difficult or impossible for the spouses of permanent residents now living in the United States to remain in the United States while they apply for a green card. It is particularly difficult for people who entered illegally, because unlike people who entered with a visa, you will not be allowed to submit your green card application in the United States even if your spouse becomes a U.S. citizen.

Nevertheless, the options outlined below will consider every possible way to get your green card in the United States and will tell you how and where to apply if you can't.

CAUTION

The six-month problem. If you've already stayed illegally in the United States for six months or more, you have a very good reason to look for a way to get your green card without leaving the United States. If you leave the country and apply for permission to come back as a legal permanent resident, you can be prevented from entering the United States for three or ten years even if you are otherwise entitled to a green card through marriage. (See Chapter 2, Section A, to review the time bar penalties for illegal stays.)

You have four options (though we don't recommend all of them, as you'll see in the subsequent discussion):

- stay in the United States illegally, hoping for a way to adjust your status to permanent residence through a local USCIS office; this option is covered in Section 2, below
- leave the United States before you have stayed illegally for six months or more, wait out your waiting period, and apply for your green card through a U.S. consulate overseas; this path is explained in Section 3
- leave the United States after you have stayed illegally for more than 180 days but less than a year, wait out your waiting period at the same time that you serve your three-year penalty for staying illegally, and apply for your green card through a U.S. consulate overseas; this possibility is explained in Section 4, or
- after you have stayed illegally for more than a year, apply for a waiver of your illegal stay before leaving for your visa interview through a U.S. consulate overseas; this option is described in Section 5.

2. Stay in the U.S. Illegally

If you've entered the U.S. illegally, it's against the law to stay in the United States while you are on the waiting list for a green card. However, a number of people take this risk.

The people most likely to risk living in the United States illegally are those who know or believe that an exception to the law allows them access to a local USCIS office to apply for their green card (adjustment of status) at the end of their wait. For these few people, taking the risk of waiting illegally may have a big payoff at the end, because there will be no penalty for their illegal entry and stay when they apply to adjust status. By contrast, any applicant who goes to a U.S. consulate to apply for a green card is exposed to potential penalties for their illegal stay—a three- or ten-year bar on returning to the United States, depending on the length of their stay. Staying in the United States illegally is a gamble that we only describe, not recommend.

CAUTION

People who attempt to stay in the United States illegally can be picked up and placed in removal proceedings at any time. Marriage to a permanent resident is not enough by itself to protect you. (For more on the risks, see Subsection 2b, below.)

There is another option, which we also don't recommend. You could wait in the United States illegally, hoping that the immigration laws will change in your favor and make you eligible to apply for a green card at a USCIS office. This is a huge gamble—recent changes in the immigration laws have made them harsher, not gentler on immigrants. But none of us has a crystal ball, and some immigrant families find it unthinkable to separate now, come what may later.

TIP

Some immigrants may become legal some other way. It is possible, although rare, for someone to enter the United States illegally and later acquire the right to be there, temporarily or permanently. For example, someone might enter illegally but apply for political asylum and be given the right to live in the U.S. while the claim is being decided. These situations are outside the scope of this book. If you are proceeding on more than one immigration application at once, you should see an attorney for help. (See Chapter 17 for tips on finding a good lawyer.)

a. A Few Who Entered Illegally Can Adjust Their Status in the U.S.

Only certain categories of immigrants are now allowed to apply for their green card in the United States using the adjustment of status procedure. People who entered the United States illegally are normally not among them. However, a very few people might be lucky enough to fall into an exception to these laws, based on having started the application process before the laws changed. The key is whether a prospective employer or a close family member of yours, even if it wasn't your spouse, filed an immigrant labor certification or petition (Form I-130 for family members) on your behalf either:

- before January 14, 1998, or
- between January 14, 1998 and April 30, 2001, if you can also prove that you were physically present in the United States on December 21, 2000.

If that labor certification or I-130 petition was approved, or if it was denied only because of a mistake by the INS (as USCIS was then called), you may be allowed to adjust your status to permanent resident at a USCIS office. People who may take advantage of one of these time windows are said to be "grandfathered in" under the old laws. (For details, see Chapter 2, Section A.) In short, if your labor certification or petition was on file as described above, you have a ticket to adjust your status in the United States, even though you entered the country illegally.

This exception only lets you use a USCIS office instead of an overseas consulate to submit and receive a decision on your green card application. It doesn't mean that you can stay in the United States while on the waiting list (before submitting the green card portion of your application). But many people take the risk of staying, in order to be with their spouse during the application process. (Immigration and Customs Enforcement or "ICE" doesn't normally search these people out, but can deport them if it happens to find them.) If you get to the end of the waiting period without having been ordered to leave, you'll be allowed apply for your green card without leaving.

The opportunity to adjust status in the United States is especially valuable to people who have already stayed illegally for more than six months. If they leave the United States, they can be kept out for three or ten years. (See Chapter 2, Section A.)

b. The Risks If You Stay Illegally

If you decide to stay in the United States illegally, you will be taking some chances. ICE has not made efforts to catch waiting spouses of permanent residents—but this could change. In addition, you could be picked up in a USCIS raid, or after someone with a grudge tips off USCIS to your whereabouts.

If you are picked up, you may be deported—and hit with a ten-year bar on returning to the United States. Your marriage to a U.S. permanent resident won't help you.

SEE AN EXPERT

If you are discovered by ICE, get a lawyer right away. The lawyer can fully evaluate your case and possibly defend you against deportation. Whatever you do, don't ignore the summons to go to court—that could destroy your chances of getting a green card later.

3. Leave Before You Have Stayed Illegally for Six Months

If you haven't stayed illegally in the United States for more than 180 days, your safest bet is to leave before that date rolls around. It is particularly important to think about when you are going to leave if you won't be allowed to submit your green card application to a USCIS office (because your situation does not fit into Subsection 2a, above).

If you must leave, it's better to do so sooner rather than later. Remember, if you leave before you have stayed illegally for six months, there are no penalties. But if you've stayed illegally for 180 to 365 continuous days, you can be barred from returning to the United States for three years. If you stay illegally for more than a year, you can be barred for ten years.

CAUTION

Make sure you can prove you stayed for less than 180 days. When the time comes to apply for your green card, the U.S. consulate will want to see proof of how long you stayed illegally in the United States. Collect and keep all evidence, such as your plane tickets, store receipts, medical records, credit card statements, and anything else that shows where you were and when.

After you are overseas and your waiting period is over, you can receive a green card through normal procedures at an overseas consulate. Obviously, this may also mean many years of separation from your spouse while you wait overseas to rise to the top of the waiting list. But five years of separation now might be better than ten years of separation (because of a time bar penalty) later.

4. Leave After You Have Stayed Illegally for More Than Six Months But Less Than One Year

If you have stayed in the United States illegally for more than 180 days (about six months) but less than one year, the law will bar you from returning to the United States for only a three-year period. If you leave the United States now, your three-year penalty period could be over by the time you reach the top of the waiting list and are allowed to apply for your immigrant visa and green card.

Leaving the United States before you have stayed illegally for a year or more might be safer than staying around for the whole green card waiting period and risking being caught by the immigration authorities. You could be deported and prevented from reentering the United States for ten years.

CAUTION

Make sure you can prove you stayed illegally by less than one year. When the time comes to apply for your green card, the U.S. consulate will want to see proof of how long you stayed illegally in the United States. Collect and keep all evidence, such as your plane tickets, store receipts, medical records, credit card statements, and anything else relevant to show where you were and when.

5. After You Have Stayed Over One Year Illegally, Apply for a Waiver

If you have stayed illegally in the United States for more than a year and cannot apply for a green card there, you could face a ten-year bar on returning to the United States after departing for your consular interview. (See Chapter 2, Section A.)

The only way to avoid the ten-year bar is to ask USCIS to forgive your illegal time in the United States. This is called asking for an I-601 "provisional" or "stateside" waiver, which allows the application to be decided before you leave the United States. This procedure is best handled by an experienced immigration attorney.

The attorney can give you a sense of how likely it is that your waiver will be approved. There are certainly no guarantees. To succeed, you will have to show that your not receiving a visa will cause extreme hardship to your spouse and parents (if they happen to be U.S. citizens or permanent residents) in the United States—and when the law says extreme, it means much more than the sadness they will feel at your being thousands of miles away. The classic case of extreme hardship is someone whose U.S. spouse or parent has severe medical problems that require the immigrating spouse's constant attention. Financial hardship will also be taken into account.

SEE AN EXPERT

These waivers are complex and paperwork-intensive. Look for an attorney who has lots of experience with them. (See Chapter 17 for tips on finding a good attorney.)

D. Step One: I-130 Petition

Regardless of whether you apply for and receive your green card overseas or in the United States, there is one thing that you should do right away. Have your spouse file a petition on Form I-130 to get you onto the waiting list. Although this petition could alert the immigration authorities that you are in the United States illegally—they don't usually use this information to track people down to deport them. The sooner your spouse files the petition, the sooner your wait to receive your green card will be over.

The I-130 petition asks USCIS to acknowledge that you're married and let you go forward with green card processing. Approval of the petition does not mean you're guaranteed approval of your green card, however. This is only the first step in the process. Like every immigrant, you will eventually have to file your own, extensive portion of the green card application. At that time, the U.S. government will take a hard look at your financial situation and other factors that might make you inadmissible.

> **CAUTION**
>
> **If the U.S. petitioner has a criminal record, see an attorney.** Under the Adam Walsh Child Protection and Safety Act of 2006, U.S. citizens and lawful permanent residents who have been convicted of any "specified offense against a minor" are prohibited from filing a family-based immigrant petition on behalf of any beneficiary (whether a child or not). USCIS will run security checks on all petitions and may call the petitioner in for fingerprinting. If the petitioner has a conviction for one of the specified offenses against a minor, then the petition will not be approved unless USCIS determines that the U.S. petitioner poses no risk to the beneficiary.

1. Line-by-Line Instructions for Petition Forms

This section will give you precise instructions for filling in the forms that are listed on the I-130 petition checklist later in this chapter. Before proceeding, see Chapter 4 for general instructions on filling in USCIS forms. Also, as you read these instructions, you should have a copy of the appropriate form in hand.

a. Form I-130

Don't be thrown off by the fact that the form addresses your U.S. spouse as "you"—after all, it's your spouse who fills in and signs this form.

 WEB RESOURCE

Form I-130 is available on the USCIS website at www.uscis.gov/i-130. Below is a sample filled-in version of the relevant pages of this form.

Part A

Question 1: Check the first box, "Spouse."

Questions 2-3: Since this petition is for a spouse, do not check any boxes here.

Question 4: If the petitioning spouse gained permanent residence through adoption, check "Yes." But no matter which box you check, it won't affect the application, since this question is mainly directed at people immigrating through parent/child relationships—something not covered in this book.

Part 2

Question 1: A U.S. permanent resident petitioner will have an A-number (Alien Registration Number), shown on the green card.

Question 2: A U.S. petitioner who has filed a past petition with USCIS may have received a USCIS Online Account Number, and should enter it here.

Question 3: A U.S. permanent resident should have a Social Security number, and fill it in here.

Question 4: The petitioning spouse should enter his/her full name. Use current married name if it was changed at the time of the marriage. See "What's Your Name?" in Chapter 4, Section B.

Question 5: The U.S. petitioner should enter any names previously used. If married before, with another name during that time, enter it here.

Questions 6-9: Self-explanatory.

Questions 10-15: Fill in U.S. permanent resident's addresses from the last five years. For more than two, enter the additional addresses in Part 9. Make sure to include the start and end dates of all addresses before the current one.

Question 16: State how many times the U.S. petitioner has been married, including this time.

Question 17: This refers only to the petitioning spouse's most recent marital status; check only married, even if there was a previous divorce.

Questions 18-19: Self-explanatory.

Sample Form I-130, Petition for Alien Relative—Page 1

Petition for Alien Relative

Department of Homeland Security

U.S. Citizenship and Immigration Services

**USCIS
Form I-130**

OMB No. 1615-0012
Expires 02/28/2021

For USCIS Use Only	Fee Stamp	Action Stamp

A-Number

A-

Initial Receipt

Resubmitted

Relocated — **Section of Law/Visa Category**

Received
- ☐ 201(b) Spouse - IR-1/CR-1
- ☐ 203(a)(1) Unm. S/D - F1-1
- ☐ 203(a)(2)(B) Unm. S/D - F2-4

Sent
- ☐ 201(b) Child - IR-2/CR-2
- ☐ 203(a)(2)(A) Spouse - F2-1
- ☐ 203(a)(3) Married S/D - F3-1

Completed
- ☐ 201(b) Parent - IR-5
- ☐ 203(a)(2)(A) Child - F2-2
- ☐ 203(a)(4) Brother/Sister - F4-1

Approved — Petition was filed on (Priority Date mm/dd/yyyy):
- ☐ Field Investigation
- ☐ Previously Forwarded
- ☐ 203(g) Resolved
- ☐ Personal Interview
- ☐ Pet. A-File Reviewed
- ☐ Ben. A-File Reviewed
- ☐ 204(a)(2)(A) Resolved
- ☐ I-485 Filed Simultaneously
- ☐ 204(g) Resolved

Returned — PDR request granted/denied - New priority date (mm/dd/yyyy):

Remarks

At which USCIS office (e.g., NBC, VSC, LOS, CRO) was Form I-130 adjudicated? _____

To be completed by an attorney or accredited representative (if any).

☐ **Select this box if Form G-28 is attached.**

Volag Number (if any)

Attorney State Bar Number (if applicable)

Attorney or Accredited Representative USCIS Online Account Number (if any)

▶ **START HERE** - Type or print in black ink.

If you need extra space to complete any section of this petition, use the space provided in **Part 9. Additional Information.**
Complete and submit as many copies of Part 9., as necessary, with your petition.

Part 1. Relationship (You are the Petitioner. Your relative is the Beneficiary)

1. I am filing this petition for my (Select **only one** box):

   ☒ Spouse ☐ Parent ☐ Brother/Sister ☐ Child

2. If you are filing this petition for your child or parent, select the box that describes your relationship (Select **only one** box):

   ☐ Child was born to parents who were married to each other at the time of the child's birth

   ☐ Stepchild/Stepparent

   ☐ Child was born to parents who were not married to each other at the time of the child's birth

   ☐ Child was adopted (not an Orphan or Hague Convention adoptee)

3. If the beneficiary is your brother/sister, are you related by adoption? ☐ Yes ☐ No

4. Did you gain lawful permanent resident status or citizenship through adoption? ☐ Yes ☒ No

Part 2. Information About You (Petitioner)

1. Alien Registration Number (A-Number) (if any)

   ▶ A- 2 2 2 3 3 4 4 5 5

2. USCIS Online Account Number (if any)

   ▶

3. U.S. Social Security Number (if any)

   ▶ 7 5 6 9 1 0 6 3 7

Your Full Name

4.a.	Family Name (Last Name)	NGUYEN
4.b.	Given Name (First Name)	Teo
4.c.	Middle Name	Thanh

Sample Form I-130, Petition for Alien Relative—Page 2

Part 2. Information About You (Petitioner) (continued)

Other Names Used (if any)

Provide all other names you have ever used, including aliases, maiden name, and nicknames.

5.a. Family Name (Last Name)

5.b. Given Name (First Name)

5.c. Middle Name

Other Information

6. City/Town/Village of Birth

Saigon

7. Country of Birth

Vietnam

8. Date of Birth (mm/dd/yyyy) 04/12/1993

9. Sex ☒ Male ☐ Female

Mailing Address

10.a. In Care Of Name

10.b. Street Number and Name 1640 Lincoln Park

10.c. ☐ Apt. ☐ Ste. ☐ Flr.

10.d. City or Town Beaverton

10.e. State OR **10.f.** ZIP Code 97006

10.g. Province

10.h. Postal Code

10.i. Country USA

11. Is your current mailing address the same as your physical address? ☒ Yes ☐ No

If you answered "No" to **Item Number 11.**, provide information on your physical address in **Item Numbers 12.a. - 13.b.**

Address History

Provide your physical addresses for the last five years, whether inside or outside the United States. Provide your current address first if it is different from your mailing address in **Item Numbers 10.a. - 10.i.**

Physical Address 1

12.a. Street Number and Name

12.b. ☐ Apt. ☐ Ste. ☐ Flr.

12.c. City or Town

12.d. State **12.e.** ZIP Code

12.f. Province

12.g. Postal Code

12.h. Country

13.a. Date From (mm/dd/yyyy)

13.b. Date To (mm/dd/yyyy)

Physical Address 2

14.a. Street Number and Name 100 N. Halsted St.

14.b. ☒ Apt. ☐ Ste. ☐ Flr. 10

14.c. City or Town Chicago

14.d. State IL **14.e.** ZIP Code 60604

14.f. Province

14.g. Postal Code

14.h. Country USA

15.a. Date From (mm/dd/yyyy) 01/01/2010

15.b. Date To (mm/dd/yyyy) 04/30/2015

Your Marital Information

16. How many times have you been married? ▶ 1

17. Current Marital Status

☐ Single, Never Married ☒ Married ☐ Divorced

☐ Widowed ☐ Separated ☐ Annulled

Sample Form I-130, Petition for Alien Relative—Page 3

Part 2. Information About You (Petitioner) (continued)

18. Date of Current Marriage (if currently married) (mm/dd/yyyy) 05/22/2019

Place of Your Current Marriage (if married)

19.a. City or Town Salem

19.b. State OR

19.c. Province

19.d. Country USA

Names of All Your Spouses (if any)

Provide information on your current spouse (if currently married) first and then list all your prior spouses (if any).

Spouse 1

20.a. Family Name (Last Name) NGUYEN

20.b. Given Name (First Name) Lea

20.c. Middle Name Nadres

21. Date Marriage Ended (mm/dd/yyyy) n/a

Spouse 2

22.a. Family Name (Last Name) n/a

22.b. Given Name (First Name)

22.c. Middle Name

23. Date Marriage Ended (mm/dd/yyyy)

Information About Your Parents

Parent 1's Information

Full Name of Parent 1

24.a. Family Name (Last Name) Nguyen

24.b. Given Name (First Name) Thanh

24.c. Middle Name

25. Date of Birth (mm/dd/yyyy) 03/01/1960

26. Sex ☒ Male ☐ Female

27. Country of Birth Vietnam

28. City/Town/Village of Residence San Francisco

29. Country of Residence USA

Parent 2's Information

Full Name of Parent 2

30.a. Family Name (Last Name) Smith

30.b. Given Name (First Name) Mary

30.c. Middle Name

31. Date of Birth (mm/dd/yyyy) 02/15/1959

32. Sex ☐ Male ☒ Female

33. Country of Birth USA

34. City/Town/Village of Residence San Francisco

35. Country of Residence USA

Additional Information About You (Petitioner)

36. I am a (Select **only one** box):
    ☐ U.S. Citizen ☒ Lawful Permanent Resident

If you are a U.S. citizen, complete Item Number 37.

37. My citizenship was acquired through (Select **only one** box):

    ☐ Birth in the United States

    ☐ Naturalization

    ☐ Parents

38. Have you obtained a Certificate of Naturalization or a Certificate of Citizenship? ☐ Yes ☐ No

If you answered "Yes" to **Item Number 38.**, complete the following:

39.a. Certificate Number

39.b. Place of Issuance

39.c. Date of Issuance (mm/dd/yyyy)

Sample Form I-130, Petition for Alien Relative—Page 4

Part 2. Information About You (Petitioner) (continued)

If you are a lawful permanent resident, complete **Item Numbers 40.a. - 41.**

40.a. Class of Admission

IR-2

40.b. Date of Admission (mm/dd/yyyy) 01/12/1996

Place of Admission

40.c. City or Town

San Francisco

40.d State   CA

41. Did you gain lawful permanent resident status through marriage to a U.S. citizen or lawful permanent resident?

☐ Yes ☒ No

Employment History

Provide your employment history for the last five years, whether inside or outside the United States. Provide your current employment first. If you are currently unemployed, type or print "Unemployed" in **Item Number 42.**

Employer 1

42. Name of Employer/Company

Oregon Brewing Co.

43.a. Street Number and Name   1000 Hops Way

43.b. ☐ Apt. ☐ Ste. ☐ Flr.

43.c. City or Town   Beaverton

43.d. State OR   **43.e.** ZIP Code 97101

43.f. Province

43.g. Postal Code

43.h. Country

USA

44. Your Occupation

Logistics Manager

45.a. Date From (mm/dd/yyyy)   05/01/2015

45.b. Date To (mm/dd/yyyy)   present

Employer 2

46. Name of Employer/Company

n/a - student

47.a. Street Number and Name

47.b. ☐ Apt. ☐ Ste. ☐ Flr.

47.c. City or Town

47.d. State   **47.e.** ZIP Code

47.f. Province

47.g. Postal Code

47.h. Country

48. Your Occupation

49.a. Date From (mm/dd/yyyy)

49.b. Date To (mm/dd/yyyy)

Part 3. Biographic Information

NOTE: Provide the biographic information about you, the petitioner.

1. Ethnicity (Select **only one** box)

☐ Hispanic or Latino
☒ Not Hispanic or Latino

2. Race (Select **all applicable** boxes)

☐ White
☒ Asian
☐ Black or African American
☐ American Indian or Alaska Native
☐ Native Hawaiian or Other Pacific Islander

3. Height   Feet 5   Inches 8

4. Weight   Pounds 1 3 5

5. Eye Color (Select **only one** box)

☐ Black   ☐ Blue   ☒ Brown
☐ Gray   ☐ Green   ☐ Hazel
☐ Maroon   ☐ Pink   ☐ Unknown/Other

Sample Form I-130, Petition for Alien Relative—Page 5

Part 3. Biographic Information (continued)

6. Hair Color (Select **only one** box)

   ☐ Bald (No hair) ☒ Black ☐ Blond
   ☐ Brown ☐ Gray ☐ Red
   ☐ Sandy ☐ White ☐ Unknown/Other

Part 4. Information About Beneficiary

1. Alien Registration Number (A-Number) (if any)

   ▶ A- 2 3 4 5 6 7 8 9 9

2. USCIS Online Account Number (if any)

   ▶ [ ][ ][ ][ ][ ][ ][ ][ ][ ][ ][ ][ ]

3. U.S. Social Security Number (if any)

   ▶ 9 8 9 9 9 9 8 9 8

Beneficiary's Full Name

4.a. Family Name (Last Name) NGUYEN
4.b. Given Name (First Name) Lea
4.c. Middle Name Nadres

Other Names Used (if any)

Provide all other names the beneficiary has ever used, including aliases, maiden name, and nicknames.

5.a. Family Name (Last Name) Pebet
5.b. Given Name (First Name)
5.c. Middle Name

Other Information About Beneficiary

6. City/Town/Village of Birth

   Quezon City

7. Country of Birth

   Philippines

8. Date of Birth (mm/dd/yyyy) 07/18/1993

9. Sex ☐ Male ☒ Female

10. Has anyone else ever filed a petition for the beneficiary?

    ☐ Yes ☒ No ☐ Unknown

    NOTE: Select "Unknown" *only* if you do not know, and the beneficiary also does not know, if anyone else has ever filed a petition for the beneficiary.

Beneficiary's Physical Address

If the beneficiary lives outside the United States in a home without a street number or name, leave **Item Numbers 11.a.** and **11.b.** blank.

11.a. Street Number and Name 1640 Lincoln Park
11.b. ☐ Apt. ☐ Ste. ☐ Flr.
11.c. City or Town Beaverton
11.d. State OR 11.e. ZIP Code 97006
11.f. Province
11.g. Postal Code
11.h. Country

   USA

Other Address and Contact Information

Provide the address in the United States where the beneficiary intends to live, if different from **Item Numbers 11.a. - 11.h.** If the address is the same, type or print "SAME" in **Item Number 12.a.**

12.a Street Number and Name SAME
12.b. ☐ Apt. ☐ Ste. ☐ Flr.
12.c. City or Town
12.d. State 12.e. ZIP Code

Provide the beneficiary's address outside the United States, if different from **Item Numbers 11.a. - 11.h.** If the address is the same, type or print "SAME" in **Item Number 13.a.**

13.a. Street Number and Name 1678 Trout Chautoco Roxas Dist.
13.b. ☐ Apt. ☐ Ste. ☐ Flr.
13.c. City or Town Q.C.
13.d. Province
13.e. Postal Code
13.f. Country

   Philippines

14. Daytime Telephone Number (if any)

   503-555-1212

Sample Form I-130, Petition for Alien Relative—Page 6

Part 4. Information About Beneficiary (continued)

15. Mobile Telephone Number (if any)

16. Email Address (if any)

lea@email.com

Beneficiary's Marital Information

17. How many times has the beneficiary been married?
▶ 1

18. Current Marital Status

☐ Single, Never Married ☒ Married ☐ Divorced

☐ Widowed ☐ Separated ☐ Annulled

19. Date of Current Marriage (if currently married) (mm/dd/yyyy)
05/22/2019

Place of Beneficiary's Current Marriage (if married)

20.a. City or Town Salem

20.b. State OR

20.c. Province

20.d. Country USA

Names of Beneficiary's Spouses (if any)

Provide information on the beneficiary's current spouse (if currently married) first and then list all the beneficiary's prior spouses (if any).

Spouse 1

21.a. Family Name (Last Name) Nguyen

21.b. Given Name (First Name) Teo

21.c. Middle Name Thanh

22. Date Marriage Ended (mm/dd/yyyy) n/a

Spouse 2

23.a. Family Name (Last Name) n/a

23.b. Given Name (First Name)

23.c. Middle Name

24. Date Marriage Ended (mm/dd/yyyy)

Information About Beneficiary's Family

Provide information about the beneficiary's spouse and children.

Person 1

25.a. Family Name (Last Name) Nguyen

25.b. Given Name (First Name) Teo

25.c. Middle Name Thanh

26. Relationship Spouse

27. Date of Birth (mm/dd/yyyy) 04/12/1993

28. Country of Birth Vietnam

Person 2

29.a. Family Name (Last Name)

29.b. Given Name (First Name)

29.c. Middle Name

30. Relationship

31. Date of Birth (mm/dd/yyyy)

32. Country of Birth

Person 3

33.a. Family Name (Last Name)

33.b. Given Name (First Name)

33.c. Middle Name

34. Relationship

35. Date of Birth (mm/dd/yyyy)

36. Country of Birth

Sample Form I-130, Petition for Alien Relative—Page 7

Part 4. Information About Beneficiary (continued)

Person 4

37.a. Family Name (Last Name)

37.b. Given Name (First Name)

37.c. Middle Name

38. Relationship

39. Date of Birth (mm/dd/yyyy)

40. Country of Birth

Person 5

41.a. Family Name (Last Name)

41.b. Given Name (First Name)

41.c. Middle Name

42. Relationship

43. Date of Birth (mm/dd/yyyy)

44. Country of Birth

Beneficiary's Entry Information

45. Was the beneficiary **EVER** in the United States?

☒ Yes ☐ No

If the beneficiary is currently in the United States, complete **Items Numbers 46.a. - 46.d.**

46.a. He or she arrived as a (Class of Admission):

F-1

46.b. Form I-94 Arrival-Departure Record Number

▶ 1 4 6 0 7 7 1 2 2 1 0

46.c. Date of Arrival (mm/dd/yyyy)   12/23/2015

46.d. Date authorized stay expired, or will expire, as shown on Form I-94 or Form I-95 (mm/dd/yyyy) or type or print "D/S" for Duration of Status

D/S

47. Passport Number

P1230007

48. Travel Document Number

49. Country of Issuance for Passport or Travel Document

Philippines

50. Expiration Date for Passport or Travel Document (mm/dd/yyyy)   05/10/2027

Beneficiary's Employment Information

Provide the beneficiary's current employment information (if applicable), even if they are employed outside of the United States. If the beneficiary is currently unemployed, type or print "Unemployed" in **Item Number 51.a.**

51.a. Name of Current Employer (if applicable)

n/a - student

51.b. Street Number and Name

51.c. ☐ Apt. ☐ Ste. ☐ Flr.

51.d. City or Town

51.e. State

51.f. ZIP Code

51.g. Province

51.h. Postal Code

51.i. Country

52. Date Employment Began (mm/dd/yyyy)

Additional Information About Beneficiary

53. Was the beneficiary **EVER** in immigration proceedings?

☐ Yes ☒ No

54. If you answered "Yes," select the type of proceedings and provide the location and date of the proceedings.

☐ Removal   ☐ Exclusion/Deportation

☐ Rescision   ☐ Other Judicial Proceedings

55.a. City or Town

55.b. State

56. Date (mm/dd/yyyy)

Sample Form I-130, Petition for Alien Relative—Page 8

Part 4. Information About Beneficiary (continued)

If the beneficiary's native written language does not use Roman letters, type or print his or her name and foreign address in their native written language.

57.a. Family Name (Last Name)

57.b. Given Name (First Name)

57.c. Middle Name

58.a. Street Number and Name

58.b. ☐ Apt. ☐ Ste. ☐ Flr.

58.c. City or Town

58.d. Province

58.e. Postal Code

58.f. Country

If filing for your spouse, provide the last address at which you physically lived together. If you never lived together, type or print, "Never lived together" in Item Number 59.a.

59.a. Street Number and Name — 1640 Lincoln Park

59.b. ☐ Apt. ☐ Ste. ☐ Flr.

59.c. City or Town — Beaverton

59.d. State — OR **59.e.** ZIP Code — 97006

59.f. Province

59.g. Postal Code

59.h. Country — USA

60.a. Date From (mm/dd/yyyy) — 05/01/2019

60.b. Date To (mm/dd/yyyy) — present

The beneficiary is in the United States and will apply for adjustment of status to that of a lawful permanent resident at the U.S. Citizenship and Immigration Services (USCIS) office in:

61.a. City or Town — Portland

61.b. State — OR

The beneficiary will not apply for adjustment of status in the United States, but he or she will apply for an immigrant visa abroad at the U.S. Embassy or U.S. Consulate in:

62.a. City or Town

62.b. Province

62.c. Country

NOTE: Choosing a U.S. Embassy or U.S. Consulate outside the country of the beneficiary's last residence does not guarantee that it will accept the beneficiary's case for processing. In these situations, the designated U.S. Embassy or U.S. Consulate has discretion over whether or not to accept the beneficiary's case.

Part 5. Other Information

1. Have you **EVER** previously filed a petition for this beneficiary or any other alien? ☐ Yes ☒ No

If you answered "Yes," provide the name, place, date of filing, and the result.

2.a. Family Name (Last Name)

2.b. Given Name (First Name)

2.c. Middle Name

3.a. City or Town

3.b. State

4. Date Filed (mm/dd/yyyy)

5. Result (for example, approved, denied, withdrawn)

If you are also submitting separate petitions for other relatives, provide the names of and your relationship to each relative.

Relative 1

6.a. Family Name (Last Name) — n/a

6.b. Given Name (First Name)

6.c. Middle Name

7. Relationship

Sample Form I-130, Petition for Alien Relative—Page 9

Part 5. Other Information (continued)

Relative 2

8.a. Family Name
(Last Name)

8.b. Given Name
(First Name)

8.c. Middle Name

9. Relationship

WARNING: USCIS investigates the claimed relationships and verifies the validity of documents you submit. If you falsify a family relationship to obtain a visa, USCIS may seek to have you criminally prosecuted.

PENAL TIES: By law , you may be imprisoned for up to 5 years or fined $250,000, or both, for entering into a marriage contract in order to evade any U.S. immigration law. In addition, you may be fined up to $10,000 and imprisoned for up to 5 years, or both, for knowingly and willfully falsifying or concealing a material fact or using any false document in submitting this petition.

Part 6. Petitioner's Statement, Contact Information, Declaration, and Signature

NOTE: Read the **Penalties** section of the Form I-130 Instructions before completing this part.

Petitioner's Statement

NOTE: Select the box for either **Item Number 1.a.** or **1.b.** If applicable, select the box for **Item Number 2.**

1.a. ☒ I can read and understand English, and I have read and understand every question and instruction on this petition and my answer to every question.

1.b. ☐ The interpreter named in **Part 7.** read to me every question and instruction on this petition and my answer to every question in

[   ],

a language in which I am fluent. I understood all of this information as interpreted.

2. ☐ At my request, the preparer named in **Part 8.**,

[   ],

prepared this petition for me based only upon information I provided or authorized.

Petitioner's Contact Information

3. Petitioner's Daytime Telephone Number

503-555-1493

4. Petitioner's Mobile Telephone Number (if any)

5. Petitioner's Email Address (if any)

teo@email.com

Petitioner's Declaration and Certification

Copies of any documents I have submitted are exact photocopies of unaltered, original documents, and I understand that USCIS may require that I submit original documents to USCIS at a later date. Furthermore, I authorize the release of any information from any of my records that USCIS may need to determine my eligibility for the immigration benefit I seek.

I further authorize release of information contained in this petition, in supporting documents, and in my USCIS records to other entities and persons where necessary for the administration and enforcement of U.S. immigration laws.

I understand that USCIS may require me to appear for an appointment to take my biometrics (fingerprints, photograph, and/or signature) and, at that time, if I am required to provide biometrics, I will be required to sign an oath reaffirming that:

1) I provided or authorized all of the information contained in, and submitted with, my petition;

2) I reviewed and understood all of the information in, and submitted with, my petition; and

3) All of this information was complete, true, and correct at the time of filing.

I certify, under penalty of perjury, that all of the information in my petition and any document submitted with it were provided or authorized by me, that I reviewed and understand all of the information contained in, and submitted with, my petition, and that all of this information is complete, true, and correct.

Petitioner's Signature

6.a. Petitioner's Signature (sign in ink)

➡  *Teo Thanh Nguyen*

6.b. Date of Signature (mm/dd/yyyy)   06/11/2019

NOTE TO ALL PETITIONERS: If you do not completely fill out this petition or fail to submit required documents listed in the Instructions, USCIS may deny your petition.

Questions 20-23: Put name of the petitioner's current spouse (the immigrant) first and any past spouses next. Leave blank or put "N/A" under the "date marriage ended" for your current marriage. USCIS wants to know when the U.S. spouse's prior marriage ended so that it can determine whether your current marriage is valid. If the petitioning spouse's prior marriage(s) ended after your present marriage began, yours is not a lawful marriage. If the petitioning spouse has just discovered that the divorce wasn't final when your marriage took place, it may not be necessary to run to a lawyer. Assuming that the divorce has since become final, you can correct the problem by remarrying. (If there was fraud involved in your hasty marriage, consult a lawyer before proceeding.)

Questions 24-35: Answer basic biographic information about the petitioning U.S. permanent resident's parents. If lacking any information about a parent, enter "unknown."

Question 36: Self-explanatory.

Questions 37-39: Leave blank since the petitioning spouse is not yet a citizen.

Question 40: Some of the information requested here is on the petitioner's green card. (See illustration below.) The date of admission shown on the older cards usually starts with the year, so that Dec. 3, 1998 would be 981203. The city is in code on the old cards: for example, SFR is San Francisco, BUF is Buffalo, and LIN is the service center in Lincoln, Nebraska. For a newer card, you'll have to figure out where the petitioning spouse entered the U.S. with an immigrant visa or were approved for a green card. Class of Admission asks for the type of visa or remedy through which the person got permanent residence, such as a Fourth Preference visa or political asylum.

Question 41: If the petitioning U.S. spouse checks "Yes" here, indicating that he or she received U.S. permanent residence through marriage, calculate how long it has been since the approval for permanent residence. A petitioning spouse who immigrated through marriage cannot petition for a new spouse for five years, unless the first spouse died or you can prove by "clear and convincing

Green Card (Front)

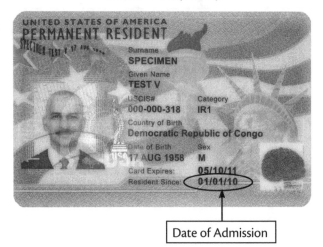

Date of Admission

evidence" that the previous marriage was bona fide (real). USCIS is concerned that the first marriage was just a sham, with the long-term goal of getting both of you into the United States by piggybacking on a sham marriage.

To prove that the first marriage was bona fide, enclose documentary evidence showing that the former spouse shared a life, such as shared rent receipts, club memberships, children's birth certificates, utility bills, and insurance agreements. As for what makes for "clear and convincing," it means a high bar to proving to do to persuade a suspicious government official that the previous marriage was bona fide.

Questions 42-49: Fill in U.S. petitioner's employment history from the last five years. If there have been more than two jobs, list ones that don't fit in Part 9.

Part 3

Questions 1-5: Provide basic biographic information on the U.S. petitioner.

Part 4

Now the questions refer to the immigrating beneficiary.

Question 1: The Alien Registration Number is an eight- or nine-digit number following a letter A, which the former INS or USCIS will have assigned. The immigrant won't have one yet without having previously applied for immigration benefits, or been in deportation/removal proceedings. (Of course, if the previous application was denied because the immigrant was found inadmissible or lied on that application, call a lawyer before going any further.)

Question 2: An immigrant who has filed a past petition with USCIS might have a USCIS Online Account Number.

Question 3: The immigrant probably won't have a Social Security number without having had a work permit, a visa allowing work, or U.S. residence. If the immigrant used a made-up or borrowed number in order to work while here illegally, consult an attorney.

Question 4: Current name.

Question 5: Enter any names the immigrant previously used, including from a past marriage.

Questions 6-10: Self-explanatory.

Question 11: Immigrant's current address.

Question 12: If it's different from Question 11, enter the U.S. address where the immigrant plans to live; hopefully with the U.S. spouse, or USCIS may raise questions.

Questions 13-16: If the immigrant has a permanent address (and phone number) outside the U.S., enter it here, plus mobile phone and email address.

> CAUTION
>
> **If the immigrant must leave the U.S. to get approval for a green card, be careful in entering address information.** This gives the government data on when the immigrant was living in the United States—perhaps unlawfully. It could lead to being punished for an illegal stay, with a three- or ten-year bar on reentry (see Chapter 2 for further discussion). It would be best to have already left the United States when the U.S. spouse sends this in, in which case there's no need to answer the question at all.

Question 17: Answer how many times the immigrant has been married, including this time.

Question 18: This refers only to your most recent marital status, so check "married," even if there was a previous divorce.

Questions 19-20: Self-explanatory.

Questions 21-24: Name current spouse first and any past spouses next. Put "N/A" under the date marriage ended for the current marriage.

The question of when prior marriage(s) ended is intended to make sure your current marriage is valid. If prior marriage(s) ended after your present marriage began, yours is not a lawful marriage. If you have just discovered that the divorce wasn't final when your marriage took place, it may not be necessary to run to a lawyer. Assuming that the divorce has since become final, you can correct the problem by remarrying. (If there was fraud involved in your hasty marriage, consult a lawyer before proceeding.)

Questions 25-44: Although the U.S. spouse is already covered in this application, it's safest to list him or her again before listing children, if any. This means all children, including any by previous relationships.

Question 45: Because the immigrant is in the U.S., you must check "Yes."

Questions 46-50: Question 46.a asks for the type of visa or other permission the immigrant entered the U.S. on. If the entry was legal, this will be on the I-94 (either a small card or data available from www.cbp.gov/i-94); as will the I-94 number for Question 46.b, and date of arrival and the expiration of stay.

Question 47: Enter the number of immigrant's passport from the home country.

Question 48: If the immigrant used some other type of travel document to enter the U.S. (such as a Refugee Travel Document or Advance Parole) enter the number here.

Questions 49-50: Self-explanatory.

Questions 51-52: Fill in current employment information. For an immigrant who is not working, enter "unemployed" or "student," if applicable.

Questions 53-56: If the immigrant has ever been in Immigration Court (removal or deportation) proceedings, consult a lawyer before continuing. A special waiver may be required in order to get U.S. residence.

Questions 57-58: If the immigrant's native language uses a non-Roman script (for example, Russian, Chinese, or Arabic), you will need to write the name and address in that script.

Questions 59-60: If you and your spouse have ever lived together, put the last address here. If not, write "N/A" or "never lived together."

Question 61: If the immigrant is eligible to adjust status, and planning to do so, enter the name of the nearest USCIS Field Office (or the one serving your area).

Question 62: If (as is more likely, particularly if the immigrant entered the U.S. illegally) the interview will be held at an overseas consulate, enter the name of the consulate with a visa processing office in the immigrant's country; or if none exists, the one with the power to handle visa requests from there. (Don't worry about getting it wrong; USCIS will redirect the application when it approves the petition.)

Part 5: Other Information.

Now we're back to questions to be answered by the petitioning U.S. spouse.

Questions 1-5: These are meant to uncover the permanent resident spouse's history (if any) of petitioning other immigrants to come to the United States. As you can probably imagine, a petitioning spouse who has a history of short marriages to people whom he/she then helped to obtain green cards can expect a major marriage fraud investigation. Consult a lawyer before proceeding.

Questions 6-9: These refer to other petitions being submitted simultaneously (for example, for children from this or other marriages), so USCIS can process the petitions together. Enter the children's names here.

Part 6

The U.S. permanent resident petitioner fills out this section with contact information and signature.

Parts 7 and 8

These are for a preparer or interpreter helping to fill out the form. If filling out the application unassisted, write "N/A" here. A little typing assistance or advice from a friend doesn't count— the only people who need to complete this line are lawyers or agencies who fill out these forms on others' behalf or offer translation services.

b. Form I-130A

 WEB RESOURCE
Form I-130A is available on the USCIS website at www.uscis.gov/i-130. Below is a sample filled-in version of the relevant pages of this form.

Part 1

Question 1: The Alien Registration Number is an eight- or nine-digit number following a letter A that USCIS (or the formerly named INS) would have assigned to an immigrant previously applied for permanent (or, in some cases, temporary) residence or been in deportation/removal proceedings. Of course, if that previous application was denied because the immigrant was found inadmissible or lied on that application, call a lawyer before going any further.

Question 2: If you've ever filed a petition with USCIS, you might have a USCIS Online Account Number.

Question 3: Enter your full, current name; your married name if you changed it at the time you wed.

Questions 4-9: Fill in all your addresses from the last five years. Any that don't fit can be included in Part 7. If you have lived at more than one address in the last five years, make sure to include the start and end dates of the other addresses.

Questions 10-23: Answer basic biographic information about your parents. If lacking any pieces of information, enter "unknown."

Part 2

Questions 1-8: Fill in your current job information (inside or outside the U.S.) for the last five years. If you are not working, state "unemployed" or "student," if applicable. If you've had more than two jobs in the past five years, attach additional information in Part 7.

Part 3

Include information about your most recent employment outside of the U.S. if it's not already listed in Part 2.

Part 4

Fill this section in with your contact information and signature.

Sample Form I-130A, Supplemental Information for Spousal Beneficiary—Page 1

Supplemental Information for Spouse Beneficiary

Department of Homeland Security

U.S. Citizenship and Immigration Services

USCIS Form I-130A

OMB No. 1615-0012
Expires 02/28/2021

To be completed by an attorney or accredited representative (if any).			
☐ Select this box if Form G-28 is attached.	**Volag Number** (if any)	**Attorney State Bar Number** (if applicable)	**Attorney or Accredited Representative USCIS Online Account Number** (if any)

▶ **START HERE** - Type or print in black ink.

The purpose of this form is to collect additional information for a spouse beneficiary of Form I-130, Petition for Alien Relative. If your spouse is a U.S. citizen, lawful permanent resident, or non-citizen U.S. national who is filing Form I-130 on your behalf, you must complete and sign Form I-130A, Supplemental Information for Spouse Beneficiary, and submit it with the Form I-130 filed by your spouse. If you reside overseas, you still must complete Form I-130A, but you do not need to sign the form.

Part 1. Information About You (Spouse Beneficiary)

1. Alien Registration Number (A-Number) (if any)
   ▶ A- 2 3 4 5 6 7 8 9 9

2. USCIS Online Account Number (if any)

Your Full Name

3.a. Family Name (Last Name): NGUYEN
3.b. Given Name (First Name): Lea
3.c. Middle Name: Nadres

Address History

Provide your physical addresses for the last five years, whether inside or outside the United States. Provide your current address first. If you need extra space to complete this section, use the space provided in **Part 7. Additional Information**.

Physical Address 1

4.a. Street Number and Name: 1640 Lincoln Park
4.b. ☐ Apt. ☐ Ste. ☐ Flr.
4.c. City or Town: Beaverton
4.d. State: OR   4.e. ZIP Code: 97006
4.f. Province:
4.g. Postal Code:
4.h. Country: USA

5.a. Date From (mm/dd/yyyy): 05/01/2019
5.b. Date To (mm/dd/yyyy): PRESENT

Physical Address 2

6.a. Street Number and Name: 918 E. Market St.
6.b. ☐ Apt. ☐ Ste. ☐ Flr.
6.c. City or Town: Boston
6.d. State: MA   6.e. ZIP Code: 02101
6.f. Province:
6.g. Postal Code:
6.h. Country: USA

7.a. Date From (mm/dd/yyyy): 06/01/2016
7.b. Date To (mm/dd/yyyy): 04/30/2019

Last Physical Address Outside the United States

Provide your last address outside the United States of more than one year (even if listed above).

8.a. Street Number and Name: 13 Dao Street, Valle Zende
8.b. ☐ Apt. ☐ Ste. ☐ Flr.
8.c. City or Town: Metro Manila
8.d. Province:
8.e. Postal Code:
8.f. Country: Philippines

Sample Form I-130A, Supplemental Information for Spousal Beneficiary—Page 2

Part 1. Information About You (The Spouse Beneficiary)

9.a. Date From (mm/dd/yyyy) `07/18/1993`

9.b. Date To (mm/dd/yyyy) `05/31/2016`

Information About Parent 1

Full Name of Parent 1

10.a. Family Name (Maiden Name) `Pebet`

10.b. Given Name (First Name) `Antero`

10.c. Middle Name

11. Date of Birth (mm/dd/yyyy) `11/23/1970`

12. Sex ☒ Male ☐ Female

13. City/Town/Village of Birth `Manila`

14. Country of Birth `Philippines`

15. City/Town/Village of Residence `Manila`

16. Country of Residence `Philippines`

Information About Parent 2

Full Name of Parent 2

17.a. Family Name (Last Name) `Martino`

17.b. Given Name (First Name) `Flores`

17.c. Middle Name

18. Date of Birth (mm/dd/yyyy) `05/02/1972`

19. Sex ☐ Male ☒ Female

20. City/Town/Village of Birth `Quezon City`

21. Country of Birth `Philippines`

22. City/Town/Village of Residence `Manila`

23. Country of Residence `Philippines`

Part 2. Information About Your Employment

Provide your employment history for the last five years, whether inside or outside the United States. Provide your current employment first. If you are currently unemployed, type or print "Unemployed" in **Item Number 1.** below. If you need extra space to complete this section, use the space provided in **Part 7. Additional Information**.

Employment History

Employer 1

1. Name of Employer/Company `n/a - student`

2.a. Street Number and Name

2.b. ☐ Apt. ☐ Ste. ☐ Flr.

2.c. City or Town

2.d. State   **2.e.** ZIP Code

2.f. Province

2.g. Postal Code

2.h. Country

3. Your Occupation

4.a. Date From (mm/dd/yyyy)

4.b. Date To (mm/dd/yyyy)

Employer 2

5. Name of Employer/Company

6.a. Street Number and Name

6.b. ☐ Apt. ☐ Ste. ☐ Flr.

6.c. City or Town

6.d. State   **6.e.** ZIP Code

6.f. Province

6.g. Postal Code

6.h. Country

Sample Form I-130A, Supplemental Information for Spousal Beneficiary—Page 3

Part 2. Information About Your Employment (continued)

7. Your Occupation

8.a. Date From (mm/dd/yyyy)

8.b. Date To (mm/dd/yyyy)

Part 3. Information About Your Employment Outside the United States

Provide your last occupation outside the United States if not shown above. If you never worked outside the United States, provide this information in the space provided in **Part 7. Additional Information**.

1. Name of Employer/Company

n/a

2.a. Street Number and Name

2.b. ☐ Apt. ☐ Ste. ☐ Flr.

2.c. City or Town

2.d. State   **2.e.** ZIP Code

2.f. Province

2.g. Postal Code

2.h. Country

3. Your Occupation

4.a. Date From (mm/dd/yyyy)

4.b. Date To (mm/dd/yyyy)

Part 4. Spouse Beneficiary's Statement, Contact Information, Certification, and Signature

NOTE: Read the **Penalties** section of the Form I-130 and Form I-130A Instructions before completing this part.

Spouse Beneficiary's Statement

NOTE: Select the box for either **Item Number 1.a.** or **1.b.** If applicable, select the box for **Item Number 2.**

1.a. ☒ I can read and understand English, and I have read and understand every question and instruction on this form and my answer to every question.

1.b. ☐ The interpreter named in **Part 5.** read to me every question and instruction on this form and my answer to every question in

[   ],

a language in which I am fluent, and I understood everything.

2. ☐ At my request, the preparer name in **Part 6.**,

[   ],

prepared this form for me based only upon information I provided or authorized.

Spouse Beneficiary's Contact Information

3. Spouse Beneficiary's Daytime Telephone Number

503-555-1212

4. Spouse Beneficiary's Mobile Telephone Number (if any)

5. Spouse Beneficiary's Email Address (if any)

lea@email.com

Spouse Beneficiary's Certification

Copies of any documents I have submitted are exact photocopies of unaltered, original documents, and I understand that USCIS may require that I submit original documents to USCIS at a later date. Furthermore, I authorize the release of any information from any of my records that USCIS may need to determine my eligibility for the immigration benefit I seek.

I further authorize release of information contained in this form, in supporting documents, and in my USCIS records to other entities and persons where necessary for the administration and enforcement of U.S. immigration laws.

I certify, under penalty of perjury, that I provided or authorized all of the information in this form, I understand all of the information contained in, and submitted with, my form, and that all of this information is complete, true, and correct.

Spouse Beneficiary's Signature

6.a. Spouse Beneficiary's Signature (sign in ink)

➡ *Lea N. Nguyen*

6.b. Date of Signature (mm/dd/yyyy)   06/27/2019

NOTE TO ALL SPOUSE BENEFICIARIES: If you do not completely fill out this form or fail to submit required documents listed in the Instructions, USCIS may deny the Form I-130 filed on your behalf.

2. Documents to Assemble for I-130 Petition

The I-130 petition asks you to submit supporting documents and payment along with the form. You're not done with your petition until you have gathered together the following:

- **Proof of the U.S. permanent resident status of your petitioning spouse.** This can be either a copy of his or her green card (front and back) or of the stamp placed in his or her passport to indicate permanent resident status.
- **Proof that you're legally married.** This should include at a minimum a copy of your marriage certificate, preferably from a government source (see Chapter 4, Section C, for details). In addition, if either you or your spouse have been previously married, you must include proof that these marriages were terminated, such as a copy of a death, divorce, or annulment certificate.
- **Proof that the marriage is bona fide.** Include a select few items of evidence to show that it is not a sham, but a real marital relationship. For instance, copies of documents showing you've spent time or lived together (such as a lease or mortgage agreement, bills sent to the house, and letters sent to the house for each spouse) are good, as are copies of joint financial accounts (bank and credit statements, loans, insurance policies). Of less weight are things like joint memberships and photos taken with friends and family; you might want to save these for your interview, when the issue of bona fide marriage will come up again.
- **Photos.** You must each submit two color passport-style photos, 2 x 2 inches in size, taken within the past six months, showing your current appearance. Passport style means that the photo shows your full face from the front, with a plain white or off-white background—and your face must measure between one inch and 1⅜ inches from the bottom of your chin to the top of your head. For more information, see the State Department website at www.travel.state.gov. However, government regulations permit you to submit a photo that doesn't completely follow the instructions if you live in a country where such photographs are unavailable or are cost prohibitive.
- **Fees.** The current fee for an I-130 petition is $535. However, these fees go up fairly regularly, so double-check this on the USCIS website at www.uscis.gov, or by calling USCIS at 800-375-5283.

3. Where to Send the I-130 Petition

After your spouse—with your help—has prepared and assembled all the forms and other items on the checklist below, he or she should make photocopies for your records. Your spouse must send the packet to the USCIS "lockbox" office serving the region where he or she lives.

The lockbox office will, after some initial processing, forward the I-130 petition to a USCIS service center, which will make the decision approving or denying it. Priority mail is typically the safest way to send anything to USCIS. The address is found below; double-check this information on the USCIS website.

If you will be adjusting your status in the U.S., you can file the Form I-130 at the same time you file your adjustment of status forms, so don't send it anywhere yet! (See Chapter 14.)

4. What Happens After Sending in the Form I-130 Petition

A few weeks after your spouse sends in your I-130 petition, he or she should get a receipt notice from USCIS. The receipt notice will tell you to check the USCIS website for information on how long the petition is likely to remain in processing. (The current average is between five and ten months.) See the sample receipt notice below. Go to "Check Case Status" then enter your receipt number to check whether any action has been taken.

As long as your petition is not beyond the "normal processing time," USCIS will ignore any inquiries from you or your spouse asking what is going on.

Where to Send the Form I-130 Petition			
If the U.S. petitioner lives in:			**Send Form I-130 to:**
Alaska American Samoa Arizona California Colorado Florida Guam Hawaii Idaho	Kansas Montana Nebraska Nevada New Mexico North Dakota Northern Mariana Islands Oklahoma	Oregon Puerto Rico South Dakota Texas Utah Virgin Islands Washington Wyoming	**USCIS Phoenix Lockbox** For U.S. Postal Service (USPS) deliveries: USCIS ATTN: I-130 P.O. Box 21700 Phoenix, AZ 85036 For courier deliveries: USCIS Attn: I-130 1820 E. Skyharbor Circle S Suite 100 Phoenix, AZ 85034
Alabama Arkansas Connecticut Delaware District of Columbia Georgia Illinois Indiana Iowa Kentucky Louisiana	Maine Maryland Massachusetts Michigan Minnesota Mississippi Missouri New Hampshire New Jersey New York	North Carolina Ohio Pennsylvania Rhode Island South Carolina Tennessee Vermont Virginia West Virginia Wisconsin	**USCIS Chicago Lockbox** For U.S. Postal Service: USCIS P.O. Box 804625 Chicago, IL 60680-4107 For courier deliveries: USCIS Attn: I-130 131 South Dearborn–3rd Floor Chicago, IL 60603-5517
If the U.S. petitioner lives outside the U.S., send Form I-130 to:			
USCIS Chicago Lockbox For U.S. Postal Service (USPS) deliveries: USCIS P.O. Box 804625 Chicago, IL 60680-4107		For courier deliveries: USCIS Attn: I-130 131 South Dearborn-3rd Floor Chicago, IL 60603-5517	

These lockboxes and service centers seem like walled fortresses—you can't visit them, and it's almost impossible to talk to a live person there. If USCIS needs additional documentation to complete your application, it will send your spouse a letter asking for it. (See Chapter 15 for what to do if you don't get a timely answer from USCIS.) Likewise, if USCIS considers denying the case based on negative evidence obtained by other means, it will send your spouse a letter informing you and giving an opportunity to respond.

Eventually your spouse will either receive a denial or an approval of the I-130 petition.

a. If the I-130 Petition Is Denied

If the petition is denied, USCIS will give you a reason for the denial. The fastest thing to do is to fix the problem and try again. For example, if the denial was because your petitioning spouse did not appear to be actually divorced from his or her previous spouse, your spouse would need to see a lawyer and obtain new and better documentation showing that there had been a final divorce. Then your spouse could file a new petition.

Sample I-130 Receipt Notice

Department of Homeland Security U.S. Citizenship and Immigration Services	**Form I-797C, Notice of Action**

THIS NOTICE DOES NOT GRANT ANY IMMIGRATION STATUS OR BENEFIT.

NOTICE TYPE Receipt		NOTICE DATE July 1, 2019
CASE TYPE I130 IMMIGRANT PETITION FOR RELATIVE, FIANCE(E), OR ORPHAN		USCIS ALIEN NUMBER
RECEIPT NUMBER MSC-19-054-00000	RECEIVED DATE JUNE 30, 2019	PAGE 1 of 1
PRIORITY DATE JUNE 30, 2019	PREFERENCE CLASSIFICATION 203(a)(2)(A) INA SPOUSE OF LPR	DATE OF BIRTH 07/18/90

ILONA BRAY
RE: LEA NADRES NGUYEN
950 PARKER STREET
BERKELEY, CA 94710

PAYMENT INFORMATION:

Application/Petition Fee:	$535.00
Biometrics Fee:	$0.00
Total Amount Received:	$535.00
Total Balance Due:	$0.00

APPLICANT/PETITIONER NAME AND MAILING ADDRESS

The I-130, Petition for Alien Relative has been received by our office for the following beneficiaries and is in process:

Name	Date of Birth	Country of Birth	Class (If Applicable)
NGUYEN, LEA NADRES	07/18/93	Philippines	

Please verify your personal information listed above and immediately notify the USCIS National Customer Service Center at the phone number listed below if there are any changes.

Please note that if a priority date is printed on this notice, the priority does not reflect earlier retained priority dates.

If you have questions about possible immigration benefits and services, filing information, or USCIS forms, please call the USCIS National Customer Service Center (NCSC) at **1-800-375-5283**. If you are hearing impaired, please call the NCSC TDD at **1-800-767-1833**. Please also refer to the USCIS website: www.uscis.gov.

If you have any questions or comments regarding this notice or the status of your case, please contact our customer service number.

You will be notified separately about any other case you may have filed.

USCIS Office Address:	**USCIS Customer Service Number:**
USCIS Nebraska Service Center P.O. Box 82521 Lincoln, NE 68501-2521	(800)375-5283 ATTORNEY COPY

If this is an interview or biometrics appointment notice, please see the back of this notice for important information.   Form I-797C 07/11/14 Y

Sample I-130 Approval Notice

Department of Homeland Security
U.S. Citizenship and Immigration Services

I-797, Notice of Action

THE UNITED STATES OF AMERICA

RECEIPT NUMBER		CASE TYPE I130 IMMIGRANT PETITION FOR
MSC-19-054-00000		RELATIVE, FIANCE(E), OR ORPHAN
RECEIPT DATE AUGUST 15, 2019	**PRIORITY DATE** AUGUST 15, 2019	**PETITIONER** NGUYEN, TEO
NOTICE DATE November 11, 2019	**PAGE**	**BENEFICIARY** NGUYEN, LEA

ILONA BRAY
RE: LEA NADRES NGUYEN
950 PARKER STREET
BERKELEY, CA 94710

Notice Type: Approval Notice

Section: Husband or wife of permanent
resident, 203(a)(2)(A)INA

This notice is to advise you of action taken on this case. The official notice has been mailed according to the mailing preferences noted on the Form G-28, Notice of Entry of Appearance as Attorney or Accredited Representative. Any relevant documentation was mailed according to the specified mailing preferences.

The above petition has been approved. The petition indicates that the person for whom you are petitioning is in the United States and will apply for adjustment of status. He or she should contact the local USCIS office to obtain Form I-485, Application for Permanent Residence. A copy of this notice should be submitted with the application.

If the person for whom you are petitioning decides to apply for a visa outside the United States based on this petition, the petitioner should file Form I-824, Application for Action on an Approved Application or Petition, to request that we send the petition to the Department of State National Visa Center (NVC).

The NVC processes all approved immigrant visa petitions that require consular action. The NVC also determines which consular post is the appropriate consulate to complete visa processing. It will then forward the approved petition to that consulate.

The approval of this visa petition does not in itself grant any immigration status and does not guarantee that the alien beneficiary will subsequently be found to be eligible for a visa, for admission to the United States, or for an extension, change, or adjustment of status.

This courtesy copy may not be used in lieu of official notification to demonstrate the filing or processing action taken on this case.

THIS FORM IS NOT A VISA AND MAY NOT BE USED IN PLACE OF A VISA.

NOTICE: Although this application/petition has been approved, USCIS and the U.S. Department of Homeland Security reserve the right to verify the information submitted in this application, petition and/or supporting documentation to ensure conformity with applicable laws, rules, regulations, and other authorities. Methods used for verifying information may include, but are not limited to, the review of public information and records, contact by correspondence, the internet, or telephone, and site inspections of businesses and residences. Information obtained during the course of verification will be used to determine whether revocation, rescission, and/or removal proceedings are appropriate. Applicants, petitioners, and representatives of record will be provided an opportunity to address derogatory information before any formal proceeding is initiated.

Please see the additional information on the back. You will be notified separately about any other cases you filed.
NEBRASKA SERVICE CENTER
U. S. CITIZENSHIP & IMMIG SERVICE
P.O. BOX 82521
LINCOLN   NE   68501-2521
Customer Service Telephone: 800-375-5283

Form I-797 (Rev. 01/31/05) N

b. If the I-130 Petition Is Approved

When your petition is approved, your spouse will receive a notice from the USCIS service center. An example of a petition approval notice is shown above. As you can see, it's nothing fancy. But it is an important document. Make a few photocopies of it and store these and the original in safe places. Note the "Priority Date" listed in the box of that name—that is the date USCIS received your I-130 petition and that date will become very important in determining your place on the waiting list, as discussed in Section E below.

At the same time that the USCIS service center notifies your spouse of the approval of your petition, it will forward your case to the National Visa Center (NVC) in New Hampshire. This office will take over and maintain your file through the waiting period.

**Checklist for I-130 Petition by
Lawful Permanent Resident**

☐ Form I-130 (see line-by-line instructions in Section D1a, above)

☐ Documents to accompany Form I-130:

　☐ Proof of the U.S. permanent resident status of your petitioning spouse, such as a copy of his or her green card (front and back) or of the stamp placed in his or her passport to indicate permanent resident status

　☐ Copy of your marriage certificate (see Chapter 4, Section C, for how to obtain such documents)

　☐ Copies of proof of termination of all previous marriages, yours or your spouse's, such as certificates of death, divorce, or annulment

　☐ Proof of bona fide marriage, such as copies of joint mortgage or rental agreements, bank and credit card accounts, insurance, and more.

　☐ Two color photos of you (passport style)

　☐ Two color photos of your spouse (passport style)

　☐ Fees: $535 currently, but double-check at www.uscis.gov/i-130

☐ Form I-130A, Supplemental Information on Spouse Beneficiary

---

5. How to Use the Checklist for Step One: I-130 Petition

This checklist lists every form, document, and other item included in the initial petition that your spouse, with your help, will need to assemble and submit to USCIS. By checking off the boxes as items are completed or found, your spouse will be able to ensure that nothing gets forgotten.

> **✓ CHECKLIST**
> **Instructions on where to obtain an online version of this checklist are available in Appendix B.**

E. The Waiting Period

Visa waiting periods are not set periods of time. Some attorneys tell their clients, "It will probably be two years." When two years go by and their green card hasn't come through, the clients worry that something has gone wrong. The truth is that waiting periods are only partly predictable. They depend on supply and demand, combined with monthly decisions by the U.S. government. You won't know for sure how long you'll have to wait until your wait is almost over.

This section will help you to understand the mechanics of this wait and how to deal with it.

1. Why You Are in Category 2A

USCIS ranks preference relatives, generally giving visas quicker to those at the top. Below, you'll see the complete list of preference relatives. As you'll see, you are in the second category down ("2A"). This means that the U.S. government has allotted a higher priority to your visa than to those of the people further down the list. That may be small comfort as the months and even years go by, however.

- **First Preference:** The unmarried sons or daughters of a U.S. citizen who are over 21 and are therefore no longer considered children. (If they were still children, they could qualify as immediate relatives, who are immediately eligible for visas.)

- **Second Preference:** The second preference category, which is where you fit, is actually made up of two subcategories, each with different waiting periods. In subcategory 2A are spouses or unmarried sons or daughters under age 21 of a permanent resident (green card holder). In subcategory 2B are the unmarried sons and daughters over age 21 of a permanent resident (they usually wait longer than 2As).
- **Third Preference:** The married sons or daughters, any age, of a U.S. citizen.
- **Fourth Preference:** The brothers or sisters of a U.S. citizen who is age 21 or older.

2. How Visas Are Allotted Year by Year

Each year, the U.S. government allots a certain number of immigrant visas in each preference category. For purposes of visa allocation, the government follows its fiscal year, which starts and ends in October. This might affect you if the government runs out of visas for your category before October. You'll know at that point that you have no chance of advancing on the waiting list until the "new year" begins October 1.

Currently, the total worldwide numbers are:

- **First Preference:** 23,400, plus any visas not used for fourth preference
- **Second Preference:** 114,200, with 77% of these going to category 2A, 23% to category 2B
- **Third Preference:** 23,400, plus any not used for first and second preference
- **Fourth Preference:** 65,000 plus any not used for the first three preferences.

This may sound like a lot of visas, but far more people want immigrant visas than can get them every year. The government gives out visas month by month, making sure never to go over the annual limit.

There are also limits on the number of visas allowed for any one country. No more than 7% of the total visas each year can go to any one country, and often the percentage turns out to be less.

There are more complexities to the allocation and numbers of these visas, but a full understanding of these numbers won't help you speed up your waiting time. The important thing to know is how to chart your own place on the waiting list.

3. How to Chart Your Place on the Waiting List

It would be nice if you could just call the government and ask how long you have to wait for your green card. No such luck. Instead, the State Department publishes a monthly *Visa Bulletin*, the one source of information on visa waiting periods. It is accessible online at www.travel.state.gov (click "U.S. Visas," then "Check the *Visa Bulletin*"). The same information is available by phone at 202-485-7699, but you have to be quick with your pencil and paper, because they talk fast.

The *Visa Bulletin* comes out monthly, around the middle of the month, but not on any particular day. Due to recent changes, it now includes two sections, instead of one: Section A ("Application Final Action Dates"), shows the "Visa Cutoff Dates" for immigrants who are eligible to receive a green card or visa (as explained below) and Section B ("Dates for Filing")shows cutoff dates for immigrants eligible to simply *begin* their portion of the application process for the green card or visa. Below is a sample of what a family-based chart in the *Visa Bulletin* looks like.

Although it's confusing at first glance, you will be able to make your way through this chart. Here's how:

1. Locate your preference category (2A) in the first column.
2. Locate your country across the top. China, India, Mexico, and the Philippines often have their own columns because of the large number of applicants—and as a result, people from these countries wait longer than others. All other countries are included in the second column called All Chargeability Areas Except Those Listed.
3. Draw a line across from your preference category (2A) and down from your country of origin. Where the two lines cross is what is called the visa cutoff or final action date —the key date which you will compare with your own Priority Date to chart your progress.

Every prospective immigrant has his or her own Priority Date—the date the INS or USCIS first received their Form I-130 petition. Your Priority Date is on the I-130 approval notice you received. Prospective immigrants whose Priority Dates are at or earlier than the cutoff or final action date listed in Section B of that month's bulletin should be ready to file their green card application, while those whose Priority Dates are at or earlier than the date listed in Section A of that month's bulletin will become eligible to receive visas or green cards. Of the former, those who entered the U.S. legally would be allowed to file for adjustment of status (see Chapter 14), even though the green card would not be immediately available to them. Still, if you are eligible to begin the adjustment of status process, you will be able to stay in the U.S. legally while your case is pending. You will also be allowed to apply simultaneously for a work permit and a travel document.

The earlier your Priority Date, the better off you are, because it means you are in line ahead of other applicants. But as you can see, the current cutoff date doesn't tell you how long it will be before your own visa or green card is issued.

Look again at the sample Approval Notice in Section D4, above. The Priority Date is in a box on the second line, with the date of August, 2019.

The following examples should help you understand how to read the *Visa Bulletin* chart.

> **EXAMPLE 1:** Toshiko is a citizen of Japan, married to a U.S. permanent resident.
>
> Toshiko's husband submitted an I-130 for her several years ago and she received a Priority Date of January 1, 2017. What does Toshiko learn by looking at the *Visa Bulletin* chart? After locating the box for Japan (under All Chargeability Areas) in category 2A, she sees that the Priority Date in Section A that is now current is January 8, 2017.
>
> That means that Toshiko is now eligible for a visa. If you're confused by the fact that Toshiko's Priority Date isn't an exact match with the *Visa Bulletin* final action date, look at it this way: Earlier is always better. Toshiko's husband actually submitted her

I-130 a few days before some other people who also became current under this month's *Visa Bulletin*. If this process were like taking a number at the bakery counter, she would have become eligible for her visa (or get to choose her doughnut) a little before the people with January 8, 2017 Priority Dates. But the *Visa Bulletin* jumps by days' and weeks' worth of Priority Dates every month, so people get lumped into larger groups. Anyone with a Priority Date of January 8, 2017 or earlier is therefore considered to have become visa eligible, or "current."

> **EXAMPLE 2:** Yumiko is also a citizen of Japan, who got married to a U.S. permanent resident more recently than Toshiko in the example above. Yumiko's husband submitted her I-130 on January 30, 2018, so that is now her Priority Date.
>
> What does Yumiko learn by looking at the *Visa Bulletin* chart? She must look at the same box as Toshiko did, to see that the current Cutoff Date is January 8, 2017. But with Yumiko's Priority Date, she is certainly not current, and not yet eligible for a visa. It's safe to say there are a number of people in line ahead of her and thus a wait of around a year ahead. However, if she looks at the box in Section B of the same *Visa Bulletin*, she will find a different "filing" date: December 8, 2017 (which is just weeks away from her Priority Date). This means she should soon be able to turn in an adjustment of status application.

If you follow the *Visa Bulletin* chart month by month, you might notice a couple of odd things. Sometimes the government gets backed up with visa applications and the final action dates just don't change. In the example above, it could be that Toshiko's Priority Date actually became current a month or two earlier—but she forgot to check it then, and the number didn't change. Sometimes the cutoff dates get stuck for months at a time, while the government deals with a backlog of visa applications. If the government hits a huge logjam, you may even see the cutoff dates go backwards.

Another odd thing you might see is a box that contains the letter C or U, instead of a date. The letter C (for "current") means there are plenty of visas in that category and no one has to wait. It's as if everyone's Priority Date suddenly were current. The letter U (for "unavailable") is the opposite, meaning that all the visas have been used up for that year. If, for example, this were February 2019, and Yumiko saw a U in her category 2A box, she'd know she could forget about getting closer to a visa until October 2019 (when the new year starts in the visa allocation process).

4. Figuring How Long You Will Wait

To roughly determine how long you will have to wait for a visa, you can subtract the final action date on the current month's *Visa Bulletin* chart from today's date. That will tell you the approximate length of time that other applicants are now waiting for a visa—though this method is complicated by the fact that they applied during a different time period than you, and demand may have risen or fallen during that time. There is no exact science to computing your probable wait.

5. How to Deal With the Long Wait

You will probably feel like nothing at all is happening during the years that you wait for your visa to become available. But in fact, the Priority Dates will be inching forward, and there are steps that you should be taking to make sure that you can claim your visa as soon as it becomes available.

a. Organizing Your Papers and Checking the *Visa Bulletin*

After your U.S. permanent resident spouse files a petition for you, you will get your own I-130 approval notice; looking much like the one shown in Section D4, above. The approval notice will show your Priority Date. Take careful note of the date and keep the notice in a safe place.

Look in the current *Visa Bulletin* to get an idea of how long your wait will be. (See Section 3, above for how to find and read the *Visa Bulletin*.) Then start checking the bulletin regularly, so you can find out as soon as you are current and can make sure that the U.S. government realizes that you are current and still alive and interested, as explained below.

> **TIP**
> **You can ask to have the *Visa Bulletin* sent to you monthly, by email.** This is a great way to make sure you don't forget to check how your Priority Date is advancing. Complete instructions can be found toward the bottom of any *Visa Bulletin*.

b. If You Change Addresses

Don't rely solely on the U.S. government to tell you when your Priority Date is current—the National Visa Center makes a fine effort, but some files may get buried in the shuffle. And, you're guaranteed not to hear from them if they don't know where to find you. Also, under rare circumstances, such as a major change in the U.S. immigration laws, the government may send out mass mailings that you also wouldn't want to miss.

Final Action Dates for March 2019					
Family-Sponsored	All Chargeability Areas Except Those Listed	CHINA—mainland born	INDIA	MEXICO	PHILIPPINES
F1	22OCT11	22OCT11	22OCT11	01AUG97	01APR07
F2A	08JAN17	08JAN17	08JAN17	15DEC16	08JAN17
F2B	01AUG12	01AUG12	01AUG12	22SEP97	22JUL07
F3	08SEP06	08SEP06	08SEP06	15JAN96	01JAN96
F4	22SEP05	22SEP05	08JUL04	08FEB98	01JAN96

If either you or your petitioning spouse change addresses, the place to contact is the National Visa Center (NVC), which keeps your case file until your Priority Date is close to being current. Advise the NVC of your new address by calling 603-334-0700 or searching for "Ask NVC" online and filling out its public inquiry form.

> ! CAUTION
>
> **In addition, within ten days of moving, you (and every immigrating member of your family) must separately advise a central USCIS office of your move.** The law requires this of all non-U.S. citizens over 14 years old who remain in the U.S. for more than 30 days— even if they're in the U.S. illegally. Failure to do so is a misdemeanor and can be punished with a jail term of up to 30 days, a fine of up to $200, or your removal from the United States. (See I.N.A. § 265; 8 U.S.C. § 1305.) The procedure is to file Form AR-11, which you can do online. Go to www.uscis.gov/ar-11. When you have finished filling out the form, you will be asked to click on "Signature," and the form will be e-filed. Print a copy for your records. It will show the date and time the form was filed, and a USCIS confirmation number as proof of filing. There is no fee required for this form.

c. What to Do When Your Priority Date Is Current

One day, your Priority Date will be current—in other words, you'll finally see the exact date of your original application, or a later date, on the *Visa Bulletin* chart. Then you'll know that it's time for you to move forward in the process of getting your visa or green card.

When you see that your Priority Date is current, don't wait for the government to call you. If you don't hear from it within a few weeks, contact the National Visa Center and ask it to send you follow-up instructions.

d. What Happens If No One Notices Your Current Priority Date

Some immigrants forget to check the *Visa Bulletin* and their Priority Date becomes current without their noticing. Sometimes, the NVC has tried to notify them, but has only an old address. Or, the NVC may have failed to keep track of the person's file. These problems can delay or destroy a person's hopes of immigrating.

You have one year after your Priority Date becomes current in Section A to pursue your visa or green card. If you do not, the government assumes you have abandoned it—and will give your visa to the next person in line. You may have an argument for getting the visa back if the government completely failed to contact you, but it's better to avoid such situations altogether. Keep track of your own Priority Date and follow the procedures in Subsection c, above, as soon as your date, or a later date, is listed in Section B of the *Visa Bulletin*. If you intend to adjust status in the U.S., you will need to inform the NVC.

6. How to Get Your Children Onto the Waiting List

Like other immigrants, you can bring certain family members along when you come to the United States. Your children who are unmarried and under age 21 qualify as what are called derivative beneficiaries by having been named on your Form I-130. (See Chapter 2, Section B, to review who counts as a child.) As a practical matter, this means that your children won't need a separate I-130 petition to start off the process. They will share your Priority Date and place on the waiting list. (Eventually, however, they will have to fill in some forms of their own.)

As you'll see in Section 8, below, children can lose their derivative beneficiary status. For example, if your spouse becomes a U.S. citizen, or if children turn 21 or get married, the children would no longer be considered derivative beneficiaries and would have to take further steps or find another way to immigrate. Section 8, below, will tell you which of these situations can be cured and how to cure them.

Be aware that if your derivative beneficiary children have children of their own, those children (your grandchildren) will not be considered your derivative beneficiaries. The law says that no one can be the derivative of someone who is already a derivative beneficiary. In this circumstance, the grandchildren would have to stay behind for at least a few years—a heartbreaking situation for some families. Unfortunately, there are no separate visas for grandchildren.

7. What Happens If Your Lawful Permanent Resident Petitioner Dies

Until recently, if you were the spouse of a permanent resident who died before you could immigrate, the petition was canceled and you could no longer become a permanent resident. In October of 2009, however, Congress changed the law. Now, under certain conditions, the petition filed by your now-deceased spouse may still go forward.

If USCIS approves the petition, you (and your children) may be able to adjust status once your Priority Date becomes current, assuming you lived in the U.S. at the time of your spouse's death and continue to live in the United States. (This assumes that there are no other bars to your adjustment of status, such as your being out of status.)

There are also provisions for allowing a substitute Affidavit of Support, given that your spouse can no longer submit one. (Unlike the spouse of a U.S. citizen, however, this new law does not allow you to petition for yourself if your spouse never filed the petition.)

USCIS has written some of the regulations needed in order to know how to process these cases, but there remains some inconsistency in how the cases are processed. If you are in the unfortunate situation of dealing with the untimely death of the petitioner in your immigration case, consult an immigration attorney.

8. Changing Visa Preference Categories

Now that you know all about life as a 2A, you need to learn how to keep or improve on your visa category. It is possible for people to move into a different preference category, which will speed up or delay their waiting time. For example, you might get a visa quicker—by moving to immediate relative category—if your spouse became a U.S. citizen. Or, life changes can push people out of their visa category, and into a lower one or out of the race altogether. Here are the most typical situations affecting married couples and their children.

a. If a Permanent Resident Petitioner Becomes a Citizen

If your spouse becomes a citizen, it is most likely good news for you. You go from category 2A straight to immediate relative. This means that you jump off the waiting list and immediately move forward with your visa processing.

If your permanent resident spouse qualifies for U.S. citizenship, he or she would be wise to apply as soon as possible. Most permanent residents can apply within five years of receiving their residence (with some exceptions). They must also be of good moral character, meet certain U.S. residency requirements, and be able to pass a test on the English language and U.S. history and government. (If you know that your spouse is going to become a U.S. citizen very soon, read Chapter 11, Spouses of U.S. Citizens, Living in the U.S.)

If your petitioning spouse becomes a citizen, advise the National Visa Center (NVC). It will upgrade your status to immediate relative.

You'll need to search for "Ask NVC" online and fill out its public inquiry form. Include your case number and be ready to provide (as a PDF or JPG file) a copy of your U.S. passport or naturalization certificate. The sample below will help you word the email.

Or, if you're eligible to adjust status in the U.S., you can just submit the entire green card application to USCIS. Include a copy of your naturalization certificate, the I-130 approval notice, and preferably a cover letter explaining that the petitioner has become a U.S. citizen. The process should move forward quickly after that, when USCIS processes the application and calls you in for an interview.

Sample Email Text Requesting Upgrade to Immediate Relative

Dear Sir/Madam:

I am the petitioner in the above case. I recently became a U.S. citizen. A copy of my citizenship certificate is enclosed. Please upgrade my wife, Marta Moscow, from category 2A to immediate relative, and proceed with processing her case. Thank you.

Sam Washington
123 Salmon Way
Seattle, WA 98105
206-555-1212

RESOURCE

For more on the eligibility and procedural requirements for obtaining U.S. citizenship: see the USCIS website at www.uscis.gov or *Becoming a U.S. Citizen: A Guide to the Law, Exam & Interview,* by Ilona Bray (Nolo).

SKIP AHEAD

If your spouse becomes a citizen, and you have children who will be immigrating with you, be sure to read Subsection h, below. For certain children, immigrating may now require extra steps.

b. If the Petitioner and Beneficiary Divorce

If you and your spouse get divorced before you apply for your immigrant visa or green card, you are out of luck. The petition is canceled and you and your derivative beneficiaries lose your green card eligibility.

There is an exception for immigrants who are victims of emotional or physical abuse by their spouse. They can file a special self-petition (Form I-360) any time until the divorce becomes final, or for two years afterward, if they can show that the divorce was related to the domestic violence. (These self-petitions are not covered in this book. Talk to a local nonprofit organization or consult an attorney. See Chapter 17 for suggestions on locating help.)

c. If a Beneficiary Dies

If you were to die, your children would lose their opportunity for a visa as well—unless your spouse has filed or can file a separate petition for them in category 2A or 2B.

If your family is in this situation, the U.S. permanent resident petitioner should ask USCIS to "recapture" the deceased parent's Priority Date when the permanent resident submits the new I-130 petitions. If USCIS assigns the deceased parent's date to the children, the children won't have to start the waiting game all over.

d. If the Petitioner Who Has Become a U.S. Citizen Dies

It's possible that, in the years since your I-130 petition was filed, your spouse became a U.S. citizen, but died before you had a chance to complete your application for a green card. Under a law passed in October of 2009, the surviving spouse of a U.S.

citizen can petition for him- or herself, regardless of the length of the marriage prior to the spouse's death. This changed the old law, which had required the couple to have been married for at least two years at the time the U.S. citizen died in order for the surviving spouse to self-petition.

If you need to self-petition, know that the petition must be filed within two years of your U.S. citizen spouse's death. The form that you will use is the Form I-360 rather than the Form I-130. You are allowed to include your children who are under 21 years old on that petition. You will still have to show that you and your spouse had a bona fide marriage, and that you have not remarried.

We recommend that you consult with an immigration attorney if you find yourself dealing with the death of your petitioner.

e. If the Petitioner Loses His Permanent Resident Status

If the permanent resident petitioner loses the right to live in the United States, the green-card applicants lose the right to live there also. In theory, permanent residence or a green card gives a person the right to live in the United States permanently—but this right can be taken away. If, for example a permanent resident spends many months overseas, USCIS may decide that he abandoned his U.S. residency and refuse to let him reclaim it. Or, if the petitioner commits certain crimes, her permanent residency could be taken away and she could be deported.

Even if a permanent resident has had a crime on record for a long time, he or she may not be safe. Recent laws have allowed USCIS to deport people for crimes that would not have made them deportable when the crime was committed. Since the goal of the law is to reunite families, it makes sense that the government would refuse to grant immigrant visas to the family members of former permanent residents.

f. What Happens When a Child Beneficiary Turns 21

If there is a chance that your child might turn 21 before his or her Priority Date becomes current, watch out! The minute a child hits age 21, he or she will automatically drop into a different visa category, from 2A to 2B. The child can, however, subtract from his or her age the amount of time it took USCIS to approve the initial petition. This is a protection created in 2002 by the Child Status Protection Act (CSPA).

Basically, you have to wait until two events have occurred: your family's I-130 petition has been approved, and the child's Priority Date has become current. At that time, you add up the number of days that the petition was pending with USCIS, and subtract it from the child's actual age. If the result of the calculation is a number less than 21, the child may continue with the green card application. (Act quickly, however; the child has only a year after becoming eligible to submit the green card application.)

> EXAMPLE 1: Nengah's mother marries a U.S. permanent resident named Frank when Nengah is 18 years old. Immediately after, Frank files a petition for the mother that includes Nengah as a derivative. USCIS takes five years to approve the petition, which happens right around the time their Priority Date becomes current. By now, Nengah is 23 years old—which, in theory, should drop her into category 2B. Fortunately, under the CSPA, she can subtract the five years that it took USCIS to approve the petition—which puts her age back at 18. As long as Nengah files for permanent residence within one year of becoming eligible, her case should be approved.

EXAMPLE 2: Kareem's father marries a U.S. permanent resident woman named Alyssa when Kareem is 17 years old. Immediately after, Alyssa files a petition for the father that includes Kareem as a derivative. It takes USCIS only one year to approve the petition. However, another five years pass before Kareem and his father's Priority Date becomes current. By this time, Kareem is 23 years old. Kareem can subtract only one year from his age of 23, which makes him legally 22 years old under the CSPA formula, and thus ineligible to adjust status under category 2A—he'll drop to category 2B and face a longer wait before immigrating.

If the CSPA doesn't help, and your child does drop into category 2B, he or she will face a wait of several years before being eligible for a visa. This problem is known as "aging out." (However, if your child turns 21 after your spouse has become a U.S. citizen, the prospects may be brighter, as discussed below in Subsection h, and in Chapter 2, Section B.)

It can be very stressful when a child beneficiary is close to getting a visa or green card and is about to turn 21. But until your family's Priority Date has become current or your spouse becomes a U.S. citizen, there's nothing you can do.

g. What Happens When a Child Beneficiary Marries

In preference categories 2A (children of permanent residents, under age 21) and 2B (children of permanent residents, over age 21), the beneficiaries must be unmarried. If your children marry, their beneficiary status is revoked forever. Their only hope is for you or your spouse to become a U.S. citizen and file a new petition for them later.

If you plan to bring along your children in either the 2A or 2B categories, make sure to advise them not to marry until after they get their green card. (USCIS may not find out about the marriage now, but it often catches such cases when the immigrant applies for U.S. citizenship—and then it strips them of their green card.)

h. What Happens to Your Children When Your Spouse Becomes a U.S. Citizen

As you remember from Subsection a above, if your spouse becomes a U.S. citizen it will help you immigrate more quickly. The same is true for your children's immigration—but there's a twist. Children of U.S. citizens need to have their own petitions (Forms I-130) on file with USCIS in order to immigrate as the children of a U.S. citizen. They can't enjoy the benefits of that parent's new citizenship if they are merely named on their immigrating parent's petition.

When this whole process began, your spouse may have simply entered your children's names on the I-130 petition for you—which would have been enough for them to immigrate if your spouse had remained a permanent resident. To put this in more technical terms, your children were eligible to immigrate as your derivative beneficiaries when your spouse was a permanent resident, but once your spouse became a U.S. citizen, they lost their derivative beneficiary status. They now need to have petitions of their own.

Fortunately, it's not too late for your spouse to file separate I-130 petitions for your children even after having become a citizen. So long as the children are still unmarried, under age 21, and are your spouse's natural children or legal stepchildren (that is, the marriage took place before they turned 18), they qualify as immediate relatives just like you. As immediate relatives, they will be able to immigrate at the same time as you. It may take around five months for the new petitions to be approved, but for most children, it should all work out in the end.

However, there are three groups of children who are, to varying degrees, still left out in the cold: those who have married, those who are not your spouse's legal stepchildren, and those who have turned 21.

Children who have married. Your children who have married could not have immigrated with you when your spouse was a permanent resident, so your spouse's citizenship doesn't actually make their situation worse. In fact, it could improve their situation if your spouse is the children's natural father or legal stepfather, because your spouse can file a petition for them in the third preference category.

Children who are not your spouse's legal stepchildren. As part of filing new visa petitions for your children, your spouse will have to prove that he or she has a direct relationship with each child, either as natural parent or legal stepparent. To be their legal stepparent, your spouse will have to show that your marriage took place before the child turned 18. If it didn't, then that child cannot immigrate until you yourself become a permanent resident and file a second preference petition for your child.

Children who have turned 21. If your child has turned 21 and no separate petition was filed for him or her, you're in for some extra work. As with your other children, your U.S. citizen spouse can file a new, separate I-130 petition if he or she is the child's natural parent or legal stepparent—but if you don't alert USCIS to the situation, your child won't become an immediate relative like you. Instead, the child will be put into the first preference visa category, which is subject to annual quotas. The child will get a Priority Date, but it will be at the very end of the first preference waiting list.

EXAMPLE: Ricardo, a U.S. permanent resident, filed an I-130 petition for his Mexican wife Soledad and their four children on January 2, 2019. Soledad got an approval notice showing her January 2, 2019 Priority Date. Because the children were named on the I-130 petition and Ricardo was a permanent resident, USCIS knew that the children were derivative beneficiaries and shared Soledad's Priority Date. But on February 3, 2020 Ricardo was sworn in as a U.S. citizen. No more derivative beneficiaries for this family; Ricardo must file a separate I-130 for each child. He does so, on February 10, 2020. That works fine for three of his children, who are under age 21—as minor, unmarried children of a

U.S. citizen, they are still immediate relatives and immediately eligible for a visa, just like their mother. But the fourth child, Jorge, has since turned 21. Jorge's Priority Date is now February 10, 2020. If you look on the *Visa Bulletin* chart in Section 3 above, you'll see that in his category, Mexico First Preference, the current Priority Date is August 1, 1997. Jorge is facing an approximate 20-year wait for a visa. If Ricardo had planned ahead and filed a separate I-130 for Jorge when he filed for the rest of the family, he could have shaved many years off Jorge's wait.

But this isn't fair! True enough. Luckily, there is a remedy for children in this situation. When your U.S. citizen spouse files the new I-130 petition, he or she can ask USCIS not to put the child at the bottom of the waiting list, but to give the child the same Priority Date as the rest of the family, even in this new category. In other words, your spouse asks USCIS to pretend that a separate I-130 petition was submitted for the over-21-year-old at the same time that the petition for the whole family was submitted, perhaps years ago.

This is called "recapturing" a Priority Date. Below is a sample letter showing how to ask for a recapture. The petitioner also needs to include complete copies of the original I-130 petition, the original USCIS approval notice showing the family's old Priority Date, and the petitioner's citizenship certificate.

Approval of recaptured dates is supposed to be automatic. Unfortunately, the USCIS service centers sometimes pay no attention to such requests—even if you write the most compelling letter and include complete documentation. You might get an approval notice showing a new Priority Date rather than your family's old one. Your only recourse would be to write many letters trying to get USCIS to correct the date (or to hire a lawyer). As a last resort, you might consider contacting the USCIS Ombudsman (www.dhs.gov/case-assistance).

TIP

Plan ahead—submit separate I-130 petitions for any children who will soon turn 21. If you are at the beginning of the immigration process, and have children who may turn 21 before the process ends, or you know that your spouse is likely to apply for U.S. citizenship, you can avoid the hassles involved in recapturing Priority Dates. Your spouse should simply file separate petitions for them from the outset.

9. Should You Wait Until Your Spouse Is a U.S. Citizen?

Applicants sometimes ask, "If I can avoid the Visa Preference System by waiting for my spouse to become a U.S. citizen, shouldn't I do so and avoid the quotas and waiting period?" The answer is no, you don't really gain anything by waiting, and you may actually lose time if your spouse's citizenship gets delayed.

You don't gain anything because your spouse will have to submit the I-130 petition sometime, even after becoming a U.S. citizen. The form is the same, no matter your spouse's status. Your approval notice will remain good even after your spouse becomes a citizen. Besides this, the longer you wait, the higher the application fee is likely to go. There is also a risk of losing time because you don't really know when your spouse will become a U.S. citizen.

You can see how things might drag on. Even after your spouse is approved for citizenship, it could be a few months more before he or she attends the ceremony to be sworn in as a U.S. citizen. By waiting for your spouse to attain U.S. citizenship, you could end up waiting even longer than you would have as a Preference Relative.

SKIP AHEAD

After examining and choosing one of the options described in this chapter, and getting your I-130 petition prepared and/or approved, see the charts below for where you'll go next.

Letter Requesting Recaptured Priority Date

---

111 Seaside Lane
Orlando, FL 32801

June 1, 20xx

USCIS ATTN: I-130
P.O. Box 21700
Phoenix, AZ 85036
[See the I-130 page of the USCIS website for the address of the service center serving your geographic region.]

RE: Petitioner: Ricardo Torres
    Beneficiary: Jorge Torres
    I-130 Petition with Priority Date Recapture
    Request

Dear Sir/Madam:

I am the Petitioner named above. Enclosed please find an I-130 petition for the above-named Beneficiary (my son) with supporting documents, including:

1. Copy of my son's birth certificate

2. Copy of his mother's and my marriage certificate

3. Copy of my citizenship certificate

4. Fee of $535 (money order).

In addition, please note that I am requesting a recapture of an earlier Priority Date for this application. My son was formerly a Derivative Beneficiary on an approved petition that I filed for his mother in 20xx, with Priority Date January 2, 20xx. I recently became a U.S. citizen, and so my son lost his derivative status. Please grant my son the earlier, January 2, 20xx, Priority Date on the approval of this I-130 petition. In support of this request, I also enclose the following:

1. Copy of original I-130, showing my son's name

2. Copy of USCIS notice approving this I-130, with January 2, 20xx, Priority Date.

Thank you for your attention to this matter.

Very truly yours,

Ricardo Torres

Ricardo Torres

Next Step If You Entered The U.S. Illegally

If you plan on staying illegally and are legally allowed to adjust status in the United States (by being grandfathered in):	When your waiting period is over and you are ready to adjust status, see Chapter 14 regarding adjustment of status application procedures.
If you plan on leaving the United States and applying for a marriage-based immigrant visa, and do not need a waiver of your illegal stay in order to return:	See Chapter 8, Section A, regarding marriage visa application procedures for overseas spouses of U.S. lawful permanent residents (or Chapter 7, Section A, if your spouse becomes a U.S. citizen).
If you cannot adjust status and will need a waiver of your illegal stay in order to return:	See an attorney; Chapter 17 contains tips on finding a good one.

Next Step If You Entered The U.S. Legally

If you can stay in the United States legally through your waiting period:	When your waiting period is over and you are ready to adjust status, see Chapter 14 regarding adjustment of status application procedures.
If you plan on staying illegally, and can change status in the United States at the end of your waiting period (by being grandfathered in, or because your spouse becomes a U.S. citizen):	When your waiting period is over and you are ready to adjust status, see Chapter 14 regarding adjustment of status application procedures.
If you are interested in leaving the United States and applying for a marriage-based immigrant visa, and will not need a waiver of your visa overstay:	When your waiting period is over, see Chapter 8, Section A, regarding marriage visa application procedures for overseas spouses of U.S. lawful permanent residents (or Chapter 7, Section A, if your spouse becomes a U.S. citizen).
If you will have to leave the United States but will need a waiver to return:	See an attorney; Chapter 17 contains tips on finding a good one.

Interviews With USCIS or Consular Officials

The final step in obtaining your visa or green card is to attend an interview with a U.S. consular or USCIS official. Until the date of your interview, it's quite possible that neither you nor your U.S. fiancé or spouse will have had any personal contact with any immigration official. For that reason, many applicants approach the interview with needless fear. Below, we guide you on what to expect and how to treat the interview as important—without suffering it as an ordeal.

With all the paperwork you've submitted by now, you might think the government should be able to approve your visa or green card without having to meet you face-to-face. However, the government views the interview as its opportunity to confirm the contents of your application after you've sworn to tell the truth (even though you represented that the answers on your application forms were true and correct when you signed them). The interview also allows the government to ask questions that will test whether your marriage is real or a sham.

Whether you're submitting your application overseas or in the United States, most of the advice in this chapter will apply to you. Overseas applicants should also read Section C regarding unique practices at U.S. consulates. U.S.-based applicants should read Section D covering practices at USCIS offices.

A. Who Must Attend an Interview?

Every hopeful immigrant can count on being required to attend an interview, whether they're applying for a fiancé visa, a marriage visa, or a green card. If you're applying for a green card at a USCIS office, your spouse will be required to attend the interview with you.

If you're applying for a fiancé or marriage visa from overseas, however, your U.S. fiancé or spouse is not required to attend the interview—but it's an excellent idea to do so. After all, one of the main topics of discussion will be a form your spouse filled out—the Affidavit of Support—showing your spouse's financial situation. If your spouse can confirm the contents of the affidavit in person, so much the better. And your spouse's willingness to travel to be with you for this part of the immigration process is a pretty good way of showing that your marriage is not a sham.

A few applicants—or more likely their U.S. fiancés or spouses—may also be asked to attend a so-called fraud interview. This happens when USCIS or the consulate has suspicions that your marriage or intended marriage is not real. Preparing for fraud interviews is covered in Section E, below.

B. Preparing for Your Interview

The key to a smooth interview is preparation. If you haven't already done so, prepare all the appropriate forms and documents. For immigrants coming from overseas, these are the ones mentioned in the mailing that you got containing your consular appointment notice. For immigrants in the United States, these are the ones discussed in Chapter 14, Section F.

1. What to Review

In order to prepare for the oral part of the interview, your most important homework task is to review your paperwork. Look at the questions and answers on every form that you've submitted or that has been submitted for you, including the ones filled out by your U.S. citizen fiancé or spouse. Though they seem to contain only boring, dry bits of information, this information is loaded with meaning to a USCIS or consular official. The dates of your visits to different places, the financial figures, and your immigration history can all add up to a revealing picture in the official's eyes.

> **EXAMPLE:** Leticia hates dealing with money issues, so she didn't read the Affidavit of Support that her husband filled out. And she didn't notice that her husband wrote on the form that he has "no

dependents." At the interview, the officer observed, "It looks like your husband doesn't earn much. How will you be supported?" Leticia replied, "Oh, I'm sure we'll make do financially. After all, my husband's aging parents and orphan nephew all live with him and don't work and he seems to support them just fine." Leticia just created a huge problem. It's now apparent that her husband lied on his Affidavit of Support and has several dependents. He is clearly less capable of supporting Leticia than it originally appeared. As a result, the consular officer may find Leticia inadmissible as a potential public charge.

The example above shows why you and your fiancé or spouse should review all the paperwork and forms carefully to be sure both of you understand them completely. If there have been any changes or if you've noticed any errors since filling out the forms, be prepared to explain the changes and provide documents confirming the new information, if appropriate.

After you've reviewed your written work, spend some time with your fiancé or spouse reviewing the facts and circumstances surrounding your relationship, such as where you met, how your relationship developed, how you've corresponded or visited and when, and why you decided to get married.

If you're applying for a fiancé visa, be ready to explain your plans for your wedding and subsequent life together. If you're already married, recall what occurred at your wedding and how you settled into your marriage. The officer will ask you about these details in order to test whether you are truly establishing a life together, not just committing a fraud in order to obtain a green card.

⚠ CAUTION

Your memory may let you down. Even if you and your fiancé or spouse think you know and remember everything about one another, you each may remember things differently. Couples have been known to disagree to the tune of a hundred people regarding how many attended their wedding ceremony. And plenty of people can't remember what they did for their spouse's last birthday. The more you know about your shared history,

the better prepared you'll be for the interview. You can make a game of testing each other on domestic facts: What color are the curtains in your house, how often do you see your in-laws, what's the name of your child's best friend? To help you with this game, take a look at the list of questions in Section F, below.

2. What to Wear

The interviewing officer's decision rests almost entirely on whether he or she believes that you're telling the truth. You'll come across as more sincere if you're dressed neatly, professionally, and even conservatively. Avoid T-shirts or jewelry with slogans or symbols that might make the officer wonder about your lifestyle or morals. We suggest that you dress as if you were going to visit your grandmother. Think about what you'll wear to your interview earlier than the night before, so that you're not up late with your ironing board.

> **EXAMPLE:** Jon showed up at his interview wearing expensive leather shoes and, around his neck, a chain with a solid gold marijuana leaf dangling from it. The officer took one look at this and went right into questioning him as to whether he had ever tried, abused, or sold drugs. When Jon wouldn't admit to anything, she referred him for another medical exam. The doctor found evidence of drug use in Jon's bloodstream, and he was denied the immigrant visa.

On this note, realize that marijuana remains illegal under U.S. federal law, despite being legal in many states. Simply working for a marijuana grower in a state where it's legal can create problems for immigrants.

3. What to Bring

You'll need to bring a number of documents to your interview, for purposes of proving your identity, the validity of your marriage, and more. You'll be given a list of the required documents when you receive your appointment notice.

Also check the chapter of this book that describes all of the applications and documents someone in your precise situation must prepare. This will give you more detail than the government's lists, particularly on the important topic of what documents to bring to prove that your marriage is the real thing.

4. Prepare for Security Screening

Most if not all U.S. consulates now have airport-style security checkpoints that screen visitors and visa applicants before they are allowed to enter. By organizing your documents in advance and making some simple preparations before going to the consulate, you can save yourself a lot of time, hassle, and unneeded stress before your interview.

- Leave any portable electronics and devices like your mobile phone, tablet, camera, music player, or similar items at home or somewhere safe.
- Don't bring any food or drink with you.
- Leave any cosmetics, perfumes or colognes, brushes and combs, and similar items at home.
- Don't bring any packages, parcels, or sealed envelopes that are unrelated to your visa application. Bring only the documents and papers you need for your visa interview.
- If possible, bring your documents and visa application materials in a clear plastic folder or envelope. This will allow consular security to easily screen your visa materials.
- Organize your materials so you can access them quickly when asked for specific documents.

C. Procedures for Consular Interviews

If you're coming from overseas, as a fiancé or spouse, your interview notice will tell you where and when to go for your visa interview.

1. Getting There Safely and On Time

If you don't live in the same city as the consulate, you'll want to arrive at least a few days in advance.

You will need time to complete your medical exam (at a clinic designated by the consulate) and to get the test results back.

On the day of your interview, it's best to arrive early, in case there's a line. Don't be surprised if you have to wait beyond your scheduled appointment time—the consulates often schedule applicants in large groups, telling all the members of each group to show up at the same time.

> **CAUTION**
> **Beware of crime around U.S. consulates.** Criminals know where the U.S. consulates are and they believe that many people going for interviews are carrying large sums of money for visa fees. Take whatever precautions are appropriate in your country. Watch out for con artists who hang around the consulate, trying to convince people that they won't get through the front door unless they hand over some money first.

2. What the Consular Officials Will Do and Say

Here's what will happen when you arrive at the consulate for your interview. First, a clerk will check the packet of forms and other items that you've brought, to make sure you've brought all that's needed.

After these preliminaries, a consular officer will meet with you, place you under oath, and review the contents of your entire application. Don't expect a cozy fireside chat in the official's office. Many consulates now conduct interviews through bulletproof glass windows that make you feel like you're in a bank or a prison.

The officer will probably start by reviewing your forms and documents. He or she may ask you questions that are identical to the ones on your forms. Since you will have reviewed these carefully, this shouldn't be a problem—but if you can't remember something, it's much better to say so than to guess at the answer.

Next, you'll have to answer questions designed to test whether your marriage or intended marriage is the real thing. The officer will probably start by asking general questions, such as how you and your U.S. citizen fiancé or spouse met, when you decided to get married, and other facts regarding your visits or correspondence. If you're already married, the official may ask how many people attended the ceremony and how you've visited or corresponded with one another in recent years. If either of you has been married before, you can expect the officer to ask about that relationship and its ending, too.

If everything looks to be in order, the officer may ask only three to five questions—but he or she can ask more. If you have children in common, the consular officer is much less likely to question whether your marriage is bona fide.

It's natural to feel embarrassed about sharing these personal details. Remember that the officers have heard it all by now. Their main interest is to see if you sound like a real fiancé or spouse. Again, it's advisable not to make guesses if you don't know the answer to a question. For example, if an officer asks you, "How many people attended your engagement party?" and you don't know or have forgotten, you could reply, "I don't remember the exact number." Even better would be to add a relevant detail that you do remember, such as, "But I can tell you that the guests drank 32 cases of champagne pretty quickly!"

If You're Pregnant at Your Fiancé Visa Interview

Don't worry if you're pregnant when you go for your fiancé visa interview—the consular officer will arrange to give the baby a separate visa if it's born before you depart for the United States. But believe it or not, before either of you are approved for the visa, the consulate will need to receive a written acknowledgment from your U.S. citizen fiancé that he is still willing to marry you. This appears to be based on the worry that your U.S. citizen fiancé may not be the father of the baby and may therefore change his mind about the engagement.

The interview can take as little as 20 minutes, in cases where the marriage is obviously real, all documents are in order, and the applicant doesn't fall into any of the grounds for inadmissibility. Don't panic if it lasts longer. If you find yourself getting nervous, remember to curb that understandable instinct to start babbling. People with real marriages have nevertheless gotten themselves into deep trouble by being unable to stop talking.

> **EXAMPLE:** Arthur, a U.S. citizen, is attending a visa interview with his immigrating wife, Natalya. He's jet-lagged and anxious to have everything go well. He starts babbling to the officer, saying, "I'm so glad to finally be getting this over with. My family thought we'd never finish up. They keep teasing me about my 'mail order bride' and acting like I don't know what I'm doing. My little brother even asked me how much Natalya was paying me to marry her, can you believe it?" Unfortunately the consular officer is in the business of believing such rumors. Arthur's little speech means that he and Natalya have to endure a whole new and harsher round of questioning before her visa is finally approved.

At the end of the interview, don't expect an immediate decision. Even if everything looks good, the consulate will need to run some final security checks with the FBI and other law-enforcement agencies. This might take only a few days or it could take several months.

Different consulates notify you that your visa has been approved (or denied) in different ways. Some just post your case number online, and you have to check. Others call you by phone, or require that you give them a return mailer, and still others allow you to email the consulate and ask. You'll find out at your interview what to expect.

3. Delayed Decisions

Even if there's a problem in your case, officers rarely deny applications on the spot. If the problem can be corrected or if you are inadmissible but are eligible to apply for a waiver, they will normally ask you to provide additional materials.

Politely ask that the officer or official put any requests for more materials in writing, stating exactly what is needed and why. If there are any questions about the validity of your marriage, the consular officer may send your file back to the United States for investigation.

> **EXAMPLE:** A U.S. consular officer in Guatemala told Estela that he couldn't approve her immigrant visa until she brought in her "sister's tax returns." What was the problem? No such tax returns existed, because the sister (who was helping sponsor Estela financially) hadn't even been working long enough to reach a tax deadline. Her lawyer in the United States wrote a letter explaining this, but the consulate continued to ask for these tax returns. Because Estela didn't have the consulate's original request in writing, this led to months of arguing back and forth, with the consular officials continually changing or forgetting what it was they were looking for.

Usually you have to return to the consulate a few days later to pick up your visa—which is actually a thick envelope stuffed full of all your supporting documents. Or, the consulate might mail the packet to you.

CAUTION
Do not open the visa envelope! You will give the envelope to the United States border officer when you arrive. The officer will examine the contents and do a last check for any problems. The border official, not the consulate, will place a stamp in your passport indicating that you are either a fiancé visa holder, a permanent resident, or a conditional resident.

D. Procedures for USCIS Interviews

Several months to a year or more after you submit your adjustment of status packet to USCIS, USCIS will schedule your interview at one of its local offices, hopefully near where you live. This could be your biggest day since your wedding: If the interview goes well—your marriage is obviously the real deal, you don't fall into any of the grounds for inadmissibility, and your documents are in order— the interview can take as little as 20 minutes. If you have children in common, USCIS is much less likely to question whether your marriage is bona fide. You will be approved for either permanent residence or conditional residence (if you've been married for less than two years or entered the United States on a fiancé visa).

The appointment notice will look much like the one below. Read the notice carefully—there's a chance that your local USCIS office has added requirements that were not covered in this book.

1. Arrange for an Interpreter

USCIS doesn't provide interpreters at interviews in the United States. A few of their officers speak Spanish or other languages, but you can't count on getting a bilingual officer, nor can you request one. If you're not comfortable in English, you'll need to bring a friend or hire an interpreter to help. Even if your spouse is capable of interpreting for you, the USCIS office probably won't allow it, because it reduces its ability to compare your answers and detect marriage frauds.

The interpreter must be over 18 and fluent in both your language and in English. Some officers also require that the interpreter be a legal resident or citizen of the United States (of course, if they're here illegally, they'd be foolish to walk into a USCIS office).

2. What the USCIS Officials Will Do and Say

In spite of the fact that hundreds of very different couples are interviewed each day across the United States, these interviews tend to follow a pattern. Here's what will probably happen at your adjustment interview, step by step.

Sample Interview Notice

Department of Homeland Security
U.S. Citizenship and Immigration Services

Form I-797C, Notice of Action

THIS NOTICE DOES NOT GRANT ANY IMMIGRATION STATUS OR BENEFIT.

REQUEST FOR APPLICANT TO APPEAR FOR INITIAL INTERVIEW	NOTICE DATE May 25, 2020
CASE TYPE FORM I-485, APPLICATION TO REGISTER PERMANENT RESIDENCE OR ADJUST STATUS	A# A 012 345 677

APPLICATION NUMBER NSC0612345678	RECEIVED DATE March 21, 2020	PRIORITY DATE March 21, 2020	PAGE 1 of 1

ANDA MIHOV
c/o ILONA BRAY
950 PARKER STREET
BERKELEY, CA 94710

You are hereby notified to appear for the interview appointment, as scheduled below, for the completion of your Application to Register Permanent Residence or Adjust Status (Form I-485) and any supporting applications or petitions. *Failure to appear for this interview and/or failure to bring the below listed items will result in the denial of your application. (8 CFR 103.2(b)(13))*

Who should come with you?

☒ If your eligibility is based on your marriage, your husband or wife must come with you to the interview.
☐ If you do not speak English fluently, you should bring an interpreter.
☐ Your attorney or authorized representative may come with you to the interview.
☐ If your eligibility is based on a parent/child relationship and the child is a minor, the petitioning parent and the child must appear for the interview.

NOTE: Every adult (over 18 years of age) who comes to the interview must bring Government-issued photo identification, such as a driver's license or ID card, in order to enter the building and to verify his/her identity at the time of the interview. You do not need to bring your children unless otherwise instructed. Please be on time, but do not arrive more than 30 minutes early. We may record or videotape your interview.

YOU MUST BRING THE FOLLOWING ITEMS WITH YOU: (Please use as a checklist to prepare for your interview)

☐ This Interview Notice and your Government issued photo identification.
☐ A completed medical examination (Form I-693) and vaccination supplement in a sealed envelope (unless already submitted).
☐ A completed Affidavit(s) of Support (Form I-864) with all required evidence, including the following, for *each* of your sponsors (unless already submitted):
    ☐ Federal Income Tax returns and W-2's, or certified IRS printouts, for the most recent tax year;
    ☐ Letters from each current employer, verifying current rate of pay and average weekly hours, and pay stubs for the past 2 months;
    ☐ Evidence of your sponsor's and/or co-sponsor's United States Citizenship or Lawful Permanent Resident status.
☐ All documentation establishing your eligibility for Lawful Permanent Resident status.
☐ Any immigration-related documentation ever issued to you, including any Employment Authorization Document (EAD) and any Authorization for Advance Parole (Form I-512).
☐ All travel documents used to enter the United States, including Passports, Advance Parole documents (I-512) and I-94s (Arrival/Departure Document).
☐ Your Birth Certificate.
☐ Your petitioner's Birth Certificate and your petitioner's evidence of United States Citizenship or Lawful Permanent Resident Status.
☐ If you have children, bring a Birth Certificate for each of your children.
☐ If your eligibility is based on your marriage, in addition to your spouse coming to the interview with you, bring:
    ☐ A certified copy of your Marriage Document issued by the appropriate civil authority.
    ☐ Your spouse's Birth Certificate and your spouse's evidence of United States Citizenship or Lawful Permanent Resident status;
    ☐ If either you or your spouse were ever married before, all divorce decrees/death certificates for each prior marriage/former spouse;
    ☐ Birth Certificates for all children of this marriage, and custody papers for your children and for your spouse's children not living with you;
☐ Supporting evidence of your relationship, such as copies of any documentation regarding joint assets or liabilities you and your spouse may have together. This may include: tax returns, bank statements, insurance documents (car, life, health), property documents (car, house, etc.), rental agreements, utility bills, credit cards, contracts, leases, photos, correspondence and/or any other documents you feel may substantiate your relationship.
☐ Original and copy of each supporting document that you submitted with your application. Otherwise, we may keep your originals for our records.
☐ If you have ever been arrested, bring the related Police Report and the original or certified Final Court Disposition for each arrest, even if the charges have been dismissed or expunged. If no court record is available, bring a letter from the court with jurisdiction indicating this.
☐ A certified English translation for each foreign language document. The translator must certify that s/he is fluent in both languages, and that the translation in its entirety is complete and accurate.

YOU MUST APPEAR FOR THIS INTERVIEW- If an emergency, such as your own illness or a close relative's hospitalization, prevents you from appearing, call the U.S. Citizenship and Immigration Services (USCIS) National Customer Service Center at 1-800-375-5283 as soon as possible. Please be advised that rescheduling will delay processing of application/petition, and may require some steps to be repeated. It may also affect your eligibility for other immigration benefits while this application is pending.

If you have questions, please call the USCIS National Customer Service Center at 1-800-375-5283 (hearing impaired TDD service is 1-800-767-1833).

PLEASE COME TO: U.S. Citizenship and Immigration Services	ON: Friday, July, 2020

630 SANSOME ST
  @ND FLOOR - ADJUSTMENT OF STATUS
  SAN FRANCISCO, CA 94710
	AT: 12:45PM

7	REPRESENTATIVE COPY

If this is an interview or biometrics appointment notice, please see the back of this notice for important information.   Form I-797C 07/11/14 Y

1. After sitting in the waiting room with dozens of other couples for so long that you're sure they've forgotten you, you'll be summoned to the inner rooms of the USCIS adjustments unit.

2. You'll be brought to the USCIS officer's desk, where your identification will be checked. Just when you're seated comfortably, you, your spouse, and your interpreter (if you've brought one) will have to stand up again, raise your right hands, and take oaths to tell the truth. The officer will ask to see all of your passports and travel documents, your work permit (if you have one), your Social Security card (if you have one), and your driver's license (if you have one). The officer will also want to see documents from your U.S. spouse, such as a driver's license, Social Security card (if available), and proof of legal U.S. immigration status.

3. The officer will start by going through your written application, asking you about the facts and examining the medical and fingerprint reports for factors that might make you ineligible for a green card. As discussed earlier, this is one of the most important parts of the interview. You'll sign the application to confirm its correctness.

4. The officer will ask you and your spouse about your married life. At this stage, the questions will be polite ones, such as where you met, when and why you decided to get married, how many people attended your wedding, or what you did on your most recent birthday or night out. You'll back up your answers with documents that illustrate the genuine nature of your marriage, such as rental agreements and joint utility bills. (Chapter 14, Section F, lists other persuasive documents you might use.)

5. If there's a problem in your application that you can correct by submitting additional materials, the officer will usually put your case on hold and send you home with a list of additional documents to provide by mail

within a specified time. For example, if your spouse's earnings are insufficient, the officer may suggest you find another family member to sign an Affidavit of Support. Rarely does USCIS deny an application on the spot.

6. If the officer suspects that your marriage is fraudulent, however, a whole new step will be added to the process. You will meet the Fraud Unit. There, an officer will interview you and your spouse separately—and intensively. The officer will compare the results of your two interviews. (For details on what to expect and how to prepare for a Fraud Interview, see Section E, below.)

CAUTION
Truly married couples get called in for fraud interviews too. If, as we hope, your marriage isn't fraudulent, you may be inclined to skip the section below that addresses fraud interviews. However, couples whose personal characteristics or living situations already raise red flags in the eyes of USCIS might need to do some extra planning. The USCIS officers are on the lookout for couples who, for example, do not seem to share a common language; have large differences in their age, religion, class, cultural, or educational background; or who don't live at the same address.

At the end of the interview, if you are approved, you will be given a letter stating that your case is approved. The letter is just for your records and cannot be used like a green card to travel in and out of the United States. Several weeks later, however, your actual green card will arrive by mail. If you receive conditional residence, you'll have to file an application about 21 months from your approval date in order to progress to permanent residency.

3. Presenting Marital Problems at the Adjustment Interview

The USCIS officer will be most likely to approve you for a green card if you're in a happy, traditional marriage. However, this doesn't mean that marital arguments or even living separately should lead the officer to deny your green card.

If you have serious problems, be reasonably open about the cause and the steps you're taking to deal with them (such as meeting with a marriage counselor or religious leader on a regular basis). Sometimes this is the strongest evidence of a real, bona fide marriage! If, however, the officer appears to wrongly believe that only happy marriages qualify you for a green card (which is not uncommon), ask to reschedule the interview so that you can bring a lawyer.

If you've actually received a legal separation (court ordered) or filed for divorce, however, your prospects for approval are dimmer. A legal separation or divorce filing may ultimately lead to a denial of your green card.

There is an exception if your U.S. citizen or permanent resident spouse is subjecting you to abuse (physical or emotional cruelty). In that case, divorce will not destroy your green card eligibility if you file what's called a self-petition on Form I-360. You must do so before the divorce decree becomes final, or within two years of the final decree if you can show that the divorce was connected to the abuse.

The self-petition declares that since you're being abused, your spouse can't be counted on to help you through the green card application process. It allows you to start or continue the process on your own. Domestic violence situations and self-petitions are not addressed in this book. Talk to your local battered women's shelter or other nonprofit or charity organization; or see a lawyer if spousal violence is holding up your application. (See Chapter 17 for more on how to find a lawyer to represent you.)

E. The Fraud Interview

If USCIS has serious doubts about whether your marriage is a real one, it will summon you and/or your fiancé or spouse for a fraud interview. A fraud interview is similar to the initial interview, but includes questions that are far more probing and intense. Such interviews are usually held only in the United States. If you are overseas, your fiancé or spouse will have to attend the interview alone, and should read Section 3, below. If you are applying within the United States, however, USCIS will no doubt call both of you in for the fraud interview.

Being called for a fraud interview is definitely not a good sign. It means that your application has been singled out because it misses facts that would prove a real marriage, contains some inconsistencies, or presents grounds for suspicion. But if your marriage really is authentic, now's the time to show them.

1. Times When a Fraud Interview May Be Required

There are various times during the application process when USCIS may call for a fraud interview. These include after your spouse files the initial petition (Form I-129F for fiancés or Form I-130 for spouses) and after your USCIS or consular interview. If you haven't reached your second wedding anniversary by the time you're ready for residence approval, you'll get conditional residency, which lasts for two years—and a fraud interview can be scheduled during or at the expiration of that time, too.

> **SEE AN EXPERT**
> **Applicants often get advance notice of a fraud interview—this is a good time to hire a lawyer.** Ask the lawyer to attend the interview. The lawyer doesn't really have much power over the questions that you are required to answer, but can be a calming influence on everyone. Also, if the lawyer attends the interview, he or she will be better prepared to deal with any follow-up matters.

2. What They'll Ask

In the classic fraud interview, a USCIS officer puts you and your spouse in separate rooms and asks each of you an identical set of questions. Later, the officer compares your answers to see if they match up. If you are applying in the United States, you can count on experiencing this type of fraud interview.

If you are applying from overseas, the USCIS officer in the United States will probably not be able to interview you—and will have to settle for speaking to your fiancé or spouse alone. In that case, the officer will want to hear your fiancé or spouse give a realistic account of the development of your relationship. The officer will also try to spot any inconsistencies within your U.S. fiancé or spouse's story or between his or her story and the application forms and documents.

The person who attends the interview should be ready for any and all types of questions, from what you gave each other for your last birthdays to the form of birth control you use. The questions vary among different officers and different years. A list of possibilities is provided in Section F, below, but no official list exists (or if it does, it's well-guarded in the government's top-secret files).

TIP

Bring matching sets of house keys if you live in the United States. USCIS officers have been known to ask husband and wife to produce their house keys. The officer then compares them to make sure that they fit the same locks.

One San Francisco officer is reputed to be obsessed with how technology fits into the couple's life, asking questions about how many TV remote controls are in the couple's shared house and who keeps the garage door opener in their car. Others might be more interested in food—asking about your favorites and who cooks what. If your fiancé or spouse lives with you, try going through your daily routine, noticing all the details, such as:

- how often and what time you call each other by phone
- how many people attended your wedding (if you're married)
- which holidays you celebrate together
- your activities the last time one of you visited the other, and
- which of your financial matters are shared, or who (if either) supports the other financially.

If you're not yet married, and applying for a fiancé visa, the questions might also cover things like:

- how your families feel about your plans
- whether the families have met you or your fiancé
- how much time you've spent together, and
- whether you had an engagement party or made a formal announcement of your engagement to family and friends.

There are no limits to the possible questions. Obviously, many of the questions in our sample list in Section F below are most suited to a couple who are already living together. For those of you who aren't yet living together, expect the officer to ask about times that the two of you have spent together.

3. How They'll Behave

Once you or your spouse gets to a fraud interview, you will have to meet with an officer whose main job is try to detect wrongdoers, not grant visas or green cards. The interviewer will not be trying to make you feel comfortable. His or her job is to push a person with questions until the person trips himself up, confesses to marriage fraud, or finally convinces the interviewer that the marriage is real.

Usually, straightforward, hard questioning is enough. Couples perpetrating a fraudulent marriage can do all the homework in the world, but when one of them forgets or doesn't know something very obvious—like where they went right after their wedding—it sticks out like a sore thumb. After that, the applicant often crumbles.

Occasionally, a hard-nosed USCIS officer will engage in harsher tactics, such as falsely telling someone that their spouse has already "confessed" that the marriage is bogus, in order to push the interviewee into confessing. Or, the officer may use flat-out intimidation, reminding the interviewee about the jail time and money fines a person faces if caught committing marriage fraud.

Sensing that the interviewee is feeling low, the officer may ask him to sign something withdrawing the petition or stating that the marriage is a fraud. If your marriage really is an honest one, don't agree to or sign anything. Ask to stop the interview and to reschedule with a lawyer present.

4. How Your Spouse Should Handle an Interview Without You

If you are overseas and are not asked to attend the fraud interview, your U.S. fiancé or spouse will have to handle it alone. He or she won't need to worry that the two of you share similar memories about your relationship—but will have to find other ways to demonstrate that your relationship is real.

A good way for your U.S. fiancé or spouse to prepare is to put him- or herself in the USCIS officer's shoes. Assume that the officer will be thinking some pretty cynical thoughts about you and your reasons for wanting to come to the United States. Your fiancé or spouse should then think about what to tell and show the officer to shatter these negative assumptions.

> **EXAMPLE:** Kevin goes in for his marriage fraud interview. As he anticipated, the officer is wearing a look on his face that says, "This guy's 20 years older than the immigrant, they probably can't even speak each other's language, so they barely know each other and she'd never marry him if there weren't a green card in it for her." Kevin has planned for this, however. He tells the officer about his and his beloved's unusual shared interest in wild horse training and describes their romantic first meeting while watching horse races on the Mongolian steppes. Kevin has mentally reviewed all the details of the time that he and she spent together and can tell the officer details about their conversations, what she wore, and the new foods that she introduced him to. And the kicker is when Kevin shows the officer his homework from the class he's taking to learn her native language. By the end of the interview, the officer's opinion has been completely turned around.

Your relationship probably didn't happen quite like Kevin's. But your fiancé can be as thorough as Kevin was in showing what makes his relationship special. With every couple, there are unusual facts and circumstances that you can use to show that the two of you are a real couple, not just a bad statistic.

F. Sample Interview Questions

These are sample questions to help you prepare for your interview, whether it's a consular, adjustment of status, or marriage fraud interview. Remember, there is no guarantee that the interviewer will ask you all or any of these questions (though many of them are drawn from actual interviews). But these should get you and your fiancé or spouse started on the process of testing each other's memory.

1. Development of Your Relationship

- Where did you meet?
- What did the two of you have in common?
- Where did you go for dates?
- When did your relationship turn romantic?
- How long was it before you decided to get married?
- Who proposed to whom?
- Why did you decide to have a [long, short] engagement?
- Did your parents approve of the match? Why or why not?

2. The Wedding

- How many people attended your wedding?
- Did each of your parents attend?
- Where was the wedding held?
- Was there music or other entertainment?
- What kind of cake (or other food) did you serve?
- Who were the bridesmaids/groomsmen?
- How late did the guests stay?
- Did the bride change clothes for the reception?
- Did you serve liquor? What kind?
- Did anyone get drunk or otherwise embarrass themselves at the reception? Who? Describe.
- What time did you and the [bride or groom] leave the reception?
- Did you go on a honeymoon? When did you leave? How did you get there? What airlines?

3. Regular Routines

- Who gets up first? At what time?
- How many alarm clocks do you set in the morning?
- Who makes breakfast?
- What do each of you eat for breakfast?
- Does your spouse drink coffee in the morning?
- What time do the working spouse or spouses arrive home?
- Do you regularly call each other during the day?
- Who cleans the house?
- What day is your garbage picked up?
- Who takes care of paying the bills?
- Do you have a joint bank account? Where?
- Do you have a cat, dog, or other pet? Who feeds it? Who walks it (or cleans its kitty litter box, cage, etc.)?
- Do you and/or your spouse attend regular religious services? Where?
- Where do you keep the spare toilet paper?

4. The Kids

- Who picks up the children at school?
- Who packs lunches for the kids?
- What are their favorite toys/activities?
- What are their least favorite foods?
- Which children (if any) still use a car seat?
- What is your usual babysitter's name?

5. The Cooking

- How many times a week on average do you eat out?
- What is your favorite restaurant for special occasions? For weekly outings?
- Who does most of the cooking?
- Who does the grocery shopping? Where?
- Is there a particular food that you eat every week?
- What is your spouse's favorite/least favorite food?
- What color are the kitchen curtains?
- Do you have a barbecue grill? Do you use it?

6. Other Family Members

- Have you met each other's parents?
- How often do you see each other's parents?
- When was the last time you saw them? Where? For how long?
- On important holidays, do you buy individual gifts for your parents-in-law? Do they buy individual gifts for you?
- How do each of you get along with your parents-in-law?
- Which other members of your spouse's family do you see frequently? When was the last time you saw them? What did you do together?

7. Home Technology

- Are any landline telephones in your house? Where are they?
- Do you have an answering machine on your telephone? Who checks the messages?
- How many televisions are in the house? In which rooms? Do you watch shows together, or separately? Name one show that you always watch together.
- Do you record any television shows?
- Do you subscribe to a DVD rental service?
- Does your spouse listen to the radio? What station?
- How many cars do you have?
- Do you have a garage? Who parks in it? Do you use a garage door opener?
- Do you have a camera? Who uses it most often? Who takes pictures at important family occasions?

8. In the Bedroom

- What size is your bed (Twin, Full, Queen, or King)?
- Do you have a regular mattress, futon, or waterbed?
- How many windows are there in your bedroom?

- What color are your spouse's pajamas?
- Who sleeps on each side of the bed?
- What form of contraception (birth control) do you use?
- When was your wife's last menstrual period?
- Where do you keep your toothbrushes? What kind of toothpaste, soap, and shampoo does each of you use?
- Do either of you read or watch television before going to sleep? Do you have lamps next to your bed?
- Have you ever had an argument that resulted in one of you sleeping in another room? Who, and which room?

9. The Rest of the House

- Do you live in a home or apartment? Who pays the mortgage or rent? How much is it?
- Is there a carpet in your front hallway? What color?
- Is your sofa a regular one or does it have a pull-out bed? Have you ever had houseguests sleep there?
- What type of curtains or window coverings are in your living room? What color?
- How many staircases are in your house?
- How many sinks, toilets, and showers are there in your house or apartment in total?
- Do you leave any lights on when you go to sleep at night?

10. Celebrations

- When is your spouse's birthday?
- What did you do for your spouse's last birthday?
- How did you celebrate your most recent wedding anniversary?
- What religious holidays do you celebrate together?
- What's the most important holiday of the year in your household? Where do you typically celebrate it?

- Have you and your spouse gone to see a movie or other form of entertainment lately? When, and what did you see?
- What did the two of you do last New Year's Eve? Fourth of July?

G. What to Do If an Interview Is Going Badly

Your chances of a smooth interview will be greatly increased by the advance preparation and organizing you're doing by using this book. Unfortunately, your efforts can't entirely guarantee a successful interview. A lot will hinge on the personality or mood of the government official.

It's important to have a balanced view of the USCIS and consular officers who will be interviewing you. They're human—and they know that part of their goal is to reunite families. Some of them can get downright sentimental as they look at your wedding photos.

Certain immigration officers have been known to go out of their way to help people—for example, spending hours searching for something in a room full of old files; or fitting a person's interview into their schedule even when the person arrived two hours late. On the other hand, some officers can get downright rude or hostile, perhaps due to their heavy caseload or the number of marriage frauds they've uncovered. Remember that they hold much of the power—getting angry will get you nowhere fast. Remain respectful and answer honestly if you don't know or remember something. Never guess or lie.

Some immigrant applicants have heard wild rumors about how to win over a U.S. government official. One showed up for his USCIS interview wearing a loud tie covered with American flags. He interjected comments about America's greatness and what a terrific member of society he would be. Not surprisingly, the officer rolled her eyes and got irritated. Most USCIS officers just want to see someone who won't waste their time, has an orderly, clean case, and is legally eligible for the green card or other benefit.

TIP

Try to get the officer's name. USCIS and consular officers often don't tell you their name, but it may be shown on their desk. The best thing to do is politely ask their name at the beginning of the interview (not when things have already started to go badly, when they may get defensive). Then write the name down. This tidbit of information may become important later. For example, if you need to file a complaint, discuss the matter with a supervisor, or consult with an attorney, you'll have an edge if you know whom you dealt with. (An experienced attorney will know all the local USCIS officers by name and can better understand your description of what happened after learning who was involved.)

Some officers are irate no matter how the applicant behaves. You might encounter an officer who makes irrelevant accusations, acts in a discriminatory manner based on your race or gender, becomes uncontrollably angry, or persists with a line of questions or statements that is completely inappropriate. If any of these things happens, ask to see a supervisor.

If things are going badly, you don't have to let the situation go from bad to worse, ending with an on-the-spot rejection of your application. To avoid letting the officer make a final, negative decision, offer to supply any information that the officer asked for, so that your case will be postponed ("pended" in USCIS lingo).

When you get home, write down as many details as you can remember of the interview, while it's fresh in your mind. Then, consider consulting an attorney about your experience to learn what you can do to improve USCIS's reaction to your application.

Even if you don't speak with a lawyer, write a letter to USCIS, asking that a supervisor consider the interviewer's conduct when making a final review of your case. Supervisors review all cases, but they will assume the officer acted appropriately unless you tell them otherwise.

Applying for a Green Card at a USCIS Office

f you are married and living in the United States, you may be one step away from becoming a U.S. permanent resident. Now you need to apply to your local USCIS office for a green card. Of course, like most things involving the USCIS bureaucracy, it's not as simple as it sounds.

The process of getting a green card in the United States is called "adjustment of status." It involves paperwork and an interview. Most of your work will happen before you have any personal contact with USCIS. You'll prepare an adjustment of status packet, including various forms, documents, fees, a medical exam, and more. Some people go screaming to a lawyer as soon as they see the mountain of forms. Take heart—much of the requested information is routine and repetitive. You'll feel like an old pro by the time you're done.

After filing the adjustment of status packet, you'll wait about one month for fingerprinting and another several months to a year (or more) for an interview with USCIS. At or soon after that interview, you should be approved for residency.

This chapter guides you through the application process, all the way from compiling your application forms to waiting for your interview, and ends with information on getting green cards for your children. It explains:

- the documents and materials, such as copies of tax returns and photos, that you will need in order to complete your adjustment of status packet (Section A)
- how to fill in the USCIS forms, line by line (Section B)
- how to turn in the forms (Section C)
- how to handle vacations or moves while you wait for your interview (Section D)
- your fingerprint appointment (Section E)
- how to start preparing for your adjustment of status interview (Section F), and
- how to obtain green cards for your children (Section G).

You'll also want to read Chapter 13, which discusses what will happen at the adjustment of status interview and what questions to prepare for.

Even though you are still months away from getting the green card, applying for it will give you some immediate rights. You can remain in the United States while USCIS works on your application, and you'll get a work permit, which will allow you to get a job during the adjustment of status process. Also, if you need or want to travel abroad, you can obtain a travel document called "Advance Parole." This helps not only with reentry, but with making sure USCIS doesn't cancel your application because you left the U.S. and "abandoned" it.

CAUTION

Do not apply to adjust status until you are sure you are eligible to obtain a green card through this procedure. The mere fact that you are in the U.S. is not enough. If you are not eligible, filing the adjustment of status papers could trigger removal or deportation procedures. Make sure you have read and followed the instructions in Chapter 11 or 12, whichever is appropriate to your situation, before applying to adjust status in the United States.

A. Documents and Information to Have on Hand

Before you begin filling in the mound of forms required by USCIS, it will be helpful to first assemble the documents and materials that must accompany the forms. Some of this requested material, such as copies of forms you've already filed, needs no explanation here; but other documentation, such as proof of your sponsor's employment, isn't so obvious. This section covers the materials that are not self-explanatory. At the end, there's a helpful checklist that shows all the documents and forms you'll need.

Applying for Immigrant Visa in the United States (Married Applicants)

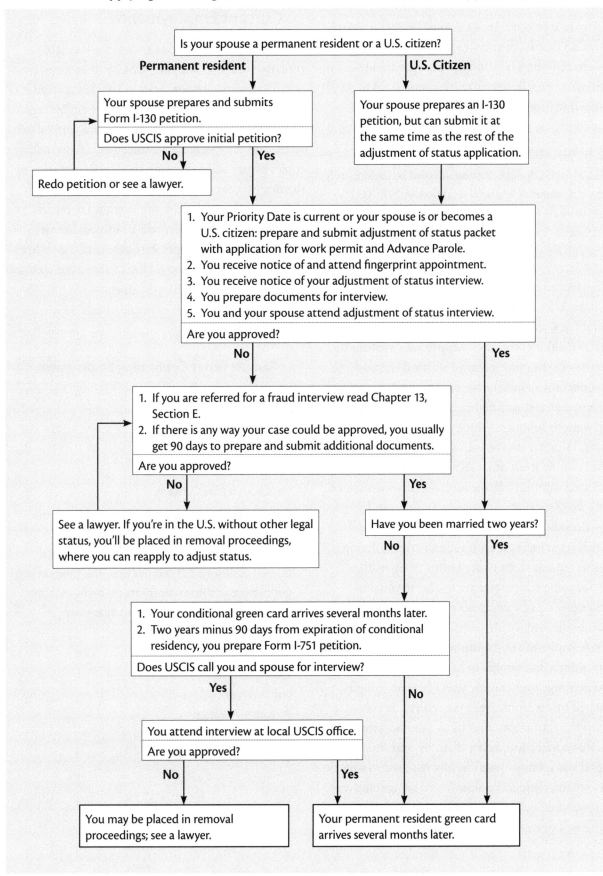

1. Your Sponsor's Tax Returns

Your spouse or other sponsor must be able to prove to USCIS that he or she (or they) can support you if necessary—and is willing to promise to do so. To fulfill these requirements, the sponsor(s) fill in an Affidavit of Support on Form I-864 or I-864EZ.

> CAUTION
> **USCIS might not be satisfied by looking only at the U.S. spouse's financial situation.** In 2018, USCIS began working on regulations that, if finalized, will shift the financial-support focus to the immigrating spouse and any children.

In order to measure your sponsor's financial situation, USCIS will ask for a copy of your sponsor's federal tax returns or transcripts for the last year. Strictly speaking, the rules require your sponsor to submit only the most recent year's tax documents, but if your sponsor's income hovered around the poverty line last year and was higher in previous years, you may want to submit all three years' worth anyway.

USCIS prefers to see your sponsor's federal tax returns in the form of an IRS transcript (an IRS-generated summary of the return that your sponsor filed). Your sponsor can request a transcript by following the instructions on the IRS website at www.irs.gov/Individuals/Get-Transcript (offering ways to request them either online or by mail).

If for some reason you are unable to obtain transcripts, it's also acceptable to photocopy the returns you filed. In that case, however, you must include copies of your sponsor's W-2s, which are small printouts from his or her employer showing total earnings over the last year (these are usually attached to the front of the tax return). If you obtain the transcripts after filing your adjustment of status application, bring them to your interview. Also, if the sponsor wasn't legally required to submit a tax return, perhaps because his or her income was too low, submit a written explanation of this.

You will not need to include state tax forms.

2. Proof of Your Sponsor's Current Employment

As further proof that your sponsor will be able to contribute to your support, USCIS likes to see proof of current employment. Start with a letter from the employer describing the dates of employment, nature of the job, wages or salary, time worked per week, and prospects for advancement. Also include copies of pay stubs covering the last six months, or the most recent stub if it shows cumulative pay.

If your sponsor is self-employed, a tax return is acceptable. If possible, add a business license, copies of current receipts, business cards, or other documents that will show USCIS that your sponsor runs a legitimate, ongoing business.

Below, you'll find an example of a good employer's letter.

Sample Letter Confirming Employment

Hitting the Road Trucking
222 Plaza Place
Outthereville, MA 90000

May 22, 20xx

To Whom It May Concern:

Ron Goodley has been an employee of Hitting the Road Trucking since September 4, 20xx, a total of over five years. He has a full-time position as a driver. His salary is $45,000 per year. This position is permanent, and Ron's prospects for performance-based advancement and salary increases are excellent.

Very truly yours,

Bob Bossman

Bob Bossman
Personnel Manager
Hitting the Road Trucking

3. Proof of Your Sponsor's Assets and Their Value

Your sponsor's tax returns and proof of employment may be enough to convince USCIS that you'll be adequately taken care of. But if they're not, Form I-864 asks the sponsor to list any assets—your sponsor's or yours—that you will be relying upon as proof of financial adequacy. For example, if your spouse owns a home or other property, it will count toward meeting the income requirement. But listing these assets will not be enough by itself—the sponsor also has to prove ownership and supply evidence of how much they're worth.

- **Proof of ownership.** You or your sponsor can establish ownership by attaching copies of deeds or bills of sale.
- **Value.** The value of an item must be the likely sale price today, not how much you or your sponsor paid for it. For real estate, a current tax assessment can be used to show the property's value. If you believe that the assessment is too low, or for property other than real estate, hire a professional appraiser to prepare an estimate and report. For cars, you can use the value listed in the *Kelley Blue Book* (online at www.kbb.com).
- **Remaining debt.** The asset-owner must also document the amount of any debt remaining on any listed asset. If no debt remains, submit proof of the final payment—most likely a receipt from a bank or lender.
- **Calculating assets' worth for immigration purposes.** Asset dollars are considered to be worth either one-fifth or one-third as much as income dollars, depending on whether the sponsor is a U.S. citizen or not. If your petitioner is a U.S. citizen, you'll need to divide each dollar of assets by three in order to arrive at its worth for purposes of sponsoring you. For all other sponsors, you'll need to divide each dollar of assets by five. To qualify based on the value of assets, the total value of the assets must equal at least five times the difference between the total household income and the current *Poverty Guidelines* amount (or at least three times the difference if the petitioner is a U.S. citizen).

EXAMPLE: Anna Marie, who is a U.S. citizen, petitions for her husband in 2019. For that year's Affidavit of Support, Anna Marie needs to show that her income is at least $21,137. Unfortunately, Anna Marie is earning only $20,000 at her current job. If she is going to use assets to make up the difference, it isn't enough for Anna Marie to show that she has $1,137 in assets. She will need to show that she has at least three times that amount in assets—that is, $3,411. (If she were a permanent resident, she would need to show that she has at least five times that amount in assets—$5,685.)

4. Eligibility of Your Sponsor's Household Joint Sponsor, If Applicable

If your spouse does not meet the financial requirements of USCIS, he or she may get help from a relative or dependent who lives in the same household. This person will be known as a household joint sponsor. If necessary, your sponsor can enlist the help of more than one. With Forms I-864 and I-864a, you'll have to attach proof that:

- **The household joint sponsor(s) live with the primary sponsor.** You can use a copy of the rental agreement or lease showing the household member's name; or you can use copies of the household joint sponsor's documents that show the same address as the sponsor, such as a driver's license, school records, utility bills, or personal correspondence, and
- **The household joint sponsors are dependents of or related to the primary sponsor.** Joint sponsors who are dependents will be listed on the main sponsor's tax return, which will be enough proof by itself. For relatives who aren't listed as dependents, however, the best proof is a birth certificate. For example, if the sponsor

and household joint sponsor are parent and child, the child's birth certificate will suffice. If they are brother and sister, the combination of both their birth certificates will work, since these certificates together show that they share the same parent or parents.

The value of this option is that it allows the petitioner and the household member to combine their incomes in order to meet the *Poverty Guidelines* requirement. By contrast, other types of joint sponsor cannot combine their income with the petitioner; theirs must be sufficient on its own.

Keep in mind that for every household joint sponsor, you will need to provide federal tax returns, proof of employment, and proof of ownership and value of the joint sponsor's assets (if you list any on the form), just as you did for your spouse and/or primary sponsor.

5. Proof That You Are Eligible to Use the Adjustment of Status Procedure

USCIS will not accept your application at all unless you can satisfy them that you are among the few immigrants allowed to have their application processed by a USCIS office within the United States. There are four ways to meet this requirement.

- **You are married to a U.S. citizen and you entered legally.** To prove that you entered legally, include a copy of your passport, visa, and I-94 (either the card or a download from the U.S. Customs and Border Protection (CBP) website at www.cbp.gov/i94). People who entered using Border Crossing Cards should photocopy both sides of the card. Proving your legal entry is extremely important. If you don't have such proof, and aren't otherwise eligible to apply from within the United States, don't risk deportation—see a lawyer before going further.
- **You entered the U.S. with a K-1 fiancé visa and have since gotten married.** Attach copies of your Form I-129F approval notice and your marriage certificate.

- **You entered the U.S. with a K-3 visa.** Attach a copy of your Form I-129F approval notice and of your passport, visa, and I-94 card.
- **You are married to a U.S. permanent resident, your Priority Date is current, you entered legally, and you have maintained lawful status.** Include a copy of your passport, visa, and I-94 (see above paragraph).
- **You didn't enter legally, but you are grandfathered in.** You might be lucky enough to be able to use the adjustment of status procedure because a petition was on file with the INS (as USCIS was then called) by one of the legal deadlines described in Chapters 2, 9, 11, and 12. (This is very rare!) To prove that you are grandfathered in, include a copy of the Form I-130 that was filed in time to grandfather you in, any proof of its mailing, and the subsequent INS approval notice. In addition, if you were grandfathered in based on an I-130 that was filed between January 14, 1998 and April 30, 2001, include proof that you were physically present in the United States on December 21, 2000. If you were in the U.S. on December 21, 2000, but don't have any documents showing your presence on that exact date, submit proof that you were in the U.S. both before and after that date. Such proof might include copies of immigration stamps in your passport, hotel or rent receipts, medical records, school records, utility bills, tax returns, car registrations, traffic tickets, employment payroll documents, and anything else you think appropriate.

6. Fees

You'll need to submit the correct fee with your application. Because the fees go up frequently, check them on www.uscis.gov/forms. (Go to the page for Form I-485, which will give you complete fee instructions.) In mid-2019 the fee for most adults was $1,225, ($1,140 plus a biometrics fee of $85). However, if you are 79 years of age or older, you don't have to pay the biometrics fee, so your fee total would be $1,140. And if you have children under age 14, they pay $750 so long as they're filing along with you. (If they're not, they pay $1,140.)

Also, if you're one of the few people who are adjusting status based on the old law Section 245(i), and submitting Form I-485A, you'll need to pay the added penalty fee of $1,000.

The application fee includes applying for a work permit (using Form I-765) and Advance Parole (using Form I-131), so don't worry when you see instructions saying some people must pay a separate fee with these forms.

Write one check or money order to cover each person's application. Checks should be made payable to "U.S. Department of Homeland Security." Or, if you prefer to pay by credit card, do so using Form G-1450, Authorization for Credit Card Transactions, available at www.uscis.gov/g-1450.

7. Using the Checklist for Adjustment of Status Packet

The checklist below lists every form, document, and other item that you and your spouse will need to gather and submit to USCIS as your adjustment of status (green card) application. As you get items ready, check off the appropriate box. That way you'll ensure that nothing gets forgotten.

CHECKLIST

The checklist for adjustment of status is available online, as well; see the instructions in Appendix B of this book.

B. Line-by-Line Instructions for Adjustment of Status Forms

Here are instructions for filling out the forms and suggestions on how to answer many of the questions. If you don't need to use one of the forms covered below, such as Form I-864A, which is filled out by a household joint sponsor, just skip it.

1. Form I-485, Application to Register Permanent Residence or Adjust Status

Form I-485 is the primary application used for immigrants adjusting status in the United States. It collects basic information about your identity and admissibility. The information on this form all refers to you, the immigrating beneficiary.

WEB RESOURCE

Form I-485 is available on the USCIS website at www.uscis.gov/i-485. Below is a sample filled-in version of the relevant pages of this form.

Part 1

This asks for basic biographic information.

Family Name is your last name, or surname. Give your real address, not a mailing address. The **c/o** line is for the name of anyone you have asked to receive mail for you (so unless you've asked someone to do this, leave this line blank). The "Alternate and/or Safe Mailing Address" section is meant for people filing without their U.S. spouse's help due to abuse, who do not want to receive mail from USCIS at their home. If that describes you, see an attorney, because the procedures are different than described here. The questions regarding your arrival refer to your most recent entry to the United States. Your **Current USCIS Status** is the type of visa or status your stay is covered by, such as F-2 (student), "overstay" if the expiration date on your visa or permitted stay has passed, or "EWI" (entry without inspection) if you crossed the border illegally but somehow became eligible to use the adjustment of status procedure.

The "Nonimmigrant Visa Number" is the one in red ink on the right side of your visa stamp; *not* the "Control Number" at the top right.

Checklist for Adjustment of Status Packet

☐ Proof that you are eligible to use the adjustment of status procedure (see Section A5, above)

☐ One of the following:

    ☐ a copy of the USCIS approval notice if you already submitted Form I-130, Petition for Alien Relative (most likely in cases where your spouse is a permanent resident), or

    ☐ a copy of your previously filed Form I-129F and USCIS approval notice (which you'll have if you entered the United States on a fiancé visa), or

    ☐ Form I-130 itself, with additional documents and forms (which you should have completed according to instructions in Chapter 11 or 12, whichever was applicable), plus Form I-130A

☐ Form I-485, Application to Register Permanent Residence or Adjust Status (see Section B2, below, for line-by-line instructions)

☐ Form I-485, Supplement A (see Section B3, below, for line-by-line instructions), (only for people who must pay a penalty fee in order to use adjustment of status as an application procedure)

☐ Form I-693, Medical Exam (unless you entered as a fiancé, in which case your earlier medical exam is all you need; USCIS will have it on file; or you wish to wait until your interview to submit this) (see Section B4)

☐ If you're exempt from the Affidavit of Support requirement, Form I-864W (to explain why you don't need to fill out Form I-864) (see Section B5, below)

☐ Form I-864 or I-864EZ, Affidavit of Support Under Section 213A of the Act (see Section B6 for line-by-line instructions)

☐ Documents to accompany Form I-864:

    ☐ U.S. spouse or sponsor's federal income tax transcripts for the last year, or a copy of the actual return with W-2

    ☐ Proof of U.S. sponsor's current employment

    ☐ A list of assets (the sponsor's and/or the immigrant's), if they're being used to prove financial capacity

☐ Proof of location and ownership of any listed assets (including the sponsor's and the immigrant's)

☐ A list of the financial need-based public benefits programs and dates of receipt, if sponsor or sponsor's dependents have used such programs within the last three years

☐ Form I-864A, Contract Between Sponsor and Household Member, if needed because primary sponsor lacks financial capacity (see Section B7, below, for line-by-line instructions)

☐ Documents to accompany Form I-864A:

    ☐ Proof that the household joint sponsors live with the primary sponsor

    ☐ Proof that the household joint sponsors are related to the primary sponsor (if they're not already listed as dependents on the primary sponsor's tax return)

    ☐ Copies of the household joint sponsors' financial information (tax transcripts for the last year, proof of employment, proof of the ownership, value, and location of assets, if any were listed, and a list of need-based public benefits programs and dates of receipt, if used in the last three years)

☐ Form I-131 Application for Advance Parole (optional; see Section D2, below)

☐ I-765, Application for Employment Authorization (see Section B8, below, for line-by-line instructions)

☐ A copy of your birth certificate, with certified translation (see Chapter 4 on how to obtain vital records)

☐ Two photos of you (passport style)

☐ Application fees (currently $1,225 for most adults, but see USCIS website, www.uscis.gov/forms), plus Form G-1450, if you wish to pay by credit card

☐ Form G-1145 (optional, in order to receive an email or text message from USCIS advising you that your application has arrived)

Sample Form I-485, Application to Register Permanent Residence or Adjust Status—Page 1

Application to Register Permanent Residence or Adjust Status

Department of Homeland Security
U.S. Citizenship and Immigration Services

USCIS
Form I-485
OMB No. 1615-0023
Expires 06/30/2019

For USCIS Use Only		
Preference Category:	Receipt	Action Block
Country Chargeable:		
Priority Date:		
Date Form I-693 Received:		

	Section of Law	
☐ Applicant Interviewed ☐ Interview Waived	☐ INA 209(a)	☐ INA 249
Date of Initial Interview: _____	☐ INA 209(b)	☐ Sec. 13, Act of 9/11/57
	☐ INA 245(a)	☐ Cuban Adjustment Act
Lawful Permanent Resident as of: _____	☐ INA 245(i)	☐ Other _____
	☐ INA 245(m)	

To be completed by an attorney or accredited representative (if any).

☐ Select this box if Form G-28 is attached.	Volag Number (if any)	Attorney State Bar Number (if applicable)	Attorney or Accredited Representative USCIS Online Account Number (if any)

▶ **START HERE - Type or print in black ink.**   A-Number ▶ **A-** ☐☐☐☐☐☐☐☐☐

NOTE TO ALL APPLICANTS: If you do not completely fill out this application or fail to submit required documents listed in the Instructions, U.S. Citizenship and Immigration Services (USCIS) may deny your application.

Part 1. Information About You (Person applying for lawful permanent residence)

Your Current Legal Name (do not provide a nickname)

1.a.	Family Name (Last Name)	Mihov
1.b.	Given Name (First Name)	Anda
1.c.	Middle Name	Marina

Other Names You Have Used Since Birth (if applicable)

NOTE: Provide all other names you have ever used, including your family name at birth, other legal names, nicknames, aliases, and assumed names. If you need extra space to complete this section, use the space provided in **Part 14. Additional Information**.

2.a.	Family Name (Last Name)	Michelski
2.b.	Given Name (First Name)	
2.c.	Middle Name	

3.a.	Family Name (Last Name)	
3.b.	Given Name (First Name)	
3.c.	Middle Name	

4.a.	Family Name (Last Name)	
4.b.	Given Name (First Name)	
4.c.	Middle Name	

Other Information About You

5. Date of Birth (mm/dd/yyyy)   06/28/1991

NOTE: In addition to providing your actual date of birth, include any other dates of birth you have used in connection with any legal names or non-legal names in the space provided in **Part 14. Additional Information**.

6. Sex   ☐ Male   ☒ Female

7. City or Town of Birth
Sofia

Sample Form I-485, Application to Register Permanent Residence or Adjust Status—Page 2

A-Number ▶ A- [ ][ ][ ][ ][ ][ ][ ][ ]

Part 1. Information About You (Person applying for lawful permanent residence) (continued)

8. Country of Birth

> Bulgaria

9. Country of Citizenship or Nationality

> Bulgaria

10. Alien Registration Number (A-Number) (if any)

▶ A- [ ][ ][ ][ ][ ][ ][ ][ ]

NOTE: If you have **EVER** used other A-Numbers, include the additional A-Numbers in the space provided in **Part 14. Additional Information**.

11. USCIS Online Account Number (if any)

▶ [ ][ ][ ][ ][ ][ ][ ][ ][ ][ ][ ][ ]

12. U.S. Social Security Number (if any)

▶ [3][8][7][3][3][8][7][7]

U.S. Mailing Address

13.a. In Care Of Name (if any)

13.b. Street Number and Name | 68 Watertown Blvd.

13.c. ☐ Apt. ☐ Ste. ☐ Flr. |

13.d. City or Town | Erie

13.e. State | PA **13.f.** ZIP Code | 19380

Alternate and/or Safe Mailing Address

If you are applying based on the Violence Against Women Act (VAWA) or as a special immigrant juvenile, human trafficking victim (T nonimmigrant), or victim of a qualifying crime (U nonimmigrant) and you do not want USCIS to send notices about this application to your home, you may provide an alternative and/or safe mailing address.

14.a. In Care Of Name (if any)

14.b. Street Number and Name

14.c. ☐ Apt. ☐ Ste. ☐ Flr. |

14.d. City or Town

14.e. State | **14.f.** ZIP Code |

Recent Immigration History

Provide the information for **Item Numbers 15. - 19.** if you last entered the United States using a passport or travel document.

15. Passport Number Used at Last Arrival

> BG0000

16. Travel Document Number Used at Last Arrival

17. Expiration Date of this Passport or Travel Document (mm/dd/yyyy) | 06/30/2025

18. Country that Issued this Passport or Travel Document

> Bulgaria

19. Nonimmigrant Visa Number from this Passport (if any)

> M1231212

Place of Last Arrival into the United States

20.a. City or Town

> New York

20.b. State | NY

21. Date of Last Arrival (mm/dd/yyyy) | 11/04/2018

When I last arrived in the United States, I:

22.a. ☒ Was inspected at a port of entry and admitted as (for example, exchange visitor; visitor, waived through; temporary worker; student):

> H-1B

22.b. ☐ Was inspected at a port of entry and paroled as (for example, humanitarian parole, Cuban parole):

22.c. ☐ Came into the United States without admission or parole.

22.d. ☐ Other:

If you were issued a Form I-94 Arrival-Departure Record Number:

23.a. Form I-94 Arrival-Departure Record Number

▶ [1][2][3][2][3][1][2][3][1][1][1]

23.b. Expiration Date of Authorized Stay Shown on Form I-94 (mm/dd/yyyy) | 09/30/2020

23.c. Status on Form I-94 (for example, class of admission, or paroled, if paroled)

> H-1B

Sample Form I-485, Application to Register Permanent Residence or Adjust Status—Page 3

A-Number ▶ A- ☐☐☐☐☐☐☐☐☐

Part 1. Information About You (Person applying for lawful permanent residence) (continued)

24. What is your current immigration status (if it has changed since your arrival)?

Provide your name exactly as it appears on your Form I-94 (if any)

25.a.	Family Name (Last Name)	Mihov
25.b.	Given Name (First Name)	Anda
25.c.	Middle Name	M

Part 2. Application Type or Filing Category

NOTE: Attach a copy of the Form I-797 receipt or approval notice for the underlying petition or application, as appropriate.

I am applying to register lawful permanent residence or adjust status to that of a lawful permanent resident based on the following immigrant category (select **only one** box). (See the Form I-485 Instructions for more information, including any **Additional Instructions** that relate to the immigrant category you select.):

1.a. Family-based

☒ Immediate relative of a U.S. citizen, Form I-130

☐ Other relative of a U.S. citizen or relative of a lawful permanent resident under the family-based preference categories, Form I-130

☐ Person admitted to the United States as a fiancé(e) or child of a fiancé(e) of a U.S. citizen, Form I-129F (K-1/K-2 Nonimmigrant)

☐ Widow or widower of a U.S. citizen, Form I-360

☐ VAWA self-petitioner, Form I-360

1.b. Employment-based

☐ Alien worker, Form I-140

☐ Alien entrepreneur, Form I-526

1.c. Special Immigrant

☐ Religious worker, Form I-360

☐ Special immigrant juvenile, Form I-360

☐ Certain Afghan or Iraqi national, Form I-360

☐ Certain international broadcaster, Form I-360

☐ Certain G-4 international organization or family member or NATO-6 employee or family member, Form I-360

1.d. Asylee or Refugee

☐ Asylum status (INA section 208), Form I-589 or Form I-730

☐ Refugee status (INA section 207), Form I-590 or Form I-730

1.e. Human Trafficking Victim or Crime Victim

☐ Human trafficking victim (T Nonimmigrant), Form I-914 or derivative family member, Form I-914A

☐ Crime victim (U Nonimmigrant), Form I-918, derivative family member, Form I-918A, or qualifying family member, Form I-929

1.f. Special Programs Based on Certain Public Laws

☐ The Cuban Adjustment Act

☐ The Cuban Adjustment Act for battered spouses and children

☐ Dependent status under the Haitian Refugee Immigrant Fairness Act

☐ Dependent status under the Haitian Refugee Immigrant Fairness Act for battered spouses and children

☐ Lautenberg Parolees

☐ Diplomats or high ranking officials unable to return home (Section 13 of the Act of September 11, 1957)

☐ Indochinese Parole Adjustment Act of 2000

1.g. Additional Options

☐ Diversity Visa program

☐ Continuous residence in the United States since before January 1, 1972 ("Registry")

☐ Individual born in the United States under diplomatic status

☐ Other eligibility

2. Are you applying for adjustment based on the Immigration and Nationality Act (INA) section 245(i)?

☐ Yes ☒ No

NOTE: If you answered "Yes" to **Item Number 2.**, you must have selected a family-based, employment-based, special immigrant, or Diversity Visa immigrant category listed above in **Item Numbers 1.a. - 1.g.** as the basis for your application for adjustment of status. Fill out the rest of this application **and** Supplement A to Form I-485, Adjustment of Status Under Section 245(i) (Supplement A). For detailed filing instructions, read the Form I-485 Instructions (including any **Additional Instructions** that relate to the immigrant category that you selected in **Item Numbers 1.a. - 1.g.**) and Supplement A Instructions.

Sample Form I-485, Application to Register Permanent Residence or Adjust Status—Page 4

A-Number ▶ A- ☐☐☐☐☐☐☐☐☐

Part 2. Application Type or Filing Category (continued)

Information About Your Immigrant Category

If you are the **principal applicant**, provide the following information.

3. Receipt Number of Underlying Petition (if any)

n/a

4. Priority Date from Underlying Petition (if any) (mm/dd/yyyy)

n/a

If you are a **derivative applicant** (the spouse or unmarried child under 21 years of age of a principal applicant), provide the following information for the **principal applicant**.

Principal Applicant's Name

5.a. Family Name (Last Name)   n/a

5.b. Given Name (First Name)

5.c. Middle Name

6. Principal Applicant's A-Number (if any)
▶ A- ☐☐☐☐☐☐☐☐☐

7. Principal Applicant's Date of Birth (mm/dd/yyyy)

8. Receipt Number of Principal's Underlying Petition (if any)
▶ ☐☐☐☐☐☐☐☐☐☐☐☐☐

9. Priority Date of Principal Applicant's Underlying Petition (if any) (mm/dd/yyyy)

Part 3. Additional Information About You

1. Have you ever applied for an immigrant visa to obtain permanent resident status at a U.S. Embassy or U.S. Consulate abroad?   ☐ Yes ☒ No

If you answered "Yes" to **Item Number 1.**, complete **Item Numbers 2.a. - 4.** below. If you need extra space to complete this section, use the space provided in **Part 14. Additional Information**.

Location of U.S. Embassy or U.S. Consulate

2.a. City

2.b. Country

3. Decision (for example, approved, refused, denied, withdrawn)

4. Date of Decision (mm/dd/yyyy)

Address History

Provide physical addresses for everywhere you have lived during the last five years, whether inside or outside the United States. Provide your current address first. If you need extra space to complete this section, use the space provided in **Part 14. Additional Information**.

Physical Address 1 (current address)

5.a. Street Number and Name   68 Watertown Blvd.

5.b. ☒ Apt. ☐ Ste. ☐ Flr.   12

5.c. City or Town   Erie

5.d. State PA   **5.e.** ZIP Code   19380

5.f. Province

5.g. Postal Code

5.h. Country

USA

Dates of Residence

6.a. From (mm/dd/yyyy)   11/01/2015

6.b. To (mm/dd/yyyy)

Physical Address 2

7.a. Street Number and Name   n/a

7.b. ☐ Apt. ☐ Ste. ☐ Flr.

7.c. City or Town

7.d. State   **7.e.** ZIP Code

7.f. Province

7.g. Postal Code

7.h. Country

Sample Form I-485, Application to Register Permanent Residence or Adjust Status—Page 5

A-Number ▶ A- ☐☐☐☐☐☐☐☐☐

Part 3. Additional Information About You (continued)

Dates of Residence

8.a. From (mm/dd/yyyy) ☐

8.b. To (mm/dd/yyyy) ☐

Provide your most recent address outside the United States where you lived for more than one year (if not already listed above).

9.a. Street Number and Name | 42, Raiska Gradina St.

9.b. ☐ Apt. ☐ Ste. ☐ Flr. ☐

9.c. City or Town | Sofia

9.d. State ☐ **9.e.** ZIP Code ☐

9.f. Province ☐

9.g. Postal Code ☐

9.h. Country | Bulgaria

Dates of Residence

10.a. From (mm/dd/yyyy) | 02/01/2010

10.b. To (mm/dd/yyyy) | 10/31/2017

Employment History

Provide your employment history for the last five years, whether inside or outside the United States. Provide the most recent employment first. If you need extra space to complete this section, use the space provided in **Part 14. Additional Information**.

Employer 1 (current or most recent)

11. Name of Employer or Company

| Berlitz Cultural Center

Address of Employer or Company

12.a. Street Number and Name | Penn Center

12.b. ☐ Apt. ☒ Ste. ☐ Flr. | 800

12.c. City or Town | Pittsburgh

12.d. State | PA **12.e.** ZIP Code | 15276

12.f. Province ☐

12.g. Postal Code ☐

12.h. Country

| USA

13. Your Occupation

| Language Teacher

Dates of Employment

14.a. From (mm/dd/yyyy) | 12/06/2017

14.b. To (mm/dd/yyyy) | present

Employer 2

15. Name of Employer or Company

| n/a

Address of Employer or Company

16.a. Street Number and Name ☐

16.b. ☐ Apt. ☐ Ste. ☐ Flr. ☐

16.c. City or Town ☐

16.d. State ☐ **16.e.** ZIP Code ☐

16.f. Province ☐

16.g. Postal Code ☐

16.h. Country ☐

17. Your Occupation ☐

Dates of Employment

18.a. From (mm/dd/yyyy) ☐

18.b. To (mm/dd/yyyy) ☐

Sample Form I-485, Application to Register Permanent Residence or Adjust Status—Page 6

A-Number ▶ A- ☐☐☐☐☐☐☐☐☐

Part 3. Additional Information About You (continued)

Provide your most recent employment outside of the United States (if not already listed above).

19. Name of Employer or Company

Czech Cultural Center

Address of Employer or Company

20.a. Street Number and Name

123 Sveta Serdika Str.

20.b. ☐ Apt. ☐ Ste. ☐ Flr.

20.c. City or Town

Sofia

20.d. State [ ] **20.e.** ZIP Code [ ]

20.f. Province [ ]

20.g. Postal Code [ ]

20.h. Country

Bulgaria

21. Your Occupation

Language Teacher

Dates of Employment

22.a. From (mm/dd/yyyy) 08/01/2011

22.b. To (mm/dd/yyyy) 10/01/2017

Part 4. Information About Your Parents

Information About Your Parent 1

Parent 1's Legal Name

1.a. Family Name (Last Name) Michelski

1.b. Given Name (First Name) Anastasia

1.c. Middle Name [ ]

Parent 1's Name at Birth (if different than above)

2.a. Family Name (Last Name) Norova

2.b. Given Name (First Name) [ ]

2.c. Middle Name [ ]

3. Date of Birth (mm/dd/yyyy) 03/10/1972

4. Sex ☐ Male ☒ Female

5. City or Town of Birth

Sofia

6. Country of Birth

Bulgaria

7. Current City or Town of Residence (if living)

Sofia

8. Current Country of Residence (if living)

Bulgaria

Information About Your Parent 2

Parent 2's Legal Name

9.a. Family Name (Last Name) Michelski

9.b. Given Name (First Name) Liski

9.c. Middle Name [ ]

Parent 2's Name at Birth (if different than above)

10.a. Family Name (Last Name) [ ]

10.b. Given Name (First Name) [ ]

10.c. Middle Name [ ]

11. Date of Birth (mm/dd/yyyy) 12/24/1968

12. Sex ☒ Male ☐ Female

13. City or Town of Birth

Sofia

14. Country of Birth

Bulgaria

15. Current City or Town of Residence (if living)

Sofia

16. Current Country of Residence (if living)

Bulgaria

Sample Form I-485, Application to Register Permanent Residence or Adjust Status—Page 7

A-Number ▶ A- ☐☐☐☐☐☐☐☐☐

Part 5. Information About Your Marital History

1. What is your current marital status?

   ☐ Single, Never Married ☒ Married ☐ Divorced

   ☐ Widowed ☐ Marriage Annulled

   ☐ Legally Separated

2. If you are married, is your spouse a current member of the U.S. armed forces or U.S. Coast Guard?

   ☐ N/A ☐ Yes ☒ No

3. How many times have you been married (including annulled marriages and marriages to the same person)?

   [1]

Information About Your Current Marriage *(including if you are legally separated)*

If you are currently married, provide the following information about your current spouse.

Current Spouse's Legal Name

4.a. Family Name (Last Name) — Mihov

4.b. Given Name (First Name) — Grun

4.c. Middle Name — Branimir

5. A-Number (if any)

   ▶ A- ☐☐☐☐☐☐☐☐☐

6. Current Spouse's Date of Birth (mm/dd/yyyy)

   03/17/1992

7. Date of Marriage to Current Spouse (mm/dd/yyyy)

   12/17/2017

Current Spouse's Place of Birth

8.a. City or Town — Hershey

8.b. State or Province — PA

8.c. Country — USA

Place of Marriage to Current Spouse

9.a. City or Town — Hershey

9.b. State or Province — PA

9.c. Country — USA

10. Is your current spouse applying with you?

    ☐ Yes ☒ No

Information About Prior Marriages *(if any)*

If you have been married before, whether in the United States or in any other country, provide the following information about your prior spouse. If you have had more than one previous marriage, use the space provided in **Part 14. Additional Information** to provide the information below.

Prior Spouse's Legal Name (provide family name before marriage)

11.a. Family Name (Last Name) — n/a

11.b. Given Name (First Name) —

11.c. Middle Name —

12. Prior Spouse's Date of Birth (mm/dd/yyyy)

13. Date of Marriage to Prior Spouse (mm/dd/yyyy)

Place of Marriage to Prior Spouse

14.a. City or Town

14.b. State or Province

14.c. Country

15. Date Marriage with Prior Spouse Legally Ended (mm/dd/yyyy)

Sample Form I-485, Application to Register Permanent Residence or Adjust Status—Page 8

A-Number ▶ A- ☐☐☐☐☐☐☐☐☐

Part 5. Information About Your Marital History (continued)

Place Where Marriage with Prior Spouse Legally Ended

16.a. City or Town

16.b. State or Province

16.c. Country

Part 6. Information About Your Children

1. Indicate the total number of ALL living children (including adult sons and daughters) that you have.

NOTE: The term "children" includes all biological or legally adopted children, as well as current stepchildren, of any age, whether born in the United States or other countries, married or unmarried, living with you or elsewhere and includes any missing children and those born to you outside of marriage.

> 0

Provide the following information for each of your children. If you have more than three children, use the space provided in **Part 14. Additional Information**.

Child 1

Current Legal Name

2.a. Family Name (Last Name)

2.b. Given Name (First Name)

2.c. Middle Name

3. A-Number (if any)

▶ A- ☐☐☐☐☐☐☐☐☐

4. Date of Birth (mm/dd/yyyy)

5. Country of Birth

6. Is this child applying with you? ☐ Yes ☐ No

Child 2

Current Legal Name

7.a. Family Name (Last Name)

7.b. Given Name (First Name)

7.c. Middle Name

8. A-Number (if any)

▶ A- ☐☐☐☐☐☐☐☐☐

9. Date of Birth (mm/dd/yyyy)

10. Country of Birth

11. Is this child applying with you? ☐ Yes ☐ No

Child 3

Current Legal Name

12.a. Family Name (Last Name)

12.b. Given Name (First Name)

12.c. Middle Name

13. A-Number (if any)

▶ A- ☐☐☐☐☐☐☐☐☐

14. Date of Birth (mm/dd/yyyy)

15. Country of Birth

16. Is this child applying with you? ☐ Yes ☐ No

Part 7. Biographic Information

1. Ethnicity (Select **only one** box)

☐ Hispanic or Latino

☒ Not Hispanic or Latino

2. Race (Select **all applicable** boxes)

☒ White

☐ Asian

☐ Black or African American

☐ American Indian or Alaska Native

☐ Native Hawaiian or Other Pacific Islander

Sample Form I-485, Application to Register Permanent Residence or Adjust Status—Page 9

A-Number ▶ A-[ ][ ][ ][ ][ ][ ][ ][ ][ ]

Part 7. Biographic Information (continued)	Dates of Membership or Dates of Involvement

3. Height   Feet [5] Inches [8]

5.a. From (mm/dd/yyyy)   [12/01/2016]

4. Weight   Pounds [1][3][0]

5.b. To (mm/dd/yyyy)   [present]

5. Eye Color (Select **only one** box)

Organization 2

☐ Black   ☐ Blue   ☒ Brown

6. Name of Organization

☐ Gray   ☐ Green   ☐ Hazel

[ ]

☐ Maroon   ☐ Pink   ☐ Unknown/Other

7.a. City or Town

[ ]

6. Hair Color (Select **only one** box)

7.b. State or Province

☐ Bald (No hair)   ☐ Black   ☐ Blond

[ ]

☒ Brown   ☐ Gray   ☐ Red

7.c. Country

☐ Sandy   ☐ White   ☐ Unknown/Other

[ ]

8. Nature of Group

Part 8. General Eligibility and Inadmissibility Grounds

[ ]

1. Have you **EVER** been a member of, involved in, or in any way associated with any organization, association, fund, foundation, party, club, society, or similar group in the United States or in any other location in the world including any military service?   ☒ Yes ☐ No

Dates of Membership or Dates of Involvement

9.a. From (mm/dd/yyyy)   [ ]

9.b. To (mm/dd/yyyy)   [ ]

If you answered "Yes" to **Item Number 1.**, complete **Item Numbers 2. - 13.b.** below. If you need extra space to complete this section, use the space provided in **Part 14. Additional Information**. If you answered "No," but are unsure of your answer, provide an explanation of the events and circumstances in the space provided in **Part 14. Additional Information**.

Organization 3

10. Name of Organization

[ ]

11.a. City or Town

[ ]

Organization 1

2. Name of Organization

[Toastmasters International]

11.b. State or Province

[ ]

3.a. City or Town

[Erie]

11.c. Country

[ ]

3.b. State or Province

[PA]

12. Nature of Group

[ ]

3.c. Country

[USA]

Dates of Membership or Dates of Involvement

4. Nature of Group

[Public speaking and leadership skills]

13.a. From (mm/dd/yyyy)   [ ]

13.b. To (mm/dd/yyyy)   [ ]

Sample Form I-485, Application to Register Permanent Residence or Adjust Status—Page 10

A-Number ▶ A-☐☐☐☐☐☐☐☐☐

Part 8. General Eligibility and Inadmissibility Grounds (continued)

Answer **Item Numbers 14. - 80.b.** Choose the answer that you think is correct. If you answer "Yes" to any questions **(or if you answer "No," but are unsure of your answer)**, provide an explanation of the events and circumstances in the space provided in **Part 14. Additional Information**.

14. Have you **EVER** been denied admission to the United States? ☐ Yes ☒ No

15. Have you **EVER** been denied a visa to the United States? ☐ Yes ☒ No

16. Have you **EVER** worked in the United States without authorization? ☐ Yes ☒ No

17. Have you **EVER** violated the terms or conditions of your nonimmigrant status? ☐ Yes ☒ No

18. Are you presently or have you **EVER** been in removal, exclusion, rescission, or deportation proceedings? ☐ Yes ☒ No

19. Have you **EVER** been issued a final order of exclusion, deportation, or removal? ☐ Yes ☒ No

20. Have you **EVER** had a prior final order of exclusion, deportation, or removal reinstated? ☐ Yes ☒ No

21. Have you **EVER** held lawful permanent resident status which was later rescinded? ☐ Yes ☒ No

22. Have you **EVER** been granted voluntary departure by an immigration officer or an immigration judge but failed to depart within the allotted time? ☐ Yes ☒ No

23. Have you **EVER** applied for any kind of relief or protection from removal, exclusion, or deportation? ☐ Yes ☒ No

24.a. Have you **EVER** been a J nonimmigrant exchange visitor who was subject to the two-year foreign residence requirement? ☐ Yes ☒ No

If you answered "Yes" to **Item Number 24.a.**, complete **Item Numbers 24.b. - 24.c.** If you answered "No" to **Item Number 24.a.**, skip to **Item Number 25.**

24.b. Have you complied with the foreign residence requirement? ☐ Yes ☐ No

24.c. Have you been granted a waiver or has Department of State issued a favorable waiver recommendation letter for you? ☐ Yes ☐ No

Criminal Acts and Violations

For **Item Numbers 25. - 45.**, you must answer "Yes" to any question that applies to you, even if your records were sealed or otherwise cleared, or even if anyone, including a judge, law enforcement officer, or attorney, told you that you no longer have a record. You must also answer "Yes" to the following questions whether the action or offense occurred here in the United States or anywhere else in the world. If you answer "Yes" to **Item Numbers 25. - 45.**, use the space provided in **Part 14. Additional Information** to provide an explanation that includes why you were arrested, cited, detained, or charged; where you were arrested, cited, detained, or charged; when (date) the event occurred; and the outcome or disposition (for example, no charges filed, charges dismissed, jail, probation, community service).

25. Have you **EVER** been arrested, cited, charged, or detained for any reason by any law enforcement official (including but not limited to any U.S. immigration official or any official of the U.S. armed forces or U.S. Coast Guard)? ☐ Yes ☒ No

26. Have you **EVER** committed a crime of any kind (even if you were not arrested, cited, charged with, or tried for that crime)? ☐ Yes ☒ No

27. Have you **EVER** pled guilty to or been convicted of a crime or offense (even if the violation was subsequently expunged or sealed by a court, or if you were granted a pardon, amnesty, a rehabilitation decree, or other act of clemency)? ☐ Yes ☒ No

NOTE: If you were the beneficiary of a pardon, amnesty, a rehabilitation decree, or other act of clemency, provide documentation of that post-conviction action.

28. Have you **EVER** been ordered punished by a judge or had conditions imposed on you that restrained your liberty (such as a prison sentence, suspended sentence, house arrest, parole, alternative sentencing, drug or alcohol treatment, rehabilitative programs or classes, probation, or community service)? ☐ Yes ☒ No

29. Have you **EVER** been a defendant or the accused in a criminal proceeding (including pre-trial diversion, deferred prosecution, deferred adjudication, or any withheld adjudication)? ☐ Yes ☒ No

30. Have you **EVER** violated (or attempted or conspired to violate) any controlled substance law or regulation of a state, the United States, or a foreign country? ☐ Yes ☒ No

Sample Form I-485, Application to Register Permanent Residence or Adjust Status—Page 11

A-Number ▶ A-☐☐☐☐☐☐☐☐☐

Part 8. General Eligibility and Inadmissibility Grounds (continued)

31. Have you **EVER** been convicted of two or more offenses (other than purely political offenses) for which the combined sentences to confinement were five years or more? ☐ Yes ☒ No

32. Have you **EVER** illicitly (illegally) trafficked or benefited from the trafficking of any controlled substances, such as chemicals, illegal drugs, or narcotics? ☐ Yes ☒ No

33. Have you **EVER** knowingly aided, abetted, assisted, conspired, or colluded in the illicit trafficking of any illegal narcotic or other controlled substances? ☐ Yes ☒ No

34. Are you the spouse, son, or daughter of a foreign national who illicitly trafficked or aided (or otherwise abetted, assisted, conspired, or colluded) in the illicit trafficking of a controlled substance, such as chemicals, illegal drugs, or narcotics and you obtained, within the last five years, any financial or other benefit from the illegal activity of your spouse or parent, although you knew or reasonably should have known that the financial or other benefit resulted from the illicit activity of your spouse or parent? ☐ Yes ☒ No

35. Have you **EVER** engaged in prostitution or are you coming to the United States to engage in prostitution? ☐ Yes ☒ No

36. Have you **EVER** directly or indirectly procured (or attempted to procure) or imported prostitutes or persons for the purpose of prostitution? ☐ Yes ☒ No

37. Have you **EVER** received any proceeds or money from prostitution? ☐ Yes ☒ No

38. Do you intend to engage in illegal gambling or any other form of commercialized vice, such as prostitution, bootlegging, or the sale of child pornography, while in the United States? ☐ Yes ☒ No

39. Have you **EVER** exercised immunity (diplomatic or otherwise) to avoid being prosecuted for a criminal offense in the United States? ☐ Yes ☒ No

40. Have you **EVER**, while serving as a foreign government official, been responsible for or directly carried out violations of religious freedoms? ☐ Yes ☒ No

41. Have you **EVER** induced by force, fraud, or coercion (or otherwise been involved in) the trafficking of persons for commercial sex acts? ☐ Yes ☒ No

42. Have you **EVER** trafficked a person into involuntary servitude, peonage, debt bondage, or slavery? Trafficking includes recruiting, harboring, transporting, providing, or obtaining a person for labor or services through the use of force, fraud, or coercion. ☐ Yes ☒ No

43. Have you **EVER** knowingly aided, abetted, assisted, conspired, or colluded with others in trafficking persons for commercial sex acts or involuntary servitude, peonage, debt bondage, or slavery? ☐ Yes ☒ No

44. Are you the spouse, son or daughter of a foreign national who engaged in the trafficking of persons and have received or obtained, within the last five years, any financial or other benefits from the illicit activity of your spouse or your parent, although you knew or reasonably should have known that this benefit resulted from the illicit activity of your spouse or parent? ☐ Yes ☒ No

45. Have you **EVER** engaged in money laundering or have you **EVER** knowingly aided, assisted, conspired, or colluded with others in money laundering or do you seek to enter the United States to engage in such activity? ☐ Yes ☒ No

Security and Related

Do you intend to:

46.a. Engage in any activity that violates or evades any law relating to espionage (including spying) or sabotage in the United States? ☐ Yes ☒ No

46.b. Engage in any activity in the United States that violates or evades any law prohibiting the export from the United States of goods, technology, or sensitive information? ☐ Yes ☒ No

46.c. Engage in any activity whose purpose includes opposing, controlling, or overthrowing the U.S. Government by force, violence, or other unlawful means while in the United States? ☐ Yes ☒ No

46.d. Engage in any activity that could endanger the welfare, safety, or security of the United States? ☐ Yes ☒ No

46.e. Engage in any other unlawful activity? ☐ Yes ☒ No

47. Are you engaged in or, upon your entry into the United States, do you intend to engage in any activity that could have potentially serious adverse foreign policy consequences for the United States? ☐ Yes ☒ No

Sample Form I-485, Application to Register Permanent Residence or Adjust Status—Page 12

A-Number ▶ A- ☐☐☐☐☐☐☐☐☐

Part 8. General Eligibility and Inadmissibility Grounds (continued)

Have you **EVER**:

48.a. Committed, threatened to commit, attempted to commit, conspired to commit, incited, endorsed, advocated, planned, or prepared any of the following: hijacking, sabotage, kidnapping, political assassination, or use of a weapon or explosive to harm another individual or cause substantial damage to property? ☐ Yes ☒ No

48.b. Participated in, or been a member of, a group or organization that did any of the activities described in **Item Number 48.a.**? ☐ Yes ☒ No

48.c. Recruited members or asked for money or things of value for a group or organization that did any of the activities described in **Item Number 48.a.**? ☐ Yes ☒ No

48.d. Provided money, a thing of value, services or labor, or any other assistance or support for any of the activities described in **Item Number 48.a.**? ☐ Yes ☒ No

48.e. Provided money, a thing of value, services or labor, or any other assistance or support for an individual, group, or organization who did any of the activities described in **Item Number 48.a.**? ☐ Yes ☒ No

49. Have you **EVER** received any type of military, paramilitary, or weapons training? ☐ Yes ☒ No

50. Do you intend to engage in any of the activities listed in any part of **Item Numbers 48.a. - 49.**? ☐ Yes ☒ No

NOTE: If you answered "Yes" to any part of **Item Numbers 46.a. - 50.**, explain what you did, including the dates and location of the circumstances, or what you intend to do in the space provided in **Part 14. Additional Information**.

Are you the spouse or child of an individual who **EVER**:

51.a. Committed, threatened to commit, attempted to commit, conspired to commit, incited, endorsed, advocated, planned, or prepared any of the following: hijacking, sabotage, kidnapping, political assassination, or use of a weapon or explosive to harm another individual or cause substantial damage to property? ☐ Yes ☒ No

51.b. Participated in, or been a member or a representative of a group or organization that did any of the activities described in **Item Number 51.a.**? ☐ Yes ☒ No

51.c. Recruited members, or asked for money or things of value, for a group or organization that did any of the activities described in **Item Number 51.a.**? ☐ Yes ☒ No

51.d. Provided money, a thing of value, services or labor, or any other assistance or support for any of the activities described in **Item Number 51.a.**? ☐ Yes ☒ No

51.e. Provided money, a thing of value, services or labor, or any other assistance or support to an individual, group, or organization who did any of the activities described in **Item Number 51.a.**? ☐ Yes ☒ No

51.f. Received any type of military, paramilitary, or weapons training from a group or organization that did any of the activities described in **Item Number 51.a.**? ☐ Yes ☒ No

NOTE: If you answered "Yes" to any part of **Item Number 51.**, explain the relationship and what occurred, including the dates and location of the circumstances, in the space provided in **Part 14. Additional Information.**

52. Have you **EVER** assisted or participated in selling, providing, or transporting weapons to any person who, to your knowledge, used them against another person? ☐ Yes ☒ No

53. Have you **EVER** worked, volunteered, or otherwise served in any prison, jail, prison camp, detention facility, labor camp, or any other situation that involved detaining persons? ☐ Yes ☒ No

54. Have you **EVER** been a member of, assisted, or participated in any group, unit, or organization of any kind in which you or other persons used any type of weapon against any person or threatened to do so? ☐ Yes ☒ No

55. Have you **EVER** served in, been a member of, assisted, or participated in any military unit, paramilitary unit, police unit, self-defense unit, vigilante unit, rebel group, guerilla group, militia, insurgent organization, or any other armed group? ☐ Yes ☒ No

56. Have you **EVER** been a member of, or in any way affiliated with, the Communist Party or any other totalitarian party (in the United States or abroad)? ☐ Yes ☒ No

57. During the period from March 23, 1933 to May 8, 1945, did you ever order, incite, assist, or otherwise participate in the persecution of any person because of race, religion, national origin, or political opinion, in association with either the Nazi government of Germany or any organization or government associated or allied with the Nazi government of Germany? ☐ Yes ☒ No

Sample Form I-485, Application to Register Permanent Residence or Adjust Status—Page 13

A-Number ▶ A- □□□□□□□□□

Part 8. General Eligibility and Inadmissibility Grounds (continued)

Have you **EVER** ordered, incited, called for, committed, assisted, helped with, or otherwise participated in any of the following:

58.a. Acts involving torture or genocide? ☐ Yes ☒ No

58.b. Killing any person? ☐ Yes ☒ No

58.c. Intentionally and severely injuring any person? ☐ Yes ☒ No

58.d. Engaging in any kind of sexual contact or relations with any person who did not consent or was unable to consent, or was being forced or threatened? ☐ Yes ☒ No

58.e. Limiting or denying any person's ability to exercise religious beliefs? ☐ Yes ☒ No

59. Have you **EVER** recruited, enlisted, conscripted, or used any person under 15 years of age to serve in or help an armed force or group? ☐ Yes ☒ No

60. Have you **EVER** used any person under 15 years of age to take part in hostilities, or to help or provide services to people in combat? ☐ Yes ☒ No

NOTE: If you answered "Yes" to any part of **Item Numbers 52. - 60.**, explain what occurred, including the dates and location of the circumstances, in the space provided in **Part 14. Additional Information.**

Public Assistance

61. Have you received public assistance in the United States from any source, including the U.S. Government or any state, county, city, or municipality (other than emergency medical treatment)? ☐ Yes ☒ No

62. Are you likely to receive public assistance in the future in the United States from any source, including the U.S. Government or any state, county, city, or municipality (other than emergency medical treatment)? ☐ Yes ☒ No

Illegal Entries and Other Immigration Violations

63.a. Have you **EVER** failed or refused to attend or to remain in attendance at any removal proceeding filed against you on or after April 1, 1997? ☐ Yes ☒ No

63.b. If your answer to **Item Number 63.a.** is "Yes," do you believe you had reasonable cause? ☐ Yes ☒ No

63.c. If your answer to **Item Number 63.b.** is "Yes," attach a written statement explaining why you had reasonable cause.

64. Have you **EVER** submitted fraudulent or counterfeit documentation to any U.S. Government official to obtain or attempt to obtain any immigration benefit, including a visa or entry into the United States? ☐ Yes ☒ No

65. Have you **EVER** lied about, concealed, or misrepresented any information on an application or petition to obtain a visa, other documentation required for entry into the United States, admission to the United States, or any other kind of immigration benefit? ☐ Yes ☒ No

66. Have you **EVER** falsely claimed to be a U.S. citizen (in writing or any other way)? ☐ Yes ☒ No

67. Have you **EVER** been a stowaway on a vessel or aircraft arriving in the United States? ☐ Yes ☒ No

68. Have you **EVER** knowingly encouraged, induced, assisted, abetted, or aided any foreign national to enter or to try to enter the United States illegally (alien smuggling)? ☐ Yes ☒ No

69. Are you under a final order of civil penalty for violating INA section 274C for use of fraudulent documents? ☐ Yes ☒ No

Removal, Unlawful Presence, or Illegal Reentry After Previous Immigration Violations

70. Have you **EVER** been excluded, deported, or removed from the United States or have you ever departed the United States on your own after having been ordered excluded, deported, or removed from the United States? ☐ Yes ☒ No

71. Have you **EVER** entered the United States without being inspected and admitted or paroled? ☐ Yes ☒ No

Since April 1, 1997, have you been unlawfully present in the United States:

72.a. For more than 180 days but less than a year, and then departed the United States? ☐ Yes ☒ No

72.b. For one year or more and then departed the United States? ☐ Yes ☒ No

NOTE: You were unlawfully present in the United States if you entered the United States without being inspected and admitted or inspected and paroled, or if you legally entered the United States but you stayed longer than permitted.

Sample Form I-485, Application to Register Permanent Residence or Adjust Status—Page 14

A-Number ▶ A- □□□□□□□□□

Part 8. General Eligibility and Inadmissibility Grounds (continued)

Since April 1, 1997, have you **EVER** reentered or attempted to reenter the United States without being inspected and admitted or paroled after:

73.a. Having been unlawfully present in the United States for more than one year in the aggregate? ☐ Yes ☒ No

73.b. Having been deported, excluded, or removed from the United States? ☐ Yes ☒ No

Miscellaneous Conduct

74. Do you plan to practice polygamy in the United States? ☐ Yes ☒ No

75. Are you accompanying another foreign national who requires your protection or guardianship but who is inadmissible after being certified by a medical officer as being helpless from sickness, physical or mental disability, or infancy, as described in INA section 232(c)? ☐ Yes ☒ No

76. Have you **EVER** assisted in detaining, retaining, or withholding custody of a U.S. citizen child outside the United States from a U.S. citizen who has been granted custody of the child? ☐ Yes ☒ No

77. Have you **EVER** voted in violation of any Federal, state, or local constitutional provision, statute, ordinance, or regulation in the United States? ☐ Yes ☒ No

78. Have you **EVER** renounced U.S. citizenship to avoid being taxed by the United States? ☐ Yes ☒ No

Have you **EVER**:

79.a. Applied for exemption or discharge from training or service in the U.S. armed forces or in the U.S. National Security Training Corps on the ground that you are a foreign national? ☐ Yes ☒ No

79.b. Been relieved or discharged from such training or service on the ground that you are a foreign national? ☐ Yes ☒ No

79.c. Been convicted of desertion from the U.S. armed forces? ☐ Yes ☒ No

80.a. Have you **EVER** left or remained outside the United States to avoid or evade training or service in the U.S. armed forces in time of war or a period declared by the President to be a national emergency? ☐ Yes ☒ No

80.b. If your answer to **Item Number 80.a.** is "Yes," what was your nationality or immigration status immediately before you left (for example, U.S. citizen or national, lawful permanent resident, nonimmigrant, parolee, present without admission or parole, or any other status)?

☐

Part 9. Accommodations for Individuals With Disabilities and/or Impairments

NOTE: Read the information in the Form I-485 Instructions before completing this part.

1. Are you requesting an accommodation because of your disabilities and/or impairments? ☐ Yes ☒ No

If you answered "Yes" to **Item Number 1.**, select any applicable box in **Item Numbers 2.a. - 2.c.** and provide an answer.

2.a. ☐ I am deaf or hard of hearing and request the following accommodation. (If you are requesting a sign-language interpreter, indicate for which language (for example, American Sign Language).):

_____

_____

2.b. ☐ I am blind or have low vision and request the following accommodation:

_____

_____

2.c. ☐ I have another type of disability and/or impairment. (Describe the nature of your disability and/or impairment and the accommodation you are requesting.)

_____

_____

Sample Form I-485, Application to Register Permanent Residence or Adjust Status—Page 15

A-Number ▶ A-

Part 10. Applicant's Statement, Contact Information, Declaration, Certification, and Signature

NOTE: Read the **Penalties** section of the Form I-485 Instructions before completing this part. You must file Form I-485 while in the United States.

Applicant's Statement

NOTE: Select the box for either **Item Number 1.a.** or **1.b.** If applicable, select the box for **Item Number 2.**

1.a. ☒ I can read and understand English, and I have read and understand every question and instruction on this application and my answer to every question.

1.b. ☐ The interpreter named in **Part 11.** read to me every question and instruction on this application and my answer to every question in

_____,

a language in which I am fluent, and I understood everything.

2. ☐ At my request, the preparer named in **Part 12.**,

_____,

prepared this application for me based only upon information I provided or authorized.

Applicant's Contact Information

3. Applicant's Daytime Telephone Number

6105551122

4. Applicant's Mobile Telephone Number (if any)

5. Applicant's Email Address (if any)

Applicant's Declaration and Certification

Copies of any documents I have submitted are exact photocopies of unaltered, original documents, and I understand that USCIS may require that I submit original documents to USCIS at a later date. Furthermore, I authorize the release of any information from any and all of my records that USCIS may need to determine my eligibility for the immigration benefit that I seek.

I understand that if I am a male who is 18 to 26 years of age, submitting this application will automatically register me with the Selective Service System as required by the Military Selective Service Act.

I furthermore authorize release of information contained in this application, in supporting documents, and in my USCIS records, to other entities and persons where necessary for the administration and enforcement of U.S. immigration law.

I understand that USCIS may require me to appear for an appointment to take my biometrics (fingerprints, photograph, and/or signature) and, at that time, if I am required to provide biometrics, I will be required to sign an oath reaffirming that:

1) I reviewed and understood all of the information contained in, and submitted with, my application; and

2) All of this information was complete, true, and correct at the time of filing.

I certify , under penalty of perjury , that all of the information in my application and any document submitted with it were provided or authorized by me, that I reviewed and understand all of the information contained in, and submitted with, my application and that all of this information is complete, true, and correct.

Applicant's Signature

6.a. Applicant's Signature (sign in ink)

➡ _Anda M. Mihov_

6.b. Date of Signature (mm/dd/yyyy)   05/19/2019

NOTE TO ALL APPLICANTS: If you do not completely fill out this application or fail to submit required documents listed in the Instructions, USCIS may deny your application.

Part 11. Interpreter's Contact Information, Certification, and Signature

Provide the following information about the interpreter.

Interpreter's Full Name

1.a. Interpreter's Family Name (Last Name)

1.b. Interpreter's Given Name (First Name)

2. Interpreter's Business or Organization Name (if any)

Part 2

Put an "X" in **the first box under 1.a** if you did not use a K-1 fiancé visa to enter the United States (in other words, if you are either an immediate relative or a preference relative with a current Priority Date and a right to use the adjustment of status procedure). Put an "X" in **the third box under 1.a** if you entered on a K-1 fiancé visa and are applying for your green card based on having married this fiancé in the United States.

Question 2 is for the Supplement A to Form I-485 described in the next section. "Information About Your Immigrant Category" does not apply if you are submitting your I-130 and I-485 together, in which case enter "N/A" in those boxes. If the U.S. spouse previously submitted the I-130, the "Receipt Number" is the 13-digit one starting with MSC, WAC, EAC, or another three-letter sequence that you'll find on the I-797 Receipt Notice USCIS sent after receiving the petition and filing fee. The Priority Date comes from the date USCIS received the I-130 petition.

Part 3

Items 1-4 in Part 3 ask about prior permanent resident applications you may have submitted. If there are none, check "no" and move on. Part 3 then asks for your residential and employment history in the U.S. and abroad.

Parts 4-7

Self-explanatory.

Part 8

Part of the purpose here is to weed out terrorists. If you've been with an organization that has a violent wing or advocates violence, even if you were only in its nonviolent subgroup, consult a lawyer. Incidentally, you can improve the USCIS officer's opinion of you by listing in Part 8, 1-13 any organizations that you have volunteered with, such as religious organizations. This shows that you are a moral person. For the rest of the questions in "Part 8"—14–80—hopefully your answers are all "no." If they aren't, don't lie—see a lawyer.

Part 9

If you need special accommodations for your interview because of a disability or impairment, explain what you need in this section.

Part 10

This is where you, the applicant, sign. There is also a place for an interpreter to sign in Part 11, if you relied on an interpreter to answer the questions.

2. Form I-485, Supplement A

You will probably not need to complete this form. Do so only if you are one of those few people who entered illegally, but are grandfathered in because you happen to possess an approved petition from a pre-January 14, 1998, or pre-April 30, 2001, filing (see Chapter 9, 11, or 12, whichever fits your current status, to review this issue).

> EXAMPLE: Danuta came to the United States by flying to Canada as a tourist, then sneaking across the Canadian border in the trunk of someone's car. She entered without inspection, or illegally. Danuta married Johan, who was then a U.S. permanent resident. Johan began the application process for Danuta by filing a petition (Form I-130) for Danuta before January 14, 1998, and the petition was approved.
>
> Luckily for Danuta, the date when Johan filed the petition is early enough that she is grandfathered into being eligible to use the adjustment of status procedure (apply for her green card in the United States). Now Danuta's Priority Date is current. Danuta must use Form I-485 Supplement A and pay an extra fee in order to do her green card processing in the United States. But Danuta is lucky—many people with later-filed applications must process in overseas consulates, where the consequence of their illegal entry and stay is that they may be prevented from returning for three or ten years.

WEB RESOURCE

Form I-485A is available on the USCIS website at www.uscis.gov/i-485supa. Below is a sample filled-in version of the relevant pages of this form.

Sample Supplement A to Form I-485—Page 1

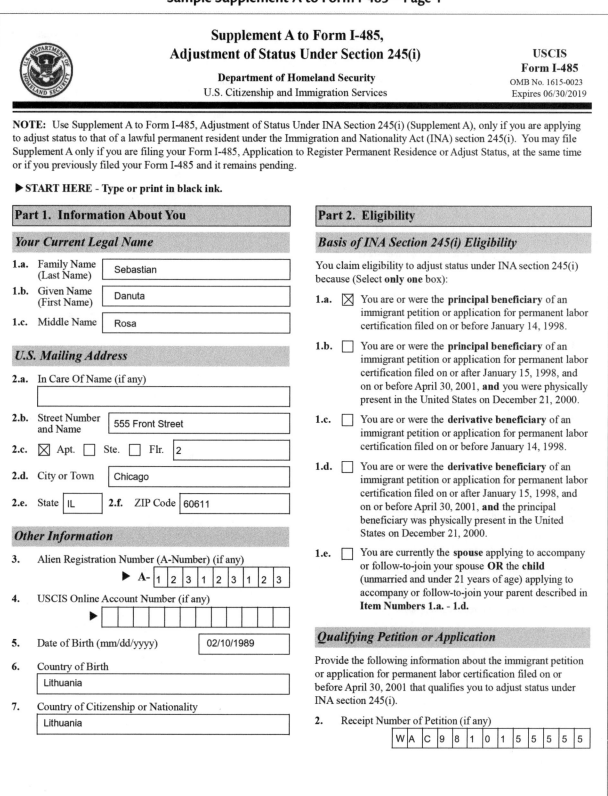

Supplement A to Form I-485, Adjustment of Status Under Section 245(i)

Department of Homeland Security
U.S. Citizenship and Immigration Services

**USCIS
Form I-485**

OMB No. 1615-0023
Expires 06/30/2019

NOTE: Use Supplement A to Form I-485, Adjustment of Status Under INA Section 245(i) (Supplement A), only if you are applying to adjust status to that of a lawful permanent resident under the Immigration and Nationality Act (INA) section 245(i). You may file Supplement A only if you are filing your Form I-485, Application to Register Permanent Residence or Adjust Status, at the same time or if you previously filed your Form I-485 and it remains pending.

▶ **START HERE** - Type or print in black ink.

Part 1. Information About You

Your Current Legal Name

1.a. Family Name (Last Name) — Sebastian

1.b. Given Name (First Name) — Danuta

1.c. Middle Name — Rosa

U.S. Mailing Address

2.a. In Care Of Name (if any)

2.b. Street Number and Name — 555 Front Street

2.c. ☒ Apt. ☐ Ste. ☐ Flr. — 2

2.d. City or Town — Chicago

2.e. State — IL   **2.f.** ZIP Code — 60611

Other Information

3. Alien Registration Number (A-Number) (if any)
▶ A- 1 2 3 1 2 3 1 2 3

4. USCIS Online Account Number (if any)
▶ [ ][ ][ ][ ][ ][ ][ ][ ][ ][ ][ ][ ]

5. Date of Birth (mm/dd/yyyy) — 02/10/1989

6. Country of Birth — Lithuania

7. Country of Citizenship or Nationality — Lithuania

Part 2. Eligibility

Basis of INA Section 245(i) Eligibility

You claim eligibility to adjust status under INA section 245(i) because (Select **only one** box):

1.a. ☒ You are or were the **principal beneficiary** of an immigrant petition or application for permanent labor certification filed on or before January 14, 1998.

1.b. ☐ You are or were the **principal beneficiary** of an immigrant petition or application for permanent labor certification filed on or after January 15, 1998, and on or before April 30, 2001, **and** you were physically present in the United States on December 21, 2000.

1.c. ☐ You are or were the **derivative beneficiary** of an immigrant petition or application for permanent labor certification filed on or before January 14, 1998.

1.d. ☐ You are or were the **derivative beneficiary** of an immigrant petition or application for permanent labor certification filed on or after January 15, 1998, and on or before April 30, 2001, **and** the principal beneficiary was physically present in the United States on December 21, 2000.

1.e. ☐ You are currently the **spouse** applying to accompany or follow-to-join your spouse **OR** the **child** (unmarried and under 21 years of age) applying to accompany or follow-to-join your parent described in **Item Numbers 1.a. - 1.d.**

Qualifying Petition or Application

Provide the following information about the immigrant petition or application for permanent labor certification filed on or before April 30, 2001 that qualifies you to adjust status under INA section 245(i).

2. Receipt Number of Petition (if any)
W A C 9 8 1 0 1 5 5 5 5 5

Sample Supplement A to Form I-485—Page 2

Part 2. Eligibility (continued)

Information on Principal Beneficiary of Petition or Application

3.a. Family Name (Last Name)   Sebastian

3.b. Given Name (First Name)   Danuta

3.c. Middle Name   Rosa

4. Principal Applicant's A-Number (if any)

▶ A- 1 2 3 1 2 3 1 2 3

Immigrant Category

5. Type or print the family-based, employment-based, special immigrant, or Diversity Visa immigrant category you selected on Form I-485, **Part 2. Application Type or Filing Category, Item Numbers 1.a. - 1.g.**

Family-based

Part 3. Bars to Adjustment

You are applying to adjust under INA section 245(i) because one or more of the following bars to adjustment apply to you (Select **all applicable** boxes):

1.a. ☐ You last entered the United States without being admitted or paroled after inspection by an immigration officer.

1.b. ☐ You last entered the United States as a nonimmigrant crewman.

1.c. ☐ You are now employed or have ever been employed in the United States without authorization.

1.d. ☒ You are not in lawful immigration status on the date of filing your application for adjustment of status.

1.e. ☒ You have ever failed to continuously maintain a lawful status since entry into the United States, unless your failure to maintain status was through no fault of your own or for technical reasons.

1.f. ☐ You were last admitted to the United States in transit without a visa.

1.g. ☐ You were last admitted to the United States as a nonimmigrant visitor without a visa under the Guam and Commonwealth of the Northern Mariana Islands Visa Waiver Program, and you are not a Canadian citizen.

1.h. ☐ You were last admitted to the United States as a nonimmigrant visitor without a visa under the Visa Waiver Program (See **travel.state.gov/content/visas/english/visit/visa-waiver-program.html**).

1.i. ☐ You are seeking employment-based adjustment of status and you are not maintaining a lawful nonimmigrant status on the date of filing your application for adjustment of status.

1.j. ☒ You have ever violated the terms of your nonimmigrant status.

Part 4. Applicant's Statement, Contact Information, Declaration, Certification, and Signature

NOTE: Read the **Penalties** section of the Supplement A Instructions before completing this part. You must file Supplement A while in the United States.

Applicant's Statement

NOTE: Select the box for either **Item Number 1.a.** or **1.b.** If applicable, select the box for **Item Number 2.**

1.a. ☒ I can read and understand English, and I have read and understand every question and instruction on this supplement and my answer to every question.

1.b. ☐ The interpreter named in **Part 5.** read to me every question and instruction on this supplement and my answer to every question in

[   ],

a language in which I am fluent, and I understood everything.

2. ☐ At my request, the preparer named in **Part 6.**,

[   ],

prepared this supplement for me based only upon information I provided or authorized.

Applicant's Contact Information

3. Applicant's Daytime Telephone Number

3125555555

4. Applicant's Mobile Telephone Number (if any)

5. Applicant's Email Address (if any)

danuta@email.com

Sample Supplement A to Form I-485—Page 3

Part 4. Applicant's Statement, Contact Information, Declaration, Certification, and Signature (continued)

Applicant's Declaration and Certification

Copies of any documents I have submitted are exact photocopies of unaltered, original documents, and I understand that U.S. Citizenship and Immigration Services (USCIS) may require that I submit original documents to USCIS at a later date. Furthermore, I authorize the release of any information from any and all of my records that USCIS may need to determine my eligibility for the immigration benefit that I seek.

I furthermore authorize release of information contained in this supplement, in supporting documents, and in my USCIS records, to other entities and persons where necessary for the administration and enforcement of U.S. immigration law.

I certify, under penalty of perjury, that all of the information in my supplement and any document submitted with it were provided or authorized by me, that I reviewed and understand all of the information contained in, and submitted with, my supplement and that all of this information is complete, true, and correct.

Applicant's Signature

6.a. Applicant's Signature (sign in ink)

➡ *Danuta R. Sebastian*

6.b. Date of Signature (mm/dd/yyyy)   06/12/2019

NOTE TO ALL APPLICANTS: If you do not completely fill out this supplement or fail to submit required documents listed in the Instructions, USCIS may deny your Form I-485.

Part 5. Interpreter's Contact Information, Certification, and Signature

Provide the following information about the interpreter.

Interpreter's Full Name

1.a. Interpreter's Family Name (Last Name)

1.b. Interpreter's Given Name (First Name)

2. Interpreter's Business or Organization Name (if any)

Interpreter's Mailing Address

3.a. Street Number and Name

3.b. ☐ Apt. ☐ Ste. ☐ Flr.

3.c. City or Town

3.d. State

3.e. ZIP Code

3.f. Province

3.g. Postal Code

3.h. Country

Interpreter's Contact Information

4. Interpreter's Daytime Telephone Number

5. Interpreter's Mobile Telephone Number (if any)

6. Interpreter's Email Address (if any)

Interpreter's Certification

I certify, under penalty of perjury, that:

I am fluent in English and _____, which is the same language specified in **Part 4.**, **Item Number 1.b.**, and I have read to this applicant in the identified language every question and instruction on this supplement and his or her answer to every question. The applicant informed me that he or she understands every instruction, question, and answer on the supplement, including the **Applicant's Declaration and Certification**, and has verified the accuracy of every answer.

Interpreter's Signature

7.a. Interpreter's Signature (sign in ink)

7.b. Date of Signature (mm/dd/yyyy)

Part 1

Review our instructions for Forms I-130 and I-485.

Parts 2-3

Check only one box under **Question 1**, but as many as fit you in Part 3. Also note the receipt number for the petition.

Part 4

Read the Declaration and Certification, then sign your name.

3. Form I-693, Medical Exam for Adjustment of Status Applicants

You'll need to have a medical exam unless you entered the United States on a K-1 fiancé visa. Applicants who entered the United States on K-1 fiancé visas and are now applying for a green card on the basis of their subsequent marriage can use the results of their earlier medical exam (done to get the fiancé visa). The results of that exam should already be in the local USCIS office's files, because they were included in the sealed packet of paperwork that served as the fiancé's entry visa.

Your medical exam can be conducted only by a USCIS-approved doctor. A list of these doctors is available at www.uscis.gov; under "Tools," click "Find a Doctor." On the next page you can find an approved doctor in your area by entering your zip code. You can also get this information by calling the Customer Contact Center at 800-375-5283. The fee varies among doctors, so you might want to call a few before choosing one.

It's often best to wait to have your medical exam done until your adjustment interview has been scheduled, since timing is an issue. When you submit the medical report to USCIS, either with your I-485 application or at the interview, it must have been signed by the civil surgeon within the previous 60 days. Then the report will remain valid for two years from when the civil surgeon signed it.

For further description of the medical exam, see Chapter 2, Section A. Once all the results are in, the doctor will fill in the Form I-693 and return

it to you in a sealed envelope. If you've given the doctor a version of the form that was photocopied or downloaded from the Internet, remind him or her to sign every page separately. Do not open the envelope—this will invalidate the results.

WEB RESOURCE

Form I-693 is available on the USCIS website at www.uscis.gov/i-693. Below is a picture of the first page of this form.

4. Form I-864W, Intending Immigrant's Affidavit of Support Exemption

Only a few lucky people will be able to use this form, namely those who are exempt from the Affidavit of Support requirement because the immigrant has either:

- worked for 40 Social Security quarters in the U.S. (approximately ten years)
- been married while the U.S. spouse worked for 40 Social Security quarters, or
- a combination of the above.

The deal is that a financial sponsor's responsibility lasts until the immigrant has (among other possibilities) earned 40 work quarters credited toward Social Security. (A work quarter is approximately three months, but it depends partly on how much you earn.) So if you've already reached the 40 quarters on your own, through lawful employment —perhaps while in the U.S. as a student or H-1B worker—there's no point in the sponsor filling out an Affidavit of Support for you. And, in an interesting twist, the immigrant can be credited for work done by the U.S. spouse during their marriage.

You'll need to prove to USCIS how many quarters of work your spouse or you has done. Contact Social Security about getting a certified statement with this information.

Because Form I-864W is fairly easy to fill out, we won't include a sample here. The form is available at www.uscis.gov/i-864w. In Part 2, you would check the first box.

Form I-693, Medical Exam for Adjustment of Status Applicants—Page 1

Report of Medical Examination and Vaccination Record

Department of Homeland Security
U.S. Citizenship and Immigration Services

USCIS
Form I-693
OMB No. 1615-0033
Expires 02/28/2019

▶ **START HERE** - Type or print in black ink.

Part 1. Information About You (To be completed by the person requesting a medical examination, **NOT** the civil surgeon)

1. **Your Full Name**

   Family Name (Last Name)   Given Name (First Name)   Middle Name

2. **Physical Address**

   Street Number and Name   Apt. Ste. Flr. Number
   ☐ ☐ ☐

   City or Town   State   ZIP Code

3. **Other Information**

   A. Sex   B. Date of Birth (mm/dd/yyyy)   C. City/Town/Village of Birth
   ☐ Male ☐ Female

   D. Country of Birth   E. Alien Registration Number (A-Number) (if any)
   ▶ A-

   F. USCIS Online Account Number (if any)
   ▶

Part 2. Applicant's Statement, Contact Information, Certification, and Signature

NOTE: Read the **Penalties** section of the Form I-693 Instructions before completing this Part. You must submit Form I-693 in a sealed envelope to USCIS as directed in the Form I-693 Instructions.

Applicant's Statement

NOTE: Select the box for either **Item A.** or **B.** in **Item Number 1.**

1. Applicant's Statement Regarding the Interpreter

   A. ☐ I can read and understand English, and I have read and understand every question and instruction on this form and my answer to every question.

   B. ☐ The interpreter named in **Part 3.** read to me every question and instruction on this form and my answer to every question in _____ , a language in which I am fluent, and I understood everything.

Applicant's Contact Information

2. Applicant's Daytime Telephone Number   3. Applicant's Mobile Telephone Number (if any)

4. Applicant's Email Address (if any)

Form I-693 10/19/17 N   Page 1 of 13

5. Form I-864, Affidavit of Support Under Section 213A of the Act

This is the place for your spouse to assure USCIS that you will be adequately provided for once you become a permanent resident. If your spouse's income is insufficient and there are no household members who can contribute, a separate sponsor from outside the household can fill in an additional Affidavit of Support on your behalf, also using the instructions below.

The instructions and sample we give below are for the long version of Form I-864. However, if the petitioner is not self-employed, is relying on earned income without help from assets or other people, and is agreeing to sponsor only one person for each affidavit, you can use a shorter version, called I-864EZ, also available at www.uscis.gov/i-864ez.

WEB RESOURCE

Form I-864 is available on the USCIS website at www.uscis.gov/i-864. Below is a sample filled-in version of the relevant pages of this form. Our sample shows a sponsor whose income and assets are not enough, and who gets help from his mother.

TIP

Need to prepare Affidavits for several family members at once? If the sponsor is bringing in more than one person using the same Form I-130 petition, such as you and your children, he or she can make copies of Form I-864 (and its supporting documents) after signing it. This will be possible for only a few applicants, however, primarily those whose U.S. spouse is a permanent resident. If your spouse is a U.S. citizen, all your children will have needed their own Forms I-130, and will also need separately filled-out Forms I-864.

Parts 1-4

These sections are self-explanatory, with the following notes:

- **In Part 1,** spouses check box 1.a; any nice friends who are separately agreeing to fill in this form as joint sponsors check either box 1.d or box 1.e.
- **In Part 2,** all the information requested refers to the immigrant, including the mailing address. If you live overseas and haven't spent time in the U.S., it is unlikely that you would have an A-Number (issued by USCIS) to enter here. For Question 6, you're unlikely to have a USCIS Online Account Number; unless, that is, you registered in order to file certain USCIS forms online.
- **In Part 3,** note that there's a place to list children. You don't need to name children who were born in the United States, because the sponsor has no obligation to support them (at least not under the immigration laws, though they will be counted elsewhere within this form to test the sponsor's overall financial capacity). The form says "Do not include any relatives listed on a separate visa petition"— that's because, if the sponsor is a U.S. citizen, the children must have been mentioned on a separate I-130 petition, and so need their own separate Forms I-864 as well.
- **In Part 4,** note that the sponsor's physical address must be in the United States in order to be eligible as a financial sponsor. If your sponsor lives outside the U.S., he or she can meet this requirement by showing the steps taken to return to the U.S. and make it his or her residence as soon as you enter. Such steps might include finding U.S. employment, locating a place to live, and registering children in U.S. schools. The sponsor should also demonstrate having made arrangements to give up residence outside the United States.

Part 5, Sponsor's Household Size

This section is self-explanatory. Remember not to count anyone twice! In other words, there's no need to put a "1" in question 3, because you've already counted your spouse.

Part 6, Sponsor's Employment and Income

The sponsor needs to fill in information about his or her employment here. Self-employment is fine. Be aware that if a self-employed sponsor has under-reported income in the past, the earnings shown may not be sufficient to support you. In that case, the sponsor will need to file an amended tax return and pay a penalty before the newly reported income is accepted as meeting the guidelines for sponsorship.

Sample Form I-864, Affidavit of Support Under Section 213A of the Act—Page 1

Affidavit of Support Under Section 213A of the INA

USCIS Form I-864

Department of Homeland Security
U.S. Citizenship and Immigration Services

OMB No. 1615-0075
Expires 03/31/2020

For USCIS Use Only	**Affidavit of Support Submitter** ☐ Petitioner ☐ 1st Joint Sponsor ☐ 2nd Joint Sponsor ☐ Substitute Sponsor ☐ 5% Owner	**Section 213A Review** ☐ MEETS requirements ☐ DOES NOT MEET requirements Reviewed By:_____ Office: _____ Date (mm/dd/yyyy): _____	**Number of Support Affidavits in File** ☐ 1 ☐ 2 **Remarks**

To be completed by an attorney or accredited representative (if any).	☐ **Select this box if Form G-28 or G-28I is attached.**	**Attorney State Bar Number** (if applicable)	**Attorney or Accredited Representative USCIS Online Account Number** (if any)

▶ **START HERE - Type or print in black ink.**

Part 1. Basis For Filing Affidavit of Support

I, [Grun] [MIHOV] ,
am the sponsor submitting this affidavit of support because (Select **only one** box):

1.a. ☒ I am the petitioner. I filed or am filing for the immigration of my relative.

1.b. ☐ I filed an alien worker petition on behalf of the intending immigrant, who is related to me as my
_____

1.c. ☐ I have an ownership interest of at least 5 percent in
_____
which filed an alien worker petition on behalf of the intending immigrant, who is related to me as my
_____

1.d. ☐ I am the only joint sponsor.

1.e. ☐ I am the ☐ first ☐ second of two joint sponsors.

1.f. ☐ The original petitioner is deceased. I am the substitute sponsor. I am the intending immigrant's
_____

NOTE: If you are filing this form as a sponsor, you must include proof of your U.S. citizenship, U.S. national status, or lawful permanent resident status.

Part 2. Information About the Principal Immigrant

1.a. Family Name (Last Name) [Mihov]

1.b. Given Name (First Name) [Anda]

1.c. Middle Name [Marina]

Mailing Address

(USPS ZIP Code Lookup)

2.a. In Care Of Name
_____

2.b. Street Number and Name [68 Watertown Blvd.]

2.c. ☒ Apt. ☐ Ste. ☐ Flr. [12]

2.d. City or Town [Erie]

2.e. State [PA] **2.f.** ZIP Code [19380]

2.g. Province
_____

2.h. Postal Code
_____

2.i. Country [USA]

Other Information

3. Country of Citizenship or Nationality
[Bulgaria]

4. Date of Birth (mm/dd/yyyy) [06/28/1991]

5. Alien Registration Number (A-Number) (if any)
▶ A- _____

6. USCIS Online Account Number (if any)
▶ _____

7. Daytime Telephone Number
[9475555555]

Sample Form I-864, Affidavit of Support Under Section 213A of the Act—Page 2

Part 3. Information About the Immigrants You Are Sponsoring

1. I am sponsoring the principal immigrant named in **Part 2.**

☒ Yes ☐ No (Applicable only if you are sponsoring family members in **Part 3.** as the second joint sponsor or if you are sponsoring family members who are immigrating more than six months after the principal immigrant)

2. ☐ I am sponsoring the following family members immigrating at the same time or within six months of the principal immigrant named in **Part 2.** (Do not include any relative listed on a separate visa petition.)

3. ☐ I am sponsoring the following family members who are immigrating more than six months after the principal immigrant.

Family Member 1

4.a. Family Name (Last Name) n/a

4.b. Given Name (First Name)

4.c. Middle Name

5. Relationship to Principal Immigrant

6. Date of Birth (mm/dd/yyyy)

7. Alien Registration Number (A-Number) (if any)
► A-

8. USCIS Online Account Number (if any)
►

Family Member 2

9.a. Family Name (Last Name)

9.b. Given Name (First Name)

9.c. Middle Name

10. Relationship to Principal Immigrant

11. Date of Birth (mm/dd/yyyy)

12. Alien Registration Number (A-Number) (if any)
► A-

13. USCIS Online Account Number (if any)
►

Family Member 3

14.a. Family Name (Last Name)

14.b. Given Name (First Name)

14.c. Middle Name

15. Relationship to Principal Immigrant

16. Date of Birth (mm/dd/yyyy)

17. Alien Registration Number (A-Number) (if any)
► A-

18. USCIS Online Account Number (if any)
►

Family Member 4

19.a. Family Name (Last Name)

19.b. Given Name (First Name)

19.c. Middle Name

20. Relationship to Principal Immigrant

21. Date of Birth (mm/dd/yyyy)

22. Alien Registration Number (A-Number) (if any)
► A-

23. USCIS Online Account Number (if any)
►

Family Member 5

24.a. Family Name (Last Name)

24.b. Given Name (First Name)

24.c. Middle Name

25. Relationship to Principal Immigrant

26. Date of Birth (mm/dd/yyyy)

27. Alien Registration Number (A-Number) (if any)
► A-

28. USCIS Online Account Number (if any)
►

Sample Form I-864, Affidavit of Support Under Section 213A of the Act—Page 3

Part 3. Information About the Immigrants You Are Sponsoring (continued)

29. Enter the total number of immigrants you are sponsoring on this affidavit which includes the principal immigrant listed in **Part 2.**, any immigrants listed in **Part 3.**, **Item Numbers 1. - 28.** and (if applicable), any immigrants listed for these questions in **Part 11. Additional Information**. Do not count the principal immigrant if you are only sponsoring family members entering more than 6 months after the principal immigrant.

> 1

Part 4. Information About You (Sponsor)

Sponsor's Full Name

1.a. Family Name (Last Name)   MIHOV

1.b. Given Name (First Name)   Grun

1.c. Middle Name   Branimir

Sponsor's Mailing Address

2.a. In Care Of Name

2.b. Street Number and Name   68 Watertown Blvd.

2.c. ☒ Apt. ☐ Ste. ☐ Flr.   12

2.d. City or Town   Erie

2.e. State PA   **2.f.** ZIP Code 19380

2.g. Province

2.h. Postal Code

2.i. Country   USA

3. Is your current mailing address the same as your physical address?   ☒ Yes ☐ No

If you answered "No" to **Item Number 3.**, provide your physical address in **Item Numbers 4.a. - 4.h.**

Sponsor's Physical Address

4.a. Street Number and Name

4.b. ☐ Apt. ☐ Ste. ☐ Flr.

4.c. City or Town

4.d. State   **4.e.** ZIP Code

4.f. Province

4.g. Postal Code

4.h. Country

Other Information

5. Country of Domicile

USA

6. Date of Birth (mm/dd/yyyy)   03/30/1992

7. City or Town of Birth

Hershey

8. State or Province of Birth

PA

9. Country of Birth

USA

10. U.S. Social Security Number (Required)

▶ 1 2 3 4 5 6 7 8 9

Citizenship or Residency

11.a. ☒ I am a U.S. citizen.

11.b. ☐ I am a U.S. national.

11.c. ☐ I am a lawful permanent resident.

12. Sponsor's A-Number (if any)

▶ A-

13. Sponsor's USCIS Online Account Number (if any)

▶

Military Service (To be completed by petitioner sponsors only.)

14. I am currently on **active duty** in the U.S. Armed Forces or U.S. Coast Guard.   ☐ Yes ☒ No

Sample Form I-864, Affidavit of Support Under Section 213A of the Act—Page 4

For USCIS Use Only	

Part 5. Sponsor's Household Size

NOTE: Do not count any member of your household more than once.

Persons you are sponsoring in this affidavit:

1. Provide the number you entered in **Part 3., Item Number 29.** `1`

Persons NOT sponsored in this affidavit:

2. Yourself. `1`

3. If you are currently married, enter "1" for your spouse.

4. If you have dependent children, enter the number here.

5. If you have any other dependents, enter the number here.

6. If you have sponsored any other persons on Form I-864 or Form I-864EZ who are now lawful permanent residents, enter the number here.

7. **OPTIONAL:** If you have siblings, parents, or adult children with the same principal residence who are combining their income with yours by submitting Form I-864A, enter the number here. `1`

8. Add together **Part 5., Item Numbers 1. - 7.** and enter the number here.

   Household Size: `3`

Part 6. Sponsor's Employment and Income

I am currently:

1. ☒ Employed as a/an
   `Chef`

2. Name of Employer 1
   `Erie Food Service`

3. Name of Employer 2 (if applicable)

4. ☐ Self-Employed as a/an (Occupation)

5. ☐ Retired Since (mm/dd/yyyy)

6. ☐ Unemployed Since (mm/dd/yyyy)

7. My current individual annual income is:
   $ `17,000`

Income you are using from any other person who was counted in your household size, including, in certain conditions, the intending immigrant. (See Form I-864 Instructions.) Please indicate name, relationship, and income.

Person 1

8. Name
   `Marta Lorita Mihov`

9. Relationship
   `Mother`

10. **Current Income** $ `30,000`

Person 2

11. Name

12. Relationship

13. **Current Income** $

Person 3

14. Name

15. Relationship

16. **Current Income** $

Person 4

17. Name

18. Relationship

19. **Current Income** $

Sample Form I-864, Affidavit of Support Under Section 213A of the Act—Page 5

For USCIS Use Only	Household Size	Poverty Guideline	Remarks
	☐ 1 ☐ 2 ☐ 3 ☐ 4 ☐ 5 ☐ 6 ☐ 7 ☐ 8 ☐ 9 ☐ Other_____	Year: _2 0___ Poverty Line: $ _____	

Part 6. Sponsor's Employment and Income (continued)

20. **My Current Annual Household Income** (Total all lines from **Part 6. Item Numbers 7.**, **10.**, **13.**, **16.**, and **19.**; the total will be compared to Federal Poverty Guidelines on Form I-864P.) $ **47,000**

21. ☒ The people listed in **Item Numbers 8.**, **11.**, **14.**, and **17.** have completed Form I-864A. I am filing along with this affidavit all necessary Form I-864As completed by these people.

22. ☐ One or more of the people listed in **Item Numbers 8.**, **11.**, **14.**, and **17.** do not need to complete Form I-864A because he or she is the intending immigrant and has no accompanying dependents.

Name

_____

Federal Income Tax Return Information

23.a. Have you filed a Federal income tax return for each of the three most recent tax years?   ☒ Yes ☐ No

NOTE: You **MUST** attach a photocopy or transcript of your Federal income tax return for only the most recent tax year.

23.b. ☐ (Optional) I have attached photocopies or transcripts of my Federal income tax returns for my second and third most recent tax years.

My total income (adjusted gross income on Internal Revenue Service (IRS) Form 1040EZ) as reported on my Federal income tax returns for the most recent three years was:

	Tax Year	Total Income
24.a. Most Recent	2018	$ 17,000
24.b. 2nd Most Recent	2017	$ 25,000
24.c. 3rd Most Recent	2016	$ 15,000

25. ☐ I was not required to file a Federal income tax return as my income was below the IRS required level and I have attached evidence to support this.

Part 7. Use of Assets to Supplement Income (Optional)

If your income, or the total income for you and your household, from **Part 6.**, **Item Numbers 20.** or **24.a. - 24.c.**, exceeds the Federal Poverty Guidelines for your household size, **YOU ARE NOT REQUIRED** to complete this **Part 7.** Skip to **Part 8.**

Your Assets (Optional)

1. Enter the balance of all savings and checking accounts.

$ _____

2. Enter the net cash value of real-estate holdings. (Net value means current assessed value minus mortgage debt.)

$ _____

3. Enter the net cash value of all stocks, bonds, certificates of deposit, and any other assets not already included in **Item Number 1.** or **Item Number 2.**

$ _____

4. Add together **Item Numbers 1. - 3.** and enter the number here.   **TOTAL:** $ _____

Assets from Form I-864A, Part 4., Item Number 3.d., for:

5.a. Name of Relative

_____

5.b. Your household member's assets from Form I-864A (optional). $ _____

Assets of the principal sponsored immigrant (optional).

The principal sponsored immigrant is the person listed in **Part 2.**, **Item Numbers 1.a. - 1.c.** Only include the assets if the principal immigrant is being sponsored by this affidavit of support.

6. Enter the balance of the principal immigrant's savings and checking accounts. $ _____

7. Enter the net cash value of all the principal immigrant's real estate holdings. (Net value means investment value minus mortgage debt.) $ _____

8. Enter the current cash value of the principal immigrant's stocks, bonds, certificates of deposit, and other assets not included in **Item Number 6.** or **Item Number 7.**

$ _____

Sample Form I-864, Affidavit of Support Under Section 213A of the Act—Page 6

For USCIS Use Only	Household Size ☐ 1 ☐ 2 ☐ 3 ☐ 4 ☐ 5 ☐ 6 ☐ 7 ☐ 8 ☐ 9 ☐ Other _____	Poverty Guideline Year: 2 0 ___ Poverty Line: $ _____	Sponsor's Household Income *(Page 5, Line 10)* $ _____ *The total value of all assets, line 10, must equal 5 times (3 times for spouses and children of USC's, or 1 time for orphans to be formally adopted in the U.S.) the difference between the poverty guidelines and the sponsor's household income, line 10.*	Remarks

Part 7. Use of Assets to Supplement Income (Optional) (continued)

9. Add together **Item Numbers 6. - 8.** and enter the number here. $ [____]

Total Value of Assets

10. Add together **Item Numbers 4.**, **5.b.**, and **9.** and enter the number here.

    TOTAL: $ [____]

Part 8. Sponsor's Contract, Statement, Contact Information, Declaration, Certification, and Signature

NOTE: Read the **Penalties** section of the Form I-864 Instructions before completing this part.

Sponsor's Contract

Please note that, by signing this Form I-864, you agree to assume certain specific obligations under the Immigration and Nationality Act (INA) and other Federal laws. The following paragraphs describe those obligations. Please read the following information carefully before you sign Form I-864. If you do not understand the obligations, you may wish to consult an attorney or accredited representative.

What is the Legal Effect of My Signing Form I-864?

If you sign Form I-864 on behalf of any person (called the intending immigrant) who is applying for an immigrant visa or for adjustment of status to a lawful permanent resident, and that intending immigrant submits Form I-864 to the U.S. Government with his or her application for an immigrant visa or adjustment of status, under INA section 213A, these actions create a contract between you and the U.S. Government. The intending immigrant becoming a lawful permanent resident is the consideration for the contract.

Under this contract, you agree that, in deciding whether the intending immigrant can establish that he or she is not inadmissible to the United States as a person likely to become a public charge, the U.S. Government can consider your income and assets as available for the support of the intending immigrant.

What If I Choose Not to Sign Form I-864?

The U.S. Government cannot make you sign Form I-864 if you do not want to do so. But if you do not sign Form I-864, the intending immigrant may not become a lawful permanent resident in the United States.

What Does Signing Form I-864 Require Me To Do?

If an intending immigrant becomes a lawful permanent resident in the United States based on a Form I-864 that you have signed, then, until your obligations under Form I-864 terminate, you must:

A. Provide the intending immigrant any support necessary to maintain him or her at an income that is at least 125 percent of the Federal Poverty Guidelines for his or her household size (100 percent if you are the petitioning sponsor and are on active duty in the U.S. Armed Forces or U.S. Coast Guard, and the person is your husband, wife, or unmarried child under 21 years of age); and

B. Notify U.S. Citizenship and Immigration Services (USCIS) of any change in your address, within 30 days of the change, by filing Form I-865.

What Other Consequences Are There?

If an intending immigrant becomes a lawful permanent resident in the United States based on a Form I-864 that you have signed, then, until your obligations under Form I-864 terminate, the U.S. Government may consider (deem) your income and assets as available to that person, in determining whether he or she is eligible for certain Federal means-tested public benefits and also for state or local means-tested public benefits, if the state or local government's rules provide for consideration (deeming) of your income and assets as available to the person.

This provision does **not** apply to public benefits specified in section 403(c) of the Welfare Reform Act such as emergency Medicaid, short-term, non-cash emergency relief; services provided under the National School Lunch and Child Nutrition Acts; immunizations and testing and treatment for communicable diseases; and means-tested programs under the Elementary and Secondary Education Act.

What If I Do Not Fulfill My Obligations?

If you do not provide sufficient support to the person who becomes a lawful permanent resident based on a Form I-864 that you signed, that person may sue you for this support.

Sample Form I-864, Affidavit of Support Under Section 213A of the Act—Page 7

Part 8. Sponsor's Contract, Statement, Contact Information, Declaration, Certification, and Signature (continued)

If a Federal, state, local, or private agency provided any covered means-tested public benefit to the person who becomes a lawful permanent resident based on a Form I-864 that you signed, the agency may ask you to reimburse them for the amount of the benefits they provided. If you do not make the reimbursement, the agency may sue you for the amount that the agency believes you owe.

If you are sued, and the court enters a judgment against you, the person or agency that sued you may use any legally permitted procedures for enforcing or collecting the judgment. You may also be required to pay the costs of collection, including attorney fees.

If you do not file a properly completed Form I-865 within 30 days of any change of address, USCIS may impose a civil fine for your failing to do so.

When Will These Obligations End?

Your obligations under a Form I-864 that you signed will end if the person who becomes a lawful permanent resident based on that affidavit:

A. Becomes a U.S. citizen;

B. Has worked, or can receive credit for, 40 quarters of coverage under the Social Security Act;

C. No longer has lawful permanent resident status and has departed the United States;

D. Is subject to removal, but applies for and obtains, in removal proceedings, a new grant of adjustment of status, based on a new affidavit of support, if one is required; or

E. Dies.

NOTE: Divorce **does not** terminate your obligations under Form I-864.

Your obligations under a Form I-864 that you signed also end if you die. Therefore, if you die, your estate is not required to take responsibility for the person's support after your death. However, your estate may owe any support that you accumulated before you died.

Sponsor's Statement

NOTE: Select the box for either **Item Number 1.a.** or **1.b.** If applicable, select the box for **Item Number 2.**

1.a. ☒ I can read and understand English, and I have read and understand every question and instruction on this affidavit and my answer to every question.

1.b. ☐ The interpreter named in **Part 9.** read to me every question and instruction on this affidavit and my answer to every question in

_____ ,

a language in which I am fluent, and I understood everything.

2. ☐ At my request, the preparer named in **Part 10.**,

_____ ,

prepared this affidavit for me based only upon information I provided or authorized.

Sponsor's Contact Information

3. Sponsor's Daytime Telephone Number

3132769940

4. Sponsor's Mobile Telephone Number (if any)

_____

5. Sponsor's Email Address (if any)

grun23@email.com

Sponsor's Declaration and Certification

Copies of any documents I have submitted are exact photocopies of unaltered, original documents, and I understand that USCIS or the U.S. Department of State (DOS) may require that I submit original documents to USCIS or DOS at a later date. Furthermore, I authorize the release of any information from any and all of my records that USCIS or DOS may need to determine my eligibility for the benefit that I seek.

I furthermore authorize release of information contained in this affidavit, in supporting documents, and in my USCIS or DOS records, to other entities and persons where necessary for the administration and enforcement of U.S. immigration law.

I certify, under penalty of perjury, that all of the information in my affidavit and any document submitted with it were provided or authorized by me, that I reviewed and understand all of the information contained in, and submitted with, my affidavit and that all of this information is complete, true, and correct.

A. I know the contents of this affidavit of support that I signed;

B. I have read and I understand each of the obligations described in **Part 8.**, and I agree, freely and without any mental reservation or purpose of evasion, to accept each of those obligations in order to make it possible for the immigrants indicated in **Part 3.** to become lawful permanent residents of the United States;

C. I agree to submit to the personal jurisdiction of any Federal or state court that has subject matter jurisdiction of a lawsuit against me to enforce my obligations under this Form I-864;

Sample Form I-864, Affidavit of Support Under Section 213A of the Act—Page 8

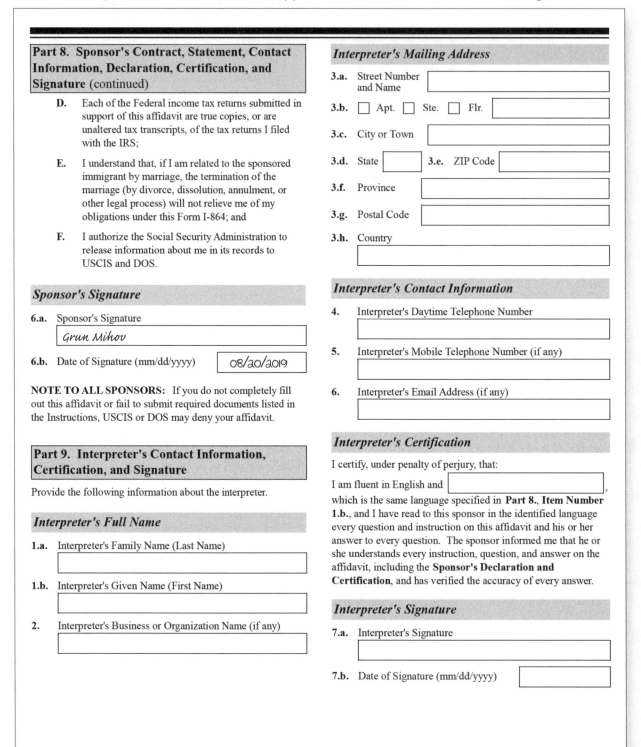

Part 8. Sponsor's Contract, Statement, Contact Information, Declaration, Certification, and Signature (continued)

D. Each of the Federal income tax returns submitted in support of this affidavit are true copies, or are unaltered tax transcripts, of the tax returns I filed with the IRS;

E. I understand that, if I am related to the sponsored immigrant by marriage, the termination of the marriage (by divorce, dissolution, annulment, or other legal process) will not relieve me of my obligations under this Form I-864; and

F. I authorize the Social Security Administration to release information about me in its records to USCIS and DOS.

Sponsor's Signature

6.a. Sponsor's Signature

Grun Mihov

6.b. Date of Signature (mm/dd/yyyy)   08/20/2019

NOTE TO ALL SPONSORS: If you do not completely fill out this affidavit or fail to submit required documents listed in the Instructions, USCIS or DOS may deny your affidavit.

Part 9. Interpreter's Contact Information, Certification, and Signature

Provide the following information about the interpreter.

Interpreter's Full Name

1.a. Interpreter's Family Name (Last Name)

1.b. Interpreter's Given Name (First Name)

2. Interpreter's Business or Organization Name (if any)

Interpreter's Mailing Address

3.a. Street Number and Name

3.b. ☐ Apt. ☐ Ste. ☐ Flr.

3.c. City or Town

3.d. State   **3.e.** ZIP Code

3.f. Province

3.g. Postal Code

3.h. Country

Interpreter's Contact Information

4. Interpreter's Daytime Telephone Number

5. Interpreter's Mobile Telephone Number (if any)

6. Interpreter's Email Address (if any)

Interpreter's Certification

I certify, under penalty of perjury, that:

I am fluent in English and   , which is the same language specified in **Part 8.**, **Item Number 1.b.**, and I have read to this sponsor in the identified language every question and instruction on this affidavit and his or her answer to every question. The sponsor informed me that he or she understands every instruction, question, and answer on the affidavit, including the **Sponsor's Declaration and Certification**, and has verified the accuracy of every answer.

Interpreter's Signature

7.a. Interpreter's Signature

7.b. Date of Signature (mm/dd/yyyy)

Questions 8-18: These questions are important for sponsors whose income is not enough by itself, but who will be using the income of members of their household to help meet the *Poverty Guidelines* minimum requirements. Unless anyone of these household members is the actual immigrant, they must plan to complete a separate agreement with the sponsor, using Form I-864A. The total income from the sponsor and household members goes in Question 20.

Question 20: Here, the sponsor is supposed to enter the income shown on his or her most recent tax return. But what if the sponsor's income has risen since filing those taxes? In that case, the sponsor should enter the more recent income figure, but put an asterisk (an *) next to it. Then find some white space somewhere on the page and write "this figure reflects present earnings, not earnings shown on tax return; see supporting documentation." The documentation the sponsor is already providing, such as an employer's letter, should be enough to show current income.

Part 7, Use of Assets to Supplement Income

The sponsor needs to complete this section only if his or her income wasn't enough by itself to meet the *Poverty Guidelines* requirements. If the sponsor needs to add assets which may include such items as a house, car, or boat, remember to subtract debts, mortgages, and liens before writing down their value. And remember that the value of these assets will later be divided by three before being used to meet the *Poverty Guidelines* minimum if your spouse is a U.S. citizen, and will be divided by five if your spouse is a permanent resident. If some of the assets being used to meet the minimum belong to the immigrant, describe these in Questions 6-8 (and of course attach documents to prove their ownership, location, and value).

If the combination of the sponsor's household available income and either one-third or one-fifth (as appropriate) of the sponsor's and/or the immigrant's assets don't yet meet the *Poverty Guidelines* minimum, you'll still need to hand in this Affidavit. But you'll definitely want to look for a joint sponsor.

Part 8, Sponsor's Contract

Unlike past versions of this form, the sponsor's signature does not need to be witnessed by a notary public.

6. Form I-864A

Not every sponsor needs to use this form. It is required only if, on the main Form I-864, the sponsor had to use the income of members of the sponsor's household to meet the *Poverty Guidelines* minimum. In that case, the sponsor will have to ask these persons to fill in portions of Form I-864A. Then both the sponsor and the household member(s) will need to sign it. The sponsor will attach Form I-864A to the main Form I-864.

If the household member whose income is being counted is you, the immigrant spouse, you don't need to sign Form I-864A unless you are agreeing to support your immigrating children as well.

WEB RESOURCE
Form I-864A is available on the USCIS website at www.uscis.gov/i-864a. Above is a sample filled-in version of this form (first six out of eight pages). The sample assumes the sponsor's mother lives with him.

Parts 1-4: Self-explanatory; filled in by the household member. For Question 8, the household member is unlikely to have a USCIS Online Account Number; unless, that is, he or she registered in order to file certain USCIS forms online.

Part 5: This part is filled in and signed by the sponsor. Self-explanatory.

Part 6: This is filled in and signed by the household member. Self-explanatory.

Sample Form I-864A, Contract Between Sponsor and Household Member—Page 1

Contract Between Sponsor and Household Member

Department of Homeland Security
U.S. Citizenship and Immigration Services

**USCIS
Form I-864A**

OMB No. 1615-0075
Expires 03/31/2020

For Government Use Only

This Form I-864A relates to a household member who:

☐ **IS** the intending immigrant　　☐ **IS NOT** the intending immigrant

Reviewed By: _____

Location: _____　Date (mm/dd/yyyy): _____

To be completed by an attorney or accredited representative (if any).	☐ **Select this box if Form G-28 or G-28I is attached.**	**Attorney State Bar Number** (if applicable)	**Attorney or Accredited Representative USCIS Online Account Number** (if any)

▶ **START HERE** - Type or print in black ink.

Part 1. Information About You (the Household Member)

Full Name

1.a. Family Name (Last Name)　Mihov

1.b. Given Name (First Name)　Marta

1.c. Middle Name　Larita

Mailing Address　　*(USPS ZIP Code Lookup)*

2.a. In Care Of Name

2.b. Street Number and Name　68 Watertown Blvd.

2.c. ☒ Apt. ☐ Ste. ☐ Flr.　12

2.d. City or Town　Erie

2.e. State　PA　**2.f.** ZIP Code　19380

2.g. Province

2.h. Postal Code

2.i. Country　USA

3. Is your current mailing address the same as your physical address?　☒ Yes ☐ No

If you answered "No" to **Item Number 3.**, provide your physical address.

Physical Address

4.a. Street Number and Name

4.b. ☐ Apt. ☐ Ste. ☐ Flr.

4.c. City or Town

4.d. State　　**4.e.** ZIP Code

4.f. Province

4.g. Postal Code

4.h. Country

Other Information

5. Date of Birth (mm/dd/yyyy)　03/28/1966

Place of Birth

6.a. City or Town　Sofia

6.b. State or Province　Sofia

6.c. Country　Bulgaria

7. U.S. Social Security Number (if any)　▶ 1 2 3 4 5 6 6 7 7

8. USCIS Online Account Number (if any)　▶

Form I-864A 03/06/18

Sample Form I-864A, Contract Between Sponsor and Household Member—Page 2

Part 2. Your (the Household Member's) Relationship to the Sponsor

Select **Item Number 1.a.**, **1.b.**, or **1.c.**

1.a. ☐ I am the intending immigrant and also the sponsor's spouse.

1.b. ☐ I am the intending immigrant and also a member of the sponsor's household.

1.c. ☒ I am **not** the intending immigrant. I am the sponsor's household member. I am related to the sponsor as his/her:

    ☐ Spouse

    ☐ Son or Daughter (at least 18 years of age)

    ☒ Parent

    ☐ Brother or Sister

    ☐ Other Dependent (Specify)

Part 3. Your (the Household Member's) Employment and Income

I am currently:

1. ☒ Employed as a/an

    Choir Director

2. Name of Employer Number 1

    Erie School

3. Name of Employer Number 2 (if applicable)

4. ☐ Self employed as a/an

5. ☐ Retired from (Company Name)

    Since (mm/dd/yyyy)

6. ☐ Unemployed since (mm/dd/yyyy)

7. **My current individual annual income is:**

    $ 30,000

Part 4. Your (the Household Member's) Federal Income Tax Information and Assets

1.a. Have you filed a Federal income tax return for each of the three most recent tax years? ☒ Yes ☐ No

NOTE: You **MUST** attach a photocopy or transcript of your Federal income tax return for only the most recent tax year.

1.b. ☐ (Optional) I have attached photocopies or transcripts of my Federal income tax returns for my second and third most recent tax years.

My total income (adjusted gross income on IRS Form 1040EZ) as reported on my Federal income tax returns for the most recent three years was:

		Tax Year	Total Income
2.a.	Most Recent	2018	$ 30,000
2.b.	2nd Most Recent	2017	$ 28,000
2.c.	3rd Most Recent	2016	$ 24,000

My assets (complete only if necessary).

3.a. Enter the balance of all cash, savings, and checking accounts. $

3.b. Enter the net cash value of real-estate holdings. (Net value means assessed value minus mortgage debt.) $

3.c. Enter the cash value of all stocks, bonds, certificates of deposit, and other assets not listed on **Item Numbers 3.a.** or **3.b.** $

3.d. Add together **Item Numbers 3.a.**, **3.b.**, and **3.c.** and enter the number here. $

Part 5. Sponsor's Promise, Statement, Contact Information, Declaration, Certification, and Signature

NOTE: Read the **Penalties** section of the Form I-864A Instructions before completing this part.

I, THE SPONSOR,

Grun Mihov ,

(Print Name)

in consideration of the household member's promise to support the following intending immigrants and to be jointly and severally liable for any obligations I incur under the affidavit of support, promise to complete and file an affidavit of support on behalf of the following named intending immigrants.

1

(Indicate Number)

Sample Form I-864A, Contract Between Sponsor and Household Member—Page 3

Part 5. Sponsor's Promise, Statement, Contact Information, Declaration, Certification, and Signature (continued)

Intending Immigrant Number 1

Name

1.a. Family Name (Last Name): Mihov

1.b. Given Name (First Name): Anda

1.c. Middle Name: Marina

2. Date of Birth (mm/dd/yyyy): 06/28/1991

3. Alien Registration Number (A-Number, if any) ▶ A-

4. U.S. Social Security Number (if any) ▶

5. USCIS Online Account Number (if any) ▶

Intending Immigrant Number 2

Name

6.a. Family Name (Last Name):

6.b. Given Name (First Name):

6.c. Middle Name:

7. Date of Birth (mm/dd/yyyy):

8. Alien Registration Number (A-Number, if any) ▶ A-

9. U.S. Social Security Number (if any) ▶

10. USCIS Online Account Number (if any) ▶

Intending Immigrant Number 3

Name

11.a. Family Name (Last Name):

11.b. Given Name (First Name):

11.c. Middle Name:

12. Date of Birth (mm/dd/yyyy):

13. Alien Registration Number (A-Number, if any) ▶ A-

14. U.S. Social Security Number (if any) ▶

15. USCIS Online Account Number (if any) ▶

Intending Immigrant Number 4

Name

16.a. Family Name (Last Name):

16.b. Given Name (First Name):

16.c. Middle Name:

17. Date of Birth (mm/dd/yyyy):

18. Alien Registration Number (A-Number, if any) ▶ A-

19. U.S. Social Security Number (if any) ▶

20. USCIS Online Account Number (if any) ▶

Intending Immigrant Number 5

Name

21.a. Family Name (Last Name):

21.b. Given Name (First Name):

21.c. Middle Name:

22. Date of Birth (mm/dd/yyyy):

23. Alien Registration Number (A-Number, if any) ▶ A-

24. U.S. Social Security Number (if any) ▶

25. USCIS Online Account Number (if any) ▶

Sponsor's Statement

NOTE: Select the box for either **Item Number 26.a.** or **26.b.** If applicable, select the box for **Item Number 27.**

26.a. ☒ I can read and understand English, and I have read and understand every question and instruction on this contract and my answer to every question.

Sample Form I-864A, Contract Between Sponsor and Household Member—Page 4

Part 5. Sponsor's Promise, Statement, Contact Information, Declaration, Certification, and Signature (continued)

26.b. ☐ The interpreter named in **Part 7.** read to me every question and instruction on this contract and my answer to every question in

_____ ,

a language in which I am fluent, and I understood everything.

27. ☐ At my request, the preparer named in **Part 8.**,

_____ ,

prepared this contract for me based only upon information I provided or authorized.

Sponsor's Contact Information

28. Sponsor's Daytime Telephone Number

3132769440

29. Sponsor's Mobile Telephone Number (if any)

3131211121

30. Sponsor's Email Address (if any)

grun23@email.com

Sponsor's Declaration and Certification

Copies of any documents I have submitted are exact photocopies of unaltered, original documents, and I understand that U.S. Citizenship and Immigration Services (USCIS) or the U.S. Department of State (DOS) may require that I submit original documents to USCIS or DOS at a later date. Furthermore, I authorize the release of any information from any and all of my records that USCIS or DOS may need to determine my eligibility for the immigration benefit that I seek.

I furthermore authorize release of information contained in this contract, in supporting documents, and in my USCIS or DOS records, to other entities and persons where necessary for the administration and enforcement of U.S. immigration law.

I certify, under penalty of perjury, that all of the information in my contract and any document submitted with it were provided or authorized by me, that I reviewed and understand all of the information contained in, and submitted with, my contract and that all of this information is complete, true, and correct.

Sponsor's Signature

31.a. Sponsor's Signature

 Grun Mihov

31.b. Date of Signature (mm/dd/yyyy)   08/20/2019

NOTE TO ALL SPONSORS: If you do not completely fill out this contract or fail to submit required documents listed in the Instructions, USCIS may deny your contract.

Part 6. Your (the Household Member's) Promise, Statement, Contact Information, Declaration, Certification, and Signature

NOTE: Read the **Penalties** section of the Form I-864A Instructions before completing this part.

I, THE HOUSEHOLD MEMBER,

Marta Mihov ,

(Print Name)

in consideration of the sponsor's promise to complete and file an affidavit of support on behalf of the above named intending immigrants.

1

(Print number of intending immigrants noted in **Part 5. Sponsor's Promise, Statement, Contact Information, Declaration, Certification and Signature**.)

A. Promise to provide any and all financial support necessary to assist the sponsor in maintaining the sponsored immigrants at or above the minimum income provided for in the Immigration and Naturalization Act (INA) section 213A(a)(1)(A) (not less than 125 percent of the Federal Poverty Guidelines) during the period in which the affidavit of support is enforceable;

B. Agree to be jointly and severally liable for payment of any and all obligations owed by the sponsor under the affidavit of support to the sponsored immigrants, to any agency of the Federal Government, to any agency of a state or local government, or to any other private entity that provides means-tested public benefits;

C. Certify under penalty under the laws of the United States that the Federal income tax returns submitted in support of the contract are true copies or unaltered tax transcripts filed with the Internal Revenue Service;

D. **Consideration where the household member is also the sponsored immigrant:** I understand that if I am the sponsored immigrant and a member of the sponsor's household that this promise relates only to my promise to be jointly and severally liable for any obligation owed by the sponsor under the affidavit of support to any of my dependents, to any agency of the Federal Government, to any agency of a state or local government, or to any other private entity that provides means-tested public benefits and to provide any and all financial support necessary to assist the sponsor in maintaining any of my dependents at or above the minimum income provided for in INA section 213A (a)(1)(A) (not less than 125 percent of the Federal Poverty Guideline) during the period which the affidavit of support is enforceable.

Sample Form I-864A, Contract Between Sponsor and Household Member—Page 5

Part 6. Your (the Household Member's) Promise, Statement, Contact Information, Declaration, Certification, and Signature (continued)

E. I understand that, if I am related to the sponsored immigrant or the sponsor by marriage, the termination of the marriage (by divorce, dissolution, annulment, or other legal process) will not relieve me of my obligations under this Form I-864A.

F. I authorize the Social Security Administration to release information about me in its records to the Department of State and U.S. Citizenship and Immigration Services (USCIS).

Your (the Household Member's) Statement

NOTE: Select the box for either **Item Number 1.a.** or **1.b.** If applicable, select the box for **Item Number 2.**

1.a. ☒ I can read and understand English, and I have read and understand every question and instruction on this contract and my answer to every question.

1.b. ☐ The interpreter named in **Part 7.** read to me every question and instruction on this contract and my answer to every question in

a language in which I am fluent, and I understood everything.

2. ☐ At my request, the preparer named in **Part 8.**,

prepared this contract for me based only upon information I provided or authorized.

Your (the Household Member's) Contact Information

3. Your (the Household Member's) Daytime Telephone Number

3135551214

4. Your (the Household Member's) Mobile Telephone Number (if any)

n/a

5. Your (the Household Member's) Email Address (if any)

n/a

Your (the Household Member's) Declaration and Certification

Copies of any documents I have submitted are exact photocopies of unaltered, original documents, and I understand that USCIS or DOS may require that I submit original documents to USCIS or DOS at a later date. Furthermore, I authorize the release of any information from any and all of my records that USCIS or DOS may need to determine my eligibility for the immigration benefit that I seek.

I furthermore authorize release of information contained in this contract, in supporting documents, and in my USCIS or DOS records, to other entities and persons where necessary for the administration and enforcement of U.S. immigration law.

I certify, under penalty of perjury, that all of the information in my contract and any document submitted with it were provided or authorized by me, that I reviewed and understand all of the information contained in, and submitted with, my contract and that all of this information is complete, true, and correct.

Your (the Household Member's) Signature

6.a. Your (the Household Member's) Printed Name

Marta Mihov

6.b. Your (the Household Member's) Signature

Marta L. Mihov

6.c. Date of Signature (mm/dd/yyyy) 08/30/2019

NOTE TO ALL HOUSEHOLD MEMBERS: If you do not completely fill out this contract or fail to submit required documents listed in the Instructions, USCIS may deny your contract.

Part 7. Interpreter's Contact Information, Certification, and Signature

Provide the following information about the interpreter.

Interpreter's Full Name

1.a. Interpreter's Family Name (Last Name)

1.b. Interpreter's Given Name (First Name)

2. Interpreter's Business or Organization Name (if any)

Sample Form I-864A, Contract Between Sponsor and Household Member—Page 6

Part 7. Interpreter's Contact Information, Certification, and Signature (continued)

Interpreter's Mailing Address

3.a. Street Number and Name

3.b. ☐ Apt. ☐ Ste. ☐ Flr.

3.c. City or Town

3.d. State

3.e. ZIP Code

3.f. Province

3.g. Postal Code

3.h. Country

Interpreter's Contact Information

4. Interpreter's Daytime Telephone Number

5. Interpreter's Mobile Telephone Number (if any)

6. Interpreter's Email Address (if any)

Interpreter's Certification

I certify, under penalty of perjury, that:

I am fluent in English and [_____],

which is the same language specified in **Part 5., Item Number 26.b.** or **Part 6., Item Number 1.b.**, and I have read to this sponsor or household member in the identified language every question and instruction on this contract and his or her answer to every question. The sponsor or household member informed me that he or she understands every instruction, question, and answer on the contract, including the **Sponsor's** or **Household Member's Declaration and Certification**, and has verified the accuracy of every answer.

Interpreter's Signature

7.a. Interpreter's Signature

7.b. Date of Signature (mm/dd/yyyy)

Part 8. Contact Information, Declaration, and Signature of the Person Preparing this Contract, if Other Than the Sponsor or Household Member

Provide the following information about the preparer.

Preparer's Full Name

1.a. Preparer's Family Name (Last Name)

1.b. Preparer's Given Name (First Name)

2. Preparer's Business or Organization Name (if any)

Preparer's Mailing Address

3.a. Street Number and Name

3.b. ☐ Apt. ☐ Ste. ☐ Flr.

3.c. City or Town

3.d. State

3.e. ZIP Code

3.f. Province

3.g. Postal Code

3.h. Country

Preparer's Contact Information

4. Preparer's Daytime Telephone Number

5. Preparer's Mobile Telephone Number (if any)

6. Preparer's Email Address (if any)

7. Form I-765, Application for Employment Authorization

Applying for employment authorization is optional, and there's no separate fee for it. But even if you're not planning to work, the employment authorization card, or work permit, is a helpful piece of photo identification. You can use it to get a Social Security card and a driver's license.

> **WEB RESOURCE**
> **Form I-765 is available on the USCIS website at www.uscis.gov/i-765.** Below is a sample filled-in version of the relevant pages of this form.

If this is your first work permit, under **"I am applying for,"** check "Initial permission to accept employment." If you've applied for a previous work permit (for example, if you're applying now as part of your green card application but previously applied for and received a work permit as a fiancé), check the box for renewals.

Questions 1-13: Self-explanatory.

Questions 14-17: Complete these if you don't have a Social Security number and wish to request one.

Question 27: Your eligibility category as an Adjustment of Status applicant is (c)(9).

Don't be confused by the various mailing addresses contained in the instructions to this form. At the adjustment of status application stage, you simply mail Form I-765 to the same address as the rest of your adjustment of status application.

> **TIP**
> **Any chance you'll travel outside the United States while awaiting your adjustment of status interview?** If so, definitely include an application for Advance Parole with your adjustment of status packet. Complete instructions are in Section D2, below.

8. Form G-1145, E-Notification of Application/Petition Acceptance

Use this form (see example below) if you want USCIS to send you an email or text message to let you know that your application has been received and accepted. (It's free!) It does not take the place of the paper receipt that you will be sent a few weeks later, which is discussed in Section C1, below.

> **WEB RESOURCE**
> **Form G-1145 is available on the USCIS website at www.uscis.gov/g-1145.**

C. Submitting the Adjustment of Status Packet

Formerly, applicants could submit their adjustment of status packet to a local USCIS district office. Now, however, you must send it to an office in Chicago. (USCIS refers to this as a "lockbox," but in fact people work there.) Your interview, however, will be handled by your local USCIS district office.

Make a complete copy (for yourself) of every form, document, photo, and check or money order in your packet, then send the packet to either:

- USCIS, P.O. Box 805887, Chicago, IL 60680-4120 (if you're using the U.S. Postal Service), or
- USCIS, Attn: FBAS, 131 South Dearborn, 3rd Floor, Chicago, IL 60603-5517 (if you're using a private delivery service such as DHL or FedEx).

1. Your Filing Receipts

Once USCIS has received and accepted your adjustment of status packet for processing, it will put you on the waiting list for an interview. Regardless of whether or not USCIS has sent you an E-Notification about your application, it will send you paper receipt notices—one for your I-485, and one each for your I-130, I-765, and I-131, if you filed those applications at the same time. (See the sample receipt below.) The receipt is a very important document. Before you risk letting the dog eat it, make several photocopies and store them in secure places.

Sample Form I-765, Application for Employment Authorization—Page 1

	Application For Employment Authorization	**USCIS**
	Department of Homeland Security	**Form I-765**
	U.S. Citizenship and Immigration Services	OMB No. 1615-0040
		Expires 05/31/2020

For USCIS Use Only

☐ **Authorization/Extension Valid From**	**Fee Stamp**
☐ **Authorization/Extension Valid Through**	
Alien Registration Number A- ⬚⬚⬚⬚⬚⬚⬚⬚⬚	
Remarks	

Action Block

To be completed by an attorney or Board of Immigration Appeals (BIA)-accredited representative (if any).	☐ **Select this box if Form G-28 is attached.**	**Attorney or Accredited Representative USCIS Online Account Number** (if any) ⬚⬚⬚⬚⬚⬚⬚⬚⬚⬚⬚⬚⬚

▶ **START HERE - Type or print in black ink.**

Part 1. Reason for Applying

I am applying for (select **only one** box):

1.a. ☒ Initial permission to accept employment.

1.b. ☐ Replacement of lost, stolen, or damaged employment authorization document, or correction of my employment authorization document **NOT DUE** to U.S. Citizenship and Immigration Services (USCIS) error.

> **NOTE:** Replacement (correction) of an employment authorization document due to USCIS error does not require a new Form I-765 and filing fee. Refer to **Replacement for Card Error** in the **What is the Filing Fee** section of the Form I-765 Instructions for further details.

1.c. ☐ Renewal of my permission to accept employment. (Attach a copy of your previous employment authorization document.)

Part 2. Information About You

Your Full Legal Name

1.a.	Family Name (Last Name)	Mihov
1.b.	Given Name (First Name)	Anda
1.c.	Middle Name	Marina

Other Names Used

Provide all other names you have ever used, including aliases, maiden name, and nicknames. If you need extra space to complete this section, use the space provided in **Part 6. Additional Information**.

2.a.	Family Name (Last Name)	Michelski
2.b.	Given Name (First Name)	
2.c.	Middle Name	
3.a.	Family Name (Last Name)	
3.b.	Given Name (First Name)	
3.c.	Middle Name	
4.a.	Family Name (Last Name)	
4.b.	Given Name (First Name)	
4.c.	Middle Name	

Sample Form I-765, Application for Employment Authorization—Page 2

Part 2. Information About You (continued)

Your U.S. Mailing Address

5.a. In Care Of Name (if any)

5.b. Street Number and Name — 68 Watertown Blvd.

5.c. ☒ Apt. ☐ Ste. ☐ Flr. — 12

5.d. City or Town — Erie

5.e. State — PA **5.f.** ZIP Code — 19380

6. Is your current mailing address the same as your physical address? ☒ Yes ☐ No

NOTE: If you answered "No" to **Item Number 6.**, provide your physical address below.

U.S. Physical Address

7.a. Street Number and Name

7.b. ☐ Apt. ☐ Ste. ☐ Flr.

7.c. City or Town

7.d. State **7.e.** ZIP Code

Other Information

8. Alien Registration Number (A-Number) (if any)
▶ A-

9. USCIS Online Account Number (if any)
▶

10. Gender ☐ Male ☒ Female

11. Marital Status ☐ Single ☒ Married ☐ Divorced ☐ Widowed

12. Have you previously filed Form I-765? ☐ Yes ☒ No

13.a. Has the Social Security Administration (SSA) ever officially issued a Social Security card to you? ☒ Yes ☐ No

NOTE: If you answered "No" to **Item Number 13.a.**, skip to **Item Number 14.** If you answered "Yes" to **Item Number 13.a.**, provide the information requested in **Item Number 13.b.**

13.b. Provide your Social Security number (SSN) (if known).
▶ 3 8 7 3 3 8 8 7 7

14. Do you want the SSA to issue you a Social Security card? (You must also answer "Yes" to **Item Number 15.**, **Consent for Disclosure**, to receive a card.) ☐ Yes ☒ No

NOTE: If you answered "No" to **Item Number 14.**, skip to **Part 2., Item Number 18.a.** If you answered "Yes" to **Item Number 14.**, you must also answer "Yes" to **Item Number 15.**

15. **Consent for Disclosure:** I authorize disclosure of information from this application to the SSA as required for the purpose of assigning me an SSN and issuing me a Social Security card. ☐ Yes ☐ No

NOTE: If you answered "Yes" to **Item Numbers 14. - 15.**, provide the information requested in **Item Numbers 16.a. - 17.b.**

Father's Name

Provide your father's birth name.

16.a. Family Name (Last Name)

16.b. Given Name (First Name)

Mother's Name

Provide your mother's birth name.

17.a. Family Name (Last Name)

17.b. Given Name (First Name)

Your Country or Countries of Citizenship or Nationality

List all countries where you are currently a citizen or national. If you need extra space to complete this item, use the space provided in **Part 6. Additional Information**.

18.a. Country
Bulgaria

18.b. Country

Sample Form I-765, Application for Employment Authorization—Page 3

Part 2. Information About You (continued)

Place of Birth

List the city/town/village, state/province, and country where you were born.

19.a. City/Town/Village of Birth

Sofia

19.b. State/Province of Birth

19.c. Country of Birth

Bulgaria

20. Date of Birth (mm/dd/yyyy)

06/28/1991

Information About Your Last Arrival in the United States

21.a. Form I-94 Arrival-Departure Record Number (if any)

▶ | 1 | 2 | 3 | 2 | 3 | 1 | 2 | 3 | 1 | 1 | 1 |

21.b. Passport Number of Your Most Recently Issued Passport

BG0000

21.c. Travel Document Number (if any)

21.d. Country That Issued Your Passport or Travel Document

Bulgaria

21.e. Expiration Date for Passport or Travel Document (mm/dd/yyyy)

06/30/2025

22. Date of Your Last Arrival Into the United States, On or About (mm/dd/yyyy)

11/04/2018

23. Place of Your Last Arrival Into the United States

New York

24. Immigration Status at Your Last Arrival (for example, B-2 visitor, F-1 student, or no status)

H-1B

25. Your Current Immigration Status or Category (for example, B-2 visitor, F-1 student, parolee, deferred action, or no status or category)

H-1B

26. Student and Exchange Visitor Information System (SEVIS) Number (if any)

▶ N-

Information About Your Eligibility Category

27. **Eligibility Category.** Refer to the **Who May File Form I-765** section of the Form I-765 Instructions to determine the appropriate eligibility category for this application. Enter the appropriate letter and number for your eligibility category below (for example, (a)(8), (c)(17)(iii)).

(c) (9) ( )

28. **(c)(3)(C) STEM OPT Eligibility Category.** If you entered the eligibility category **(c)(3)(C)** in **Item Number 27.**, provide the information requested in **Item Numbers 28.a - 28.c.**

28.a. Degree

28.b. Employer's Name as Listed in E-Verify

28.c. Employer's E-Verify Company Identification Number or a Valid E-Verify Client Company Identification Number

29. **(c)(26) Eligibility Category.** If you entered the eligibility category (c)(26) in **Item Number 27.**, provide the receipt number of your H-1B spouse's most recent Form I-797 Notice for Form I-129, Petition for a Nonimmigrant Worker.

▶ | | | | | | | | | | | |

30. **(c)(8) Eligibility Category.** If you entered the eligibility category (c)(8) in **Item Number 27.**, have you **EVER** been arrested for and/or convicted of any crime?

☐ Yes ☐ No

NOTE: If you answered "Yes" to **Item Number 30.**, refer to **Special Filing Instructions for Those With Pending Asylum Applications (c)(8)** in the **Required Documentation** section of the Form I-765 Instructions for information about providing court dispositions.

31.a. **(c)(35) and (c)(36) Eligibility Category.** If you entered the eligibility category (c)(35) in **Item Number 27.**, please provide the receipt number of your Form I-797 Notice for Form I-140, Immigrant Petition for Alien Worker. If you entered the eligibility category (c)(36) in **Item Number 27.**, please provide the receipt number of your spouse's or parent's Form I-797 Notice for Form I-140.

▶ | | | | | | | | | | | |

31.b. If you entered the eligibility category (c)(35) or (c)(36) in **Item Number 27.**, have you **EVER** been arrested for and/or convicted of any crime?

☐ Yes ☐ No

NOTE: If you answered "Yes" to **Item Number 31.b.**, refer to **Employment-Based Nonimmigrant Categories**, **Items 8. - 9.**, in the **Who May File Form I-765** section of the Form I-765 Instructions for information about providing court dispositions.

Sample Form I-765, Application for Employment Authorization—Page 4

Part 3. Applicant's Statement, Contact Information, Declaration, Certification, and Signature

NOTE: Read the **Penalties** section of the Form I-765 Instructions before completing this section. You must file Form I-765 while in the United States.

Applicant's Statement

NOTE: Select the box for either **Item Number 1.a.** or **1.b.** If applicable, select the box for **Item Number 2.**

1.a. ☒ I can read and understand English, and I have read and understand every question and instruction on this application and my answer to every question.

1.b. ☐ The interpreter named in **Part 4.** read to me every question and instruction on this application and my answer to every question in

[_____] ,

a language in which I am fluent, and I understood everything.

2. ☐ At my request, the preparer named in **Part 5.**,

[_____] ,

prepared this application for me based only upon information I provided or authorized.

Applicant's Contact Information

3. Applicant's Daytime Telephone Number

[6105551122]

4. Applicant's Mobile Telephone Number (if any)

[_____]

5. Applicant's Email Address (if any)

[_____]

6. ☐ Select this box if you are a Salvadoran or Guatemalan national eligible for benefits under the ABC settlement agreement.

Applicant's Declaration and Certification

Copies of any documents I have submitted are exact photocopies of unaltered, original documents, and I understand that USCIS may require that I submit original documents to USCIS at a later date. Furthermore, I authorize the release of any information from any and all of my records that USCIS may need to determine my eligibility for the immigration benefit that I seek.

I furthermore authorize release of information contained in this application, in supporting documents, and in my USCIS records, to other entities and persons where necessary for the administration and enforcement of U.S. immigration law.

I understand that USCIS may require me to appear for an appointment to take my biometrics (fingerprints, photograph, and/or signature) and, at that time, if I am required to provide biometrics, I will be required to sign an oath reaffirming that:

1) I reviewed and understood all of the information contained in, and submitted with, my application; and

2) All of this information was complete, true, and correct at the time of filing.

I certify, under penalty of perjury, that all of the information in my application and any document submitted with it were provided or authorized by me, that I reviewed and understand all of the information contained in, and submitted with, my application and that all of this information is complete, true, and correct.

Applicant's Signature

7.a. Applicant's Signature

[*Anda Mihov*]

7.b. Date of Signature (mm/dd/yyyy) [5/19/19]

NOTE TO ALL APPLICANTS: If you do not completely fill out this application or fail to submit required documents listed in the Instructions, USCIS may deny your application.

Part 4. Interpreter's Contact Information, Certification, and Signature

Provide the following information about the interpreter.

Interpreter's Full Name

1.a. Interpreter's Family Name (Last Name)

[_____]

1.b. Interpreter's Given Name (First Name)

[_____]

2. Interpreter's Business or Organization Name (if any)

[_____]

Sample Form G-1145, E-Notification of Application/Petition Acceptance

e-Notification of Application/Petition Acceptance

Department of Homeland Security
U.S. Citizenship and Immigration Services

USCIS
Form G-1145

What Is the Purpose of This Form?

Use this form to request an electronic notification (e-Notification) when U.S. Citizenship and Immigration Services accepts your immigration application. This service is available for applications filed at a USCIS Lockbox facility.

General Information

Complete the information below and clip this form to the first page of your application package. You will receive one e-mail and/or text message for each form you are filing.

We will send the e-Notification within 24 hours after we accept your application. Domestic customers will receive an e-mail and/or text message; overseas customers will only receive an e-mail. Undeliverable e-Notifications cannot be resent.

The e-mail or text message will display your receipt number and tell you how to get updated case status information. It will not include any personal information. The e-Notification does not grant any type of status or benefit; rather it is provided as a convenience to customers.

USCIS will also mail you a receipt notice (I-797C), which you will receive within 10 days after your application has been accepted; use this notice as proof of your pending application or petition.

USCIS Privacy Act Statement

AUTHORITIES: The information requested on this form is collected pursuant to section 103(a) of the Immigration and Nationality Act, as amended INA section 101, et seq.

PURPOSE: The primary purpose for providing the information on this form is to request an electronic notification when USCIS accepts immigration form. The information you provide will be used to send you a text and/or email message.

DISCLOSURE: The information you provide is voluntary. However, failure to provide the requested information may prevent USCIS from providing you a text and/or email message receipting your immigration form.

ROUTINE USES: The information provide on this form will be used by and disclosed to DHS personnel and contractors in accordance with approved routine uses, as described in the associated published system of records notices [**DHS/USCIS-007 - Benefits Information System and DHS/USCIS-001 - Alien File (A-File) and Central Index System (CIS),** which can be found at **www.dhs.gov/privacy**]. The information may also be made available, as appropriate for law enforcement purposes or in the interest of national security.

Complete this form and clip it on top of the first page of your immigration form(s).

Applicant/Petitioner Full Last Name	Applicant/Petitioner Full First Name	Applicant/Petitioner Full Middle Name
Mihov	Anda	Marina

Email Address	Mobile Phone Number (Text Message)
mihov123@email.com	5061235555

Among other things, the receipt will contain your A-number, which you'll need if you have to correspond with USCIS about your case. (USCIS is a big bureaucracy—your number will become more important than your name.)

Soon after getting your receipt(s) you should receive an Application Support Center (ASC) Appointment Notice. The notice schedules you for an appointment to have your fingerprints, photo, and signature taken. The photo and signature are used to create your work permit and your Advance Parole travel document (described in Section D2, below), if you requested those. Your fingerprints are taken for processing your application for adjustment of status.

The work permit is good for one year. Once your case is approved and you become a permanent resident, you no longer need a work permit. Your right to work is evidenced by your permanent resident card. In case your application is delayed for some reason, however, you can renew the work permit for one-year periods for as long as you are still waiting for a decision on your adjustment of status application.

D. Moving or Traveling While Waiting for Your Interview

After you've submitted your adjustment of status packet you will wait several months to a year or more before your interview is scheduled. Of course, your life continues on and you may want to move your residence or make travel plans. Read the material below before you do.

1. If You Change Addresses

You do not have to live in one place while waiting for your green card. However, your application will go most smoothly if you and your spouse settle yourselves at a stable address and stay there. This will help ensure that you receive notices of important USCIS appointments (first for fingerprints, then for the interview).

If you do move, then within ten days of moving, you (and every immigrating member of your family) must advise USCIS. The law requires this of all non-U.S. citizens over 14 years old and remaining in the U.S. for more than 30 days—failure to do so is a misdemeanor and can be punished with a jail term of up to 30 days, a fine of up to $200, or your removal from the United States. (See I.N.A. § 265; 8 U.S.C. § 1305.)

The procedure for advising USCIS of your move is to use Form AR-11. To file the AR-11 online, go to www.uscis.gov/ar-11 and click "File Online" Follow the instructions. When finished, click "Submit" to e-file the form. Print a copy for your records. It will show the date and time the form was filed, and will contain a USCIS confirmation number. There is no fee for this form. One advantage to e-filing your AR-11 is that you will be asked whether you have applications pending, so that the office that will interview you will automatically be informed of your address change (a big improvement over the old system, in which you had to separately advise each office handling your application).

How Long Will You Wait Until Your Interview?

The easiest way to find out how long you will likely have to wait for your interview is to go to the USCIS home page at www.uscis.gov. Click "Check Case Status," then click the link at the bottom of the page entitled "USCIS Processing Times Information." On the next page, first choose "I-485 family based" for the application type, and then choose the name of the district office where your file is pending. You'll see a broad range of processing times, such as 11-36 months, and a case inquiry date. Once your filing date is on or before the latter date, you can call or submit an inquiry via the USCIS website.

Sample Adjustment of Status Application Receipt Notice

| Department of Homeland Security
U.S. Citizenship and Immigration Services | **Form I-797C, Notice of Action** |

THIS NOTICE DOES NOT GRANT ANY IMMIGRATION STATUS OR BENEFIT.

NOTICE TYPE Receipt	NOTICE DATE April 12, 2019
CASE TYPE I-485, Application to Register Permanent Residence or Adjust Status	USCIS ALIEN NUMBER 12345677
RECEIPT NUMBER MSC-19-006-000	RECEIVED DATE April 05, 2019	PAGE 1 of 1
PRIORITY DATE March 21, 2019	PREFERENCE CLASSIFICATION 201 B INA SPOUSE OF USC	DATE OF BIRTH JUNE 28, 1991

ANDA MIHOV
68 WATERTOWN BLVD.
APT.12
ERIE, PA 19380

PAYMENT INFORMATION:

Application/Petition Fee:	$1,140.00
Biometrics Fee:	$85.00
Total Amount Received:	$1,225.00
Total Balance Due:	$0.00

NAME AND MAILING ADDRESS

The above application/petition has been received by our office and is in process.

Please verify your personal information listed above and immediately notify the USCIS National Customer Service Center at the phone number listed below if there are any changes.

Please note that if a priority date is printed on this notice, the priority does not reflect earlier retained priority dates.

Next Steps:
- USCIS will schedule a biometrics appointment for you to have your biometrics electronically captured at a USCIS Application Support Center (ASC). You will be receiving a biometrics appointment notice by mail with the specific date, time, and place where you will have your fingerprints and/or photographs taken.
- You must wait to receive your biometrics appointment notice before going to the ASC for biometrics processing.
- This notice does not serve as your biometrics appointment notice.

If you have questions about possible immigration benefits and services, filing information, or USCIS forms, please call the USCIS National Customer Service Center (NCSC) at **1-800-375-5283**. If you are hearing impaired, please call the NCSC TDD at **1-800-767-1833**. Please also refer to the USCIS website: www.uscis.gov.

If you have any questions or comments regarding this notice or the status of your case, please contact our customer service number.

You will be notified separately about any other case you may have filed.

USCIS Office Address:	USCIS Customer Service Number:
USCIS National Benefits Center P.O. Box 648003 Lee's Summit, MO 64002	(800)375-5283 ATTORNEY COPY

If this is an interview or biometrics appointment notice, please see the back of this notice for important information.

Form I-797C 07/11/14 Y

If you prefer to file your AR-11 by regular mail, print out the form from the USCIS website and mail it to the address shown on the form. It's best to file by Priority Mail and retain copies of the filed forms and proof of mailing. Realize, however, that if you mail your AR-11, you will still have to send an additional letter to the USCIS interviewing office to notify it of your address change.

If you move to another city, your entire file may have to be sent to a different USCIS office. This always results in long delays. If you know before you file your adjustment of status application that you'll be moving to a different city, it's wise to wait until after your move to file your application.

Also keep in mind that your sponsor and any joint sponsor must inform USCIS of their new addresses; either online as explained above, or by submitting Form I-865 by mail. It's available at www.uscis.gov/i-865.

2. Traveling While Waiting for Your Interview

While waiting for your adjustment of status interview, you may want or need to visit your home country, to visit family or continue arranging your move to the United States, for example. You can travel, but must use great care. If you simply get up and go without getting official permission, the law says you will have given up (or abandoned, in USCIS terminology) your adjustment of status application. You will need to start all over.

There are a few narrow exceptions. If you arrived in the United States on a K-3 visa (a so-called "fiancé visa" designed especially for already-married couples), you can use these to reenter the United States as many times as you like until a decision has been made on your green card application.

Similarly, if you entered the U.S. on an H-1B or L-1 visa (which are types of employment-based visas), you can use your visa to reenter the U.S. as long as it is still valid and you are returning in order to resume the same employment.

To protect yourself (if you don't have a K-3, H-1B, or L-1 visa), ask USCIS for advance permission to leave (called "Advance Parole"). You can either file the Advance Parole application together with your adjustment of status application, or you can file it separately, along with proof that your adjustment of status application has already been filed.

Once you've received Advance Parole, your adjustment of status application will be preserved, including its place in line. Your trip shouldn't delay the processing of your application. In fact, you may be granted a multiple entry Advance Parole document, meaning you can take many trips within a certain time period.

a. Qualifying for Advance Parole

USCIS grants Advance Parole fairly readily to adjustment applicants, recognizing the hardship caused by its own processing delays. The Form I-131 Instructions warn you that USCIS will grant Advance Parole only for "urgent humanitarian reasons" or a "significant public benefit" (including personal or family emergencies or bona fide business reasons). USCIS strictly follows these criteria when deciding whether to grant expedited (speedy) processing requests.

The form you'll complete will ask you to attach a page explaining how you qualify for Advance Parole and why your application deserves to be approved. This explanation doesn't need to be very long. You can simply write your name and A-number at the top of a page and then say something like this: *"I qualify for Advance Parole because I am the spouse of a U.S. citizen awaiting my adjustment of status interview. I would like to travel during this time to visit family."*

However, if you are traveling because of an emergency, it may help or speed up your application to explain and substantiate the crisis. For example, if it's a family medical emergency, provide a letter from your family member's doctor explaining your family member's condition and the need for your visit. (If the letter is in another language, be sure to have it translated; see Chapter 4, Section C, on how to translate documents for USCIS.)

b. Be Cautious About Leaving

The Advance Parole document is your ticket back into the United States, but it is not a guaranteed ticket. Its function is to keep your adjustment of status application alive while you're gone—but it won't necessarily protect you from being found inadmissible for any of the reasons on the list in Chapter 2, Section A—though it will, at least, protect you from the time bars, according to B.I.A. Interim Decision #3748. So if you have any doubts about your admissibility to the United States, don't leave at all, or consult a lawyer first.

Don't be alarmed, however, if upon returning to the United States, you are pulled into a separate line. This is called "secondary inspection," and it is the normal procedure for anyone returning with an Advance Parole document.

WEB RESOURCE

Form I-131 is available on the USCIS website at www.uscis.gov/i-131. A sample filled-in version is below.

c. Using the Checklist for Applying for Advance Parole

The checklist below details what you'll need to apply for Advance Parole. Mark off the relevant items as you complete or obtain them to make sure that you haven't forgotten anything. If you didn't include this with your I-485 adjustment application already, note that USCIS requires that you send in your I-131 application well before you plan to travel. As of 2019, some applications are taking six months or more to be approved.

The form you'll use for Advance Parole is Form I-131, Application for Travel Document. This form is largely self-explanatory. However, it is also used by applicants applying for other immigration benefits, so there are some portions that don't apply to you. The only parts that you need to fill in are Parts 1, 2 (put an "X" in **box 1.d**), 3, 7, and 8. Enter "TBD," which means "to be determined," if you don't yet know your travel dates.

When you're done, make a complete copy of your paperwork (for your records). If you are filing it at the same time as the I-485, just send the original with the I-485 to the lockbox that accepts filing of your I-485. If you are filing it after having filed your I-485, then where you send the original depends on the first three letters of the receipt number on your I-485 receipt notice. Check the Form I-131 instructions for the correct addresses.

If you are asking that your application be handled more speedily because of an emergency, it's best to use the courier address rather than the P.O. Box address.

Previously, it was possible to submit the application form online through the USCIS website. However, USCIS discontinued this "e-Filing" system in 2015.

Checklist for Applying for Advance Parole

☐ Form I-131

☐ A separate sheet of paper, in accordance with Part 7 of the application form, explaining how you qualify for Advance Parole and why your application deserves to be approved (no need to spend too much time on this—most requests are approved without question unless you're requesting expedited processing)

☐ If you are traveling because of an emergency, evidence to prove it

☐ Copy of the receipt notice you got when you filed your adjustment of status packet (if you are filing your I-131 after already having filed your I-485)

☐ Copy of a photo ID, such as a driver's license

☐ Two color photos of you, passport style

☐ Fee: there is no fee as long as your I-485 is pending

WEB RESOURCE

This checklist is also available online; to obtain an RTF version, see the instructions in Appendix B.

Sample Form I-131, Application for Travel Document—Page 1

Application for Travel Document

Department of Homeland Security
U.S. Citizenship and Immigration Services

**USCIS
Form I-131**
OMB No. 1615-0013
Expires 12/31/2018

For USCIS Use Only	Receipt	Action Block	To Be Completed by an *Attorney/Representative*, if any.

☐ **Document Hand Delivered**

By: _____ Date: _____ / _____ / _____

☐ Fill in box if G-28 is attached to represent the applicant.

Document Issued

☐ Re-entry Permit *(Update " Mail To" Section)* ☐ Refugee Travel Document *(Update " Mail To" Section)*

☐ Single Advance Parole ☐ Multiple Advance Parole *Valid Until:* _____ / _____ / _____

Mail To *(Re-entry & Refugee Only)*

☐ Address in *Part 1*

☐ US Consulate at: _____

☐ Intl DHS Ofc at: _____

Attorney State License Number:

_____

▶ **Start Here.** Type or Print in Black Ink

Part 1. Information About You

1.a. Family Name *(Last Name)* | Mihov

1.b. Given Name *(First Name)* | Anda

1.c. Middle Name | Marina

Physical Address

2.a. In Care of Name

2.b. Street Number and Name | 68 Watertown Blvd

2.c. Apt. ☒ Ste. ☐ Flr. ☐ 12

2.d. City or Town | Erie

2.e. State | PA   **2.f.** Zip Code | 19380

2.g. Postal Code

2.h. Province

2.i. Country | USA

Other Information

3. Alien Registration Number (A-Number)

▶ A- ☐☐☐☐☐☐☐☐☐

4. Country of Birth

Bulgaria

5. Country of Citizenship

Bulgaria

6. Class of Admission

H-1B

7. Gender ☐ Male ☒ Female

8. Date of Birth *(mm/dd/yyyy)* ▶ 06/28/1991

9. U.S. Social Security Number *(if any)*

▶ 3 8 7 3 3 8 8 7 7

Sample Form I-131, Application for Travel Document—Page 2

Part 2. Application Type

1.a. ☐ I am a permanent resident or conditional resident of the United States, and I am applying for a reentry permit.

1.b. ☐ I now hold U.S. refugee or asylee status, and I am applying for a Refugee Travel Document.

1.c. ☐ I am a permanent resident as a direct result of refugee or asylee status, and I am applying for a Refugee Travel Document.

1.d. ☒ I am applying for an Advance Parole Document to allow me to return to the United States after temporary foreign travel.

1.e. ☐ I am outside the United States, and I am applying for an Advance Parole Document.

1.f. ☐ I am applying for an Advance Parole Document for a person who is outside the United States.

If you checked box "1.f." provide the following information about that person in 2.a. through 2.p.

2.a. Family Name *(Last Name)*

2.b. Given Name *(First Name)*

2.c. Middle Name

2.d. Date of Birth *(mm/dd/yyyy)* ▶

2.e. Country of Birth

2.f. Country of Citizenship

2.g. Daytime Phone Number (☐☐) ☐☐ - ☐☐☐

Physical Address (If you checked box 1.f.)

2.h. In Care of Name

2.i. Street Number and Name

2.j. Apt. ☐ Ste. ☐ Flr. ☐

2.k. City or Town

2.l. State ☐ **2.m.** Zip Code

2.n. Postal Code

2.o. Province

2.p. Country

Part 3. Processing Information

1. Date of Intended Departure *(mm/dd/yyyy)* ▶ TBD

2. Expected Length of Trip *(in days)* TBD

3.a. Are you, or any person included in this application, now in exclusion, deportation, removal, or rescission proceedings? ☐ Yes ☒ No

3.b. If "Yes", Name of DHS office:

4.a. Have you ever before been issued a reentry permit or Refugee Travel Document? *(If " Yes" give the following information for the last document issued to you):* ☐ Yes ☒ No

4.b. Date Issued *(mm/dd/yyyy)* ▶

4.c. Disposition *(attached, lost, etc.):*

If you are applying for a non-DACA related Advance Parole Document, skip to Part 7; *DACA recipients must complete Part 4 before skipping to Part 7.*

Sample Form I-131, Application for Travel Document—Page 3

Part 3. Processing Information *(continued)*

Where do you want this travel document sent? *(Check one)*

5. ☐ To the U.S. address shown in **Part 1 (2.a through 2.i.)** of this form.

6. ☐ To a U.S. Embassy or consulate at:

6.a. City or Town _____

6.b. Country _____

7. ☐ To a DHS office overseas at:

7.a. City or Town _____

7.b. Country _____

If you checked "6" or "7", where should the notice to pick up the travel document be sent?

8. ☐ To the address shown in **Part 2 (2.h. through 2.p.)** of this form.

9. ☐ To the address shown in **Part 3 (10.a. through 10.i.)** of this form.:

10.a. In Care of Name _____

10.b. Street Number and Name _____

10.c. Apt. ☐ Ste. ☐ Flr. ☐ _____

10.d. City or Town _____

10.e. State _____ **10.f.** Zip Code _____

10.g. Postal Code _____

10.h. Province _____

10.i. Country _____

10.j. Daytime Phone Number (___) ___ - ____

Part 4. Information About Your Proposed Travel

1.a. Purpose of trip. *(If you need more space, continue on a separate sheet of paper.)*

_____
_____
_____
_____

1.b. List the countries you intend to visit. *(If you need more space, continue on a separate sheet of paper.)*

_____
_____
_____
_____

Part 5. Complete Only If Applying for a Re-entry Permit

Since becoming a permanent resident of the United States (or during the past 5 years, whichever is less) how much total time have you spent outside the United States?

1.a. ☐ less than 6 months **1.d.** ☐ 2 to 3 years
1.b. ☐ 6 months to 1 year **1.e.** ☐ 3 to 4 years
1.c. ☐ 1 to 2 years **1.f.** ☐ more than 4 years

2. Since you became a permanent resident of the United States, have you ever filed a Federal income tax return as a nonresident or failed to file a Federal income tax return because you considered yourself to be a nonresident? *(If "Yes" give details on a separate sheet of paper.)*

☐ Yes ☐ No

Sample Form I-131, Application for Travel Document—Page 4

Part 6. Complete Only If Applying for a Refugee Travel Document

1. Country from which you are a refugee or asylee:

If you answer "Yes" to any of the following questions, you must explain on a separate sheet of paper. Include your Name and A-Number on the top of each sheet.

2. Do you plan to travel to the country named above? ☐ Yes ☐ No

Since you were accorded refugee/asylee status, have you ever:

3.a. Returned to the country named above? ☐ Yes ☐ No

3.b. Applied for and/or obtained a national passport, passport renewal, or entry permit of that country? ☐ Yes ☐ No

3.c. Applied for and/or received any benefit from such country (for example, health insurance benefits)? ☐ Yes ☐ No

Since you were accorded refugee/asylee status, have you, by any legal procedure or voluntary act:

4.a. Reacquired the nationality of the country named above? ☐ Yes ☐ No

4.b. Acquired a new nationality? ☐ Yes ☐ No

4.c. Been granted refugee or asylee status in any other country? ☐ Yes ☐ No

Part 7. Complete Only If Applying for Advance Parole

On a separate sheet of paper, explain how you qualify for an Advance Parole Document, and what circumstances warrant issuance of advance parole. Include copies of any documents you wish considered. *(See instructions.)*

1. How many trips do you intend to use this document? ☐ One Trip ☒ More than one trip

If the person intended to receive an Advance Parole Document is outside the United States, provide the location (City or Town and Country) of the U.S. Embassy or consulate or the DHS overseas office that you want us to notify.

2.a. City or Town

2.b. Country

If the travel document will be delivered to an overseas office, where should the notice to pick up the document be sent?:

3. ☐ To the address shown in **Part 2 (2.h. through 2.p.)** of this form.

4. ☐ To the address shown in **Part 7 (4.a. through 4.i.)** of this form.

4.a. In Care of Name

4.b. Street Number and Name

4.c. Apt. ☐ Ste. ☐ Flr. ☐

4.d. City or Town

4.e. State

4.f. Zip Code

4.g. Postal Code

4.h. Province

4.i. Country

4.j. Daytime Phone Number ( ) -

Sample Form I-131, Application for Travel Document—Page 5

Part 8. Signature of Applicant *(Read the information on penalties in the Form instructions before completing this Part.)* If you are filing for a Re-entry Permit or Refugee Travel Document, you must be in the United States to file this application.

1.a. I certify, under penalty of perjury under the laws of the United States of America, that this application and the evidence submitted with it is all true and correct. I authorize the release of any information from my records that U.S. Citizenship and Immigration Services needs to determine eligibility for the benefit I am seeking.

Signature of Applicant

➡ *Anda M. Mihov*

1.b. Date of Signature *(mm/dd/yyyy)* ▶ 05/09/2019

2. Daytime Phone Number (3 1 4) 2 7 6 - 9 4 4 0

NOTE: If you do not completely fill out this form or fail to submit required documents listed in the instructions, your application may be denied.

Part 9. Information About Person Who Prepared This Application, If Other Than the Applicant

NOTE: If you are an attorney or representative, you must submit a completed Form G-28, Notice of Entry of Appearance as Attorney or Accredited Representative, along with this application.

Preparer's Full Name

Provide the following information concerning the preparer:

1.a. Preparer's Family Name *(Last Name)*

1.b. Preparer's Given Name *(First Name)*

2. Preparer's Business or Organization Name

Preparer's Mailing Address

3.a. Street Number and Name

3.b. Apt. ☐ Ste. ☐ Flr. ☐

3.c. City or Town

3.d. State

3.e. Zip Code

3.f. Postal Code

3.g. Province

3.h. Country

Preparer's Contact Information

4. Preparer's Daytime Phone Number   Extension

( ) -

5. Preparer's E-mail Address *(if any)*

Declaration

To be completed by all preparers, including attorneys and authorized representatives: I declare that I prepared this benefit request at the request of the applicant, that it is based on all the information of which I have knowledge, and that the information is true to the best of my knowledge.

6.a. Signature of Preparer

6.b. Date of Signature *(mm/dd/yyyy)* ▶

NOTE: If you require more space to provide any additional information, use a separate sheet of paper. You must include your Name and A-Number on the top of each sheet.

E. Your Fingerprint Appointment

About one month after submitting your adjustment of status packet to USCIS, you'll get an appointment for fingerprinting (called "biometrics"). USCIS will require that you be fingerprinted at a USCIS-authorized site. In some nonurban areas of the United States, USCIS also offers mobile fingerprinting vans. If you can't make it at the scheduled time, you can ask to be rescheduled.

Your fingerprints will be reviewed by the U.S. Federal Bureau of Investigation (FBI), which will check them against records held by the police as well as by USCIS (which often takes the fingerprints of people caught crossing the border illegally). The FBI will send a report to USCIS to confirm your identity and to show whether you have committed any crimes or immigration violations that might make you inadmissible.

> **SEE AN EXPERT**
>
> **If you think you might have a criminal record but aren't sure, consult a lawyer.** You won't discover until you get to your adjustment of status interview what the FBI report says about you. The lawyer can help you request a separate fingerprint report from the FBI and deal with whatever it shows, to help you get your green card.

F. Advance Preparation for Your Adjustment of Status Interview

Although you will probably wait many months or a year or more for your adjustment of status interview, when the appointment letter finally comes it will give you a date only around four weeks away. For this reason, it is important to prepare yourself and your documents well in advance.

> **TIP**
>
> **Remember to read Chapter 13 for your final interview preparation.** It will give you a complete picture of what will happen at the interview and describe how to make it a success.

1. Positioning Yourself for a Good Interview

Your adjustment of status interview is most likely to go smoothly if you and your spouse live together. Also, the two of you should combine as many practical aspects of your life as possible, including bank accounts, insurance policies, electric, plumbing, and other utility accounts, club memberships, and the ownership of cars, houses, and other major property. You can refer to all of these to prove that your marriage is real.

As you combine these parts of your life, pay attention to the paperwork that comes with them. Save those important contracts, receipts, and other forms of documentation. You'll want to take copies to your interview.

> **TIP**
>
> **If you've had to live apart, think about how you'll prove that you are still a true couple.** For example, if one of you has a job and the other is attending college ten hours away, living together won't be possible. While USCIS understands that such situations occur and won't automatically deny your green card on this basis, they will require additional proof that your marriage is real. You could show USCIS evidence that you spent holidays and vacations together and regularly communicate with one another.

2. Assembling Documents for Your Interview

Preparation is the key to a smooth interview. You will want to arrive with a number of documents and other items in hand, as explained in the following subsections. Keep track of these items in the months leading to the interview and reread this section a few days before your interview. You'll also find a checklist below, to help you make sure you've assembled the right material.

a. Photo Identification and Passport

You and your spouse will each need to present photo identification. Your passport is best. If you don't have a passport, use a separate form of photo identification for the interview. The U.S. citizen or permanent resident spouse usually presents a driver's license.

b. Original Documents and All INS or USCIS Permits

Assemble the originals of the documents you used to enter the United States, and any other documents you've received from U.S. consulates or INS or USCIS offices (for example, an Advance Parole travel permit). Also, if you've mailed copies of documents to USCIS, such as your marriage and birth certificates, bring the originals for the USCIS officer to see.

Your spouse will need to bring the original proof of his or her U.S. citizenship status (a birth certificate, naturalization certificate, or passport) or permanent resident status (a green card or stamp in his or her passport).

The officer may not ask for all of these, but you'll be glad you brought them if he or she does ask.

c. Updates to Materials in the Application

Has anything important in your life changed since filing the adjustment of status paperwork? If, for example, you or your spouse have a new or different job, bring a letter from the new employer and copies of recent pay stubs. (Of course, your spouse's income still needs to be high enough to deal with the Affidavit of Support requirements. If it has gone down, you, the immigrant, may be able to help by bringing proof that you are now working in the United States.)

If you and your spouse have reached the two-year anniversary of your marriage since filing the application, be ready to remind the officer of this, so you'll be approved for permanent, not conditional, residency. If a tax year has passed, bring a copy of your latest tax returns (or better yet, an IRS transcript of these returns).

And even if nothing has changed, prove that fact with a recent pay stub showing that the financial sponsor is still bringing in the income.

d. Proof That Your Marriage Is Real

The interview is an important opportunity for the USCIS officer to decide whether your marriage is bona fide, or "for real." The documents that you show are important factors in the decision. They should show that you and your spouse's lives are intertwined and that you trust each other with your financial and personal matters.

Below is a list of documents most immigrants present. However, this list isn't engraved in stone. Use your imagination and be ready to do some organized "show-and-tell." No need to flood the officer with paper—copies of six items from this list would be a reasonable amount.

- rental agreements, leases, or mortgages showing that you live together and/or have leased or bought property in both spouses' names
- your mutual child's birth certificate or a doctor's report saying that one of you is pregnant or seeking fertility treatment
- utility bills in both your names
- joint bank statements
- joint credit card statements
- evidence that one spouse has made the other a beneficiary on his/her life or health insurance or retirement account
- auto registrations showing joint ownership and/or addresses
- joint club memberships
- receipts from gifts that you purchased for one another (these should be typical gift purchases, such as jewelry, flowers, or candy)
- letters from friends and family to each or both of you mailed to your joint address, or
- photos of you and your spouse taken before and during your marriage, including photos from your wedding. (USCIS knows wedding pictures can be faked, but many officers enjoy

seeing them anyway.) The photos should, if possible, include parents and other relatives from both families. Write the date taken and a brief description of what the photo shows on the back (or underneath, if you're photocopying them). Don't bother with videos of the wedding or other events—there won't be time or a space to view them.

> **TIP**
>
> **It's not necessary for every single document to show both of your names.** You can instead, for example, bring separate pieces of mail that show matching addresses or that you've divided up responsibility for household bills.

3. Using the Checklist for Adjustment of Status Interview

The checklist below lists all of the documents and other items that you are normally required to bring to your adjustment of status interview. By checking off each item as you collect it, you'll be sure that nothing gets left at home on your interview day.

> **CHECKLIST**
>
> **Instructions on where to obtain an online version of this checklist are available in Appendix B at the back of this book.**

Checklist for Adjustment of Status Interview

☐ Photo identification/passport

☐ Original documents for review/comparison with copies

☐ Updates to material in the application

☐ Proof that your marriage is bona fide

☐ Sealed envelope with medical exam report if not submitted with I-485

> **TIP**
>
> **Photocopy every document you intend to bring.** If there are new items you want to show the officer, such as bank statements or utility bills, the officer probably won't consider them unless you're willing to leave the document behind. You won't want to turn over your original documents to a USCIS file. Bring a copy along with the original.

G. Green Cards for Your Children

This section contains an overview of the procedures for submitting adjustment of status applications for your children, but complete details (especially line-by-line instructions on filling out the forms for your children) are outside the scope of this book. But having filled out all the paperwork required for your own green card, you'll be well-positioned to complete these forms for your children. Of course, you might be more comfortable using a lawyer.

1. The Form I-130

If your spouse is a lawful permanent resident, then you have probably already dealt with Form I-130, and can skip to Section 2.

However, if your spouse is a U.S. citizen you will accordingly need to fill out a separate I-130 petition for each child.

The exception is if you entered on a K-1 fiancé visa, and your children are in K-2 status (and still unmarried and under age 21). Your child remains your derivative, and can file his or her adjustment of status application with no need for a Form I-130 petition. However, USCIS must approve the child's adjustment of status application before the child turns 21, or the child will "age out" (lose eligibility under this visa category). The Child Status Protection Act (CSPA) will not help your child in this situation, since CSPA does not apply to K-2 visas. To include your child under CSPA, you could ask your spouse to file a separate Form I-130 before your child's 21st birthday. Otherwise, you'll need to request that USCIS expedite (speed up) your case to avoid the age-out problem. Include a written request within your cover letter on top of your adjustment of status packet, and write in red letters "Request for expedite—age-out problem" on top of the letter.

Your child's application will be submitted to the same place as yours.

For the documents accompanying Form I-130, you'll be happy to hear that your children do not need to fill out Form I-130A, nor do they need to include their photos. Include copies of your and your spouse's marriage certificate, as well as copies of the children's birth certificates, to show the family relationships.

2. The Remainder of Your Children's Adjustment of Status Packet

Each unmarried child under 21 who wishes to get a green card along with you will have to submit a separate adjustment of status packet. (This includes some children who are actually over 21, but who remain legally under that age because of the Child Status Protection Act.) This packet will be nearly identical to yours.

Children who are derivatives on your petition (that is, didn't have a separate I-130 filed for them) won't need a separately signed and notarized Affidavit of Support (Form I-864). They can submit a photocopy of yours. Of course, you'll want to make sure that the children's names are listed in your Form I-864 and that your spouse or other sponsor has shown enough income and assets to cover all the children. And children who had their own I-130s need a separate I-864, too.

Children under 14 need not be fingerprinted. Pay close attention to the fees; while a separate set of fees needs to be paid for each immigrant, the rates are sometimes reduced for children.

As long as you submit your adjustment of status packet together with those of your children—that is, in the same envelope—you can expect to be interviewed at the same time. The children probably won't have to answer more than one or two questions at the interview.

3. If You Have Children Already Over 21 or Married

In some situations, your children may be unable to adjust status right away. For example, if your spouse is a permanent resident (not a citizen) and your child turns 21 before his or her Priority Date becomes current, then your child drops into a different visa category (2B) and must return to the waiting list before becoming eligible to adjust status.

Or, if your child entered on a K-2 visa and you were unable to both submit an adjustment of status application and get it approved before the child's 21st birthday, the child loses his or her eligibility to carry on with the process. (Your spouse could have filed a separate I-130 to preserve your child's eligibility at the outset, but it's too late now.)

Even more complex, if your child entered on a K-4 visa and your U.S. citizen spouse didn't or couldn't file a Form I-130 on the child's behalf before the child turned 21 (thereby gaining the protection of the Child Status Protection Act) the child will lose his or her eligibility to immigrate on the same schedule as you. (If a K-4 child's I-130 is filed after the child's 21st birthday, the child will be placed in the family first preference category, which has a wait, but moves fairly quickly.)

Similarly, if your child has gotten married, he or she drops to a lower visa category if your spouse is a U.S. citizen, and becomes completely ineligible for a green card if your spouse is a permanent resident.

Do not even try to submit an adjustment of status packet for your children at the same time as yours under any of these circumstances. The children could be placed in deportation proceedings if they are not in the United States legally.

But don't give up on your child's immigration prospects. Hopefully your spouse has already submitted separate Forms I-130 to a USCIS service center for any children eligible to immigrate (see discussion of eligibility in Chapter 2), thereby placing them on a waiting list for a future green card.

Unfortunately, if your spouse is a U.S. citizen and is not the child's biological parent, then he or she can file Form I-130 only if he or she qualifies as a "stepparent"—and that will work only if your marriage occurred before the child's 18th birthday. But you do have the option of filing a petition for the child yourself, as soon as you are approved for permanent residence, placing the child in category 2A (if the child is under 21) or 2B (if the child is over 21) of the family preference system (meaning an approximate wait of a year and a half under category 2A and five to ten years under category 2B). Even when you're a permanent resident, however, you can't file petitions for your children who are already married—you'll need to wait until you're a U.S. citizen to do that.

CAUTION

Children on a K-2 or K-4 visa who can't or don't want to adjust status must leave the U.S. when their permitted stay expires. Regardless of the expiration date on the visa itself, their status runs out either when the date on their Form I-94 passes, they turn 21, or you become a permanent resident (which means the child is no longer your derivative). Failure to leave on time could result in the child spending illegal time in the United States, and thereby becoming subject to the time bars discussed in Chapter 2.

SEE AN EXPERT

A lawyer can help you evaluate the rights of your children over 21 to immigrate, and prepare the applications if necessary. Chapter 17 tells you how to find a good lawyer.

CAUTION

Your approval for U.S. residency is cause for celebration, but not necessarily the end of your dealings with USCIS. If you were given conditional, not permanent residency, you will need to apply for permanent residency in approximately 21 months (see Chapter 16 for instructions). Also read Chapter 16 on how to protect and enjoy your U.S. residency.

Dealing With Bureaucrats, Delays, and Denials

If you think your I-130 petition or green card application is taking too long, welcome to the crowd. You are one of thousands of people applying for immigration benefits, and all of you are simultaneously dealing with governmental agencies that are often slow and inefficient. And if you think your application has been unfairly denied, you're not alone in this, either.

Fortunately, there are steps you can take—before, during, and after the application process—that will minimize the chances for delay or denial. This chapter discusses

- how to anticipate and deal with problems during any part of the immigration process (Section A), and
- how to respond to negative decisions (Sections B and C).

A. Anticipating and Dealing With Delays

In view of the number of people applying for visas and green cards, it's almost guaranteed that your application will spend some time in processing limbo. Although you can't prevent delays, you can anticipate them and be ready to deal with them when the time comes.

1. Plan Ahead for Lost or Wayward Papers

Knowing the likelihood of problems in advance, you can minimize them by keeping a copy of everything you send and (in the United States) sending everything by Priority Mail. If you're mailing from your own country, use the safest method available, preferably with some form of tracking.

No matter where you are, be aware that many USCIS addresses are Post Office boxes, where services like FedEx will not deliver. (These delivery companies need an actual person at the destination to sign for the article.) The USCIS website offers alternate addresses for courier services.

By taking these steps, you'll have the evidence you need in case you must show immigration authorities that it was their fault that a file was delayed or mislaid.

CAUTION

Don't even think of bribing a U.S. government official. Although there are countries where the only way to get anything from a government official is to offer cash or other gifts, the United States is not one of them. Personnel at USCIS and the consulates may sometimes be difficult, but it's generally not because they're expecting money. In fact, most of them are proud of the fact that the United States operates strictly according to the rule of law. Offering a bribe will most likely hurt or ruin your chances of getting a green card or visa.

2. When Should You Start Inquiring About Delays?

When it comes to delays, how long is too long? That is the million-dollar question. Processing times for USCIS and consular applications vary depending on the number of people applying.

a. How Long Should You Wait for Your Initial Receipt?

If you are waiting for an initial receipt (Form I-797C), such as one for an I-129F or I-130 petition that your fiancé or spouse filed with USCIS, six weeks is the longest you should wait. After that, you should probably make an inquiry.

First, check with your bank to see whether the check you submitted with the application was cashed. If it was, try to read the receipt number on the back of the check. Then call USCIS Customer Service at 800-375-5283. Even without a receipt number (which USCIS usually likes to use to track a case), they may be able to track your application using your other identifying information, such as your A-number, date of birth, and address.

b. How Long Should You Wait for a Decision on Your Case From USCIS?

Before you submit your applications to USCIS, you will probably want to know how long most people wait for a decision. You can usually get this information from the USCIS website.

The first thing to know is what type of petition or application you submitted. For family cases, it's likely to be an I-129F, I-130, I-485, I-765, or I-131. Next, review the posted processing times at USCIS. gov (click "Check Processing Times"). This will give you a rough idea of how long USCIS will need to decide on your petition or application under regular processing.

Second, you can click "Check Case Status" and enter your case number (the 11-digit number on the I-797 Receipt Notice that begins with EAC, LIN, MSC, WAC, or YSC) to get some information on where you are in the system. You can also, through the case status system, sign up to get email or text updates whenever USCIS takes action on your case. Be aware that these notification services sometimes are sporadic and delayed.

Finally, if you see that your petition's or application's "received date" is before the "Receipt date for an inquiry" noted alongside the posted processing time range on the USCIS website, you can call or write to ask USCIS to take action on the petition or application. The case inquiry link is on the case status page of USCIS's website. Or call the Contact Center number at 800-375-5283. Be ready with the case number and names and addresses of the persons referenced in the petition or application.

Keep in mind that processing times change. Although you may have checked the processing time several months earlier when you submitted your application, check it again before contacting USCIS. Once the USCIS office has gone beyond its normal processing time, it's time to contact the agency.

c. How Long Should You Wait to Be Scheduled for an Interview at the Consulate?

Some consulates post information about average wait times on their website. Go to the U.S. Department of State website at www.usembassy.gov, and select your consulate. If you don't find the processing times listed, you may need to call its public information number.

Many consulates now rely on the National Visa Center (NVC) to schedule appointments for them. If your case is at the NVC, you can call 603-334-0700 or go to https://travel.state.gov and click "U.S. Visas," then "Immigrate," then "The Immigrant Visa Process," then "After Your Petition is Approved," then "When and how to contact NVC."

The NVC does not provide general information about average wait times, but will respond to your specific questions about your case. Be ready to provide your NVC case number, which is on all correspondence from them.

3. Information Needed for an Inquiry

At some point, you will be sent a receipt notice (Form I-797C) with a case processing number. You'll recognize it because it starts with a three-letter abbreviation. The main ones are WAC, LIN, EAC, TSC, MSC, and YSC. These refer to the service center that issued the receipt. The receipt notice processing number is your single most important piece of information for tracking your application and making inquiries.

If you are processing your case at a consulate, once the National Visa Center gets your case, it assigns you a case number. The first three letters of that number refer to the consulate that will process your case. Once your case is at the NVC or the consulate, the case number is your single most important piece of information for tracking your application and making inquiries.

4. Emergency Attention

If there is some reason that your application really should be given immediate attention—that is, put ahead of all the other waiting applications—be sure to highlight this, most likely in a letter. It's better to attach this letter to your application than to send it later, asking that your application be moved out of the normal processing category into expedited processing.

If you have to send such a letter later, be sure to include your application's receipt number. You can also make a note on the outside of your envelope, in large, bold letters, saying: "URGENT! PLEASE EXPEDITE!" That way, you'll alert the people in the mail room to the fact that you need your request to get to an adjudicating officer as quickly as possible. But limit your cries for help to true emergencies, such as:

- a family member is dying in your home country and you need permission to leave the country during your green card processing to visit them, or
- you have scheduled surgery on the same day as an important USCIS appointment.

If possible, include proof of any claimed emergency, such as a letter from a doctor.

5. How to Inquire About Delays

Once you've determined that USCIS or a consulate is taking longer than it should, the question is what you can do about it. Your best course of action depends on where your application is.

a. Delays at a USCIS Office

If any USCIS office has your application, and it has been there beyond the normal processing time there are two ways to inquire: online or by phone. (The system for making in-person appointments to visit a USCIS office was phased out in 2019.) Call USCIS at 800-375-5283. Although the person you speak with will most likely not be able to tell you anything useful during that call, he or she will start an inquiry and tell you when to expect a response.

An often-easier possibility is to use USCIS's online inquiry function, available at www.uscis.gov. Click "Check Case Status," then look for "Submit a Case Inquiry." You will probably want to click the box titled "Case outside normal processing time." After entering your information, you can submit an explanation of the problem. Whether and how soon you get a reply, however, is questionable—people (including attorneys) who've tried it report mixed results and generic, unhelpful answers. But at least you'll avoid a long wait for someone to answer the phone.

The least useful course of action is to write a letter to USCIS. You are unlikely to get a response, except perhaps a boilerplate letter. The one exception is if you were already interviewed and were told that you should expect to receive a decision by mail. In this situation, if you do not want to make an inquiry online or use the Customer Contact number, you can write directly to the office where you were interviewed and ask for a decision on your case.

Although you may feel frustrated by delays in your case, remember to be polite. The officer you are speaking with is not the one who caused your delay; in fact, this officer is the one you are relying on to help you. You may be justifiably outraged by USCIS's action or inaction, but never insult or threaten the officer with whom you are speaking. At best, such behavior is never helpful; at worst, it could be interpreted as a threat, which could lead to criminal prosecution as well as a quick denial.

b. Delays at the NVC

If the NVC delays in something like sending your case to the consulate, you can submit an online inquiry (go to https://travel.state.gov and click "U.S. Visas," then "Immigrate," then "The Immigrant Visa Process," then "After Your Petition is Approved," then "When and how to contact NVC.", or call 603-334-0700. Be ready with your NVC case number, which you'll find on all correspondence from the NVC.

Sample I-129F Receipt Notice

Department of Homeland Security
U.S. Citizenship and Immigration Services

I-797C, Notice of Action

THE UNITED STATES OF AMERICA

RECEIPT NUMBER		CASE TYPE	I129F
WAC-19-041-00000			PETITION FOR FIANCE(E)
RECEIVED DATE	PRIORITY DATE	PETITIONER	
November 18, 2019		ANDERSON, CHRISTA	
NOTICE DATE	PAGE	BENEFICIARY	
December 1, 2019	1 of 1	CUEVAS, BERNARDO	

ILONA BRAY
RE: BERNARDO CUEVAS
950 PARKER ST.
BERKELEY, CA 94710

Notice Type: Receipt Notice

Amount received: $535.00

Receipt notice - If any of the above information is incorrect, call customer service immediately.

Processing time - Processing times vary by kind of case.
- You can check our current processing time for this kind of case on our website at **uscis.gov**.
- On our website you can also sign up to get free e-mail updates as we complete key processing steps on this case.
- Most of the time your case is pending the processing status will not change because we will be working on others filed earlier.
- We will notify you by mail when we make a decision on this case, or if we need something from you. If you move while this case is pending, call customer service when you move.
- Processing times can change. If you don't get a decision or update from us within our current processing time, check our website or call for an update.

If you have questions, check our website or call customer service. Please save this notice, and have it with you if you contact us about this case.

Notice to all customers with a pending I-130 petition - USCIS is now processing Form I-130, Petition for Alien Relative, as a visa number becomes available. Filing and approval of an I-130 relative petition is only the first step in helping a relative immigrate to the United States. Eligible family members must wait until there is a visa number available before they can apply for an immigrant visa or adjustment of status to a lawful permanent resident. This process will allow USCIS to concentrate resources first on cases where visas are actually available. This process should not delay the ability of one's relative to apply for an immigrant visa or adjustment of status. Refer to **www.state.gov/travel** <http://www.state.gov/travel> to determine current visa availability dates. For more information, please visit our website at www.uscis.gov or contact us at 1-800-375-5283.

Always remember to call customer service if you move while your case is pending. If you have a pending I-130 relative petition, also call customer service if you should decide to withdraw your petition or if you become a U.S. citizen.

Please see the additional information on the back. You will be notified separately about any other cases you filed.
U.S. CITIZENSHIP & IMMIGRATION SERVICES
P.O. BOX 68005
LEE'S SUMMIT, MO 68005
Customer Service Telephone: (800) 375-5283

Form I-797C (Rev. 08/31/04) N

c. Delays at the U.S. Consulate

If your case is delayed at the consulate after the interview, you will need to find out how that particular consulate prefers to receive inquiries. The possibilities are: visiting, calling, or writing a letter. Be sure to provide your NVC case number.

6. Incomplete or Lost Portions of Your Application

If USCIS or the NVC needs something to complete your application, such as further evidence of your bona fide marriage, or a missing financial document, they will usually mail you a Request for Evidence (RFE).

If you receive a request for more documentation, try to gather whatever was asked for and get it in the mail as soon as possible, and definitely before the deadline (likely 87 days, which is the regulatory maximum). Don't forget to include the original notification form as a cover sheet—but make a copy for yourself first.

It's also helpful to write a cover letter explaining what's in your submission. This letter should be organized similarly to the RFE, to demonstrate to the officer handling your case that you provided all of the requested information.

> **CAUTION**
> **You get only one chance to respond to a USCIS RFE.** The agency's regulations require that you submit all the requested materials at the same time, not in separate mailings. If you send back the RFE and later remember that you failed to include other documents—even if you send these documents prior to the deadline—USCIS will likely not consider these when deciding your case. However, if you are unable to locate certain documents and the deadline for your reply is looming, at least send USCIS what you have.

What should you do if you're asked for something that you know you've already sent? This is a surprisingly common occurrence If the requested item is something inexpensive or easy to come by, don't even

try arguing with USCIS or the NVC—even if you have photocopies proving that you already sent the item. Just assume it's been lost and send another one.

Lost checks or money orders are a different matter. Don't send USCIS another check or money order until you've found out what happened to the first draft. If you sent a check and haven't received information about it with your monthly bank statement, ask your bank to tell you whether your check has been cashed. If so, get the check and send USCIS a copy of both sides, so that USCIS officials can see their own stamp and processing number.

If you sent a money order and kept the receipt with the tracer number, call the company that issued the money order to find out whether it's been cashed. Ask for a copy of the cashed money order or other evidence that you can use to prove to USCIS that they were the ones who cashed it. If you can't get a copy of the cashed money order, send USCIS a copy of your receipt and an explanation. Hopefully, they will stop bugging you for the money.

B. What to Do If an Application Is Denied

First, a word of reassurance: Neither USCIS nor the NVC or consulates like to deny visas to eligible applicants. Unless you are clearly ineligible, they will usually give you many chances to supplement your application and make it worthy of approval. Maybe this is the good side of a slow-moving bureaucracy—every decision takes time, even a negative one. (But don't use this as an excuse to be sloppy in putting your application together the first time.)

> **SEE AN EXPERT**
> **If your visa or green card has been denied, it's time to think about getting a lawyer.** This advice is particularly important if the denial was due to something more serious than a bureaucratic mistake or a lack of documentation on your part. You'll definitely need a lawyer for the complicated procedures mentioned below, including removal proceedings and motions to reopen or reconsider. (See Chapter 17 on finding a lawyer.)

1. Denial of Initial Fiancé or Immigrant Petition

If USCIS denies your initial I-129F fiancé petition or I-130 petition, the best thing for your U.S. fiancé or spouse to do is to start over and file a new one. This is true even if a lawyer is helping you. There is an appeal process, but hardly anyone ever uses it. You'll probably spend less time starting over, and the fee is about the same. Besides, no government agency likes to admit it was wrong, so there is a tactical advantage to getting a fresh start.

If you feel your case is being treated unfairly, consider contacting the USCIS Ombudsman (www.dhs.gov/case-assistance).

2. Denial of Visa or Green Card

If USCIS or the consulate denies an application further along in the process, your response will depend on where you are—in the U.S. or overseas.

a. Denial of Green Card After Applying for Adjustment of Status in the U.S.

If you are applying for adjustment of status in the United States, there is technically no appeal after a denial. If, as is likely, you have no other legal right to be in the United States when the application is denied (such as a pending political asylum application), you may be placed in removal proceedings in Immigration Court. There, you will have the opportunity to renew your marriage-based green card application before an immigration judge. In rare circumstances, you might need to file a motion to have your case reopened or reconsidered; or you may need to file a separate suit in federal court.

> CAUTION
>
> **Never ignore a notice to appear in Immigration Court.** Attorneys regularly receive questions from immigrants who were scheduled for a hearing in Immigration Court and either forgot, couldn't make it, or just hoped the problem would go away. Failing to appear for

a court date is the worst thing you can do to your hopes of immigrating. It will earn you an automatic order of removal (deportation), which means that USCIS can pick you up and put you on a plane home anytime, with no more hearings. You'll also be hit with a prohibition on returning to the United States for many years and further punishments if you return illegally. The fact that your spouse is a U.S. citizen or resident won't be worth much after an order of removal has been entered.

b. Denial of Fiancé Visa at U.S. Consulate

If you are applying for a fiancé visa through a consulate overseas, you have no appeal after a denial. The consulate is at least required to tell you the reason for the denial, and often the fastest thing is to fix the problem and reapply.

In some cases, the consular officer raises a question as to whether USCIS should have approved the underlying petition in the first place, and sends the petition back to USCIS for another look. This is called a "consular return," and kicks off a lengthy waiting period. It could be six months or more before USCIS receives the petition back from the consulate and contacts you to tell you what's wrong.

At that point, USCIS will send you a Notice of Intent to Revoke (NOIR), which essentially says that new information brings into question whether USCIS approved the petition in error. The NOIR will outline the specific issues and give you a limited time to respond. If you find yourself in this unlucky situation, talk to a lawyer before proceeding. Once you have resolved all the issues, and USCIS is satisfied, it will again send the petition back to the consulate. The foreign-born fiancé can then pick up the process where it halted the last time.

If the issue was whether you truly intended to get married, it might be wise to marry in your home country and work on gathering evidence that your marriage is the real thing before you apply for an immigrant visa.

c. Denial of Marriage-Based Visa at U.S. Consulate

If you are applying for an immigrant (marriage-based) visa, the consulate will give you one year after the denial of your visa application to provide information aimed at reversing the denial. If you feel you are being treated unfairly, this is a good time to get the U.S. spouse's local Congressperson involved (see Section C, below). At the end of the year, your application will close and you must start all over again. There is no appeal from the denial or the closure.

> ! **CAUTION**
> **Don't attempt multiple, inconsistent applications.** The U.S. government keeps a record of all your applications. If you come back five years later with a new U.S. citizen fiancé or spouse and a new visa or green card application, USCIS or the consulate will be happy to remind you of any past fraud or other reasons for inadmissibility. (Changing your name won't work—by the end of the application process, USCIS will have your fingerprints.)

C. When All Else Fails, Call Your U.S. Congressperson

If your case turns into a true bureaucratic nightmare or a genuine miscarriage of justice, your U.S. citizen or permanent resident spouse can ask a local Congressperson for help. Some of them have a staff person dedicated to helping constituents who have immigration problems. A simple inquiry by a Congressperson can end months of USCIS or consular stonewalling or inaction. In rare cases, the Congressperson's office might be willing to put some actual pressure on USCIS or the consular office.

> **EXAMPLE:** Rodrigo, a U.S. citizen, was trying to get permission for his wife Sandra to immigrate from Mexico. She attended her visa interview and was told to come back with more proof that she would be financially supported and not become a public charge. Although Rodrigo's income was already over the *Poverty Guidelines,* he found a joint sponsor, who submitted an additional Affidavit of Support for Sandra. The consulate still wasn't willing to grant the visa. Rodrigo consulted with an attorney, who wrote letters to the consulate—but got no reply. Finally his attorney wrote a letter to Rodrigo's Congressperson asking for help. They submitted copies of all the relevant documents, so that the Congressperson would fully understand the problem. The visa was granted—with no explanation—a week after the Congressperson's inquiry.

Your Congressperson probably won't be surprised to hear from you. Illinois Congresswoman Janice Schakowsky once reported that eight out of ten calls from her constituents were complaints about the INS (as USCIS was then called). (See "Unchecked Power of the INS Shatters American Dream," by Kim Christensen, Richard Read, Julie Sullivan, and Brent Walth, *The Oregonian*, Sunday, December 20, 2000.)

After You Get Your Green Card

I f you're reading this after becoming a permanent or conditional resident, congratulations! But don't stop reading. This chapter will give you some important tips on how to protect and enjoy your new status, and how to turn conditional residence into permanent residence.

It's Not Too Early to Plan for U.S. Citizenship

If your spouse was a U.S. citizen when you were approved for U.S. residency, and you remain married and living together, you can apply for U.S. citizenship 90 days before your three-year anniversary of approval. Immigrants who were initially approved as conditional residents don't have to wait any longer. Your two years of conditional residence count toward the three years' wait for citizenship, as long as you did eventually become a permanent resident.

Take a look at your permanent resident card to identify your initial approval date. For example, if you were approved for residency on April 1, 2019, you can apply for citizenship anytime after January 1, 2022.

The time period changes to *five* years minus 90 days if you are married to a *permanent resident*, or if you were married to a U.S. *citizen* but you divorce or stop living together during the required three years.

To become a U.S. citizen, you'll need to learn English, prove that you've lived in the United States for much of your time as a permanent resident, prove that you're of good moral character, and pass a test in U.S. history and civics. For more information, see *Becoming a U.S. Citizen: A Guide to the Law, Exam & Interview,* by Ilona Bray (Nolo), and the USCIS website at www.uscis.gov.

A. How to Prove You're a U.S. Resident

Your best proof that you are either a conditional permanent resident (if you had been married for less than two years when approved) or a permanent

resident is your permanent resident card—known as the green card. Usually, you will receive it in the mail within a few weeks of your application being approved.

Sample Green Card

If you enter the U.S. after being granted an immigrant visa at a U.S. consulate, you will also get a stamp in your passport when you enter. This stamp serves as temporary evidence of your permanent residence while you are waiting for your green card to be mailed to you. You can show this stamp to employers or use it to travel in and out of the United States.

If you get permanent residence by adjusting your status (within the U.S.), the USCIS officer may be reluctant to put a stamp in your passport. If you know you will need proof of your permanent residence before you get your green card, however —for example if you need to leave the U.S.—the officer will likely give you the temporary stamp.

After your case is approved, but before you get the actual green card, you will receive an Approval Notice and a Welcome Notice. It's always a relief to see these notices, but don't try to use them as if they were your green card. If you leave the U.S., you cannot use them to get back in. If you're over the age of 18, the law requires you to carry your green card or other evidence of your status at all times. But keep a photocopy of it in a safe place, in case it's lost or stolen—this will make it much easier to get a replacement card from USCIS.

Sample Notice of Approval for Residency

Department of Homeland Security U.S. Citizenship and Immigration Services	**Form I-797C, Notice of Action**

THIS NOTICE DOES NOT GRANT ANY IMMIGRATION STATUS OR BENEFIT.

Receipt Number		Case Type I485 - APPLICATION TO REGISTER PERMANENT RESIDENCE OR ADJUST STATUS
Received Date 01/11/2018	Priority Date 09/01/2017	Applicant A 123456789
Notice Date 01/14/2019	Page 1 of 1	Anda Mihov

Ilona Bray
950 Parker St.
Berkeley, CA 94701

Notice Type: Approval Notice
Section: Adjustment as direct beneficiary
of immigrant petition, Form I-485
COA: IR1

We have mailed an official notice about this case (and any relevant documentation) according to the mailing preferences you chose on Form G-28, Notice of Entry of Appearance as Attorney or Accredited Representative. This is a courtesy copy, not the official notice.

<u>What the Official Notice Said</u>

WELCOME TO THE UNITED STATES OF AMERICA

This is to notify you that your application for permanent residence has been approved. It is with great pleasure that we welcome you to permanent resident status in the United States.

At the top of this notice you will see a very important number. It is your USCIS A# (A-number). This is your permanent resident account and file number. This permanent account number is very important to you. You will need it whenever you contact us.

We will soon mail you a new *Permanent Resident Card*. You should receive it within the next 3 weeks. You can use it to show your new status. When you receive your card you must carry it with you at all times if you are 18 or older. It is the law.

Please call us at (800) 375-5283 if any of the information about you shown above is incorrect, if you move before you receive your card, or if you don't receive your card within the next 3 weeks. If you call us, please have your A# and also the receipt number shown above available. The receipt number is a tracking number for your application.

Please read the notice that comes with your card. It will have important information about your card, about your status and responsibilities, and about permanent resident services available to you.

Your new card will expire in ten years. While card expiration will not directly affect your status, you will need to apply to renew your card several months before it expires. When the time comes and you need filing information, or an application, or if you ever have other questions about permanent resident services available to you, just call our *National Customer Contact Center* at **1-800-375-5283** or visit the USCIS website at www.uscis.gov. (If you are hearing impaired, the NCSC's TDD number is **1-800-767-1833**.) The best days to call the NCSC are Tuesday through Friday.

Once again, welcome to the United States and congratulations on your permanent resident status.

THIS FORM IS NOT A VISA AND MAY NOT BE USED IN PLACE OF A VISA.

NOTICE: Although this application or petition has been approved, USCIS and the U.S. Department of Homeland Security reserve the right to verify this information before and/or after making a decision on your case so we can ensure that you have complied with applicable laws, rules, regulations, and other legal authorities. We may review public information and records, contact others by mail, the internet or phone, conduct site inspections of businesses and residences, or use other methods of verification. We will use the information obtained to determine whether you are eligible for the benefit you seek. If we find any derogatory information, we will follow the law in determining whether to provide you (and the legal representative listed on your Form G-28, if you submitted one) an opportunity to address that information before we make a formal decision on your case or start proceedings.

Please see the additional information on the back. You will be notified separately about any other cases you filed.

National Benefits Center
U. S. CITIZENSHIP & IMMIGRATION SVC
P.O. Box 648004
Lee's Summit MO 64064

USCIS Contact Center: www.uscis.gov/contactcenter

If this is an interview or biometrics appointment notice, please see the back of this notice for important information.   Form I-797C 06/07/18

Applying for a Social Security Number

With your U.S. residency, you are eligible for a Social Security number. This is a number given to all people legally living and working in the United States, to identify them and allow them to pay into a system of retirement insurance. You may have already applied for a Social Security number if you received a work permit before getting your green card. If not, now is the time to apply. You'll need this number before you start work—your new employer will ask for it in order to file taxes on your behalf.

To apply for your number, visit your local Social Security office. You can find it on the Social Security Administration's website at www.ssa.gov.

B. Traveling Abroad

There's no question about it—travel outside the United States is one of your rights as a conditional or permanent resident. But don't stay away too long. As the term "resident" suggests, you are expected to reside—that is, make your home—in the United States. If you make your home outside the United States, you could lose your green card.

Border officers are on the front lines of deciding whether returning green card holders are living outside the country. The officer will ask when you left the U.S., what you were doing while you were away, and where you make your home. If you were outside the U.S. for more than one year, and did not get advance permission before leaving, the law presumes that you abandoned your permanent residence. To challenge that presumption, you will probably have to attend Immigration Court and convince an Immigration Judge that you did not intend to abandon your status.

Even if you stay out of the U.S. for less than a year on each particular trip, making many trips outside the U.S. creates a risk of being found to have abandoned your residency if, over the course of several years, you spend more time outside the U.S. than within it. Trips outside the U.S. for more than six months are treated more seriously

than shorter trips, but even shorter trips can raise questions if you make so many that it looks like you are merely visiting the U.S. instead of living there.

If the border officer wonders whether you abandoned your permanent resident status, in addition to your length of time outside the U.S., the officer may consider whether you:

- pay U.S. taxes
- own a home or apartment or have a long-term lease in the United States
- were employed in the foreign country
- took your family to the foreign country
- are returning to the U.S. with a one-way ticket or a round-trip ticket back to the foreign country, and
- maintain other ties with the United States.

If you're coming back after a trip of several months, you can make your entry to the United States easier by bringing copies of documents that show that your home base is still in the United States. These documents could include your U.S. tax returns, home lease, evidence of employment, or other relevant documents.

In case you have a problem convincing a border official that you did not abandon your permanent residence, know that you do not have to accept the officer's decision as final. You have the right to present your case in Immigration Court. Only an Immigration Judge has the authority to make a final decision about whether you abandoned your status. For help with this, contact an attorney.

TIP

Get permission before leaving. If you know in advance that you're going to have to spend more than a year outside the United States, apply for a reentry permit. Use Form I-131, Application for Travel Document, available at www.uscis.gov/i-131. You will want to check Box 1.a in Part 2 for reentry permits. You will have to explain to USCIS the purpose of your trip and how much time you've already spent outside the United States. You don't need to wait for the permit to be approved before you leave the U.S., but it would be best to get your biometrics taken for the permit before you leave (a process that typically takes three to four weeks from the time you submit the I-131). It's also possible to make a quick trip back to the U.S. to attend your biometrics appointment.

C. Your Immigrating Family Members' Rights

If children immigrated with you, their legal status will pretty much match yours. If you received conditional, rather than permanent residency, so did they—and they will also have to apply for permanent residency 90 days before the second anniversary of the date they won conditional residency (see Section G, below, regarding application procedures).

One difference between your children's status and yours may be the number of years that they must wait before they apply for U.S. citizenship.

If your spouse was a permanent resident when you were approved, then you as well as your children must wait five years before applying for U.S. citizenship.

However, if your spouse was a U.S. citizen when you were approved, then there's a small chance that your children are on a fast track to U.S. citizenship. A U.S. citizen's biological and adopted children automatically become U.S. citizens upon entry to the U.S., on the condition that the children live within the U.S. and in the custody of their U.S. citizen parent. This right comes from the Child Citizenship Act of 2000, but it applies only to biological and adopted children, not to the stepchildren of U.S. citizens.

The children who benefit from this law will automatically receive a certificate of citizenship from USCIS by mail, within about six weeks of entering the United States. Children who would qualify for automatic citizenship except for the fact that they are over 18 when they become permanent residents will have to wait five years before applying for citizenship (despite the fact that you, their parent, need wait only three years).

RESOURCE
Want more information on how to obtain citizenship through family members? Talk to a lawyer or local nonprofit organization, or see Nolo's free online immigration articles at www.nolo.com.

D. Sponsoring Other Family Members

Once you are a permanent (not conditional) resident, you have limited rights to petition or sponsor other members of your family to immigrate. After you become a U.S. citizen, the law adds a few more family members to the list of those for whom you can petition.

The chart below, "Bringing the Family Over," shows the relatives whom you can help immigrate. (This chart does not discuss which relatives can immigrate immediately and which will have to wait until a visa is available.)

Bringing the Family Over

If you are a permanent resident, you can bring:
- Unmarried children
- Spouse.

If you are a U.S. citizen, you can bring:
- Parents
- Spouse
- Children (unmarried or married)
- Brothers and sisters.

The pathways represented in the chart above work only within your own family line—even if your spouse is a U.S. citizen he or she cannot bring in *your* parents, brothers, or sisters. Put another way, no one can petition for their in-laws.

Your children are another matter, however—as discussed in Chapter 2, Section B, your U.S. citizen spouse can (if he or she hasn't already) petition not only for children who are his or her own biological offspring, but also for his or her legal stepchildren (if your marriage took place before they turned 18).

1. Your Unmarried Children

Your unmarried children under 21 probably immigrated with you. If they didn't, you have a few options. First, if you came directly from overseas, it may not be too late to use the application you filled out, which resulted in your permanent residency. Adding children to an existing application is called "following to join." Ask your consulate about the procedures for doing this.

Your second option is to look again at whether your U.S. spouse can file a visa petition for your children. If they are your U.S. spouse's biological children, this will be no problem. If your spouse is a U.S. citizen, the children under 21 are considered immediate relatives; if your spouse is a U.S. permanent resident, the children go in category 2A of the Preference System. Either way, your U.S. spouse can follow the same procedures in petitioning for them to immigrate as he or she did for you.

If the children are not your U.S. spouse's biological children, he or she can petition for them only if they are his or her legal stepchildren. To be legal stepchildren, your marriage must have taken place before their 18th birthday.

Your third option is, as a lawful permanent resident, to file a visa petition for your children yourself. However, this won't get them a visa for at least a few years. As children of a permanent resident, they will be in the second preference category (2A) of the Visa Preference System, meaning that quotas limit how many such people are given visas each year. Your children will have to be on a waiting list for several years before becoming eligible to immigrate. (See Chapter 8, Section A2, for more details on the Visa Preference System.)

If you have unmarried children over 21, look again at whether your U.S. spouse can petition for them. If he or she is a U.S. citizen and the children's biological parent or legal stepparent, they will be placed in the first preference category of the Visa Preference System. That also means they will have to be on a waiting list.

You too could file a visa petition for your unmarried children over 21, but that would put them in category 2B of the Visa Preference System, and it will be a many-years-long wait for them.

2. Your Married Children

If your children are married and neither you nor your spouse are U.S. citizens, you cannot apply for them to immigrate. When one of you becomes a citizen, that person can file a petition to place the children in the third preference category, which moves rather slowly—often ten or more years. If your spouse is going to file the petition, the children must be his or her biological children or legal stepchildren.

3. Parents, Brothers, and Sisters

You are not permitted to file a petition for your parents until you are a U.S. citizen. When you get your citizenship, they will be considered immediate relatives and won't face any waiting periods.

When you are a U.S. citizen, you will also be able to file petitions for your brothers and sisters, but they will have to wait in the Visa Preference System (as members of the fourth, and last, preference). Their wait will be longer than anyone's—averaging 16 years for most applicants and 24 years for applicants from the Philippines. To make matters worse, Congress keeps threatening to do away with the fourth preference category.

E. Losing Your Permanent Resident Status

You can lose your U.S. permanent resident status by violating the law (committing a crime) or violating the terms of your residency, such as by staying out of the United States and living abroad for too long, as explained above in Section B. If you are in the United States, a violation of the law could make you deportable, in which case USCIS might start Immigration Court proceedings against you and eventually send you away. If you attempt to return to the United States, you could be found inadmissible and kept out.

You Can Be Deported for Not Telling USCIS You've Changed Your Address

In 2002, the Immigration and Naturalization Service (INS, now called USCIS) shocked immigrants and their advocates by starting to enforce little-known provisions of the immigration law that make it a crime for immigrants not to submit immediate notifications whenever they change their address.

The potential punishments include fines, imprisonment, or deportation. While the immigration authorities largely ignored these legal provisions in the past, their post-September 11th security focus changed this. Unfortunately, a number of innocents may be caught in the trap.

As a green card holder, you must take steps to protect yourself. Within ten days of your move, send USCIS a notice either online at www.uscis.gov or by mail using Form AR-11. Note that you can't just send one form per family—every member of your household needs to have a separate form submitted for him or her.

Form AR-11 itself is fairly self-explanatory. The question about your "last address" refers only to your last address in the United States, not overseas. The address you supply should be where you actually live, not a P.O. Box or work address. There is no fee for filing Form AR-11.

To file Form AR-11 online, go to www.uscis.gov/ar-11, and click "Online Change of Address." Follow the instructions. You will be asked whether you have any applications pending with USCIS. Be sure to check off all appropriate applications, so as to prompt USCIS into passing your new address to the right places. When you have finished, click "Submit."

Print a copy of the filed form for your records. It will show the date and time the form was filed, and will contain a USCIS confirmation number.

If you prefer to file your AR-11 by regular mail, you can print out the form from the USCIS website and mail it to the address shown on the form. For proof of filing, it's best to file by a courier such as FedEx or DHL or by certified or Priority Mail and retain copies of the filed forms and proof of mailing.

If you have any applications pending with USCIS and you file your AR-11 by mail, USCIS has no mechanism to send your change of address to all the appropriate offices, and you will have to inform them separately. Call the USCIS Contact Center at 800-375-5283 to provide your new address for all pending petitions or applications.

If you have a case in Immigration Court or at the Board of Immigration Appeals, or if your case is at the National Visa Center or a consulate, these places are separate from USCIS, and Form AR-11 information is not shared with them. Be sure to contact these places separately to let them know about your change of address. Whenever you mail a change of address to any of the agencies, make copies of the notification, and mail everything by a courier service or certified or Priority Mail with return receipt. Put your copies and the return receipt in a safe place.

What if more than ten days have already passed and you've only just discovered your responsibility to file Form AR-11? Most attorneys advise that you fill out the form now, to show USCIS you made an attempt to comply and to assure that it has your current address. USCIS can forgive failures to notify it that weren't willful (intentional).

CAUTION

Even in states where medical or recreational marijuana use is legal, immigrants must be careful. Your immigration status is governed by federal law, which makes any marijuana use illegal. So, even though your state may not convict you for certain uses of marijuana, the federal government can. Green card holders convicted of a violation of a federal law relating to marijuana (other than a single offense involving possession for their own use of 30 grams or less) are deportable. You may also be found deportable if you are a "drug abuser or addict." Also, a green card holder who travels outside the U.S. and then attempts to return could face inadmissibility problems based on medical marijuana usage. Finally, even working for a state-approved marijuana grower or dispensary can land you in hot water under federal drug trafficking laws. See a lawyer for a personal analysis.

Men 18–26 Must Register for the Military Draft

Lawful U.S. resident males (green card holders) between the ages of 18 and 26 are required to register for military service, otherwise known as the Selective Service. USCIS won't deport you if you don't register, but it will hold up your eventual citizenship application. As of the year 2000, immigrants who apply to adjust status in the United States were supposed to be registered automatically, but don't count on this. It's easy to make sure you are registered. Go to the Selective Service website at www.sss.gov, click "Check Registration," and enter the requested information. If you are not yet registered, you can do so on the same website. From the home page, click "Register." If you prefer to register by mail, pick up the Selective Service form at any U.S. Post Office or download it from the Selective Service website.

A full discussion of inadmissibility and deportability is beyond the scope of this book. Very briefly, you become removable or deportable if you:

- are involved in document fraud or alien smuggling

- go on public assistance (become a public charge or receive "welfare") within the first five years of entry, unless you need public support because of something beyond your control, such as a disabling accident (see I.N.A. § 237(a)(5); 8 U.S.C. § 1227(a)(5))
- fail to comply with a condition of your green card (such as failing to follow a course of treatment to cure an illness you had when you were approved for residency)
- commit crimes, or
- violate the immigration laws (for example, participate in a sham marriage or immigrant smuggling).

You probably aren't planning on a crime spree as soon as you get your green card. But the message to take from these criminal grounds is that you have to be extra careful. Your U.S. citizen friends might not worry too much about engaging in certain illegal activities, such as shooting a gun at the sky on the Fourth of July or sharing a marijuana cigarette among friends. But if you are caught participating in these same activities, you could lose your green card and be deported.

F. How to Renew or Replace Your Green Card

This section is about the green card itself—the little laminated card that shows you're a resident. If something happens to the card—if it expires or gets lost—you don't ordinarily lose your status. (The only exception is that when the cards of conditional, not permanent residents expire, their status expires along with it, as discussed in Section G, below.)

However, the law requires you to have a valid green card in your possession, and it's a good thing to have on hand in case you travel, get a new job, or get picked up by an overeager government officer who thinks you "look" illegal.

1. Renewing Expiring Green Cards

If you are a permanent resident (not a conditional resident), your status does not expire—but your green card *does* expire, every ten years. When the expiration date on your green card is six months away, you will need to apply to renew it.

Use Form I-90, available on the USCIS website at www.uscis.gov/i-90. You can also submit this form electronically, or through the USCIS website—though you'll still have to mail in the supporting documentation. Instructions are not included in this book, but Form I-90 comes with a fairly complete set of instructions, and you can read more on the USCIS website.

Alternately, if you are ready and eligible to apply for U.S. citizenship, you can submit the citizenship application instead of renewing the green card. USCIS doesn't mind if you carry around an expired green card in this circumstance. If you need to change jobs or travel, however, you will probably want to renew the green card, to prove to the rest of the world that you are still a permanent resident.

2. Replacing Lost or Stolen Green Cards

If your green card is lost, stolen, accidentally dropped into a blender, or otherwise destroyed, you will need to apply for a new one. Like renewal, this is done using Form I-90 (see instructions in Section 1, above, on where to obtain the form).

TIP

Report all stolen green cards to the police. Green cards are a hot item, and there is always a possibility that yours will be stolen and sold. If this happens to you, be sure to file a police report. You may not get your card back, but when you apply for a replacement card, the report will help convince USCIS that you didn't sell your own card.

G. Converting From Conditional to Permanent Residence

If you were married for less than two years at the time of your approval for residency, or if you entered the United States as a K-1 fiancé, you will be given conditional residence. This means that not only your card, but your underlying legal status will expire in two years. USCIS will take a second look at whether your marriage is indeed real (bona fide) before it allows you to stay permanently.

During your two years of conditional residency, you'll have all the day-to-day rights of a permanent resident. You'll be able to work, travel in and out of the United States, and even count your time toward the three or five years you'll need to accumulate before applying for U.S. citizenship.

But if, during this period, USCIS discovers that your marriage was not real in the first place, it can place you in removal proceedings and take away your green card and your immigration status.

1. When Will Your Conditional Residence Expire?

If you've just been approved for residency and you are not sure whether you're a conditional resident or when your residency will expire, take another look at the stamp in your passport. It should look much like the one below.

The notation CR-1 in this passport indicates that its holder received only conditional residency. The date on the top is when he entered: July 23, 1987. The date below the CR-1, July 22, 1989, shows when his two years of conditional residency will end. (When this person eventually got permanent residency, a separate stamp was placed on another page of his passport.)

Don't be confused by the other date you see on the sample, October 22, 1987. This is the date when the *stamp* in the passport expired, meaning that its holder should have received his separate green card by then. Every immigrant's passport stamp will have its own expiration date, even the immigrants who receive permanent, not conditional residency. If the passport holder from our sample hadn't received his green card by the October 1987 date, he could have gone to a USCIS office for a new passport stamp. Your initial green card will also show a two-year expiration date if you receive conditional residency.

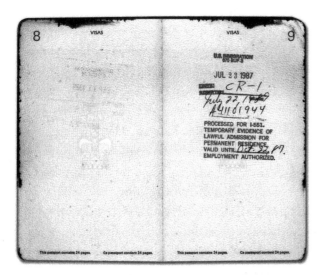

Sample Conditional Residence Stamp

2. The Application Procedures

To convert your conditional status to permanent status, you will need to submit a Petition to Remove the Conditions on Residence (Form I-751), complete with documents and fees, to USCIS up to 90 days before the date your conditional residence status expires. Below, you'll find a checklist for this petition.

If you send this petition too soon, that is, earlier than 90 days before your conditional residence expires, you'll get it right back. But if the petition is not filed by your card's expiration date, it and your conditional residence status will both expire and you could be deported. So you see, you have a three-month window in which to complete and file your I-751 application.

Keep track of the deadline. USCIS will not always tell you when the petition is due. Put the due date on every calendar you own; tape it to your refrigerator, bedroom mirror, or forehead—do whatever you need to do to remember the date.

SEE AN EXPERT

If you miss the deadline by a short time, don't just give up. If you're late by only a few weeks, mail the application with a cover letter, explaining the delay. The regulations allow you to file late for "good cause" (see 8 C.F.R. § 216.4(a)(6)). Good cause might mean a family or medical crisis, a move, or changes at your job—whatever the issue, back up your explanations with documentary proof. If it's been longer, see a lawyer right away. You've probably got about three to six months before USCIS puts you into removal proceedings, at which point continuing with your application becomes much harder.

The information you need to have on hand is fairly straightforward, as you can see by looking at the checklist, below. One item merits mention, however—evidence of your marital relationship. This key portion of the application should be nothing new—remember the types of documents you had to provide for your adjustment of status or consular interview? These might include copies of rent receipts, joint bank or credit card statements, and children's birth certificates. Include documents covering only the last two years (don't resubmit items that USCIS has already seen).

3. What If Your U.S. Spouse Won't Sign the Joint Petition?

A lot of things can happen to a marriage in two years. People can get divorced or separated or the petitioning spouse might die. In some cases, the immigrant becomes the victim of domestic violence at the hands of a spouse who will no longer help with the immigration paperwork.

Any of these circumstances will make it impossible to submit the Petition to Remove Conditions on Residence in its standard and simplest form, as a joint petition signed by both spouses. But you're not necessarily out of luck. In fact, Form I-751 allows you to check boxes showing that you are divorced after a good faith marriage, widowed, the victim of being battered or extreme cruelty in a good faith marriage, or cannot file the petition jointly with your spouse for some other reason, but would suffer extreme hardship if you were denied permanent residency. If you check any of these boxes, you will still submit the form, but you won't have your spouse's signature.

Extreme hardship. This is the most general ground for a waiver—and you technically don't even need to prove a good faith marriage—but it's also considered the hardest to qualify for. You must show that political or economic changes have arisen in your country since the time you became a conditional resident that would cause you extreme hardship if you were to return. (See I.N.A. § 216(c)(4)(a); 8 U.S.C. § 1186a(c)(4)(a).) For example, if you've recently become an outspoken public critic of a repressive government's policies and might be persecuted upon your return, you'd have a good case.

Divorce. This ground is more clear-cut; except that the divorce must actually be final before you can be approved for this waiver. And, depending on where you live, the courts may take many months to grant you a divorce. This means you may want to file the divorce papers yourself in order to get the process going, instead of waiting for your U.S. spouse. On the other hand, the longer you stay married, the better your chances of showing that the marriage was bona fide in the first place. If the timing gets tight, you should file your waiver request without the divorce decree (in order to preserve your status) with a promise to send it later. Include a copy of the divorce filing, as well as proof that the marriage was entered into in good faith. USCIS should issue a request for evidence ("RFE") giving you 87 days in which to respond. By then, hopefully, the termination of your marriage will be final, and you can return the appropriate paperwork. File your waiver request late, arguing that the upheaval in your life caused by your marital troubles was good cause for your lateness.

Battery or extreme cruelty. You might qualify for this section of the waiver if you've been the victim of "any act or threatened act of violence [by your U.S. spouse], including any forceful detention, which results in physical or mental injury. Psychological or sexual abuse or exploitation, including rape, molestation, incest (if the victim is a minor), or forced prostitution shall be considered acts of violence."

(See 8 C.F.R. § 216.5(e)(3)(i).) You don't have to be divorced or even separated from your spouse.

The main challenge here will be documenting the good faith marriage (particularly if you've had to quickly leave the home where you and your spouse lived), as well as documenting the abuse (with things like police and medical reports, photos, psychological evaluations, witness statements, letters from shelters, and more). And don't worry—USCIS will not advise the abusive spouse about the application.

You'll need substantial documentation of your eligibility for approval under the category you marked—including both documents showing that your marriage was entered into in good faith (similar to what you supplied when you got your conditional residence) and documents proving the divorce, spouse's death, abuse, or hardship. A complete explanation of this process is outside the scope of this book. Consult a lawyer, a local nonprofit that serves immigrants, or a battered women's shelter for help.

4. Line-by-Line Instructions for Form I-751

Use this form to convert your conditional residency to permanent residency.

WEB RESOURCE

Form I-751 is available on the USCIS website at www.uscis.gov/i-751. For a sample filled-in form (relevant pages only), see below.

Part 1, "Information About You, the Conditional Resident": This means the immigrating spouse. For Question 9, you're unlikely to have a USCIS ELIS Account Number; unless, that is, you registered in order to file certain USCIS forms online. However, the ELIS system is largely nonfunctional at the moment. For Question 18, you will probably know if you are in **"removal or deportation proceedings."** You'll be in this situation if you've done something—or the government thinks you've done something—that gets you into Immigration Court. Common examples include being convicted of a crime or giving USCIS reason to believe that your marriage

Sample Form I-751, Petition to Remove the Conditions on Residence—Page 1

Petition to Remove Conditions on Residence
Department of Homeland Security
U.S. Citizenship and Immigration Services

USCIS
Form I-751
OMB No. 1615-0038
Expires 12/31/2019

For USCIS Use Only	Receipt	Action Block	Remarks

	Reloc Sent	Reloc Received
	Date (mm/dd/yyyy) / /	Date (mm/dd/yyyy) / /
	Date (mm/dd/yyyy) / /	Date (mm/dd/yyyy) / /

☐ Petitioner interviewed on (mm/dd/yyyy) ____ / / ____   ☐ Approved under INA 216(c)(4)(C) Battered Spouse/Child

To be completed by an attorney or accredited representative (if any).	☐ Select this box if Form G-28 is attached.	Attorney State Bar Number (if applicable)	Attorney or Accredited Representative USCIS ELIS Account Number (if any)

▶ **START HERE - Type or print in black ink.**

Part 1. Information About You, the Conditional Resident

1.a. Family Name (Last Name)   Hollis

1.b. Given Name (First Name)   Nigel

1.c. Middle Name   Ian

Other Names Used

List all other names you have ever used, including aliases, maiden name, and nicknames. If you need extra space to complete this section, use the space provided in **Part 11. Additional Information**.

2.a. Family Name (Last Name)

2.b. Given Name (First Name)

2.c. Middle Name

3.a. Family Name (Last Name)

3.b. Given Name (First Name)

3.c. Middle Name

Other Information

4. Date of Birth (mm/dd/yyyy)   08/18/1988

5. Country of Birth
UK

6. Country of Citizenship or Nationality (provide all that apply)
UK

7. Alien Registration Number (A-Number) (if any)
▶ A- 1 2 3 4 5 6 7 8 9

8. U.S. Social Security Number (if any)
▶ 8 8 8 1 1 8 8 8 8

9. USCIS ELIS Account Number (if any)
▶

Marital Status

10. Marital Status
☐ Single   ☒ Married   ☐ Divorced   ☐ Widowed

11. Date of Marriage (mm/dd/yyyy)   11/05/2017

12. Place of Marriage
New York, NY

13. If the marriage through which you gained conditional residence has ended, provide the date it ended (date of divorce or date of death) (mm/dd/yyyy)
n/a

14. Conditional Residence Expires On (mm/dd/yyyy)
11/10/2019

Form I-751   12/05/17 N

Page 1 of 11

Sample Form I-751, Petition to Remove the Conditions on Residence—Page 2

Part 1. Information About You, the Conditional Resident (continued)

Mailing Address

15.a. In Care Of Name

15.b. Street Number and Name — 114 Fulton Street

15.c. ☒ Apt. ☐ Ste. ☐ Flr. — 6E

15.d. City or Town — New York

15.e. State — NY   **15.f.** ZIP Code — 10038

16. Is your physical address different than your mailing address?   ☐ Yes   ☒ No

If you answered "Yes" to **Item Number 16.**, provide your physical address below.

Physical Address

17.a. In Care Of Name

17.b. Street Number and Name

17.c. ☐ Apt. ☐ Ste. ☐ Flr.

17.d. City or Town

17.e. State   **17.f.** ZIP Code

Additional Information About You

18. Are you in removal, deportation, or rescission proceedings?   ☐ Yes   ☒ No

19. Was a fee paid to anyone other than an attorney in connection with this petition?   ☐ Yes   ☒ No

20. Have you ever been arrested, detained, charged, indicted, fined, or imprisoned for breaking or violating any law or ordinance (excluding traffic regulations), or committed any crime which you were not arrested in the United States or abroad?   ☐ Yes   ☒ No

If you answered "Yes" to **Item Number 20.**, provide a detailed explanation in **Part 11. Additional Information** or on a separate sheet of paper, and refer to the **What Initial Evidence Is Required** section of the Form I-751 instructions to determine what criminal history document to include with your petition.

21. If you are married, is this a different marriage than the one through which you gained conditional resident status?   ☐ Yes   ☒ No

22. Have you resided at any other address since you became a permanent resident?   ☐ Yes   ☒ No

If you answered "Yes" to **Item Number 22.**, provide a list of all addresses where you have resided since becoming a permanent resident and the dates you resided at those locations in the space provided in **Part 11. Additional Information**.

23. Is your spouse or parent's spouse currently serving with or employed by the U.S. Government and serving outside the United States?   ☐ Yes   ☒ No

Part 2. Biographic Information

1. Ethnicity (Select **only one** box)
   ☐ Hispanic or Latino
   ☒ Not Hispanic or Latino

2. Race (Select **all applicable** boxes)
   ☒ White
   ☐ Asian
   ☐ Black or African American
   ☐ American Indian or Alaska Native
   ☐ Native Hawaiian or Other Pacific Islander

3. Height   Feet 5   Inches 11

4. Weight   Pounds 1 6 2

5. Eye Color (Select **only one** box)
   ☐ Black   ☐ Blue   ☐ Brown
   ☐ Gray   ☐ Green   ☒ Hazel
   ☐ Maroon   ☐ Pink   ☐ Unknown/Other

6. Hair Color (Select **only one** box)
   ☐ Bald (No hair)   ☐ Black   ☐ Blond
   ☐ Brown   ☐ Gray   ☐ Red
   ☒ Sandy   ☐ White   ☐ Unknown/Other

Sample Form I-751, Petition to Remove the Conditions on Residence—Page 3

Part 3. Basis for Petition

Joint Filing

My conditional residence is based on my marriage or my parent's marriage to a U.S. citizen or lawful permanent resident, and I am filing this joint petition together with (Select **only one** box):

1.a. ☒ My spouse.

1.b. ☐ My parent's spouse because I am unable to be included in a joint petition filed by my parent and my parent's spouse.

OR (Select **all** applicable boxes in the next section.)

Waiver or Individual Filing Request

My conditional residence is based on my marriage or my parent's marriage to a U.S. citizen or lawful permanent resident, I am unable to file a joint petition with my spouse or my parent's spouse, because:

1.c. ☐ My spouse is deceased.

1.d. ☐ My marriage was entered in good faith, but the marriage was terminated through divorce or annulment.

1.e. ☐ I entered the marriage in good faith, and, during the marriage, I was battered, or was the subject of extreme cruelty, by my U.S. citizen or lawful permanent resident spouse.

1.f. ☐ My parent entered the marriage in good faith, and, during the marriage, I was battered, or was subjected to extreme cruelty, by my parent's U.S. citizen or lawful permanent resident spouse or by my conditional resident parent.

1.g. ☐ The termination of my status and removal from the United States would result in an extreme hardship.

Part 4. Information About the U.S. Citizen or Lawful Permanent Resident Spouse. If Filing as a Child Separately, Information About the U.S. Citizen or Lawful Permanent Resident Stepparent Through Whom You Gained Your Conditional Residence.

Relationship

1.a. ☒ Spouse or Former Spouse

1.b. ☐ Parent's Spouse or Former Spouse

Other Information

2.a. Family Name (Last Name) `Beach`

2.b. Given Name (First Name) `Sandra`

2.c. Middle Name `Leah`

3. Date of Birth (mm/dd/yyyy) `12/20/1990`

4. U.S. Social Security Number (if any)
▶ `1` `2` `3` `4` `5` `6` `7` `8` `9`

5. A-Number (if any)
▶ A- ☐☐☐☐☐☐☐☐☐

Physical Address

6.a. Street Number and Name `114 Fulton Street`

6.b. ☒ Apt. ☐ Ste. ☐ Flr. `6E`

6.c. City or Town `New York`

6.d. State `NY` **6.e.** ZIP Code `10038`

6.f. Province

6.g. Postal Code

6.h. Country `USA`

Part 5. Information About Your Children

Provide information on all of your children. If you need extra space to complete this section, use the space provided in **Part 11. Additional Information**.

Child 1

1.a. Family Name (Last Name) `Hollis`

1.b. Given Name (First Name) `Nadine`

1.c. Middle Name `Ann`

2. Date of Birth (mm/dd/yyyy) `12/02/2017`

3. A-Number (if any)
▶ A- ☐☐☐☐☐☐☐☐☐

4. Is this child living with you? ☒ Yes ☐ No

5. Is this child applying with you? ☐ Yes ☒ No

Sample Form I-751, Petition to Remove the Conditions on Residence—Page 4

Part 5. Information About Your Children (continued)

Physical Address

6.a. Street Number and Name: 114 Fulton Street

6.b. ☒ Apt. ☐ Ste. ☐ Flr. 6E

6.c. City or Town: New York

6.d. State: NY **6.e.** ZIP Code: 10038

6.f. Province:

6.g. Postal Code:

6.h. Country: USA

Child 2

7.a. Family Name (Last Name):

7.b. Given Name (First Name):

7.c. Middle Name:

8. Date of Birth (mm/dd/yyyy):

9. A-Number (if any) ▶ A-

10. Is this child living with you? ☐ Yes ☐ No

11. Is this child applying with you? ☐ Yes ☐ No

Physical Address

12.a. Street Number and Name:

12.b. ☐ Apt. ☐ Ste. ☐ Flr.

12.c. City or Town:

12.d. State: **12.e.** ZIP Code:

12.f. Province:

12.g. Postal Code:

12.h. Country:

Child 3

13.a. Family Name (Last Name):

13.b. Given Name (First Name):

13.c. Middle Name:

14. Date of Birth (mm/dd/yyyy):

15. A-Number (if any) ▶ A-

16. Is this child living with you? ☐ Yes ☐ No

17. Is this child applying with you? ☐ Yes ☐ No

Physical Address

18.a. Street Number and Name:

18.b. ☐ Apt. ☐ Ste. ☐ Flr.

18.c. City or Town:

18.d. State: **18.e.** ZIP Code:

18.f. Province:

18.g. Postal Code:

18.h. Country:

Child 4

19.a. Family Name (Last Name):

19.b. Given Name (First Name):

19.c. Middle Name:

20. Date of Birth (mm/dd/yyyy):

21. A-Number (if any) ▶ A-

22. Is this child living with you? ☐ Yes ☐ No

23. Is this child applying with you? ☐ Yes ☐ No

Sample Form I-751, Petition to Remove the Conditions on Residence—Page 5

Part 5. Information About Your Children (continued)

Physical Address

24.a. Street Number and Name

24.b. ☐ Apt. ☐ Ste. ☐ Flr.

24.c. City or Town

24.d. State

24.e. ZIP Code

24.f. Province

24.g. Postal Code

24.h. Country

Child 5

25.a. Family Name (Last Name)

25.b. Given Name (First Name)

25.c. Middle Name

26. Date of Birth (mm/dd/yyyy)

27. A-Number (if any)

▶ A-

28. Is this child living with you? ☐ Yes ☐ No

29. Is this child applying with you? ☐ Yes ☐ No

Physical Address

30.a. Street Number and Name

30.b. ☐ Apt. ☐ Ste. ☐ Flr.

30.c. City or Town

30.d. State

30.e. ZIP Code

30.f. Province

30.g. Postal Code

30.h. Country

Part 6. Accommodations for Individuals With Disabilities and/or Impairments

NOTE: Read the information in the Form I-751 Instructions before completing this part.

1. Are you requesting an accommodation because of your disabilities and/or impairments? ☐ Yes ☒ No

2. Are you requesting an accommodation because of your spouse's disabilities and/or impairments? ☐ Yes ☒ No

3. Are you requesting an accommodation because of your included children's disabilities and/or impairments? ☐ Yes ☒ No

If you answered "Yes" to **Item Numbers 1. - 3.**, select any applicable box for **Item Numbers 4.a. - 4.c.** Provide information on the disabilities and/or impairments for each person.

4.a. ☐ I am deaf or hard of hearing and request the following accommodation. (If you are requesting a sign-language interpreter, indicate for which language (for example, American Sign Language).):

_____

_____

_____

4.b. ☐ I am blind or have low vision and request the following accommodation:

_____

_____

4.c. ☐ I have another type of disability and/or impairment. (Describe the nature of your disability and/or impairment and the accommodation you are requesting.):

_____

_____

_____

Sample Form I-751, Petition to Remove the Conditions on Residence—Page 6

Part 7. Petitioner's Statement, Contact Information, Acknowledgement of Appointment at USCIS Application Support Center, Certification, and Signature

NOTE: Read the information on penalties in the **Penalties** section of the Form I-751 Instructions before completing this part.

NOTE: If you selected **Box 1.a.** in **Part 3.**, your spouse must also read and sign the petition in **Part 8.** Signature of a conditional resident child under 14 years of age is not required; a parent may sign for a child.

Petitioner's Statement

NOTE: Select the box for either **Item Number 1.a.** or **1.b.** If applicable, select the box for **Item Number 2.**

1.a. ☒ I can read and understand English, and have read and understand every question and instruction on this petition, as well as my answer to every question. I have read and understand the **Acknowledgement of Appointment at USCIS Application Support Center**.

1.b. ☐ The interpreter named in **Part 9.** has also read to me every question and instruction on this petition, as well as my answer to every question, in

_____,

a language in which I am fluent. I understand every question and instruction on this petition as translated to me by my interpreter, and have provided complete, true, and correct responses in the language indicated above. The interpreter named in **Part 9.** has also read the **Acknowledgement of Appointment at USCIS Application Support Center** to me, in the language in which I am fluent, and I understand this Application Support Center (ASC) Acknowledgement as read to me by my interpreter.

2. ☐ I have requested the services of and consented to

_____,

who ☐ is ☐ is not an attorney or accredited representative, preparing this petition for me. This person who assisted me in preparing my petition has reviewed the **Acknowledgement of Appointment at USCIS Application Support Center** with me, and I understand the ASC Acknowledgement.

Petitioner's Contact Information

3. Petitioner's Daytime Telephone Number

2225551212

4. Petitioner's Mobile Telephone Number (if any)

2225551212

5. Petitioner's Email Address (if any)

nigelh@email.com

Acknowledgement of Appointment at USCIS Application Support Center

I, | Nigel | Ian | Hollis | ,

understand that the purpose of a USCIS ASC appointment is for me to provide fingerprints, photograph, and/or signature and to re-affirm that all of the information in my petition is complete, true, and correct and was provided by me. I understand that I will sign my name to the following declaration which USCIS will display to me at the time I provide my fingerprints, photograph, and/or signature during my ASC appointment.

> *By signing here, I declare under penalty of perjury that I have reviewed and understand my application, petition, or request as identified by the receipt number displayed on the screen above, and all supporting documents, applications, petitions, or requests filed with my application, petition, or request that I (or my attorney or accredited representative) filed with USCIS, and that all of the information in these materials is complete, true, and correct.*

If conditional residence was based on a marriage, I further certify that the marriage was entered into in accordance with the laws of the place where the marriage took place and was not for the purpose of procuring an immigration benefit.

I also understand that when I sign my name, provide my fingerprints, and am photographed at the USCIS ASC, I will be re-affirming that I willingly submit this petition; I have reviewed the contents of this petition; all of the information in my petition and all supporting documents submitted with my petition were provided by me and are complete, true, and correct; and if I was assisted in completing this petition, the person assisting me also reviewed this **Acknowledgement of Appointment at USCIS Application Support Center** with me.

Sample Form I-751, Petition to Remove the Conditions on Residence—Page 7

Part 7. Petitioner's Statement, Contact Information, Acknowledgement of Appointment at USCIS Application Support Center, Certification, and Signature (continued)

Petitioner's Certification

Copies of any documents I have submitted are exact photocopies of unaltered, original documents, and I understand that USCIS may require that I submit original documents to USCIS at a later date. Furthermore, I authorize the release of any information from any and all of my records that USCIS may need to determine my eligibility for the immigration benefit that I seek.

I furthermore authorize release of information contained in this petition, in supporting documents, and in my USCIS records to other entities and persons where necessary for the administration and enforcement of U.S. immigration laws.

I certify under penalty of perjury, that the information in my petition, my responses to each question, and any document submitted with my petition were provided by me and are complete, true, and correct.

Petitioner's Signature

6.a. Petitioner's Signature

Nigel I. Hollis

6.b. Date of Signature (mm/dd/yyyy)   08/12/2021

NOTE TO ALL PETITIONERS: If you do not completely fill out this petition or fail to submit required documents listed in the Instructions, USCIS may deny your petition.

NOTE: If you are filing based on claims of having been battered or subjected to extreme cruelty waiver or individual filing, you are not required to have the spouse's or individual listed in **Part 4's** signature.

Part 8. Spouse's or Individual Listed in Part 4.'s Statement, Contact Information, Acknowledgement of Appointment USCIS Application Support Center, Certification, and Signature (if applicable)

Provide the following information about the spouse or individual listed in **Part 4.**

NOTE: Read the information on penalties in the **Penalties** section of the Form I-751 Instructions before completing this part.

Spouse's or Individual's Statement

NOTE: Select the box for either **Item Number 1.a.** or **1.b.** If applicable, select the box for **Item Number 2.**

1.a. ☒ I can read and understand English, and have read and understand every question and instruction on this petition, as well as the petitioner's answer to every question. I have read and understand the **Acknowledgement of Appointment at USCIS Application Support Center.**

1.b. ☐ The interpreter named in **Part 9.** has also read to me every question and instruction on this petition, as well as the petitioner's answer to every question, in

_____ ,

a language in which I am fluent. I understand every question and instruction on this petition as translated to me by my interpreter, and have provided complete, true, and correct responses in the language indicated above. The interpreter named in **Part 9.** has also read the **Acknowledgement of Appointment at USCIS Application Support Center** to me, in the language in which I am fluent, and I understand this Application Support Center (ASC) Acknowledgement as read to me by my interpreter.

2. ☐ I have requested the services of and consented to

_____ ,

who ☐ is ☐ is not an attorney or accredited representative, preparing this petition for me. This person who assisted me in preparing my petition has reviewed the **Acknowledgement of Appointment at USCIS Application Support Center** with me, and I understand the ASC Acknowledgement.

Spouse's or Individual's Contact Information

3. Spouse's or Individual's Daytime Telephone Number

2225551212

4. Spouse's or Individual's Mobile Telephone Number (if any)

2225551212

5. Spouse's or Individual's Email Address (if any)

sandra@email.com

Sample Form I-751, Petition to Remove the Conditions on Residence—Page 8

Part 8. Spouse's or Individual Listed in Part 4.'s Statement, Contact Information, Acknowledgement of Appointment USCIS Application Support Center, Certification, and Signature (if applicable) (continued)

Acknowledgement of Appointment at USCIS Application Support Center

I, | Sandra   Leah   Beach |,
understand that the purpose of a USCIS ASC appointment is for me to provide my fingerprints, photograph, and/or signature and to re-affirm that all of the information in my petition is complete, true, and correct and was provided by me. I understand that I will sign my name to the following declaration which USCIS will display to me at the time I provide my fingerprints, photograph, and/or signature during my ASC appointment.

> *By signing here, I declare under penalty of perjury that I have reviewed and understand my application, petition, or request as identified by the receipt number displayed on the screen above, and all supporting documents, applications, petitions, or requests filed with my application, petition, or request that I (or my attorney or accredited representative) filed with USCIS, and that all of the information in these materials is complete, true, and correct.*

I also understand that when I sign my name, provide my fingerprints, and am photographed at the USCIS ASC, I will be re-affirming that I willingly submit this petition; I have reviewed the contents of this petition; all of the information in my petition and all supporting documents submitted with my petition were provided by me and are complete, true, and correct; and if I was assisted in completing this petition, the person assisting me also reviewed this **Acknowledgement of Appointment at USCIS Application Support Center** with me.

Spouse's or Individual's Certification

Copies of any documents I have submitted are exact photocopies of unaltered, original documents, and I understand that USCIS may require that I submit original documents to USCIS at a later date. Furthermore, I authorize the release of any information from any and all of my records that USCIS may need to determine my eligibility for the immigration benefit that I seek.

I furthermore authorize release of information contained in this petition, in supporting documents, and in my USCIS records to other entities and persons where necessary for the administration and enforcement of U.S. immigration laws.

I certify under penalty of perjury, that the information in my petition, my responses to each question, and any document submitted with my petition were provided by me and are complete, true, and correct.

Spouse's or Individual's Signature

6.a. Spouse's or Individual's Signature

Sandra Leah Beach

6.b. Date of Signature (mm/dd/yyyy) | 08/12/2021

NOTE TO ALL SPOUSES OR INDIVIDUALS: If you do not completely fill out this petition or fail to submit required documents listed in the instructions, USCIS may deny your petition.

Part 9. Interpreter's Contact Information, Certification, and Signature

Provide the following information about the interpreter.

Interpreter's Full Name

1.a. Interpreter's Family Name (Last Name)

1.b. Interpreter's Given Name (First Name)

2. Interpreter's Business or Organization Name (if any)

Interpreter's Mailing Address

3.a. Street Number and Name

3.b. ☐ Apt. ☐ Ste. ☐ Flr.

3.c. City or Town

3.d. State | | **3.e.** ZIP Code

3.f. Province

3.g. Postal Code

3.h. Country

Interpreter's Contact Information

4. Interpreter's Daytime Telephone Number

5. Interpreter's Email Address (if any)

is fraudulent. If you are in court proceedings, you should already have a lawyer. If you don't, see Chapter 17 on how to find a good one.

If you check "Yes" to Question 19, about whether a fee was **"paid to anyone other than an attorney in connection with this petition,"** you haven't done anything wrong, but that person needs to enter his or her name and other information in Part 10. The rest of this Part should be self-explanatory.

Part 2: Self-explanatory.

Part 3: If you are still married and your spouse is cooperating with the process of applying for your permanent residency, put an "X" in Box 1.a.

Part 4: Mostly self-explanatory. Fill in information about the U.S. spouse.

Part 5: List both U.S. citizen and immigrating children.

Part 6: If you are requesting an accommodation at your interview (which may or may not be required) because of a disability or impairment—such as having a sign-language interpreter—explain that here.

Checklist for Filing Joint Petition to Remove Conditions on Residence

Here's what you'll need to assemble for your joint petition to remove the conditions on your residency and become a permanent resident:

☐ Form I-751

☐ Copy of both sides of your green card

☐ Required supporting documents, including evidence that marriage is ongoing and bona fide, such as lease or mortgage documents showing both spouses' names, children's birth certificates, joint bank and credit card account statements, and so on

☐ Application fee (currently $595, but fees change often so double-check this at www.uscis.gov, or by calling 800-375-5283); you can mail a check or money order or pay by credit card using Form G-1450

☐ Biometrics fee (for photos and fingerprints; currently $85)

Parts 7 and 8: It is very important that both of you remember to enter your names and contact information and to sign. (The "Petitioner" is the immigrant for purposes of this form.) Your two signatures are an indication of the ongoing validity of your marriage.

Parts 9 and 10: Don't worry about these sections—they're for the interpreter and attorney or other legal representative who assist with this application.

5. Where to File the Joint Petition

When you and your spouse are finished preparing the joint petition, make a complete copy for your files. Then send the packet of forms and documents to USCIS—the address is in the online instructions—or call the USCIS information number at 800-375-5283.

As you may have learned by now, USCIS Service Centers, which handle forms I-751, are different than the local USCIS offices that you can actually visit. All contact with the service center will have to be by mail.

Priority Mail, certified mail with return receipt requested, or a courier such as FedEx is highly recommended—these service centers receive a huge volume of mail. You may need the tracking information as proof that USCIS received your petition if it gets misplaced.

6. Your Receipt Notice

Once your application is received and the USCIS service center has reviewed it to see that you've included all the appropriate documents and fee, you'll get a receipt notice. It may be several weeks before you get this receipt notice.

This notice is an important document. It extends your residency for a period of 18 months. It will be your only proof of your legal status at this time—it's a bit awkward to show to employers, border patrol officers, and others, but it really is an official document. You must, however, also carry your expired green card at the same time (since the card, unlike the receipt, has your photo on it).

During this time period, you will also be sent an appointment notice stating when and where you must appear for biometric processing. (It's usually at a USCIS Application Support Center.) Biometric processing includes taking your photograph, signature, and index fingerprint, for use in generating your new green card. If you're between ages 14 and 79, it also includes taking your fingerprints, in order to do another criminal background check.

Most people receive their permanent resident cards before the expiration of their 18-month extension. If you fall into the group of people who do not get their cards in a timely manner, don't worry that this will affect your legal status in the United States—you will remain a conditional resident until USCIS makes a decision on your application. If, however, you need evidence of your legal status, you'll need to call the USCIS Contact Center at 800-374-5283 to request an appointment to visit your local USCIS field office.

Bring an unexpired passport, your old green card, and your receipt notice. The USCIS officer will take your green card, and in return give you what's called an I-551 stamp in your passport. This stamp will serve as evidence of your status, and will be valid for another year.

> CAUTION
>
> **Do not travel with an expired receipt notice!**
> If you don't get your permanent resident card by the time your receipt notice expires, request an appointment from USCIS (as noted above) and get a temporary stamp in your passport before you leave the United States—otherwise, you may not be let back in.

7. Approval by Mail

With any luck at all, USCIS will approve your permanent residence by mail. If you don't receive an approval by the time your 18-month extension expires, take your receipt notice and your passport and visit your local USCIS office (after making an appointment). If no decision has been made, USCIS will stamp your passport, extending your conditional residence. If you request it, the information officer will also send an inquiry to the service center handling your case, pointing out that your case has gone beyond normal processing time.

8. Approval After Interview

You and your spouse may be called in for an interview regarding the joint petition. If so, it probably means USCIS has some doubts about your marriage being real (although they also seem to regularly choose a few couples at random).

Try to figure out why you're being called for an interview. Are you and your spouse living in different places? Did issues arise at your earlier USCIS or consular interview (when you got your conditional residence)? If so, think about how you can overcome these issues.

For example, if you and your spouse are living separately because one of you is in school, bring school transcripts and copies of documents showing that you often phone or visit one another. Or, if you are temporarily separated, get a letter from your marriage counselor or religious advisor confirming that she or he sees you regularly and is helping you face problems in your relationship and work them through.

Don't be surprised if the service center informs you that you'll be interviewed but the local USCIS office takes many months before scheduling an appointment. This delay doesn't have anything to do with the merits of your application. It just means that the local offices have numerous other applicants to interview before you.

> SEE AN EXPERT
>
> **Being called in for an interview at this stage is somewhat unusual.** You might want to ask a lawyer to help you prepare and to attend the interview with you. (See Chapter 17 for tips on finding a good lawyer. Also see Chapter 13 for practice questions.)

9. After You Are Approved or Denied

If you are required to attend a USCIS interview, and your case is approved at or after the interview, you will receive your permanent resident card in the mail a few weeks later. If you don't receive your green card within six months, however, call the USCIS Contact Center.

If your application is denied, you will be placed in removal proceedings, unless you are lucky enough to have an alternate legal status.

SEE AN EXPERT

If you are placed in removal proceedings and you haven't already found a lawyer, do it now. (For tips on finding a good one, see Chapter 17.) Whatever you do, don't skip a court date. Failure to appear results in an automatic order of deportation and could permanently ruin your chances of immigrating.

CHAPTER

17

Legal Help Beyond This Book

You are not required to have a lawyer when applying for an immigrant visa or green card in the United States or overseas. In fact, if you are overseas, lawyers cannot attend consular interviews with you, though they are allowed to prepare the paperwork and have follow-up communications with the consulates.

However, there are many times when you may need or want a lawyer's help. Because immigration law is complicated, even a seemingly simple case can suddenly become nightmarish. If so, you'll need good legal help, fast. And you can avoid some problems by hiring a lawyer from the get-go. In this chapter, we'll explain:

- when applicants typically need to consult an attorney (Section A)
- how to find suitable counsel (Sections B, C, and D)
- hiring, paying, and (if necessary) firing your lawyer (Sections E, F, and G), and
- how to do some legal research on your own (Section H).

CAUTION

If you are or have ever been in deportation (removal) proceedings, you must see a lawyer. If the proceedings aren't yet over or are on appeal, your entire immigration situation is in the power of the courts—and you are not allowed to use the procedures described in this book. Even if the proceedings are over, you should ask a lawyer whether the outcome affects your current application. A past order of removal can make you inadmissible.

A. When Do You Need a Lawyer?

Again, the ideal is to hire a lawyer from the outset, to help you spot issues, avoid complications, and deal with all the paperwork. But if you couldn't afford to do this, or decided against it, bringing a lawyer in later is likely still possible.

The most common legal problem encountered by would-be immigrants is the claim by USCIS or the consulate that they are inadmissible for one or more of the reasons listed in Chapter 2, such as having spent unlawful time in the U.S., committed a crime, or previously lied to the U.S. government. If you already know that any of these grounds apply to you, it definitely makes sense to get legal help before you begin the application process.

Another circumstance that often drives people to lawyers is the failure of USCIS or the consulate to act on or approve the application, for reasons that have more to do with bureaucracy than law. For example, an applicant who moves from Los Angeles to San Francisco after filing the green card application might find that the application has disappeared into a bureaucratic black hole for several months. Delays at the USCIS service centers are also ridiculously common.

Lawyers don't have a lot of power in such circumstances. But at least the lawyer may have access to inside inquiry lines, where they can ask about delayed or problematic cases. Unfortunately, even lawyers have trouble getting answers to such inquiries, but it's often worth a try. An experienced lawyer may have contacts inside USCIS or the consulate who can give information or locate a lost file. But these lawyers can't use this privilege on an everyday basis, and long delays are truly an everyday occurrence.

The bottom line is that a lawyer may be able to help, but has no magic words that will force the U.S. government into taking speedier action.

CAUTION

Don't rely on advice by USCIS information officers. Would you want the receptionist in your doctor's office to tell you whether to get brain surgery? Asking USCIS information officers for advice about your case (beyond basic procedural advice such as where to file an application and what the fees are) is equally unsafe. The people who staff USCIS phone and information services are not experts. USCIS takes no responsibility if their advice is wrong—and won't treat your application with any more sympathy. Even following the advice of officials higher up in the agency may not be safe. Always get a professional second opinion.

B. Where to Get the Names of Good Immigration Lawyers

Finding a good lawyer can involve a fair amount of work. Immigration law is a specialized area—in fact it has many subspecialities within it—so you obviously don't want to consult the lawyer who wrote your best friend's will. And whatever you do, don't just open the telephone book and pick the immigration lawyer with the biggest advertisement. Even bar association referral panels (lawyer listing services run by groups of lawyers) tend not to be very helpful. Such services tend to assume that any one of their lawyer-members is qualified to handle your case, and they may simply refer you to the next lawyer on their list with no prescreening.

It is far better to ask a trusted person for a referral. You probably know someone in the United States who is sophisticated in practical affairs and has been through an immigration process. Perhaps this person can recommend his or her lawyer, or can ask that lawyer to recommend another.

Local nonprofit organizations serving immigrants can also be excellent sources for referrals. A nonprofit organization is a charity that seeks funding from foundations and individuals to help people in need. Since they exist to serve others rather than to make a profit, they charge less and are usually staffed by people whose hearts and minds are in the right places. In the immigrant services field, examples include the Northwest Immigrant Rights Project (Seattle), El Rescate Legal Services (Los Angeles), the International Institutes (nationwide), and Catholic Charities (nationwide).

The department of Justice offers a list of "Pro Bono Legal Service Providers" at www.justice.gov/eoir in the "Action Center" box on the right, (click "Find Legal Representation" then "List of Pro Bono Legal Service Providers"). This list includes both attorneys and nonprofits. But despite what "pro bono" means, don't be surprised to find that they're not all really free. Many attorneys at least charge a nominal consultation fee, and many nonprofits must charge fees to cover their costs as well.

Also check out Nolo's Lawyer Directory at www.nolo.com (under "Find a Lawyer," enter "Immigration Law" and the city or zip code where you live, or the nearest large city). This allows you to view lawyers' photos, and personal profiles describing their areas of expertise and consultation fees.

Yet another good resource is the American Immigration Lawyers Association (AILA), at www.ailalawyer.com. AILA offers a lawyer referral service. Membership is limited to lawyers who have passed a screening process, which helps keep out the less scrupulous practitioners. But not all good immigration lawyers have joined AILA (membership is a bit pricey).

Try to get a list of a few lawyers whom you've heard do good work, then meet or talk to each and choose one. We'll talk more about lawyers' fees below.

C. How to Avoid Sleazy Lawyers

There are good and bad immigration lawyers out there. Some of the good ones are candidates for sainthood—they put in long hours dealing with a difficult bureaucracy on behalf of a clientele that typically can't pay high fees.

The bad ones are a nightmare—and there are more than a few of them. They typically try to do a high-volume business, churning out the same forms for every client regardless of their situation. Such lawyers can get clients into deep trouble by overlooking critical issues in their cases or failing to submit applications or court materials on time. But the one thing they never seem to forget is to send a huge bill for their supposed help. Some danger signs to watch for are:

- **The lawyer approaches you in a USCIS office or other public location and tries to solicit your business.** This is not only against the lawyers' rules of professional ethics, but no competent lawyer ever needs to find clients this way.
- **The lawyer makes big promises, such as "I guarantee I'll win your case," or "I've got a special contact that will put your application at the front of the line."** The U.S. government

is in ultimate control of your application, and any lawyer who implies that he or she has special powers is either lying or may be involved in something you don't want to be a part of.

- **The lawyer has a very fancy office and wears a lot of flashy gold jewelry.** A high-rent office or a $2,000 outfit aren't necessarily signs of a lawyer's success at winning cases. These trappings may instead be signs that the lawyer charges high fees and counts on impressing clients with clothing rather than results.

- **The lawyer encourages you to lie on your application.** This is a tricky area. On the one hand, a good lawyer can assist you in learning what information you don't want to needlessly offer up, and can help you present the truth in the best light possible. But a lawyer who coaches you to lie—for example, by telling you to pretend you lost your passport and visa when in fact you entered the United States illegally—isn't ethical. There's every chance that USCIS knows the lawyer's reputation and will scrutinize your application harder because of it.

You might think that the really bad lawyers would be out of business by now, but that isn't the case. Sad to say, neither the attorney bar associations nor the courts nor even the police take much interest in going after people who prey on immigrants. Occasionally, nonprofits devoted to immigrants' rights will attempt to get the enforcement community interested in taking action. Unfortunately, this threat of official scrutiny isn't much of a deterrent.

TIP

If you are the victim of an unscrupulous lawyer, complain! Law enforcement won't go after lawyers who prey on immigrants until there is enough community pressure. If a lawyer, or someone pretending to be a lawyer, pulls something unethical on you, report it to the state and local bar association and the local district attorney's office. Ask your local nonprofits if anyone else in your area is collecting such information.

Watch Out for Nonlawyers Practicing Immigration Law

Because much of immigration law involves filling in forms, people assume it's easy. They're wrong. Be careful about whom you consult with or hand your case over to. Unless the person shows you certification that he or she is a lawyer or an "accredited representative," or a paralegal working under the direct supervision of a lawyer, this person should be thought of as a typist. (An accredited representative is a nonlawyer who has received training from a lawyer and been recognized by USCIS as qualified to prepare USCIS applications and represent clients in court.) And this is true even for those who go by fancy names such as "immigration consultant" or "notary public"—these people do not have a law degree.

To check on whether someone is really a lawyer, ask for their Bar Number and call the state bar association.

Hiring a nonlawyer or nonaccredited representative is appropriate only if you want help with the form preparation, and no more. But as you know from reading the information on filling out forms in Chapter 4, even the address you enter can have legal consequences. Don't just turn your case over and let the consultant make the decisions.

If you feel you've been defrauded by an immigration consultant, you may want to sue in Small Claims Court; see *Everybody's Guide to Small Claims Court*, by Cara O'Neill (Nolo).

D. How to Choose Among Lawyers

Once you've got your "short list" of lawyers, you'll want to speak to each one. How much a lawyer charges is bound to be a factor in whom you choose (see Section F, below). But it shouldn't be the only factor. Here are some other important considerations.

1. Familiarity With Cases Like Yours

As mentioned above, immigration law is a specialized area. And some immigration lawyers spend much of their time in subspecialities, such as helping people obtain political asylum or employment-based visas. To learn how much experience a lawyer has in fiancé or marriage-based visas, ask some very practical questions, such as:

- How long do you expect my case to take?
- What is the reputation of the officers at the USCIS or consular office who will handle my case?
- How many marriage-based cases did you handle this year?

An experienced lawyer should be able to provide detailed, insightful answers to your questions and should be regularly handling marriage-based cases.

2. Client Rapport

Your first instinct in hiring a lawyer may be to look for a shark—someone you wouldn't want to leave your child with, but who will be a tough fighter for your case. This isn't necessarily the best choice in the immigration context. Since you may need to share some highly confidential issues with your lawyer, you'll want to know that the person is discreet and thoughtful. Also, realize that a lawyer's politeness goes a long way in front of immigration officials— sharks often produce a bureaucratic backlash, whereas the lawyers with good working relations with USCIS may have doors opened to them.

3. Access to Your Lawyer

You'll want to know that you can reach your lawyer during the months that your application winds its way through the USCIS or consular bureaucracy. A lawyer's accessibility may be hard to judge at the beginning, but try listening to the lawyer's receptionist as you wait in his or her office for the first time. If you get the sense that the receptionist is rude and

trying to push people off or give them flimsy excuses about why the lawyer hasn't returned their calls or won't talk to them, don't hire that lawyer.

Many immigration lawyers are sole practitioners and use an answering service or voicemail rather than a receptionist. In that case, you'll have to rely on how quickly they answer your initial calls. In your first meeting, simply ask the lawyer how quickly he or she will get back to you. If the lawyer regularly breaks promises, you'll have grounds on which to complain. Of course, you too have a responsibility not to harass your lawyer with frequent calls. The lawyer should be available for legitimate questions about your case, including inquiries about approaching deadlines.

4. Explaining Services and Costs

Take a good look at any printed materials the lawyer gives you on your first visit. Are they glitzy, glossy pieces that look more like advertising than anything useful? Or are they designed to acquaint you with the process you're getting into and the lawyer's role in it? Think about this issue again before you sign the lawyer's fee agreement, described in the section immediately below. Being a good salesperson doesn't necessarily make someone a good lawyer.

E. Signing Up Your Lawyer

Many good lawyers will ask you to sign an agreement covering their services and the fees you will pay them. This is a good idea for both of you, and can help prevent misunderstandings. The contract should be written in a way you can understand; there's no law that says it has to be in confusing legal jargon. The lawyer should go over the contract with you carefully, not just push it under your nose, saying, "Sign here." Some normal contract clauses include:

- **Scope of work.** A description of exactly what the lawyer will do for you.

- **Fees.** Specification of the amount you'll pay, either as a flat fee (a lump sum you pay for a stated task, such as $1,200 for an adjustment of status application) or at an hourly rate, with a payment schedule. If you hire someone at an hourly rate, you can ask to be told as soon as the hours have hit a certain limit.

> **TIP**
> **Don't pay a big flat fee up front.** Since the lawyer already has your money, he or she will have little incentive to please you. And if you don't like the lawyer later on, chances are you won't get any of your money back. Instead, pay for a few hours' service—then if you don't like the lawyer's work, end the relationship.

- **Responsibility for expenses.** Most lawyers will ask you to cover not only the application fees charged by the U.S. government, but the incidental expenses associated with the work that they do, such as phone calls, postage, and photocopying. This is fair. After all, if your case requires a one-hour phone call to the consulate in Brunei, that call shouldn't eat up the lawyer's fee. But check carefully to be sure that the lawyer charges you no more than a reasonable markup on these items. Some lawyers have been known to turn a tidy profit by charging, for example, 25 cents a page for a photocopy job that really costs only three cents a page.
- **Effect of nonpayment.** Many lawyers charge interest if you fail to pay on time. This is normal and probably not worth making a big fuss about. If you have trouble paying on time, call the lawyer and ask for more time—he or she may be willing to forgo the interest if it's clear you're taking your obligation seriously.
- **Exclusion of guarantee.** The lawyer may warn you that there's no guarantee of winning your case. Though this may appear as if the lawyer is looking for an excuse to lose, it is actually a responsible way for the lawyer to protect against

clients who assume they're guaranteed a win; or who later accuse the lawyer of having made such promises. After all, USCIS or the consulate is the ultimate decision maker on your case.

- **Effect of changes in case.** Most lawyers will warn you that if there is something you didn't tell them about (for example, that you are still married to another spouse) or a significant life change affects your case (for instance, you get arrested), they will charge you additional fees to cover the added work these revelations will cause. This too is normal; but to protect against disputes, make very sure that the contract specifies in detail all the work that is already included. For example, a contract for a lawyer to help you with a green card application within the United States might specify that the lawyer will be responsible for "preparation of petition and adjustment of status packet, filing all applications with USCIS, representation at interview, and reasonable follow-up with USCIS." If the lawyer agrees to include work on any special waivers or unusual documents, make sure these are mentioned in the contract (for example, a waiver or an extra Affidavit of Support from a joint sponsor).

F. Paying Your Lawyer

You may have to pay an initial consultation fee as well as a fee for the lawyer's services. The initial consultation fee is usually around $100 to $200. Some good lawyers provide free consultations. But many have found that they can't afford to spend a lot of their time this way, since many immigrants have no visa or remedy available to them, which means the lawyer gets no work after the initial consultation.

Be ready to pay a reasonable fee for your initial consultation, but do not sign any contracts for further services until you're confident you've found the right lawyer. This usually means consulting with several lawyers first.

1. Flat Rates and Hourly Rates

Many lawyers charge flat rates for green card applications. That means you can compare prices. The current range in the United States for a basic fiancé visa is between $700 and $2,000, and a marriage-based application runs anywhere from $800 to $3,000. If the lawyer quotes an hourly rate instead, expect to pay between $100 and $350 per hour.

A higher rate doesn't necessarily mean a better lawyer. Those who charge less may be keeping their overhead low, still making their name in the business, or philosophically opposed to charging high fees. But an extremely low fee may be a sign that the person isn't really a lawyer, as covered in "Watch Out for Nonlawyers Practicing Immigration Law," above.

2. If All the Rates Are Too High

If the prices you are being quoted are beyond your reach but you definitely need legal help, you have a couple of options. One is to ask the lawyer to split the work with you. With this arrangement, the lawyer consults with you solely about the issue causing you difficulty, reviews a document, or performs some other key task, at the hourly rate; while you do the follow-up work, such as filling out the application forms and translating or writing documents, statements, letters, or more.

Be forewarned, though, that while many lawyers will sell you advice on an hourly basis, most won't want to get into a mixed arrangement unless they are sure they won't end up cleaning up after anything you might do wrong. For example, a lawyer might not agree to represent you in a USCIS interview if the lawyer wasn't hired to review your forms and documents before you submitted them to USCIS.

Another option is to look for a nonprofit organization that helps people with family visa cases. A few provide free services, while most charge reduced rates. But don't get your hopes too high. The U.S. government does not fund organizations that provide services to immigrants (except for very limited types of services), which means that most nonprofits depend on private sources of income, and are chronically underfunded. The result is that many nonprofits will have long backlogs of cases and may not be able to take your case at all.

G. Firing Your Lawyer

You have the right to fire your lawyer at any time. But before you take this step, make sure that your disagreement is about something that is truly the lawyer's fault. Many people blame their lawyer for delays that are actually caused by USCIS or the consulates. You can always consult with another lawyer regarding whether your case has been mishandled. Ask your lawyer for a complete copy of your file first (to which you have a right at any time). If it appears that your case was mishandled, or if relations with your lawyer have deteriorated badly, firing the lawyer may be the healthiest thing for you and your immigration case.

You will have to pay the fired lawyer for any work that has already been done on your case. If you originally paid a flat fee, the lawyer is permitted to keep enough of the fee to cover the work already done, at the lawyer's hourly rate, limited by the total flat fee amount. Ask for a complete list of hours worked and how those hours were spent. Don't count on getting any money back, however—flat fees are often artificially low, and it's very easy for a lawyer to show that your fee got used up on the work that was done.

Firing your lawyer will not affect the progress of your applications with USCIS or the consulate. However, you should send a letter to the last USCIS or consular office you heard from, directing them to send all future correspondence directly to you. (Your new lawyer can do this, too.)

H. Do-It-Yourself Legal Research

With or without a lawyer, you may at some point wish to look at the immigration laws yourself. If so, we applaud your self-empowerment instinct—but need to give you a few warnings. A government spokesperson once called the immigration laws a "mystery, and a mastery of obfuscation" (spokeswoman Karen Kraushaar, quoted in *The Washington Post*, April 24, 2001). She couldn't have said it better.

The result is that researching the immigration laws is something even the experts find difficult— which means you may be wading into treacherous waters if you try it on your own. Figuring out local USCIS office procedures and policies can be even more difficult. Lawyers learn a great deal through trial and error, or by attending meetings and reading articles written by other lawyers who tried something first or who learned important information from USCIS or State Department cables, memos, or other instructions. Unfortunately, you won't have ready access to these sources.

Does all this mean that you shouldn't ever look further than this book? Certainly not. And some research inquiries are quite safe—for instance, if we've cited a section of the law and you want to read the exact language or see whether that section has changed, there's no trick to looking up the law and reading it. But in general, be cautious when researching, and look at several sources to confirm your findings.

Immigration laws are federal, meaning they are written by the U.S. Congress and do not vary from one state to another (however, procedures and priorities for carrying out the laws may vary among USCIS offices in different cities or states, and federal courts in the various circuits may interpret the laws differently). Below we give you a rundown on the most accessible research tools—and not coincidentally, the ones that immigration lawyers most often use.

1. The Federal Code

The federal immigration law is found in Title 8 of the United States Code. Any law library (such as the one at your local courthouse or law school) should have a complete set of the U.S. Code (traditionally abbreviated as U.S.C.). The library may also have a separate volume containing exactly

the same material, but called the Immigration and Nationality Act, or I.N.A.

Unfortunately, the two sets of laws are numbered a bit differently, and not all volumes of the I.N.A. cross-reference back to the U.S. Code, and vice versa. For this reason, when code citations are mentioned in this book, we include both the U.S.C. and I.N.A. numbers.

2. USCIS and State Department Regulations and Guidance

Another important source of immigration law is the Code of Federal Regulations, or C.F.R. Federal regulations are written by the agencies responsible for carrying out federal law. The regulations are meant to explain in greater detail just how the federal agency is going to carry out the law. You'll find the USCIS regulations at Title 8 of the C.F.R., and the Department of State regulations (relevant to anyone whose application is being decided at a U.S. consulate) at Title 22 of the C.F.R. The USCIS and Department of State regulations are helpful, but certainly don't have all the answers. Again, your local law library will have the C.F.R.s, as does the USCIS website.

If you are applying from overseas, you may also wish to look at the State Department's *Foreign Affairs Manual*. This is primarily meant to be an internal government document, containing instructions to the consulates on handling immigrant and nonimmigrant visa cases. However, it is available for public researching as well; your local law library may be able to find you a copy, or go to https://fam.state.gov.

3. Information on the Internet

It is worth familiarizing yourself with the USCIS and State Department websites. The addresses are www.uscis.gov and www.travel.state.gov. The USCIS website offers advice on various immigration benefits and applications, downloads of most immigration forms, and current fees.

On the State Department website, most of the useful information is found under "Get U.S. Visas," including the monthly *Visa Bulletin,* links to U.S. embassies and consulates overseas, and downloads of consular forms.

The Internet is full of sites put up by immigration lawyers as well as immigrants. Because the quality of these sites varies widely, we don't even attempt to review them here. Many of the lawyers' sites are blatant attempts to give out only enough information to bring in business. The sites by other immigrants are well-meaning and can be good for finding out about people's experiences; but they're not reliable when it comes to hard legal or procedural facts.

4. Court Decisions

Immigrants who have been denied visas or green cards often appeal these decisions to the federal courts. The courts' decisions in these cases are supposed to govern the future behavior of USCIS and the consulates. However, your marriage-based visa case should never get to the point where you're discussing court decisions with a USCIS or State Department official, arguing that your case should (or should not) fit within a particular court decision.

For one thing, the officials are not likely to listen until they get a specific directive from their superiors or the court decision is incorporated into their agency's regulations (the C.F.R.). For another thing, such discussions probably mean that your case has become complicated enough to need a lawyer. We do not attempt to teach you how to research federal court decisions here.

Internet Resources

This list summarizes the useful Internet sites that have been mentioned in this book.

- U.S. Citizenship and Immigration Services (USCIS): www.uscis.gov
- The U.S. Department of State: www.travel.state.gov
- U.S. consulates and embassies abroad: www.usembassy.gov.

Words You Will Need to Know

A-Number. An eight- or nine-digit number following the letter A (for Alien) that USCIS assigns to you when you apply for your green card. People who apply for certain other immigration benefits, or who are placed in removal proceedings, also receive an A-number. Once you are assigned this number, USCIS uses it to track your file. You should include it on any correspondence with USCIS.

Adjustment interview. Normally the final step in applying for adjustment of status or a green card within the United States. A USCIS officer personally reviews the application, speaks with the applicant, and approves or denies the application.

Adjustment of status. The procedure for becoming a lawful permanent resident without having to leave the United States. Adjustment of status is available only to immigrants who fit certain eligibility criteria. Many immigrants will have to use the traditional method of gaining permanent residence, even if they already live in the United States, that is, applying for an immigrant visa at a U.S. consulate or embassy abroad (consular processing).

Alien. USCIS uses this term to refer to "a foreign-born person who is not a citizen or national of the United States." I.N.A. Section 101(a)(3); 8 U.S.C. Section 1101(a)(3). In other words, the word covers everyone from illegal aliens to green card holders. We don't use the term much in this book, but you'll need to get used to the word if you do additional research.

Beneficiary. A person intending to immigrate to the United States, for whom a U.S. family member (a citizen or permanent resident) or employer has filed a petition in order to sponsor the would-be immigrant.

Border Patrol. See Customs and Border Protection (CBP), below.

Citizen (U.S.). A person who owes allegiance to the U.S. government, is entitled to its protection, and enjoys the highest level of rights due to members of U.S. society. People become U.S. citizens through birth in the United States or its territories, through their parents, or through naturalization (applying for citizenship and passing the citizenship exam). Citizens cannot have their status taken away except for certain extraordinary reasons. (See Nolo's website at www.nolo.com for more information.)

Citizenship exam. The test that a lawful permanent resident must pass before he or she can become a U.S. citizen, covering the English language as well as U.S. civics, history, and government.

Conditional resident. A person whose status is almost identical to that of a lawful permanent resident, except that the status expires after two years. Immigrants whose marriages to U.S. citizens haven't reached their second anniversary by the time they're approved for residency or enter the U.S. on their immigrant visa become conditional residents. After another two years, they must apply to USCIS for permanent residency. On rare occasions where it becomes apparent even before the two-year expiration date that the marriage was a sham, USCIS can terminate a conditional resident's status immediately (see I.N.A. Section 216(b)(1); 8 U.S.C. Section 1186a(b)(1)).

Consular interview. Normally the final major step in the process of applying for an immigrant visa and from overseas. At the interview, a U.S. consular officer personally reviews the application, speaks with the applicant, and approves or denies an immigrant entry visa. (The U.S. border officer has the final say, however, in whether the entry visa can be exchanged for entry and the green card or lawful permanent resident status.)

Consular processing. The green card application process for immigrants whose final interview and visa decision will happen at an overseas U.S. embassy or consulate.

Consulate. An office of the U.S. Department of State located overseas and affiliated with a U.S. embassy in that country's capital city. The consulate's responsibilities usually include processing visa applications.

Customs and Border Protection (CBP). Part of the Department of Homeland Security (DHS). Its primary functions include keeping the borders secure from illegal crossers, and meeting legal entrants at airports and border posts to check their passports and visas and decide whether they should be allowed into the United States.

Department of Homeland Security (DHS). A government agency created in 2003 to handle immigration and other security-related issues. DHS became the umbrella agency encompassing USCIS, ICE, and CBP.

Department of Justice. An agency of the U.S. federal government that oversees the Immigration Courts.

Department of State. An agency of the U.S. federal government that oversees U.S. embassies and consulates.

Deport/Deportation. See Removal, below.

Deportable. An immigrant who falls into one of the grounds listed at I.N.A. Section 237; 8 U.S.C. Section 1227, is said to be deportable, and can be removed from the United States after a hearing in Immigration Court. Even a permanent resident can be deported.

EAD. See Employment Authorization Document (EAD), below.

Embassy. The chief U.S. consulate within a given country, usually located in the capital city. This is where the U.S. ambassador lives. Most embassies handle applications for visas to the United States.

Employment Authorization Document (EAD). Often called a work permit, this is a card with one's photo on it that indicates that the card holder has the right to work in the United States. Green card holders no longer need an EAD.

Executive Office for Immigration Review. See Immigration Court, below.

Expedited removal. The procedures by which Customs and Border Patrol officers at U.S. borders and ports of entry may decide that a person cannot enter the United States. (See I.N.A. Section 235(b); 8 U.S.C. Section 1225(b).) The officers can refuse entry when they believe the person has used fraud or is carrying improper documents. People removed this way are barred from reentering the United States for five years.

Family Unity. A special program for spouses and children of people who received residency through Amnesty or Cuban/Haitian Adjustment in the late 1980s. (Amnesty was a one-time program, benefiting people who had been living or doing farm work illegally in the United States.) Through the Family Unity program, these family members receive a temporary right to live and work in the United States while waiting to become eligible for permanent residence through a family petition.

Field Office. One of many USCIS offices in the United States that serves the public in a specified geographical area. Field Offices are where most USCIS field staff are located. These offices usually have an information desk, provide USCIS forms, and accept and make decisions on some—but not all—applications for immigration benefits. For a list of locations, see the USCIS website at www.uscis.gov and click "Find an Office."

Fraud interview. A specialized USCIS interview in which one or both members of an engaged or married couple are examined separately to see whether their marriage is real or just a sham to get the foreign-born person a green card. If both are interviewed, they will separately be asked the same set of questions, and their answers compared. Also called a "Stokes interview."

Green card. This slang term refers to the green identification card carried by lawful permanent residents of the United States. In this book, we also use it to refer to the card received by conditional residents. The USCIS name for the green card is an "I-551" or "Permanent Resident

Card." Don't confuse it with the other card often carried by noncitizens, the work permit or Employment Authorization Document.

Green card holder. This is the common slang term, used widely in this book, for an immigrant or a lawful resident, whether permanent or conditional.

I-94. A document showing the date when a person's authorized stay expires. It is prepared by CBP when someone enters the U.S. on a visa or other permitted entry. Once issued as a small card, most entrants must now download it from www.cbp.gov (click "Get Your I-94 Admission Number"). Many people wrongly believe that they can stay until the expiration date in their original visa. Unfortunately, it's the date in the I-94 that controls (although if the visa remains valid, the person may leave and reenter the United States).

Illegal alien. Illegal alien is more of a slang term than a legal term, usually referring to people who have no permission to live in the United States. The preferred term is "undocumented person."

Immediate relative. An immediate relative is the spouse, parent, or unmarried child under age 21 of a U.S. citizen. Immediate relatives can apply for green cards without worrying about quotas or waiting periods. "Spouses" include widows and widowers who apply for the green card within two years of the U.S. citizen spouse's death. Parents must wait until their U.S. citizen child is age 21 to apply. Children can include stepchildren and adopted children (subject to further requirements).

Immigrant. Though the general public usually calls any foreign-born newcomer to the United States an immigrant, USCIS prefers to think of immigrants as including only those persons who have attained "lawful residency" or a green card.

Immigration Court. Also known as the "Executive Office for Immigration Review" or "EOIR." This is the first court that will hear your case if you are placed in removal proceedings. Cases are heard by an "Immigration Judge," who doesn't hear any other type of case. USCIS has its own crew of trial attorneys who represent the agency in court.

Immigration and Customs Enforcement (ICE). This agency of the Department of Homeland Security handles enforcement of the immigration laws within the U.S. borders.

Immigration and Nationality Act (I.N.A.). A portion of the federal code containing all the immigration laws. The I.N.A. is also contained in the United States Code (U.S.C.) at Title 8. You can find the I.N.A. at www.uscis.gov.

Immigration and Naturalization Service (INS). Formerly, a branch of the United States Department of Justice, responsible for controlling the United States borders, enforcing the immigration laws, and processing and judging the cases of immigrants living in the United States. However, in 2003, the INS was absorbed into the Department of Homeland Security, and its functions divided between U.S. Citizenship and Immigration Services (USCIS), Customs and Border Protection (CBP), and Immigration and Customs Enforcement (ICE).

Inadmissible. A person to whom the U.S. government will deny a visa, green card, or admission to the United States because he or she falls into one of the categories listed at I.N.A. Section 212; 8 U.S.C. Section 1182. Broadly speaking, these categories of inadmissibility cover people who might be a burden on or risk to the U.S. government or public for health, security, or financial reasons. Replaces the formerly used term "excludable." Green card holders who leave the United States for 180 days or more can also be found inadmissible upon attempting to return.

K-1 visa. The State Department's name for a fiancé visa.

K-2 visa. The State Department's name for the visa given to unmarried children under age 21 who accompany someone on a K-1 fiancé visa.

K-3 visa. The State Department's name for a visa created in December 2000 for already-married persons who would prefer to use a so-called fiancé visa as a mode of entering the United States. They then apply to adjust status.

K-4 visa. Given to children of K-3 visa holders.

Lawful permanent resident. See Permanent resident, below.

National Visa Center (NVC). An intermediary office responsible for receiving the files of approved petitions from USCIS, sending the applicants instructions and requests for forms and fees, and ultimately transferring the cases to overseas U.S. consulates. In some cases, the NVC may hold onto an applicant's files for years, while the immigrant is on the waiting list for a visa.

Naturalization. When an immigrant succeeds in attaining U.S. citizenship through submitting an application and passing the citizenship exam, he or she is said to have "naturalized."

Nonimmigrant. A broad term meant to cover people who come to the United States lawfully, but temporarily. Most nonimmigrants have a specific expiration date attached to their stay. Some others may stay for the "duration of status," or "D/S," such as students, who can stay until they complete their education.

NVC. See National Visa Center(NVC), above.

Permanent residence. The status of being a permanent resident; see below.

Permanent resident. A "green card holder." Also called a "lawful permanent resident." This is a person who has been approved to live in the United States for an unlimited amount of time. However, the status can be taken away for certain reasons, such as having committed a crime or made one's home outside the United States. Though the green card itself needs to be renewed every ten years, the actual status doesn't expire. After a certain number of years (usually five), a permanent resident can apply for U.S. citizenship. But many people remain in the United States for decades without applying for citizenship. Although they cannot vote, permanent residents enjoy many other rights, such as the right to work and travel freely.

Petition. In the context of this book, the first application filed by a U.S. citizen or lawful permanent resident petitioner, which starts the process of bringing their family member to the United States as an immigrant. This application is sometimes referred to by its form number, I-130.

Petitioner. Someone who has filed a petition in order to sponsor someone to immigrate to the United States.

Provisional waiver. A new waiver introduced in 2013, allowing some applicants whose only ground of inadmissibility is unlawful presence in the U.S. to apply for a waiver of this inadmissibility before departing the U.S. (most likely for a consular interview) in order to receive an answer before taking the risk of departing and being barred from return if the waiver is denied.

Public charge. The immigration law term for an immigrant who has insufficient financial support and goes on welfare or other need-based government assistance. Likelihood of becoming a public charge is a ground of inadmissibility.

Removal. A new immigration law term combining the former terms "exclusion" and "deportation." Removal means the process of sending an alien back to his or her home country because he or she is (or has become) inadmissible or deportable. (Before the laws changed some years ago, "exclusion" meant sending a person back before they'd entered the United States, and "deportation" meant sending someone away who was already in the United States. Now these terms have been combined.)

Resident. Someone who is residing legally in the United States, whether temporarily, permanently, or conditionally.

Service Center. A USCIS office responsible for accepting and making decisions on particular applications from people in specified geographical areas. Unlike USCIS Field Offices, Service Centers are not open to the public; all communication must be by letter, or email, with limited telephone access. Though inconvenient to work with, you often have no choice—an application that must be decided by a Service Center will not be accepted or decided by a Field Office. For information on Service Center locations, call the USCIS information line at 800-375-5283 or see the USCIS website at www.uscis.gov.

Sponsor (noun). The traditional but nonlegal term for a petitioner. In this book, we use "sponsor" more narrowly to refer to someone who is sponsoring an immigrant financially (by signing an Affidavit of Support on the immigrant's behalf).

Sponsor (verb). To "sponsor" an immigrant is the traditional term for "petitioning" the person to come to the United States—that is, initiating a process allowing the immigrant to apply for legal admission and/or status by virtue of a family relation to the sponsor.

Status. In the USCIS's vocabulary, to have "status" means to have a legal right (temporary or permanent) to remain in the United States. For example, green card holders have "permanent resident" status; people on student visas are in student status.

Summary exclusion. See Expedited removal, above.

Time bars. The common name for the three or ten years that a person may have to spend outside the United States as a penalty for having previously been present there unlawfully for six months or more. (See Chapter 2, Section A, for details.)

United States Code. See Immigration and Nationality Act (I.N.A.), above.

Unlawful time. "Unlawful" is a legal term referring to time spent in the United States without either documents, an unexpired visa, or any other legal right to be here. How much time a person has spent in the United States unlawfully has become extremely significant within immigration law, for reasons explained in Chapter 2, Section A.

Visa. A right to enter the United States. Physically, the visa usually appears as a stamp in the applicant's passport, given by a U.S. consulate overseas. The visa is used only to enter the United States, at which time the visa is immediately exchanged for a "status" (such as that of permanent resident or tourist or student). Sometimes, however, you'll hear the terms "visa" and "status" used as if they were interchangeable—in part reflecting the fact that immigrants switching to a new status within the United States might technically granted a visa, or at least a visa number, although they may never see it. Different types of visas have different names, usually with letter codes. For example, a "B" visa is a visitor visa; an "F" visa is a student visa.

Visa Waiver Program. A program that allows citizens of certain countries to enter the United States without a visa and stay for up to 90 days. For details and a list of countries, see www.travel.state.gov, or talk to your local U.S. consulate.

Waiver. An application that a hopeful immigrant files with USCIS, usually on Form I-601, asking it to overlook, or forgive, something that would normally make that person inadmissible, ineligible for an immigration benefit or for entry to the United States. Only certain problems can be waived.

Work permit. See Employment Authorization Document (EAD), above.

Table of Visas and Immigration Benefits

Immigrant Visas (for Permanent Resident Status)	
Type of Visa or Benefit	**Basis for Eligibility**
Family Based	
Immediate Relative	Minor unmarried children or spouses of a U.S. citizen; parent of an over-21-year-old U.S. citizen.
First Preference	Unmarried adult child of a U.S. citizen.
Second Preference: 2A	Spouses and unmarried sons and daughters of lawful permanent residents.
Second Preference: 2B	Unmarried sons and daughters, over the age of 21, of lawful permanent residents.
Third Preference	Married sons and daughters of U.S. citizens.
Fourth Preference	Brothers and sisters of U.S. citizens.
Employment Based	
First Preference	Priority workers who have "extraordinary ability" or are "outstanding professors and researchers" in their field. Also certain multinational executives and managers.
Second Preference	"Members of the professions holding advanced degrees" or "aliens of exceptional ability" in their field.
Third Preference	Skilled workers (2 years' training or experience), professionals, and "other workers" (capable of performing unskilled, but not temporary or seasonal labor).
Fourth Preference	Special immigrants including ministers, religious workers, former U.S. government employees, and others.
Fifth Preference	Investors in job-creating enterprises in the U.S. ($500,000 to $1 million).
Other Benefits or Remedies	
Refugees and Asylees	People who fear persecution in their home country based on their race, religion, nationality, political opinion, or membership in a particular social group. Refugees are processed overseas, asylees within the United States.
"NACARA" for Nicaraguans and Cubans	An amnesty-like program for Nicaraguans and Cubans who entered the United States before December 1, 1995.
"NACARA" Suspension of Deportation	For Salvadorans, Guatemalans, and nationals of several former Soviet and Eastern European countries who entered the United States before 1990 (exact date varies by country) and who applied for asylum, "ABC," or Temporary Protected Status by certain dates; they can apply for "suspension of deportation," described below.
Suspension of Deportation	A remedy normally only available to persons placed in deportation proceedings before April 1, 1997. If the person can prove that he or she has lived in the United States for seven continuous years, has had good moral character, and that the person's deportation would cause extreme hardship to his or her self or his or her spouse, parent, or children who are U.S. citizens or permanent residents, a judge can grant the person permanent residency.

Immigrant Visas (for Permanent Resident Status) (continued)	
Type of Visa or Benefit	**Basis for Eligibility**
Other Benefits or Remedies (continued)	
Cancellation of Removal	An immigration benefit allowing an immigrant in removal proceedings to ask the immigration judge to grant permanent residence. The judge's decision will be a matter of discretion. In the case of undocumented immigrants, the applicant must prove 1) having lived continuously in the U.S. for at least ten years; 2) good moral character during those years; 3) that he or she isn't statutorily barred from entry based on having violated certain U.S. security or criminal laws; and 4) that his or her U.S. citizen or permanent resident spouse, parent, or children would face "extraordinary and exceptionally unusual hardship" if the applicant were forced to leave the United States. In the case of immigrants who already have U.S. permanent residence, but are in removal proceedings because of having committed a crime, the applicant must prove that he or she has 1) been a lawful permanent resident for at least five years; 2) lived in the U.S. for at least seven years in any status; and 3) not been convicted of an aggravated felony.
"VAWA" Cancellation of Removal	For spouses and children of U.S. citizens and permanent residents who have been battered or been victims of extreme cruelty. If such persons can prove that they not only fall into this category but have lived continuously in the United States for three years, have been of good moral character and not committed certain crimes, and that their removal would cause extreme hardship to them, their child, or (if the applicant is a child), their parent, a judge may approve them for permanent residency.
Registry	People who have lived in the United States continuously since January 1, 1972 can apply to adjust status to permanent residence.
Temporary Protected Status	People from certain Congressionally designated countries experiencing war or civil strife; they may apply for a temporary right to stay in the United States until conditions in their home country have improved.

Nonimmigrant Visas (Summary List)	
Type of Visa or Benefit	**Basis for Eligibility**
A-1	Diplomatic employees
A-2	Officials or employees of foreign governments
B-1	Business visitors
B-2	Tourists or visitors for medical treatment
C-1 "Transit visa"	For passing through at a U.S. airport or seaport
D-1 "Crewmember"	For people serving on a ship or plane, landing or docking temporarily
E-1	Treaty Traders
E-2	Treaty Investors
F-1, F-2	Students (academic), including at colleges, universities, seminaries, conservatories, academic high schools, other academic institutions, and in language training; and their spouses and children
F-2	Spouses and children of F-1 visa holders
F-3	Citizens or residents of Mexico or Canada commuting to the U.S. to attend an academic school
G-1	Employees of international organizations who are representing foreign governments; and their spouses and children
H-1B	Temporary professionals (for specialty occupations such as doctors, engineers, physical therapists, computer professionals; must have at least a bachelor's degree)
H-1C	Nurses who will work for up to three years in areas of the U.S. where health professionals are recognized as being in short supply
H-2A	Temporary agricultural workers coming to the U.S. to fill positions for which a temporary shortage of American workers has been recognized by the U.S. Department of Agriculture
H-2B	Temporary agricultural workers
H-3	Trainees coming for temporary job training
I-1	Representatives of international media
J-1, J-2	Exchange visitors; and their spouses and children
K-1, K-2	Fiancées and fiancés of U.S. citizens and their children
K-3, K-4	Spouses of U.S. citizens awaiting approval of their marriage-based petition and a green card, and their children
L-1, L-2	Intracompany transferees working as executives, managers, or persons with specialized knowledge; and their spouses and children
M-1, M-2	Vocational students; and their spouses and children
M-3	Citizens or residents of Mexico or Canada commuting to the U.S. to attend vocational school
N-8	Parents of certain special immigrants

Nonimmigrant Visas (Summary List) (continued)	
Type of Visa or Benefit	**Basis for Eligibility**
N-9	Children of certain special immigrants
NATO-1, NATO-2, NATO-3, NATO-4, and NATO-5	Associates coming to the U.S. under applicable provisions of the NATO Treaty; and their spouses and children
NATO-6	Civilians accompanying military forces on missions authorized under the NATO Treaty
NATO-7	Attendants, servants, or personal employees of NATO-1 through NATO-6 visa holders
O-1, O-2	People with extraordinary ability in sciences, arts, business, athletics, or education, and their support staff
P-1	Internationally recognized entertainers, performers, and athletes, and their support staff
P-2	Cultural exchange entertainers
P-3	Artists and entertainers in groups presenting culturally unique programs
P-4	Spouses and children of P-1, P-2, and P-3 visa holders
Q-1	Exchange visitors in cultural exchange programs
Q-2	Participants in the Irish Peace Process Cultural and Training Program (Walsh visas)
Q-3	Spouses and children of Q-1 visa holders
R-1, R-2	Religious leaders and workers; and their spouses and children
S-5	Witnesses in a criminal investigation
S-6	People coming to the U.S. to provide information about a terrorist organization
T-1, T-2, T-3	Women and children who are in the United States because they are victims of human trafficking, cooperating with law enforcement; and their spouses and children
U-1, U-2, U-3	Victims of criminal abuse in the United States who are assisting law enforcement authorities; and their spouses and children
V	Spouses and unmarried sons and daughters (2A) of U.S. lawful permanent residents who have already waited three years for approval of their I-130 petition or the availability of a green card, and whose petition was on file by December 21, 2000

How to Use the Downloadable Forms on the Nolo Website

This book comes with downloadable checklists that you can access online at: **www.nolo.com/back-of-book/IMAR.html**

To use these files, your computer must have specific software programs installed.

We've put the checklists into RTF format, meaning you can open, edit, print, and save them with most word processing programs such as Microsoft *Word*, Windows *WordPad*, and recent versions of *WordPerfect*.

Although the checklists' primary purpose is to allow you to mark off boxes as you gather the necessary materials for your application, the RTF format might come in handy if you'd like to customize them, perhaps subtracting or adding items based on the specific requirements of your case.

Every word processing program uses different commands to open, format, save, and print documents, so refer to your software's help documents for help using your program. Nolo cannot provide technical support for questions about how to use your computer or your software.

CAUTION
In accordance with U.S. copyright laws, the forms provided by this book are for your personal use only.

List of Checklists Available on the Nolo Website

To download any of the files listed below, go to **www.nolo.com/back-of-book/IMAR.html**

Title	File Name
Checklist for K-1 Fiancé Petition	K1VisaPetition.rtf
Checklist for Fiancé Appointment Package	AppPackage.rtf
Checklist for Marriage-Based I-130 Immigrant Petition	MarriagePetition.rtf
Checklist for Immigrant Visa Forms and Documents (U.S. Citizen Spouse)	VisaFormsDoc.rtf
Checklist for I-130 Petition by Lawful Permanent Resident	LawfulPermRes.rtf
Checklist for Immigrant Visa Forms and Documents (LPR Spouse)	VisaFormsDocLPR.rtf
Checklist for I-130 Petition by U.S. Citizen for Immigrant Living in U.S.	VisaPetUSCitizen.rtf
Checklist for Adjustment of Status Packet	StatusPacket.rtf
Checklist for Applying for Advance Parole	AdvanceParole.rtf
Checklist for Adjustment of Status Interview	StatusAdjustment.rtf
Checklist for Filing Joint Petition to Remove Conditions on Residence	Conditions.rtf

Index

F

H

H-1B visas, temporary professionals, 26, 144, 204, 346, 372, 434

Household members. *See* Relatives

House keys, matching, 314

Humanitarian reinstatement, 34, 185

I

I-94 card. *See* Form I-94

I-551 stamps, on passports, 413

ICE (Immigration and Customs Enforcement), 266–267, 270

Illegal entry

EWIs, 216, 232–233

expedited removal, 93

fiancés in the U.S. engaged to U.S. citizens, 216, 220–223, 224

fiancés in U.S. engaged to permanent residents, 226, 228–229, 230

inadmissibility due to, 16

permanent bars and, 19, 20, 25

spouses of permanent residents, 262, 268–271

spouses of U.S. citizens, 232–233, 236–238, 260

See also Time bars

Illegal stays (overstaying visas)

adjustment of status and, 23, 24

consequences, 19–20, 266–268, 283

documenting history of U.S. visits, 220, 236, 267, 271

expiration of K-1 fiancé visa, 102

fiancés in U.S. engaged to permanent residents, 227

fiancés in U.S. engaged to U.S. citizens, 218, 220–223, 224

inadmissibility due to, 16

legal assistance, 270

paperwork to document, 26–27, 220, 222, 238

spouses of permanent residents, in the U.S., 263, 265

spouses of U.S. citizens, in the U.S., 232, 265–268

tourist visas and, 57, 106–107, 234

"unlawful" definition, 19

Visa Waiver Program and, 7, 23, 24, 216, 226, 232, 233–234

waivers/forgiveness of, 7, 267–268, 271

See also Time bars

Immediate relatives, defined, 232

See also Children; Relatives

Immigrants

anti- and pro-immigrant sentiments, 2

USCIS focus on immigrant's finances, 322

Immigrant visas, table of visas or benefits, 432–433

Immigration and Customs Enforcement (ICE), 266–267, 270

Immigration and Nationality Act, 16

Immigration Court, 46, 102, 124, 172, 250, 391, 403–404

Immigration Equality website, 31

Immigration fraud. *See* Marriage fraud; Visa fraud

Immigration laws

changed while waiting for Priority Date, 187

Congressional amendments, 2

inadmissibility due to violation of, 18

information resources, 10, 227

nonlawyers practicing immigration law, 418

researching, 422

Section 245(i), 24–25

See also Lawyers, issues for consultation

Inadmissibility, 16–27

information resources, 16

legal assistance, 18, 21, 22

losing permanent resident status, 398

medical exams, 18–19, 208

nationals under Trump travel ban, 17

organization affiliations, 342

overview of grounds for, 6, 16

permanent bars and, 19, 20, 25

spouses of U.S. citizens, living in the U.S., 232

visa fraud and, 18, 216, 392

See also Time bars

Incest, marriage to blood relations, 30, 31

⚖ NOLO

More from Nolo

Nolo.com offers a large library of legal solutions and forms, created by Nolo's in-house legal editors. These reliable documents can be prepared in minutes.

Create a Document Online

Incorporation. Incorporate your business in any state.

LLC Formation. Gain asset protection and pass-through tax status in any state.

Will. Nolo has helped people make over 2 million wills. Is it time to make or revise yours?

Living Trust (avoid probate). Plan now to save your family the cost, delays, and hassle of probate.

Provisional Patent. Preserve your right to obtain a patent by claiming "patent pending" status.

Download Useful Legal Forms

Nolo.com has hundreds of top quality legal forms available for download:

- bill of sale
- promissory note
- nondisclosure agreement
- LLC operating agreement
- corporate minutes
- commercial lease and sublease
- motor vehicle bill of sale
- consignment agreement
- and many more.

Nolo's Bestselling Books

U.S. Immigration Made Easy
$44.99

How to Get a Green Card
$39.99

Becoming a U.S. Citizen
A Guide to the Law, Exam & Interview
$29.99

Legal Research
How to Find & Understand the Law
$49.99

Nolo's Encyclopedia of Everyday Law
$34.99

Every Nolo title is available in print and for download at Nolo.com.

www.nolo.com

NOLO **Save 15%** *off your next order*

Register your Nolo purchase, and we'll send you a **coupon for 15% off** your next Nolo.com order!

Nolo.com/customer-support/productregistration

On Nolo.com you'll also find:

Books & Software

Nolo publishes hundreds of great books and software programs for consumers and business owners. Order a copy, or download an ebook version instantly, at Nolo.com.

Online Forms

You can quickly and easily make a will or living trust, form an LLC or corporation, apply for a provisional patent, or make hundreds of other forms—online.

Free Legal Information

Thousands of articles answer common questions about everyday legal issues, including wills, bankruptcy, small business formation, divorce, patents, employment, and much more.

Plain-English Legal Dictionary

Stumped by jargon? Look it up in America's most up-to-date source for definitions of legal terms, free at Nolo.com.

Lawyer Directory

Nolo's consumer-friendly lawyer directory provides in-depth profiles of lawyers all over America. You'll find information you need to choose the right lawyer.

IMAR10